EDIBLE FOREST GARDENS

EDIBLE FOREST GARDENS

❧ VOLUME ONE ❧
Ecological Vision and Theory
for Temperate Climate Permaculture

DAVE JACKE
with Eric Toensmeier

CHELSEA GREEN PUBLISHING COMPANY
WHITE RIVER JUNCTION, VERMONT

The field research for, and writing of, portions of this manuscript were undertaken under the auspices of the New England Small Farm Institute, Inc., Belchertown, Massachusetts.

RECYCLED PAPER STATEMENT
Chelsea Green sees publishing as a tool for cultural change and ecological stewardship. We strive to align our book manufacturing practices with our editorial mission, and to reduce the impact of our business enterprise on the environment. We print our books and catalogs on chlorine-free recycled paper, using soy-based inks, whenever possible. Chelsea Green is a member of the Green Press Initiative (www.greenpressinitiative.org), a nonprofit coalition of publishers, manufacturers, and authors working to protect the world's endangered forests and conserve natural resources. Edible Forest Gardens was printed on Silva Enviro Scholar, a 100-percent post-consumer recycled, chlorine-free paper supplied by Marquis Book Printing.

Project Editor: Collette Leonard
Developmental Editor: Ben Watson
Copy Editor: Cannon Labrie
Proofreader: Nancy Ringer
Indexer: Peggy Holloway
Illustrator: Elayne Sears
Book design by Peter Holm, Sterling Hill Productions.
Printed in Canada on recycled paper.
First printing, July 2005
11 10   4 5 6 7 8 9 10

Library of Congress Cataloging-in-Publication Data
Jacke, Dave.
Edible forest gardens / Dave Jacke with Eric Toensmeier.
     p. cm.
Includes bibliographical references and index.
ISBN 1-931498-79-2
1. Edible forest gardens. 2. Edible forest gardens--North America. I.
Toensmeier, Eric. II. Title.
SB454.3.E35J24 2005
635'.0915'2--dc22

                         2004029745

Chelsea Green Publishing
P.O. Box 428
White River Junction, VT 05001
(800) 639-4099
www.chelseagreen.com

To my father,
STANLEY EMIL JACKE,
February 10, 1925–May 3, 1999.
You never understood what I've been up to in my life,
but you supported me anyway. May I pass on a
gift as great, or greater, to my own.

And to my daughter, and my father's namesake,
EMILY.
May this book help make your world and your
children's world a more beautiful, enlivening, and joyful place.

Edible Forest Gardens is complete in two volumes. *Volume One: Ecological Vision and Theory for Temperate Climate Permaculture* offers a holistic vision for forest gardening and explains the underlying ecological principles. *Volume Two: Ecological Design and Practice for Temperate Climate Permaculture* covers the practical considerations of forest gardening, including design, maintenance, and a uniquely valuable "plant matrix" describing hundreds of edible and useful species.

Volume One, ISBN 1-931498-79-2, $75
Volume Two, ISBN 1-931498-80-6, $75
Volumes One and Two as a Set, ISBN 1-890132-60-8, $150

www.chelseagreen.com
802-295-6300

CONTENTS

LIST of TABLES and FIGURES

PREFACE

This book defies easy categorization. Is it a gardening book? An ecology text for teachers and students? A visionary testament? A manual for hard core eco-designers and back-to-the-landers? A manifesto for the next two centuries of agroforestry research and breeding work? It is all these and more. I know all too well the benefits and drawbacks of wide skills and interests, broad knowledge, and integrative, cross-discipline thinking. While such attributes can be exciting, illuminating, holistic, and even healing, pulling it all together and trying to take it somewhere useful can get maddening at times.

When Eric and I began this journey in 1997, we thought we would put together a relatively brief explication of forest gardening in a North American context for the "educated suburban gardener." He would do the Plant Species Matrix and related appendices, and I would write the prose. While that division of labor remained basically intact, I found it impossible to write the 150-page manual I originally envisioned. As any author knows, there is often a great paradox in the craft of writing: at the same time that the writer is in complete control of the environment he creates with the written word, every writing project has a life of its own, which the author ignores at his peril.

Every time I sat to compose chapter 3 (now chapters 3, 4, 5, and 6 of volume 1) I found myself stuck. I couldn't do the subject justice in a short span. I didn't want to regurgitate permaculture cofounder Bill Mollison, as so many others have—had I done that I would not have been able to live with myself. I needed to go back to ground in scientific ecology to see what people had learned since I was in college and first got involved with permaculture in the late 1970s. Despite the value and genius embedded within permaculture, to which I

owe great debt, I wanted even more solid footing for an integration of vision, ecology, design, and practice the likes of which I have strived for all my life, and which I felt the world still lacked. So, Eric had to listen over the phone to a thousand pages of manuscript in the ensuing effort. It has been a grueling seven years, and the most difficult thing I have ever chosen to do. I am glad the process now moves into its outward phase. It will be interesting to see what bounces back onto the radar screen from this big "ping" that is now going out into the world.

This book would not have been possible without many people, a large number of them absolutely key to our success in this endeavor. My gratitude must first go to Eric, with whom I have traveled, labored, laughed, and grappled for all these many years. Thanks for sticking with me through thick and thin, for committing and surrendering, for going away and always coming back, for being who you are, and for your good humor and your enthusiasm. Appreciations also go to numerous and nameless other friends and acquaintances, my parents, my siblings, and perfect strangers, too, who gave moral support. To our editor, Ben Watson, thanks for opening and holding the space for this book at Chelsea Green, and for enlarging that space as the book became what it is. My humble apologies and love to Emily, Eric, Ben, and any others who suffered as a result of my book mania.

Money makes the world go round, it seems, and many people invested their faith in us through their generosity. This project was funded entirely by private donations and personal resources. Donors shall remain nameless, but you know who you are—a huge kiss to you all. Thanks to the brave souls (almost two hundred!) who bought book subscriptions through our "Community-Supported

Authoring" (CSA) program when this project began, and as it continued. Your graciousness and patience have been marvelous, and the cash flow helped greatly. Gratitude is also due Judy Gillan and the New England Small Farm Institute of Belchertown, Massachusetts, who made much of the research possible. *Invaluable* is the only word to describe their assistance.

Professional and "lay" readers added tremendously to the process. My appreciation goes to forest ecologist Dr. David Perry; landscape architect, permaculturist, and LSU Professor Emeritus Dan Earle; garden writer Miranda Smith; the amazing Linda Scott (you helped me over the big humps); Lisa Stocking and her partner Joel; Peter Buhl; and other friends, cohorts, random contacts, and the members of the CSA review group. Your feedback really fed us, and the thinking and writing here is much better for your critiques. I am also grateful to researchers, writers, and professionals to whom I have spoken or whose work fed my quest for knowledge: Dr. David Perry; Dr. Paul Colinvaux; Dr. Elaine Ingham; Ted St. John; J. Philip Grime; John Weaver; Bill Mollison; David Holmgren; Steward Pickett and Mark McDonnell; Christopher Alexander and associates; Roget and his heirs; and many others. I'm glad I have such good shoulders to stand on. Of course, none of these people hold responsibility for any mistakes, inaccuracies, or scandalous statements in this work. That responsibility is entirely mine.

Finally, I give my gratitude to my teacher, Gurumayi Chidvilasananda, for the great blessings she has offered to me and to the world. The inner spark burns more brightly because of you.

May this book—in both its volumes—and its ideas serve you, dear reader, and your highest purposes on this planet, not to mention the planet itself. Thank you for accepting the invitation. Now get out there and start gardening!

DAVE JACKE
October 1, 2004
Keene, NH

In 1989, fresh out of high school, I read Mollison and Holmgren's *Permaculture One*. Since then my drive to learn about the elegant, perennial, integrated ecosystems for human food production it describes has never ceased. Though permaculture broadened its range to cover energy, shelter, and a wide range of food production issues in the following years, my fascination with its original focus has never wavered. My work in writing this book has been my best effort to provide information to help exploration of this (originally temperate Australian) model here in my own home, the eastern forest region of North America.

I am immensely grateful to Dave Jacke for the opportunity to take on this task, which has shaped my life these past seven years. Thanks to Dave for taking the extra time in writing, despite all the pain and frustration it caused us both. The result is a new permaculture testament reflecting the latest in science's understanding of eastern forest ecology. Dave's persistence has made this book a serious contribution to the future of ecological food production. Thanks also to Dave for an intellectual comradeship like no other in my life. Our minds continually challenge and build on each other's ideas, and our work on these books has been made so much stronger because of our collaboration. Thanks to Dave for his strong friendship, and for his drive and determination.

Thanks to my family for their belief in me. Their support was essential at every stage of writing. Thanks especially to my mother for assisting me through several "crunch" phases of writing, as she has since elementary school, and to my father for teaching me his love of plants and gardening in the forest.

Thanks to our editor Ben Watson, and our publisher, Chelsea Green, for their patience and tolerance. They stood by us as the book stretched years beyond schedule and many times longer than projected. The results are well worth it! Also, my sincere gratitude to Ben and Chelsea Green for their commitment to works on permaculture.

A special thank-you to the generous people whose financial support made this work possible. Without you the project could never have gotten off the ground. I also want to recognize the New England Small Farm Institute. In addition to their fiscal sponsorship, their library has been a critical research resource. In my "day job" working for NESFI, I have learned much of what I know about writing, designing tables and worksheets, and especially editing.

Thanks to those who have taught and inspired me. My summer apprenticeship with Jerome Osentowski of the Central Rocky Mountain Permaculture Institute was a chance to live and learn in a site that demonstrated the principles of permaculture as well or better than anywhere I have seen. It has been my great privilege to work for and count as my friend Steve Breyer of Tripple Brook Farm. He has generously shared his time and amazing collection of plants with me since I first worked for him in 1994. Our visits with Robert Hart, Patrick Whitefield, Joe Hollis, and Charlie Headington were extremely helpful. I would like to give special appreciation to Ken Fern and the crew from Plants for a Future. Their online database has been an incredibly valuable tool, and our visit to their plant collection gave me an opportunity to sample many interesting new species. Our visit to Martin Crawford, who took a whole day out of his very busy schedule, was to me the most important of all our visits. Martin's garden is a remarkable achievement, and his numerous publications have been one of the most important foundations on which we have written this book. Other writers and thinkers who have been important for my research are J. Russell Smith, Robert Kourik, Bill Mollison and David Holmgren, Stephen Facciola, the researchers of the Land Institute (notably Wes Jackson, Judith Soule, and Jon Piper), Paul Stamets, Carol Deppe, and Alan Kapuler. A special thanks to David Theodoropoulos, whose bold, challenging ideas came at a critical time in the development of this work.

A special thanks to my friend, housemate, and gardening partner Jonathan Bates. The case study in the design section of volume 2 is a design we developed together and are implementing in our garden. His patience, reliability, hard work, and enthusiasm are the reason I have a forest garden today. Special thanks to him for all his hard work in the final hours as we raced to rework the design chapters into a workbook and finalize our design using the newly developed process.

Thanks to all my friends who have supported me along the way: Michelle Wiggins, Kaycie D'Auria, Arthur Lerner and Emily Kellert, the whole Rodriguez-Ross clan, Craig Hepworth, Erin Royster, Walter Hergt, and Rob Fetter. Miranda Smith has been a great friend and an important helper in teaching me about the world of garden writing and editing. Thanks to my alma mater, the Institute for Social Ecology, for the opportunity to teach and for setting aside part of their farm for an experimental superhardy forest garden. Appreciations to my cocounselors Betsy Feick, Susan Munkres, and Jennie Sheeks for helping me keep my life together during the past seven years. To those I have forgotten to mention, my gratitude and apologies. Despite the best efforts of the people listed above, I have doubtless made many mistakes. These are mine alone.

Finally, thank you to the forest gardeners (present and future), the plant geeks, the backyard breeders, the adventurous seed companies and nurseries, and all the people who give of their time to make the world greener and more interesting. For my part I dedicate this book to you.

ERIC TOENSMEIER
October 1, 2004
Holyoke, MA

FIGURE 0.1. Inside Robert Hart's forest garden in Shropshire, England, the oldest known temperate-climate forest garden in the world. Though planted too densely, it evokes forest character while producing large amounts of food with minimal maintenance. *Photo by Dave Jacke.*

Introduction:
An Invitation to Adventure

Come among the unsown grasses bearing richly, the oaks heavy
with acorns, the sweet roots in unplowed earth . . .

—Ursula K. LeGuin, *Always Coming Home*

Picture yourself in a forest where almost everything around you is food. Mature and maturing fruit and nut trees form an open canopy. If you look carefully, you can see fruits swelling on many branches—pears, apples, persimmons, pecans, and chestnuts. Shrubs fill the gaps in the canopy. They bear raspberries, blueberries, currants, hazelnuts, and other lesser-known fruits, flowers, and nuts at different times of the year. Assorted native wildflowers, wild edibles, herbs, and perennial vegetables thickly cover the ground. You use many of these plants for food or medicine. Some attract beneficial insects, birds, and butterflies. Others act as soil builders or simply help keep out weeds. Here and there vines climb on trees, shrubs, or arbors with fruit hanging through the foliage—hardy kiwis, grapes, and passionflower fruits. In sunnier glades large stands of Jerusalem artichokes grow together with groundnut vines. These plants support one another as they store energy in their roots for later harvest and winter storage. Their bright yellow and deep violet flowers enjoy the radiant warmth from the sky.

WHAT IS AN EDIBLE
FOREST GARDEN?

An edible forest garden is a perennial polyculture of multipurpose plants. Most plants regrow every year

without replanting: perennials. Many species grow together: a polyculture. Each plant contributes to the success of the whole by fulfilling many functions: multipurpose. In other words, a forest garden is an edible ecosystem, a consciously designed community of mutually beneficial plants and animals intended for human food production. Edible forest gardens provide more than just a variety of foods. The seven Fs apply here: food, fuel, fiber, fodder, fertilizer, and "farmaceuticals," as well as fun. A beautiful, lush environment can be a conscious focus of your garden design, or a side benefit you enjoy (see figure 0.1).

Forest gardens mimic forest ecosystems, those natural perennial polycultures once found throughout the world's humid climates. In much of North America, your garden would soon start reverting to forest if you were to stop tilling and weeding it. Annual and perennial weeds would first colonize the bare soil. Shrubs would soon shade out the weeds. Then, sun-loving pioneer trees would move in and a forest would be born. Eventually, even these pioneers would succumb to longer-lived, more shade-tolerant species. It can take many decades for this process, called succession, to result in a mature forest.

We humans work hard to hold back succession—mowing, weeding, plowing, and spraying. If the successional process were the wind, we would be constantly motoring against it. Why not put up a sail and glide along with the land's natural tendency to become forest? Edible forest gardening is about expanding the horizons of our food gardening across the full range of the successional sequence, from field to forest, and everything in between.

Besides the food and other products, you should design your forest garden for self-renewing, self-fertilizing self-maintenance. For a self-renewing garden, plant mainly perennials and self-sowing annuals. Allow a healthy soil community to develop by mulching and leaving the soil undisturbed. Build soil fertility with plants that fix nitrogen, amass soil minerals, act as mulch sources, or a blend of these. Reduce or eliminate your pest control work by providing food and shelter for insectivorous birds and predatory and parasitic insects. Fragrant plants, such as onions, may confuse insect pests and slow their march toward your crops. In fact, you can reduce pest and disease problems simply by mixing things up, rather than planting in blocks of the same species! All these things, and more, reduce the amount of maintenance your garden needs and increase its yields. When we mimic how nature works and design well, we can reduce the work of sustaining ourselves to mulching, some pruning, occasional weeding, and minimal pest and disease management (depending on the crops you grow). Oh, and then there's the harvesting!

Essentially, edible forest gardening is the art and science of putting plants together in woodlandlike patterns that forge mutually beneficial relationships, creating a garden ecosystem that is more than the sum of its parts. You can grow fruits, nuts, vegetables, herbs, mushrooms, other useful plants, and animals in a way that mimics natural ecosystems. You can create a beautiful, diverse, high-yield garden that is largely self-maintained.

GARDENING *LIKE* THE FOREST VS. GARDENING *IN* THE FOREST

Edible forest gardening is not necessarily gardening *in* the forest. It is gardening *like* the forest. You don't need to have an existing woodland if you want to forest garden, though you can certainly work with one. Forest gardeners use the forest as a design metaphor, a model of structure and function, while adapting the design to focus on meeting human needs in a small space. We learn how forests work and then participate in the creation of an ecosystem in our backyards that can teach us things about ecology and ourselves while we eat our way through it. Gardening *like* a forest is what this book is all about.

Gardening *in* the forest is different. We can transform an existing piece of woodland into an edible forest garden, and this book will explain how, but there are many other ways to garden in the forest. These include the restoration of natural woodlands, ecological forestry, and the creation of primarily aesthetic woodland gardens. The latter forms of gardening *in* the forest are *not* what this book is about. If you want to garden *in* the forest in any of those ways, see the resources listed in the appendix. If you want to grow food in a garden *like* a forest, read on.

WHERE CAN YOU GROW A FOREST GARDEN?

Forest gardens are viable in small urban yards and large parks, on suburban lots, or in a corner of a rural farm. We have seen examples ranging from a 2-acre (0.8 ha) rural research garden, to a jungle of food plants on a quarter-acre lot, to a heavily planted 30-by-50-foot (9 by 15 m) embankment behind an urban housing project. Smaller versions are definitely possible; the same principles and ideas still apply, though it might stretch the word *forest* rather far. Despite the name *forest garden,* it is best if your site has good sun. Of course, if your land is shady and wooded, this book has plenty of ideas and information you can use.

You can most easily grow forest gardens where forest, especially deciduous forest, is the native vegetation. This means a climate with ample rainfall during the growing season and relatively mild winters. This book focuses on the lands now and formerly covered by the eastern deciduous forest between USDA plant hardiness zones 4 and 7, with some overlap into zones 3 and 8 (see figure 0.2). However, the information presented applies to all of Earth's moist temperate habitats, and beyond. Eric researched plants from similar climates the world over for inclusion in the "Top 100" species (see appendix 1) and the Plant Species Matrix (in volume 2's appendices). The principles of ecology still apply in other locales. Those of you in drier climates, such as the prairies and the desert Southwest, can grow forest gardens too, if you provide irrigation and wind protection. You should, however, look to your native habitats as models for sustainable agriculture. Those of you in the north, say, plant hardiness zone 3 and colder, have more limited species options, but you can still play the game.

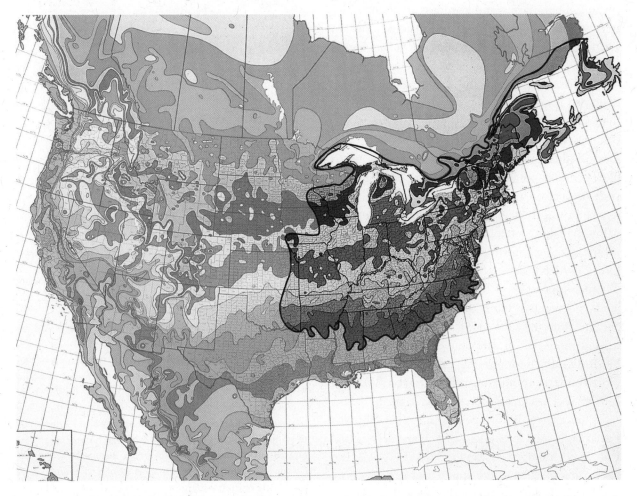

FIGURE 0.2. While this book focuses on the geographic range outlined in black above, the vision and ecology discussed here apply in many regions. We also discuss species that offer the best opportunities for human uses and ecosystem function in humid, temperate climates anywhere. This geographic range of focus runs from the Atlantic coast to the prairies, and from plant hardiness zones 4 through 7, with some overlap into zones 3 and 8. *Map courtesy of the U.S. Department of Agriculture.*

THE GARDEN OF EDEN: IT SOUNDS GREAT, BUT IS IT PRACTICAL?

We like to think of edible forest gardening as recreating the Garden of Eden. The introduction's first paragraph makes it sound like it is. Is such an abundant, low-maintenance food garden really possible? Let's take a few lessons from history.

The notion of edible forest gardening is ancient in many ways but relatively new to modern Western culture, especially in North America. The peoples of tropical Africa, Asia, and Latin America have a long tradition of multistoried agriculture. Their farms and gardens often integrate trees, shrubs, livestock, and herbaceous crops in various ways—a set of strategies called agroforestry. Fodder trees in pastures provide windbreaks, livestock forage, and shade. Some of these trees also improve the soil by fixing nitrogen from the air and putting it into the soil. Alley cropping systems combine rows of nitrogen-fixing and food-producing trees with strips of annual crops like corn and potatoes. Multistoried "food forest" systems used in many tropical regions mimic the rain forest, growing crops such as coconut, oil palms, bananas, coffee, pineapples, and ginger. The Javanese have grown village- and home-scale forest gardens since at least the tenth century. These compose 15 to 50 percent of village croplands.[1] Obviously, forest gardens work in tropical climates, and have for a long time. Similar systems existed in cooler climates hundreds of years ago. We'll discuss the forest-management practices of North American Indians in chapter 1, but Western culture also has an agroforestry heritage.

An intensive land-use system called coppice forestry was used throughout Britain and continental Europe beginning at least in the Middle Ages. Many trees can sprout from the stump and regrow vigorously after being cut down. These stump sprouts, called coppice, can provide fuel, fiber, fodder, or mulch, depending on the species (figure 0.3). In medieval Europe, coppice plots produced logs, poles, saplings, and brush for use in crafts, industry, and building construction. Cut on seven- to twenty-five-year rotations, they offered excellent habitat for wild game, as well as for wild edible and medicinal plants essential to the medieval diet. Coppicing dramatically prolongs a tree's life, so coppice stumps can produce material for generations. British researchers have

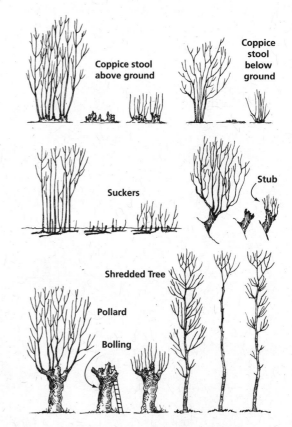

FIGURE 0.3. Coppice management of woody plants formed the foundation of medieval European land use and economics. How we manage these eternally springing species depends on their biology and uses. Plants with adventitious buds under their bark can be coppiced (top), pollarded (bottom), or stubbed (center right) aboveground by cutting growth back to the trunk. Coppicing leaves a short stool or stump for resprouting. Pollarding off a high stump or bolling keeps new growth out of reach of large livestock until it is needed for fodder. Mid-sized stubs are for shorter animals. Some species form suckers from underground roots or rhizomes, allowing cutting at ground level (center). Shredding involves pruning resprouting branches off a tall specimen (bottom right). The illustration shows each technique just before cutting, just after cutting, and one year after cutting. *Adapted from Rackham, 1993.*

proven that several continuously coppiced stumps, known as stools, are five hundred to eight hundred years old, two to three times a tree's normal life span.[2] Talk about sustainability! Unfortunately, coppice forestry systems almost disappeared during the Industrial Revolution, but they are experiencing a budding revival, at least in Britain.

The record certainly shows that forest-garden-like systems have been viable and practical in temperate climates. Isn't it possible for us to do far better now if we put our hearts and minds to it? A small but growing number of people in the cold climates of the world have been developing these ideas for the current era.

J. Russell Smith's seminal 1950 work *Tree Crops: A Permanent Agriculture* first sparked renewed interest in the potential of agroforestry throughout the world. However, tropical countries and large-scale tree-crop systems received most of the resulting research attention. Bill Mollison and David Holmgren also studied tropical and subtropical ecosystems, along with arid lands. As cofounders of the permaculture concept in late 1970s Australia,[3] they gathered ideas for designing "permanent agricultures" using ecological principles and dispersed them to virtually every continent. Tree crops and agroforestry systems were a large part of permaculture's initial toolbox. Permaculture practices now extend beyond agriculture into all aspects of human culture and range from regional to household scales. Unfortunately, permaculture's subtropical origins and the overwhelming need for these ideas in lower latitudes has led most permaculture literature to focus outside of temperate climates, at least until recently.

Robert Hart pioneered temperate agroforestry at a home scale with his inspirational 1991 book *Forest Gardening*.[4] Hart's insights arose from his tropical agroforestry work,[5] his Gandhian beliefs, and his experiments on a tiny smallholding in Shropshire, England, where he started his garden in 1981. That makes it the oldest known temperate-climate forest garden in the world (see our case study on page 110). His forest garden was a beautiful testament to his vision. Unfortunately, last we knew it was in legal limbo after his death in March 2000. Permaculture designer and teacher Patrick Whitefield followed Hart's book with his more practical *How to Make a Forest Garden*,[6] a solid book

FIGURE 0.4. Forest gardens can grow and produce even at 7,000 feet (2,100 m) in the Rocky Mountains. This path, winding among apple trees at Central Rocky Mountain Permaculture Institute, Basalt, Colorado, USA, is bordered by numerous plants offering ecological functions and human uses. These include borage (*Borago officinalis*), a self-sowing annual with edible lavender flowers and greens that provides beneficial insect habitat, nectar for pollinators, and medicinal uses; nitrogen fixers such as the yellow-flowered groundcover bird's-foot trefoil (*Lotus corniculatus*) and the shrubby Siberian pea shrub (*Caragana arborescens*) with its drying pods full of seeds edible by humans and chickens; garlic and perennial onions; and the perennial, edible-tubered sunflower Jerusalem artichoke (*Helianthus tuberosus*). *Photo by Dave Jacke.*

with a British focus. These two books, combined with numerous works on permaculture, sparked widespread planting of forest gardens in Britain. These gardens and books all demonstrate the potential of edible forest gardens, if not the actual benefits.

Forest gardens have spread more slowly in North America. Fewer people have heard of the idea, so examples are farther between—but they do exist. Forest gardeners have achieved at least moderate success in maritime Washington State; at 7,000 feet (2,100 m) in the cold, dry Colorado Rockies (figure 0.4); in the hot, humid city of Greensboro, North Carolina; and in chilly southern New Hampshire.

AN INVITATION TO ADVENTURE

We have yet to work out many practical considerations for this "new idea" of forest gardening, especially in North America. British forest-garden plants and experiences may not translate well to this continent. Many of our native plants have good forest-gardening potential, but we have tested few of them. Strong evidence supports the forest garden idea, yet this information lies scattered across many different references on farming, gardening, agroforestry, and ecology. We have seen good on-the-ground examples on two continents. We have also created enough of these gardens and grown enough of the species to know they can work. Still, we believe the practice can work better than anyone has yet achieved. Successful forest gardens stand within reach of many people throughout the temperate world—as long as they can find clear thinking, accurate knowledge, and solid information on the ecology of useful plants. But there is still much to learn, and this is where you come in.

You hold in your hands the first manual spelling out key concepts of forest ecology and how to apply them to a North American forest garden. Our intent is to provide you with a comprehensive guide to forest garden theory and practice; give a signifi-

cant push to the state of the art; and get as many people as possible involved in experimenting with this idea. The purpose of *Edible Forest Gardens* is to offer you the inspiration, information, and tools you need to successfully grow your own forest garden.

The book comes in two volumes, covering the vision, ecological theory, design, and practice of forest gardening. Volume 1 has two parts, and part 1, "Vision," includes two chapters. Chapter 1 looks at the ecological and cultural context for forest gardening, focusing on eastern North America. Chapter 2 lays out a vision of forest gardening's potential for reintegrating ourselves into the natural world, and goals for edible forest garden design arising from that vision. Four chapters in part 2, "Ecology," explore the ecology of the forest and the forest garden. They build solid theoretical foundations from which to derive guidelines for forest garden design and management. When we create edible forest gardens, we consciously create both visible and invisible structures to fulfill the goals discussed in the vision. Throughout these first two parts of the book, you will find boxes and feature articles that go into greater depth on particular topics of interest. In addition, three case studies scattered through the text provide concrete examples of forest gardens we visited in our research travels.

Volume 1 concludes with three appendices. The first describes forest gardening's "Top 100" species to whet your appetite for the nitty-gritty and give you a sense of forest gardening's food-production potential. Plant hardiness zone maps for North America and Europe follow this, as well as a list of publications and organizations that can help you learn more about forest ecology and forest gardening. The glossary, bibliography, and index should also assist you in using volume 1 effectively.

Volume 2 is essentially a forest gardener's "tool kit" and constitutes part 3 of this work. It contains seven chapters explaining how to design, plant, and manage your forest garden. These chapters place all the implications of the ecological analysis in part 2 into a gardening and garden-design context. The second volume also includes five appendices that offer detailed information and resources to help you map your site, select and find plants, and create beneficial animal habitat. This first volume sometimes refers to various parts of volume 2 because we want you to understand how the theory explored here guides the practical aspects of forest gardening discussed there.

Please note that though this work comes in two volumes, we have tried to make each volume able to stand alone. However, for optimal understanding and application of the ideas and practices presented, we strongly recommend that you read both volumes. Like the elements that compose an ecosystem, these two volumes are separate but interrelated and function most effectively when used in tandem.

So we invite you to join in a lifetime of quiet adventure. Ecological systems at their essence operate on simple principles yet have endlessly fascinating intricacies. Many tasty and useful plants stand ready for use in forest gardens. Many more exist with great potential for selection and development. We know much about the basics of edible forest garden design and management, but there is still much more to learn. It seems we have many lifetimes' worth of creative interest and fulfilling enjoyment ahead.

We seek to learn—from our own fields, thickets, forests, and wetlands—the ways in which living things have adapted to our climate and land. We want to mimic these habitats with productive garden ecosystems. The goal is to create mutually beneficial communities of multipurpose plants for our own sustenance, and thereby to include ourselves in the natural world. We seek to recreate the Garden of Eden, and, as Bill Mollison and David Holmgren say, "Why not?"

1. Reijntjes et al., 1992, page 38.
2. Rackham, 1993.
3. *Permaculture One* (Mollison and Holmgren, 1978) and *Permaculture Two* (Mollison, 1979), the first books on permaculture, are no longer in print, but they have been succeeded by *Introduction to Permaculture* (Mollison and Slay, 1991) and *Permaculture: A Designer's Manual* (Mollison, 1988, now with several newer editions), both from Tagari Publications (Tyalgum, Australia.)
4. Hart, 1991.
5. Douglas and Hart, 1984.
6. Whitefield, 1996.

PART ONE

Vision

The ultimate goal of farming is not the growing of crops, but the cultivation and perfection of human beings.

—MASANOBU FUKUOKA, *The One-Straw Revolution*

We cannot solve the significant problems we face at the same level of thinking we were at when we created them.

—ALBERT EINSTEIN

How we garden reflects our worldview. When we see the world as a collection of independent and isolated elements, it is difficult, if not impossible, for us to grasp the interconnectedness of natural systems. How could we then garden ecologically, or live and act responsibly in an interdependent world?

Western culture, for all its benefits, has created immense problems for the forests of North America, for the people living in the lands once occupied by them, and for anyone who wants healthy food to eat in the twenty-first century. We can solve these problems only with significantly different ways of thinking. The ultimate goal of forest gardening is not only the growing of crops, but also the cultivation and perfection of new ways of seeing, of thinking, and of acting in the world.

1

The Forest and the Trees

We all have the forest in our blood.

—Robert A. de J. Hart

In 1964, two scientists cut down a red maple tree in a North Carolina forest. They had with them a bottle containing a solution of radioactive calcium and phosphorus, two important plant nutrients. The two researchers placed the bottle so the solution would soak into the fresh stump but could not get directly into the surrounding soil, water, or air. Eight days later, 43 percent of all species within 22 feet (7 m) of the stump—almost twenty different tree, shrub, vine, and herb species—showed radioactivity in their leaves.[1] What might explain this observation?

The scientists believed that strands of fungi in the soil connected the plants to one another. They were right. Certain kinds of soil-dwelling fungi actually grow into the roots of plants, sometimes right into the cells of the roots. These fungi trade sugars made by the plants for nutrients and water brought to the roots by the fungi. This ecological deal making is a special cooperative relationship called a mycorrhiza (literally "fungus root," figure 1.1). Some mycorrhizal fungi have specific plant hosts. Others associate with a variety of plant species. Researchers have shown that mycorrhizas dramatically increase plant health and survival. They also link forest plants through their underground network of fungal threads.

Root grafting is another way plants connect. Roots from different plants often meet one another as they roam the soil. In the mid-1960s, two other

FIGURE 1.1. When fungi and plants form a mutualistic relationship we call them a mycorrhiza (literally "fungus root"). Mycorrhizas link forest plants together in a mutual support network that effectively makes the root mass of the forest a single functional unit. Mycorrhizas play critical roles in developing and maintaining ecosystem health, and the vast majority of plants form them. *Photo by Dr. Elaine Ingham, Soil Foodweb, Inc., used with permission.*

scientists found that more than 160 tree species can form root grafts with other plants of the same species when their roots meet. About one-fifth of those can form root grafts with other species in the same genus—white birch with yellow birch, for example. Some of these grafts can even occur between different genera—such as between birch and maple, or birch and elm.[2] The evidence shows that root-grafted plants form a mutual aid network. They share nutrients, water, and even hormones. The benefits? Sharing hormones can help ensure cross-pollination between trees by synchronizing the trees' flowering time, for example.

These two observations should radically change our view of forests, and forest gardens. As the first two scientists concluded, "It would seem logical to regard the root mass of the forest . . . as a single functional unit" creating "a 'mutual benefit society' . . . in which minerals and other mobile materials are exchanged between roots."[3] Imagine the eastern deciduous forest before European colonization: perhaps a single functional root mass from southern Canada to the Gulf Coast, and from the Atlantic to the prairies!

THE PRIMEVAL FOREST: A REMEMBRANCE

Now imagine this: You are walking through the primeval forest of eastern North America on a warm spring day, years before European settlers began cutting it down. Sunlight filters through leafless branches. The canopy arches far overhead. Trees of all ages surround you. In some cases, these beings tower to heights of over 100 feet (30 m), with ages of three hundred or more years. Trees 1 to 2 feet (30 to 60 cm) in diameter abound; mature by our standards, they are still young for this forest. Saplings and small trees wait in the shade for a chance to grow, or reach for the sun where one of the ancients has crashed down, dead from old age or storm.

The different kinds of trees amaze you. Craggy old oaks are dying back or broken in places. The ground under the straight-trunked hickories is littered with the remains of last year's nuts. Massive maples hover protectively over their many progeny: few of these thickly sown maple seedlings and saplings will survive to maturity. You see spreading butternuts, towering hemlocks, huge white pines, and chestnuts—chestnuts, those glorious trees whose presence is felt everywhere, whose nuts are the most important food for many of the forest inhabitants.

Small trees adapted to live their whole lives in the shade fill the space under the canopy: hop hornbeam with its flaky bark; clumps of ironwood with its smooth, muscled, bluish gray stems; and stands of witch hazel, still wearing the remnants of their small yellow fall flowers. Shade-tolerant trees such as beech and hemlock patiently wait for another gap to form near them so they can spurt another step closer to the canopy before the gap closes. Here and there you find clumps of shrubs, occasionally thick stands of them, all beginning to flower and leaf out before the trees take the sunlight away. The ground has an undulating, rough, hummocky appearance. This stems from the lifting, and then decay, of big root masses when trees fall. As a result, up to fourteen different wildflowers grow in every square yard of forest floor.[4] Each of these species has adapted to slightly different soil, light, and moisture conditions created by this "pit and mound" terrain.

It turns out that many of the herbaceous plants you see are even older than the aged trees scattered about. What looks like a colony of many plants is actually one living organism with numerous stems, many hundreds of years old. Each of these wildflowers comes to prominence and maturity at different times throughout the growing season. They make the best of the sun and space while they can, then make room for later bloomers. As you look closer, you see mushrooms popping up here and there. These are the only visible sign of the complex web of life below the ground that makes this system

FIGURE 1.2A. Contrary to popular belief, old-growth forest contains trees of varied sizes, species, and ages arranged at varying densities depending on site quality and successional history. Disturbance by natural forces and indigenous peoples also add to this natural variation. This figure shows a location in Petersham, Massachusetts before European colonization. Figures 1.2b and 1.2c show the same location in later years. *Photo of the Harvard Forest Dioramas by John Green, used by permission of Fisher Museum, Harvard Forest, Petersham, Massachusetts.*

function. The earth is soft and spongy. You grab some topsoil out of the leaf litter. You find worms, insects, salamanders, and roots of all kinds in the moist and musty leaf mold.

You keep walking. You become aware of the incredible variety in the structure of the woods. In some places, huge old-growth trees shelter thin shrub and herb layers in the dimness. Most people imagine the primeval forest like this: a dark forest of big trees. However, patches of many kinds surround these dark woods—open clumps of bigger trees, dense stands of younger trees, big areas with trees of many ages, and glades at large openings in the canopy. Curiously, there are occasional pure patches of white pine. This is unusual because white pine is sun loving. A large area would need to have been completely cleared at some point for a patch like this to grow. There are large, light-filled savannas of old oaks, butternuts, and hickories—well spaced so they have rounded crowns and their canopies cover less than half the ground—with shrubs, grasses, and wildflowers growing in the sun between them. Wet soils grow thickets, often with white cedar, red maple, and other wet-tolerant trees emerging from the brush. In a few places, large meadows open before you, full of grasses and wildflowers. Occasionally, some fields appear to be returning to forest. Here, young white pines in abundance, shrubs, and sapling trees are overtaking the grasses and flowers that share the space.

You come upon a recently burned savanna, the ground blackened and charred. The air is warmer here in the spring light. You look up—and the butternut trees are in full bloom! Why has this place been burned? You realize that the forest floor has been relatively open and passable, not thick with brush, wherever you have gone, except in the swampy thickets you have avoided. Could fire be the reason?

GARDENING THE FOREST

Recent studies indicate that the "wild, untamed landscape" we imagine the earliest colonists found was, at minimum, strongly human influenced. In fact, the primeval forest was probably a *managed ecosystem*.[5] Some authors go even further. They suggest that the eastern forest "was, and is (except in its remotest parts) a cultural phenomenon," even before European colonization.[6] The native peoples had widespread influence on their habitat besides the direct impacts of their farming. They managed the forest to increase and diversify their food supply, and to improve their living conditions in general.

Researchers have increased their estimates of the precontact North American population from 1 million to between 9.8 and 12.25 million. They think the majority of these people lived in the eastern forests, mainly in the Mid-Atlantic region and the South. "In 1492, parts of the eastern seaboard had population densities in excess of those of the closely settled parts of Western Europe."[7] Clearly, populations at such densities will have major influence on the landscape.

Many of these peoples used "swidden" (also known as "slash-and-burn") techniques to clear forest patches and grow corn, beans, squash, and other crops. After a few years of cultivation exhausted the soil, they would let the clearings revert to forest to rebuild its fertility. Sometimes they returned to clear and replant after a ten- to twenty-year fallow cycle. If not, fast-growing white pine could become dominant in these areas, creating the almost-pure stands mentioned earlier. Some studies estimate that slash-and-burn management would have affected between 22 and 28 million acres (9 to 11 million ha) of land at any one time. That's nearly 20 percent of the total land area currently farmed in the easternmost thirty-one states of the United States.[8] We should not overlook the importance of these cultivated crops in the native diet, or their effects on the forest. However, researchers have most frequently ignored native agroforestry practices, and we know the least about them.

Native agroforestry yielded a whole host of products from trees and their plant and animal associates with relatively low labor requirements. Temperate deciduous forests are, or were, the home of "a range of species second only to the tropical rain forest" in their diversity.[9] The first white settlers were astonished by the abundance of fish, game birds, large mammals, and "wild" foods found here, at least during the growing season. American Indians used much of this diversity in their diets on a seasonal basis. How was this abundance generated and maintained, particularly in the face of the population densities we now know existed?

Research shows that fire was a major management tool of the native peoples of North America.[10] Some reports suggest that New England Indians burned groves of butternuts and hickories in the spring on a three-year rotation to blacken the ground and increase air temperatures at flowering time.[11] This increased the number of pollinated flowers, producing more nuts. The savannas and prairies the colonists found in the midst of the forest were probably also intentionally created with fire. "One school of thought . . . suggests that most of the prairie openings and even large anomalous areas like the Kentucky Blue Grass country [were] a consequence of Indian burning."[12] These openings provided great habitat for vital native foods, including nuts and acorns produced by savanna trees, not to mention blueberries, raspberries, filberts, and large game. Fire also reduced the prevalence of human and plant diseases and pests. It reduced the amount of brush cluttering the forest floor, improving the ability of hunters to catch their prey. Fire also created more patches and "edge" habitat, which produces abundant deer browse, and therefore more deer for harvest. In fact, many of the game species most frequently used by the Indians prefer habitats that are dependent on or enhanced by fire. These facts appear to be true across North America. In California, for example, we now know that the highly productive oak woodlands found by colonial settlers degrade without careful burning. They therefore lose productivity, diversity, wildlife value, beauty, and usefulness to humans.[13] These oak groves were the primary source of staple crops for the California Indians, who ate acorns in abundance.

Much more acreage was probably under agroforestry management using fire than was affected by swidden agriculture. Then again, the two areas probably overlapped, with fallow clearings providing berries, hazelnuts, useful herbs, and wild game habitat, among other things. It is easy to imagine the difficulty the colonists would have had even *seeing* this form of agriculture, given their cultural mind-set. But, agriculture it was.

Clearly, this continent's aboriginal peoples strongly influenced the ecology of their homes. They deliberately altered the ecosystem to provide more tree crops and other "wild" crops, to make hunting easier and game more plentiful, and to eliminate pests and diseases. They created varied habitats for themselves and other forest dwellers. They caused the land to produce abundant and diverse foodstuffs, medicines, fibers, fuel, and animal food—everything they needed to survive. In essence, the native North Americans were *gardening* on a grand scale. They were participants and "guiders of change" in their ecosystem. Their "garden" was beautiful, productive, and sustainable over the long haul.

FOREST REMNANTS

These images of a healthy forest and its human inhabitants contrast starkly with current reality. We have fragmented and divided the "single, functional root mass" of eastern North America with our roads, our fields, our dwellings, and our places of manufacture, commerce, and leisure. In some places, only remnants remain. We have transformed a wooded landscape into the urban landscape and suburban yards of the country we all know.

The precolonial forest was a mosaic of many different patches. Yet it had a lot of "forest interior" habitat. It changed slowly and had only periodic, mostly small-scale disturbances. Even the indigenous people's influence, larger than previously thought, preserved the forest as the dominant ecosystem. The most radical change within the eastern deciduous forest, and most other forests the world over, is this: rather than humans living in a forested context, forest remnants stand as stressed and disconnected islands within a human cultural context. Today's forests consist mostly of second- or third-growth stands. These smaller, generally less healthy trees grow in degraded soil and plant communities. The fragments contain diminished biological diversity. They cannot as easily absorb and hold rainfall or perform other essential ecological functions. Atmospheric changes due to human impacts also threaten forest health.[14]

Between the 1600s and the 1800s, settlers cut about 80 percent of the forest east of the Appalachian Mountains. They turned this land into fields, pastures, villages, and cities. In the 1800s, the wave of deforestation moved west across the Appalachian Mountains into the Ohio and Mississippi River valleys. The East then began undergoing succession, a process in which plant communities successively change from field back to mature forest. However, it takes centuries for forests to recover from intense deforestation through natural succession. Even the "large" tracts of forest that now exist are mere shreds of the former fabric. Most areas were farmed at one

FIGURE 1.2B. Forest clearing by European settlers eventually resulted in 80 to 90 percent of precolonial forests being cut. Pasture management and cultivation largely destroyed the seed banks of native flora. This is the same location as that shown in figures 1.2a and 1.2c. *Photo of the Harvard Forest Dioramas by John Green, used by permission of Fisher Museum, Harvard Forest, Petersham, Massachusetts.*

time. Cultivation, planting of pasture species, and grazing destroyed whatever seed banks of native plant species the soil once held. Herbaceous diversity is therefore low in most second-growth forests. In addition, some biologists estimate that to have real wilderness, contiguous undisturbed habitat (with no roads, fields, and so on) must amount to more than 1 million acres (400,000 ha). Otherwise there isn't enough forest interior habitat to support the species required. No such areas of unfragmented forest remain in the eastern United States.

Fragmentation increases forest edge, in a pattern different from native agroforestry. The contrasts are greater, and the edges more abrupt. The openings are larger, and the remaining forest smaller. All this results in more sunlight, drier conditions, stronger winds, and different animal, insect, and plant populations. Frequent major disturbances discourage species adapted to less disturbance and shadier and moister conditions—generally natives. They favor disturbance-adapted opportunist species, mostly nonnatives (see page 18). For instance, sometimes plant communities will now shift from forest or preforest conditions to a community dominated by vines, such as Oriental bittersweet (*Celastris orbiculatus*) or kudzu (*Pueraria lobata*). These vigorously expansive and highly dispersive vines thrive in edge environments and forest remnants and can shade out trees, young or old.

Loss of forest cover also alters the local and regional climate, increasing temperature and moisture extremes in the landscape. Forests significantly

FIGURE 1.2C. After farmland abandonment in the 1800s, successional development began once again. In many parts of the eastern forest, white pine (*Pinus strobus*) spread rapidly due to its light, wind-dispersed seed and sun-loving niche. This was then cut in the early 1900s, allowing hardwood trees to take over. Despite the relatively rapid reestablishment of native forest trees, the herbaceous flora has not yet fully recovered from colonial clearing. This is the same location as that shown in figures 1.2a and 1.2b. *Photo of the Harvard Forest Dioramas by John Green, used by permission of Fisher Museum, Harvard Forest, Petersham, Massachusetts.*

moderate winter temperatures and winds and reduce summer temperatures. Forests store water in the soil and in their biomass, or living matter. They release large amounts of water into the atmosphere, thereby increasing rain and dewfall downwind. Forests thus moderate both flood and drought. They help sustain "base flow" in streams and rivers. The great deforestation of the nineteenth century caused many streams and springs to dry up and disappear from the face of the land.

In addition, more edge habitat favors animals such as deer. Ecologists call deer a "keystone species," because their population can determine the species composition and vegetation architecture of the plant communities within which the deer live. Many suburban areas now support deer populations as high as ten times that of rural forests. High deer populations do major damage to farms, gardens, and landscape plantings. Worse, in some cases these beautiful animals "have literally browsed away the next generation of the forest by consuming all the seedlings of many trees, shrubs, and herbaceous species."[15] Squirrels share a similar story, except that they eat the seeds of many trees. High squirrel populations may thereby reduce or prevent forest regeneration.

Another probable keystone species that most people know nothing about is now absent from

Feature Article 1:
Natives and Exotics: Definitions and Questions

In this book, we will use the words *native, exotic, nonnative,* and *opportunist* many times. It is appropriate, therefore, that we define these words as best we can.

For the purposes of this book, a *native* species is one that established itself on the North American continent before European contact. We may also call these species *precolonial.* An *exotic* or *nonnative* species is therefore one that arrived in North America since European contact. For practical reasons, the latter definition includes species that arrived as imported species (intentionally brought by humans) and as immigrants (arriving "naturally" under their own steam or through accidental introduction). We will use the term *opportunist* to denote plants that tend to:

- disperse quickly and widely using agents such as wind- or animal-borne seed (dispersive plants);
- vigorously expand in size or area covered through vegetative propagation (expansive plants); or
- combine the above two traits.

Plants that persist strongly in the face of our attempts to eradicate them (persistent plants) can also cause us problems, especially when combined with opportunism. However, persistence is not necessarily an indicator of opportunism. Opportunist species may be either native or exotic, but the opportunists of most concern these days are those that people call "invasive exotics."

If you think about it, you will doubtless realize that these definitions of *native* and *exotic* leave much to be desired. They define as "native" a plant that arrived on a bird's back and established itself the week before Columbus landed. Meanwhile, one that arrived the same way the week after would be "exotic." They classify as "native" plants grown by American Indians, such as corn, squash, or other crops, when they actually originated in Central America. They also define horses as nonnative here, even though the horse, and the camel, originally evolved in North America. Luckily for both these species, they migrated to other continents before becoming extinct here. These definitions also beg the question whether five hundred years from now we might reasonably consider species we now call exotic to be native, or whether exotics will always be exotics, no matter how long evolutionary history goes on from here. The fact is that species disperse into new habitats all the time, even across large expanses of ocean. They also naturalize and integrate into new ecological communities all the time, and they do so at different rates depending on the characteristics of the species, the environment, and the ecosystem's other inhabitants.

Clearly, for these and other reasons, the terms *native, exotic,* and *nonnative* have scientific and practical problems that make their value and meaning doubtful. Nonetheless, they are in widespread use. They acknowledge a key event in North America's geological and ecological history: the "invasion" and dominance of European colonists, cultures, and plant and animal species. Whether these words and their definitions blind us or lead us to greater understanding is, we currently believe, open to question. We need a scientifically functional definition of nativeness, not an arbitrary one with questionable usefulness. Unfortunately, this is well beyond the scope of this book, if it is possible at all.

We use the word *opportunist* rather than *invasive* for a number of reasons. The most important is that the word *invasive* assigns to plants alone a set of behaviors that clearly can arise *only* from the interaction between plants and their environment. The word *opportunist*, however, directs some attention to the role played by the context in which the plant finds itself. *Opportunist* also removes the unconscious sense of threat from the discussion; if you look in the dictionary, you will see that *invasion* at least implies aggression, attack, injury, and encroachment. Such insinuations muddy the waters of inquiry into what is really going on. They confuse unspoken human values with biological phenomena. We cannot credit these behaviors to plants: they are projections of human consciousness. This is why we use the terms *dispersive* and *expansive* to describe the behaviors of plants: they are more accurate and more useful, and they are free of bias and insinuation.

We raise these issues because of exploding concern over native plant conservation and the rise of "invasive exotic" species. We share these concerns. However, just before publication, we read a series of books (see page 156) that raise serious questions about the paradigm now used to describe and define native, exotic, and invasive plants. We cannot resolve the questions raised before publication of this work. Consequently, we have settled on the definitions above and dropped the word *invasive* from general use until further notice. We discuss some of these questions later, after clarifying some key ecological concepts (see feature articles 3 and 5, pages 156 and 282). In the meantime, know that when we say "opportunist" we are talking about at least some of the same plants that others call "invasive," and recognize the words *native*, *exotic*, and *nonnative* as red flags for an area of our learning, and of ecology, that is ripe with opportunities for deeper knowledge. And stay tuned! Not only are ecosystems dynamic and ever changing, but so is our understanding of them.

North America. Before European colonization, the passenger pigeon (*Ectopistes migratorius*) population reached perhaps three to five billion birds—25 to 40 percent of the bird population of the United States.[16] They traveled in flocks so huge that early European explorers wrote that their passing overhead would darken the sky for hours—even days, according to John James Audubon. When they found an area with abundant food, these flocks would select a roosting area in a forest stand and leave droppings on the forest floor that reached several inches in thickness in short order.[17] Imagine the nutrient value such deposits represented! Even if a flock had roosted in a given spot once every ten or twenty or fifty years, the effects on forest health and productivity would have been enormous, completely altering soil ecology and fertility over the long run. Some authors believe that the decimation of the passenger pigeon population could account for much of the general decline in forest health throughout eastern North America. It stands to reason that increased susceptibility of various tree species to insects and diseases could result at least partly from poorer tree nutrition caused by the extinction of this species.

Of course, decreasing air quality probably also plays a major role in reducing forest health. Too much ozone in the lower levels of the atmosphere resulting from pollution damages plants and plant communities, particularly in the Southeast. Not enough ozone in the upper atmosphere resulting from chlorinated hydrocarbon releases degrades forest health, as well as human health, by causing higher ultraviolet radiation from the sun. Acid rain has negative impacts on soil and plant health. Few of us realize, though, that the nitrogen compounds ("NO_x") that help cause acid rain also enrich soil nitrogen levels to as much as three times the normal amount. This reduces the lignin content, and therefore the strength, of woody plant tissues. It increases their susceptibility to diseases and insects. It amplifies the ability of fast-growing opportunist species to survive and reproduce compared to slow-growing

Box 1.1: Shifting the Burden to the Intervenor[18]

*The burden of maintenance and ongoing functional integrity
shifts to those who intervene in self-regulating systems.*

This principle applies to any system, be it agricultural, ecological, physiological, psychological, or social. An "intervenor" stands outside an existing system and doesn't respect or understand how the system works. The intervenor therefore interferes in the system's healthy functioning, sometimes unknowingly or for fun or profit, but often in an attempt to "fix" perceived problems. The unintended consequences of this intervention throw the system out of balance, disrupt essential functions, and increase the system's reliance on intervention to maintain balance. The intervenor then bears the burden of maintaining the system's integrity. If the intervenor does not take on this responsibility, the system degenerates. Even if the intervenor *does* take on the responsibility, the system's ability to maintain itself may *still* degenerate. The interventions required to maintain balance thus often become increasingly intensive. The illusion of separation and lack of understanding cause increased work, reduced richness, and the loss of natural capital.

A good example of shifting the burden is the use of pesticides in agriculture. A farmer perceives a pest problem and intervenes in the system by spraying chemicals. This kills not only the "target" pest but also other insects and microbes in the soil and vegetation. The ability of the system to maintain balance and control on its own then decreases. So another pest problem crops up, the farmer sprays again, and the cycle continues. For a time things seem better. In reality they get worse and worse. More pesticides, and stronger ones, become necessary over time. If the farmer stops spraying, the pests will increase out of control, and he or she will lose the crop, so addiction has set in. It takes time, effort, and understanding to rebuild a self-maintaining system. However, it takes much more effort to keep intervening over the long run.

Our interventions in the forests of eastern North America occurred for different reasons, but the results are the same. Disrupted ecological function has reduced the ecosystem's ability to maintain itself. In this case, however, we have not taken on the burden of caring for the community. The resulting declines in natural capital have been enormous. By gardening responsibly, each in our own yards, we can rebuild healthy ecological systems in our neighborhoods. By designing and creating forest gardens that mimic forest ecosystems, we can learn how to rebuild and reinhabit a self-maintaining landscape.

species. Research also shows that excessive soil nitrogen increases the succulence of vegetation. This increases deer populations, further contributing to the deer problems discussed earlier.

The combination of these and other issues has led Leslie Jones Sauer, in her book *The Once and Future Forest*, to state that "the forest of five centuries past is largely gone, and the recoverability of its remnants is, in fact, very much in question. . . . Despite the remarkable resilience of nature and the repeated seeming recovery of the landscape, the forest is losing its ability to replenish itself."[19] As the species that intervened in these ecosystems, we humans now carry the burden of responsibility to maintain and restore the ecosystem that sustains us (see box 1.1). Whether we proactively pick up that responsibility and carry it out faithfully will decide the course of history and evolution for many species for many generations to come. Unfortunately, we seem not to be doing this in the places where we now live, work, and garden. In fact, quite the opposite is true.

SUBURBAN ECOLOGY

Human-created landscapes now dominate large areas of the planet, particularly in the industrialized nations. Despite that fact, little serious ecological study has taken place in the world's suburban ecosystems.[20] Even in these days of relatively strong environmental concern, we design these landscapes with a completely different set of goals in mind than ecological health and food production. All of the issues discussed concerning forest remnants apply to suburban woodlands. But what of the cultural landscape? What kind of ecosystem have we created there?

Imagine the typical suburban scene. Each home has its separate lot, whether big or small. The homes usually sit far from the street. The street is often the only space owned in common by the community. Surrounded by other homes, the residences are separated from commercial and manufacturing "zones." The property lines and streets are laid out such that the only, or the safest, way to get to work or school or to meet basic needs is via gasoline-powered transport. This results in a much greater need to pave over the land. Unburned hydrocarbons and other air pollutants from auto exhaust fall back to the earth and lead to "oiling" of urban and suburban soils, making them more resistant to rainfall absorption, among other things.[21]

Rain falls and runs off roofs, pavement, compacted lawns, and "oiled" soils. It flows into gutters and street sewers, then into streams and rivers, with little making its way into the groundwater. Water is pumped in from across town, with a large proportion of it used for irrigation (30 to 60 percent of urban water)[22] and for flushing toilets (40 percent of average residential use). Sewage is pumped out to somewhere else, the nutrients dumped into streams or rivers after partial treatment. Sometimes the sewage is partially treated and the nutrients flow into groundwater via septic systems. Leaves are raked up and burned, landfilled, or piled away from the soil and plant roots that need them. Fertilizer is produced far away, shipped to the area, and purchased before application to the soil. Consumer goods are manufactured outside the region, shipped in, and purchased. Garbage (and recyclables) are placed on the street and taken "away."

Small woodland islands are surrounded by roads, cars, and buildings, or trees are scattered, often with only lawn beneath them ("woodlawns"). The houses are surrounded by landscapes full of plants mostly from distant places with little or no evolutionary history in their current locale. Many offer little food or shelter for beneficial insect populations or birds, among other things. Insecticides, herbicides, and so on, whether "organic" or "chemical," are produced far away and shipped in for purchase. Garden plants are propagated outside the region and shipped in. Most plants are "ornamentals," "weeds," or unattended escapees, almost all inedible. Food is produced elsewhere and shipped

FIGURE 1.3. As the human population grows and people move out of the cities, suburban development is fragmenting the second- and third-growth forests that have grown since the previous century. This land use tends to introduce exotic species, increase the amount of edge, and otherwise alter the overall landscape mosaic. It also gives each family access to a small piece of land with which to grow food, experiment with forest gardening, and attempt to restore healthy ecosystem function. *Photo by Dave Jacke.*

in. When people have food gardens, they usually are tucked out of sight, out of mind, and out of view of the neighbors. They rely on external inputs of energy, nutrients, insect and disease controls, and water and are based primarily on annual plants. For some reason, growing food is considered unsightly, unseemly, possibly antisocial, and in some towns and cities, illegal!

The tremendous infrastructure we have built in our cities and towns reflects a culture and horticulture of separation and isolation. Disconnection is a major theme of suburban life. Forest remnants are disconnected from each other. Both native and exotic plants are disconnected from their prior ecological context. People are disconnected from land. Residences are disconnected from work, commerce, and school. Television and the automobile disconnect people from each other. Culture is disconnected from agriculture. As we cut down and bulldozed the ecological communities that were here before us, we designed and built a human ecosystem that also militates against human community.

To create and maintain an ecosystem like this, homogeneity and standardization, that is, monocultures, are required. The gardens we find tend to be similar in species composition, no matter what the site conditions: "across a continent of breathtaking biological diversity, we have planted two or three dozen plants."[23] The plants in the well-kept lawns and landscapes are mostly genetically identical hybrids and cultivars, many sterile and not self-reproducing. Lot sizes are similar, even if ground conditions are not. The people in the houses tend to be of one class and ethnic group. The same foods are eaten everywhere across huge climate, landform, vegetation, and other landscape variations. We try to prevent dynamic change in our environment, so the monoculture extends even into the dimension of time. Finally, and probably most importantly, we apply the monoculture mindset to the uses or functions of things. We see and design systems in which each element has only one perceived relationship to the world around it, usually a single purpose for human profit, need, comfort, or convenience.

The scale and degree of monoculture and of the disconnections between design elements in suburban ecosystems is awe inspiring, and highly unnatural. While this may *look* like an orderly system to us, it is in fact *an extremely disordered system* from an ecological perspective.[24] Even if our gardens *look* like a forest, they probably don't *function* like a forest. Natural systems tend to be more diverse, more dynamic, and more variable. They must be if they are to survive and thrive. Materials, nutrients, and water in human systems tend to flow in linear fashion. In ecosystems things flow in cycles and circles. Every living and nonliving thing has a whole universe of functions in the natural world: trees function as soil holders, wildlife homes, air cleaners, rainmakers, organic matter sources, nutrient cyclers, soil porosity improvers, microclimate moderators, and thousands of other things, not just as lumbermakers or shadegivers. The disorder we continue to create requires absolutely huge amounts of energy and work to maintain. It also creates tremendous amounts of pollution and waste. Just the nutrients wasted in the system described above are amazing, not to mention the energy, the water, the labor, the intelligence, the lives, and so on. All this because we simply fail to see each part of the ecosystem as multifunctional, interconnected, dynamic—and worthy of respect.

Our biggest mistake is that we see ourselves as separate from the natural world. We then project that sense of separation onto every other living and nonliving thing with which we interact.

GARDENING IN THE INDUSTRIAL IMAGE

The farms upon which we all depend for food rely almost exclusively on crops requiring intensive inputs of seed, fertilizer, energy, and equipment.

These inputs all come from distant parts of the planet. Our food is shipped back and forth across the globe at high ecological cost. Almost always there is bare soil in the farm fields, and bare soil is damaged soil. These fields usually contain just one plant species at worst, at best ten or twenty. All or virtually all of these are annual plants, and almost all of them are genetically identical hybrids produced far away and "engineered" to require inputs of industrial energy, chemicals, tools, and techniques. Ecologically, the toll of modern agriculture includes:

- lost topsoil (some say topsoil is the largest U.S. export by weight);
- lost genetic diversity in seed crops;
- depleted water resources;
- chemical contamination (of water, soils, food, workers, and wildlife);
- increasingly pesticide-resistant "pests" and "weeds";
- and ten or more calories of energy expended for every calorie of food produced.[25]

The same orderly disorder, disconnected thinking, and monoculture mind-set pervades modern industrial agriculture and creates work, waste, and pollution.

Most home food gardens are miniature versions of large-scale farms, with large inputs of energy, labor, and materials. More people are composting now than were two decades ago. This is an improvement, but it still doesn't change most of the basic picture. If our far-flung industrial system crashed down around us, most gardeners would be left in the lurch without fertilizers, pesticides (organic or chemical), pumped water, and, most importantly, seeds. In addition, look at the structure of our gardens. Have you ever seen a natural temperate-climate ecosystem where everything was laid out in straight rows? Where everything was an annual plant, or even where annuals made up more than 20 percent of the plant community? Where vertical space was used sparingly, if at all? Large areas of a single species occupying a space in nature are very uncommon, and when found such a space rarely excludes all other species.

This is not to say that straight rows, for example, are necessarily bad. The point is to look at the assumptions behind the choices we make. We must look at the question of how we design our landscapes and grow our food from an ecological perspective. Home food gardening is an important means for reconnecting people to land. Unfortunately, the way we grow food most often further reflects the same design principles we have used, with devastating effect, in replacing the forests with suburbs, and in our large-scale agriculture system. These modern landscapes are all a direct result of the same linear, monoculture mind-set, a mind-set that flies in the face of ecological realities.

LESSONS LEARNED

What can we learn from all of the foregoing? Our first glimpse of fungi and plants working together points to our first lesson: the amazing interconnection inherent in healthy ecosystems. Cooperation between organisms is an essential aspect of how ecosystems work. The extent of that cooperation is much wider than most of us knew. Reverence and respect are natural responses to the awesome interconnections we now know to be present in nature.

Next, we find that most of our images of "old growth" forest were wrong. These forests were composed not only of large, old trees. They included mixed-age woods of all kinds and patches of different plant communities, including savannas and meadows. They were not homogeneous. The primeval forest was also dynamic, fluid, and changing, influenced heavily by human actions. In fact, native peoples were a keystone species in the primeval forest. Their behaviors created the forest as they knew it in significant ways, and vice versa. The humans and the forest were coevolving, mutually supporting participants in each other's lives.

When we contrast this participatory involvement with the way our culture has influenced the forest, we see total opposites. They cocreated interdependence, dynamically stable abundance, and functional diversity; we have created fragmentation, imbalanced excesses, and simple variety. We are still a keystone species in the forests of North America. Our actions and inactions are primary determinants of ecosystem health and evolution. When we look at how we have structured our own communities, we see the same disconnection we have created in the forest taken to an extreme. Hence, we have the attendant problems of waste, work, and pollution. The root of these design patterns lies in our monocultural way of seeing and thinking of things in space, in time, and in terms of function.

As Einstein said, we cannot solve these significant problems at the same level of thinking we were at when we created them. We must move beyond the monoculture mind-set, the world of separation. We must move into a world of participatory involvement and cocreative evolution with our ecosystem. We have to see both the forest *and* the trees. We all have the forest in our blood. We must begin to think like, act like, and garden like the forest.

1. Barbour, Burk, and Pitts, 1987, pages 139–40.
2. Barbour, Burk, and Pitts, 1987, pages 139–40.
3. Barbour, Burk, and Pitts, 1987, pages 139–40.
4. Sauer and Andropogon Assoc., 1998, page 12.
5. Cronon, 1983.
6. Williams, 1993.
7. Williams, 1993, page 29.
8. Williams, 1993, page 31.
9. Campbell, 1983, page 60.
10. Martin, 1996.
11. Davies, 1984.
12. Williams, 1993, page 31.
13. Martin, 1996.
14. Much of the information on the ecology of forest remnants is derived from Sauer and Andropogon Assoc., 1998. References for this section will be provided only for specific quotes.
15. Sauer and Andropogon Assoc., 1998, page 35.
16. Dept. of Vertebrate Zoology, National Museum of Natural History. 2001. The Passenger Pigeon. http://www.si.edu/resource/faq/nmnh/passpig.htm (accessed Setember 2, 2004).
17. Audubon, 1827–1838.
18. The name for this principle and its general definition came from Senge et al., 1994, page 139.
19. Sauer and Andropogon Assoc., 1998, pages 9 and 35.
20. One good treatise on the topic: McDonnell and Pickett, 1993.
21. Sauer and Andropogon Assoc., 1998.
22. Marinelli, 1998, page 26.
23. Marinelli, 1998, page 11.
24. Thank you Bill Mollison for this insight!
25. Soule and Piper, 1992, chapter 1. This is only one of many books cataloging the ecological crises of modern agriculture, but it's a good one. Other sources cite twenty calories of energy used per calorie of food.

Visions of Paradise

A thing is right when it tends to preserve the integrity, stability, and beauty of the biotic community. It is wrong when it tends otherwise.

—Aldo Leopold, *A Sand County Almanac*

By mimicking a natural vegetation structure, farmers can copy a whole package of patterns and processes that have developed and worked in an ecological or evolutionary time frame. With this structural approach, a multitude of beneficial processes can be incorporated into agroecosystems.

—Judith Soule and Jon Piper, *Farming in Nature's Image*

The ultimate goals of forest gardening are the growing of an abundant diversity of tasty, nutritious, and healthy foods and the cultivation and perfection of ecological ways of seeing, thinking, being, and acting in the world. The more we perfect these new ways of being, the better we will become at growing food in this new way. Ecology is the basis of edible forest garden design. Mimicry of forest structure and function is the essential strategy. What do these things mean?

This chapter's purpose is to explore in more detail the vision and purpose of edible forest gardening, both philosophically and practically. To do so, we will look at ecology in general, and mimicry in particular. We will outline the advantages and limitations of mimicry as a strategy, especially in terms of mimicking forests. What might such an approach look like? What does it require of us? What are we trying to achieve by doing it? What do we need to achieve to make it work? In this chapter, we will clarify our purposes, spell out our objectives, and review some images of what forest gardens might look like in different contexts. Then, in part 2, we can go on to examine the specifics of

what we can adapt from the structure and function of forests for our own purposes.

STUDY OF THE HOUSEHOLD: ECOLOGY DEFINED

People who analyze dreams often say that any house in a dream represents the self. In this spirit, let's define *ecology* from its Greek root words *oikos*, meaning "household," and *logia*, meaning "study of." Ecology studies the world of nature that is our household. It studies how we and other organisms make our homes in the world. It also studies the households of our bodies and how they relate to the world around us: what we eat, what we need, what we give back, and how we do these things. Technically speaking, ecology is "a branch of science concerned with the interrelationship of organisms and their environments" or "the totality or pattern of relations between an organism and its environment."[1] The first definition concerns the field of study itself. The second concerns the realm of the reality "in the field," and how a particular organism makes its way in the world. In this book, we will draw from the branch of science called ecology to understand the pattern of relationships that make up the forest, so we can create a similar pattern of relationships called a forest garden. If ecology is the basis of design, then what is the basis of ecological systems? The chapters that follow cover this topic, but we will summarize some key ideas here.

The first idea is that every organism on the earth is intimately and irrevocably connected to every other and to the nonliving elements of the planet. We unite with our environment to form communities and ecosystems, whether we know it or not. We cannot escape this reality any more than we can run from our feet. We can pretend our feet aren't there, but that does not alter the reality.[2] Species interrelate in varied ways, with varying degrees of intimacy and interaction. Later in the book we will discuss some of these relationships, and how to design the forest garden to make use of these interactions.

The second essential idea is that the structure of ecosystems gives them stability and resilience. These structures both cause and result from the way the system works. Many ecosystem structures remain invisible to us because they arise from the relationships between species, and between species and their environment. Not all are a physical structure we can see. We'll see it when we believe it, or rather, when we understand it. Once we see it, we can work with it.

The third key idea is that ecosystems change discontinuously and are complex beyond our understanding. Evolution occurs over long time scales (hundreds to thousands to millions of years), but ecosystems also change over the shorter frame of "ecological time." Each kind of change influences the other. Neither of these necessarily occurs at a constant rate. Discontinuous change means that periods of stability may be followed by major transformations in short order at any scale in time or space. In addition, the number of relationships among ecosystem elements is staggering, and

beyond our rational capacities to comprehend. We cannot understand ecosystems simply by breaking things down into their constituent parts and seeing how they work. Though analysis is an important and useful process, we must use additional tools to look at how the pieces relate to each other, and we must always bow to the awesome mystery of which we are a part. Therefore, we are participants in an ever-varying dance with an enigmatic partner. Sometimes we take the lead; sometimes we follow nature's lead. This dance can be harmonious and fun, if we follow certain guidelines. It can also turn into a riot. But we have to figure out the guidelines ourselves—our partner will only give us a few hints and respond to our moves. What kinds of hints do we have to go on?

Given the vast complexity of interconnection and the invisibility of many of the key structures of ecological systems; given the evolutionary timescales it takes for systems to generate these stabilizing structures; and given the short timescales in which we can act to make a difference in our own lives, it makes sense for us not to try to reinvent the wheel. Hence the idea of mimicry, an age-old strategy used by species across the globe for various reasons.

TALES OF MIMICRY

What is mimicry? Let's look at a couple of examples of mimicry in natural and human-manipulated ecosystems. Then we'll explore its advantages and limitations.

MONARCH AND VICEROY

The monarch butterfly (*Danaus plexipus*) is a beautiful orange-and-black native American butterfly of wide renown. Monarch caterpillars feed exclusively on plants of the milkweed genus (*Asclepias* spp.). The thick, milky sap of milkweeds contains highly toxic chemicals that defend the plants against generalist herbivores—plant-eaters that feast on pretty much whatever they can find.

Monarchs have evolved with the milkweeds so that the caterpillars can eat the poison, survive it, store it, and become toxic themselves: they turn the plant's defense to their own advantage. After achieving this feat, it becomes advantageous to have a bright, distinctive appearance. That way, birds, being visual predators, can identify the nasty-tasting monarch by its "warning coloration" and avoid attacking it. And so it evolved.

The viceroy butterfly (*Limenitis archippus*) is another beautiful orange-and-black native American butterfly. It is less common and a little smaller than the monarch. It has a slightly different pattern on its wings but is otherwise similar in coloration. The viceroy does not feed on milkweed and is not poisonous to its flying predators. However, natural selection has favored butterflies that look similar to the monarch, because this decreases their chances of being eaten by birds. Having lived for millennia in the same regions, the viceroy has evolved to imitate the monarch's coloration. It looks the same, so it gains some of the same advantage the monarchs have. What we can learn from this?

First, exact duplication of the monarch is not necessary to achieve the advantage sought. Sufficiency is the only test. Second, the mimic has its own purposes, which are different from those of the model, though similar. A key question then becomes how much mimicry, and of what kind, is enough to gain the desired advantages. Third, there are limits to mimicry. If the viceroy were to become too successful and too abundant, both the monarch and the viceroy would lose the protection offered by the monarch's warning coloration, and the system would evolve in some other direction.

The forest is our monarch. To design a forest garden, we must first know what a forest is and how it operates. Then we can gain its advantages without taking on qualities not suited to our purposes. We must therefore get clear on our purposes. We must also keep sight of the fact that we must keep the natural forests we have healthy. Their abundance is essential to ours. We cannot replace forest ecosystems and their functions with our limited capacities and different purposes. Neither can we expect our forest gardens to thrive without healthy forest around. Our garden ecologies need species from nearby natural areas if they are to maintain balance. We also need our models close at hand, so we can study and learn from them.

Our forest gardens are the viceroy. Based on our research and experience, Eric and I believe that we humans can design gardens that produce abundant food while maintaining the ecological benefits that natural systems confer. Our approach is to mimic the structure of the forest, for "when the whole structure is imitated, certain emergent properties that are expressed only at the ecosystem level can appear in agroecosystems."[3] A case study from the tropics demonstrates this.

Mimicking Forest Succession

When you cut down any forest, especially tropical forests, the soil's nutrients become more mobile. They rapidly become available during decomposition, wash away in the rain, and burn away in the sun. Intact ecosystems, on the other hand, tend to maintain their fertility over long periods, unless disturbed. While individual plants may be able to absorb and store nutrients, they cannot conservatively cycle them through the ecosystem on their own; the processes that exhibit the property of fertility maintenance emerge from the whole ecosystem (see "The Anatomy of Self-Renewing Fertility" in chapter 5 for details). Can a mimic of a natural successional community develop the emergent property of self-renewing fertility like the model?

To answer this question, a team of scientists clear-cut a tropical forest. They then measured the root mass of five different treatment plots of the resulting successions. The five treatments included:

- a control plot, where they prevented any regeneration;
- a natural succession, where they just let the forest grow back;

- an enriched succession, where they added seed stock to the natural successional sequence, but took no plants away;
- a maize and cassava crop treatment, where they grew each species in monoculture;
- and, of most interest to us, an *imitation* of the natural succession created by the researchers.

"The imitation of succession was an attempt to build an ecosystem that resembled the natural secondary growth of the area structurally and functionally, but using different species. In this study, the investigators replaced, as the plants appeared on the site, the naturally occurring species with morphologically similar ones (that is, annual for annual, herbaceous perennial for herbaceous perennial, tree for tree, vine for vine) not native to the site."[4] The control plot allowed them to compare the rates of nutrient loss and root growth for the full range of treatments.

This study showed that "the species-rich [natural] successional vegetation was effective in maintaining soil fertility." The mimic worked comparably, especially with regard to holding soil nutrients. "In general, the imitation of successional vegetation had the same structural and functional attributes as the diverse, naturally occurring successional vegetation. After four years, fine root surface area, which is critical to site restoration after disturbance, was very similar between the native and the successional mimic. . . . The successional vegetation and the imitation of succession had no species in common, yet they did not differ with respect to their impact on soil fertility."[5] The enriched succession performed better than any other treatment, retaining more nutrients and producing more root mass. Meanwhile, the corn and cassava monocultures and the barren control plot did the worst.

This work supports the idea that we can create working mimics of naturally occurring forest successions that exhibit similar properties, at an ecosystem level, as their models. Granted, this study focused primarily on soil fertility and root mass, and we intend to meet a more robust list of goals. However, we propose mimicry far more sophisticated than the relatively simple replacement of "annual for annual, herbaceous perennial for herbaceous perennial, tree for tree, and vine for vine." We suggest choosing plants that will perform specific functions within the mimic ecosystem to gain specific advantages. We also suggest mimicking specific structures at an ecosystem level to gain specific advantages. What are some of these advantages?

THE ADVANTAGES OF FOREST MIMICRY

To understand what we can gain from forest mimicry, let us compare some characteristics of "natural" ecosystems and modern agriculture using the Nature-Agriculture Continuum (see figure 2.1).[6]

Agriculture		Nature
High ——————— Fragility ———————		Low
Low ——————— Resilience ———————		High
Low ——— Species & Genetic Diversity ———		High
Low ——— Degree of Functional Interconnection ———		High
High ——————— Rate of Nutrient Flux ———————		Low
Fertilizers ——————— Nutrient Source(s) ——— Local, Recycled		
Solar/Fossil Fuels ——— Energy Source(s) ———————		Solar
High ——— Amount of Management Required —— Low/None		
High ——— Amount of Waste/Pollution ——— Low/None		
High ——— Amount of Food Produced ———————		Low

FIGURE 2.1. The Nature-Agriculture Continuum shows the characteristics of natural ecosystems and conventional agricultural ecosystems at the two ends of the spectrum. Agriculture's only redeeming characteristic is that it produces large amounts of food. Natural systems, on the other hand, have numerous desirable qualities but produce relatively less food. Organic agriculture attempts to move agriculture toward the "nature" end of the continuum, maintaining high food yields while reducing negative characteristics. Forest gardening starts at nature's end and attempts to increase yields while maintaining all of nature's desirable qualities. *Adapted from Soule and Piper, 1992, page 122.*

Box 2.1: The Principle of Functional Interconnection

The purpose of a functional and self-regulating design is to place elements or components in such a way that each serves the needs, and accepts the products, of other elements.[7]

Wild ecosystems contain webs of cooperation and interdependence that help generate the emergent system properties of stability, resilience, and harmony. Such healthy systems create no waste and generate no pollution because the inherent by-products of every living thing become food for some other living thing. They take no outside work to maintain because the networked system of elements regulates fluctuations in the ecosystem and its populations.

Our goal in forest garden design is to generate such self-maintaining, networked ecosystems. If the members of the garden ecosystem meet one another's needs and use one another's products, then we don't have to meet those needs or deal with those products, unless we want to. This is how we reduce our workload and place the maintenance and regulation of the system back into the system's own hands. In contrast, when the elements in our garden do not meet one another's needs, we must meet those needs ourselves, creating extra work for us. When these elements aren't using one another's products, those unused products become waste or pollution.[8] Applying the principle of functional interconnection shifts these burdens back to the garden, turns the burdens into benefits, and takes us out of the role of intervenor. We will discuss these ideas in more detail in part 2 of this volume and also in volume 2.

THE NATURE-AGRICULTURE CONTINUUM

Modern agriculture lacks resilience and displays fragility: it will not regenerate itself if disturbed (without effort on our part), and it is easily disturbed by drought, excess rainfall, insect population explosions, or, for that matter, a loss of fossil fuels. The monocultural lack of diversity militates against the system's ability to generate functional interconnection (see box 2.1), where different parts of the living system interact in a mutually supportive way. Nutrients move through current farm ecosystems at a high rate: "our modern agricultural practices break open nutrient cycles so that farmers must intervene and supply lost nutrients to prevent agroecosystems from running down."[9] We supply these nutrients with fertilizers. Farms therefore require fossil fuels to keep running, in addition to solar energy. They also require much work, not only on the farm, but also to mine resources in distant parts of the world and get them to the fields. Vast amounts of waste and pollution result. The saving grace is that modern agriculture produces a lot of food per acre—as long as fossil fuels remain available.

Natural ecosystems, particularly forests, show less fragility and more resilience than agricultural systems. They tend to develop high species and genetic diversity and a high degree of functional interconnection as they mature. Nutrients cycle and move more slowly through the system, at least in mature ecosystems. Only the sun powers natural ecosystems, with no input from fossil energy sources, except perhaps dead biomass. Natural systems require little or no management. They create little or no waste or pollution. We hope to gain all these advantages by mimicking forest ecosystems. The problem is that natural ecosystems—at least the disturbed ecosystems we now have—tend to produce relatively small amounts of human food per acre.

Conventional agriculture forms the conceptual basis for organic farming. In response to the drawbacks of industrial agriculture, organic farming attempts to move closer to nature on the continuum. Organic farmers apply selected natural processes to their work. Using composting, crop rotations, nitrogen-fixing plants, intercropping, biological pest control, and so on, organic agriculture begins to recreate nutrient cycles, functional interconnection, and species diversity without losing the high food yields. However, many drawbacks of modern agriculture persist in organic farming and gardening. The worst include dependence on fossil fuels and high maintenance requirements.[10] Organic farming does not mimic the structure of natural systems, only selected functions. Hence, many of the functions inherent in those structures are not available to organic farmers without humans doing the work somehow. Clearly, organic agriculture is still pretty close to the "agriculture" side of the continuum, but it is moving toward the "nature" side.

The American Indians based their agriculture on natural systems. Early settlers wrote in their journals about how hard it was to tell that food was growing in the Indians' cultivated fields. The complex mix of crops looked like a tangled mess to European eyes. The Indians' agroforestry systems—woodlands managed for increased food production and improved wild game habitat—were so integrated into their environment that we can barely call their work "agriculture." Few if any colonists recognized it as such. Therefore, the natives' strategy of "gardening the forest" was clearly way over on the "nature" side of the continuum. Though their sustainable form of land management exhibited the characteristics of natural systems described above, it produced only enough food for an estimated 100,000 people to live in all of New England,[11] compared to the millions who live there now.

We can creatively adapt from natural systems models. We can also go further than the Native Americans did. We can invent a wide range of forest gardens, from wild or semiwild foraging gardens to completely domesticated gardens that still behave like natural ecosystems. We have plant resources from around the world available to us. We have more tools. We have greater knowledge of breeding techniques, soil fertility, and so on. Edible forest gardens can therefore cover a wide range of the Nature-Agriculture Continuum, always favoring the natural end of the spectrum since they arise from natural models. Mimicking the forest should confer upon our gardens the qualities of low fragility, high resilience, diversity, functional interconnection, recycling and conservation of nutrients, solar economy, low management requirements, and minimal or no waste or pollution. The big question that remains, however, is whether we can create forest gardens that have these desirable characteristics *and* produce more food. How productive can a forest garden be? We don't really know. The idea is so new to the modern, nontropical world that we have found no published data documenting the productivity of temperate-climate perennial polycultures like forest gardens. Although we know of no studies, we do have some indicators.

FOREST PRODUCTIVITY

Plant photosynthesis turns solar energy into chemical energy in the form of complex carbohydrates. Ecologists call the total amount of sunlight captured by plants gross primary production, because plants function as the primary producers of any ecosystem. The energetic "costs of production" and "costs of living" are deducted from the total captured. The energy "profit" left over after paying these costs is called net primary production (NPP). It represents how much solar energy the plants transform into living matter, or biomass. Those of us who eat for a living know biomass in one form or another as "food." So the more sunlight plants turn into biomass, the more food is available to support all the nongreen species in the ecosystem, including us.

The estimated NPP of plant communities around the world varies tremendously (figure 2.2). The essential, intuitively obvious fact is that the better the growing conditions, the higher the NPP of the ecosystem. Deserts, limited by severe lack of water, and tundra, limited by severe cold and short

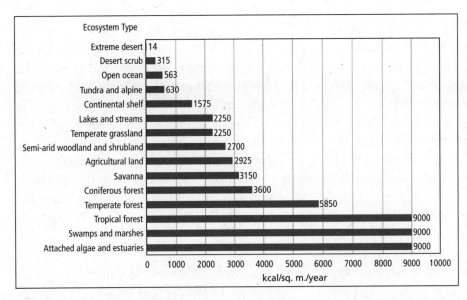

FIGURE 2.2. The net primary productivity (NPP) of different ecosystems on planet Earth. The numbers after the bars represent the amount of solar energy converted to biomass in thousands of calories per square meter per year (kcal/m²/yr). Notice that agricultural land captures only half the energy of temperate forest, and less than savanna. Woodland and shrubland here refers to communities limited by aridity to such open habitats, not the midsuccession stage in humid, temperate climates. *Adapted from Kormondy, 1976; data from Whittaker, 1970.*

growing seasons, have very low productivity. Tropical rain forests, with plentiful water and consistent warm temperatures, have the highest productivity. Even most of the moderately productive ecosystems—from temperate grasslands to conifer forests—have some form of limitation, climatic or biological, on their NPP. The thing to notice, though, is that agricultural land nets around 3 million calories per square meter per year, while temperate forests net *twice as much energy.*

Even a brief look at figure 2.2 demonstrates that temperate forests are among the most productive ecosystems in the world. Agricultural land cannot share that distinction. This is especially true because the net energy production of agricultural land turns negative (that is, more energy goes in than comes out) when we include the energy cost of fossil fuels in the equation. Yet the *yield* of agricultural land is high in terms of food. Just think: if we can get even half the percentage of useful energy—or yield—out of temperate forest ecosystems as we get out of farmland, we will get the same yield in calories per acre. Alternatively, we can keep our energy inputs low and get lower yields, but higher net production—more yield per amount of energy expended. Clearly, each forest gardener will make different choices about how much energy to put into his or her forest garden,

and how much he or she will get out. However, we contend that the amount of intelligence invested in the design and management of the forest garden has more effect on yield and net production than many other factors. Chapter 4 further discusses the fate of energy in forest ecosystems.

COOPERATION AND ADDITIVE YIELDS IN POLYCULTURES

We must make another shift in our thinking to see the value of forest gardening. We must change our concept of yield.

Let's say you grow raspberries in full sun as well as in partial shade under nearby fruit or nut trees. Your yield of raspberries per square foot will be higher in full sun. However, in the forest garden, we need to evaluate the yield of the *whole system*, rather than the yield of only one part of the system. In the forest garden, you may harvest raspberries, apples, pecans, hazelnuts, and various vegetables and herbs, for example. You may also "harvest" labor-saving "yields" like weed control, beneficial insect attraction, and soil fertility improvement from the garden community. This diversity of yields is fundamental to the forest garden idea. We must consider this when comparing forest gardening to other ways of growing food. Diverse yields in time and character offer "crop insurance" (rarely will the whole system fail even if one crop does). They also offer a steadier supply of food and other products throughout the year. Most importantly, diverse crops can result in higher net yields from the agricultural system. This is called additive yielding or overyielding.

The "three sisters" system used by the Iroquois exemplifies additive yielding. Professor Jane Mt. Pleasant of Cornell University studied these polycultures of corn, pole beans, and squash. She found that three-sisters plots grown in the Iroquois way yielded about 25 to 40 bushels of corn per acre (360 to 570 l/ha). This compares poorly to the 100-bushels-per-acre (1,400 l/ha) average for modern New York State farmers. Then she added the value of the beans and squash from the same plots. The total yield of the three-sisters system was 4.02 million calories per acre (9.93 million calories/ha), compared to monoculture corn's yield of 3.44 million calories per acre (8.50 million calories/ha). That's 17 percent higher, and a more balanced diet, we might add! In addition, the three-sisters crop had multiple benefits. The beans fixed atmospheric nitrogen to help feed the corn, or at least to reduce their competition with it. The squash, with its broad leaves, acted as a weed-limiting, soil- and water-conserving cover crop between the cornstalks. In a 1993 study, Mt. Pleasant adapted the three-sisters system to modern equipment. She found that per-acre corn yields were the same as yields of monoculture-cropped corn on the same soils, so there is a possibility of even greater additive yielding with current technology.[12]

The trick in creating additive yielding is finding plants that can live together without competing or that actually cooperate with each other. Competition lowers the yield of the system, while cooperation can result in additive yields like those we seek in our forest gardens. We will discuss cooperation and competition more fully in chapter 4.

The inherent advantages of natural ecosystems and forests in particular are clear: they generate emergent properties including resilience, diversity, interdependence, nutrient conservation, low maintenance, and lack of pollution. The productivity of temperate forest ecosystems, on the whole, cannot be discounted. All we have to do is find ways of using enough of the energy forests capture to make the effort worth our while without losing the ecosystem advantages outlined by the continuum concept. The key to maintaining the ecosystem advantages is to mimic the structure of forests. The key to making the natural productivity of forests available to us is to find a diversity of yields, including the cutting of labor and other costs, from the ecosystem. These two goals are mutually compatible and reinforcing.

THE LIMITATIONS OF FOREST MIMICS

The biggest limitation to forest gardening at this time is the relative lack of sufficient field trials demonstrating how to make it reach its full potential in different regions. The existing demonstrations show that forest gardens can work, and that they can probably work better than anyone has yet achieved. Hence, this book focuses on offering theory to back up and guide your practice. We hope you will join us in exploring and sharing what we learn with other practitioners.

Also, as stated earlier, we should not consider replacing natural forests with forest mimics. We need natural forests to help fill the gaps in our designs, to supply species, and to act as our models. We need them to express their own intrinsic value and purpose in a way we can never mimic or replace. To think we can supplant natural forests with artificial ones is a recipe for disaster—both for us and for all the other species that live in the forest. How we interact responsibly with natural forests to maintain, restore, and enhance them is a topic for discussion elsewhere.

Finally, we do not expect forest gardening to replace regular gardening or the foods we know and love. Just how far we can take forest gardening in supplying food for ourselves is not yet determined. Many of the foods we eat and enjoy come from sun-loving plants not bred to produce well in semi-shady or shady environments. Even the Native Americans grew annual crops in concert with their agroforestry systems. Forest gardening is another option for growing food and other products for human use. It is an option that can teach us things that may change the way we garden, the way we live, and the way we view ourselves in relation to our world. It's fun, too! Rediscovering and "improving" the plants that thrive in such environments remains one of our major tasks.

There is also something oxymoronic about the notion of forest gardens. We all know intuitively that a forest covers a large area. Contrast this with the word *garden*. It connotes something small—smaller than a farm even, which is usually still smaller than a forest, at least in New England. Whether or not the million-acre figure is truly the minimum viable size for a healthy forest, certainly the minimum viable size of a forest is much larger

than anything we would call a garden. Even large forest gardens will be too small to support healthy, genetically stable, reproducing populations of many plants and animals as a true forest should. Our gardens will rely on us, and on nearby natural areas, for some of those functions. Also, forest gardens will tend to have a lot more "edge" than will a healthy, mature forest, with little or no true interior habitat. Neither of these things is necessarily bad. In fact, the increased light from the edges should help increase the productivity of the forest garden (see chapter 3 for more on the "edge effect").

This brings us to another oxymoron about forest gardens. It turns out that the successional stage with the highest NPP is not the forest. The most productive stage is intermediate succession, before the tree canopy totally closes in, when trees, shrubs, herbs, and vines all live together (we'll discuss this further in chapter 6; see figure 2.3). If you want to design your forest garden for highest yield, technically

FIGURE 2.3. Midsuccession environments—from oldfield mosaics such as this through stages dominated by sun-loving pioneer trees—have higher net primary productivity than mature forests. Luckily, most of our developed woody crops, including apples, pears, peaches, apricots, cherries, persimmons, raspberries, hazelnuts, walnuts, and so on, are adapted to such habitats.

speaking, you will likely design and manage to maintain a *preforest* stage of succession. You can still create a "foresty" forest garden if you want. That might be beneficial for some crops, such as nut trees. But if what we design and plant isn't even going to be a *forest*, then why call it a forest garden?

Again, we are using the forest as a metaphor and a model. We intend to mimic natural plant communities in our agriculture. Forest gardens are most appropriate in regions where forests naturally grow. Some forest gardens will be in the forest. Some will not. Some will look like forests, some will look like shrub and small tree communities, and others will look like gardens. Some will be big; some will be small. What will tie them all together is the principles that underlie their design and management. They will embody the structure and function of forests at one stage of succession or another, and they should exhibit those qualities discussed in the Nature-Agriculture Continuum section: resilience, diversity, functional interconnection, self-maintenance, self-renewing fertility, solar economics, and food production. How might all this look in practical terms?

SPANNING THE GAMUT: IMAGES OF FOREST GARDENS

Forest gardens can come in a multitude of sizes, shapes, and habitats, from rural to urban, from open

FIGURE 2.4. An existing forest interior such as this has decent forest gardening potential. One should proceed carefully, however. We suggest using only native species if possible, especially if no opportunist plants are already in evidence. Also check out the uses and functions of all the existing species before you thin or clear, and watch for rare or endangered species.

shrubland or woodland to dense forest. Let's explore some of the possible permutations so you can have some pictures in your mind's eye as you learn the ecology that lies behind all of them. We intend what follows to be suggestive rather than prescriptive or comprehensive. Chapter 2 in volume 2 offers many more patterns and images for your forest garden.

FOREST GARDENS IN THE WOODS

If you already have woodland on your property (figure 2.4), you should first carefully inventory it. Then you can respectfully add to and subtract from the existing plant community to make your forest garden. If you choose minimal change in the existing woods, the main task might be the under-planting of perennial vegetables and medicinals such as edible violets (*Viola* spp.), ginseng (*Panax quinquefolia*), ramps (*Allium tricoccum*), giant chickweed (*Stellaria pubera*), and the like. Going a little further, you could thin the existing woods of understory plants that are less useful and add useful shrubs and shade-tolerant trees (figure 2.5), as well as woodland perennials. You could also create canopy openings and plant a successional sequence that will refill the gaps with useful species from the bottom up (figure 2.6). Such planting schemes can vary from wild, essentially unmanaged plantings, to semiwild, partially managed plantings, to highly maintained gardens-in-the-woods. It all depends on your goals, site preparation, species selection,

FIGURE 2.5. You can create a forest garden in existing woods by selectively thinning the current vegetation, then planting useful and functional woody and herbaceous understory plants. These could include edibles such as ostrich fern (*Matteuccia struthiopteris*), ramps (*Allium tricoccum*), and giant Solomon's seal (*Polygonatum biflorum* var. *commutatum*) or medicinals like ginseng (*Panax quinquefolia*). Woody plants that fruit at least a little in partial shade are currants (*Ribes* spp.), pawpaw (*Asimina triloba*), redbud (*Cercis canadensis*), and Oregon grape (*Mahonia aquifolium*).

FIGURE 2.6. A forest gap garden is another option in existing woods. Here, you cut a gap or clearing in the forest and replant with a range of plants, including species you hope will grow into the canopy such as northern pecan (hardy selections of *Carya illinoinensis*), persimmon (*Diospyros virginiana*), or mulberry (*Morus* spp.). The understory plantings can be sun-loving or partial-shade-tolerant species grown until the shade gets too deep or shade-tolerant edibles planted for the long haul.

and existing vegetation. An understanding of gap dynamics in mature forest succession will help you manage some such systems (see "Gap Dynamics" in chapter 6). In such cases, we strongly urge using primarily, if not only, native species to support and restore native ecosystem integrity—if natives will meet your design goals. See the discussion of natives and exotics in feature article 3 (page 156) for more information.

WOOD'S-EDGE FOREST GARDENS

An abrupt line usually marks the edge between forest and field in cultivated landscapes (figure 2.7). In this case, woods with tall trees stop right at the edge of a mown or cultivated area, with little or no transitional vegetation. In most natural landscapes, broad transition areas typify the edges between drastically different habitats such as field and forest. These "edge zones" usually contain myriad microclimates in a small space, which creates highly productive and highly diverse ecosystems. We can use such edges to advantage by planting both in the woods and in the field to create broad areas of transition with diverse useful species (figure 2.8).

"INSTANT SUCCESSION" FOREST GARDENS

When presented with an open field or lawn in which to plant your edible forest garden, you can

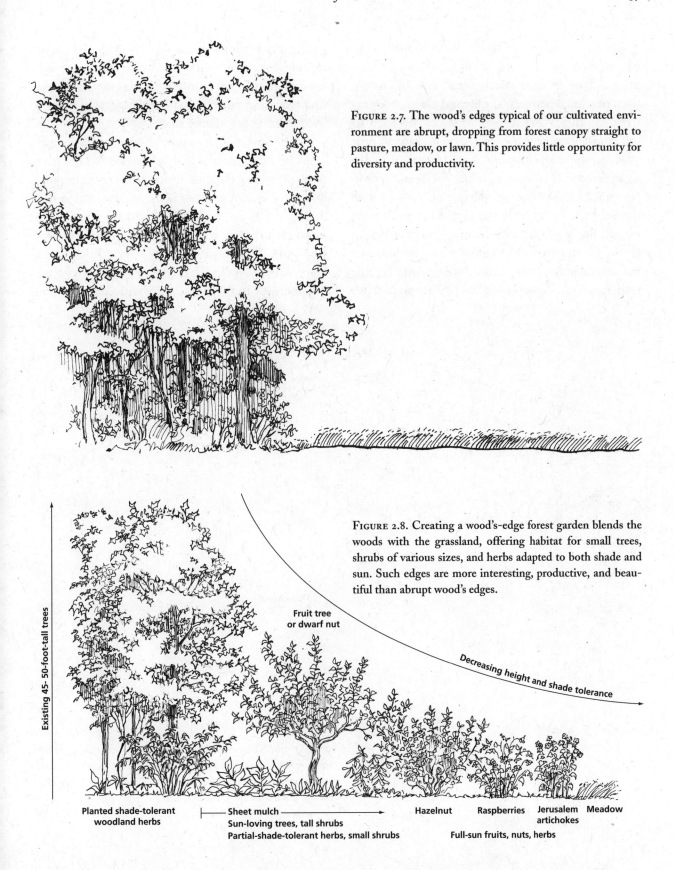

FIGURE 2.7. The wood's edges typical of our cultivated environment are abrupt, dropping from forest canopy straight to pasture, meadow, or lawn. This provides little opportunity for diversity and productivity.

FIGURE 2.8. Creating a wood's-edge forest garden blends the woods with the grassland, offering habitat for small trees, shrubs of various sizes, and herbs adapted to both shade and sun. Such edges are more interesting, productive, and beautiful than abrupt wood's edges.

Existing 45- 50-foot-tall trees

Fruit tree or dwarf nut

Decreasing height and shade tolerance

Planted shade-tolerant woodland herbs

Sheet mulch
Sun-loving trees, tall shrubs
Partial-shade-tolerant herbs, small shrubs

Hazelnut   Raspberries   Jerusalem artichokes   Meadow

Full-sun fruits, nuts, herbs

design the garden as an "instant succession."[13] In an instant succession, you plant all the species for each stage of the garden's successional development—from perennial herbs, to shrubs and herbs, to young trees, to "climax forest"—all at once. You then let the forest garden grow on its own, with a little guidance here and there to keep it headed in the right direction. Of course, to get the spacing right you must design backward in time step-by-step toward the present from the climax stage, or what we call the "successional horizon." You can then fit all the shorter-lived, sun-loving plants for the earlier stages around the longer-lived plants for the later stages as shown in figures 2.9 through 2.12.

Such a dense planting should need minimal maintenance for many years. Just make sure you plant enough groundcovers and sun-loving plants for the first years and put all the plants, especially longer-lived ones, at reasonable spacings.

Instant successions require a large initial investment of time, money, and information. They also need a lot more hands-on research to determine how they work best, but they are fun and interesting, too. If you have a large space to convert to forest garden, then you must be ambitious to undertake this all-at-once strategy. See "Microforest Gardens and Nuclei That Merge" on page 42 for a different way to fill a large space with forest garden.

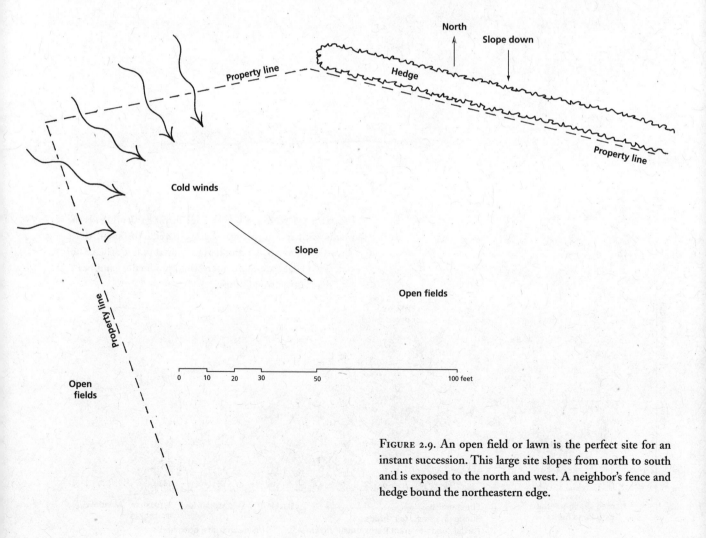

FIGURE 2.9. An open field or lawn is the perfect site for an instant succession. This large site slopes from north to south and is exposed to the north and west. A neighbor's fence and hedge bound the northeastern edge.

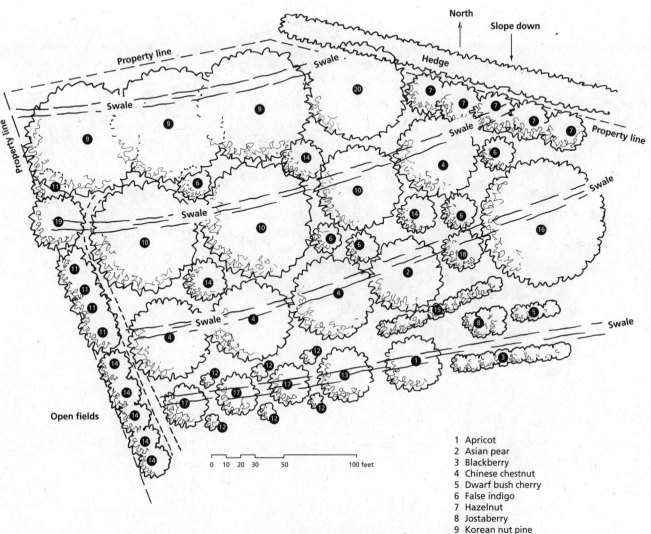

FIGURE 2.10. To design an instant succession you must begin at the end: the "horizon habitat." This helps you place the future canopy trees with proper spacing and end up with the habitat conditions you want. This plan expresses what you might expect in twenty-five years or more. The layout of a series of runoff infiltration swales, a windbreak of Korean nut pines, and the spacing of the main trees are the key factors determining the planting pattern. The smaller trees between the crop trees are nitrogen-fixing species.

1 Apricot
2 Asian pear
3 Blackberry
4 Chinese chestnut
5 Dwarf bush cherry
6 False indigo
7 Hazelnut
8 Jostaberry
9 Korean nut pine
10 Kaki persimmon
11 Northern bayberry
12 New Jersey tea
13 Peach
14 Pea shrub
15 Raspberry
16 Red mulberry
17 Semidwarf apple
18 Semidwarf European pear
19 Smooth alder
20 Swiss stone pine

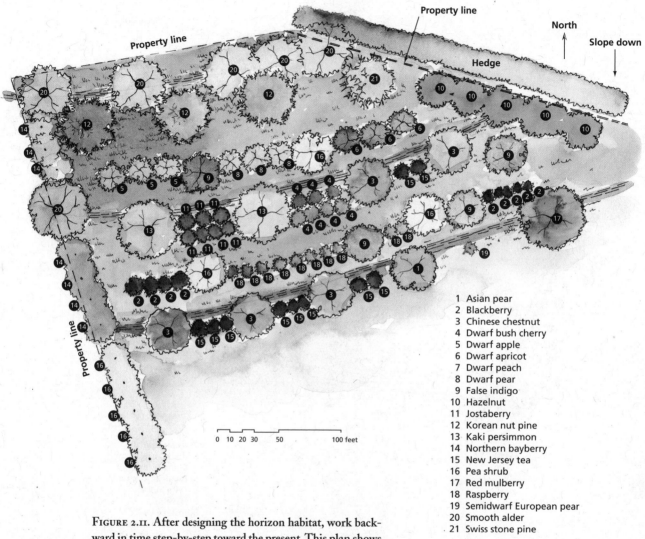

Property line

Property line

North

Slope down

Hedge

1 Asian pear
2 Blackberry
3 Chinese chestnut
4 Dwarf bush cherry
5 Dwarf apple
6 Dwarf apricot
7 Dwarf peach
8 Dwarf pear
9 False indigo
10 Hazelnut
11 Jostaberry
12 Korean nut pine
13 Kaki persimmon
14 Northern bayberry
15 New Jersey tea
16 Pea shrub
17 Red mulberry
18 Raspberry
19 Semidwarf European pear
20 Smooth alder
21 Swiss stone pine

Property line

0 10 20 30   50   100 feet

FIGURE 2.11. After designing the horizon habitat, work backward in time step-by-step toward the present. This plan shows
the forest garden at about fifteen years, with midsuccession
well underway. Short-lived and easily transplanted species
grow between the enlarging future canopy in spaces previously
planted in cover crops. The planting includes nitrogen-fixers
for soil improvement as well as intermediate-stage crops. The
Korean nut pines are beginning to shade out the faster-
growing soil-improving alder windbreak that served initially.

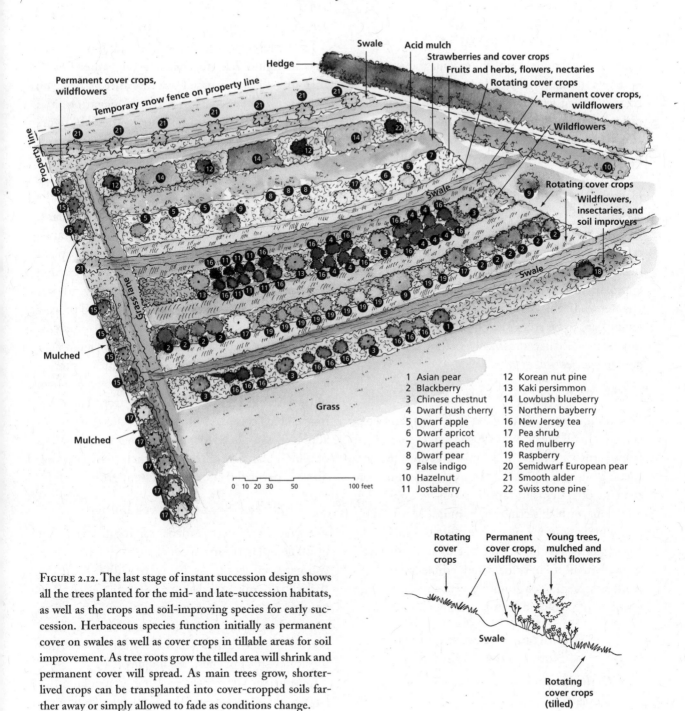

Permanent cover crops, wildflowers

Temporary snow fence on property line

Property line

Hedge

Swale

Acid mulch

Strawberries and cover crops

Fruits and herbs, flowers, nectaries

Rotating cover crops

Permanent cover crops, wildflowers

Wildflowers

Rotating cover crops

Wildflowers, insectaries, and soil improvers

Swale

Swale

Grass lane

Mulched

Mulched

Grass

1 Asian pear	12 Korean nut pine
2 Blackberry	13 Kaki persimmon
3 Chinese chestnut	14 Lowbush blueberry
4 Dwarf bush cherry	15 Northern bayberry
5 Dwarf apple	16 New Jersey tea
6 Dwarf apricot	17 Pea shrub
7 Dwarf peach	18 Red mulberry
8 Dwarf pear	19 Raspberry
9 False indigo	20 Semidwarf European pear
10 Hazelnut	21 Smooth alder
11 Jostaberry	22 Swiss stone pine

0 10 20 30   50   100 feet

FIGURE 2.12. The last stage of instant succession design shows all the trees planted for the mid- and late-succession habitats, as well as the crops and soil-improving species for early succession. Herbaceous species function initially as permanent cover on swales as well as cover crops in tillable areas for soil improvement. As tree roots grow the tilled area will shrink and permanent cover will spread. As main trees grow, shorter-lived crops can be transplanted into cover-cropped soils farther away or simply allowed to fade as conditions change.

Rotating cover crops

Permanent cover crops, wildflowers

Young trees, mulched and with flowers

Swale

Rotating cover crops (tilled)

Relay Plantings

Another option for establishing your forest garden is to plant sun-loving, early-succession species at first, and then let them grow and mature. As conditions change, you can plant more shade- and stress-tolerant species in the garden or replace functional, fertility-building plants with more useful crops. We call this style of succession relay planting because it is like a relay race, with the first set of plants "passing the baton" to the next set as the site becomes shadier or more fertile. This method is especially useful when the site has been highly disturbed by heavy equipment or otherwise approximates "primary succession" conditions (see chapter 6). In this case, the land needs much tender loving care to be at its most productive, and conditions must change drastically before some forest garden species will grow well.

Suburban Landscape Mimics

Urban and suburban dwellers with aesthetic concerns can still create a forest garden, even in their front yards (figure 2.13). In this situation, the aesthetic goals will influence the garden design more than in other circumstances, so make your plant selections with this criterion in mind. Many edible and otherwise useful plants are quite beautiful. The forest garden can fit into a range of aesthetic styles from formal to informal, and edible plants can work as screening or ground covers and can fit into a variety of color and texture schemes.

Microforest Gardens and Nuclei That Merge

If you have a tiny urban yard, or even a rooftop, you can still plant a forest garden. It might stretch the word *forest* to the breaking point, but you can apply the same design principles to a small space. You can use as few as two or three semidwarf trees and associated plants that fill a 30-foot (9 m) circle (figure 2.14). You could make such a minigarden almost any shape.

For larger spaces, you can use a pattern such as that in figure 2.14 to create forest garden nuclei that quickly achieve self-maintenance. Then you can grow them outward by propagating and dividing plants so they eventually merge (figure 2.15). You can propagate many forest garden plants by layering. This entails burying branches of the plant so that the middle of the branch is belowground and the end sticks out of the soil while the base is still attached to the mother plant. Eventually the belowground section of the branch will grow roots. You can then cut off the new plant and move it elsewhere, or leave it there to expand your planting. Other species spread by underground runners, and you can let this natural process occur to expand your forest garden nucleus. Practices like these mimic the overall development pattern of many plant communities during succession, and they can be great ways to grow your own nursery stock. They also reduce up-front labor and investment compared to instant successions. In addition, you can adapt your scheme to the realities of which plants you like and which plants do well on your particular site as the system grows.

Large-Scale Forest Garden

We have seen forest gardens ranging from 30 feet by 50 feet (9 by 15 m) to over 2 acres (0.8 ha). Once you get over about one-half acre (2,000 sq. m) in size, broad-scale establishment techniques come in handy. At the Agroforestry Research Trust in Devon, England, Martin Crawford has established a research and demonstration forest garden that illustrates some of these techniques.

Given that Martin was working all alone on this large-scale project, he figured it would take him ten years or so to fully plant the understory. Since he was going to propagate his own understory planting stock to save money, what he planted would depend on what he had available. He also figured that he would learn more about the best planting combinations for shrubs and herbs as he went through that

FIGURE 2.13. Forest gardens can serve perfectly well as ornamental gardens. When it is carefully designed, you can have your landscape and eat it too. This garden at Copia in Napa, California, includes a prune plum tree (*Prunus domestica*), a currant bush (*Ribes* sp.), borage (*Borago officinalis*), bronze fennel (*Foeniculum vulgare*), perennial kale (*Brassica oleracea*), and a ground cover of sweet woodruff (*Galium odoratum*) with a few coral bells (*Heuchera* sp.) mixed in. *Photo by Jonathon Bates.*

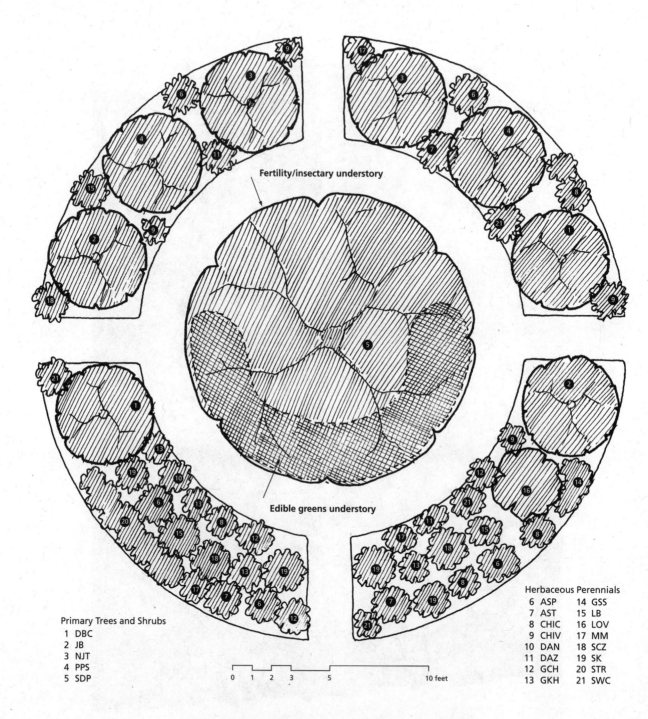

Fertility/insectary understory

Edible greens understory

Primary Trees and Shrubs
1 DBC
2 JB
3 NJT
4 PPS
5 SDP

0 1 2 3   5   10 feet

Herbaceous Perennials
6 ASP   14 GSS
7 AST   15 LB
8 CHIC   16 LOV
9 CHIV   17 MM
10 DAN   18 SCZ
11 DAZ   19 SK
12 GCH   20 STR
13 GKH   21 SWC

FIGURE 2.14. You can apply forest garden concepts at virtually any scale. A "microforest garden" can be as small as a single semidwarf fruit tree and its required rooting zone. Here multi-purpose plants abound in an attempt to meet as many ecosystem and human needs as possible in a 30-foot (9 m) circle. The suggested species shown are listed in table 2.1.

TABLE 2.1. Species list for the microforest garden shown in figure 2.14. Abbreviations for species shown on the plan appear in the first column. Abbreviations after the species names denote ecological functions and human uses as follows: APC=aromatic pest confuser; CUL=culinary; DA=dynamic accumulator; EF=edible fruit; EG=edible greens; ER=edible roots; ES=edible shoots; GC=groundcover; GN=generalist nectary; IS=invertebrate shelter; MED=medicinal; N2=nitrogen fixer; SN=specialist nectary; T=tea.

1. Paths, between Stones:

chamomile DA, GC, MED, SN, T
pussytoes GC, SN
thymes CUL, GC, GN, MED, T
white clover DA, GC, GN, IS, N2, T
white tansy yarrow GC, IS, MED, SN

2. Primary Trees and Shrubs:

DBC   dwarf bush cherry (*Prunus x jacquemontii* Joy, Jan, or Joel) EF
JB   jostaberry EF
NJT   New Jersey tea GN, N2
PPS   pygmy pea shrub N2
SDP   semidwarf pear, with multiple varieties grafted onto one rootstock for cross-pollination EF

3. Under Pear Tree:

• Edible Greens Understory:

chickweed DA, EG, GC, GN
miner's lettuce EG, GC
ramps APC, EG, ER, spring ephemeral
sorrels (*Oxalis, Oxyria,* and *Rumex* spp.) EG, GC, MED
spring beauty EG, ER, GN, spring ephemeral
strawberry saxifrage EG, GC, SN
violets DA, EG, GC, GN, edible flowers

• Fertility/Insectary Understory:

comfrey, large-flowered DA, GC, GN, IS, MED
Mahala mat GC, GN, N2
mountain avens GC, N2, T
pussytoes GC, SN
white clover DA, GC, GN, IS, N2, T

4. Herbaceous Perennials in Borders:

ASP   asparagus ES, GN, MED
AST   aster, New England IS, SN
CHIC   chicory DA, EG, GN, IS, MED, T
CHIV   chives APC, CUL, DA, EG, ER, GN, MED
DAZ   daisy, English EG, GC, IS, MED, SN
DAN   dandelion, thick-leaved DA, EG, GN, IS, MED, T
GCH   garlic chives APC, CUL, DA, EG, ER, GN, MED
GKH   good King Henry EG, MED
GSS   giant Solomon's seal EG, ER, MED
LB   lemon balm APC, CUL, DA, GC, GN, MED, T
LOV   lovage CUL, EG, IS, MED, SN
MM   musk mallow EG, GN, IS, MED
SCZ   scorzonera EG, ER, IS, SN
SK   skirret ER, IS, SN
STR   strawberries DA, EF, GC, GN, MED, T
SWC   sweet cicely CUL, EG, ER, IS, SN, T

5. Runners to Fill In around Herbs:

Any listed under "Edible Green Understory" or "Paths Between Stones" above, plus bellflower, Dalmation EG, GC, GN

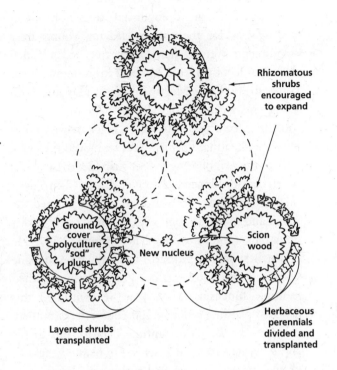

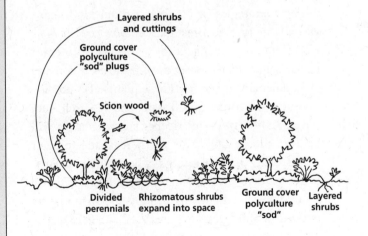

FIGURE 2.15. You can use a pattern such as the microforest garden in figure 2.14 to develop "nuclei that merge." Choosing plants that grow rapidly and divide or otherwise propagate easily can allow you to get one nucleus established in self-maintenance mode and then expand to other nuclei with the extra plants the system produces. This saves money, though it takes longer to get the whole system established.

process. Therefore, Martin planned the planting pattern only for his canopy trees ahead of time.

Martin first planted about 250 trees from about 150 species for the canopy, leaving young trees standing in a grassy field. Each tree had a mulch zone of 6 feet by 6 feet (2 m by 2 m) to reduce grass competition. Then, Martin killed the grass in a strip along the garden's edge 8-feet (2.5 m) wide by mulching for a year with heavy, black, woven polyethylene sheeting. The next year he moved the black poly to the neighboring 8-foot strip (2.5 m) and laid down coarse chipped bark mulch 1 inch (3 cm) deep on the bare area. Afterward, he heavily planted the killed and mulched zone with vigorous, mostly rhizomatous ground-cover plants (figure 2.16). He chose these species primarily to fill the ground plane with vegetation other than grass, but many had multiple functions. Each year he continued this process, planting about 6,500 square feet (600 sq. m) per year. In the meantime, Martin put in his shrub crops across the 2 acres. He planted these in clusters under the trees and within the already converted ground layer using the sheet-mulch technique (see volume 2, chapter 6).

These strategies enabled Martin quickly to convert a large field to forest garden *completely by himself*. The sun-loving and semi-shade-tolerant herbaceous understory species improve the soil and attract beneficial insects. These plants also provide products for consumption, sale, and research purposes. As the trees cast deeper shade, Martin will convert the ground layer to more shade-tolerant plants using relay plantings. The result is a large forest garden with an increasingly diverse, dense ground layer and growing canopy and shrub layers over a few short years (figures 2.17 and 2.18).

GOALS OF FOREST GARDENING

The above images of different forest gardens lead us to ponder the underlying goals forest gardeners might have in common. Of course, each person will have different aims for his or her forest garden. At the same time, we must be clear about the goals most will share and those that are fundamental to the forest garden idea. Here are six to keep in mind.

Grow an abundant diversity of tasty, nutritious food and other useful products. Despite Masanobu Fukuoka's assertion that the ultimate goal of farming is the cultivation of human beings, food production is the acid test of forest gardening. We want to maximize the yield for the energy expended. We want to grow crops diverse in their time of growth, harvest, and maintenance, diverse in which spaces they use in the garden, and diverse in their character. We urge you to design your forest garden around foods you like, foods that give you joy and fulfillment and that nurture a healthy body. However, we also urge you to try new foods. Expand the range of tastes you find acceptable. Experiment with ways of cooking and eating plants that will grow well in your forest garden, but which you have not yet eaten. Putting too much emphasis on the new and different can lead to disappointment, but sticking with the same old stuff will not move the yardstick ahead as much.

The biggest risk relative to this goal is that we will throw the baby out with the bathwater. As we have said, edible forest gardening is a new idea for modern North America. We have much to learn and to prove "on the ground," despite the successes we have seen. Please learn from our mistakes, and the mistakes of others, as we present them. That way, you can make newer and better mistakes while failing less significantly.

Create a stable, resilient garden ecosystem, driven by solar energy, that largely maintains and renews itself. The word *stability* can have a wide range of meanings in ecology.[14] *Stability* in this case, and throughout this book, means constancy of function, as well as inertia and persistence, or in other words, longstanding functioning and resistance to loss of function. We want our gardens to produce useful yields over a long

FIGURE 2.17. Stepping back a bit, one can see the far end of Martin's forest garden as it looked in 1997. One section of the garden has already been strip-mulched and planted, and the black poly is doing its thing on the next section. *Photo by Martin Crawford.*

FIGURE 2.16. When working on a large scale, special tactics may be necessary. Martin Crawford planted his 2-acre (0.8 ha) site in Devon, England, with all his intended trees and shrubs in one go. He then used black woven polyethylene to kill 8-foot (2.5 m) strips of grass before planting with vigorous ground covers and soil improvers. In this way he got his trees going and then methodically planted the ground layer while propagating the herbaceous materials he needed to save money. In the background you can see part of the 2-acre field Martin began converting to forest garden in 1994. The current year's herbaceous plantings are left of the strip mulch, shown near the end of the growing season. *Photo by Dave Jacke.*

FIGURE 2.18. The same area of Martin's garden is transformed only four years later, in 2001. The trees are growing more rapidly now because the herbaceous plants are improving soil conditions rapidly, pest problems are minimal, and maintenance has decreased. *Photo by Martin Crawford.*

period, maintain and renew themselves, and meet the other goals we set for them. Resilience is the ability of a system under stress to return to its previous state after the stress is removed.[15] So, we would like our gardens to bounce back in yields and ecosystem functioning if they become stressed. The forest is what bounces back after we stop stressing the landscape in most of the humid temperate world. Perennials are usually more resilient than annuals. Generalists are

more resilient than specialists. Using these components helps our gardens achieve resilience.

But what does *self-maintenance* mean? We should distinguish here between self-maintenance (which includes self-regulation) and self-management. Maintenance is the grunt labor of running an ecosystem: getting nutrients where they're needed when they're needed, supplying water, harvesting crops, planting plants, and so on. When we propose a "largely self-maintaining" ecosystem, we mean that many or most of these tasks are in the hands of the system itself. For example, we don't have to worry about providing the nutrients and water; the system does these tasks itself. It's like teaching your children to brush their own teeth, comb their own hair, and tie their own shoes. Clearly, we will need to harvest the crops, since the system won't do that for us. We propose a goal of *largely* self-maintained gardens because we feel that goal is achievable.

Self-regulation is somewhat more involved than self-maintenance. It is akin to our children learning to regulate their own behavior—not to shout in quiet restaurants, not to whine, but instead to say what they need, ask and thank, and eat well. In the garden, this involves regulating the behavior of populations and keeping things in balance: keeping pests and diseases under control, preventing weeds from taking over and diminishing community diversity, and so on. Largely self-regulating forest gardens are also achievable in this sense. Because weeding and pest control are typical maintenance activities in most gardens, we lump them in with self-maintenance.

Self-management is a completely different ballgame. Management involves envisioning the future and marshalling the forces required to get there. In the forest-gardening context, that means guiding the succession and evolution of the garden, and perhaps breeding new plant varieties to enhance system performance and productivity. This is more like our children deciding what they want to be when they grow up, deciding which job to take, choosing whether to go to college or which college to go to, and figuring out how to achieve these things. Self-managing forest gardens are a great ideal. However, we humans have limited experience with the dynamics of growing species polycultures that have yet to be tested, much less invented. Hence, we feel that self-management is a less realistic goal at this time, though it is something toward which we should strive. In the meantime, we'll stick with reasonable, achievable goals.

The term *low maintenance* is often bandied about these days in the landscaping field, though often there are few clear indications of what it means. Self-maintenance goes beyond low maintenance. The functional interconnection inherent in forest gardening means that the garden takes more care of itself because each garden element provides some useful function to support the whole system. In the case of forest gardening, the intent is to reduce the amount of human labor and energy spent on yearly soil preparation and fertility maintenance, planting, thinning, weeding, mowing, and insect and disease control. This is possible because either the plants and animals within the garden do not need such care or other plants or animals supply those needs. At least, this is the ideal.

Regular forest garden tasks will likely include cutting back selected plants, encouraging others, mulching, harvesting, and paying attention. Supposedly, Robert Hart's tool kit for managing his forest garden in England consisted of only five tools: a wheelbarrow, a bucket for carrying harvested produce, a sickle, a pair of pruning shears, and a bag of mulch. In addition, depending on the crops grown, some specialized pest management may be needed. On a yearly basis, you may need to prune or cut back one plant or another to keep things in balance and to do minimal propagating or planting. At some point, you may decide to become a force of nature and create gaps in the canopy, followed by replanting, to renew or redirect successional sequences as the forest garden matures. "Largely self-maintaining" means that there is still gardener involvement in these tasks, but the primary roles of humans are as observers, designers, and guiders of change. However, *complete* self-maintenance is likely to remain a holy grail in forest gardening for the most part. With conscious design and good management, we can certainly greatly reduce the amount of work we must do to keep the system running. Complete elimination of work is not what we are claiming here!

Self-renewal is a key piece of the self-maintenance

game. Using perennials starts the process in more than one way: perennials not only renew themselves yearly without effort on our part, they also capture and recycle nutrients leaching from the soil more effectively than annuals (see chapter 5). Excess vegetation is easily cut back and used as fertilizing mulch. It is simple to propagate many perennials to increase the garden's size or fill gaps made by occasional forces of nature, and a good mix of plants is likely to fill any such gaps by themselves. All of these characteristics make it much easier to keep a forest garden from requiring outside inputs of fossil energy or nutrient sources, except perhaps in the establishment phase. Ongoing care and "coevolution" of the forest garden is discussed in more detail in chapter 7 of volume 2.

Designing the garden to generate functional interconnection is a means to the above ends. Minimizing competition and maximizing cooperation includes selecting plants that fill particular niches and functions in the garden and then placing them appropriately.

Protect and restore ecosystem health. Aldo Leopold once said that ecosystem health is "the capacity of the land for self-renewal."[16] Edible forest gardens can protect and restore the health of the ecosystem in myriad ways. These include:

- stabilizing and increasing habitat for endangered wildlife, beneficial insects, and plants in urban, suburban, and rural landscapes;
- improving ecosystem processes such as rainwater infiltration, air and runoff purification, nutrient conservation, soil conservation and development, and biomass storage;
- reducing the impact of landscaping activities by reducing resource use, reducing toxic chemical use, and minimizing the abundance of opportunistic species; and
- providing locally grown foods, medicines, and other products that reduce the impact of global industrial agriculture.

Embody beauty, elegance, and spirit in the landscape. Some of the most beautiful plant communities on the earth are mature forests and fields undergoing succession (oldfields). Robert Hart's forest garden, though seemingly disorganized, felt captivating, mysterious, and larger than it really was. Oldfield successions express palpable dynamism in slow motion. The varied, usually colorful vegetation patterns often result in a connected series of outdoor "rooms" one can explore and inhabit. These aesthetic environments differ from what most people have or want in their front yard. No matter: once you have tasted the spirit of natural regeneration embodied in these communities, you will never forget them. Perhaps you will realize that you already have a forest garden outside your door. Even if this kind of beauty does not captivate you, you can still adapt the forest garden idea to more formal aesthetic sensibilities.

Improve economic sustainability. Growing your own food and medicinal plants reduces the expense of buying these items. Forest gardening promises to lower the cost of gardening over the long run, so that the cost of homegrown food should be lower. Forest gardening usually requires a large initial investment of time and materials, depending on how you start your garden, and this can cost money. Once a garden is established, however, the expenses should drop substantially. Better nutrition, moderate exercise, and the garden atmosphere of beauty and ease will promote better health. You can also design forest gardens conducive to creating viable small businesses that can help improve the family bottom line.

Cultivate a new paradigm for human participation in the ecology of cultural and natural landscapes. Last, but certainly not least, we come to Fukuoka's ideal: the cultivation and perfection of human beings. Since the way we garden manifests our worldview, it stands to reason that gardening in a new way will reflect and stimulate changes in that worldview. Are humans separate from or part of nature? How can or should we interact with our environment to meet our needs and respect the integrity and inherent value of our planet-mates? How do we cooperate? What is our role in the ecosystem? What is sacred, and what is not? How do we embody that sacredness in our everyday interactions with the world? All of these questions, and more, have bearing on our relationship to the edible forest garden. The edible forest garden also has things to say about each of these questions, if we will only look, listen, think, feel, and heed the signs.

REVISION—THE GARDEN OF EDEN?

That last forest gardening goal urges us to step back and look at the bigger picture. How might forest gardening help us reenvision and revise our world, our worldview, and our sense of ourselves?

SUBURBAN FOREST ECOLOGY OF THE FUTURE

Imagine that you live in a typical suburb in the late twenty-first century. You and your neighbors all across town have turned your back, front, or side yards into forest gardens of various sorts. Fruits and nuts swell on trees everywhere. Berry bushes lean over fences. You can walk down the sidewalk and nibble along the way. Various green, red, blue, brown, and multicolored foods grow along your path—you even know all their names and how to use them. Flowers bloom all over the place. The scent-filled air buzzes with insects on their appointed rounds. The whole landscape has transformed into an edible paradise. Some of the earliest forest gardens have now been growing for over fifty years, and those who study them are learning much about designed ecosystems and their development.

Some people created low-key, low-effort, but still productive and beautiful forest gardens. Most of these provide diverse yields, in terms of kinds of products, when the products are harvested, and what part of the forest garden they come from.

However, different gardeners focus on different purposes. One focuses on berry production, another on different kinds of nuts. Others prefer perennial vegetables and shade-tolerant medicinal plants. Many like their regular "graze through the garden" evening walk after work. For everyone, though, it's about living in a place of beauty and reconnecting with nature and with their true self.

Other people intensively design and manage their gardens. They gain higher yields of food, herbal medicinals, and other products. Some useful plant or another fills every niche in these gardens. These gardeners spend much of their time harvesting, processing, and giving away or selling the products of their labors, not weeding and planting. In some cases, different people manage and use the same garden for different purposes: one for food, one for bees and honey, one for medicinal plants, one for dye plants. Some of these forest gardens approach farm scale as they grow and link with other gardens. New cottage industries have sprung up based on cooperative small-scale production, processing, and marketing using locally grown products. However, the links being built go well beyond economic ties.

As more people put in forest gardens, restored useful and ecologically appropriate species to their yards, and made the soil healthier, a number of interesting things happened ecologically. First, more birds began reinhabiting the human-made landscape, as did more insect life. As ecosystem balance began to reemerge with our help, the amphibians and reptiles came back too. Then people noticed they had fewer pest imbalances in their landscapes, and pesticides became even less necessary than they were before. As the soils improved, the plants got healthier, and less runoff flowed into street sewers. People needed less fertilizer and irrigation as time went on. The health of the streams, lakes, ponds, and rivers improved as fewer nutrients washed into them from what had previously been mostly compacted lawns receiving strong doses of fertilizer. The fishing got better.

Previously isolated forest fragments linked to

each other as home gardens came into ecological balance and spread through town. People's yards became pathways for plants and animals to interact across neighborhoods that had previously blocked them. Sometimes this was "good," and sometimes it was "bad," but most folks understood that it meant the web of life was reweaving itself.

Eventually, people around the country grasped the forest garden idea. Edible forest gardens sprang up in urban, suburban, and rural areas. Experimentation by the interested public increased. Research by government agencies and universities began—after some commotion. This resulted in the development of new plant varieties for perennial polycultures throughout all the climate and soil regimes of North America. Our human habitat started looking, feeling, and acting more like a natural ecosystem. Agriculture as we knew it was transformed. So were the suburban, urban, and rural places where we lived, and the way we saw ourselves in the context of the natural world. As the forests, meadows, and waterways of the world became more diverse, healthier, and more alive, we felt healthier, more alive, more connected, and less alone than we had for generations. Things were better in the world since forest gardening came to North America at the end of the twentieth century!

It's a nice vision, isn't it?

ECOLOGICAL RESTORATION, ECOLOGICAL REFORMATION

To many, the scenario envisioned above may appear far-fetched, idealistic, or so close to the mythical Garden of Eden as to seem bogus. Let's talk about that.

The role that edible forest gardening can play in restoring the ecology of our cultural landscape is large. This arises not only from the potential for low-maintenance productive food systems in people's yards and public spaces and from the wide variety of forest gardens we can create. This powerful role exists because of the interconnections we can create throughout our neighborhoods and towns on an ecosystem scale, and because of the

changes of hearts and minds necessary for edible forest gardeners to succeed.

Bill Mollison, cofounder of permaculture, has said that the suburbs represent one of the best opportunities for sustainable design and living. There are more people with a little bit of land in these habitats than in any other. In the cities, people have far fewer opportunities to connect with any semblance of the natural world, much less to be self-supporting in any major way. Rural areas have too few people for high productivity without machinery driven by fossil fuels. We can, however, reunite the shreds of ecological fabric that still exist in the suburbs. We can restore and link natural areas, though humans will manage many, as in precolonial times. More importantly, we can turn the cultural landscape of our communities into an ecosystem that works by designing, planting, and tending our yards in accord with nature's way, overlaying our purposes onto the landscape appropriately. Creating edible and otherwise useful forests, savannas, meadows, thickets, and wetlands in our yards can do this. It can also recreate strands that will help weave the remaining forest fragments back into a more healthy and stable ecosystem. With thoughtful action on the part of thousands, if not millions, this is completely achievable. That's the ecological restoration part. But this can happen only with a deep and ongoing change in the hearts and minds of those who are responsible for the world we have created and can create—and that's all of us. This change of heart is the ecological reformation of which we speak.

Gardening writer Janet Marinelli explores what she calls "gardening in the age of extinction" in her book *Stalking the Wild Amaranth*. After reviewing the history and philosophies of garden styles from Greece to the present day and discussing the ecological realities we humans face in the coming years, she writes:

What is the place of landscape design in such a world? As William Howard Adams points out in

Nature Perfected, the presence of massive overpopulation and monstrous cities has raised critical questions about the form, the function, and even the very survival of gardens. "Concocting bogus images of lost paradise," in his view, "only exposes our impoverishment." It seems that we are being forced back to something akin to the "walled gardens of some barbarous medieval town," he writes, "but without any of the metaphysics to transform our isolation into a civilized, revitalizing environment." Is there any way out of this horticultural—and metaphysical—abyss?[17]

First, there is nothing wrong with exposing our impoverishment. Indeed, such is the first step of any healing or transformational process, as difficult or painful as it might be. The way we think, eat, live, and garden has contributed to this impoverishment. Take it in and own it: *we are all responsible for this.*

Second, there is at least one way out of the abyss: the metaphysics are out there in the Garden itself. Adam and Eve left the Garden of Eden after eating the fruit from the Tree of Knowledge, when they became self-conscious and realized a sense of separateness between themselves and God or Nature. The history of Western civilization is the story of our increasing knowledge, and our application of that knowledge to meet the needs originally met with ease in the Garden of Eden. Meanwhile the natural world became "other," objectified, simply a means to an end, a tool or resource for us to meet our goals, an object with no intrinsic value of its own. We now find our knowledge leading us back to an understanding of unity, and of sacredness.

The boundaries we saw between our world and ourselves are breaking down. Physics shows us that what we thought were particles are also waves, and that the act of observing something changes the observed. Physicists don't mention that it changes the observer, too! Ecology shows us that our limiting and false beliefs that we are separate from "nature," and that it is possible to study "pristine" ecosystems in their "natural state," threaten our own survival and that of many other species. We cannot go back to the boundaryless, unself-conscious union of children, to the Garden of Eden we imagined, and possibly experienced, before. Now is the time for us to create the kind of partnership with the natural world that only mature adults can create, based on self-knowledge, humility, and respect. We humans are both particles *and* waves. We are separate individuals *and* we are interacting and interdependent with all of creation at many levels. We have creative power, but not creative dominion. We can take, but we must also give. We cannot go back to the primeval forest we have destroyed, but we can recreate the primal forest, at least metaphorically, in the here and now. We can create a new Garden of Eden, but we can't do it alone. We need nature's help, and she needs ours.

This metaphysics involves envisioning ourselves as part of the natural world and acting in accord with that vision, not in the same way as the native peoples of this continent did before us, but as participants in ways appropriate for our time in history, for our culture, for the ecosystems that exist now. Now is the time to restore ourselves to the ecosystem, and thereby to restore the ecosystem itself. To do that we must reform ourselves: reform our sense of who we are, of what is right and wrong, of how the world works, and how we operate within it socially, economically, ecologically, and spiritually. This radical undercurrent flows through this whole book and the whole edible forest garden idea. Since the word *radical* literally means "of, relating to, or proceeding from a root," it is an appropriate word to use. Let's get to the root of the issue, or the "weed" will still come up.

So, the edible forest garden requires us to be open. To listen and look. To hone our skills of observation and discernment. To use these skills before we intervene in our gardens, and in our world. To act with respect, humility, and as much wisdom as we can muster. To expand our sense of where our gardens begin and end to include the neighbor's yard, the town, the region, and the planet, with all of the inhabitants therein. We must challenge our assumptions and sacred cows. We must be committed to truth. And we must spend time in our hammocks, hanging out in the Garden.

Edible forest gardening requires us to learn ecology, not just theoretically, but with our bodies outside in the field. What principles guide the behavior and design of natural ecosystems? Only by understanding these can we consciously design edible forest gardens that mimic how nature works. Then we must coevolve with these systems. In that process we learn and change. We embody these principles in ourselves; they become part of us. How can we not change the way we think and live as a result?

As we discuss the principles of ecology and design in the chapters that follow, please also read the subtext: the implications these principles have for the reformation of our society. For we must not only place all of ourselves back into the Garden, and our gardens back into nature, we must also welcome nature back into ourselves.

We see things not as they are. We see things as *we* are.

—The Talmud

As far as possible, men are to be taught to become wise not only by books, but by the heavens, the earth, oaks and beeches.

—Comenius, *Great Didactics*, 1632

Case Study 1

Charlie's Garden

Size: 0.1 acre (50 ft by 90 ft; 15 m by 27 m) ◆ Location: Greensboro, NC, USA ◆ Designed 1993, planted 1994 to 2002 ◆ USDA Hardiness Zone: 8 ◆ Latitude: 36° N ◆ Growing Season: 200 days

> Domestic gardens as we have known them through the centuries were valued mostly for their habitableness and privacy, two qualities that are conspicuously absent in contemporary gardens. . . . The house-gardens of antiquity furnish us, even in their fragmentary and dilapidated state, perfect examples of how a diminutive and apparently negligible quantity of land can, with some ingenuity, be transformed into an oasis of delight. . . .
>
> —BERNARD RUDOFSKY, *"The Conditioned Outdoor Room"*

When we design forest gardens as outdoor living rooms (pattern #6, in volume 2, chapter 2), they become spaces that live, because we live in them. Charlie Headington's garden in urban Greensboro, North Carolina, exemplifies this principle. Charlie's ingenuity transformed this small bit of land into an "oasis of delight," complete with habitableness and privacy. The integration of forest gardening with landscape design demonstrates that good guiding principles, native talent, keen observation, and intuition can create a highly productive, functional, very low-maintenance and beautiful garden. With a little more information and a few more plants, Charlie's garden can become even more rich and productive.

CHARLIE'S GOALS

Charlie has a hard time articulating exactly what he was after when he started his garden, beyond general statements. He had little gardening experience then. Having taken a permaculture course, he mainly planned to use the design principles and ideas he had learned. He had also read *The Integral Urban House* and wanted to make something similar: a huge garden with water catchment, using many perennials to make life easier. His satisfaction with his garden indicates that he likes annual crops as well as perennials, that he prefers fruits to nuts, and that he was loathe to cut major trees already on the property. Low maintenance was an ideal, but he was unsure how far he could push that.

Charlie started his garden in 1990 on the fly: he designed minimally, if at all, before creating it (don't try this at home!). He admits he knew little when he started. "As it evolved," he says, "I realized in the midst of it what I was doing, how the parts nest inside each other in organized systems. I understand the whole better after doing my own garden." Now he designs before creating gardens for other people, using the understanding he gained from his own place.

GARDEN DESCRIPTION

Charlie is a supportive man with a relaxed manner and a ready smile, open yet slightly reserved, charming and unpretentious. The gardens have a similar feel, but they obviously make a splash in the neighborhood just for being what they are. Informality rules and plants are almost everywhere, though there is order inherent in the lushness. On the surface, this garden looks almost as full as Robert Hart's. Looking deeper, however, shows that though Charlie may have planted more densely than we now recommend, Charlie has in no way gone to Robert's extremes.

Charlie's house squeezes onto its small 50- by 180-foot (15 by 55 m) lot without much room to spare, except in back. You can't miss it once on the right street—it's the only one with a meadow between the street and the sidewalk rather than the customary lawn. The house sits at the east end of the lot near the street. The south lot line splits the driveway shared by Charlie's family and their neighbors. The north lot line brings the neighbor's shady lawn within a few feet of the living room windows. This leaves about half the lot for garden west of the house, in the back. We focused our mapping and will focus this discussion on the back-yard, but the whole place is so nice we have to say a few things about the front and the south.

A colorful meadow, interrupted by sidewalk, sweeps up from the street into the modest east-facing front yard (figure C1.1). There, densely packed small trees and shrubs, flowering away, offer privacy with a view and a modicum of scented shade to the front porch. The sweeping line started by the plants continues up the porch roof to the top of the house, visually melding house with earth. Since it is all within 30 feet (9 m) of the road, there is not much edible on this side of the house, but it sure feels comfortable and welcoming.

The house's high south wall used to drop abruptly down to the shared driveway, with little privacy and only 4 to 5 feet (1.2 to 1.5 m) between the wall and the pavement. The resulting heat made the rooms on this side intolerable for much of the year. Now, a bamboo-and-nylon-mesh trellis leaning against the wall up to the tops of the second-story windows

FIGURE C1.1. The suburban forest ecology of the future—now. Charlie Headington's forest garden begins in front with a meadow between the street and the house. *Photo by Dave Jacke.*

supports deciduous vines for summer shade and winter sun (originally they were hardy passion-flowers and annuals, but now they are muscadine grapes; see figure C1.2). Three 15-foot (5 m) columnar semidwarf pear trees (varieties 'Warren' and 'Magness') shade the house wall east of the trellis. These fit the space well, pollinate each other, and taste delicious. Window boxes on the house further increase the growing area and drape the walls with more vegetation.

FIGURE C1.2. The 4-foot-wide (1.2 m), sunny, hot, south-facing driveway and house wall prove that forest gardening is viable virtually anywhere. Narrow, columnar pears and herba-ceous vines on the trellis provide food and beauty as well as welcome relief from the heat. The roof runoff collection tanks provide automatic trickle irrigation to the toasty soil through soaker hoses. Note the bamboo fence at left. It continues west to screen the driveway from the gardens and supports espaliered apples, too. *Photo by Eric Toensmeier.*

Most of the gutters slope toward the south side of the house. Charlie hooked the downspouts to stacked 55-gallon (210 l) plastic drums to catch the runoff. Attached soaker hoses allow rain to fill the drums and then slowly trickle into the soil next to the sun-baked drive. "These work great for minimizing my watering," he says. "They really help the plants thrive." All this has made the south wall much shadier and more tolerable in the hot summers, as well as more private and productive of food. This shows that you can forest-garden virtually anywhere, even in a 4- by 25-foot (1.2 by 7.5 m) space between a house and a driveway.

In back, trellises, fences, and pergolas carry the house into the garden and the garden onto, into, and almost over the house, until the building seems virtually alive. This is the heart of the forest garden, and in some ways the heart of the whole living space (see figure C1.3). The land slopes up from the house to the west, gently at first, then more steeply before flattening by the western fence line. Charlie terraced the steeper portion of the slope so he could place his main annual garden where the steepest slope used to be. The terrace divides the space into upper and lower gardens, with the terrace wall and the area just below it forming a central, more functional space. Large ash, elm, and red maple trees along the north boundary cast significant shade there. These trees, the house, the western fence, and the garage and driveway frame the back yard. They define an east–west oriented, moderately sloping, 50- by 90-foot (15 by 27 m) yard with large sunny areas in the upper and lower gardens and deep shade along the north edge. A small redbud tree in the center of the space by the garage provides some shade in the central portion of the garden, as well.

THE LOWER GARDEN

The lower garden contains several different microclimates, from sun to shade, and performs a number of social, horticultural, and practical functions. The main path between the kitchen porch

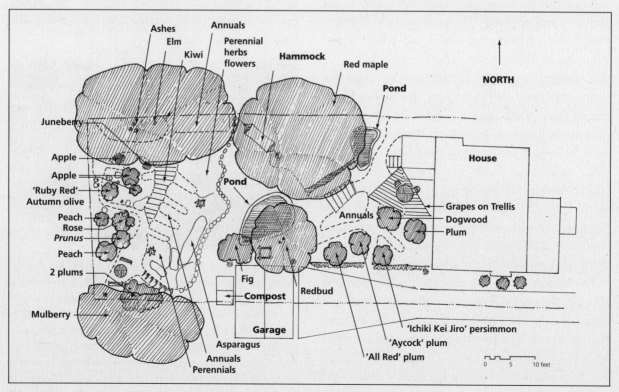

FIGURE C1.3. Site plan of Charlie's backyard in Greensboro, North Carolina.

FIGURE C1.4. This bamboo arbor frames the main path from car to kitchen door and divides the lower garden into sunny beds (at right) and shady patches (at left). Though not a living structure, it represents another example of using vertical space—definitely a forest gardening principle. *Photo by Dave Jacke.*

FIGURE C1.5. One of the sunny annual beds (at left) in Charlie's forest garden lies adjacent to the bamboo arbor in figure C1.4. The path here is another way you can get from the car to the kitchen door, picking salad greens on the way. On the right herbs and flowers grow under small plum and persimmon trees that make the space feel more like a midsuccession environment than an annual garden. Barely visible in the shade in back is a table and chairs under a bamboo grape trellis. *Photo by Dave Jacke.*

and the garage and parking area diagonally divides the space into shady northern areas and sunny southern areas and provides a direct link from the kitchen to the central and upper gardens. The path passes a large garden pond and under a pergola on its way (figure C1.4). Against the house, a pergola-covered patio offers a table and chairs so you can sit in the shade sipping a fruit smoothie while enjoying the garden with friends. Grapes growing on the pergola enhance the Eden-like atmosphere. A woven bamboo fence defines the edge between the sunny lower garden area and the driveway. This fence supports dwarf apple trees grown as cordons—tied at the stake, as it were, to prevent the trees from toppling over, to increase productivity, and to provide screening (see figure C1.2).

A second path meanders through the sunny garden south of the main path (see figure C1.5).

FIGURE C1.6. This 'All Red' purple-leaf plum is one of Charlie's delights, both visually and to the palate. *Photo by Eric Toensmeier.*

The beds here contain annual crops, tree crops, and diverse perennial herbs, insectary flowers, medicinals, and ornamentals. Right behind the espalier fence, reinforcing the separation between the garden and the driveway, are three stunning trees:

an 'All Red' purple-leaf plum (figure C1.6), an 'Aycock' green-leaf plum, and an oriental persimmon 'Ichi Ki Kei Jiro'. The All Red plum shines with its red leaf and fruit color, prolific high-quality fruit, self-pollination, disease resistance, and vertical growth habit. The Aycock plum (zones 5–8) combines well with the All Red due to its horizontal growth habit (up to 12 ft/4 m high), tasty purple fruit, and need for All Red pollen. Both plums flower abundantly in spring. The Ichi Ki Kei Jiro (zones 6–10) produces large, delicious persimmons on a small (10 ft/3 m high), self-fertile tree with great orange fall color.

On the north side of the main path and its pergola, the shade from the pre-existing red maple and the neighbor's trees grows deep. This shady patch, like other shady spots at Charlie's, has much lower diversity and interest than the rest of the garden (except for the lower garden pond, described below). The main plant growing in the shade there is myrtle (*Vinca* spp.), which represents an opportunity for enrichment and increased productivity.

THE NEXUS

The central area, north of the garage, forms the nexus of the garden. Paths and terrace converge and diverge here, and flows of water cross and gather. The garage roof provides the primary source of this water flow. The garage gutters drain into a 10- by 16-foot (3 by 5 m) teardrop-shaped pond next to the garage (figure C1.7). Though at ground level on the uphill side, the pond edge stands at sitting-wall height on the downhill side. A woven bamboo-wattle fence supports the pond's plastic liner, with a buffer of soil and rock to prevent the bamboo from puncturing the liner. This pond overflows by a pipe under the main path into a stone-lined ditch that also captures runoff from up the hill. The ditch directs both flows into a smaller, lower garden pond sunk into the earth in the deep shade nearer the house (figure C1.8). The lower pond also receives runoff from the house via a bamboo gutter built into the trellis on the north

FIGURE C1.7. Early morning illuminates the central nexus and the upper garden. The pond in the foreground provides beauty and beneficial animal habitat. The mix of plants in back includes annual vegetables, fruit trees, hardy kiwis, asparagus, culinary herbs, and other mouthwatering enchantments. *Photo by Dave Jacke.*

side of the back deck. This little pond does much to save the shady space mentioned above from barrenness and provides a modicum of amphibian habitat for the lower garden.

The larger upper pond and its resident plants and animals provide diversity, beauty, and interest to the garden, forming a centerpiece to the space. Mints and strawberries, heal-all (*Prunella vulgaris*), irises, and hostas grow in the soil-wattle walls, softening its edges. Cattails (*Typha* spp.), iris, pickerelweed, lotus, and water hyacinths provide habitat and flowers in the water. Charlie has noticed a dragonfly population increase since he

FIGURE C1.8. This plastic-lined, gravel-filled trench directs overflow from the upper garden pond to the lower one. It also collects overland runoff from the upper garden. Notice the vertical piece of bamboo in back; this carries roof runoff from the house into the lower pond. These catchment systems reduce the need to manually fill the pond, while also maintaining habitat for beneficial organisms that use the pond, such as frogs and dragonflies. These reduce pest populations in the garden. This picture was taken about 20 feet (6 m) north of figure C1.4, looking in the same compass bearing. Notice the difference in light conditions. *Photo by Dave Jacke.*

FIGURE C1.9. Between the upper pond and the garage lies this little nook of utility, with a redbud arching overhead. Charlie keeps his mushroom logs in this shady spot near the pond so he can water them easily. Their location along the main path allows daily inspection and harvest. The same applies to the nursery transplants and other tender plants he keeps here. *Photo by Dave Jacke.*

installed this pond. These flying predators keep down mosquitoes, among other things. The pond's uplifted form on three sides probably makes it more difficult for frogs and toads to get out for garden insect patrols. However, the ground-level uphill side directs such traffic toward the upper garden, which has no other pond to supply this need. Charlie frequently fills watering cans in the upper pond.

In the shade of the redbud tree between the upper pond and the garage, and right next to the main path from the kitchen to the driveway, Charlie has a small nursery space and some oak logs inoculated with shiitake mushrooms (figure C1.9). The redbud (*Cercis canadensis*) produces edible young pods, and offers brilliant spring flowers and a pleasing form and texture. Its shade keeps the pond cool, helping maintain the pond's health. A fig tree also grows just west of the redbud, further hiding the compost bins tucked out of sight behind the garage. A well-used hammock, strung in the shade between the red maple and the neighbor's shed on the north edge of the lot, completes the garden's central nexus.

THE UPPER GARDEN

The upper gardens form a space to themselves, a getaway from the house and yard. The terraced grade change and roundabout access pattern support this ambience, as do the overall planting scheme and two or three other simple elements. The bulk of the most "foresty" garden space grows here, packed between the main back path and the western fence line.

The main back path divides the upper garden between mainly perennials to the west and mainly annuals to the east. This path is covered by a pergola with a hardy kiwi vine growing on it (figure C1.10). The hardy kiwi variety 'Issai' (*Actinidia arguta* 'Issai') is the only self-pollinating hardy kiwi around (all others have male and female flowers on separate plants). This makes it a perfect choice for a small pergola such as this. It yields well, tastes great, and has few insect problems (but only in warmer climates, as Issai appears less hardy than other varieties). The pergola turns the pathway into a food-producing space and the whole back of the upper garden into a private paradise. It also forms a backdrop to the annual garden beds just above the terrace wall.

This annual garden used to take the shape of keyhole beds with a large asparagus patch in front, but runoff problems resulted from the keyhole paths running up and down the hill. The asparagus didn't do well, either, for unknown reasons. Charlie took out the asparagus and converted to cross-contour beds that work much better for water catchment. Various herbaceous perennials surround and mingle with these annual beds, providing fruit, flowers, herbs, and insect habitat.

When we visited, the tree crop area behind the kiwi pergola consisted of closely planted dwarf fruit trees mixed with a variety of herbs and some shrubs, and more outdoor living space. All the dwarf trees are full size now, and their crowns touch. This has reduced the annual garden area among the trees,

FIGURE C1.10. The kiwi trellis (at left) defines the back garden as an "away" spot for escape from life's pressures. With table, chairs, and fresh nibbles close at hand, the kitchen only a few steps away, and the garden's nooks beckoning, the forest garden becomes an oasis of delight worthy of living long and prospering. *Photo by Dave Jacke.*

which was Charlie's plan (it also makes the area difficult to photograph well). However, he did not leave enough room between the trees for the shrubs to get sufficient light. If he were to do it over, he says he would space the trees farther apart to give his shrubs more sun.

Trees here include diverse varieties of dwarf apples, peaches, apricots, and plums, primarily, along with individual 'Ruby Red' autumn olive (*Eleagnus umbellata* var. *orientalis* 'Ruby Red', an opportunist nitrogen-fixer with edible fruit) and juneberry (*Amelanchier* sp.) plants. Charlie has come close to getting rid of his apricots and plans to replace his peaches with persimmons. The stone fruits just haven't done well consistently, and he has come to love persimmons.

Shrubs include thornless blackberry and other *Rubus* species, a few 'Pixwell' gooseberries, roses, and buffaloberry (*Shepherdia canadensis*, another nitrogen-fixer). Violets, comfrey, mints, bee balm, strawberries, Egyptian onions, anise hyssop, lovage, and tansy are the most prominent useful species in the herb layer, along with annuals, a few ornamentals, and other less abundant species. Most of these, though, are sun-loving herbs. Less diverse and productive patches of ground were, and still are, evident in the shady areas under both the big, mature, preexisting trees, as well as under the dwarf trees Charlie planted. He is aware of these bare patches but hasn't decided how to fill those niches.

There used to be a small garden pond and bench in the southern corner of the upper garden, which Charlie has now replaced with a flat area for a table and chairs. The pond was too small and not self-sustaining, since it was not fed by roof or overland runoff. The space was also too valuable as a getaway to keep it as it was. This change increased the family's use of the back garden area, making it a more removed counterpart to the patio by the house. Consequently, you can sit back there sipping a fruit smoothie in complete peace and privacy if you don't want to be social.

MAINTENANCE AND YIELDS

On the maintenance front, Charlie was surprised by how little work his garden takes now that it has matured. He put in much work to alter the landform, plant and mulch the plants, and establish the water systems. There was some weeding and watering in the early years until things established, but that is minimal now. He fertilized with rock powders when he built the garden, but the only fertilizer he uses now is mulch, maybe some goat manure in the fall, and throwing nutrient-rich comfrey into his compost piles. On an annual basis, he has to put in only about ten hours per week for two

weeks in spring, and the same for two weeks in the fall. This includes mulching (usually in the fall), and pruning, thinning, and spreading compost around younger trees and bushes in spring, occasionally with some replanting or revising of his landscape scheme. He says he is "not good" with spray programs for his fruit trees, but this seems to reduce to his yields minimally, if at all. Other than his spring and fall activity bursts, he puts in up to an hour per week during the eight-month growing season, mainly to care for his annual vegetables. He uses hand tools for most of this maintenance. If you add up the numbers, Charlie spends only about sixty-eight hours per year working in quite pleasant surroundings with simple tools managing his garden!

Charlie says it took four or five years to start getting significant amounts of food from the perennials. In the meantime, he grew many annual vegetables. Now that his system has matured, he gets "humongous numbers of plums, pears, figs, kiwis, oriental persimmons, apples," and on and on. He gets flowers for his table, flavorful teas, culinary herbs, fresh lettuce, fresh scallions, and other vegetables. He gets mint for his salads and his iced tea. He gets strawberries, blueberries, raspberries, and blackberries. He gets colorful dragonflies flitting by eating mosquitoes, frogs croaking at night, and birds and their songs. He gets a cooler, more comfortable, colorful, quiet, enchanting, ever-changing and fascinating place to live. That's eight months of fresh fruit, vegetables, and herbs and numerous other benefits for sixty-eight hours of labor annually, and rather little ongoing expense for fertilizer, tools, equipment, seeds, machinery, or chiropractic bills. What more could you ask for?

ASSESSMENT

How can we say that Charlie's garden is anything but a success? He has created a rich oasis, a place that is comfortable, enlivening, and nourishing—physically, mentally, and emotionally. He gets great yields with minimal work and constantly refines his system, as any designer would. Though the space contains a fair number of annual crops, it still qualifies as a forest garden because the context is wooded, many of the plantings are small trees and shrubs, and it contains plants in numerous vegetation layers. The garden contains many stages of succession, from annually disturbed soil to meadow, oldfield habitat, and small tree polycultures. Only the latest stages of succession, with unbroken expanses of larger trees, are missing.

Notwithstanding Charlie's broad and deep success, he can take his system even further. He can certainly increase the diversity of yields, and the total system yield, probably without lowering the yields of most existing crops. Some of the changes below could reduce his work even more.

First, and most important, Charlie's lack of clearly articulated goals has probably hampered his design's potential and caused him to work more than he might. Stronger and more detailed intentionality, especially in the design and management of guilds and polycultures in the herbaceous layer, could significantly increase the garden's productivity. Charlie should blend his articulated goals, his analysis and assessment of the situation on the ground, and his vision of the garden's future in his ongoing design choices. The following discussion assumes a desire for more food of whatever kind, less work of any kind, and less reliance on external inputs of nutrients and organic matter.

We expect most of the productivity increase will come from the herb layer, and some from the shrub layer. We did not map the herbaceous vegetation in detail or make lists of every herbaceous perennial Charlie had growing. The latter would allow one to analyze the plants' niches, uses, and functions, figure out what niches might still be open, and select useful species to put in them. Charlie could then ensure, for example, a season-long progression of blooming insectaries. Since we do not have that data, we will proceed with an assessment based on our observations.

As mentioned in the description, the shady environments had few useful plants and lower diversity. In discussing his garden recently, Charlie acknowledged there were bare patches under his fruit trees now that they have grown to full size. We noticed a relative lack of perennial vegetables in general, and of shade-tolerant perennial vegetables and herbs in particular. We also noticed that most of the perennial herbs present were clumpers or mat-formers, and there were fewer runners. Therefore, most of his herb layer patches were single-species patches rather than true plant mixtures. In addition, there were few nitrogen-fixers and only a few known broad-spectrum dynamic accumulator species (mainly comfrey). The garden did have insectary plants, but we doubt it had a succession of strong beneficial insect nectar plants blooming throughout the year.

We suggest first considering a list of shade-tolerant herbaceous species that fill the various functions just discussed (table C1.1). Most of these are perennial vegetables, most are multifunctional, and many are ground covers. Many of these will fill in between existing large clumpers in the garden, improving the polycultures already present. In the shadiest areas under the large yard trees, we suggest planting spring-ephemeral perennial vegetables such as ramps, spring beauties, and toothwort along with a summer-green shade-tolerant ground cover such as foamflower, perhaps with licorice fern, great Solomon's seal, or ostrich fern arching above. Alternatively, Charlie could grow ostrich fern and dwarf comfrey in the deep shade and harvest nutrients and fiddleheads from this currently unproductive area. Other interesting combinations are possible. Many of the other species in table C1.1 could grow underneath the fruit trees where the shade is less intense.

Nitrogen-fixers are scarce in table C1.1 because they need full sun to fix much nitrogen, and sun-loving nitrogen-fixers are commonly available. Those shown have edible uses and make good ground-cover plants to reduce Charlie's need to

TABLE C1.1. Useful herbaceous perennials for shady niches in Charlie Headington's forest garden, Greensboro, NC. Sun: ○ = full sun, ◐ = part shade, ● = full shade; N_2 = nitrogen fixers; DA = dynamic accumulator of calcium and other nutrients; I = attracts beneficial insects; GC = ground-cover plant; native region: ENA = eastern North America, WNA = western North America, APP = Appalachia; EUR = Europe, EURA = Eurasia. See appendix 1 for more information.

Species	Common Name	Edible Parts	Sun	N_2	DA	I	GC	Native Region	Comments
Allium canadense	wild garlic	all	○◐					ENA	self-sows, persistent
Allium cernuum	nodding wild onion	all	○◐					ENA	tasty
Allium tricoccum	wild leek, ramp	all	◐●					ENA	tasty spring ephemeral
Amphicarpaea bracteata	hog peanut	tubers	○●	N_2			GC	ENA	sprawls
Apios americana	groundnut	tubers	○◐	N_2			GC	ENA	aggressive, sprawls
Asarum canadense	wild ginger	roots	◐●				GC	ENA	beautiful
Beta vulgaris maritima	sea beet	leaves	○◐					EUR	
Ceanothus prostratus	prostrate ceanothus	none	○◐	N_2			GC	WNA	aggressive, tea (leaves)
Chamaemelum nobile	chamomile	none	○		DA	I	GC	EURA	tea, (flowers)
Chenopodium bonus-henricus	good King Henry	leaves	○◐					EURA	self-sows, tasty
Chrysogonum virginianum	green and gold	none	○◐			I	GC	ENA	
Cichorium intybus varieties	chicory varieties	leaves	○◐		DA			EURA	tea (roots), windblown seed
Claytonia spp.	spring beauties	leaves, roots	◐●				GC	ENA, WNA	spring ephemeral
Crambe maritima	sea kale	leaves, shoots	○◐					EUR	
Dentaria diphylla	toothwort	roots	◐●				GC	ENA	spicy spring ephemeral
Equisetum spp.	horsetails	none	○◐		DA		GC	ENA	in ponds, aggressive
Galax urceolata	galax	none	◐●				GC	APP	evergreen, slow-growing
Matteuccia struthiopteris	ostrich fern	fiddleheads	◐●					ENA	aggressive
Mentha 'Marilyn's Salad'	Marilyn's salad mint	leaves	○◐			I	GC	cultivar	mild flavor
Montia spp.	miner's lettuces	all	varies				GC	varies	self-sows, tasty
mushrooms in mulch	mushrooms in mulch	mushrooms	○◐		DA			varies	throughout the garden
Myrrhis odorata	sweet cicely	leaves, seeds	○◐			I		EUR	self-sows, anise flavor
Nasturtium officinale	watercress	leaves	○◐		DA			EURA	in ponds
Oxyria digyna	mountain sorrel	leaves	○◐					ENA	self-sows
Polygonatum biflorum var. *commutatum*	great Solomon's seal	shoots, roots	○●					ENA	beautiful
Polypodium glycyrrhiza	licorice fern	roots	◐●					WNA	flavored roots
Pycnanthemum spp.	mountain mints	tea	○◐			I	GC	ENA	some aggressive
Rubus tricolor	creeping raspberry	fruit	○●				GC	ASIA	aggressive
Rumex spp.	sorrels	leaves	○◐		DA		GC	EURA	some self-sow
Symphytum grandiflorum	dwarf comfrey	leaves	○◐		DA		GC	EURA	medicinal, persistent, aggressive
Taraxacum officinale	dandelion	leaves, roots	○◐		DA	I		EURA	self-sows, cultivars, tea (roots)
Tiarella cordifolia	foamflower	none	◐●			I	GC	ENA	aggressive
Vaccinium crassifolium	creeping blueberry	fruit	○◐				GC	APP	below blueberries
Zizia spp.	Alexanders	none	○◐			I		ENA	beautiful

mulch. Their vigor also makes them suitable for cutting to use as mulch. Groundnut (*Apios americana*), in particular, would fit well into Charlie's many-pergola'd garden, with its vigorous twining vine, beautiful purple flowers, and nutritious tubers. Some developed varieties now yield tubers the size of a child's fist.

Charlie has many fruit trees. Most fruit trees have high demand for calcium. He lives in an urban area in the humid eastern United States, where acid rain is likely to rapidly leach nutrients like calcium (as well as potassium). While his heavily mulched garden probably has high soil fungi levels, and this will help conserve calcium (see chapter 5), more calcium accumulators may be in order. Charlie already has a number of calcium-accumulating species in his garden (table C1.2). Some of the others should work well in his shady areas while also offering additional yields. Inoculating his mulch with edible fungi can only help, for example. We suggest he increase the numbers of all the listed species and use the leaf litter from his flowering dogwoods as the valuable resource it is.

Charlie could also develop guilds of plants to help conserve and cycle the other key nutrients besides nitrogen and calcium in his garden. His strategy of throwing comfrey into his compost piles is good, and he can do the same with other dynamic accumulators. Growing the plants where the nutrients are needed and letting them drop their leaf litter there is even easier, though. All of the dynamic accumulators in table C1.2 accumulate calcium as well as other nutrients.

Charlie's policy of not spraying his fruit has worked so far, probably because of the species diversity, the insectary plants he already has, and his selection of disease-resistant crops and varieties. However, it may be only a matter of time before the bugs start getting something. A full complement of insectary plants could help keep the balance longer, or limit the damage if it does tip the wrong way. Listing the blooming times of

TABLE C1.2. Selected calcium accumulators and their accumulated nutrients.

Species Name	Common Name	Nutrients
Acer saccharum	sugar maple	Ca, K
Allium schoenoprasum	chive	Ca, Na
Carya spp.	hickories, pecan	Ca, K
Carya ovata	shagbark hickory	Ca, K, P
Chamaemelum nobile	chamomile	Ca, K, P
Cichorium intybus	chicory	Ca, K
Cornus florida	flowering dogwood	Ca, K, P
Equisetum spp.	horsetails	Ca, Co, Fe, Mg, Si
Nasturtium officinale	watercress	Ca, F, Fe, K, Mg, Na, P, S
Plantago spp.	plantains	Ca, Cu, Fe, K, S, Si

all the insectary plants present, and then filling the gaps, offers the best means of ensuring beneficials have nectar sources all season long. Evaluating habitat needs besides nectar is a good idea, too (see appendix 5 in volume 2).

The above are the most important recommendations we offer. We'll note just a few more to round out this assessment.

- Provide more room for fruiting shrubs to increase crop diversity by increasing the spacing of trees in the next round of plantings, creating shrub polyculture patches in specific locations, or finding niches to tuck individual shrubs into what is already there. Most of Charlie's shrubs were runners (e.g., *Rubus* and *Rosa* species). More clumping shrubs could tuck into small spaces nicely or create better polyculture patches.
- Include some nut-producing species to provide protein. These would have to be small-stature or slow-growing species, such as hazelnuts, filberts, nut pines, or some of the dwarfing chestnut family plants (*Castanea pumila, C. seguinii* x *mollissima, C. pumila* x *hybrida*, or *C. crenata*).

- If he wanted to get radical, Charlie could cut down one or more of the preexisting mature ash, elm, or maple trees and replace it with a large nutproducer, such as a pecan, hickory (both calcium accumulators!), or chestnut, or a large fruit tree, such as a good-quality mulberry or full-size apple, pear, plum, or persimmon. Even if he doesn't want to go there intentionally, he might want to consider what he would do if one died or blew down in a storm.

All these recommendations are optional and depend on Charlie's goals. Does he want nuts? Is he concerned about reducing his labor even more by increasing the number of fertility plants, or are the annuals, ornamentals, and herbs he has now more important to him? How much does he want to experiment, and how much does he want to just have a working system he can let hum along? He plans to take out his remaining stone fruits and replace them with the persimmons he loves. Perhaps experimenting with other fruits, nuts, or herbs is less important to him now.

As you can see, the design process never ends. Charlie's garden reminds us that things always change. You learn that you like persimmons and the stone fruits are not performing well. So what do you do? Well, what do you want? What is the site like now? What is your scheme and scenario? How can you implement it? Just keep applying the design process in a conscious way, and you will get there.

CONCLUSION

Charlie's garden succeeds on many levels, first simply because it exists. The first lesson from Charlie's garden, therefore, is simply to start. Do not let lack of knowledge or experience stop you. Even if you don't "design" your garden on paper, keep in mind good design principles and specific strategies or patterns that you like. You can still succeed, even if you are not an experienced gardener or designer, if you think things through.

The second lesson after starting is to continue! You will learn along the way and change your garden repeatedly, no matter how much design you do up front. You are just less likely to have to make major changes and fix big mistakes if you design it more thoroughly first. No matter, though: persistence pays off. Keep going, with an open mind and at least one observant eye.

Charlie's garden also succeeds horticulturally: it grows much food with little labor and low cost in a healthy, even a beautiful, environment. One reason it succeeds horticulturally is that it succeeds socially and psycho-physiologically. Charlie and his family obviously spend much time in their garden, whether they are working, harvesting, hanging out talking, or doing homework on the patio. This ongoing *and multifunctional* relationship with his garden allows Charlie to observe the results of his choices and actions, to revise and refine his garden, and simply to enjoy its nourishment. Perhaps the biggest lesson of Charlie's garden, indeed of all the forest gardens we have seen, is that forest gardens should meet human needs. Your forest garden should meet your needs. If it meets your needs in many realms, you will find yourself fulfilled, strengthened, encouraged, and motivated to continue playing with it. The more habitable and private you can make your garden, the more comfortable in different seasons, at different times of day, and in different social situations, the more time you will spend in your little corner of paradise. After all, spending time in paradise is what forest gardening is all about.

1. Webster's New Collegiate Dictionary. Springfield, MA: Merriam Co., 1981.
2. Thank you Doug Kraft for this analogy!
3. Soule and Piper, 1992, page 127.
4. Soule and Piper, 1992, pages 143–44.
5. Soule and Piper, 1992, pages 143–44.
6. We are indebted to Soule and Piper, 1992, for this analysis.
7. Mollison, 1988, page 69.
8. Mollison, 1988, page 38.
9. Soule and Piper, 1992, page 116.
10. These drawbacks are discussed more fully in chapter 4 of Soule and Piper, 1992.
11. Cronon, 1983. Presumably population densities were higher farther south.
12. Wolkpomir, 1995, page 104.
13. Bill Mollison, thanks.
14. See Kimmins, 1997, pages 439–41 for an excellent discussion of the various meanings of stability.
15. Colinvaux, 1986, page 681.
16. Leopold, 1949, quoted in Sauer and Andropogon Assoc., 1998.
17. Marinelli, 1998, page 73.

PART TWO

Ecology

"Don't give me academic theory; give me practical advice and actions!" That's what I heard, appropriately, in the certainty of the 1970s. But at a time of confusion, such as the 1990s, promising and relevant theory is the only antidote to dated ideology or belief. . . . Oddly, one of the most practical things we could recommend now is massive support for the expansion of new theory.

—C. S. HOLLING, *The Renewal, Growth, Birth, and Death of Ecological Communities*

The map is not the territory.

—ERIC BELL

At its simplest, edible forest garden design involves choosing plants and deciding when and where to place them in the garden. These seemingly simple choices must generate the forestlike structures that achieve our design goals. However, simply creating a physical structure resembling the forest is probably not sufficient to fulfill all the goals we seek. We must also mimic the forest's invisible "social structures" and how forests change through time. Practical strategies for edible forest garden design, planting, and management arise from promising and relevant theories about these fundamental aspects of forest ecology.

The conceptual tools we present in the following chapters may prove more essential to good forest garden design and management than your shovel, pruners, and wheelbarrow. The well-equipped forest gardener must be able to observe well and to understand and interpret what he or she observes. At the same time, it is essential to recognize that the map is not the territory, the concept is not the reality, and plants don't read books. The ideas presented in this section are gateways through which we can pass to a deeper understanding of the forest, of our gardens, and, let's hope, of ourselves. If we get stuck at the gateway, we will never get into the Garden itself.

The first two chapters in part 2 examine the five elements of the forest's physical architecture and the social structures of the forest and the garden. These help us create diverse yields, self-maintenance, and high productivity. The next chapter explores the interrelationships of soils, nutrients, roots, and microbes that help us generate self-renewing fertility. The last chapter explores the changes in these elements as forests move through successional processes.

. . . theory gives fresh meaning to old places, connects the seemingly unrelated, and guides action.

—ANNE WHISTON SPIRN, *The Language of Landscape*

The Five Elements of Forest Architecture

The five elements of the forest's visible, physical architecture help make the forest what it is—in our eyes, hearts, and minds and on the ground. These fundamental components—vegetation layers, soil horizons, vegetation density, patterning, and diversity—define the physical structure of forest ecosystems as they change through time and anchor the invisible social structures that make the system work. We pattern these five elements when we select plants and choose where and when to place them in the forest garden.

VEGETATION LAYERS

The vertical structure of the forest is one of its defining attributes. Ecologists commonly categorize this structure into between four and seven layers in temperate forests. Robert Hart describes seven "stories" in his forest gardening scheme: the canopy; the low tree layer; shrubs; herbaceous plants; the soil surface; the root zone or rhizosphere; and the vertical or vine "layer."[1] Patrick Whitefield simplifies this to four—trees, shrubs, vegetables, and vertical—partly due to the challenge of differentiating between layers, and partly because most people in Britain have small lots where large trees are generally unsuitable. Despite

the difficulty of categorizing vegetation in this way, it is helpful both in understanding forest ecology and in designing forest gardens.

THE LAYERS DEFINED

Our layer definitions are either relative or absolute (see table 3.1 and figures 3.1 and 3.2). Relative terms include those whose meaning depends on their relationship to other layers of vegetation, and they relate to ecological function. Absolute terms define height categories and the kinds of plants that tend to inhabit them.

Almost any layer of plants can be the overstory, as long as there is a plant layer below it; we define a canopy as any overstory over 12 feet (4 m) in height—small to very large trees, large or very large shrubs, or high vines. For example, we do not consider a mass of dwarf fruit trees a canopy, though it could be an overstory, since such trees are usually 8 or 10 feet (2.4 to 3 m) high at most. Similarly, a highbush blueberry patch is not a canopy, but the blueberries could form either an overstory or a woody understory in the shrub layer.

The kinds of plants (herb, shrub, and tree, for example) only loosely relate to specific heights. Some shrubs (in a botanical sense) extend into the low tree layer, some herbs extend into the shrub layer if they are of sufficient height, and many shrubs mature in the herb layer, or even in the

TABLE 3.1. Forest garden layers and horizons

Layer Relative	Height (feet)	Height (m/cm)	Definition / Plant Forms Included
Overstory	Any	Any	The topmost layer of any two or more layers of vegetation
Canopy	12–150+	4–45 m	Any overstory higher than 12 feet (4 m): trees, shrubs, vines
Understory	Any	Any	Any layer of vegetation under an overstory
Root Zone	<0	<0	The litter, humus, leaching, and deposition layers of the soil (O, A, E, and B horizons); the "true soil"*
Absolute			
Tall Tree	50+	15+ m	Trees and vines
Low Tree	12–50	4–15 m	Trees, large shrubs, and high vines
Shrub	6–12	2–4 m	Trees, shrubs, vines, and very large herbs
Herb	0.5–6	0.15–2 m	Herbs, shrubs, trees, and scrambling vines
Ground	0–0.5	0–15 cm	Any plants, woody or herbaceous, plus the current year's leaf litter or mulch
Vine	0.5+	15 cm+	Woody or herbaceous climbing vines
Topsoil	Variable	Variable	The uppermost, fertile, organic layers of the soil, including the litter, humus, and leaching layers (O and A horizons)*
Subsoil	Variable	Variable	The lowest layer of true soil, where leached nutrients and humus are deposited (E and B horizons)*
Substratum	Variable	Variable	The nonliving parent material, that is, mineral soil and bedrock (C and D horizons)*

* See figure 3.5 and the discussion of soils in the next subsection for more information.

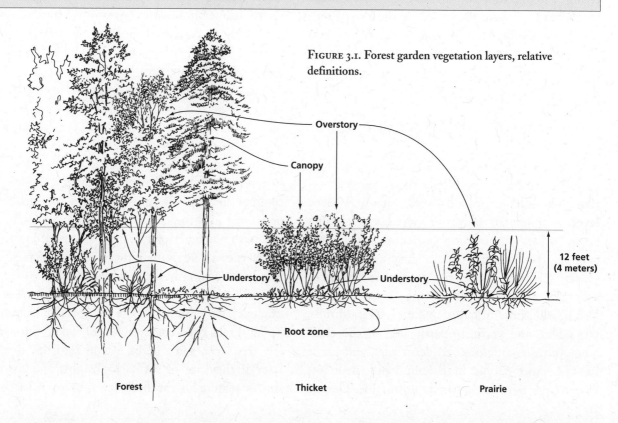

FIGURE 3.1. Forest garden vegetation layers, relative definitions.

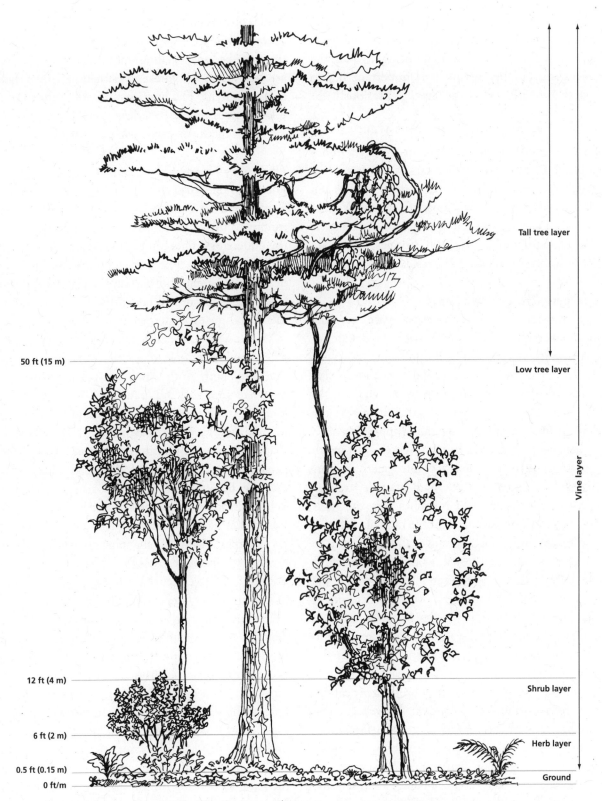

50 ft (15 m)

12 ft (4 m)

6 ft (2 m)

0.5 ft (0.15 m)
0 ft/m

Tall tree layer

Low tree layer

Vine layer

Shrub layer

Herb layer

Ground

FIGURE 3.2. Forest garden vegetation layers, absolute definitions.

ground layer. While we know that these layer names might be confusing, the terms help one visualize and understand what might be going on in the ecosystem. For this reason it is important not to take the specifics about the layers too seriously.

THE FUNCTIONS OF THE LAYERS

Each vegetation layer has different ecological functions, and affects the other layers in the ecosystem in various ways. Understanding these functions and effects will help us design most effectively. We discuss some species for each layer below. Appendix 1, "Forest Gardening's 'Top 100' Species," discusses the best forest gardening species, layer by layer.

Overstory: Tree or Shrub Canopy

The overstory takes up the most space, gets the most sun, and uses the most nutrients and water of any layer in the community. It dominates photosynthesis and biomass creation and therefore greatly influences the soil environment by the character of its nutritional needs and leaf litter. It affects the biology and chemistry of the rain dripping through it: lichens and bacteria in an Oregon old-growth forest canopy fix the majority of nitrogen that enters the soil ecosystem; leaves and branches release nutrients, hormones, and microbes into the raindrip.[2] The canopy also patterns the rainfall: different tree shapes and branching angles direct raindrip to the edges of the tree crown, or down the trunk to the soil, or they may scatter it evenly under the branches. And, of course, the overstory determines the amount of sunlight passing to lower layers of plants. All understory layers must therefore adapt to the conditions created by the overstory.

In a forest situation, numerous species fill the role of canopy tree, and a number of useful trees can fill that role in the forest garden. However, some canopy trees are sun loving and shade intolerant, tending to reach the canopy early in a forest's life or when there is a major disturbance. Most fruit and nut trees fall into this category, having been selected and bred for orchard situations. Other trees are shade tolerant and can germinate and live below the canopy while they wait for an opportunity to break through the "green ceiling" into the sun. These trees are well suited to a forest gap situation, where there is less sunlight. The best examples of useful shade-tolerant trees are the American beech (*Fagus grandifolia*) and the sugar maple (*Acer saccharum*).

Understory Tree and Shrub Layers

Forest understory trees usually tolerate shade. Some need to eventually make their way to the canopy to thrive, while others live and reproduce in the understory. Those in the first group back up the canopy, ready to take over should disturbance or death create a gap. Both groups add vertical diversity, and therefore habitat, to the forest, as well as increasing the ecosystem's net primary productivity.

Most useful understory trees produce more fruit when they have more sun, although some are fully shade tolerant. Both American persimmon (*Diospyros virginiana*) and pawpaw (*Asimina triloba*; figure 3.3), for example, grow fine and produce fine in full sun. However, pawpaw will also grow in shade and can even produce in partial shade, while persimmon will not produce very well in shade. This may be because the pawpaw's native habitat is floodplain forest, while persimmon is a midsuccession suckering tree. Both have tasty, nutritious fruit. As another example, shadblow serviceberry (or juneberry, *Amelanchier* spp.) can take either a tree or a shrub form, tolerates shade or sun, and yields fruit of varying quality depending on the selection.

The understory shrub layer is similar in that it contains some young trees or shrubs that will regenerate the canopy. It also adds vertical structure and increases the net primary productivity of the ecosystem as a whole. However, being at a lower height, the shrub layer offers ground-dwelling animals (that's us) opportunities for food that the understory tree layer does not.

Most useful shrubs love sun and evolved in intermediate succession or forest-edge environments. Many spread by means of suckers or underground

FIGURE 3.3. Pawpaw (*Asimina triloba*) is a shade-tolerant floodplain forest understory tree native to North America. It produces tasty, highly nutritious fruit, coppices, and has interesting chemical properties currently being explored for pesticide and medicinal uses. *Photo by Dave Jacke.*

runners, such as American plum (*Prunus americana*), or from multistemmed shrubs that send up new stems from the root crown to replace older stems, like hazelnuts (*Corylus* spp.) or juneberries. The shrubs that survive under a forest canopy generally produce fewer fruits and nuts than the earlier succession species unless they, too, grow in full sun or close to it. Exceptions exist, though, especially among the gooseberries and currants (*Ribes* spp.; see feature article 2 on page 76). If you want, you can develop a shrubby canopy that resists invasion by trees.[3] This requires dense, sun-loving, and sun-hogging species that self-regenerate, often from root sprouts.

Herb and Ground Layers

Plants in these layers often conserve and cycle large quantities of critical nutrients, especially in the early spring (see chapter 5). With up to fourteen species per square yard (12 per sq. m) in old-growth forests, they contribute greatly to plant diversity and strongly support insect diversity. The herb and ground layers tend to exhibit higher productivity because of their proximity to the soil, which gives off large amounts of carbon dioxide. The ground layer also offers a home to fallen logs, leaf litter, and other debris that are critical components of structural diversity and overall system stability. We humans find these layers the easiest to observe, manage, and harvest, and we know the most about them.

We can choose from a number of useful shade-loving or shade-tolerant edible herbaceous perennials. The wild leek, or ramp (*Allium tricoccum*), reigns as the king of the edible spring ephemerals. It is one of the tastiest and easiest-to-grow spring greens (see figure 3.4). Food, however, isn't the only good yield from a shady understory. Many important medicinal plants love the shade or tolerate it, including famous ones like ginseng (*Panax quinquefolia*) and goldenseal (*Hydrastis canadensis*). A number of plants that attract beneficial insects evolved in the shade, as did some good soil-improving plants. We discuss herbaceous species in more detail in feature article 2 (page 76).

Vines

The vine "layer" can develop in any of the other vegetation layers or in all of them, depending on the vine and host species. Though frequently simple freeloaders, vines may become parasitic if they end up reducing their host's health and productivity. This seems to happen most often with opportunistic exotic vines. When we choose to host vines, we take on the work of providing structural support in return for their fruit, usually using trees, dead or alive. The vine layer is rather adaptable to our needs and the kind of system we choose to create.

FIGURE 3.4. The leaves and bulbs of the ramp or wild leek (*Allium tricoccum*) are one of the most delicious spring edibles around. As spring ephemerals ramps come and go quickly, but they are worth waiting and looking for. Easily propagated from seed or bulb transplants, they like moist, rich soil and grow well in hardwood forests where they are shaded in summer and can gather early spring sunshine. *Photo by Dave Jacke.*

Grapes (*Vitis* spp.) are the most common vine crop, and they require full sun and warm temperatures for best production. In the wild, grapes grow all the way to the canopy to meet this need. Vines that can produce in partial shade, such as hardy kiwis, may be more useful.

Hardy kiwis (*Actinidia arguta* and relatives) evolved in forest-edge habitats in northeastern China. These delicious fruits are high in vitamin C. We have not yet selected and bred them much for vineyard conditions, so they still tend to possess some good shade-adapted qualities. Michael Dolan

of Burnt Ridge Nursery in southwest Washington State grows hardy kiwis on trellises between rows of Turkish tree hazels (which are fairly tall trees) and up the north side of a huge spruce tree. He gets good yields in both environments. In southern New Hampshire, Doug Clayton tried growing hardy kiwis in the shade of red oaks at a west-facing forest edge and did *not* get good yields. Whether this was because of shade, root competition, or a mismatch in soil microbiota or chemistry is hard to say. Kiwis are vigorous vines, with one plant covering a large area quickly. A few biologists have said they are "invasive," but we have seen no evidence that they disperse readily.

THE FUNCTIONS OF THE LAYERS AS A WHOLE

In addition to their different individual functions and effects, the layers all share certain characteristics that are valuable to keep in mind when we design.

Layers are an aspect of plant niche. Different plants use different strategies for making a living, make use of different resources at different times of the year, have different tolerances and different abilities to compete, and ally themselves with different partners in the process. We call the sum of all of a plant's or animal's unique characteristics, tolerances, form, functions, and behaviors its niche. Which layer(s) a plant inhabits is a basic part of its niche. Is the plant a canopy or understory tree? A canopy or understory shrub? An understory herb? As you imagine these and other plant niches, you might get a sense of some of the plants' other characteristics, such as shade tolerance, plant associates, or successional stage. We solve the puzzle of how to locate a plant in space and time in part by examining a plant's layer adaptations.

More layers means more opportunities for yield. Plants need not occupy all the layers for a stand to be a forest or a forest garden. One could design a garden that had two useful layers, say a fruit tree canopy and a diverse herbaceous layer; however, such a system would not take full advantage of the opportunities that vertical structure offers. Depending on what you are trying to achieve, we would advocate finding space for additional plants in additional layers. A garden with plants in all its layers captures the maximum possible solar energy and offers more opportunities to produce yields. We must balance this against the benefits of "lumpy texture" (see "Diversity" on page 101) and the limits to vegetation density (see "Vegetation Density" on page 84).

More layers mean more bird species. More bird species make their home in plant communities with more layers than in those with fewer layers,[4] probably because more resources and habitats exist in multi-layered communities. A similar correspondence presumably exists for insects and other invertebrates, because many birds depend upon them for food. Since well over 90 percent of birds and insects are beneficial, increasing their diversity helps us reach our goal of maintaining low and balanced pest populations. The upshot: more layers will increase bird diversity generally, and possibly insect diversity. However, if you want to attract specific species, you will need to create specific habitat features, since the requirements of each species vary (see volume 2, appendix 5).

Mixed age stands stabilize the ecosystem. According to some foresters, if a forest doesn't have at least three layers, it isn't a forest, or at least it isn't a stable or healthy one.[5] This has to do with the forest's ability to regenerate itself: if there is only a high canopy and an herb layer, for example, the canopy will have nothing to replace it. Mixed-aged stands are therefore usually more stable over the long run than even-aged stands. Uneven-aged structure shows up in the lower vegetation layers as seedling and sapling trees and polewood. A mixed-aged stand can benefit orchards and forest gardens by evening out yields over the years, always providing at least some young and vigorous trees, and preventing a sudden turnover of trees that can leave you fruitless until younger trees mature.

SOIL HORIZONS

> The soil profile is an instant indicator of important ecosystem processes. These processes proceed with remarkable independence of the parent rock.
>
> —Paul Colinvaux, *Ecology*

Soils are a mystery. If you dig a hole in undisturbed forest, you will exhume distinct layers of soil with different colors, textures, and consistencies as your shovel descends. You will find roots, worms, and other critters living in the upper layers, with less life, less brown soil, and more olive, yellow, or red soil as you go deeper. If you probe far enough you may hit water, and the soil will have changed color there, usually to a grayish hue. Eventually, you will hit bedrock and will be able to dig no further. What do these layers, or soil horizons, mean? Why are they there? What do they have to do with forest gardening?

When life interacts with mineral particles, soil is born. Essential ecological processes occur in different parts of the soil column to different degrees, and these different processes affect the character of the soil differently. Soils express these differences in the visible patterns of their horizons, known collectively as the soil profile.

By now, it is practically a cliché: healthy soil generates healthy plants, healthy forests, and healthy forest gardens. Less well known is the fact that plants are essential to the creation and maintenance of a healthy soil community, and in some surprising ways. We improve our ability to design, plant, and manage forest gardens by understanding the functions of soils, how the soil profile expresses these functions, and how plants support healthy soil biology.

The following discussion assumes a deep, well-drained forest soil in a humid, temperate zone.

Feature Article 2:
With All These Layers, What Do I Grow in the Shade?

This, understandably, is one of the questions people most frequently ask about forest gardening. It has several answers.

Forest Gardens Aren't Necessarily Deeply Shaded

Forest gardens rarely mimic the scale, density, and late-succession character of true forests. Therefore, many forest gardens will never have deep shade even with plants growing in every layer, and those that will often won't have deep shade for many years. In addition, there will be edges, crop rotations, and disturbances that create sunnier places. So there are plenty of opportunities to use sun-loving and partial-shade-adapted plants, to bank on the additive yields of many species that each yield less than they would in the full sun, and to design gaps and clearings that allow for at least some sun-loving crops within the forest garden.

Some Sun-Loving Crops Still Produce in Partial Shade

Most typical garden crops originally evolved in the sunny habitats of early succession. We have since bred these annuals for high production in full sun, with no selection or breeding for production in shade. Even the woody perennial crops—fruit trees, small fruits, and many herbs—probably evolved as early to midsuccession species and have been selected and bred for sun-filled growing spaces. As a result, these crops will not yield well in full shade.

Sun-loving plants have a high capacity to use bright light—they can kick into high gear—but in return cannot produce much in low light. Also, many sun-loving plants burn their stored energy faster in the dark than do shade-tolerant plants (i.e., they have a higher dark respiration rate).[6] However, even sun-loving plants are easily oversaturated with light well beyond their capacity to use it: most plants reach their maximum rate of photosynthesis—known as light saturation—at between 16 percent and 50 percent of full sunlight (for shade-adapted and sun-adapted plants, respectively).[7] This means that a number of sun-loving plants may tolerate partial shade and still produce effectively, though perhaps not exuberantly.

Many greens, for example, can be healthy and productive in partial shade and even manage fairly well at the darker end of partial shade. In fact, plants often grow larger leaves in shade than in full sun! The annual greens at my former homestead in New Hampshire were happy in the partial morning shade of a birch tree, then two to three hours of full sun, followed by the diffuse sky light and solid afternoon shadow of the house. They needed less water and each plant lasted longer as a cut-and-come-again crop without going bitter. Perennial greens such as French sorrel and its relatives can grow fine crops in partial shade. Also, the farther away from the Poles one goes, the stronger the light gets, so sun-loving plants have more tolerance for partial shade in the southern United States than in the dimmer light of northern areas.

We recommend experimenting with different crops, especially greens, in partial shade to see which ones do best for you and your site. We also strongly suggest that you select for and develop the partial-shade production capacity of your favorite crops. Selection and breeding are easier and more fun than you might think (see chapter 7 in volume 2).

Grow Plants Adapted to Shady Conditions

If you want to grow the most food in a shady forest-garden understory, you must grow plants adapted to shady conditions. The most useful shade-tolerant plants tend to be herbaceous perennials, especially native ones. Native herbaceous plants tend to have more specific ecological requirements than do their canopy cohorts. Learning the native plant communities in your area is fundamental to understanding how plants have adapted to the climate and soils of your region, and to finding out which native plants, or similar nonnatives, may serve your goals. It is therefore necessary to know your shade, soils, and plants well. Observing different kinds of shade in different environments feeds your plant selection process, especially when you get to know a plant's native habitat and its strategy for dealing with shady conditions.

Unfortunately, while we could define numerous kinds of shade, it is impossible to get consistent, reliable information on plant shade preferences beyond full sun, partial shade, and full shade. We know little on a broad basis about which specific kinds of shade specific plants prefer. Nonetheless, we can still work with this variety by understanding the strategies plants use to adapt to shade. What strategies do plants use to deal with these different kinds of darkness? In addition to the slower dark respiration rate mentioned earlier, shade-loving herbaceous plants have two basic strategies that allow them to grow and reproduce in the dimness. Let's characterize these two strategies as the "slow-and-steady" approach and the "hurry-up-and-wait" approach.

Slow-and-Steady: Summer Greens and Evergreens
"Slow-and-steady" plants tend to stay leafed out over the entire growing season or year-round ("summer green" plants and evergreens). Evergreens in particular photosynthesize a large portion of their total production before the upper layers of vegetation leaf out or after their leaves fall, but all slow-and-steady plants can also slowly accumulate energy all season long.

Shade-loving plants can achieve 40 to 60 percent of their photosynthesis from moving sunflecks—small patches of intense sunlight shining through small holes in the canopy. They can rapidly switch their photosynthetic process on and off, unlike sun-adapted plants, using even 5- to 10-second-long sunflecks efficiently.

The occurrence of many small sunflecks increases the average light intensity in lower layers, so that small-leaved trees can have high crown density while enabling plants that use light efficiently to photosynthesize effectively.[8] Long exposure to the bright light and heat of direct sun can easily overwhelm many slow-and-steady plants. These plants also usually grow slowly, so they cannot compete well with sun-tolerant species when in full sun. The slow-and-steady strategy is most appropriate for uniform or fractured partial shade or for part-day shade conditions.

Hurry-Up-and-Wait: Ephemerals
The "hurry-up-and-wait" species, also known as ephemerals or spring ephemerals, leaf out, gather energy for a while, reproduce, and then go dormant. Most importantly, this strategy allows some of them to grow in virtually full sun, since their leaves emerge before those of the canopy trees. It also provides them with access to abundant spring moisture and the first flush of soil nutrients, minimizes their expenditure of energy on respiration and risk of being eaten, and limits competition. Ephemerals generally require cool, moist soil during dormancy, so they may not do well out in the open. Plants using the hurry-up-and-wait strategy work fine in almost all shade conditions except deep building shadows where there is no spring sunshine to be had. Hurry-up-and-wait may be the only viable strategy for understory herbs in densely layered or densely canopied deciduous forests with uniform deep shade.

Many forests display a yearly round of herbaceous perennials that share the same space at different times of the growing season, one suite of ephemeral plants coming and going after another. Though we may struggle to recreate such an herbaceous perennial tag team with useful plants, it seems a good ideal to strive for, since it is an effective way to minimize competition and maximize diversity and yield.

How else can we make use of the shade for food production? Not only should we choose plants adapted to shady conditions, but we also need to think about what plant parts we harvest.

Seek Yields Appropriate to Shade: Roots, Shoots, Leaves, and Fungi

Plants have a limited amount of energy they can use to meet their needs for immediate metabolism, resource gathering, building and repairing their bodies, alliances and defense, next year's reserves, and reproduction. Flowers, fruits, and seeds are the last items on a plant's energy budget wish list, unless it thinks it is about to die. Trying to grow fruit, seed, and nut crops in the shade will generally be an uphill struggle with a few small successes, though there are some significant exceptions. Instead, we should focus our attention on yields that coincide with the strategies shade-tolerant plants use.

Roots, Shoots, and Leaves

Most temperate forest herbs spread primarily by vegetative reproduction, rather than by seed, because low light conditions limit their seed production. Therefore, we typically use the roots, stems, or leaves of shade-tolerant plants like wild ginger (*Asarum canadense*), rosybells (*Streptopus roseus*), and wild leeks, rather than the fruits. Since the plants need to store energy for the following year's growth, harvesting these plant parts directly reduces the future viability of the plant. Signs of overharvesting could take several years to show up. Yields from these plants will generally be seasonal, and may be low on a per-square-foot basis. Luckily, most wild edibles are highly nutritious and can contribute significantly to our diet even if their caloric content is low.

Fungi and Medicinals

Mushrooms are a completely new world for most people. The moist, shady environment of the forest garden is ideal for many fungal friends, and a number of these species grow with minimal effort, such as the king stropharia (*Stropharia rugoso-annulata*; see volume 2, appendix 2 for more species). Yields of mushrooms can be extremely high, and they can grow on materials considered waste or mulch by most gardeners. The side effects of mushroom production on nutrient cycling and biological balance benefit the garden as a whole.

Many shade-tolerant plants are useful farmaceuticals. Again, though yields may be low in some cases, their total impact on our lives can be significant. A small quantity of leaves or roots can create a large amount of tincture, for example. Classic medicinals like goldenseal and ginseng are great forest garden species, but many less-well-known plants also do well in the shade. Tuberous chickweed (*Pseudostellaria jamesiana*) is one lesser-known shade-tolerant medicinal plant and superfood, its mineral-rich leaves providing healing to all tissues, especially the lungs and skin. Its tasty tubers and lettucelike leaves are also good edibles, while its flowers attract beneficial insects.

Fruits and Nuts in the Shade

If you have more of an interest in fruit crops or nuts, then the shade productivity potential is probably lower than for herbaceous crops. Some exceptions exist, however.

Research by Martin Crawford at the Agroforestry Research Trust in Devon, England, shows that gooseberries and red currants grown under 40 percent shade cloth showed no decrease in yield over plants grown in the full sun.[9] Many currants and gooseberries evolved in semishady and shady environments. I have seen wild gooseberries and currants in New England fruiting moderately in full shade below thick canopies, such as young maple trees. Another example is the pawpaw, a tree that grows wild in the understory of mature floodplain forests in the Southeast and Mid-Atlantic states and out into the Midwest and yields tasty, nutritious fruit in partial shade or full sun, though we have never seen heavy crops in full shade. Again, a plant's native habitat is a decent guide to its shade tolerance and potential shade productivity, though this is not foolproof. Luckily, the additive yielding of forest garden systems provides some insurance against low yields of any particular crop.

Surprisingly, time, climate, and vegetation type influence the characteristics of the soil profile more than does geology. Hence, temperate deciduous forests all have similar soil profiles, so the dynamics discussed are similar across the temperate forest region, though there will be differences from site to site. This discussion is not accurate for boreal, subtropical, semiarid, or arid regions, including most of the prairies. We will discuss details of how to work toward soil health and self-renewing fertility in chapter 5. What follows is essential background for that discussion.

Each of the six typical temperate-forest soil horizons reveals the preeminence of certain inner workings, when one knows what to look for (figure 3.5). The basic pattern is this: climatic and life processes dominate at the surface, and geology, chemistry, and physics dominate at the bottom. Each horizon in between reflects differing degrees of influence of these two interacting sets of forces.

Soil scientists used to recognize only four horizons: the topsoil, subsoil, substratum, and bedrock (called the A, B, C, and D horizons, respectively). In recent years, they have separated the organic and eluviation horizons (labeling them O for organic and E for eluviation, which means "leaching") from the A and B horizons because of the distinctive processes that dominate there. Mimicking the naming of the O and E horizons, we have named each of the original four horizons based on its letter designation in soil science and its reigning ecological process.

TOPSOIL: THE ORGANIC (O) AND ASSIMILATION (A) HORIZONS

The living topsoil is home to uncounted trillions of organisms essential to terrestrial life, many of which scientists have never seen or named. It contains more usable nutrients than any other horizon because it has enough organic matter and oxygen to fuel the earthen economy. This, then, is also where the most plant roots grow, seeking physical and biochemical support and adding to the tumult of life in these few spare inches of ground.

Topsoil depths in the temperate deciduous forest region range from 3 inches (8 cm) or less on steeper hillsides to 2 feet (60 cm) or more in floodplain soils. Construction and farming activities often disrupt or mix the organic and assimilation horizons, so that we cannot always tell them apart in agricultural or suburban areas. Even in shallow or disturbed topsoils there's a lot going on—more than we can ever know or imagine.

The Organic Horizon

Fresh and partially rotted organic matter lying on the soil surface, not yet mixed with mineral soil, forms the O horizon. This mulch layer absorbs and conserves moisture, protects the soil from compaction by rainfall and footsteps, and provides habitat for insect predators. It moderates soil temperatures, which prevents frost-heaving of plants and root winterkill (tree roots die below 20° to 25°F/-4° to -7°C). Mulch sometimes allows roots to continue growing all winter long if the soil temperature remains above 38°F/3°C.[10] The leaf litter also represents a big reserve of both nutrients and energy, and it acts as the "town dump" at the beginning of the community's nutrient recycling system.

Many living things make their home in the O horizon, at least part-time. Networks of fine-textured, short-lived tree roots grow into the organic layer when conditions are right, dying back when things turn sour. Spiders, mites, and predatory insects hide, search, and destroy. Snakes, toads, small mammals, and birds give birth, hunt, eat, nest, and die there. Fungi, bacteria, nematodes, and protozoa move in and out as conditions allow, trying to be the first to get their favorite foods, and the last to be eaten by someone else.

The usual human activities easily disturb these communities. They need time to develop their community structure, the right conditions, a diversity of organic matter foods, and maybe a little tender loving care in order to be there and stay there. When we eliminate the O horizon by tilling it under or raking up all the debris, we interrupt the

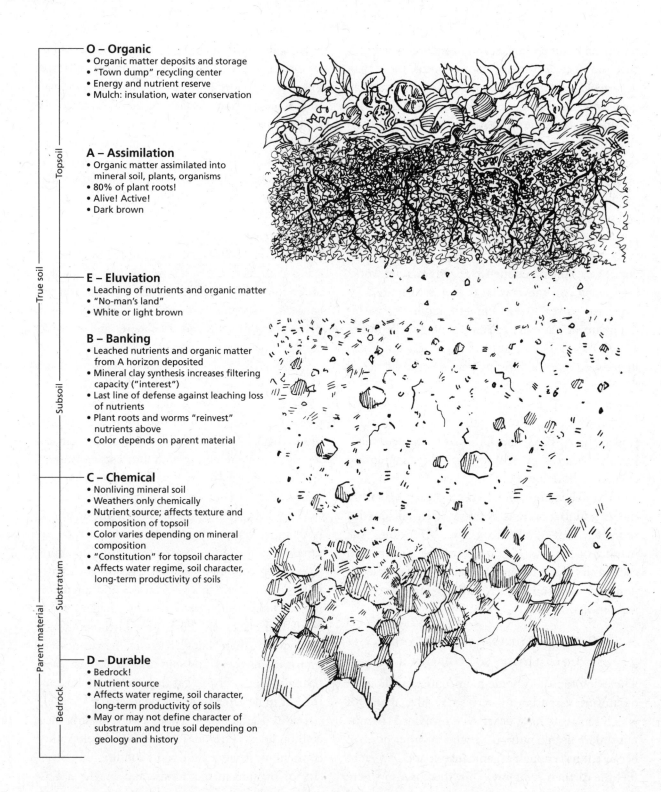

O – Organic
- Organic matter deposits and storage
- "Town dump" recycling center
- Energy and nutrient reserve
- Mulch: insulation, water conservation

A – Assimilation
- Organic matter assimilated into mineral soil, plants, organisms
- 80% of plant roots!
- Alive! Active!
- Dark brown

E – Eluviation
- Leaching of nutrients and organic matter
- "No-man's land"
- White or light brown

B – Banking
- Leached nutrients and organic matter from A horizon deposited
- Mineral clay synthesis increases filtering capacity ("interest")
- Last line of defense against leaching loss of nutrients
- Plant roots and worms "reinvest" nutrients above
- Color depends on parent material

C – Chemical
- Nonliving mineral soil
- Weathers only chemically
- Nutrient source; affects texture and composition of topsoil
- Color varies depending on mineral composition
- "Constitution" for topsoil character
- Affects water regime, soil character, long-term productivity of soils

D – Durable
- Bedrock!
- Nutrient source
- Affects water regime, soil character, long-term productivity of soils
- May or may not define character of substratum and true soil depending on geology and history

Topsoil

True soil

Subsoil

Substratum

Parent material

Bedrock

FIGURE 3.5. The six soil horizons and their ecological character and functions.

processes by which nature builds this soil community and make the soil dependent upon our activities for its continued vitality. Such disruptions can also make the habitat inhospitable for the beneficial organisms, while encouraging the fungi, bacteria, or insects we don't want. We humans must then work harder to keep things in balance—another example of shifting the burden to the intervenor.

The Assimilation Horizon

Assimilation happens in the A horizon in many ways: microbes, invertebrates, and larger animals assimilate energy and nutrients from the organic matter, the soil assimilates organic matter into its structure, the roots of plants assimilate water and nutrients into their bodies, and the soil ecosystem assimilates energy from the plants. At the same time, organic material washes into the A horizon from above, and clay, nutrients, and chemicals wash out of the A horizon whenever water moves through it.

Percolating rainfall and a host of organisms mix organic materials into the mineral soil below. There, the decomposer community attacks the organic matter from all sides, breaking it down further. More or less predictable sequences of microbes and invertebrates eat different kinds of organic matter on the forest floor at specific stages of decay.[11] The energy and nutrients locked up in the organic matter stoke the fires of this decomposer community, and the decomposers tie up the nutrients from the organic matter, preventing the nutrients from washing away in the rainfall. The decay-resistant humus that results from decomposition has many beneficial effects on the soil: it increases aeration, as well as water-holding capacity and nutrient-storage capacity; it aggregates soil particles; and it decreases soil density while improving its structure. Humus and other forms of organic matter give the A horizon its typical dark brown, coffee-bean color.

Healthy topsoil hosts a highly complex living community of many sizes, shapes, and habits, with each element having a role to play in this mysterious theater of death and rebirth. About half of plant biomass lives belowground, mainly in the topsoil horizons, with a higher percentage there in droughty or less fertile soils where the importance of roots to plant survival increases.

The biomass of insects, worms, and other invertebrates in forest soils is equivalent to that of between 4 and 13 sheep per acre (10 to 33 per hectare), and it accounts for the vast majority of animal biomass in forests. Scientists once estimated that soil microbe biomass in a British wheat field equaled the weight of about 40 sheep per acre (100 per hectare), and that was a wheat field, not a healthy forest soil.[12] In contrast, a friend of mine runs about 3 sheep per acre (7 per ha) on fairly poor New Hampshire land, while good soils under intensive management can support an average of 5 or 6 sheep per acre (12 to 15 per ha) year-round on a low-input, sustained-yield basis.[13] Soil biology consultant Elaine Ingham talks about farmers needing to "manage their belowground microherds."[14] How true! Plants play a key role in this.

Plant roots add considerably to the dynamics of the A horizon by loosening it, sloughing off rich organic material as they grow and die, and secreting all manner of chemicals into the soil environment. Each plant species gives off a characteristic complex of compounds into the soil environment to support and manage the microbes in its root zones, even varying its secretions at different times of the year to favor different organisms (see chapter 5).

The constant addition of organic matter from above keeps the A horizon rich with nutrients and energy, and the dynamic soil ecosystem uses that energy and thereby traps nutrients in the A horizon as long as possible. But while these processes build the topsoil, percolating water is tearing it down by washing components of the topsoil into the subsoil, and sometimes beyond.

SUBSOIL: THE ELUVIATION (E) AND BANKING (B) HORIZONS

In these horizons the soil begins its shift from a living, moving, breathing ecosystem toward a relatively lifeless mineral realm. The subsoil serves as the last best chance for nutrients leached out of the topsoil to be captured and recycled back to the surface. Spongy or friable subsoils present little restriction to water flow, oxygen movement, and root growth. Compact, fine-textured, or solid subsoils restrict rooting depth and water and oxygen movement and can lead to loss of health and productivity in your garden. The subsoil ranges from less than 6 inches (15 cm) to several feet in thickness.

The Eluviation Horizon

When it rains and the topsoil can't hold any more water, the excess water seeps downward, carrying fine particles and chemical compounds from the topsoil with it. This is eluviation, or leaching, the same process that occurs in making coffee.

Technically speaking, eluviation occurs in the O and A horizons frequently; however, other soil processes dominate in those layers. Here, the process of eluviation exceeds the process of assimilation to the point that, when it exists, the E horizon has less organic matter and fewer nutrients than the horizon above, and less clay than the horizon below. Its lighter, bleached color stands in significant contrast to the color of the topsoil. Eluviation dominates and characterizes the E horizon; hence its name. Whether or not the horizon exists or shows itself by a strong color shift, eluviation happens wherever rainfall exceeds evapotranspiration. The eluviation horizon ranges from zero to many inches in thickness. It can begin from a few inches below the soil surface to 2 or more feet down.

The E horizon verges on being a no-man's land. Lacking organic matter and depleted of clays, it has only limited nutrient-storage capacity. Its proximity to the soil surface means there are still significant amounts of water pulling away what materials it has and carrying through it the materials that come in from above. Luckily, below the E horizon there is often more soil where these nutrients are deposited, so they have a chance to be "loaned back" into the soil economy above.

The Banking Horizon

The B horizon begins from several inches to several feet below the surface. It "is a zone where minerals are strongly weathered and materials leached from the A and E layers tend to accumulate."[15] Like the interest a bank earns to increase its wealth, a mysterious process of synthesis in the B horizon creates "secondary minerals" or mineral clays from deposited material.[16] These tiny, honeycombed particles possess a very great amount of surface area, about one million times the surface area of a solid cube the same size. Their negative electrical charges catch and hold passing nutrients, increasing the "wealth" in this underground bank. Plant roots can then make "withdrawals" from the bank's nutrient assets, cycling them back into the aboveground community. Our earthworm friends also carry these clays up into the topsoil, increasing the topsoil's ability to hold nutrients and water. Feeding the earthworms with organic matter increases this mixing process.

The B horizon therefore supports the long-term nutritional health of the ecosystem. If there were no "bank" where leached nutrients were deposited, they would pass into soil layers too deep for plant roots to use or wash out of the soil completely and go downstream. This trickle-down scheme can work to the benefit of the biotic masses only as long as there is a means to recycle the accumulated "assets" back into the economy of the surface.

PARENT MATERIAL: CHEMICAL (C) AND DURABLE (D) HORIZONS

The "parent material" constitutes the matrix that gives birth to a soil. That matrix is the bedrock if the soil is very young or if there is a substratum of mineral particles weathered from the bedrock over time. Where glaciers, rivers, or gravity have laid down deep, fine-grained deposits, the substratum becomes the parent material and the bedrock minimally affects conditions near the surface.

Like our own parents, the parent material provides the "genetic basis" or constitution of the overlying soil, influencing its texture, structure, consistence, drainage, acidity, and mineral composition. The ecological processes in the horizons above then modify this constitutional foundation tremendously. The influence of life is so great that the mineral balance of the upper soil layers is usually radically different from that of the parent materials. However, any nutrients lacking in the parent material will probably be in short supply in the aboveground and topsoil ecosystems.

Substratum: The Chemical Horizon

The mineral particles in this horizon weather chemically, not biologically. Water does most of this work, but organic acids leached from the upper layers help out, too. The C horizon can also accumulate the nutrients from the upper horizon that are more soluble, such as calcium, magnesium, potassium, and sodium. Only a small percentage of plant roots reach into the substratum, but when they do, they significantly enhance the water and nutrient balance of the plants and the aboveground ecosystem (see "Deeply-Rooted Trees Do It Better" in chapter 5, page 201). The substratum can start within a foot of the surface on the poorest soils or several feet below the surface in deep bottomland soils. It may be well over a hundred feet thick in glaciated or alluvial areas or in erosional valley bottoms.

The texture, structure, and consistence of the substratum help determine the drainage characteristics of the topsoil and subsoil: how well drained are the upper layers, how much water the soil profile can store, and whether that water can move upward in the soil by capillary action to supply the vegetation above. If the substratum is too compact, fine grained, or solid, then the growth and movement of plant roots and water will be limited.

Bedrock: The Durable Horizon

Bedrock changes only very slowly. It is weathered generally only by water and leached acids, but occasionally by plant roots or ice if it is close enough to the surface. Like the substratum, the kind of bedrock a site has will tend to influence the texture, structure, and consistence of the overlying soil. For example, slate usually weathers to yield fine silt and clay particles, whereas sandstone weathers to yield sandy soils.

The kind of bedrock in a region influences the water regime below the ground, and this affects the drainage characteristics of the surface layers. Whether the bedrock fractures or is otherwise able to drain or collect water affects plant survival, especially in shallow soils.

TABLE 3.2. Summary of soil horizon functions.

Topsoil:
- Stores and recycles energy, nutrients, and water; processes organic matter
- Moderates soil temperatures
- Primary physical and biochemical support for plants
- Loses nutrients, organic matter, and clays to lower horizons by leaching
- Economy fueled by organic matter decomposition and plant root exudates
- Location of the bulk of animal and microbial biomass and diversity in forest ecosystems, and about half of plant biomass
- Hosts formation of soil aggregates that improve soil texture and structure; water- and nutrient-holding capacity; soil porosity, drainage, and aeration; and microbial habitat diversity
- May limit productivity if too wet, dry, thin, compact, clayey, and so on

Subsoil:
- Captures and stores some nutrients leached from topsoil
- Secondary physical and biochemical support for plants
- Synthesizes nutrient-grabbing mineral clays
- Stores water, and passes it up to topsoil when texture and roots allow
- May limit rooting depth if too wet, dry, compact, clayey, and so on

Substratum and Bedrock:
- Provide constitutional basis for long-term soil fertility
- In younger soils, an important nutrient reserve
- Provide deep water and nutrient storage accessible by some plants
- May limit rooting depth if too wet, dry, shallow, compact, clayey, and so on

VEGETATION DENSITY

Every person possesses a unique, variable, and mostly unconscious sense of personal space. Plants are no different. When plants get too close to each other, they don't thrive. How close is too close depends, frequently, on specific, knowable resource needs, but plants often need space for reasons unknown to us. The opposite is true, too: sometimes they need to be closer together.

We will discuss three interacting kinds of density. Coverage or percent cover strongly influences light and shade, as well as the overall character and resource demands of the plant community. The crown density of individual species also influences these factors. Root density determines the level of belowground competition between plants. We will focus primarily on percent cover and root density and then integrate all three as we begin to explore how to space plants reasonably in complex polycultures. Vegetation density defines ecosystems. Complete canopy closure makes a forest a forest, but do we want such high density in our forest gardens?

COVERAGE DEFINES COMMUNITY CHARACTER

The terms *coverage*, *cover value*, and *percent cover* all simply mean the percentage of the ground covered by a given plant, plant species, or forest layer. Ecologists assume that comparing the coverage of layers or of different species in a given layer will indicate those layers' or species' relative importance to, and influence on, the ecosystem. They consider the topmost layer with coverage over 50 percent the dominant layer. A species with cover values over 50 percent in a given layer is considered dominant in that layer, or in the stand as a whole if the layer is the overstory. Three species each with 20 to 30 percent coverage would be considered codominant, as long all other species are sparsely represented.

For example, imagine part of a forest garden (figures 3.6a and b). You can estimate the coverage of each layer using a simple evaluation system: Look at the plan view of the forest garden (figure 3.6a)

and ask yourself which of the following categories applies to the percentage of the area in the garden covered by, for example, the tree layer:

- Does the layer cover 75 to 100 percent of the horizontal area?
- Does it cover 50 to 75 percent of the horizontal area?
- Does it cover 25 to 50 percent? If it does, does it appear that the average distance between crowns is equal to the average radius of crowns?
- Or does the layer cover less than 25 percent of the horizontal area?

Just take your best guess for each layer using these categories. Once you are done, look at table 3.3, which shows the measured coverage of each layer in this bed. Notice that "cover" includes the gaps in a plant's crown (figure 3.6c): scientists consider the gap area to be under the influence of the crown. Well, maybe. This makes it easier to estimate cover values and design them, and it ignores crown density differences between species.

Despite this fact, percent cover more or less defines plant community character. The coverage of the top layers determines, in large part, the conditions in the layers below. And the coverage of all the layers combined affects the amount of water and nutrients required to support the community as a whole, and vice versa.

TABLE 3.3. Cover values of the plants shown in figure 3.6a. Cover is in square feet and percent of total. The percentage is taken relative to the horizontal area of the space, not the total cover of plants.

Vegetation Layer	Actual Cover	Percent Cover
Tree	1,241	50%
Shrub	564	23%
Herb	1,515	61%
Bare Ground	6	<1%
Total Cover	3,326	134%
Horizontal Area	2,500	100%
Overlap	826	34%

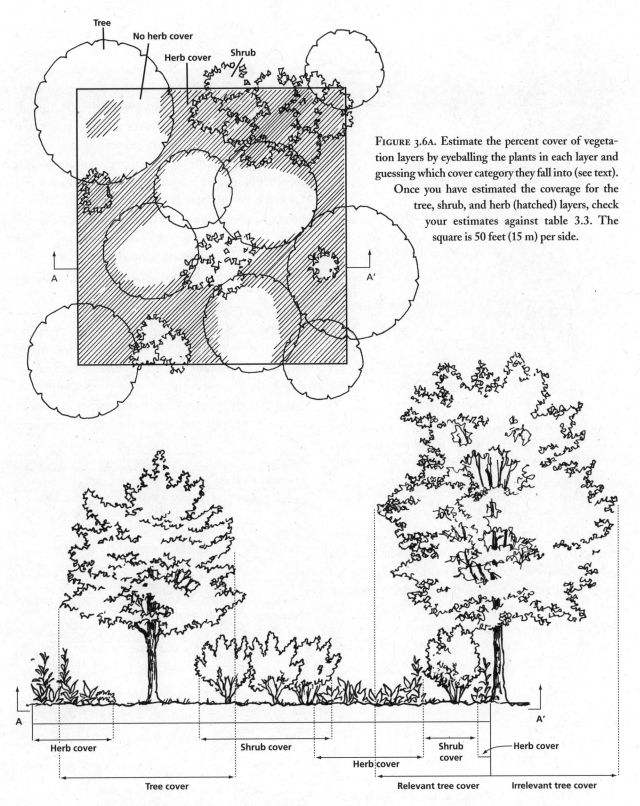

FIGURE 3.6A. Estimate the percent cover of vegetation layers by eyeballing the plants in each layer and guessing which cover category they fall into (see text). Once you have estimated the coverage for the tree, shrub, and herb (hatched) layers, check your estimates against table 3.3. The square is 50 feet (15 m) per side.

FIGURE 3.6B. Section A-A' of figure 3.6a, showing how coverage bubbles are drawn or imagined.

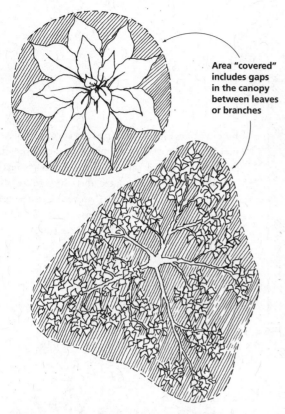

Area "covered" includes gaps in the canopy between leaves or branches

FIGURE 3.6c. When estimating cover, gaps in the canopies or spaces between leaves are considered part of the coverage area because they are said to be "under the influence" of the canopy, as shown.

We don't expect you to use coverage as a precise tool, getting uptight about measuring what percent cover you have in each layer. However, it is a useful lens through which to view the community, and to keep in mind when designing. So let's quickly visit the realm of numbers to explore the impact of coverage on a few different plant communities. Then you can take what you like and leave the rest. As we discuss these different examples, imagine how you might mimic such communities in your forest garden.

Coverage in Various Plant Communities

Naming plant communities is about as arbitrary, and necessary, as naming vegetation layers: you have to draw the line somewhere so you know what you are talking about. We will here define as a forest those tree communities with 100 percent canopy coverage and interlocking tree crowns (table 3.4, figures 3.7a and b). Any tree stand without interlocking crowns we will call a woodland (figure 3.7c and d), unless tree coverage is less than 40 percent. Below 40 percent tree coverage, the plant community is considered a shrub thicket, shrubland, or grassland, depending on which other layer has more than 40 percent coverage. The 40 percent cover value is fairly easy to estimate in the field: when the average distance between tree crowns equals the mean radius of tree crowns, coverage is about 40 percent (figure 3.7c).[17]

Natural Forest

In a forest with interlocking crowns (figures 3.7a and b), each tree is hemmed in by its neighbors, unable to reach its full potential form and spread. Trees in the shadiest corners must spend extra resources to grow, and then keep alive, the branches needed to reach out of their way to get sunlight. Let us note

TABLE 3.4. Definitions of plant community types based on cover values of the different layers. *Adapted from UNESCO, 1973.*

Community Type	COVERAGE IN EACH LAYER		
	Tree	Shrub	Herb
Forest	100%	any	any
Woodland	40–99%	any	any
Thicket	<40%	100%	any
Shrubland	<40%	40–99%	any
Savanna	25–40%	<40%	100%
Grassland	<25%	<40%	100% >50% grasslike
Forb community	<25%	<40%	100% >50% forbs

Coverage Guidelines:

100% = all crowns interlock, usually with crowns in irregular shapes

40% = average distance between crowns equals average crown radius

Notes:

Heath communities are shrub thickets or shrublands with dominant shrubs (>50% cover) growing to less than 18 inches (50 cm).

Grasslands must have at least 50% total cover by grasslike species; grasslike species include sedges, rushes, grasses, and so on.

Forb communities include fern thickets, wildflower meadows, farm fields, and so on with more than 50 percent total cover of nongrassy herbs.

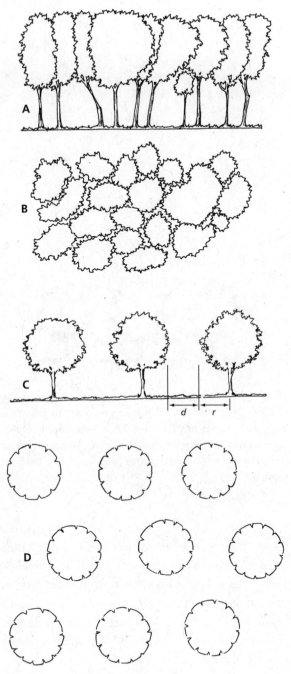

FIGURE 3.7A–D. Forest has 100 percent canopy cover, as shown in plan and section views (a and b). Notice the odd shapes of the interlocking tree crowns; if you look in a forest, they are rarely circular the way we tend to draw them. This density causes high stress and competition and lowers net productivity. Any wooded ecosystem with 40 to 99 percent cover is a woodland (c and d). When the distance (*d*) between crowns equals the radius (*r*) of tree crowns, cover is 40 percent. Woodlands have higher net production than forests.

here that the roots of the plants spread farther than the crowns. One hundred percent canopy coverage means that the trees' roots intermingle intensely. The trees are certainly competing for light, probably for water and nutrients depending on the soils and climate, and maybe for carbon dioxide in the air at times if the vegetation is dense enough.

This situation is typical of high-stress, high-competition-for-resources forest life. Ecologists call the individual plants that can survive and reproduce successfully in this environment "stress tolerators." This level of competition is one of the main aspects of forest ecosystems we definitely do *not* want to mimic in our forest gardens, except in special circumstances. This means that most forest gardens will not have 100 percent tree cover. Technically speaking, they will instead be woodland gardens. (See pages 2 and 32–34 for why we still call them "forest gardens.")

The coverage of forest understory layers varies tremendously. One can find forests with a dense canopy and little else, forests with every layer full or close to it, and every combination in between. Each has a different character, and each responds to and creates different conditions in and around itself.

Orchards

The woodlands we call orchards generally have two layers of vegetation: an herbaceous ground layer, commonly grass, and the tree canopy. Orchardists frequently plant the trees as far apart as their crowns will spread, so the tree crowns touch but don't interlock. Canopy cover values therefore range from 78 to 90 percent (for square and hexagonal patterns, respectively; figure 3.8). Compared to 100 percent coverage, as in forests, such spacing reduces light competition, allows the trees to reach their full potential form and spread, and maximizes the amount of leaf area relative to stem mass. This maximizes possibilities for gathering sunlight and minimizes the amount of energy going into maintaining stem biomass. At the same time, it achieves the greatest tree cover within those limits, and

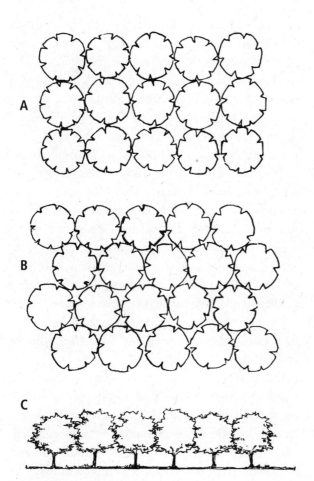

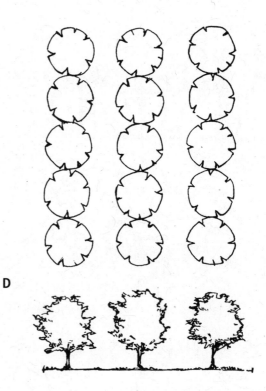

FIGURE 3.8A–D. Typical square-grid orchards result in coverage of about 78 percent (a), while hexagonal orchard geometries bring cover values to 90 percent (b). In section view, both of these crowns-touching arrangements look like figure c. When you add an 8-foot (2.3 m) lane, tree cover drops to 55 to 65 percent (d).

hence the greatest quantity of fruit produced per acre. Even so, the canopy does not cover 10 to 22 percent of the area, and sometimes more, leaving small patches of sun that might provide a home for other crops.

Many orchardists increase the distance between rows, as shown in figure 3.8d, to make maintenance access easier. Typical tree cover values can then range from 55 to 65 percent. A greater between-row distance also improves air circulation, quite important in reducing disease problems, and can allow frosty air to drain downhill. Finally, greater tree-to-tree distances further reduce competition between the trees for light, as well as for water and nutrients.

While the reduced competition of wider spacing should increase per-tree yields, the greater distance will, at some point, decrease per-acre yields because fewer trees are planted per acre. Professional orchardists most often want high per-acre yields of a single crop. Home orchardists more likely have an interest in high per-tree yields and high system yields of diverse crops. There's a big difference between the two, but in either case, the question of spacing is always a balancing act.

Oldfield Succession: Mosaics, Shrublands, and Woodlands

The cover values of all layers during oldfield succession vary over a wide range depending on age, history, and developmental pattern. We offer here images of some of the environments created with various cover values in different layers at a few

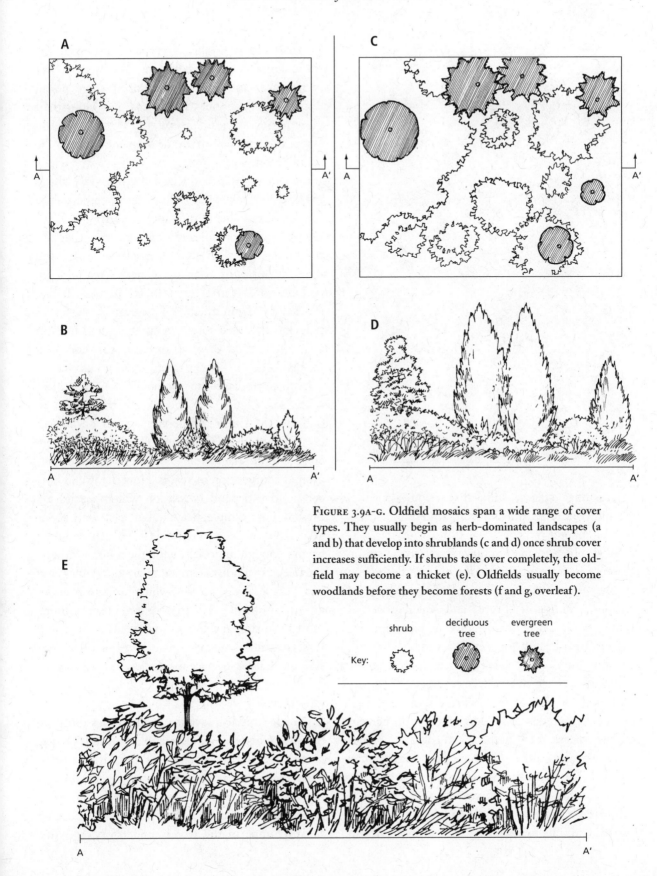

FIGURE 3.9A–G. Oldfield mosaics span a wide range of cover types. They usually begin as herb-dominated landscapes (a and b) that develop into shrublands (c and d) once shrub cover increases sufficiently. If shrubs take over completely, the old-field may become a thicket (e). Oldfields usually become woodlands before they become forests (f and g, overleaf).

Key:

| shrub | deciduous tree | evergreen tree |

F

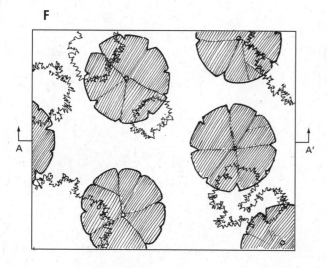

G

successional stages. This discussion also lays groundwork for our in-depth treatment of succession in chapter 6.

As shrubs and trees achieve a relatively strong presence in early succession, the oldfield becomes a mosaic of vegetation types, including patches of meadow, clumps of shrubs, and small groves of young trees. These sunny, diverse environments express great beauty. Figures 3.9a and b show such a community, with half the area dominated by herbaceous cover, shrub layer coverage of 25 percent, and 15 percent tree cover. Please note that though herbaceous cover dominates in 50 percent of the space, total herbaceous cover is higher because grasses and forbs (nongrassy herbs) grow beneath the shrubs and trees, too.

Once shrub coverage increases to 40 percent, a shrubland is born (figure 3.9c and d). As the shrub clumps continue to expand by root suckering or tip

layering and new shrubs sprout from seed, the shrub clumps begin to converge. Usually tree cover increases at the same time and, at some point, begins to shade out the shrubs and slow their growth. Sometimes, however, the shrubs grow too fast or the trees do not invade soon enough, and the stand becomes a thicket.

Like in forests, in thickets the overstory shrub crowns interlock at 100 percent cover, perhaps with the occasional tree lording over it all (figure 3.9e). Dense thicket canopies can create deeper shade in the understory than some tree canopies can, and they can resist invasion by pioneer trees for long periods—over thirty years so far in one thicket studied in Connecticut.[18] This can be useful in reducing the need to cut or spray sapling trees in power-line right-of-ways or view corridors and may be handy in some garden situations as well.

In the woodland environments of mid- to late succession (figure 3.9f and g), the trees begin to outgrow the shrub and herb layers but do not yet create an interlocking canopy. The more trees there are, the more shade is created, and the more below-ground competition increases. How shady and how competitive depend greatly on which species are present. For example, black walnut casts only about 50 percent shade even in full leaf. This shade is still bright enough to overwhelm the photosynthetic capabilities of most temperate-zone legumes and cool-season forage grasses, which saturate at about one-third of full sun.[19] In addition, black walnuts, most hickories, and bur as well as other oaks—all typical savanna species—tend to grow deep root systems that leave space for shallow-rooted species.

Savanna

In North America, savanna communities form the transition between forests and grasslands at the northern and eastern edges of the Great Plains, where average evaporation just begins to exceed average precipitation. Savannas have continuous grass and forb cover in the herb layer, scattered shrub clumps in the woody understory, and tree

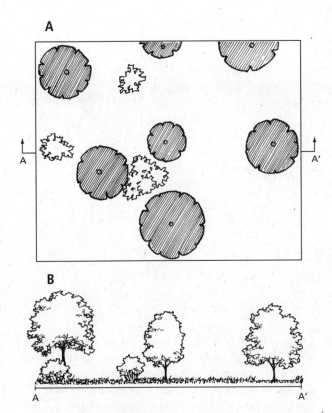

A

B

FIGURE 3.10A-B. Savannas consist of widely scattered trees or tree clumps in a grassland context. In this example, tree cover is 22 percent, about the minimum to be considered savanna at all.

and silvopastoral systems that mix trees with annual crops or pastures are two examples. However, in climates that are more humid, savanna is appropriate only on dry, fire-maintained, cultivated, or grazed sites. Otherwise "weed" trees and shrubs are likely to colonize your "savanna" and turn it into forest.

Coverage Summary

Estimating the cover value of the different vegetation layers is a handy way of characterizing the structure and conditions of the plant community, of conveying a picture of it, and of designing forest garden structure. It does not, however, express the fullness of vegetation density. We must consider at least two other elements that relate to vegetation density: crown density and root patterns.

CROWN DENSITY MODIFIES COVERAGE EFFECTS

Coverage ignores differences in the density of the actual plant crowns themselves. Hence, a Norway maple 50 feet (15 m) in diameter has the same cover value as a 50-foot-diameter black walnut, despite the fact that black walnut casts only about 50 percent shade in full leaf, while Norway maple casts up to 90 percent shade. Clearly, the overstory species' crown density makes a great deal of difference to what can grow in the understory, especially at high overstory cover values. Herbaceous species' crown density also matters, particularly if you intend them to be a weed-limiting ground cover. For that job, you obviously want a dense crown to outcompete any weeds that might try to sprout below the plants you want. Though genetics mostly determines crown density, stressed or unhealthy plants will show thinner growth. Light conditions and site fertility also affect leaf and branch abundance.

We have found little crown density information for trees other than natives (see volume 2, table 3.25; we have no data for shrubs). More data on this topic would be useful for serious edible forest garden design. Data showing winter (leafless) density would

cover between 25 and 40 percent[20] (figures 3.10a and b). They exhibit drought-tolerant prairie plants as well as deep-rooted, fire-resistant woody plants. Some computer models indicate that this vegetation type may expand as our global climate changes in the coming decades.

Bur oak (*Quercus macrocarpa*) dominates many oak savannas, but other oaks also occur in this type, predominantly post oak and blackjack oak (*Q. stellata* and *Q. marilandica*, respectively), especially in the south. In the north, hickories can be major players in the oak savanna as well. These trees all cast a light shade. Savanna trees tend to clump together rather than spacing evenly apart, and in dry and windy climates, they tend to clump in moister soils.

Mimicking such an ecosystem should be relatively easy with such useful trees as models. Alley cropping be useful when considering solar gain on buildings or light levels for spring ephemerals. Many trees still cast 50 percent or more shade even when bare in the winter! You can estimate the density of an existing tree crown by observing it yourself. The best way to do this is to use broad density categories such as those in volume 2's table 3.25, and then estimate how much sky you can see between leaves from the ground. A rough estimate is fine.

Root Density Determines Belowground Competition

> The space arrangement of those parts of trees which are above the soil is mainly decided by their roots and the competition existing between them for water and food in the ground.
>
> —V. T. Aaltonen, "On the Space Arrangement of Trees and Root Competition"

We should take the arrangement of plant roots more seriously in landscape design than we do generally, but this is especially true in edible forest garden design. Selecting and locating plants so they partition soil resources will minimize competition and maximize production. Most tree root research in humid climates has focused on apples, with some work on other fruits and a little on nuts and wild forest trees. These studies make some useful conclusions possible, some of which we will discuss here, with more in chapter 5.

European, Russian, and U.S. researchers have found that apple-tree root systems spread from 1.5 times the tree canopy diameter in fertile, fine-textured soils, and up to 3 times the canopy width in poorer, sandier soils where resources are more scarce (figures 3.11a and b). Most work on other fruit trees confirms this observation, with average root area diameters of 2.25 times the crown diameter.[21] This means that the total area covered by a tree's roots ranges from being 2 times larger than the crown area in good soils to being 9 times the crown area in poor soils, being on average about 5 times the horizontal area of the crown. Wild North

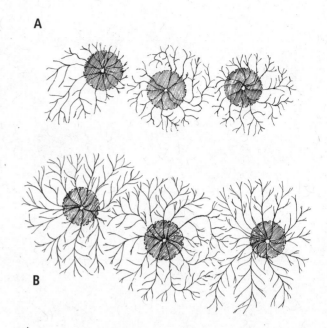

Figure 3.11a–b. In fertile, moist soils (a), fruit tree roots usually spread to 1.5 times the crown diameter, yielding a total horizontal root area that is 2.25 times the crown area. In infertile, dry, or shallow soils (b), fruit trees spread their roots to 3 times the crown diameter, yielding a total root area that is 9 times the crown area! So the question is, on your site, which resource(s) are most limiting: water, nutrients, or light? This should have a major influence on your plant spacing.

American forest tree roots spread well beyond the drip line of the canopy, covering 4 to 7 times the canopy area and often having a total diameter up to twice the *height* of the tree! We have found very little data to shed light on root patterns among nut trees in orchard situations. A study of young pecan tree root systems in "soils typical of Georgia" shows a root spread more in line with that of wild forest trees: 2 to 3 times tree height and 3 to 4 times canopy width (figure 3.12).[22] These data pretty well dispose of the common myth that tree roots spread only to the drip line of the tree canopy!

Additional research indicates that at least some trees, such as apples, peaches, and persimmons, don't like to intermingle their roots with those of other trees of their own species. Since competition is highest between individuals of the same species, this makes some sense, though other factors may

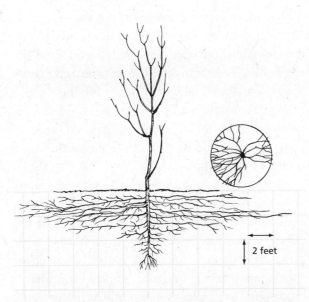

FIGURE 3.12. This pecan tree in Georgia was six years old when dug up for this diagram. It had a branch spread of 5.5 feet (1.6 m) and was 13 feet (4 m) high, but its roots were 6 feet (2 m) deep and 24 feet (7 m) wide. The circle shows the orientation of the eleven largest lateral roots. *Adapted from Woodruff, 1934.*

play into it. Little research appears to have been published on most other crop trees in this regard.

These points taken together have some interesting implications. Root competition between trees planted at a normal orchard spacing (crowns touching) will be high, particularly if the orchard is all one species, more so if the trees of the species don't like their roots intermingling, and especially in poorer soils. In poor soils—shallow, dry, infertile, or with high water tables—the controlling factor in tree spacing should be the diameter of the root spread, not of the crown. In deep, fertile, moist, well-drained soils this is less of an issue, because soil resources are less limiting. In any case, close spacing will probably work best when the planting is a mix of species that are more likely to share the soil by intermingling their root systems.

THE LIMITS TO DENSITY

A given piece of land can support no more than a certain total amount of vegetation at any given time. Water, light, and nutrients frequently become primary limiting factors. Vegetation density directly affects the level of competition among plants for these resources. If there is more vegetation than the site can support, all the plants will be stressed, and some will die in order to maintain the balance. How much is too much?

The total leaf area in natural temperate deciduous forests rarely exceeds 8 times the ground area, and most deciduous forests have between 4 and 6 times the leaf area.[23] We cannot easily measure or even estimate this. Coverage is the best gauge of this factor for the layperson, inexact as it is. Chances are that if you design a forest garden with every layer 100 percent full of vegetation, you are pushing the vegetation density limits for your land (unless crown densities are low and you have a very fertile, well-watered site). On poorer soils, the site will support less. Your plants will therefore be under stress, will not thrive or produce as well, and some may die. Even without too much total vegetation, spacing plants too closely can have the same effects. Planting trees too close together is the biggest, most common mistake we have seen in all our forest garden travels!

PATTERNING

The patterns we find in natural and managed ecosystems both build and reflect the ecological functions and relationships in the system. Straight rows of crops resulting from the requirements of large-scale industrial agriculture reflect the relationships between people, beliefs, equipment, crops, and landscape, for example. These industrial patterns feed back into the system to cause new kinds of landscapes, crops, equipment, beliefs, and people to evolve.

The patterning of natural systems results from myriad factors interacting similarly, some of which we shall discuss below. Understanding the functions of forest ecosystem patterns helps us choose our garden patterns more wisely. What patterns might we want to mimic, and why? Which might we want to avoid mimicking, and why? In addition, many patterns in our forest gardens will not be found in natural forests, for they arise from our goals, needs, and desires. In like fashion, these patterns both build and reflect the relationships between and among us and our gardening partners—plants, birds, insects, and microbes. All such patterns exist at regional, neighborhood, and backyard scales.

The following section will only begin discussing patterning by addressing a few key ideas at large and small scales. Chapter 6 extends the discussion of patterns as part of understanding plant succession, and chapter 2 in volume 2 develops a whole language of patterns for us to use in forest garden design.

Patterns *of* the Forest

North America's forests used to cover many acres with relatively unbroken canopy, subsuming any patches, gaps, and edges within them. Edge zones were minimal, while interior forest was maximal. Today the reverse is true: the forest exists primarily as patches and edge zones within an open context. Forest interior is minimal or nonexistent, while edge zones are maximal. Some ecologists say the effects of these edges extend into the forest 100 yards (90 m), others say over a mile.[24] This means that the overwhelming majority of forest gardens, even those in existing woods, will be edge environments to at least some degree. Our forest gardens are also likely to be islands of unique biology in a sea of less unique biology. What might these larger patterns mean for our gardens?

Classic Edge Effects

The "edge effect" theory states that the transition zones, or edge environments, between different communities, such as between field and forest or pond and upland, have higher diversity, population density, and, according to some, productivity. In theory, this is because they contain species from the environments on both sides of the edge, as well as species adapted to and found only in the edge environment.[25] In the past two decades, many ecological designers, ourselves included, have touted the edge effect as a means to increase farm and garden diversity and productivity by increasing the amount of edge farms and gardens contain.[26] Of course, it turns out it is not as simple as that. We need to tease apart the theory to find the pieces that have more or less validity.

There is no substantiation for higher edge-zone *productivity* except in wetlands and midsuccession environments where the edge effect may not be the cause. In addition, evidence of increased edge-zone plant *diversity* and *density* is spotty: some edges show more diversity or density than adjacent habitats, some less. Classic edge effects occur most often in wide edge zones (tens of meters to hundreds of kilometers) rather than narrow ones.[27] This restricts the usefulness of the theory for small-scale design. Higher edge-zone diversity at a small scale is most clearly documented in bird populations. Finally, when edge zones interconnect and dominate, as they do today, they become perfect migration routes for disturbance-adapted opportunist species. These species can actually *decrease* the diversity of edges and of adjacent forests because they can sometimes outcompete many plants they encounter (see feature articles 3 and 5).

Despite these facts, the increased diversity and population density in certain edge environments should cause us to sit up and take notice. These effects can be good for our gardens, depending on what we want to grow. While we are aware of the possible benefits of edge zones, we must beware of the potential drawbacks. The challenge is to get the benefits while discouraging the negative effects.

The complex vegetation mosaic of midsuccession habitats (see figure 3.9) is a classic edge-habitat model that we can use in our forest gardens. Diversity and vegetation density are typically high in these habitats, and net primary productivity (NPP) is higher than for climax forest (see "Changes in Ecosystem Characteristics through Succession" in chapter 6, page 265). The edges between land and water, such as marshes and wet meadows, are among the most productive habitats in the world (see figure 2.2)—up to 70 percent more productive than temperate forest and three times more productive than agricultural land. Midelevation sites on mountains often have higher species diversity than lower and higher elevations, because species from both the highlands and lowlands can survive there. Certainly it is true that a sharp edge between forest and field is less diverse than a wide edge zone with a diversity of shrubs, small trees, grasses, and herbs. Since this is similar to the midsuccession habitats mentioned above, wide forest edges are probably more productive, too.

Surface Area Effects

We should not confuse edge effects in the classic ecological sense, as above, with the effects of increased surface area. Sometimes having maximal edge, or surface area, is ideal. Our lungs and intestines are perfect examples: to get maximal interchange of gases and liquids from one side of a membrane to another, increase the edge. For maximum surface area to capture sunlight, increase the edge (figure 3.13). For maximum blueberry planting space along the edge of a pond, increase the edge (figure 3.14). For maximum access to the interior of a garden bed, increase the edge (figure 3.15). Just remember that if you have more edge to work with, so too do the weeds that want in! As Martin Crawford says, "Forest gardens are not infinite and edges are a permanent feature. The inevitable consequence of having permanent edges is work! . . . The key, then, is not to go for maximum edge at all costs, but to come to a compromise."[28]

Alternatively, if you want to create dark forest-interior habitat in the smallest possible area, you want to minimize the edge or surface area of the forest. If you want to fence your garden at the least expense, then you want a compact shape with the least amount of edge. If you want a ground-cover patch with minimal opportunity for invasion by

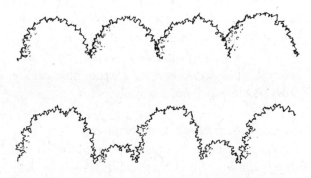

FIGURE 3.13. The cross-sectional canopy surface area of trees spaced so their crowns touch (top) is one-third less than the canopy surface area of trees planted more widely and interplanted with shrub crops (bottom).

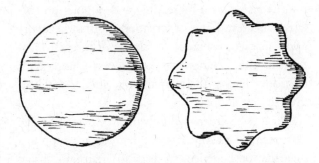

FIGURE 3.14. These two ponds have the same flat surface area, but the one on the right has 20 percent more edge because of its undulations. It therefore provides more habitat for blueberries on the edge, as well as more shallow water for fish or crustaceans.

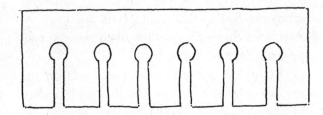

FIGURE 3.15. Keyhole patterns in garden beds, made famous by Bill Mollison, mimic the structure of our intestines and lungs. All these patterns are designed to maximize the surface contact between two environments, in this case between garden bed space and path space. This maximizes opportunities to move materials and energy across the boundary, while minimizing the space required to do it.

perennial weeds, then you want to plant in a circle. Think about what you are trying to achieve, and then consider the shapes and sizes that will best help you achieve it. Edges are a fact of physical life and a possible tool, not a panacea.

Fragmentation, Islands, and Corridors

The fragmentation of once enormous forests has led to patches of forest that act like islands in a sea of fields and suburbs. Ecologists studying Pacific Ocean islands figured out a long time ago that the smaller an island is, the harder time it has maintaining high diversity and stable populations of any given species: out-migration increases, in-migration decreases, and inbreeding and population collapse threaten. These observations of island ecology apply just as reasonably to islands of forest amidst the suburbs. Connecting these forest islands with corridors helps them maintain stable, healthy, diverse populations.

Our forest gardens will rely in large part upon the existence of nearby natural habitat to supply a diversity of beneficial insects to maintain insect population balances. Therefore, consider the context of your forest garden. What natural habitats exist nearby? Are there corridors that connect your garden to these habitats, or can you create one? Will your forest garden be an island or part of a web? Whether or not you can change whatever reality you face in this regard, it is important to know what that reality is. Only then can you take appropriate action in the face of it.

What makes a good corridor depends on the species you want to attract. For beneficial insects, the best corridor will be a mix of trees, shrubs, and flowering herbaceous plants that is permanent and unsprayed with pesticides and has a year-round litter or mulch layer on the ground and a season-long supply of nectary flowers from the families Apiaceae, Asteraceae, and some Lamiaceae (umbels, asters—i.e., composites—and some mints). Roadsides can offer such corridors for birds and beneficial insects, depending on how they are

managed. Many birds will require a larger territory than most backyards can offer. Finding out which bird species are already around will help you determine which ones you might want to attract to your yard to help control pests, and how.

Once you have determined the pattern of nearby habitats and connecting corridors, you will need to make the garden a haven for these friends of our crops. If your forest garden will be an island, with no significant habitats nearby or no corridors to connect to them, you had better make your garden a paradise—and the bigger the better! To some degree it is true that "if you build it, they will come." And with the right habitat elements in place, they will stay. Even if they don't come, though, you will have what you need to make a home for any beneficial insects you may buy or relocate to inhabit your garden. In the meantime, get your neighbors to start forest-gardening, or thoughtfully seed some good, tough, native habitat plants around the neighborhood guerrilla-style. Expanding your biological island will increase the balance and sustainability of your gardens and your neighborhood. We discuss the habitat requirements of insects and birds in chapter 4 of this volume and in appendix 5 of volume 2. Please also read the discussion of natives and exotics (feature articles 1, 3, and 5) before you consider planting *any* plants in your neighborhood (or your yard, for that matter). It is possible to throw ecosystems out of balance, even with the best of intentions.

PATTERNS *in* THE FOREST

Patterns within forests relate mostly to the distribution of plants. Three basic patterns of plant distribution appear in nature: random, regular, and clumped (figure 3.16). Knowing the reasons behind these patterns of plant distribution can help us design our forest gardens.

Random patterns. When a species has a random distribution, plants of that species are as likely to be near one another as they are to be far from one another—the location of one plant has no influence

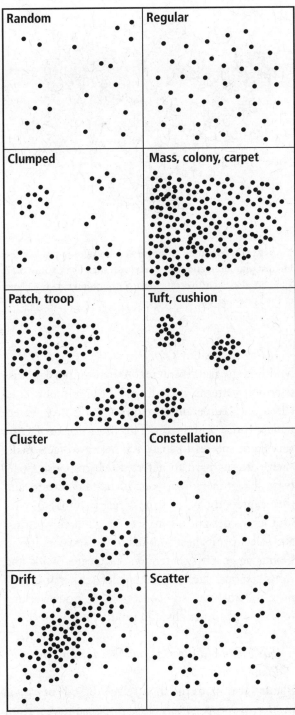

TABLE 3.5. Clumped pattern definitions.

Clump: a dense, compact grouping with fairly definite edges; frequently one plant with many stems, or a plant and its daughters; somewhere between a tuft and a patch or troop in size

Mass, colony, carpet: a large, dense grouping with fairly definite edges; a huge clump, or many clumps or numerous individuals growing densely over a large area

Patch, troop: a dense, medium-size grouping with fairly definite edges; a medium clump, or several clumps, or many individuals growing in a clump

Tuft, cushion: a small, dense grouping with fairly definite edges; a small clump, or a few individuals growing closely together

Cluster: a loose clump, less compact, but still with fairly definite edges; often roundish, usually with fewer individuals than a clump

　Constellation: a very loose cluster with few individuals, but still in a definite group; may take any shape

Drift: a grouping where the spacing between elements varies from dense near the middle to scattered at the edges; often in an overall pattern that is somewhat linear, curvilinear, or elliptical

Scatter: a helter-skelter accumulation; similar to a drift, but less dense, with no consistent pattern of density and not in an overall linear or curvilinear pattern; may cover a larger area than a drift

FIGURE 3.16. Basic distribution patterns in nature. The many meanings of *clumped* are organized from most dense and distinct to least (see also table 3.5). Different plants tend to end up in one or more of these patterns because of the way they disperse themselves. Mimicking these patterns can lead to elegant and functional design.

on the location of another plant. Truly random patterns are rare, even with wind-distributed seed, but randomness is always a factor in plant distribution.

Regular Patterns. Regular patterns can be human geometries, as in an orchard, or they can be the result of severe competition for a scarce resource. Some plants in the desert Southwest exhibit a natural regular distribution because water shortage causes the plants to spread themselves apart at approximately equal distances to each other. Regular patterns do not often develop in humid temperate forests unless humans are involved.

Clumped Patterns. Most plants distribute themselves in clumped patterns of one kind or another: in stands, patches, or drifts; in radial or linear patterns; in colonies, mats, carpets, troops, tufts, or cushions (see figure 3.16 and table 3.5). As many a landscape designer will tell you, clumps or drifts of

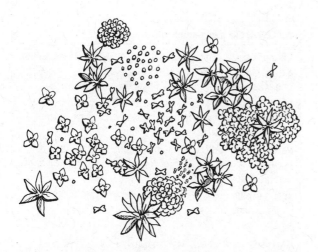

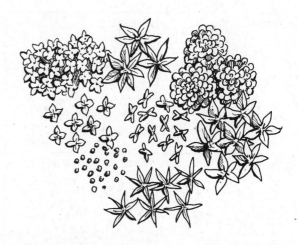

FIGURE 3.17. Mixing the distribution patterns shown in figure 3.16 provides great interspecies contact and a natural look. Compare to figure 3.18.

FIGURE 3.18. Mixtures of single-species masses provide less interest and interaction than mixtures such as in figure 3.17. They are also likely to create more competition between plants of the same species.

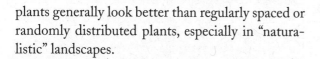

plants generally look better than regularly spaced or randomly distributed plants, especially in "naturalistic" landscapes.

Species Mixtures. When plant species mix in natural polycultures, the above patterns overlay each other (figure 3.17). Drifts and clumps of different species may interweave or may spread out into scatters or clusters to make room for each other. Masses of one species may grow in a patch next to masses of other plants, with clumps, drifts, or scatters of another species mixed into one or the other or both of the masses. Many combinations are possible. Note that species mixtures patterned as interwoven drifts, clumps, and scatters have more opportunities for interspecies interaction than do neighboring single-species masses (compare figure 3.18 with figure 3.17).

Functions of Patterns in Forests

Patterns are both causes and effects of ecological functions in ecosystems. Here are a few examples of how patterns can aid us in design and management.

A Response to Site Conditions

Multiple site factors interact to determine plant distribution patterns, including soil pH and nutrients, elevation, temperature regimes, moisture, water-table depths, and so on. The most critical factors vary from species to species. These two facts make such patterns hard to detect. Such responsive patterns take time to sort out in natural forests, and they express themselves most clearly in old growth. Our job as designers is to second-guess this process and select plants best adapted to the site conditions. Going against these tendencies creates work and stress for ourselves and our plants, either from the need to "improve" site conditions or from working to keep a plant healthy and productive, or both.

The Result of Dispersal and Propagation Methods: Plant Habits

Plants also pattern themselves based on their means of propagation and dispersal (see "Run, Rhizome, Run" in chapter 5, page 207). These two fundamental aspects of plant niche reflect both a plant's "choices" about how best to survive and the environment in which the plant evolved. Therefore, these functions and patterns may have value to us or our plants of which we are not aware. When possible, we urge you to allow plants their natural functions or patterns unless they are clearly detrimental to your own interest. Again, going against these functions and patterns tends to create work and stress for both you and the plant.

In this book, we will use specific terms to denote particular aspects of plant growth and dispersal patterns. *Dispersive* plants spread their seed rapidly, in great numbers or to great distances, usually via wind or animals. This often, but does not always, result in successful establishment of seedlings over large areas. The pattern of dispersal depends upon the means of dispersal: birds tend to deposit seeds and manure under perches, resulting in clumped distributions. Wind patterns and landscape structure influence the deposition of wind-dispersed seeds, and usually create drifts and scatters of one form or the other.

Plants exhibit a number of vegetative propagation methods. Rhizomatous plants—whether herbaceous or woody—spread by means of underground runners, called rhizomes (which are actually modified stems), from which secondary shoots and roots arise. Root suckers are also secondary shoots; however, they develop from true roots, not rhizomes, and mostly occur in woody plants. Plants may also spread by stolons, which, like rhizomes, are modified stems, but these spread aboveground. Technically, such plants are called stoloniferous plants. Any of these three vegetative expansion methods may result in shoots arising near or far from a plant's main stem, depending on the species and its tendencies. We call especially vigorous rhizomatous, root-suckering, or stoloniferous plants *expansive* plants.

Which of these dispersal techniques a plant uses, and how far from the stem new shoots arise, influence the plant's dispersal pattern in the field and help define the plant's habit or behavior. Plant habits are a key element of polyculture design, so let's review a few more definitions, mainly concerning vegetative propagation.

Box 3.1:
The Principle of Relative Location

To enable one community member to functionally connect to another appropriate community member, we must put each in the right place relative to the other.[29]

Patterning and placement play major roles in creating, allowing, or preventing interaction between individual organisms and nonliving elements in ecosystems. Exactly what role they play depends on the elements involved and the kind of interactions they have. Consideration of the character of each component and the kind of relationship desired between them is fundamental to understanding optimal placement patterns for a given objective. This can get to be a complex business, but there are ways to simplify it. Natural systems appear to generate various patterns repeatedly for specific reasons, and we can mimic and alter these patterns for our own purposes. We lay out some functions of these patterns in this section. Thorough consideration of the patterns already existing in any site also aids this process. Later chapters here and in volume 2 will cover all of these aspects of determining the optimal relative location for each design element in your forest garden.

At the broadest level, plants fall into either of two categories: clumpers or runners. Within these categories, plants separate based on their form (tree, shrub, herb, vine, and their height) and how far apart shoots arise from each other. Most trees are singular, standard trees with one main trunk, for example. However, some trees put up shoots near their base, whether from the crown, root suckers, or rhizomes; we call these sprouting trees. Others grow shoots from rhizomes or root suckers at a distance from the trunk; these we call suckering trees. Multistemmed shrubs put up multiple shoots from the crown.

Rhizomatous, stoloniferous, and root-suckering shrubs are either thicket forming or mat forming, depending on their height. These shrubs may be either running or clumping thicket or mat formers, depending on whether they spread indefinitely. Herbs may also be mat-forming clumpers or runners, or they may be just simple clumpers or runners. This depends on how closely spaced the new shoots are and the height of the plants.

The variations in pattern that these plant forms and habits can create are manifold. We will discuss how to design with these variations in volume 2, chapter 4.

Defense Against Herbivory and Parasitism

Plants disperse themselves to minimize herbivory and parasitism and to maximize their offspring's chances of creating further generations. The "resource concentration hypothesis" states that "insect pests, particularly species with a narrow host range [i.e., specialist herbivores], have greater difficulty in locating and remaining upon host plants in small, dispersed patches as compared to large, dense, pure stands."[30] When a plant species scatters or is randomly dispersed, herbivores and parasites spend more time and energy finding their host and less time and energy eating and reproducing, and they have a greater chance of being eaten themselves. "Seedlings have the highest probability of establishing and surviving to adulthood when they 'escape' from herbivores and pathogens that are harbored by other trees of the same species. There seems to be little question that trees can 'hide' from natural enemies in species-rich forests."[31] This concept applies mostly to sexual reproduction and seed dispersal, since vegetative reproduction generally does not send offspring far from the parent plant.

Animal- and wind-dispersed seeds tend to travel the farthest of any dispersal strategy. Simply observing the seed or fruit structure will allow you to guess which dispersal strategy a plant uses. Some of our most disease- and pest-prone crops, such as apples, evolved to disperse long distances via animals to escape from their enemies.

Patterning to Facilitate Alliances

Patterns also can facilitate alliances between different species in the forest and the forest garden. Two of the key alliances in this regard are pollination interactions and soil-based food-web relationships such as mycorrhizas.

Clumped distributions aid pollination. The wind pollinates most nuts, and almost all need pollen from another variety within the same species to produce (i.e., they are *not* self-fruitful), so clumped distribution aids the nut grower in the same way that planting corn in blocks aids the gardener. Insects pollinate most fruits and berries, whose self-fruitfulness varies considerably. If compatible cross-pollinating varieties grow nearby and the right pollinating insects are around, cross-pollination happens.

It helps to fill your forest garden with appropriate flowers to keep the pollinators going. If you clump these flowers near the crops you want pollinated, the insects will be in the habit of visiting your yard. Other pollinator habitat elements should also be nearby (see chapter 4 and volume 2, appendix 5).

Clumping of more than one normally associated species helps individual plants find their mycorrhizal and other root-zone partners, improving individual plant performance. It also helps the plants form the mutual-aid network discussed at the beginning of chapter 1.

A Means of Reducing Competition or Increasing Advantage

A regular pattern can reduce competition between individuals by partitioning resources to make sure everyone gets their share, as in bird nesting territories or the regular spacing of orchard trees. Similarly, dispersing seed far and wide using animals or wind reduces competition between parents and their offspring. Even so, clumped distributions can be a means of increasing competitive advantage through mutual aid, as in the case of shrubs that use underground root runners to support young clones as they invade new habitat.

DIVERSITY

Political correctness has grabbed hold of this word in a big way and isn't likely to let go anytime soon (for good reason). Yet discussions of diversity in social and political terms tend to remain harrowingly narrow-minded. The same holds true in environmental circles: when most people think of diversity in an ecological context they are talking about species diversity, which is a combination of both the number of species in an area and the abundance of each species there. Is that really enough? Diversity itself is more diverse than most people realize.

An old argument in ecology questions whether diversity leads to ecosystem stability. In some cases it does, but in other cases it does not. Given the diverse kinds of ecosystem diversity (and the varied meanings of the word *stability*), it is not surprising that this argument could become somewhat muddled. As David Perry says in *Forest Ecosystems*: "Does diversity stabilize ecosystems? Yes, but . . ." Ultimately, it is not diversity per se that creates stability. Only the right kinds of diversity, put together in the right way, create stability, resilience, and work-minimizing self-maintenance. What kinds of diversity do we find in forests, what causes them, and what are their effects? How should we mimic them in our forest gardens, and why?

The following discussion begins the transition from examining the architecture of forests and forest gardens to exploring the social structure of these ecosystems.

SCALES OF DIVERSITY

Just as we must ponder the context to see how our gardens fit into larger patterns, so we must study different scales of diversity in and around our gardens to know where our gardens stand, and how to respond. At each scale there are several kinds of diversity to consider.

Within-Habitat Diversity

A habitat is a place or a type of place that provides food, water, and refuge for a species or individual. By definition, a given habitat exhibits relative consistency in its soil, elevation, aspect (the direction a slope faces relative to the sun), and successional stage, but any habitat also includes some amount of variation.

Within-habitat diversity is akin to the diversity of your backyard—the area under your direct control or subject to your forest-gardening efforts. Then again, you may have or want to develop two or more different habitats in your yard, and you will then need to think about the diversity within each of those habitats. For example, if you own a plot of flat, sandy soil with nothing but grass growing on it, you have essentially one habitat. If the neighboring plot has some of the same flat, sandy lawn, but half of it suddenly drops to a lower floodplain, the neighbor has at least three habitats: the level lawn, the floodplain, and the slope between them. The basic question here is, given relatively consistent conditions within a habitat, how diverse a system has nature attained? This will be some guide to what you can do in your forest garden.

The most diverse ecosystems usually develop in large habitats with a warm climate, moderate moisture and nutrient levels, and frequent small- to moderate-scale disturbances. Habitats that are smaller, drier, wetter, less or more fertile, less or more disturbed, or more northerly generally exhibit less diversity. Temperate deciduous forests growing on moist soils in eastern North America exhibit fairly high tree canopy richness (numbers of species), with fairly even representation of the species, that is, with no one species dominating to excess. Whether we can attain such diversity in isolated forest gardens is questionable: requirements for cross-pollination will mean that we have to double or triple up on species not also found locally.

TABLE 3.6. Species richness in moist temperate deciduous forests.

Forest layer	Approx. Maximum Species Richness
Tree canopy	10–18 species per 0.1 hectare (± 0.25 acre)[i]
Shrub layer	10 species per 0.1 hectare[ii]
Herb layer	14 species per square yard (17 per sq. m)[iii] 35–40 species per habitat[iv]

i Robertson. et al. 1978, page 263.
ii Ibid.
iii Sauer, 1998, page 12.
iv Parnall, 1998.

The 0.1-hectare (0.25 acre) plots in natural forests shown in table 3.6 do not need to do this, since the larger forest context meets such needs. Once your whole neighborhood is forest gardening, though, higher diversity becomes more feasible! This is why we need to look at diversity over the larger scale.

Note that the species diversity of the herb layer in table 3.6 is higher than in the upper layers. This is typical not only in natural temperate forests but also in tropical forest gardens. Traditional *pekarangan* (home forest gardens) in Java usually include one hundred or more useful species, with the highest diversity in the lower layers.[32] We may not achieve that level of diversity of edible or directly useful plants in a temperate-climate forest garden, but we can easily get two to several dozen useful species. When we add beneficial plant allies for outcompeting weeds, attracting insects, and accumulating nutrients, not to mention plants for beauty, our forest gardens will easily exceed fifty species, and may approach one hundred, again with the highest species diversity in the lower layers.

Landscape Complexity: Diversity between Habitats
Imagine that you own a small acreage that contains a gravelly hillock amidst rolling silt soils, a pond and shore environment, and a small stream and floodplain. Here you have many habitats to consider, each with a characteristic set of species living in it. While each habitat may be low in diversity by itself, the diversity of species across the landscape may be much greater than that of a same-size uni-

form acreage could ever have. Between-habitat diversity represents landscape complexity, or the rate of change in species composition across the landscape.

Herbaceous plants usually demonstrate higher diversity between habitats than trees. Trees' large size and dominant community roles favor adaptation to broad soil and site tolerances. Small variations in microclimate, topography, soils, and disturbance history strongly influence herbaceous understory composition.

Landscape complexity also strongly influences animal diversity. "A homogenous forest may support diverse fauna if it is set up within a heterogeneous landscape, and [conversely], animal diversity may be relatively low in a heterogeneous forest that exists as an isolated island within a sea of farms, suburbs, or forest monocultures."[33] Relatively barren or homogenous surroundings will reduce your ability to develop a balanced forest garden, and you will have to make extra effort to attract and keep beneficial animals. A more diverse landscape context allows you to relax a little and focus on attracting the species you want. What kinds of diversity do you need to look for in that context?

KINDS OF DIVERSITY

If species diversity isn't enough, then what is? Diversity of composition, structure, and function all influence the behavior, stability, and productivity of forest gardens. We will discuss compositional and structural diversity below. Though introduced here, functional diversity relates most clearly to the social system of the forest and is the subject of chapter 4.

Compositional Diversity: Building Blocks
Aldo Leopold once said something like "The first rule of intelligent tinkering is to keep all the pieces."[34] In many people's minds, animals, insects, fungi, and microbes are either uninvited but tolerated guests or outright unwelcome visitors among our private plant collections. This "us and them"

mentality has to go: we're all in this together, and we need each other.

What are the building blocks of the forest? Compositional diversity includes all the living and nonliving components of the ecosystem. The more diverse these building blocks, the broader will be the foundation of the forest and the garden.

Organisms and Species

Diverse kinds of organisms are essential to healthy ecosystems. The diversity of plants forms the basis for the diversity of all other forms of life: the higher the plant diversity, the higher the diversity of other life forms. Yet forests contain thousands of species besides plants, the vast majority of which live belowground.

Vertebrates (mammals, birds, reptiles, and amphibians) compose no more than 2 percent of *known* terrestrial animal species. The rest are "arthropods, nematodes, worms of one kind or another, and other small things."[35] Ecologists working in Oregon old-growth forests estimate that up to 16,000 individual invertebrate animals live under the area of one footstep. By 1998, scientists there had identified about 3,500 soil-dwelling arthropod species (insects, spiders, and mites) and estimated that the total number was about 8,000. This compares to a combined total of 143 vertebrate species in the same forest.[36]

The number of soil microbe species (bacteria, fungi, and protozoa) could vastly overshoot that of soil arthropods, but microbial diversity is unknown. Interestingly, mycorrhizal fungi are an exception to the general rule that diversity tends to decrease as one moves from tropical ecosystems toward the Poles. Temperate forests represent a peak in mycorrhizal diversity: tropical lowland forest may contain several hundred species of mycorrhizal fungi, while many temperate forests contain several thousand.[37]

Like soil ecology, tree canopy ecology is a new science, while the ecology of leaf surfaces is barely even born. "New" species are being discovered there, too, some of them microbes that live on leaves and bark or actually live *in* leaves or bark as endophytes (literally "within plants"). Fungal endophytes in leaves make a deal similar to their mycorrhizal cousins: you give me sugars, and I'll protect you from pathogens and herbivores (more on this later).

The vast majority of all these species and different kinds of organisms play beneficial or even essential roles in the ecosystem.

Genetic Diversity within Species

While plant-species diversity is high in the tropics and decreases as one moves toward the Poles, tropical trees tend to be genetically uniform, while temperate trees are not. "Studies of temperate and boreal tree species have found that on the order of 75 percent to 90 percent of all species-wide genetic variability resides within populations and only 10 percent to 25 percent between populations."[38] Temperate forests are almost as diverse as tropical forests when you include variation within the species. In other words, when we use a single genetic variety of a single species—one genotype—over large areas, we eliminate the majority of diversity in our home ecosystem, even if we are planting one genotype of a native species. Genetic diversity is one of the temperate forest's key defenses against wholesale loss from pests and disease at an ecosystem level. We should mimic this by staffing our forest gardens with diverse varieties of each species we grow, if possible.

Legacies: Soils and Deadwood Diversity

Ecologically speaking, a legacy includes anything handed down from previous generations of an ecosystem, especially a predisturbance ecosystem. Legacies include soil chemistry and biology, soil aggregates and organic matter, the soil seed bank, and deadwood. Loss of any of these legacies is a major blow to a healthy, stable ecosystem and slows or alters recovery after disturbance.

Dead trees, both standing and downed, support a whole food web involving microbes, invertebrates, reptiles, amphibians, small mammals, and birds. Cavity-nesting and snag-foraging birds depend on standing deadwood to survive, and many birds use standing deadwood as perches. Rotten logs store large quantities of water that can mean survival for trees (whose roots frequently invade fallen logs), their microbial associates, and numerous insects, earthworms, tree frogs, and small mammals during dry times or catastrophes. These biological islands help forests recover from fire, cutting, and other disturbances by providing a center of microbial diversity, storing organic matter and water, preventing erosion, and more. Rotten logs provided safe haven for large numbers of species of all sizes that quickly regenerated after the devastating eruption of Mount Saint Helens in 1980.

Minerals, Gases, and Chemicals

The mineral content of soil parent materials, the gas composition of the soil profile, and chemicals falling in rainfall or generated by plants and other organisms all play key roles in supporting or limiting system processes.

When considering compositional diversity we essentially ask, "What is here in what quantities?" or "What components does this system include?" This inventory offers vital information, but it doesn't go far enough. We also need to understand the placement patterns of these elements.

Structural Diversity: Patterns of Building Blocks

The pattern within which you place building blocks, whether concrete blocks or elements of ecosystem compositional diversity, determines the kind of structure you end up building, its form, and its functions. "A forest with complex architecture is like a house with many rooms. It provides greater opportunity to find a space providing protection from enemies, and it allows the evolution of unique niches that effectively reduce conflicts over resources."[39] Structure translates into niches: the more diverse the structures, the more diverse the niches.

Structural diversity includes both the physical architecture and the social structure of an ecosystem. Here we are concerned with variation in the overall physical architecture, as well as variation in topography and soil conditions. Diversity in the social structure helps balance and stabilize the system against shocks and loss.

Soil and Microclimate

While high plant-species diversity tends to generate higher diversity of all other forms of life, greater diversity in soil and microclimate conditions tends to generate greater plant-species diversity. For example, pit-and-mound topography, which typifies old-growth forest floors, radically increases the diversity of soil and microclimate conditions. This diversity in soil structure contributes mightily to high herbaceous understory diversity in these forests. Could it be that the biblical notion of "making the rough places plain" is exactly the wrong idea for recreating the Garden of Eden? Spirit works in mysterious ways.

Aspect is a major microclimate determinant that, in turn, determines habitat diversity, especially in the herbaceous understory. In the Northern Hemisphere, north-facing aspects get less sun, and their cool, moist microclimates foster late springs, slowly changing temperatures, and short growing seasons. West-facing slopes or the west sides of buildings tend to be the hottest, driest places, because maximum solar gain in the space coincides with peak midafternoon air temperatures. This causes wide day–night temperature swings and high stress from repeated freezing and thawing of woody tissues and soil. Southerly aspects are the next hottest and driest and have the longest growing season of any microclimate. East and southeast-facing aspects are the best microclimates in much of the temperate zone: sunny in the cool morning hours, shaded in the hot afternoons. Combine that with summer sun, good cold-air drainage to reduce frost, good cold-wind protection, and moist soil conditions, and you have the ideal conditions for people and most common crops.

Of course, each of these microclimates suits specific species better than others, so not everyone needs southeast-facing spaces! For instance:

> The leaves of even the hardiest herbaceous plants suffer from too rapid thawing in sun after a freezing night; hence the winter woods displays, in its ground layer, some differing slope aspects. Herbaceous plants which retain their leaves in winter, as *Hepatica, Hydrophyllum, Tiarella,* are often localized on northerly slopes where [daily] temperature changes are slow. The green leaves of these plants and the semi-evergreen *Smilax hispida* stand out conspicuously in the brown and gray background of the winter woods.[40]

Therefore, even small areas of varying slope aspect can allow you to plant a higher diversity of plants. So observe your microclimates carefully and design them thoughtfully!

Lumpy Texture: Age Structure and Disturbance

Old-growth forests typically vary in density tremendously from place to place, presenting a lumpy texture like that of hearty vegetable stew, while young forests and some forest gardens we have seen manifest a texture as smooth as split-pea soup (figures 3.19, 3.20, and 3.21). Frequent disturbances of low to moderate scale and intensity create this structural complexity in forests by creating gaps in the canopy that then go through a process of succession. These gaps change the age structure of the forest, the microclimate, and the species composition, the effects of which can last for generations. Tree death from old age or storm is a classic example of this kind of disturbance, as is fire in some regions.

Canopy Structure and Understory Diversity

Light intensity varies under a canopy with uneven density, height, and leaf sizes. Different trees leaf out at different times in spring and drop their leaves earlier or later in the fall, affecting the success of spring ephemerals and late-summer bloomers. Trees with drooping branches tend to concentrate rainfall at the edges of their crowns (gathering up to twice the precipitation as falls in forest gaps), while erect branching leads to rain running down tree trunks, and horizontal branches distribute precipitation more evenly. The leaves of different trees decompose at different rates and contain different chemicals and nutrients.[41]

All of these and other variations translate into

FIGURE 3.19. "Lumpy texture" versus "split-pea soup" in vegetation layers. We want both high diversity of foliage height and low evenness of texture (as on the left), not high foliage height diversity and high evenness (as on right). Such structural diversity appears to enhance bird and insect diversity regardless of plant species composition.

FIGURE 3.20. An Appalachian cove forest in North Carolina's Smoky Mountains offers a great example of lumpy texture. Notice the dense shrub and herb vegetation in the foreground, and the lack thereof at left and farther back. Also note the variation in density of the tree trunks in different areas of the woods. *Photo by Dave Jacke.*

FIGURE 3.21. Robert Hart's forest garden in Shropshire, England, is more like split-pea soup than chunky vegetable stew. Plants of many heights grow together, but every layer is equally packed throughout most of the garden. This reduces lumpy texture and air circulation and increases pest and disease potential and the general hassle of getting around the garden. *Photo by Dave Jacke.*

more niches for plants, animals, and microbes to fill. More niches mean more opportunities for yield, and also for interconnection, resource partitioning, and reducing competition.

Diverse Structure and Arthropod Diversity

As discussed earlier, bird diversity increases as the number of layers in a plant community increases, and *this pattern tends to occur independent of plant-species diversity.* In other words, the structural diversity alone seems to account for increased bird diversity. Since arthropods (such as spiders, mites, and insects) compose the largest portion of animal biomass in ecosystems and many of our pest problems are mite- and insect-related, it behooves us to look a little more at how these creatures respond to structural diversity.

Work in Oregon and North Carolina has shown that sucking herbivores (such as aphids) constitute the vast majority of arthropods in young forests,

while predators, decomposers, and flower or seed predators are absent (table 3.7). Old-growth forest arthropod populations exhibit more balance, with predators and herbivores almost equally represented, and smaller but significant numbers of other arthropod groups. Examination of the data in detail also shows that the old-growth forest canopies contained more species within each functional group of arthropods. While we know little about the forces that shape these patterns, the structural and compositional diversity of the older forests and the larger number of niches therefore available probably contribute considerably to the situation.[42] Other research supports this thesis, and may indicate that species composition and diversity in lower vegetation layers may be as important to insect diversity as structural diversity, perhaps more so.[43]

Having explored both the diverse building blocks with which we must interact and the diverse structure that creates "a house with many rooms," we

TABLE 3.7. Biomass of arthropods in canopies of young and old-growth conifer forests. Note the imbalance of sucking herbivores (such as aphids) in young forest and the balance between defoliators (such as caterpillars) and predators in old-growth forests. Data from H. J. Andrews Experimental Forest, Oregon (Schowalter, 1989).

Functional Group	BIOMASS, grams per hectare	
	Old-Growth Forest	Young Forest
Defoliating herbivores	180	0
Sucking herbivores	10	370
Predators	160	50
Others	30	0
Total	380	420

now need to discuss the diverse functions necessary to run this house.

Functional Diversity: Patterns of Influence

Functions are the "normal or characteristic action[s] of anything"[44]—behaviors, effects, or influences inherent in something because of its structure or way of being. Any ecosystem element can influence other parts of its community, the structure of its community as a whole, or internal community processes such as nutrient cycling, succession, and photosynthesis. The community as a whole influences other communities and processes external to itself, such as the climate or the water cycle. The functional diversity of these elements and their communities has four dimensions.

First, at the organism level, functional diversity expresses itself by the fact that every living thing has a diversity of inherent functions: needs, products, behaviors, tolerances, characteristics, and influences. These multiple functions define an organism's species niche.

Second, at the community level, every ecosystem is composed not only of "things" as discussed under "Compositional Diversity," but also of diverse sets of functions or roles, such as producer, herbivore, pollinator, browser, canopy tree, or spring ephemeral herb. These functions represent community niches, or community roles or "professions," which are filled by species with the proper "equipment" or "training" and which we can examine separate from the species that fill them. A primary segment of these community roles relates to the food-web structure of the community—who eats whom—and therefore who influences whom.

Third, not only must the system perform a diverse set of functions—fill diverse community niches—to remain viable, but stability and resilience depend upon the system containing diverse sets of organisms that perform each function—in other words, redundancy of function. If the ecosystem has only one species performing each community role, and one of those species is lost, then the community loses that function, not just the species. Thus, the fabric of the web begins to unravel, as important processes and links that keep the community running are lost.

Finally, we must distinguish between diversity that is functional and diversity that is not. Functional diversity in this sense means diversity that works, diversity in which the elements functionally interconnect to create an operational system, as opposed to simple variety. Simple variety is a mere collection of things, flotsam and jetsam, adrift and directionless. Functionally interconnected systems have drive, energy, and integrity: functional diversity, diversity that is going somewhere. Edible forest gardening is about creating this kind of functional diversity, achieving our goals using clear understanding of the multiple functions of species, the functional roles needed in systems, and how we might interconnect them. Given the limits of our understanding, to do this we probably also need a dash of luck, the grace of God, or the help of Mother Nature, however you want to say it. Nonetheless, in our forest gardens we must aim for diversity that works.

WHAT DIVERSITY DOES

Diversity provides more niches. Diversity begets diversity. Greater diversity in the elements composing the system adds more structure and more functions, which create more niches for more species to inhabit, which allows more elements . . . With evolutionary time, niche specialization increases, species partition resources more finely, and the ecosystem adds more niches.

Diversity reduces competition. Greater diversity through specialization leads to less competition for resources and creates new resources for other species to exploit. In addition, as more species participate, such as, say, herbivores that limit plant populations, competition declines at the plant level, and more diversity is possible at that level. This is called the cropping principle (see box 4.5, page 134).

Diversity increases productivity and yield. More niches mean increased efficiency in use of resources, which increases productivity. Increased productivity means increased opportunities for yield. Functional diversity, that is, diversity that works, can be directed to increasing yields by increasing the diversity of yields from the system. On a more mundane level, we find that stands of trees with a mixture of species tend to show greater cycling of nutrients than monoculture stands. This could be because the different species use and move different nutrients, because the variation in leaf litter increases soil microbe diversity, or because the different litter types assist in each other's decomposition somehow.[45]

Diversity generates functional interconnection. Linking the needs and products of different ecosystem components creates social structure in the system. In nature, this functional interconnection increases resource-use efficiency, increases productivity, and further increases diversity. In design, functional interconnection reduces work, waste, and pollution and increases yield.

Diversity generates stability and resilience. Species in the same community whose niches overlap use the same resource in a similar way. This redundancy supports stability and resiliency by providing backup services should one species drop out of the community role it plays. Stability is more a result of the system's structure than of diversity per se. However, diversity helps ensure that the structures that create stability and resilience are there.

Diversity reduces herbivory. A mix of species and genotypes with little dominance by any one has an interesting effect on herbivores and diseases: they spend more time and energy finding their host plants and less time and energy eating and reproducing. This is most true for specialist herbivores, but even generalist herbivores have their preferences. It also makes it easier for predators to find their prey, as the herbivores have to move around and expose themselves for longer periods. In the case of scab spores or other diseases, a mixed-plant matrix reduces the chance of infection by reducing the chance these spores have of landing on their host. "Herbivores and pathogens almost always do best when their food plants are concentrated rather than dispersed."[46] Not only diversity but also the length of time the diverse components live together affect insect populations: "studies suggest that the more diverse the agroecosystem and the longer this diversity remains undisturbed, the more internal links develop to promote greater insect stability."[47]

Diversity creates beauty. Highly diverse ecosystems are beautiful, awe inspiring, interesting, and fun. It's nice to know that our aesthetic sense supports our ecological goals, even though it is often an unconscious agreement.

Dominance militates against diversity. When one species or genotype dominates an ecosystem, diversity declines. This principle achieves its extreme expression in the monocultures typical of our industrial age.

SUMMARY

The five elements of forest architecture are visible aspects of forest structure and manifestations of the invisible "social structures" of the forest and the forest garden. The layers of the forest garden express primary aspects of the different niches or life strategies of plants, and how they partition resources above- and belowground. The soil horizons reveal the changing balances between living processes (of organic accumulation, decomposition, and recycling) and the nonliving realities of leaching and the mineral realm as depth increases. Vegetation density influences the intensity of interaction between individuals and species in the ecosystem and greatly defines the character of the ecosystem. Patterning facilitates or inhibits interactions between species because relative location is fundamental to many of these interactions, whether they are pollination, protection from herbivory or disease, or access to resources or allies. The diversity of the forest occurs at different scales and includes the full range of organisms in the forest, the various structural patterns of those organisms, and the functional interactions between them. This functional diversity is essential to the strength, resilience, and longevity of the ecosystems we cocreate with our plant, animal, and microbial allies.

Having begun to examine the visible structures of the forest, let's apply what we've learned to a specific garden, in this case, Robert Hart's forest garden in Shropshire, England. Then we can explore the invisible structures that lie behind the five elements of architecture.

Case Study 2

Robert's Garden

Size: 3,200 sq ft (40 ft by 80 ft; 12m by 24m) ◆ Location: Church Stretton, Shropshire, England ◆ Planted 1979 and onward ◆ USDA Hardiness Zone: 8 ◆ Latitude: 52.5° N

The first time we create something worthwhile, we usually make mistakes. This is, after all, the purpose of prototypes. You try out an idea, see how it works, and improve on it the next time around. In forest gardens, though, it can take years for our design errors to show up. This is why on-paper design is so critical to forest gardening if you want a good product. We need to think through the implications of our plant placements as best we can over time, make at least some mistakes on paper, correct them, and take it from there. Even so, we will likely make some mistakes, but, to slightly revise an old saying, anything worth doing is worth doing poorly. This is how we learn to do it well.

Robert Hart's forest garden in Shropshire, England, was the first known temperate-climate forest garden in the world. As the prototype of temperate forest gardens, it can teach us much, both what to mimic and what to avoid. Hart's willingness to defy traditions in service to his ideals and vision, and to simply start and find out what worked over time, are certainly exemplary. His pioneering role, evolving process, and lack of design or horticultural training meant that Robert didn't design his garden on paper and imagine how it would look as the plants grew. That one step could have made a big difference. Yet even without it, he created a basic planting pattern that worked reasonably well on his site. With a few easy adjustments, that basic pattern could have worked far better and for far longer than it did.

The discussion below concerns only Robert's original forest garden. You can read about this and the other parts of Robert's homestead in his book *Forest Gardening*. Compare his pictures of the garden in its earlier stages of development with the pictures we include here from 1997. The area we discuss appears as "Forest Garden 1" on the illustration beginning chapter 5 in the 1996 U.S. edition, and as "Forest Garden" in figure 1 of the 1991 U.K. edition.

ROBERT'S GOALS

Robert's primary goal was self-sufficiency, "a system of land-use capable of supplying all basic human needs, consisting mainly of trees and other perennial plants with no livestock component."[48] As a primary means to that end, Robert designed his garden "to achieve the utmost economy of space and labor,"[49] in other words, to require minimal maintenance. He sought to maximize his own health through a diverse diet of nutritious home-grown foods. He wanted to create a garden of natural beauty, where one could see that he had "moulded the earth to his necessity without violating it."[50] This aesthetic also plays well into his low-maintenance aims. Interestingly, Robert does not directly mention high yields as a key goal, except in reference to generating a diversity of highly nutritious crops. He often discusses the abundance of foodstuffs his garden offered, but he never indicates high yields as a major motivator for his design.

Beyond these general goals, most of which we all seek in forest gardening, Robert does not explicitly lay out his aims or guiding design concept for patterning his specific forest garden. Even in conversation, he either waxed poetic about his lofty ideas and ideals or discussed the brilliant details of what he

FIGURE C2.1. The patch of trees in the midground is Robert's forest garden. His house is the white building at right. From the outside, Robert's forest garden doesn't look like it could feel as much like a forest as it does. But compare this image with the feeling evident inside the garden in figure 0.1 or the other images throughout the book. *Photo by Dave Jacke.*

had done to achieve them. This is fine as far as it goes, and probably results from the evolving, design-as-you-go nature of his project. However, many designers get into trouble by glossing over the middle levels of specificity in articulating their goals.

GARDEN DESCRIPTION

We spent four full days with Robert and his garden in September 1997. The forest garden was then eighteen years of age, though some of the trees were much older, most notably the damson plums planted over a century ago and still bearing prolifically. While eighteen is young in terms of most tree life spans, one could say the forest garden as a whole was succession-ally mature or perhaps even overmature. At the time,

Robert was eighty-four and increasingly frail (he died less than three years later, in March 2000, and last we heard his garden was in legal limbo owing to an inheritance dispute). The garden had gotten minimal attention from him for the previous three years. It was in surprisingly good shape for having had little management for so long, but we certainly were not seeing the garden in its prime. This gave us a sense of what happens when management declines.

Even so, Robert's garden was strikingly beautiful, in a way that is hard to describe. It did not have the hallmarks of typically beautiful landscaping: bright colors, views and focal points, neatness, and a trimmed appearance. Quite the opposite on all counts. Its beauty derived from something deeper and more primal. It shimmered with a special sort of energy. It felt safe, enclosing, and enfolding (see

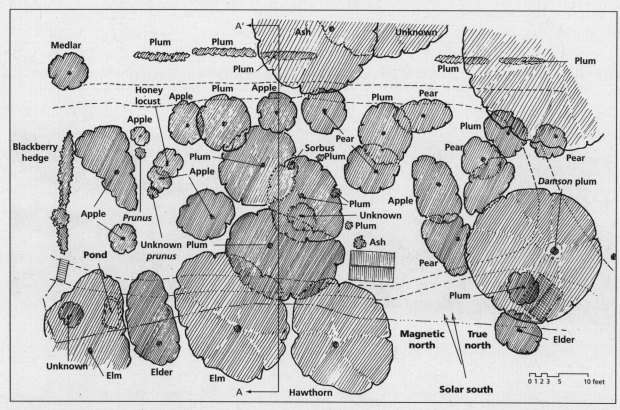

FIGURE C2.2. This map of Robert's forest garden shows the basic layout and the trees but, given the garden's complexity, does not include the shrubs and herbs. Note the density of planting: the shapes of the tree crowns indicate many are trying to get out of each other's way or away from large shrubs nearby. The numerous young trees also lead one to conclude that without thinning the garden would get even more dense over time.

figure 0.1, page xviii). It was wild, in a mild-mannered sort of way. It felt like a forest, but it also felt like a garden. This combination truly holds a special magic. Some of that magic may have also been due to the history of the site (see Robert's book). From the outside, it hardly looked like a forest at all (figure C2.1), and it is surprising that the ambience inside this small garden could feel so foresty in such an open context.

The main forest garden was about 45 feet wide by 80 feet long (a total of 3,800 square feet or less than 1/10 acre; about 14 m by 24 m, or 353 sq. m). To some this may seem a large area, but compared to large trees it is a small patch: one mature black walnut tree could have covered the entire forest garden! The garden's long axis was oriented almost east–west (figure C2.2). It occupied a gentle west-

facing slope, losing perhaps 3 to 4 feet (0.9 to 1.2 m) of elevation along its long axis, from damson plums to raspberry hedge. Soils were loamy in nature, with a significant proportion of clay. They seemed to hold fertility well, though they did not drain as well as one might desire in such a moist climate.

The garden's only two paths ran along the long sides, the north path wide enough for a good-size cart, the south path just wide enough to walk single file. We saw no defined access to the garden interior, or evidence there had ever been any. No distinct planting beds guided our footsteps outside the main paths. Vegetation hung into the paths, especially the narrower south path, getting us wet as we walked around in the damp weather, and potentially spreading disease.

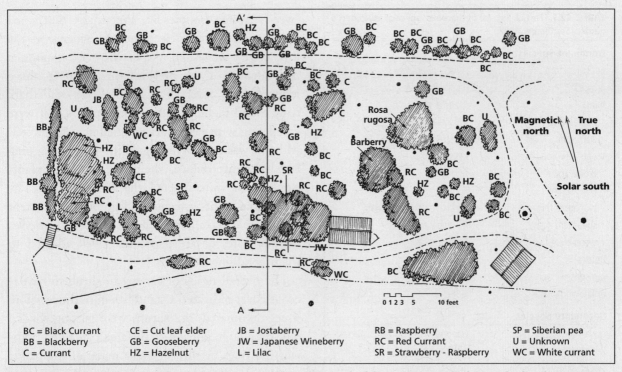

BC = Black Currant   CE = Cut leaf elder   JB = Jostaberry   RB = Raspberry   SP = Siberian pea
BB = Blackberry   GB = Gooseberry   JW = Japanese Wineberry   RC = Red Currant   U = Unknown
C = Currant   HZ = Hazelnut   L = Lilac   SR = Strawberry - Raspberry   WC = White currant

FIGURE C2.3. The shrub layer in Robert's garden covered about 30 percent of the area in a more or less regular distribution pattern. Many of the shrubs were in shade under trees. There was no apparent relationship between shrub patterning and tree patterning on this site. Luckily, most of the shrubs were *Ribes* species (currants, black currants, and so on), which can still produce in shade.

The garden essentially had three main vegetation layers. When we visited, the low tree canopy covered about 60 percent of the garden in a clumped distribution, forming fingers extending mainly from the south to the north (figure C2.2). The north edge of the garden was fairly open and free of major tree cover. The openings extended toward the south like spaces between the fingers of canopy. In places, this allowed light to enter the shrub and herb layers fairly well, even under the canopy, but in other places the canopy was very dense and the understory extremely shady. Small shrub clumps and individual shrubs covered about 30 percent of the area, spread out in a regular pattern (figure C2.3). However, half the shrub layer stood underneath the canopy. This left about 25 percent of the garden area for herbaceous plants directly under the sky.

Canopy species mainly included fruit trees: fourteen plums, eight apples, six pears, one rowan (*Sorbus aucuparia*), and one rare rowan relative (*S. arra-*nensis). Some adjacent European elder (*Sambucus nigra*), elm (*Ulmus* spp.), ash (*Fraxinus excelsior*) and hawthorn (*Crataegus* spp.) trees overhung the garden from the edges.

The shrub layer consisted mostly of *Ribes* species (gooseberries and red, white, and black currants), with *Rubus* species (raspberries, blackberries, and so on), hazels (*Corylus* spp.), roses (*Rosa* spp.), young fruit trees, and Siberian pea shrubs (*Caragana arborescens*) filling out most of the rest. A few single specimens included cut-leaf elder (*Sambucus nigra* 'Laciniata'), lilac (*Syringa* spp.), and a few shrubs neither Robert nor we could identify. Half these shrubs received moderately deep shade under the tree canopy. The balance had direct sunlight overhead but still received significant shade from neighboring trees. It is a good thing *Ribes* dominated the shrub layer, since it can still fruit in the shade. Most everything else was less than vigorous, especially the shaded hazels, as they required more sunshine.

TABLE C2.1. Partial list of herbaceous species at Robert's garden, September 1997.

Dominant Species:

garlic mustard	*Alliaria petiolara*
grasses	Family Poaceae
mints	*Mentha* spp.
apple mint	*M. suaveolens*
curly mint	*M. sp.*
eau-de-cologne mint	*M. sp.*
ginger mint	*M. sp.*
peppermint	*M. x piperita*
pineapple mint	*M. suaveolens* 'Variegata'
spearmint	*M. spicata*
water mint	*M. aquatica*
nettles	*Urtica dioica*
ramsons	*Allium ursinum*
unknown "weeds"	

Secondary Species:

good King Henry	*Chenopodium bonus-henricus*
lemon balm	*Melissa officinalis*
sweet cicely	*Myrrhis odorata*
woundwort	*Stachys* spp.

Minor Species:

bistort	*Polygonatum bistorta*
broccoli, 'Nine-Star Perennial'	*Brassica oleracea*
cardoon	*Cynara cardunculus*
chives	*Allium schoenoprasum*
comfrey	*Symphytum officinale*
lovage	*Levisticum officinale*
sorrel	*Rumex acetosa*

Unfortunately, we were unable to undertake a detailed herb layer inventory when we were there (see table C2.1 for a partial list of species). The most abundant useful herbaceous species in evidence at the time included apple mint (*Mentha suaveolens*), nettles (*Urtica dioica*), garlic mustard (*Alliaria petiolara*), ramsons (*Allium ursinum)*, sweet cicely (*Myrrhis odorata*), lemon balm (*Melissa officinalis*), woundwort (*Stachys* spp.), comfrey (*Symphytum officinale*), and good King Henry (*Chenopodium bonus-henricus*). Numerous grasses and unidentified "weeds" were also present. We expect that some useful species present were not in evidence at the time of year we visited. We also expect the minimal maintenance of the previous three years to have reduced herb layer diversity. Robert's trademark daily round included cutting back plants that were competing with neighbors and pulling a few weeds while he was out harvesting. Without such ongoing low-level disturbance, the more vigorous plants would have outcompeted the less vigorous. The herbaceous plants listed are all vigorous or persistent species, able to compete well and fend for themselves without care, or are particularly well adapted to shady conditions, or both.

The overall ratios of canopy to shrub to herbaceous cover indicated a stand late in midsuccession. Trees dominated, the shrubs were getting shaded out, yet a large portion of the area contained herbs with no trees or shrubs. Since many of the plants were still relatively young, shrub and tree cover have probably increased since then, unless a disturbance took place. Shrub crop production likely has declined since our visit, and some of the shrubs, notably the hazels, probably have gotten little chance to produce at all given their age, size, and location relative to canopy trees. We also believe the garden's increasing successional age was contributing to the decline in herb-layer diversity, as the shade grew deeper in the bulk of the garden.

Late midsuccession was also indicated by the density of tree stems (figure C2.4). In natural late midsuccession stands, a stage called "understory repression" often sets in, at which point the extremely dense growth of pioneer tree saplings cuts out virtually all light to the herb layer. The sun-loving herbs die out, and the herbaceous understory becomes barren for a time. Eventually, woodland herbs move in as the canopy thins. Robert's forest garden was not as dense as that, but he planted his trees far too close together and the effect was similar.

FIGURE C2.4. Spring in Robert's garden demonstrates the succession of green that occurs through the season. This view from the east end of the garden looking west shows that herbaceous perennials are first to bare their heads, making use of the sun while they can. Next come the shrubs, which are already displaying some green. The trees leaf out last. This picture also clearly indicates the high density of Robert's plantings. *Photo by Chuck Marsh*.

ASSESSMENT

One can easily say this garden achieved Robert's primary goals. While he kept no records of his yields as far as we know, Robert had no question that the forest garden gave him all he asked of it, if not more. Even if one were to take the most jaundiced view of his work, the garden in its prime clearly provided large quantities of diverse crops for many months each year. Even having provided little or no maintenance for three years, he was still eating out of his garden on a daily basis when we visited. What annual crop grower can say that? Self-sufficiency, low maintenance, natural beauty, and decent-enough yields were successful products of this tiny piece of earth lightly cultivated by a humble, "nonhorticultural"

man. Surely, this makes forest gardening a viable option within reach of millions.

With these major successes duly noted and acknowledged, let us take a more critical look at Robert's garden design. Remember, though, that Robert told us a number of times while we were there that "he didn't know much about plants." While we initially took this as a statement of humility from a master, we came to see that he was right. Nor was Robert a designer per se. We do not mean the comments below to denigrate Robert or his accomplishments in any way. We intend them only to shed light on a subject dear to his heart, and to improve your chances of making a better forest garden than the Man himself!

Good path design was a major oversight in this

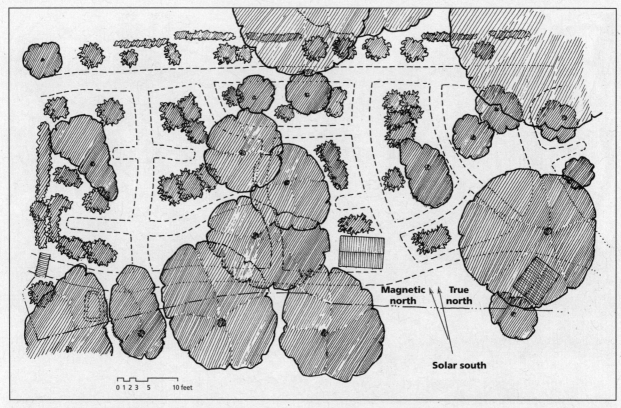

FIGURE C2.5. A revised planting pattern for Robert's forest garden could involve creating better path access to the garden's core and rearranging the shrubs to get more light. Though this scheme would be more functional, it would look less like a forest—and this is where value judgments enter the fray.

garden. Gaining access to the garden's core to monitor, maintain, and harvest crops was problematic, requiring walking on soils that were frequently wet due to the weather, and that stayed wet due to the soil's texture. The vegetation jungle was certainly partly due to the lack of maintenance over the previous three years, but narrow pathways, extremely close spacing, and eccentric planting patterns contributed mightily. Though a much more forestlike ambience resulted, practical concerns were lost. Ultimately, such design choices are a value judgment on each gardener's part, but we would opt for wider main paths, additional access to the garden's core, and better definition of planting beds and planting patterns. This would facilitate management and minimize soil compaction and disease spread. How might we achieve this?

The tree cover pattern created north–south linear canopy openings. However, the shrub and herb planting pattern did not take advantage of this, nor did the path pattern relate to it. Robert spread the shrubs evenly around the garden, with no apparent relationship between shade conditions then or in the future and the kinds of shrubs planted in a given spot or their overall planting scheme (see figure C2.3). The same appeared true of the herbs, though the herb patch compositions changed in response to conditions to some degree; more grasses grew in the sunnier areas, for example. Secondary paths following the spaces between canopy fingers would have eased management and organized the planting pattern as well. Sun-loving herbs could grow along the secondary cross paths, with shrubs behind them and woodland herbs

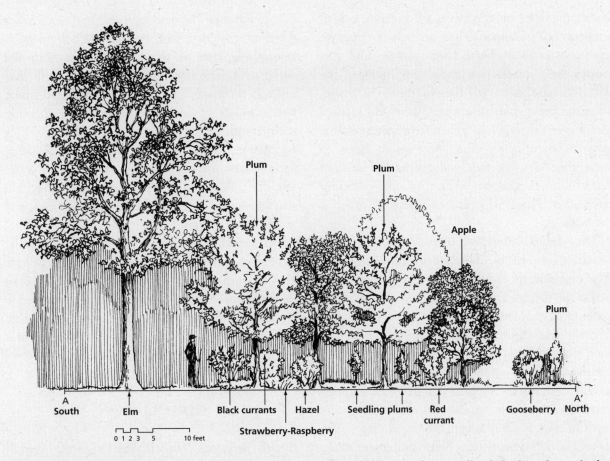

Plum

Plum

Apple

Plum

A
South

Elm

Black currants

Strawberry-Raspberry

Hazel

Seedling plums

Red currant

Gooseberry

A'
North

0 1 2 3 5   10 feet

FIGURE C2.6. A north–south cross section of Robert's garden reveals the arrangement of trees to allow light along the north edge of the garden, with taller trees to the south and shorter ones to the north. Unfortunately, the northern apple tree will grow to shade the north edge eventually.

growing under the trees that compose the canopy fingers (see figure C2.5).

Extending the canopy fingers from the south and leaving the north edge of the garden more open as Robert did is a good way to maximize sunlight in the northern clearing while creating deeper shade to the south. This works best and lasts longest only if the taller trees are all placed at the south edge and the shorter trees toward the north, as Robert's garden was arranged at the time (figure C2.6). However, the growth of his trees will eventually cause the loss of more of his sunny habitat than he might have wished sooner than might be desirable. He did have other sunny areas to cultivate, so perhaps he did not care. However, this situation is a

good reminder to us all to sketch our designs in section views as well as plan views to help us envision the plan ahead of time.

Robert also made the same mistake that almost every other forest gardener we have met has made: he planted woodies too close together. You can see evidence of this in figure C2.2. Notice the odd shapes of the tree crowns, indicating how the trees have grown to avoid each other. Notice the seedling and sapling plums planted right at the crown edge of the plum smack in the middle of the garden. The plum's neighbors already crowded it, and then Robert planted more seedlings right next to it. Also notice the tiny honey locust in the western third of the garden, and imagine it three or four times that crown diameter as it achieves adolescence, not to mention full adulthood! These are only the trees we are talking about here! Overplanting like this causes early understory repression, reduces the effective life span of the successional stage, increases plant competition and stress, and reduces yields over the long run. When trees are small, it is easy to plant more than you need, hard to remember how big they will eventually get, and hard to cut them down when they start crowding each other. This is why planning on paper makes a lot of sense.

The shrubs often had more shrub-free room around them, because of their scattered distribution. The problem: the shrubs usually got in the way of access to the fruit trees or blocked the available paths back and forth through the core of the garden. Perhaps this shrub distribution made the garden look forestlike, but it was a major hassle to move around the place, not to mention to prune, harvest, and monitor insects. The few nitrogen-fixing shrubs present were wholly shaded. Since nitrogen-fixers need full sun to fix nitrogen, the pea shrubs might as well have not been there. Shrub placement made little sense in any way, except that *Ribes* will produce fruit in some shade, and this group dominated the shady shrub layer present.

Despite Robert's claims of growing over one hundred species and varieties in his forest garden, diversity in this garden was low, especially in the shrub layer. Robert likely grew the trees most worth growing in his garden, and he had diverse varieties of what he did have. In a garden this small, he really should have had fewer trees at a more reasonable spacing. The shrub and herb layers, with their smaller plants, provide more opportunities for easily increasing species diversity. Robert did love his *Ribes*, though: currants, black currants, and gooseberries were certainly his main crop, or one of them, and he had diverse species and varieties within his main crop, which is good. However, he could have grown many other species, particularly had he patterned his shrub layer to respond to the

canopy pattern. The herb layer also had much lower diversity than we had expected. There was an astonishing lack of nitrogen-fixers in both the shrub and herb layers, for example. It is also unlikely there was a succession of beneficial-insect nectar plants blooming throughout the growing season, with no gaps. The same probably goes for bee plants. Robert had only two major dynamic accumulator species in his garden that we could tell. The presence of weeds indicates unfilled niches that he might have been able to fill with more, and more useful, species.

Despite all of the foregoing, however, we must remember that Robert devised the first temperate-climate forest garden known on the planet in modern times. Of course he made mistakes. We are grateful to him for making them, and for sharing his garden so openly with us so we could learn from them. We hope you learn from them too.

CONCLUSION

By all accounts, Robert Hart's forest garden achieved much. It surely met his aims, and more. Those few square feet of ground spurred a world-wide movement, not to mention having fed one English gentleman and his many visitors both food and soul nourishment for a good many years with minimal labor and great satisfaction. In fact, the whole forest garden idea resulted from Mr. Hart's desire to limit his needs and wants to something he could achieve on his own land, without violating that land's inherent nature. This is what Plato meant when he said, "It is the wise restraints that make men free." If we apply this idea even more fully to our forest gardens, restraining ourselves from planting long enough to plan just a little (or even a lot) more, and limiting the number of woody species we plant to maintain better spacing, our gardens will easily achieve for us as much as Robert's did for him, if not more.

1. Hart, 1991.
2. Luoma, 1999.
3. Niering et al., 1986; Niering and Goodwin, 1974.
4. MacArthur and MacArthur, 1961.
5. Greg Cox, Massachusetts Forestry Foundation, Belchertown, MA, personal communication, October 14, 1998.
6. Barbour, Burk, and Pitts, 1987, pages 370–71.
7. Barbour, Burk, and Pitts, 1987, page 369; Perry, 1994, page 313. C4 photosynthetic pathways can allow plants never to reach saturation, even at full sun.
8. Barkman, 1992.
9. Martin Crawford, AgroForestry Research Trust, personal communication, September, 1997.
10. Luoma, 1999, page 118.
11. Packham et al., 1992, chapter 8.
12. Perry, 1994, page 277.
13. Ellen Dumas (née Marie), Greenfield, New Hampshire, sheep farmer, personal communication, January 21, 2000.
14. Soil Foodweb, Inc., 1999.
15. Perry, 1994, page 270.
16. Colinvaux, 1986, page 487.
17. UNESCO, 1973.
18. Niering et al., 1986.
19. Gordon and Newman, 1997, page 37.
20. Barbour, Burk, and Pitts, 1987, page 530.
21. Atkinson, 1980a; Rogers and Vyvyan, 1934; Biswell, 1935; Kourik, 1986; Kolesnikov, 1971.
22. Woodruff and Woodruff 1934.
23. Perry, 1994, page 312.
24. Sauer and Andropogon Assoc., 1998, page 17.
25. Odum, 1971, page 157.
26. This has been most prominent in the literature and teachings of permaculture.
27. See Odum, 1971, pages 157–9, and Perry, 1994, page 68.
28. Crawford, 1995, page 13.
29. Adapted from Mollison, 1988, page 5.
30. Liebman, 1995, page 212.
31. Perry, 1994, page 212.
32. Liebman, 1995, page 259.
33. Perry, 1994, page 207.
34. Perry, 1994, page 225.
35. Perry, 1994, page 54.
36. Luoma, 1999, pages 96–97.
37. Perry, 1994, page 54.
38. Perry, 1994, page 190.
39. Perry, 1994, page 172.
40. Braun, 1950, page 4.
41. Barkman, 1992.
42. Perry, 1994, pages 202–3.
43. Watt, 1992, and Young, 1992.
44. *Webster's Dictionary*, quoted in Perry, 1994, page 172.
45. Binkley, 1992.
46. Perry, 1994, page 212.
47. Altieri, 1995, pages 275–76.
48. Hart, 1991, pages 15–16.
49. Hart, 1991, page 2.
50. D. H. Lawrence, quoted in Hart, 1991, page 31.

℮4℮

Social Structure: Niches, Relationships, Communities

> Ecological communities are not as tightly linked as organisms, but neither are they simply collections of individuals. Rather, the community is a unique form of biological system in which the individuality of the parts (i.e., species and individuals) acts paradoxically to bind the system together.
>
> —David Perry, *Forest Ecosystems*

Everybody is just trying to make a living. The result of different organisms making a living together is social structure: "patterns in the way that individuals, species, or groups of species relate to one another and to the system as a whole."[1] The interplay between the freedom to evolve as an individual species and the reality of communal interdependence results in "diversity that works": an incredible variety of life forms—each with unique needs, "equipment," and "training"—performing interconnecting "job-roles" that create an evolving, self-maintaining, self-renewing social structure.

Relationships build social structures. In ecosystems, these relationships are born primarily of organisms' needs for energy and resources, and as a result, they determine the flows of energy, nutrients, and influence within the community. When we work skillfully with social structures, we participate in creating the resilient, self-maintaining garden system we want, and we get the abundant diversity of foods we need.

The purpose of this chapter is to help you understand forest garden social structure and how to work skillfully with it to achieve your goals. We cannot hope to understand all the interactions in our gardens as they take place, and we don't need to. We need only develop anchors and strategies to design a fundamental framework of relationships and conditions, and then remain observant. As we grow with our gardens, we will find ways to guide and refine the structure and support its self-maintenance. The ideas presented in this chapter should help you design more stable, resilient, and productive polycultures. They should also help you observe more carefully, interpret what you observe, and modify your choices and behavior to support and steer your forest garden as you travel together through time.

The concept of niche is fundamental to our discussions in this chapter. In ecology, this word has three related meanings. As discussed in chapter 3, a community niche defines an organism's relationship to its sources of food or energy and its functions in the community, or its basic way of making a living. A community niche is akin to a job-role in a village, such as a priest, blacksmith, teacher, or farmer. The various individuals who fill these village roles each bring their unique training, skills, personality, and experience to their "community niche." In a similar way, the species niche defines the unique characteristics, behaviors, and adaptations of a particular species. Finally, for a species to make a living filling its community niche, the environment must have the right combination of resources and characteristics. The environment niche is "that set of ecological conditions under which a species can exploit a source of energy effectively enough to be able to reproduce and colonize further such sets of conditions."[2] An analogous example: if a village doesn't have many horse owners, a blacksmith will have a hard time making a living there by making only horseshoes.

This chapter focuses primarily on species and community niches in its exploration of ecosystem social structure. We will explore environment niches in volume 2, chapter 3, since undertaking site analysis and assessment during the design process builds a basic understanding of the environmental niches available in your landscape. Here in chapter 4, we will explore ecosystem social structure by building from the species level. Once we understand species niches, we will examine social structure at the community level. The final section of this chapter looks at the strategies we can use to anchor social structure in our forest gardens.

SPECIES, SPECIES NICHES, AND SPECIES RELATIONSHIPS

How species interact depends on who they are: species and species niches act as building blocks of social structure, and of forest garden design. Once we have gained a clear understanding of species niches, we will explore relatively simple two-species interactions and the principles that govern them. This will help us begin envisioning what we are trying to create in our forest gardens.

Species Niche: The Strategies and Multiple Functions of Species

Every person possesses a unique set of qualities, equipment, and training that prepares her or him for certain lines of work. A species niche resembles these inborn and developed characteristics. When we ponder the growth requirements of a plant—its climate tolerance, soil requirements, and moisture

preferences—we are pondering aspects of its species niche. The same goes for its human uses, aesthetic values, and ecological functions. These all express inherent characteristics of the plant as an organism, and these characteristics all constitute parts of its species niche. The concept of species niche contains important implications for our design process, and for understanding how species interact and ecosystems operate.

An organism's species niche includes an infinitude of functions and characteristics. Many of these characteristics and functions appear discrete, and we can measure or estimate them them. Some we cannot measure, but we can observe or intuit them. Some we can never know. However, we have to start somewhere. By classifying some of the major elements of species niches (table 4.1 and figure 4.1), we can analyze the niches of plants and other species for design purposes. Niche analysis is a critical tool for design that most of us use all the time (box 4.1). Yet while analyzing species niches can be quite useful, we must not only see these species characteristics piecemeal. We also need a unifying vision that helps us see the organism as a whole and puts it into its context. The concept of species strategies embodies this unifying vision. We elucidate the idea of niche analysis more fully in box 4.1, throughout the rest of both volumes of this book, and especially in appendix 1 of volume 2. Therefore, this section focuses on species strategies and observations we can make to help us understand them.

The diversity of species functions at the organism scale underlies the principle of multiple functions, a key ecological design principle. Nothing serves only one function. Indeed everything has multiple interactions with its environment and multiple characteristics (see box 4.2). Yet we must go further. How can we grasp the essence of an organism's species niche?

An organism's characteristics, behaviors, and functions affect its survival in its environment. As such, a species niche reflects the sum total of the organism's ongoing attempts to remain adapted and adaptive, or its ways of interacting with the world.

TABLE 4.1. Some elements of species niches.

Core Strategy
- Key mode of adaptive success (e.g., spring ephemeral herb; canopy tree; large, hoofed browser; ground-nesting insectivorous bird; etc.)
- Ruderal, competitor, or stress tolerator (see below)

Context
- Ecogeography (climate, native region, habitat)
- Associates (coevolutionary neighbors)
- Predators

Needs
- Tolerances and preferences (water, soil, light, pH, hardiness, etc.)
- For animals: food and shelter (nesting habitat, winter habitat, etc.)
- Allies (pollinators, dispersal agents, nutrient gatherers, etc.)

Products
- Products directly useful to humans: fruit, leaves, fiber, dye, etc.
- Products useful to other species: nectar, shelter
- Other products (often considered "wastes"): dead leaves, twig and bark sheddings, etc.)

Characteristics
- Evolutionary history/genetics (taxonomy)
- Form (morphology): size, shape, habit, root pattern, etc.

Functions, Behaviors, and Influences
- Rate and means of spread and establishment, growth rate
- Nutrient dynamics: nitrogen fixation, dynamic accumulation
- Seasonal behaviors (time of flowering, leaf drop, etc.; for animals: time of emergence, number of larval stages, length of gestation, etc.)
- Nuisances, poisonousness

EUROPEAN PEAR (*Pyrus communis*)

Core strategy: An animal dispersed competitive stress tolerator of sunny mid- to late-succession woodland canopies.

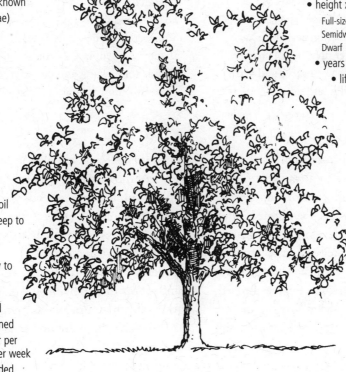

Context:
- native region: temperate Europe, W. Asia
- native habitat: unknown
- native associates: unknown
- family: Rose (Rosaceae)

Predators:
- generalist herbivores
- codling moth
- pear psylla
- fireblight
- pear scab

Needs, tolerances:
- full sun
- soil pH 6.0–6.5
- hardiness zones 4–9
- moist, well-drained soil
- prefers moderately deep to deep soils
- tolerates clay
- prefers soils with low to moderate nitrogen content
- high calcium demand
- yields best when pruned
- needs 2–3 gal. water per sq. ft. of root zone per week
- cross-pollinators needed

Characteristics:
- form: upright tree
- habit: standard tree, flat-rooted with sinkers
- height x width:

	feet	meters
Full-size:	25–40 x 25–30	8–12 x 8–9
Semidwarf	15–20 x 15–20	5–6 x 5–6
Dwarf	10–15 x 15	3–5 x 5

- years to bearing: 4–7
  - life span:

    Full-size: 50–75 years
    Dwarf: 15+

Products:
- fruit: pome; late summer and fall ripening
- yield:

	bushels	liters
Full-size:	2–4	70–140
Semidwarf	0.5–1.5	18–36

- white flowers: spring
  - glossy green foliage
  - moderately dense to dense shade

Functions, behaviors:
- animal dispersed
- can naturalize
- flowers may die in early frosts
- leafs out after flowering
- drops leaves midautumn

FIGURE 4.1. Niche analysis of the European pear (*Pyrus communis*).

Box 4.1: Niche Analysis: Everybody Does It

Every gardener we have ever met does niche analysis in one form or another, either in their heads, in their hearts, with books, or on paper. It often takes the form of a simple assessment of a plant's hardiness, sun or shade needs, and tolerance for acid, alkaline, dry, moist, or wet soil. Quick and dirty assessments like this work fine for conventional gardening. However, a more robust niche analysis becomes essential when designing productive, self-maintaining forest gardens using novel combinations of uncommon plants over a broad range of climates, habitats, and gardener goals.

Niche analysis fulfills key functions in species selection and design, especially with less well-known species. It allows us to select plants that have the greatest chance of performing well on our site. It facilitates the noncompetitive combining of species. It helps ensure that our plant selections fulfill all the functions we know our edible ecosystems require. A large database of plants and their niche characteristics allows us purposefully to use a greater diversity of species. Finally, niche analysis helps us observe and learn more quickly, keenly, broadly, and deeply.

While we can measure or observe only a small portion of any species' infinite number of niche characteristics, this portion still constitutes a huge array of characteristics. In addition, we can define each characteristic any number of ways. We must select the most important characteristics for our purposes when we analyze niches. We must carefully define the characteristics and categorize species with reasonable consistency. Contextual information, such as native habitats, balances the detailed data, often helping fit the puzzle pieces together.

The Plant Species Matrix and its associated tables in appendix 1 of volume 2 represent our catalog of niche characteristics of useful plant species based upon this ecological view of plants and their multiple functions. We discuss the organization of the matrix in more detail in that appendix. We also provide some information on the niche requirements of various animals useful in the forest garden in volume 2, appendix 5. Chapter 3 of volume 2 discusses how to do niche analysis for existing and desired species, and how to use this information in forest garden design.

Every surviving organism must marshal these characteristics and inner resources in a way that blends its inherent character with its environmental context. We all must choose how to spend our limited time and energy. When we develop habits in that regard, we have adopted a strategy to get us through life. In plants and animals, these strategies are genetically coded to at least some degree. Indeed, the myriad species characteristics we might analyze or observe can develop into a pattern illuminating that species' strategy for gaining its needed energy and material resources and continuing into the next generation within its context.

An organism's strategy constitutes the core of its species niche—how it makes its living. It unifies and organizes the disparate details of the organism's tolerances, preferences, needs, and yields into a coherent whole. It reflects the organism's evolutionary "choices" about how to spend its energy to adapt to its environment. Does a given plant allocate its energy mostly to reproduction, to growth and competition, or to defense and maintenance? Does it have broad environmental tolerances, or does it have specific, narrow requirements? Is a given predatory insect a specialist or a generalist, feeding on, for example, only one species of aphid, or on any species of aphid, or on any small, soft-bodied insect? Which strategy a plant or animal chooses will determine in

Box 4.2: The Principle of Multiple Functions

Every component of a design should function in many ways.

—BILL MOLLISON, *Permaculture: A Designer's Manual*

This principle derives from at least two realities. First, when we examine living beings, we find that each has an infinitude of inherent needs, products, roles, behaviors, and characteristics. Each of these aspects of living things helps define its niche. The same is true of nonliving things: they interact in multiple ways with their environment. We can therefore say that any organism or thing has multiple functions. Second, there is an old saying that "in nature you can never do just one thing." The complex, inter-linked systems of the universe mean that Newton was wrong: every action has many unequal and diverse reactions.

This principle itself offers multiple benefits. First, when we apply the principle of multiple functions we find ways to take advantage of the inherent functions or gifts of a species or object in multiple ways without creating stress (see box 4.3). This allows us to get more yield for any given amount of energy and materials invested in a system (to use a nuclear-era cliché, more "bang for the buck"). Second, when we know that

everything has more than one function, we are more likely to go looking for various interactions we might be able to use. Therefore, we are more likely to catch any possible negative consequences or interactions that may exist. We then have the opportunity to avoid, mitigate, or transform those negative consequences. Finally, this principle combines with the principles of stress and har-mony, self-regulation, and redundancy to create networks of mutual support within the garden. The garden can therefore become a stable, resilient, self-maintaining system rather than a set of isolated elements we have to maintain all by ourselves.

On a practical level, what this means is that the best forest-garden plants are those that will have more than one function for us or our garden ecosystems, such as edible, nitrogen-fixing ground covers. It also means that we must accommodate this reality in our design process. Focusing on functions, not things, as we design helps us select or design our garden elements to meet multiple needs.

which environments it will perform the best. It will also influence its usefulness to us, both in kind and quantity and in how, where, when, and why we can use that species in our forest garden.

So strategies unify the details of species niche characteristics into an orchestrated whole. Yet the details help us learn and choose the plants as we design. We need to work with both of these aspects of species niches to work effectively. The balance of this section discusses various aspects of plant strate-gies and how we can think about, "read," and learn about the plants and their species niches.

Species Strategies

A strategy is an "evolutionarily developed (geneti-cally-based) pattern of response to the elements of the environment that are likely to be encountered in the [organism's] habitat."[3] For plants, it deals with the plant's core relationship to resources, com-petitors, enemies, and associates—how, when, and where it places itself in the environment. The idea integrates many aspects of plant niche, including plant physiology, population ecology, and commu-nity ecology. For example, one scientist has called shade-tolerant trees of late succession such as sugar maple and American beech "small-gap specialists." They cannot tolerate rapid shifts from understory conditions to strong sun (as occurs in large clearings) without stress or damage, yet they require two or more gaps in the canopy during their life if they are to reach the topmost layer.[4] So strategies don't concern only whether a plant is shade tolerant, what its moisture tolerances are, and whether it can survive in infertile soils. Strategies involve how these realities come together into a modus operandi that works to sustain and reproduce the species in a certain context in time and space.

When we choose a plant for our garden, we choose to use that plant's strategy. Managing and using plants in ways that harmonize with their essential strategies in life offers us some significant benefits. For example, plants whose strategy emphasizes reproduction will likely yield more seed than those that emphasize maintenance or growth and competition. Trying to force high yields of fruit from plants using maintenance as a primary strategy will be an uphill battle, whereas harvesting stems and leafy greens from a plant emphasizing growth and competition makes sense. Strategies influence not only the kinds and quantities of yield we may expect from a given species, but also where and when we may optimally place a species in our gardens. Plant breeding often alters a plant's fundamental strategy, and therefore alters its ecology, successional role, and resource or maintenance demands.

Since plant strategies came to the fore as a key aspect of plant ecology and succession, ecologists have developed a number of conceptual frameworks to classify them. The problem is that, as of yet, there seems to be no clearly "right," optimal, or generally accepted framework. The way people define plant strategies reflects the perspective of the beholders and their realm of interest or study as much as it does the diversity of the biological world. A plant's form expresses part of its strategy. So do its means of dispersal, its rate of growth, its seasonality, its breadth of tolerances, its defense mechanisms, and so on. What we need is a way of pulling together these different aspects of resource allocation by plants into a more generalized pattern to help us understand how everything fits together. Let us look at a model that does that.

Basic Plant Strategies: Ruderals, Competitors, and Stress Tolerators

According to a model developed by British ecologist J. P. Grime, plants use three basic niche strategies. Any given species can possess features of more than one of these strategies.

Ruderal species derive their name from *rudus*, the Latin word for "rubble," because these plants depend upon disturbance for habitat and cannot tolerate competition. Fecundity and dispersal form the core of this strategy, providing the ability to escape to uncontested habitat in disturbed areas and rapidly dominate space. These "weedy" plants, which include mainly annuals (such as lamb's-quarter, *Chenopodium album*) as well as biennials (like wild carrot or Queen Anne's lace, *Daucus carota*), therefore exhibit rapid growth and produce many seeds, often wind borne, that can lie dormant in the ground for years waiting for another disturbance to trigger germination. The majority of our food plants and common weeds use this early-succession strategy.

Competitor plants tend to dominate midsuccession. They put most of their resources into competing with other species, using root suckers and rhizomes, overtopping, chemical warfare against impinging neighbors (allelopathy, discussed later in this chapter), nutrient hoarding, and dense, fibrous, exclusionary root systems to do so. These species put somewhat less energy into reproduction than ruderals in any given year. Their intermediate life spans afford them more opportunities to regenerate successfully in future years, but not a lot more. Many dynamic accumulators and nitrogen fixers fall in this category, as do most fruit trees and shrubs and pioneer trees such as poplar and white pine. Though they can rebound from moderate disturbance, most competitors do not deal well with intense disturbance or with prolonged stress.

Stress tolerators divide their resources between competition and stress resistance, because stress limits the resources available for competing. These species tend to live in environments where total community demand for resources is high or resources are low. Resisting stress therefore means dealing with lack of light, nutrients, or water (by storing them, cooperating with other species to get them, or by needing less), with herbivore attacks (often by chemical defense), and with long periods of minimal shifts in community position followed by sudden changes that must be rapidly exploited. Most forest species use this strategy, including most timber and nut trees, as do many useful perennial herbs. Reproduction follows the long-term plan here, with minimal seed production, multiyear cycles of seed production, and life spans in the hundreds or even thousands of years.

Take some time to consider plants you know and love in light of this model. Which of these strategies do these plants use? Are they almost purely one, a combination of two, or a combination of all three? Get used to thinking of plants in this regard for a while before we discuss these three strategies further in chapter 6.

Specialist and Generalist Strategies in Beneficial Insects and Spiders

The forces of natural selection cause living beings to adapt over evolutionary time. In that process, different species become specialized relative to their critical resources to a greater or lesser degree. We use the terms *generalist* and *specialist* to denote the two extremes of the specialization spectrum. We can therefore speak of specialist or generalist plants, or specialized insect predators, such as parasitic wasps, and generalist insect predators, such as spiders.

Specialists like the tiny braconid or ichneumon wasps may have extremely narrow niches, laying their eggs only on the larvae of one particular species

of aphid or other insect. When the eggs hatch, the wasp larvae eat the aphid. If the exact aphid species isn't around, neither is the wasp. However, if the wasp cannot meet its other needs it will not remain, even if the aphid *is* present. Parasitic wasps tend to be minute insects, and their adults need frequent doses of concentrated food energy, which they get from flower nectar. Yet their short mouthparts allow them to get nectar only from small, open, short-tubed flowers, such as those in the composite, umbel, and mint families (Asteraceae, Apiaceae, and Lamiaceae, respectively). They need these plants around so they can get the energy to find their host species so they can reproduce and keep working for us. One plant species may attract many different specialist predators: researchers in Massachusetts found that sweet fennel (*Foeniculum vulgare*) attracted forty-eight species of ichneumon wasps, including species that attack codling moth (a pest of apples, apricots, pears, and quince) and grape berry moth. Many specialized nectarivorous predatory and parasitic insects visit common chickweed (*Stellaria media*) flowers (and chickweed tastes great to humans, too).[5]

Spiders are extremely important in ecosystems. If you find yourself pulling spiderwebs out of your face when walking through your forest garden, apologize, rejoice, and give thanks! You have encountered a sign that you have generalist predator friends and allies at work around you. Research indicates that excluding spiders from agroecosystems can result in exponential growth of insect pests.[6] No single spider species is critical: "generalist predators including the spiders . . . control prey largely through the assemblage effect: species of varied sizes and habits need to be present throughout the growing season of the pest species to limit the growth of associated pest populations."[7] Some spiders build webs, and some hunt. As generalist predators, spiders are not selective about what they catch and eat. They will eat beneficials as well as pests and "indifferent" species, so some researchers disregard them. Yet this "cast a wide net" strategy is precisely what makes spiders so important: whichever insects are most abundant are the ones they will catch the most. This prevents insect population explosions, as long as the spider's other needs are met.

Spiders' soft bodies leave them vulnerable to drying out. They regulate their water content by selecting environments high in humidity, with cool temperatures, out of the sun. Bare, hot soil will kill them quickly if they don't leave. They like mulch better. They like grass hay mulch more than leaf litter or bark mulch.[8] They like vegetation and shade. "Tall and diverse vegetation with sufficient interspaces is likely to enhance numbers of most web-building spiders,"[9] not only because of the shade, but also because of the architectural possibilities for web building and the diverse niches and prey available. Some spiders live more than one year, so winter headquarters are also important: they like hollow stems, empty seed capsules, dead flower heads, bark crevices, and so on (volume 2, appendix 5 contains information on how to increase arthropod predator overwintering success). Some hibernate in the soil, near certain plants. Swiss researchers found the highest concentration of hibernating spiders under comfrey: 240 spiders per square meter of soil!

Spiders disperse far and wide by ballooning after they hatch in the spring: tiny spiders let out long silk threads, the wind picks them up, and away they go. Imagine thousands of little spiders floating around hoping to land in a good habitat—if you're squeamish you may not believe it, but this is good news! If they land somewhere habitable, they will stick around. If they land somewhere too hot and dry, with nowhere to build a web or hunt, they will let out more silk and float somewhere else. Forest gardens make perfect habitats for them. Unmulched gardens or farmland make terrible habitats for them, and if the mulch isn't there in the spring when the spiders are on the move, they won't stay to see if the mulch will arrive later. Therefore, even generalist species have specific niche requirements that must be met if they are to survive and thrive.

Moreover, we need to encourage both the generalist and the specialist predators by meeting their niche requirements.

Niche Breadth and Successional Stage

Generalists and specialists exist in the plant world, too, only here ecologists speak of wide niche breadth and narrow niche breadth. One aspect of niche breadth is a plant's tolerance to environmental variables. Interestingly, research on the tolerance ranges of plants from both early- and late-succession environments indicates that both herbs and trees exhibit the same pattern of niche breadth relative to successional stage. "In every case, early-successional species had broader and more overlapping response than did late-successional species, whether the comparisons were made among herbs or among trees."[10] Herbs adapted to early-succession environments (annuals) had wider tolerances for water, nutrients, underground space, and pollinators than herbs from late-succession environments (prairie perennials). Trees from early succession had wider tolerances for nutrients and water than trees from late succession. Having overlapping responses and tolerances among early-succession plants (broader, more overlapping niches) means they will tend to have stronger competitive interactions. Greater specialization (narrower niches) among late-succession species allows them to minimize competition and stress.[11] If this relationship holds across the board, *we should generally find it easier to create low-competition, overyielding polycultures using late-succession species rather than early-succession species.* In other words, forest gardens likely have more opportunities for good polyculture design than annual crop systems.

Niches in Time

The preceding discussion shows how plant strategies vary over successional time scales. However, strategies relating to niches in time exist on seasonal and multiyear scales, too. Spring ephemeral wildflowers perfectly illustrate this. They use the bright sunshine and abundant nutrients available in

Box 4.3: The Principle of Stress and Harmony

Stress is the prevention of natural function or the existence of unfulfilled needs or forced function. Harmony is the permission of chosen and natural functions, the supply of essential needs, and the absence of forced unnatural functions.[12]

For a species to survive and reproduce, it must be able to meet its essential needs. For a species to thrive, it must perform its essential functions. Preventing the fulfillment of essential needs and repressing natural, inherent functions causes stress, as does forcing functions that are unnatural. Allowing a species its natural expression and meeting its needs creates harmony. What functions, behaviors, and tolerances come naturally to a species or individual? Which don't?

If you think about which jobs in your life have

been most stressful, which have been least, and why, you will begin to understand your "niche" in the world. Obviously, we are happier and most productive in those situations that meet our needs most effectively and allow us to operate in those ways that are natural to us. The same is true for plants, animals, and microbes, as well as nonliving objects. Our goal is to design ecosystems where stress is low or absent and harmony is high. Understanding the niches of plants and animals helps us achieve this goal.

spring to grow, store energy, and flower before the canopy leaves break bud, then die back shortly thereafter. Many spring ephemerals contain very high nutrient levels. They therefore make especially good foods for us animals to use to detoxify and rebuild after a long winter—a useful coincidence of needs and yields. Time niches come in other forms as well:

- Time niches are critical to the successful sexual reproduction of any plant species. Fruit trees that need cross-pollination must have cross-pollenizers that flower at the appropriate time, or all is lost.
- Many nut trees bear seed on alternate-year or longer cycles to limit the growth of herbivore populations—a reverse time niche, or a time of no niche for the plant's predators. Then, when the trees bear large crops in a so-called mast year, the herbivores cannot eat it all, and the seeds have a better chance of surviving. When we breed nut trees for consistent annual bearing

we shift the burden of nut defense to the intervenors—us.
- Apricot flowers often bud too early and get killed by frost in the northern part of their hardiness range. They must grow somewhere with good cold-air drainage or where the soil and air temperatures will remain cool in the spring to delay flowering. This is an example of modifying a time niche using a spatial niche.
- If a garden yields abundantly all at once, the workload can rise to the breaking point and significantly reduce your ability to use it all (like squirrels in mast years!). Analyzing yield *timing* is often as important as yield *quantity* in assessing system stability and sustainability.

We must therefore ponder how the characteristics we discover in plants, such as alternate-year bearing, relate to plant strategies. This may help us make breeding, design, and management choices that are more effective.

Form Follows Function: Structure Is a Guide to Species Niche

An organism's structure reflects its niche, because that form gives the organism the equipment that allows it a specific livelihood, as well as certain inherent capacities and limitations. Bats and birds reflect this nicely: insectivorous bats evolved to eat night-flying insects using ultrasonic navigating and prey-finding equipment; hence their big ears. Insectivorous birds forage in daytime, so they possess well-developed eyes. We can observe the physical structure of various species and make guesses about their niche requirements from the structures we find.

Tall, straight-stemmed trees with few side branches have obviously evolved to live in the canopy of the forest. Short trees with many side branches, or multistemmed shrubs, usually grow in early-successional situations or possess other adaptations that allow them a livelihood in full or partial shade. As a high-quality timber tree, American chestnut exemplifies the former, while Chinese chestnut, an orchard tree, illustrates the latter. This is one reason why Chinese chestnut cannot replace American chestnut in our forests.

The root patterns of plants indicate their niche, too: from shallow, fibrous roots to deep laterals and taproots, each reflects how the plants acquire and use their key resources—as organic soil feeders, deep mineral and water prospectors, or what-have-you.

Plant Structure Affects Interactions

If the structure of a plant helps us understand its niche, then it would logically follow that the structure of plants has much to do with how they interact:

> Recently it has become clear that the placement of plant parts in space and their mode of display (plant architecture) are very important in plant–plant interactions. . . . [For example,] in some situations, architecture may be even more critical than physiological processes (such as photosyn-

thesis rates) in determining competitive interactions between neighbors.[13]

For example, F. A. Bazzaz and his cohorts studied interactions between perennial herbs such as *Aster lanceolatus* and several *Solidago* species (goldenrods) in oldfield environments.[14] Once established, these plants propagate vegetatively using underground runners, a common midsuccession plant strategy. Goldenrods usually replace asters in oldfield successions partly because the aster's longer runners result in loose, open clumps, whereas the goldenrod's short runners form dense clumps that effectively resist other species. The aboveground architecture also influences their relative competitive abilities: The goldenrods cast denser shade. Accordingly, goldenrod seedlings can sprout underneath asters, but not the reverse. The ability of shrubs and trees to overtop herbaceous competitors also shows how plant architecture influences plant niches in both space and time.

Environment Niche Completes Species Niche: Indicator Plants

If a niche is a property of a species it must yet be exercised in a suitable environment. Specialization for food resources is possible only where that food resource is present. A bird with feet adapted to perching on small twigs can live only where there are small twigs, and so on.[15]

Obviously, we need to understand the resources and conditions of the garden environment so we can match species to the site. We must therefore examine the site thoroughly as we design, as well as work to understand the niches of our desired species.

Environment niche is the complement of species niche. If we want to grow taprooted crop trees but our soils are shallow, the environment will not support the crop very well, if at all. Conversely, if a species thrives on a given site, the site must meet its niche requirements well. Theoretically, then, if we know the niche requirements of the species already growing on a site, we can use them as indicators of the site conditions or environmental resources available in our garden (see volume 2, chapter 3 for tables of indicator plants). Theoretically.

Plants usually try to grow wherever they or their propagules land. Plant tolerances range from very narrow to very wide. Every species population contains some genetic diversity. Complex interactions occur between different resources and conditions that may alter the tolerance ranges for a particular resource or condition. Throw in the empirical and anecdotal nature of the current information on plant indicators, and it is clear we should move cautiously.

Therefore, you should never consider only one plant or species an accurate indicator. Use several species or plants indicating the same conditions. Plants with narrow tolerance ranges for a resource or site condition make the best indicators, and those with wide tolerance the worst. Plant health is also an indicator of site conditions. If a plant thought to indicate fertile soils looks sickly or feeble, it may indicate infertility!

Also, base your interpretations on how reliably plants can indicate the various resources or conditions. Roughly, from most reliable to least, you can use plants as indicators to:

- determine successional stage and estimate future successional trajectory;
- gauge soil moisture or, by examining root systems, the water table depth;
- estimate the recentness of soil disturbance (e.g., cultivation);
- indicate soil tilth or texture;
- estimate the abundance of soil nutrients, specifically or generally; and
- estimate pH.[16]

However, you should back up plant indicators with other forms of observation, especially when the indicators give mixed signals or the issue is critical, potentially costly, or has long-term implications.[17]

Of course, species do not live in isolation, especially in forests or forest gardens. If we are to design workable forest gardens, we must understand the kinds of interactions our garden inhabitants may have with each other. In this way, we can work to maximize beneficial interactions and minimize harmful relationships.

TWO-SPECIES INTERACTIONS: BUILDING BLOCKS OF SOCIAL STRUCTURE

Interactions between two species reflect the nature of the species involved. Each interaction is a way for each participant to meet a need or to make use of the natural products or by-products of another species' way of life, or it simply results from the participants' inherent characteristics. Hence, observing species interactions also provides us with clues about the niches of the actors involved.

Species interact in six basic kinds of pairwise relationships (table 4.2): predation (including herbivory and parasitism); competition; mutualism; facilitation; inhibition; and neutralism. These interactions differ in their beneficial, neutral, or detrimental effects on the species involved.

More than one of these interactions can take place at the same time between the same two individuals

TABLE 4.2. Interactions between two species. *Adapted from Perry, 1994, page 226.*

Type of Interaction	Species 1	Species 2	Nature of Interaction
Predation, parasitism, herbivory	+	–	Species 1 benefits at the expense of species 2.
Competition	–	–	Both species suffer.
Mutualism, cooperation	+	+	Both species benefit.
Facilitation	0	+	Species 1 helps species 2 and is unaffected.
Inhibition	0, +	–	Species 1 benefits or is unaffected as it inhibits species 2.
Neutralism	0	0	Neither species affects the other.

0 = no interaction; + = a positive effect on this species; – = a negative effect on this species

or species, or one interaction can transform into another. For example, species may simultaneously compete for water resources while they cooperate to support pollinator populations they both depend upon. As larvae, monarch butterflies prey upon milkweed plants (*Asclepias* spp.) that they later help to pollinate as adults. The facilitation of vines by supporting trees can turn into a parasitic relationship as the vine begins to harm its host.

As we briefly discuss each of these two-species interactions, we will look at how each influences social structures and our forest gardens, focusing on competition and mutualism.

Predation, Parasitism, and Herbivory

Parasites are smart little buggers. They have usually found a way to get a meal without killing it, so they need only find their meal once and then hang on. Herbivores are little different: their meals do not move around much, but they usually do not completely kill their host either. Predators, on the other hand, take big bites and then have to find another meal "on the hoof." Although the individual hosts and prey probably don't appreciate it, these ways of being eaten ultimately benefit species and ecosystems.

Predatory interactions as a group constitute one of the most direct and powerful pairwise interactions in ecosystems. They shape the direction of species evolution to a great degree: those being eaten keep evolving new strategies to avoid that prospect, while the eaters find new ways to get their meals. Plants create toxic defenses against herbivores or grow thorny leaves and stems. They find ways to disperse themselves and "hide" amid the foliage, or they simply root deeply and regrow rapidly after each meal. Animals, especially insects, play a numbers game to ensure their species continue. They also hide, startle their attacker and flee, become poisonous, and take any number of other defensive strategies. On offense, the possible countermeasures are legion. However, these defensive and offensive strategies are of less import than the effects of pre-

dation, herbivory, and parasitism on the social structure at large, which we shall discuss when we talk about the food web later in this chapter.

Competition

When two species or individuals living near each other need the same resource, and that resource is scarce, they compete for that resource. Three points follow from this.

First, competition takes place *only when a resource is in short supply*. An understanding of limiting factors in the environment is therefore essential to understanding competition (see box 5.1, page 176). Community niche also influences whether species compete. Plants frequently compete with each other because they often fully use the available light, water, and nutrients. On the other hand, predators and climatic factors, rather than a limited food supply, often hold down insect herbivore populations. When that happens, different insect species can consume the same food without competing among themselves.[18]

Second, since the two species or individuals need the same resource, their species niches overlap in this arena. As a result, we can see that the most competition is likely to occur between individuals or species whose niches are similar, or whose niches overlap the most. Competition is therefore high between individuals of the same species because their niches are likely to be the same. In the case of vegetatively propagated plants, since their genetics are precisely alike, their niches are precisely alike, and they will compete with each other the most. Similarly, species compete more with other species that play the same role in the food web: herbivore with herbivore, carnivore with carnivore, and so on. Plants compete more with other plants in the same layer of vegetation than with those in different layers because their niches are more similar.

Finally, contrary to our culture's popular rhetoric, competition is a negative interaction for both species or individuals involved in it. Ecologists used to think competition was the primary force driving

Box 4.4: The Competitive Exclusion Principle

Stable populations of two or more species cannot continuously
occupy the same niche . . . one species: one niche.

—Paul Colinvaux, *Ecology*

Whenever two or more species attempt to occupy the same niche, one species always has an advantage. The advantage might be inborn, or it might arise by chance, such as "who got there first." The species with the greatest advantage, even if it is only a small one, will drive the other to extinction: competitive exclusion. This creates a tendency over evolutionary time for species to diverge in their use of resources to avoid competition. In the shorter frame of ecological time, however, competitive exclusion is a powerful force—as the dominance of vigorous plants such as kudzu, quackgrass, and other species shows.

Several factors can modify the predicted extinction. If the weaker species has an escape, or a third force modifies the interaction, the weaker species may survive. Coexistence may result if both species compete weakly—that is, they use different resources or the same resource at different times or places. Coexistence may also result if they benefit each other in a way that limits the competition's impact. Generally, populations of different species can coexist because they avoid competition by occupying different niches or because the many facets of interaction include cooperative as well as competitive aspects. One primary goal of edible polyculture design, then, is to find useful species that fill different niches or that cooperate and thus can coexist indefinitely with minimal competition.

We should note that competitive exclusion generally occurs faster in resource-abundant conditions, and more slowly when resources are limited.[19] Presumably, the advantaged species can multiply its advantage more rapidly when resources are abundant. This may be why highly fertile sites tend to exhibit lower diversity than moderately fertile sites.

---

evolution; most now see it as only one evolutionary force among several. Competing is a stress, and it inhibits productivity in ecosystems. Because competition causes suffering for those involved in it, species evolve to avoid competition whenever they can, or to mute it with other helpful interactions. In other words, species evolve to differentiate their niches, to partition resources, and to have different ways of making a living. In many cases, they evolve to cooperate.

Reducing Competition: Increasing Scarce Resources or Reducing Demand

We can reduce competition by increasing the supply of resources (water, nutrients, light, carbon dioxide) or by reducing demand, for example, by proper spacing. Both of these standard agricultural strategies work. Plant spacing is one of the fundamental aspects of any kind of farming or gardening. We will talk about plant spacing further in chapters 1 and 4 of volume 2.

Increasing resources conventionally means importing them from elsewhere at high cost. Increasing nutrient supplies ecologically means using deep-rooted and otherwise nutrient-accumulating plants, mulches, and good soil biology to improve nutrient cycling, storage, and supply—though these take time. Short-term fertilizing may be necessary as the biological systems develop in your garden. Making use of existing water resources (such as

Box 4.5: The Cropping Principle

Heavy predation gives opportunity for increased [prey] diversity by reducing competition among the prey.

—PAUL COLINVAUX, *Ecology*

When predation is heavy, the principle of competitive exclusion cannot operate between prey because the stronger competitor gets cropped. This is one of the principles behind weeding, or behind controlling opportunist exotic plants. If a superplant is competitively excluding all other plants from a patch of ground, hacking it back heavily allows the diversity of the patch to remain by reducing the competition. In our forest gardens, hacking back vigorous plants is one of the more common management tasks, and an effort to maintain the diversity of the whole system by limiting competition. Fire can play this role in some ecosystems, as can heavy herbivore feeding, both allowing greater plant diversity. In theory, government "crops" big business to allow greater diversity in the marketplace. One needs to be careful, though: cropping can *increase* competition at times, depending on the resource situation. For example, cutting back plants may increase demand for soil nutrients. In poor soils, regrowth may cause stronger competition for those nutrients than if the plants had not been cut back.

roof runoff) efficiently through garden placement, grading, drainage, and storage systems and the use of mulches and dry-tolerant plants can reduce demand or increase effective supply. Properly designed drip irrigation systems very efficiently use water. These systems are most time- and labor-efficient in perennial plantings where the system can stay in place year-round.

Minimizing Competition: Polycultures

Monoculture cropping essentially maximizes competition in the ecosystem, since niche overlap and competition are highest among individuals of the same species. The only ways to reduce competition in monocultures are to increase resources and to space plants farther apart. It would follow, therefore, that polycultures would at least have the chance to exhibit less competition in a dense array of plants given the right mix of species, though there is also a chance for competitive exclusion to reign. The right mix of species is the trick. We'll talk about that later in the chapter.

In most cases, we seek to minimize competition in our forest gardens, and so increase the productivity of the whole system. Increasing scarce resources, spacing plants properly, using the cropping principle, and creating polycultures are three good ways to do this. In some cases, we may want to use competition to prevent plants or animals we don't want from taking root in our forest gardens. The fact that species evolve to avoid competition is a good hint for us, though: cooperation and mutual aid are just as important, if not more important, in the creation of self-maintaining, balanced, productive gardens.

Mutualism

Mutual aid, or mutualism, abounds in ecosystems and may be the most common form of two-species relationship in nature. "Plants, animals and . . . microbes that do *not* participate in at least one mutualism are rare—and in all likelihood do not exist."[20] Mutualism appears to occur mainly between species on different trophic levels. For instance, technically speaking, a mycorrhizal fungus is an herbivore, since it feeds on energy produced by its plant ally.

Individuals or species may depend upon cooperation for survival (obligate mutualism), or the cooperation may help species or individuals thrive, but they can survive and reproduce without it (facultative mutualism). Mutualisms can be either pairwise, meaning that only two particular species cooperate with each other, or diffuse, meaning that a species can cooperate with many possible partners. Most cooperative relationships are facultative and diffuse, because obligate and pairwise relationships limit flexibility in a constantly changing environment. In addition, many of these interactions are on-again, off-again: they take place only when it is in the participant's best interest, like a limited partnership.[21]

The known forms of mutualism most important to forest gardeners fall into several categories: harvest, protection, pollination, and dispersal mutualisms.

Harvest Mutualisms

"Those related to resource acquisition are the most ubiquitous and diverse of nature's mutualisms."[22] Harvest mutualisms include those between digestive organisms in animal guts and their hosts, and also "farming" mutualisms, such as those between aphids and the ants that guard, herd, and disperse them in return for "honeydew" excreted from the aphids' backsides. Some ants cultivate and eat fungi, carting fungus foods down into their "climate-controlled" growth chambers. We have previously mentioned mycorrhizas and the other root-zone microbes, and these are perhaps the most critical for us to work with, along with nitrogen-fixing mutualisms. Since much more is generally known about nitrogen-fixing organisms, let's look more closely at mycorrhizas (see figure 1.1 on page 11).

"Roughly 90 percent of the world's plant species form mycorrhizas with at least one (and frequently many) species of fungi."[23] Mycorrhizas appear to be obligate for all wild conifers, and probably for all kinds of trees. Of the over 6,500 flowering plants studied so far, more than 70 percent are obligate mycorrhizal plants, and another 12 percent have facultative mycorrhizas. A large proportion of the world's worst weeds are facultative with fungi, *but not obligate*. Other weeds are nonhost plants that do not associate with fungi at all.

What do mycorrhizas do for plants? They can:

- gather water and nutrients;
- extend the life of plant roots;
- protect plant roots from predators, pathogens, salt, and toxic heavy metals;
- biodegrade toxic organic chemicals;
- aggregate soil particles;
- weather minerals and organic matter;
- mediate plant-to-plant interactions; and
- evolve faster than their hosts, helping their tree allies cope with change.[24]

When soil fertility is high, plants form many fewer mycorrhizal relationships than in poor soils, though it appears to be extremely rare that a plant in the wild ever goes completely without fungal partners.

Three kinds of mycorrhizal fungi prefer different environments and appear to perform somewhat different functions:[25]

- Arbuscular mycorrhizal (AM, formerly called VAM or vesicular-arbuscular mycorrhizal) fungi enter the cells of plant roots and appear to be the most common of the three types, especially in fertile soils. Most plants form this type of mycorrhiza. AM fungi always release their spores belowground, never forming mushrooms. Most AM fungi do not appear to be able to directly break down organic matter, so they rely on a healthy decomposer community to function well. Several companies sell diffuse, facultative, generalist AM fungal inoculants that seem to greatly enhance the performance of a wide variety of plants (see "Managing Mycorrhizas" in chapter 5, page 228 and "Mycorrhizal Inoculation" in chapter 5 of volume 2).
- Ectomycorrhizal (EM) fungi coat and enter the roots of plants but do not penetrate the cells, instead remaining in the spaces between them. These fungi appear able to directly strip nutrients out of organic matter, and they consequently

become more numerous on poor sites, especially those low in phosphorus. All truffles are EM fungi, as are a number of aboveground mushrooms. Some of these are obligate and pairwise mutualists with specific trees, which makes their cultivation much more difficult.

• Ericoid and arbutoid mycorrhizal fungi also penetrate the root cells of their hosts, but they frequent only the roots of plants related to blueberries and rhododendrons (family Ericaceae). These plants inhabit highly acidic soils with especially weak decomposer communities, low nitrogen levels, and very poor nutrient cycling. As a result, these fungi, especially fungi associated with *Arbutus* and *Arctostaphyllos* species, decompose organic matter quite adeptly, gathering nitrogen quickly.

The "Soil Food Web" section of chapter 5 (page 216) discusses mycorrhizas and their ecological functions further, but before moving on, a couple of additional comments are necessary. When two trees or other plants engage in competition, the addition of mycorrhizal fungi into the mix seems to transform the plant-to-plant interaction into a neutral interaction, if not outright cooperation! Mycorrhizas even appear to take carbon compounds from canopy trees and feed them to trees in the understory, so that the canopy tree supports the shade-limited individual.[26] Finally, pollution appears to be harming mycorrhizal communities in the soil, particularly the increased acidity and nitrogen content of rainfall—yet another reason to stop acid rain.

Protection Mutualisms

Unlike the Mob, protection mutualisms create mutual benefit without force or threat of retaliation: one species protects another from predation or pathogens, with food or shelter as common return gifts. For example, ants appear to be essential to the protection and establishment of many native woodland wildflowers, as well as to the dispersal of their seeds, receiving food in return. The trumpet creeper vine (*Campsis radicans*) has evolved four different nectary organs with which it feeds ants in return for protection from herbivores.[27] Fungal endophytes, mycorrhizal fungi, and microbes on leaf surfaces and in the root zone all make similar deals, and we need to encourage them.

Fungal endophytes (literally, "within plants") live inside plant leaves and stems and appear to protect plants from pathogens and herbivores. These diverse, short-lived fungi can adapt more quickly to changes in herbivore and pathogen strategies than can longer-lived plant hosts. Though they have been discovered mainly in grasses and conifer needles so far, one researcher believes we will eventually find them to be as common as mycorrhizas—the rule rather than the exception.[28] It would be interesting to know how many perennial crops have fungal endophytes, especially in comparison to their wild cousins, and how we can encourage this relationship. The endophytic lawn grasses introduced in the 1980s and 1990s appear to work well in protecting grasses from diseases and insects.

Evidence exists that microbes living on the surfaces of plant leaves help protect plants from pathogens, and that sprays containing "tea" made from compost of good biological quality can help support these microbes.[29] See chapter 5 in volume 2 for more details.

Acid rain can kill or inhibit both endophytes and leaf microbes.

Pollination Mutualisms

In their excellent treatise *The Forgotten Pollinators*, dealing with a previously unheard-of subject, Stephen Buchman and Gary Paul Nabhan said:

It now appears that the majority of plants studied to date show evidence of natural pollinator limitation. That is to say, under natural conditions, 62 percent of some 258 kinds of plants studied in detail suffer limited fruit set from too few visits by effective pollinators. If this condition is the norm in the natural world, to what extent is the regeneration of plants jeopardized by human disruption of the interactions between plants and their pollinators?[30]

Until recently, most pollination studies related to agricultural systems. Thus, we know relatively little about pollination of unconventional crops or in forest ecosystems. However, the fact that pollinators appear to be a limiting resource in natural ecosystems, and that plants therefore probably compete for pollinators, indicates the seriousness and importance of the pollinator mutualisms we usually take for granted. Habitat and native plant loss have decimated native pollinator populations. Various imported diseases and pests have been decimating populations of the imported and naturalized European honeybees we have relied upon for decades to pollinate our crops. We need to learn the habits and habitats of the native pollinators in our regions so we can support these allies to do their work, make their livings, and help us do the same. We'll discuss this further in volume 2, appendix 5.

The wind pollinates most nut crops and many native North American trees (for example, alder, beech, chestnut, chinkapin, filbert, ginkgo, hazelnut, hickory, jojoba, oak, pecan, pine, and walnut, among others).[31] Vertebrate pollination (by birds or bats, for instance) is rare in north temperate zones. Therefore, insects dominate the pollination of most forbs here, but native plants often have pollinators other than bees.[32] Ants, beetles, flies, moths, butterflies, and other species all may pollinate specific plants. They do this in return for the plants offering the animals nectar. Hence, we call nectar-offering plants nectary plants. Most plant-pollinator mutualisms are diffuse, but members of the same taxonomic group (bees, beetles, or moths and butterflies) tend to pollinate the same kinds of flowers. Different pollinator groups tend to prefer certain flower colors, while a flower's structure governs who can actually gather nectar and pollen from it (see table 4.3).

Flower types and pollinators may stratify according to vegetation layers: many ant- and beetle-pollinated flowers appear to occur in the ground layer, while flowers built for fly, wasp, bee, and butterfly pollination may occur more in the middle and upper layers.

It pays to foster compositional diversity, both to ensure pollination of your plants and to attract the pollinators using the plants. Knowing who pollinates your particular crops can help you choose associated plants that will benefit the same pollinators to keep them around.

Dispersal Mutualisms

The dispersal of seeds, fungal spores, and other microorganisms by insects, birds, and mammals large and small amplifies the impact of the small amounts of nutrients animals cycle in their manures. It also affects our management and harvest strategies.

Birds and mammals carry seeds and microbes in their guts and deposit them into the right environments with soluble fertilizers, assisting soil biology diversity. Ground-dwelling rodents propagate fungal spores, especially of truffles and other fungi that fruit belowground, many of which are mycorrhizal. Thank a chipmunk today.

Ants disperse the seeds of a large number of woodland wildflowers that have evolved specific ant-feeding adaptations for this purpose. Ant nests contain aerated soils and decomposing organic matter that support the seedlings' establishment. The ants also protect the seedlings. Ant-dispersed plants are

TABLE 4.3. General pollinator preferences. *Adapted from Perry, 1994, pages 236–237.*

Pollinator	Flower Color	Flower Structure
birds (uncommon)	green, red	large, usually long tubes
butterflies, moths	none known	not easily accessible tubes
bees	yellow, blue	easily accessible, or if not, bees specialize by size for specific flower sizes
flies, wasps, beetles, ants	brown, drab colors	unspecialized, open dish bowls, often "smelly"

notoriously slow to reestablish themselves in disturbed areas, as are ants: "as hard as they are to eject from your kitchen, ant populations of the forest are exterminated by clearcutting and return very slowly, if at all."[33] Forest herbaceous diversity could take considerably longer than five hundred years to rebound from cutting to primeval forest levels unless a local seed source of ant-dispersed plants is nearby.[34]

Over 60 percent of temperate tree species possess nuts and fleshy fruits that encourage animal dispersal of the seeds they contain. One-third of temperate forest birds eat fruit at one time or another. "In one study, 50 jays were estimated to transport and cache 150,000 acorns from 11 pin oak trees over 28 days," carrying the seeds up to 22 kilometers and burying them below the soil surface near their nest sites.[35] "Birds are very skilled at selecting only sound, viable nuts from trees,[36]—in other words, the best ones of the crop. This is what we are up against! Yet it is exactly what the trees want the birds to do, despite our wishes to the contrary. Maybe we need to become jaybird mutualists and teach the birds to do our bidding in return for guaranteed food. This is probably possible! If we don't co-opt the competition, we shall be forced to compete strongly for our nuts.

Co-optation is exactly the story concerning mice. According to nurseryman Steve Breyer at Tripple Brook Farm in Massachusetts, some Midwestern Indian customers of his recently found that mice will hoard several quarts of edible hog-peanuts (*Amphicarpaea bracteata*) in belowground storage chambers.[37] Apparently, the Indians were able to gather plenty of hog-peanuts for themselves, while leaving sufficient amounts for the mice. Harvesting the small subterranean pods of the native, nitrogen-fixing, shade-tolerant hog-peanut plants is not easy, so cooperating with mice makes a great deal of sense if you choose to grow and eat these tasty plants.

Facilitation

Facilitation happens when one species benefits from an interaction, but the facilitator is unaffected. We discuss many examples of these interactions in other parts of the book, so we will simply list types of facilitation here. One plant may facilitate another by:[38]

- modifying microclimate (light, moisture, air movement);
- offering physical support;
- modifying the soil;
- encouraging beneficial, or discouraging harmful, soil fauna;
- distracting or deterring predators or pathogens;
- reducing the impact of competitors; or
- attracting pollinators, herbivore predators, or dispersal agents.

It seems hard to believe that the facilitator could *not* be affected by such interactions, at least in some way. Facilitation is probably frequently a short-lived phenomenon that evolves to some other interaction, such as parasitism, competition, or mutualism over either ecological or evolutionary time. For example, during succession, shrubs may shift a meadow ecosystem from a bacterial-dominated soil toward the fungal-dominated soil that trees appear to prefer, therefore facilitating the trees. However, in most cases the trees ultimately outcompete the shrubs, ending the facilitative relationship.

Another example, lichens, themselves a mutualistic interaction between algae and fungi, frequently receive facilitation from trees, on whose bark lichens grow. However, this may at times not be facilitation at all but mutualism. Some lichens can fix nitrogen from the atmosphere, and it turns out that nitrogen leaches from lichens into stem flow or raindrip during rainstorms. Though difficult to measure, the importance of this phenomenon to forests can range from lichens making a small but significant contribution to their becoming a major nitrogen source.[39]

Inhibition

Inhibition occurs when one party to an interaction suppresses another and either benefits from or is unaffected by the interaction.

The most commonly discussed form of inhibition involves allelochemicals, compounds plants use to defend against pathogens, feeding animals, and other plants. Most plants produce allelochemicals; as of 1974, scientists had identified twelve thousand of these compounds, with more being discovered at a rate of about one thousand per year within the whole plant world. Though we know little of their various effects and potential uses, the medicinal and psychoactive properties of plants come from these chemicals. Animals create allelochemicals, too—think of skunks!

The most widely known example of this chemical warfare (called allelopathy) among plants is the compound juglone, which members of the genus *Juglans* (walnuts) use to inhibit other plants from growing nearby. Walnuts secrete juglone from their roots, it washes from their leaves in the rain, and their decaying nut husks release the chemical, the effects of which last for years in the soil even after the trees have been removed. Juglone does not affect all plants equally: see volume 2, appendix 3 for a listing of known susceptible and compatible species. The allelopathic strategy helps reduce the competition walnuts face in the deep, fertile soils they seem to prefer.

Many plants produce in their foliage chemicals that inhibit the growth, fertility, or digestion of their herbivores or pathogens or else are outright poisonous to them. We have selected or bred many of our food plants for reduced allelochemical properties, leaving the plants defenseless on their own. In some cases this is good. In other cases, it unnecessarily increases our workload as gardeners and farmers. Breeders seem to be paying more attention to creating inherently disease-resistant varieties these days, and it seems there is much room for improvement in this regard. It behooves all of us to look for varieties that use allelochemical defenses against the more common or destructive pests and diseases.

Many allelochemicals aimed at herbivores and pathogens sometimes also inhibit the germination or growth of other plants. The phenols, terpenes, and tannins in fresh peat moss, pine or cedar chips, leaves, sawdust, or bark mulch can damage growing plants when used as mulch. Before spreading these materials on actively growing plants, you should first allow rain to leach these materials for several months—as when leaves fall in the autumn and begin breaking down over the winter—or let fungi digest the complex compounds that cause the problems by growing edible mushrooms in the mulch pile.[40]

Inhibition can play a major role in the soil ecosystem, as well. Decomposing and living grass roots release chemicals that inhibit mycorrhiza formation in many woody plants. Bacteria called *Streptomyces* appear to grow more abundantly in clear-cuts and in between islands of regenerating shrubs and trees than in forests or within regenerating islands. *Streptomyces* can allelopathically inhibit specific plants, bacteria, mycorrhizas, or plant pathogens, depending on which strain grows (a few *Streptomyces* stimulate mycorrhizas).[41] While inhibition may thus slow the progress of succession, invading shrubs also use allelopathy to inhibit grasses and herbaceous perennials and so outcompete them. These realities have major impact on the patterns and strategies of successional plants.

Neutralism

Adjacent species participate in neutralism when they have no positive or negative effects on each other, either as a whole or with respect to a specific resource or function. Though neutrality may not be as beneficial as mutualism, it is certainly much better than competition. In these cases, clearly the species have very different niches, with little or no overlap in resource use or community role. Remember, though, that a pair of plants, for example, may have a neutral relationship with respect to one resource, such as pollinators, while competing heavily with respect to another resource, such as water. However, neutralism with respect to universal needs like water may occur if the species draw from different soil horizons, use the resource at different times, or if water is not in short supply. Relative neutrality is often one of the

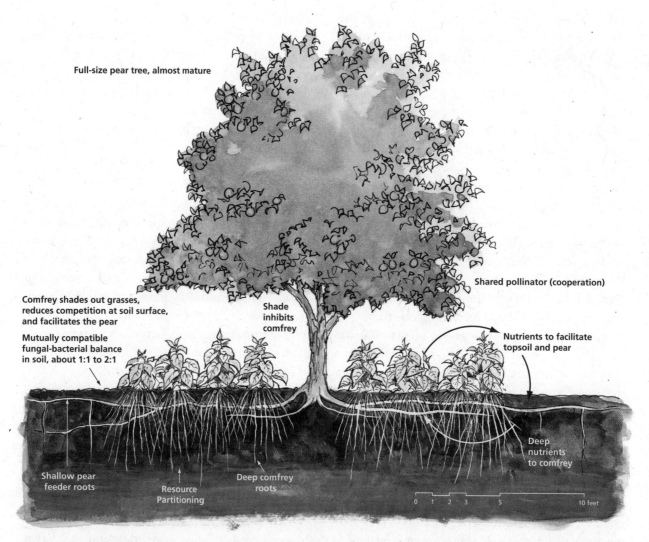

Full-size pear tree, almost mature

Shared pollinator (cooperation)

Comfrey shades out grasses, reduces competition at soil surface, and facilitates the pear

Shade inhibits comfrey

Mutually compatible fungal-bacterial balance in soil, about 1:1 to 2:1

Nutrients to facilitate topsoil and pear

Deep nutrients to comfrey

Shallow pear feeder roots

Resource Partitioning

Deep comfrey roots

0 1 2 3   5   10 feet

FIGURE 4.2. Some of the multiple interactions in a biculture of European pear (*Pyrus communis*) and comfrey (*Symphytum officinale*). The pear shades and therefore inhibits the comfrey, reducing its aggressiveness. The comfrey shades out grasses under the pear, reducing grass competition. The comfrey and the pear prefer a similar fungal–bacterial balance in the soil. The comfrey dynamically accumulates many nutrients from the deep soil and feeds them to the topsoil, aiding the pear. The two plants share pollinators but flower at different times, so they support each other's pollination needs. Deep-rooted comfrey partitions the soil resources with shallow-rooted pear.

goals for the desired species in our designed polycultures if mutualism or facilitation between them is not possible.

The Multiple Facets of Paired Interactions

These six kinds of interactions between species pairs can take place at different times between the same two species, and some may take place at the same time with respect to different resources. For example, imagine a patch of comfrey plants growing beneath a pear tree (figure 4.2). The shade of the pear may inhibit the comfrey, though well-pruned pears have a more open canopy than unpruned trees. Meanwhile, the two species share

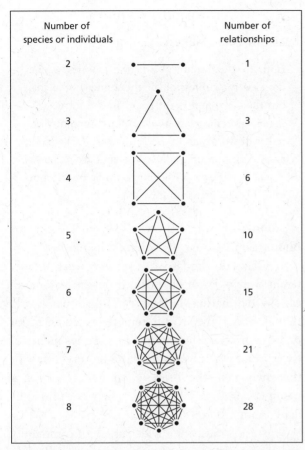

Number of species or individuals		Number of relationships
2		1
3		3
4		6
5		10
6		15
7		21
8		28

FIGURE 4.3. The number of relationships within a constellation of interacting elements increases rapidly as elements are added to that constellation. We need to keep things on the simple side in forest garden design as much as is feasible!

the same bee pollinators, and since they flower at different times of the year they cooperate in supporting those allies. The pear is a heavy nutrient feeder with mainly shallow roots that spread wider than the tree canopy. Meanwhile, the comfrey is a potent deep-rooted dynamic accumulator of many nutrients planted closer to the trunk. Therefore, the comfrey facilitates the pear when the comfrey leaves fall to the ground and rot. The comfrey also facilitates the pear tree by shading out competitive grasses that allelopathically foster the wrong soil biology balance. This is probably good, though we know little about the soil biology of comfrey. On the other hand, during drought years, the comfrey may compete with the pear for water, and the

potential exists for it to compete with the pear for nutrients as well if soils are poor. On balance, however, this would appear to be a favorable combination and pattern of plants, and the experience of forest gardeners indicates that it is.

As if that weren't complex enough, though, that's just two species! When two individuals or species interact, there is only one relationship between them, multifaceted though it is. If we add a third element to the set, the number of relationships climbs to three (figure 4.3). Add a fourth element and the number of relationships jumps to six. By the time we get to ten interacting elements, there are forty-five pairwise relationships, each multifaceted—complex beyond the ability of most human minds to rationally comprehend. How can we reasonably understand and work with these multifaceted interactions in communities of plants, animals, and microbes? We must come at it from the perspective of the whole community and how it is put together, as well as from the pieces and how they relate to each other.

MULTISPECIES INTERACTIONS: FRAMEWORKS OF SOCIAL STRUCTURE

Our goal in forest gardening is to create stable, resilient, self-maintaining communities. Such communities arise from interactions between free individual species, each acting in its own best interest based on its inherent needs and characteristics. How does the individuality of these parts, as David Perry says, "act paradoxically to bind the system together" so the system maintains balance of its own accord? A self-regulating social structure doesn't emerge from a random collection of simple pairwise relationships. We need diversity that works—functional diversity.

We discussed the first aspect of functional diversity, the multiple functions of species, when we discussed species niches at the start of this chapter.

These multiple functions possess generative potential for interconnection, since the specific needs and products of each species create possibilities for specific forms of relationship with others. The additional aspects of functional diversity—diversity of functions, redundancy of function, and functional interconnection—also grow from species niches and pairwise relationships.

In this section, we will discuss several different kinds of multispecies interactions. Community niches express the diverse job-roles or ecosystem functions that organisms must perform to make any given ecosystem work. Food webs constitute the primary expression of community niches, since food-web positions form the essence of the functional roles that species play (decomposer, herbivore, producer, and so on). Groups of species can act as guilds in two ways: by partitioning resources among species with similar community niches to avoid competition, and by forming networks of mutual support among species with different niches. The former (resource-partitioning guilds) represents redundancy of function, because the species all fill the same niche and therefore back up their community role, while the latter (mutual-support guilds) represents a secondary expression of functional interconnection, the primary interconnections being those in the food web. While food webs and community niches manifest themselves rather quickly by the ecosystem's sheer existence, guilds take more time to develop. For all these frameworks of social structure to develop to their fullest expression, species must adjust to each other over evolutionary time. Community niches, food webs, and guilds thus form the frameworks of community social structure. How these guilds form within ecosystems and how community niches are filled are questions whose answers will guide our efforts at recreating these social structures in our forest gardens. Unfortunately, whether the answer involves the process of coevolution, of evolutionary adjustment, or of convergent evolution will likely remain unanswered for a long time.

COMMUNITY NICHES

Ecologist Paul Colinvaux said:

> Both the [community] and the [species] niches describe the profession of the animal [or plant], but the viewpoint is different. In the former, the American robin plays a role in the community as a puller of worms and food for hawks; in the latter, an American robin pulls worms and avoids hawks as part of a program working to thrust more robins into the next generation.[42]

Community niches result from organisms finding similar ways of making a living. Just as all accountants do similar work yet may work for different companies or clients in different regions, all canopy-defoliating herbivores do similar work, though it may be in different tree species, forest types, or parts of the canopy. The species niches of those canopy herbivores may also be very different: they may take the form of an insect, a bird, a mammal, or a microbe, though they perform similar community roles.

Organisms must fill a wide variety of community niches to make an ecosystem work, and work well. There is energy from the sun to capture, store, and distribute throughout the community. Nutrients must be gathered, transformed, stored, used, and made available again after use. There are populations to regulate to keep the balance and the peace. All these functions and more need to be performed in different places and times and under different conditions. In addition, each function is performed only because it represents an opportunity to make a living.

We can define community niches in a number of ways. Position in the food web is one central aspect of community niche (see below); layer position is another. Community roles also include life form (e.g., tree, shrub, herb), specific food preferences or habits (e.g., browser, grazer, gleaner, sun loving, shade tolerant), means of reproduction (e.g., mast producing, fruit bearing, ground nesting), or other characteristic qualities or functions. No fixed rules exist to guide us. We define community niches partly by what is relevant to the discussion or problem at hand. The common denominator is the role in the community, a role generic enough that a number of species could fill it, and specific enough to be useful as an analysis and design tool. A couple of examples should help clarify what we mean when we say "community niche."

Ecologists studying arthropod diversity in young and old-growth forest canopies used community niches to understand the structure of these communities (see the example on page 106, "Diverse Structure and Arthropod Diversity"). Here is how they described some of the community niches of canopy arthropods:

- sucking herbivores;
- defoliating herbivores;
- flower or seed predators;
- predators; and
- decomposers.

The researchers could have segregated the predator niches more finely, if needed, into categories such as leaf-gleaning predators, stem-gleaning predators, flying predators, and so on.

We can look at plant niches in the community the same way: community niches relate not only to who eats what or whom, but also to how plants place themselves in relation to resources and reproduction. So forests provide niches for mast-producing canopy trees, understory fruiting shrubs, berry-producing canopy vines, shade-tolerant understory trees, spring ephemeral wildflowers, and spreading summer ground covers, among others. Oldfields changing back to forest have niches for clumping grasses and rapidly spreading grasses, for sun-loving suckering shrubs, for pioneer trees, and so on. As ecosystem designers, we will likely have some specific roles we want filled in the garden to optimize the system and reduce our workload. These include fertility plants, beneficial insect and wildlife habitat, ground covers for weed control, and useful yields for us. These are all kinds of community niches (see table 4.4).

Diversity of Function in Community Niches

Any healthy ecosystem needs a diverse array of community roles filled to function well. When the arthropod community in the canopy of a young forest consists almost entirely of sucking herbivores, with few other community niches represented, diversity of function is low and the system is out of balance (see "Diverse Structure and Arthropod Diversity" and table 3.7 on page 107). When the old-growth forest exhibits a balance of predators and defoliating herbivores, and other kinds of arthropods live there too, diversity of function is higher and the system is more in balance. The predators help regulate the herbivore populations, and the other arthropods perform vital roles in helping to maintain balance as well. More community niches filled means more diversity of function, which in turn helps stabilize the community.

TABLE 4.4. Some aspects of the community niches of plants.
Trees and Shrubs
Ruderal, competitor, or stress tolerator
Canopy or understory (sun or shade loving)
Pioneer, climax, or gap phase (see chapter 6)
Deciduous or evergreen
Nut, mast, fruit, or seed bearing
Singular, clumping, suckering, or coppicing
Heart, flat, or tap rooted
Herbs
Ruderal, competitor, or stress tolerator
Annual, biennial, or perennial
Sun, partial shade, or full shade loving
Evergreen, ephemeral, or summer green
Singular, clumping, spreading, or matting
Forb, grass, fern, or moss
Bulb, corm, tuber, rhizome, tap, or fibrous root
Functions or Uses
Nitrogen-fixer or dynamic accumulator
Insectary plant
Ground cover
Wildlife habitat (food, shelter)
Food, fuel, fiber, fodder, farmaceutical, fun

Community Niche Sets Numbers

As ecologist Paul Colinvaux has said, "There cannot be more individuals in a species population than there are opportunities to practice its niche."[43] If one compares a species niche to a human occupation, one can see how this works. If a region has a limited number of churches, only a certain number of ministers will have a way to make a living in that profession. If more ministers graduate from divinity school, the region's total number of ministers is unlikely to change because the opportunities for ministering, at least in that form, are limited. "Opportunities set numbers in a human occupation. Niche sets numbers for a species population."[44]

Tendency Toward Filled Niches

As the saying goes, "nature abhors a vacuum." Whenever there is an unused resource, someone will come along to make use of it: "ecological communities tend towards filled niches."[45] The longer a community exists, the more time it has to fill more of its community niches, either by evolution or by immigration of new species. The more species diversity there is in an ecosystem, the more of its niches are filled.

It takes work to prevent the ecosystem from following this natural tendency—which is what weeding is all about. Weeds take advantage of unfilled niches in the garden. So one might think of the need to weed as a symptom of poor ecosystem design. Obviously, from this perspective, it makes sense to try to fill every niche with useful species so that the amount of work to maintain the system goes down while the yield of the system as a whole goes up. The process of succession also expresses this tendency toward filled niches.

Community niche defines a species' role in its community from the community's perspective. For the system to function well, organisms must fill a diverse set of interconnecting community niches in diverse ways so that stability, redundancy, resilience, and self-maintenance reign. The kinds of relationships that species build in ecosystems help determine that diverse set of niches. Primary among these relationships is predation, because predation leads to the formation of food webs.

FUNCTIONAL INTERCONNECTIONS: THE DIVERSE FUNCTIONS OF THE FOOD WEB

Food webs constitute the most elemental and influential part of social structure in ecosystems; they are the primary infrastructure of functional interconnection. Food-web positions also form the core of community and species niches, the essence of diverse community functions. Food-web structure determines the flow of nutrients and energy as well as the balance of species populations, and it influences the evolution of every member of "society." As we design our forest gardens, we must remain conscious that we are designing a food web and use that knowledge to help create a high-yield, self-maintaining system. When we "follow the energy" (as opposed to the money), we find opportunities to create more yields to support our livelihoods and more ways to allow the system to maintain itself.

"Who feeds whom" is one of the primary determinants of the flows of energy, materials, and influence through ecosystems. Note that we did not say who *eats* whom: energy and materials can flow from one organism to another without killing and eating being involved. Predation, parasitism, and herbivory constitute a major portion of the links that create the food web and play a major role in regulating populations, managing competition, cycling nutrients, and dispersing energy both above- and belowground. However, mutualism and cooperation play major roles in the food web as well.

Food Web Basics

Solar energy enters all ecosystems as food only through plants, the producers. The rest of us are consumers: herbivores eat plants, primary carnivores eat the herbivores, secondary carnivores eat primary carnivores, and so on. Though often

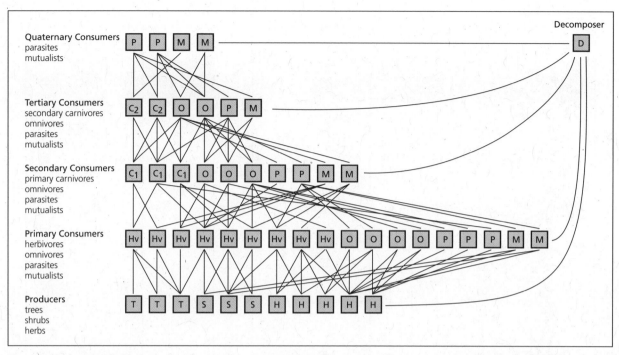

FIGURE 4.4. A simplified hypothetical food web for an aboveground ecosystem. Notice the typical spindle shape of the web, with the widest level occurring at the primary consumer level. Each of the upper trophic levels includes mutualists and parasites, as well as the more familiar herbivores and carnivores, such as cows, tigers, birds of prey, and so on.

ignored, decomposers play key roles in any ecosystem by recycling nutrients and energy from the wastes and dead bodies of all other living things. Each of these basic roles in the food web is called a trophic level, the word *trophic* being Greek for "nursing," since the members of each trophic level "operate on a common feeding plan."[46] However, many species feed at more than one trophic level; such omnivores include many birds, insects, and mammals. These trophic levels begin to define the niche of each species in the ecosystem.

Each trophic level contains not only the typical herbivores and carnivores we might expect, but also pathogens or parasites that feed on the level below, as well as mutualists (such as mycorrhizal fungi or bacteria in termite or human digestive tracts) that benefit from cooperative relationships with species at the next lower trophic level (see figure 4.4). Decomposers feed on all levels of the food web.

Figure 4.4 illustrates a simplified hypothetical

food web. Figure 4.5 shows an attempt to estimate the amount of energy flowing between the different links in an actual deciduous forest's food web in New Hampshire. The following discussion relates to these two diagrams. We will discuss the soil food web in more detail in chapter 5.

Food Webs Regulate Populations

It should be intuitively obvious that the higher trophic levels regulate the populations of the lower trophic levels by eating them. The reverse is also true: lower trophic levels influence the upper levels by determining the amount of energy available to support them and the range of niche strategies available for garnering food and energy. Carnivores at the upper levels of the food web therefore play a major role in controlling herbivore populations, along with weather and plant defense mechanisms.

Irregularities in these population-balancing factors create a dynamic in which forest insect herbivores

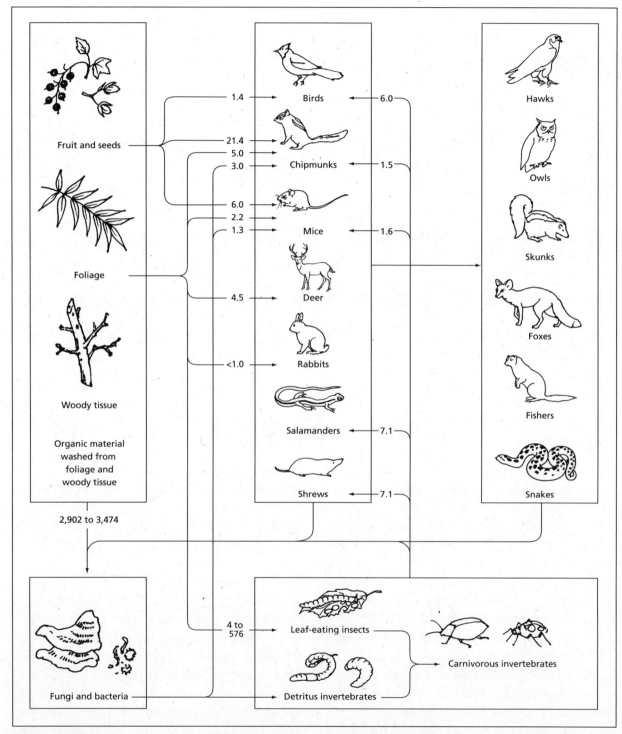

FIGURE 4.5. Food-web energy flow in a northern hardwood forest. Numbers shown are thousands of calories per square meter per year flowing from one compartment to another. The vast majority of energy produced by forests goes to rot in the soil. Insect herbivore populations can sometimes explode, hence the wide range of energy flows to them. Note that significant amounts of energy emerge from the box at the bottom to act as the primary support for populations of birds, salamanders, and shrews, all key pest control allies. *Adapted from Gosz et al., 1978.*

tend to experience major population explosions on a periodic or infrequent basis. As figure 4.5 shows, the amount of energy consumed by these species can increase by a factor of 100 or more at these times, with over 40 percent of yearly plant biomass production being eaten. As we shall see below, the system responds to regulate even these population eruptions.

Insects and Microbes Dominate Middle Trophic Levels

The majority of biomass in the herbivore and primary carnivore roles consists of insects and microbes, with the majority of microbe "herbivores" being plant mutualists—allies of our allies. Higher carnivores tend to be larger animals and birds, because it pays to be able to put your food into your mouth whole. We therefore must learn to manage not only our microherds belowground, but also the insect herds aboveground.

Carnivore Diversity Depends on Plant Diversity

When we examine the number of species at each trophic level, we find that food webs tend to be spindle shaped (narrow at the top and bottom and wide in the middle, as in figure 4.4). The number of herbivore species is higher than the number of plant species, but the number of species decreases with each jump to higher trophic levels. There are many strategies for making a living from plants and a relative abundance of available energy to support diverse herbivore species. However, the second law of thermodynamics ("no energy transfer is 100 percent efficient," i.e., energy is always wasted when transformed) means that fewer numbers of species can live off each succeeding trophic level, so diversity must go down. Lower food-source diversity at the higher trophic levels leads most carnivore species into omnivory.

This means, therefore, that we and our plant allies will *always* have many kinds of "enemies" to deal with. Thinking we can kill them all off is ecological folly, for there are just too many niches

available. If we limit the diversity of plants in the system, then we limit the diversity of predators that make a living helping our allies. If we increase plant-species diversity, there should be a corresponding increase in predator diversity. Most predators are omnivores using different strategies to eat whatever they can get, which yields redundancy in function. More redundancy and diversity at the predator levels provide regulation of the herbivores more consistently.

Research in Swiss vineyards in 1990 demonstrates these points. Researchers analyzed insect populations in vineyards with varying plant diversity in the ground layer. They found that as botanical diversity and the quantity of flowering plants increased, the diversity of insects increased overall, but not evenly within the trophic levels. While the diversity of beneficial and "indifferent" arthropods increased as botanical diversity increased, *the diversity of pests remained the same, while their populations fell to lower levels*. The predators were able to use the diverse resources of the plant community, including pollen, nectar, shelter, and overwintering sites, to meet their diverse needs, so they were available to reduce the pest-insect populations. Many of the additional arthropods in the diverse vineyards were spiders, which were attracted not by specific plant species but by the structural features of the diversified ecosystem. More plants meant more variation in texture, height, and density, allowing more niches for these generalist predators, whether web builders or hunters.[47] A similar story is told by research in apple orchards, where parasitism of tent caterpillar and codling moth eggs and larvae was eighteen times higher in orchards with rich floral undergrowth than those with sparse undergrowth.[48]

We will always have an "herbivore hump" to get over. The bigger and wider the springboard there is at the producer level, the better the landing will be on the other side.

Carnivore Population Stability Depends on Prey Population Stability

While it may seem obvious that carnivores need their prey available if they are to stick around, this fact does not seem to influence how most farmers and gardeners run their operations. The goal is most often complete eradication of a pest insect, which then results in the absence of the controlling predators! Counterintuitive though it may seem, to keep pests in balance we need to maintain their populations and not let them disappear completely. This keeps the food web intact. Balance is the goal, not eradication.

The Vast Majority of Plant Material Goes to Rot!

One quick look at the amount of energy flowing from the plants to various food-web compartments in figure 4.5 makes this point very clearly. *About sixty-five times more energy goes to decomposers than goes to all herbivores combined*, except when leaf-eating insect populations explode. How can we take advantage of this huge decomposer energy flow to increase our yields? In one word: mushrooms.

While we will talk about this more in chapter 1 of volume 2, let us rant enthusiastically here for a moment. Numerous species of mushrooms are simple to grow, very tasty, rather nutritious, and even medicinal. We are not talking about the sorry, bland button mushrooms most people know from the grocery store. We mean king stropharia, shiitake, oyster, chicken-of-the-woods, reishi, wood ear, lion's mane, and shaggy mane mushrooms. These and other species can grow in beds of wood chips or straw used as mulch, in logs, and some even in freshly cut tree stumps. Yields from small beds and logs can be tremendous, up to 25 percent of the mulch or log substrate (wet weight) in mushrooms![49] Species sequencing and polycultures can yield higher amounts if well managed, as each species degrades different constituents of the organic matter. Mushroom gardening is tasty, fun, and relatively unexplored territory for most gardeners.[50] In the

meantime, the importance of the decomposer food web goes beyond the potential yields.

The Soil Food Web Feeds Aboveground Carnivores

So much energy gets dumped into the soil food web, both from rotting vegetation and from plant root secretions, that a significant portion makes its way back aboveground. Here it takes the form of large invertebrates living on the forest floor, such as those flies and beetles whose larvae live in the leaf litter but whose adults live in the trees, and so on. These animals become the primary foods of shrews, salamanders, and birds and provide significant parts of the diet of mice and chipmunks (figure 4.5). Birds are especially important here: In most years, the bulk of bird food (about 80 percent) consists of insects deriving energy from the soil food web. However, if leaf herbivore populations explode, birds shift their food supply to take advantage of the aboveground food source then readily available. By supporting bird populations in most years, *a healthy soil food web is a significant contributor to maintaining the balance of aboveground insects!* Organic farmers have it only partly right: feeding the soil does not just feed the plants, it feeds the whole ecosystem!

Nutrients Follow Energy in the Food Web

As plants and animals transfer body parts through the food web via predation, both energy and nutrients go with them. Managing the food web is therefore a critical aspect of creating self-renewing fertility. Since most of the forest's energy goes belowground, the soil food web is the most important food web to manage in this regard. See chapter 5 for more on this.

Food webs perform many functions in ecosystem social structure. The functional interconnections within the food web generate self-regulation of species populations. These connections also disperse energy and nutrients to the community's members. The diversity of plants significantly affects the diversity of predators, as does the health of the soil food web. Though the food web forms the primary interconnections in the community, guilds perform other important functions.

GUILDS: PARTITIONING RESOURCES AND BUILDING MUTUAL SUPPORT

People don't use the word *guild* much these days. It possesses a bit of medieval flavor, and rightly so, for it derives from Old English and Old Norse terms referring to payment, tribute, or yield, as well as to the medieval associations of craftsmen and merchants who played a major role in the social structures of their time. Ecologists have used the word in two ways: one denotes a set of mutually interdependent plants and animals; the other describes "groups of species that have similar food requirements (e.g., the guild of insect-eating birds)."[51] In permaculture circles, the word *guild* has more of an association with the former mutual-support network. Mollison defines a guild as a "harmonious assembly of species clustered around a central element (plant or animal) . . . [that] acts in relation to this element to assist its health, aid our work in management, or buffer adverse environmental effects."[52]

Rather than dispense with one or the other of the useful meanings, and to further clarify exactly what we are trying to accomplish in forest garden design, we have decided to use the following phrases and definitions:

- *Resource-sharing guild* or *resource-partitioning guild* denotes groups of species with a similar way of making a living (i.e., the same community niche) that partition resources so they compete minimally.
- *Mutual-support guild* denotes groups of species with dissimilar community niches that form networks of mutual aid. These may or may not focus on a central element.
- *Guild* in general means groups of species that exhibit one or both of the above characteristics.

Redundancy of Functions: Resource-Sharing Guilds

Resource-sharing guild members perform a similar function, fill the same niche, or divide a shared resource among themselves. The species that eat canopy-foliage herbivores—be they birds, insects, spiders, or bacteria—compose such a guild. They use the same resource in the same community in a similar way. Canopy trees form a guild. Hummingbird-pollinated flowering plants compose a guild, with the hummingbirds as the shared resource.[53] Nut-storing and nut-dispersing animals (squirrels, blue jays, and humans) are potentially a guild. These species groups each have a similar niche characteristic, and their niches overlap. Niche overlap often leads to competition.

The thing about resource-sharing guilds, though, is that usually individual guild members don't use the shared resource in exactly the same way. Either they eat at different times of the day or they forage at different locations in the canopy, or at different times of the year, or faster or slower, or some other variation on the theme (figure 4.6). In this way, the guild members partition the resource they share and minimize competition. However, should one species drop out of the guild, the others can expand their activities or range to fill the gap, take advantage of the extra resources, and maintain the performance of their community function (see box 4.6).

Resource-sharing guilds therefore confer stability and resilience on ecosystems, because they represent redundancies in community function. Redundancies also offer flexibility to the system, giving it multiple pathways to respond to imbalances and reinforce vital processes. If only one species were eating canopy-foliage herbivores, and that species died out for some reason, canopy-foliage herbivores would have no population-reducing predators. If this were the case in our orchard, we would have to take on the job of predator of canopy-foliage herbivores or suffer the consequences. Is this a job that we particularly want?

A set of plants sharing the same pollinators by flowering at different times throughout the growing

FIGURE 4.6. A native plant polyculture from a New England old-growth forest includes horseshoe-shaped wild ginger (*Asarum canadense*), upright arching wild oats (*Uvularia sessilifolia*), and fernlike squirrel-corn (*Dicentra canadensis*), among others. We can learn from observing natural polycultures such as these. For example, the arching form of the wild oats works well with the other two mat-forming species to avoid light and space competition. *Photo by Dave Jacke.*

season is a resource-sharing guild, and these plants probably also partition light, water, and nutrients since they dominate at different times. Plants that partition the soil column vertically and horizontally to minimize nutrient competition provide another example. A set of plants fruiting at different times in the growing season is also a guild if the plants rely on the same animals to disperse their seed. The various organisms in the soil food web that decompose woody organic matter, including fungi, bacteria, earthworms, and beetles, compose a guild.

Frequently, species share resources in a number of different guilds at the same time, creating a complex network of interconnection. These intersecting resource-sharing guilds create patchworks of species that simultaneously share a community niche in one dimension (say pollination) yet live in divergent community niches in other dimensions (such as flowering time or rooting pattern).

Functional Interconnection, the Sequel: Mutual-Support Guilds

Functional interconnection creates networks of mutual support between elements: the inherent

Box 4.6: The Principle of Redundancy

Every essential function should be supported by many components.

—BILL MOLLISON, *Permaculture: A Designer's Manual*

Our observation that the redundancy of functions in resource-sharing guilds builds ecosystem stability and resilience leads us to a design principle along the same lines. If we have only one crop that meets an essential need, such as food protein, and that crop fails, we are in trouble. Having more than one way of filling essential needs reduces that trouble, especially if the alternatives have different niches and requirements. For example, walnut production may be somewhat susceptible to cold weather during pollination. Chestnuts tolerate these conditions but have more disease and insect problems. Chickens produce eggs most of the year, but predators of one sort or another may eat them. Using all these means of meeting our protein needs assures a supply of protein under more conditions than relying on only one. Things change and disaster does strike! Don't put all your eggs in one basket. Build redundancy of essential functions into your forest garden.

functions of one element—an organism's natural products, characteristics, or influences—meet the needs of one or more other organisms or create conditions that help those organisms flourish. Food webs express the primary infrastructure of functional interconnection in ecosystems, where one organism meets its needs by partaking of the body or inherent by-products of another. Mutual-support guilds incorporate the food web as well as other forms of functional interconnection. Though it may be useful to think of mutual-support guilds as multispecies mutualisms, these guilds may include any of the pairwise interactions discussed earlier.

In natural forests, mutual-support guilds link

across trophic levels: one plant attracts predatory insects, another plant or animal benefits from that interaction. For example, a mutual-support guild built around trumpet creeper vines (*Campsis radicans*) includes the vine itself; the ants that feed on the vine's nectar and protect it from herbivores; the hummingbirds that pollinate and feed on the vine's flowers; the other birds that nest in the viney tangle; the tree the vines grow on; and the soil organisms associated with the vine's roots.

You can find shreds of guild ideas in many living gardens and in many pieces of literature, including scattered throughout this book. Here are a few more:

- Canopy trees facilitate shade-loving understory herbs by creating conditions appropriate for their success, while the herbs improve nutrient cycling in a number of ways (see "A Few Comments on the Roles of Plants in Nutrient Cycling" in chapter 5, page 183), or they support predatory insects.
- Simply growing a crop amid a mix of plant species and varieties offers defensive benefits, as insect pests find it harder to locate their host prey.
- Herbalist and author Steven Foster says that one nettle plant (*Urtica dioica*) planted among ten herbs will increase the oil content of the herbs, hence increasing their medicinal and culinary value.[54]
- Researchers suspect that strongly aromatic plants like onions, garlic, mints, and others confuse the chemical signals pests use to locate their prey. We call these plants "aromatic pest confusers."
- A multitude of flowers in orchards reduces the number of insect pests by increasing the effectiveness of parasitoids and predators.[55]
- The varroa mites that kill honeybees do not like menthol. Some beekeepers claim that mints planted near beehives offer the bees a means of killing the mites. Apparently, they land on the mints and fan themselves with the minty air to rid themselves of the parasites.[56]

Mutual-support guilds build social structure in ecosystems. The relationships involved can include such diverse interactions as pollination support, inhibition of competitors, physical support of vines, microclimate modification, providing habitat for critical animals, or any number of other functions.

One of the challenging things about mutual-support guilds in particular is that the species elements in them can be widely separated in space. For example, in California, wild blackberries (*Rubus ursinus*) and wild grapes (*Vitis californica*) often grow twining together in floodplain habitats, but not always. Each species falls prey to a different species of leafhopper, which can do significant damage to the plants. A single insect (*Anagrus epos*) parasitizes the eggs of both leafhoppers, which appear first on the early-leafing blackberries and later on the grapes. The grapes growing amid the blackberries get maximum control of their leafhoppers by *Anagrus*, but grapes *up to 4 miles (6 km) away* can also get effective leafhopper control from the same *Anagrus* population. Despite the distance, blackberries and grapes miles apart are both members of the same mutual-support guild because of a mobile parasitoid. Though we cannot say what the effective distances would be for predator species in other instances, clearly plants can be "functionally interdependent with respect to their herbivores" in circumstances we might not expect.[57]

Guilds in the general sense may incorporate both resource-partitioning functions and mutual-support functions. The redundancy of functions that resource-sharing guilds embody supports stability and resilience in the ecosystem. The functional interconnection of mutual-support guilds helps create a self-maintaining ecosystem. However, neither of these kinds of multispecies interactions develops overnight. It takes time—evolutionary time—for species to generate these characteristics. Knowing how ecosystems generate these two kinds of guilds will guide us in generating them, too.

Coevolution, Evolutionary Adjustment, and Convergent Evolution

Function reforms form, perpetually.

—Stewart Brand, *How Buildings Learn*

Organisms that inhabit similar environments in different geographical localities often resemble each other even though their evolutionary backgrounds differ. . . . Form and function converge under the mantle of similar selective forces in the environment.

—Robert E. Ricklefs, *Ecology*

The topics of coevolution, evolutionary adjustment, and convergent evolution launch us into controversial and cutting-edge areas of ecology. Whether these theories reflect actual factors in ecosystems, or how much of a factor they are, influences how we design and manage forest gardens, how we select species and species polycultures, and how we breed plants that are more useful. Unfortunately, these controversies are still unresolved, so we may not be able to get clear answers to these questions: we have to acknowledge our ignorance and the limits of our understanding. Yet the questions themselves are instructive.

Coevolution in the narrow sense is the reciprocal evolutionary influence of two closely interacting organisms upon each other, leading to each species changing genetically from the interaction. Coevolution in this sense is hard to prove scientifically in any case, but it appears most likely in some predator-prey "arms races," in obligate, pairwise mutualisms,[58] and in the divergence of species niches through competition.[59] Yet influence flows in many directions within natural systems. So many species interact at any one time that strict two-species coevolution is probably significantly diluted in most cases. At the same time, each coevolving species needs to preserve flexibility for future changes and situations where it may not find its current partners around it. This is why most mutualisms are diffuse and facultative, and why specialist herbivores and predators are more rare than are generalists. Some ecologists argue, therefore, that diffuse coevolution is probably more characteristic of ecosystems than pairwise coevolution. "Diffuse coevolution implies that many species, on the same or different trophic levels, may simultaneously exert selective pressures on one another and be affected by changes in other component members."[60] It makes intuitive sense that a species would evolve in response to all the other species in its environment, and that all species would do this to some degree, making the influence reciprocal, though in a diffuse way.

Assuming this is true, it would follow that as communities of species live together through evolutionary time, interacting species adjust to each other and find their niches in the social structure as best they can, given the ever-changing nature of that structure. Diffuse coevolution in this sense would take the random flotsam and jetsam of natural species associations and forge functioning guilds and communities from them. Theoretically, the longer a group of interacting species evolves together, the more mutually adjusted they become, the less they compete, and the more they cooperate. They evolve to partition resources in time, in space, and by kind; they adapt to depend upon different resources or to use the same resources at different times, in different places, or under different conditions. Links would develop between species, creating mutual-support guilds. Holes in the community niche structure would fill. Diffuse coevolution, in theory at least, leads to niche differentiation, functional interconnection, niche saturation, community stability, and efficiency. If this theory were true, then long-standing natural communities would be good models for us to mimic, not just generally, but specifically, right down to the species, if possible. It provides a reason to protect and plant native flora in its native associations as much as possible, so we can have the highest chance of creating a stable, healthy, interconnected garden ecosystem with minimal competition.

We can raise a number of challenges to the above theory. We will discuss only two of them here. First, the concept of "diffuse coevolution" is perhaps stretching the word *coevolution* a bit far. Clearly some interactions have more evolutionary influence on a species than others, so the selective pressures will vary from species to species, altering the reciprocity of the interactions. In some (unknown) number of cases, it is likely that reciprocity does not exist: the more genetically flexible and short-lived species (e.g., microbes, insects) would likely evolve to adapt to longer-lived or more genetically stable species (e.g., trees) present in their environment. Perhaps this is why some ecologists use the term *evolutionary adjustment* when discussing such concepts. However, in this context we can still say that "community efficiency and stability increase in direct proportion to the degree of evolutionary adjustment between associated populations."[61] Coevolution and evolutionary adjustment theoretically lead to essentially the same result on a community scale, and our response of mimicking native communities and using native plants as much as possible would still hold.

The second argument against coevolution, and even evolutionary adjustment, is that species move a lot. According to some researchers, pollen records indicate that North American trees were in quite different associations during the last ice age than they are now. The trees' varying postglacial migration rates and patterns over the last fifteen thousand years indicate that species move as individuals, not as plant associations.[62] Hence, these folks claim, the trees cannot have lived together long enough for coevolution to occur, for species to have partitioned niches and built webs of cooperative relationships. Given the life spans of trees (150 to 300 years), it would take many, many thousands of years for significant genetic change to occur in a species, if one is to believe the "gradual change" theory of evolution.[63] However, perhaps these researchers are not looking back far enough.

For example, the oaks, as a genus, were already in existence 40 to 50 million years ago, along with chestnuts, beech, and walnuts.[64] This means that the basic reproductive strategies of acorn, beechnut, and walnut production and dispersal had already developed by that time. Leaf shapes from 65 million years ago are similar to those of today, suggesting that "some of these tree lineages have hardly changed through 65 million years of Earth history."[65] Even some of the species associations appear to have long-term history, at least according to some researchers: "it is clear, however, that after the [most recent Pleistocene] glaciations the Mixed Helophytic forest of eastern North America was not very different from that of Middle to Late Tertiary times" (2.5 to 30 million years ago).[66] If this is the case, might not some of these species, genera, or families have coevolved over a long and distant history? Nonetheless, if it is difficult to prove coevolution in present-day ecosystems, then we can let go of trying to prove it occurred 30 million years ago, at least for now! If coevolution does not create the guilds and other social structures we observe in ecosystems, then how might they have manifested, and how might that influence how we design our forest gardens?

Assuming plants move around too much to coevolve or adjust to each other, then perhaps convergent evolution plays a role in forging functioning guilds and communities. Convergent evolution is the evolution of two or more geographically and evolutionarily distant species or communities living in comparable environments to similar form and function. For example, convergent evolution appears in the case of the North American meadowlark and the African yellow-throated longclaw, two species that look and function alike though they live on different continents and have different evolutionary histories. The most amazing example may be a group of cave-dwelling insects that mistakenly became known as one species, the collembolan *Pseudosinella hirsute*. A researcher discovered that this "species" is actually composed of four separate evolutionary lines that evolved to virtually indistinguishable form as they specialized for the same living conditions in different places.[67] While many examples of convergent evolution in the animal world are known, instances from the plant world are less widely recognized, though perhaps no less common. New World cacti and the similar African euphorbias may be the most familiar example. The challenge is distinguishing between convergent evolution and taxonomic relatedness.

Convergent evolution cannot have happened if the species in question are taxonomically related, that is, if they came from related evolutionary or ancestral lines. For example, many species in the temperate forests of eastern North America are taxonomically related to species from the temperate forests of eastern Asia, many of them belonging to the same family, if not the same genus. There is strong evidence that these species evolved from the same ancestors or lived together tens of millions of years ago when the temperate forest was circumpolar and subtropical and tropical habitats covered most of what is now temperate North America and Asia.[68] These species' similarities derive from their common ancestry, not convergent evolution. Nevertheless, research indicates that convergent evolution occurs at the species level, and work has been done exploring convergent evolution at the community scale as well.

In his book *The Eternal Frontier*, Tim Flannery discusses the amazing similarities between the species living on the American savanna of 15 million years ago and those now living in the African savanna, even though the two sets of fauna arose from distinct taxonomic groups. Such examples suggest there may be a limited range of viable adaptive options available to species living within certain environments—that the kinds of resources available in a given environment drive the most adaptive strategies in certain directions. "One reason for expecting convergence is that available energy is limited and must be allocated to competing functions such as feeding, locomotion, defense, growth, reproduction, and maintenance. If environments in two localities are similar, the best allocation patterns

of resources among these competing functions may also be similar."[69] If this were true, then evolution would drive whatever genetic stock is available toward giraffelike, hippolike, and zebralike animals, for example, in a savanna environment.

Widely separated plant communities in similar environments with species from different evolutionary lines often have similar vegetation structure, patterns of productivity over time, plant growth forms, bird guild structure, and phenology (seasonal cycles of flowering, fruiting, bud break, leaf fall, and so on). Interestingly, ecologists do not consider plant-species richness (an aspect of diversity) to be a characteristic that converges.[70] One can easily observe the similarities between chaparral vegetation in Chile, southern Australia, California, the Mediterranean, and South Africa, for example. *Similar* is a relative term, however, and studies have shown significant differences as well, apparently caused by variation in fire regime, human disturbance, and other factors.[71] Yet these differences still prompt some questions. In a given environment, are there limited sets of optimal solutions for plant form and function toward which species evolve? How do these "optimal solutions" relate to the concept of community niche? Are they essentially the same? Is the community, then, composed of sets of species that are muddling toward these optimal solutions, such that the community as a whole ends up looking similar and working comparably in analogous environments the longer the species have to adapt to the given conditions?

Debates about questions like these continue to this day, and they always bring us back to the debate between the concept of plant communities as some sort of superorganism versus the individualistic view of plants. Some researchers, even today, still stand at one or the other extreme.[72] However, as stated in this chapter's opening quote, the evidence seems clear that this is not an either-or question; instead, ecosystems are some odd, variable, and dynamic combination of each. Coevolution, both pairwise and diffuse, clearly occurs in some instances.

Evolutionary adjustment is likely happening as well, and convergent evolution with its "optimal solutions" or community niches may play some role. Diffuse coevolution almost certainly plays a larger role than pairwise obligate coevolution, and species with shorter life spans probably adjust more rapidly to those with longer life spans, as evidenced by the fungal endophytes discussed earlier in this chapter. Meanwhile, species reserve the right or ability to act as individuals to a degree varying by species. And yes, it does appear that there are a limited (though potentially large) number of community niches or "optimal solutions" that plants and animals gravitate toward in given environments.

So it would seem that plant communities, like human ones, combine free association and simple "overlapping of ranges" on an individualistic basis with a mix of constantly varying levels of commitment, interaction, and association between members. Some of these interactions have a reciprocal intensity that causes community members to adapt to each other over time. Other interactions are such that one member adapts to another while the other remains more or less the same. Some interactions are such that there is no influence, and everyone goes about their business, adapting only to the system at large given whatever specific skills and training they have. And all of this happens in a context where there are a relatively limited set of options for how to make a living successfully in a given environment, yet within those limits there is freedom and creativity to try new ways of doing things. This amounts to what one writer on ecology and politics called "macroconstraints and microfreedoms."[73]

The thoughts above work to our advantage as we go about mimicking natural ecosystems in our gardens. They theoretically give us the flexibility to substitute species within certain limits while maintaining functional community social structure and interactions. They should also give us pause, though, because we probably cannot know all of the interactions going on in an ecosystem. We may miss critical functional elements if we mess around too much or leave out strands in the web. As Aldo Leopold once said, "The key to intelligent tinkering is to keep all the pieces." However, to make it tinkering, we have to give ourselves room to tinker, to substitute, to play with new pieces, and to use the old pieces in new ways. We discuss more specifically how all this plays out in practice in feature article 3, and in the following sections of this chapter.

Species niches and pairwise interactions offer valuable insights into the building blocks of social structure. Meanwhile, community niches, food webs, guilds, coevolution, and convergent evolution provide equally valuable understanding of the ways these building blocks work together. Ecosystem social structure is admittedly more fluid and less visible than physical architecture. How can we anchor and stabilize the fluid and ephemeral social structures of ecosystems? What strategies shall we use to create and maintain them in our forest gardens?

SOCIAL STRUCTURE DESIGN: ANCHORS AND STRATEGIES

The invisible social structure of ecosystems is challenging to design and manage. When we include a crop in our garden, the crop's multiple inherent products create potential connections between the crop and other organisms, and so begin building a food web. The herbivores we'd prefer to keep in check come of their own accord when we provide the resources they need to make a living. We need to work harder at including the allies of our allies in our designs, providing the resources *they* need to make a living.

Various ecosystem elements appear able to moor these fluid social systems, so we must focus on these anchors: diverse plants, a healthy soil ecosystem, and predator habitat elements. Broad strategies, such as diversifying the plant species to diversify the predators and feeding the soil ecosystem to feed the aboveground predators, can definitely help, but these are blunt instruments, useful though they may

Feature Article 3:
Natives and Exotics, Opportunists and Invasives

We see things not as they are. We see things as *we* are.

—THE TALMUD

Concern and alarm about exotic and so-called invasive plants have grown rapidly in recent years. This alarm arises partly from pictures like figure 4.7, and also from widely quoted statistics and ideas such as these:

- Some researchers have estimated that current *annual* environmental and economic losses, damage, and control costs associated with "invasive" plants exceed *$136 billion* in the United States alone! About a third of this cost occurs in agriculture, raising food prices and leading to greater pesticide use. Costs of invasives in home landscapes exceed $5 billion per year.[74]
- Exotic plants now plague over 100 million acres (40 million ha) of public and private land, with that area increasing by 20 percent—twice the size of Delaware—each year.[75]
- This rate of change overwhelms the evolutionary mechanisms of natural systems and may soon lead to what one author called a "planet of weeds."[76]
- Invasive species decrease habitat diversity.
- Invasive exotic plants cause the extinction of native plants.
- Exotics do not support healthy ecosystem function because native insects and other wildlife cannot use them for food or to meet other needs.

We have also experienced distress about these issues, based not only on thoughts such as those above, but also our own experiences of seeing beloved New England habitats become more and more dominated by species such as Oriental bittersweet (*Celastrus orbiculatus*), Norway maple (*Acer platanoides*), Japanese knotweed (*Reynoutria japonica*), and so on. As a result, when we began

writing this book we initially emphasized protecting native species, discouraging the use of nonnative species whenever possible, and warning readers of the dangers of invasive plants.

Then we came across a series of excellent books that expanded our vision of plants, animals, humans, and the North American continent. These included:

- Tim Flannery's *The Eternal Frontier*, an ecological history of North America from 65 million years ago to the present;
- Jared Diamond's *Guns, Germs and Steel*, a multidisciplinary exploration of the ecological factors leading to the global dominance of Western culture;
- Connie Barlow's *Ghosts of Evolution*, an engaging examination of evidence for the missing animal partners that dispersed the seed of plants she dubs "ecological anachronisms"; and
- finally and most significantly, David Theodoropoulos's *Invasion Biology: Critique of a Pseudoscience*, a hard-hitting exposé of issues apparently avoided in conservation biology, and the potential social and emotional factors that lead to what he calls "invasion hysteria."

The first three books provide excellent background for reading Theodoropoulos. The perspective gained from them helps one see past the intense, definitive style and highly challenging content of *Invasion Biology*, which one might otherwise dismiss out of reactionary impulses.

After reading these books, we began reevaluating our positions on a number of issues—a process that will take more time than we had to finish this book. Our initial review changed the reasons for our native

FIGURE 4.7. Kudzu (*Pueraria lobata*) overtaking a home in Virginia, the classic example of "invasive" species behavior. Further north, Oriental bittersweet (*Celastrus orbiculata*) plays a similar role, though perhaps not so exuberantly. *Photo by Eric Toensmeier.*

and exotics policy some, and it decreased our pronative and antiexotics stridency, but the result of our deliberations in terms of on-the-ground choices is pretty much the same, at least so far. What follows is a snapshot of our current take on the issues. While we do not agree with everything Theodoropoulos has to say, we believe his critique deserves serious consideration and discussion, for it raises many important issues. We will discuss "invasiveness" as an ecosystem process further in feature article 5 (page 282).

First, Theodoropoulos and other writers strongly object to statistics such as those cited in the first and second bullets in this article. They say such figures are grossly inflated and unrealistic, even though they

are frequently quoted and appear to form the basis for much of the recent "hysteria," as they call it.

Second, notice the use of the word *plague* in the second bullet. Invasive plant literature and journalism frequently use emotion-laden, reaction-triggering words and phrases such as *infestation, invasion, overrunning, planet of weeds,* and so on. This is a disservice to the public, and a discredit to the writers who use such phrases, even if they help sell the story. We must stop this fear-mongering if we are to think clearly and act from our highest principles rather than our lowest common denominator. When you see trigger words such as these, put a red flag on the information coming at you, and dig deeper into the issues. Incidentally, we could level this same criticism against some of Theodoropoulos's writings, which one might at times describe as "antihysteria hysteria."

However, Theodoropoulos also strongly disputes the idea that there is an "invasive species crisis" with ecological theory and numerous references. He claims that the last several points in the first bulleted list are completely untrue and unsubstantiated, and that the studies supporting such claims are based on bad science. Many of his arguments are logical, and the references appear valid, though some of his statements of ecological fact we consider theories still in dispute, such as the individualistic theory of plant communities. He cites examples of how the belief in this crisis has led some people to illogical actions, such as spraying herbicides in habitats containing "invasives" that are otherwise healthy, and declaring a species "exotic" simply because it is 50 miles outside its "natural range" as biologists define it. His argument that human disturbance is the preeminent cause of invasiveness strikes home, especially when coupled with the human tendency to point the finger of blame outside ourselves and not take responsibility for our own effects on the world. The simple act of calling a species "invasive" when this behavior can *only* arise from the interaction between organism and environment provides the clearest evidence in support of this idea.

It does seem clear that in at least some cases, if not many or most, "invasive" species are convenient and visible scapegoats for problems created by human activity. Theodoropoulos presents evidence that the great majority of nonnative opportunists are adapted to disturbed sites. "Development," conventional agriculture, industrial pollution (notably acid rain), industrial forestry, habitat fragmentation, and global warming represent intense disturbances to worldwide ecosystems. Why should we be surprised, then, that disturbance-adapted species are increasing in population? We might do well to treat underlying causes, and not symptoms. Spraying herbicide in

natural areas to kill unwanted plants is not going to solve the environmental crisis! Such responses will only mask the problem, helping us pretend we are doing something useful when we are actually making it worse. In addition, proposed regulatory changes in the United States would make the importation of new species extremely difficult. Under this "white list" regulation, a new species would be guilty until proven innocent, and only species on the white list would be legal to import. Testing to prove noninvasiveness can have only dubious scientific credibility. It would also be so incredibly expensive as to make enormous corporations the only ones who could import new species, further consolidating their control over the world's seeds and plants.

While Theodoropoulos builds his critique around the evolutionary, ecological, and psychological issues involved, Australian permaculture founder David Holmgren arrives at similar conclusions from another angle. Holmgren states that in densely planted home food gardens with limited space, priority must be given to the most productive species—and that most native Australian species don't fit the bill. A similar, though less extreme situation confronts us here in North America. Diamond's book provides excellent context for this argument. Holmgren also believes that we must measure the ecological changes brought by naturalizing exotics against the benefits useful plants provide by increasing local self-reliance and reducing the need for fossil fuels. To create towns and gardens that produce most of their own food, fuel, fiber, fodder, fertilizer, farmaceuticals, and fun, Holmgren says we "need to design human ecologies from the widest range of genetic materials available."[77] For example, while nitrogen-fixing plants have the potential to naturalize into disturbed landscapes, they reduce the need for petroleum-based fertilizers, with their associated environmental hazards from drilling, manufacturing, transportation, and even war. Like Theodoropoulos, Holmgren does not see the naturalization of nonnative species as an environmental crisis, but rather as the dawn of "ecosynthesis": nature's way of adapting life to the new conditions created by human activity by generating new ecosystems from the materials at hand, including both native and exotic species.[78] (Holmgren will explore these issues further in his forthcoming book *Weeds or Wild Nature: Migrant Plants and Animals in Australia.*)

Wherever you stand in the natives versus exotics debate, we urge you to read and consider both Holmgren and Theodoropoulos, among others. Take what they say under advisement, and let this be the beginning of the exploration, not the end. The issues they raise touch on important areas of ecology, human ecology, and evolutionary biology where consensus has not yet developed, but where such a consensus is vitally important.

In the meantime, we propose the following "policies" to forest gardeners to deal with this situation:

Give native plants preference when selecting species for your forest garden. Use native plants whenever they can fulfill your design purposes, for at least three reasons.

First, natives of all kinds have had a tough time of it in the past five hundred or more years; they need all the friends and help they can get. We strongly urge native plant protection, conservation, propagation, and planting as a way of supporting this threatened flora. Ideally, plant conservation will include planting natives in associations as close as possible to those in which they were last known to have grown naturally, as well as trying them in new combinations of both natives and exotics in our home garden ecosystems and elsewhere. Given the pace of change in today's and tomorrow's world, this is the most likely means of keeping species alive. This can succeed *only* if we manage the disturbance regimes of our landscapes to suit the species we are trying to grow. Forest gardening can play a key role in helping us do that while meeting our own needs.

Second, coevolutionary theory suggests that using natives will yield benefits for the stability and health of your garden ecosystem. Using *any* set of plants with a clear sense of purpose, and of species and community niche functions, should help build effective guilds and webs of interrelationships. However, natives may be more likely than nonnatives to have *unintended benefits*, and less likely to have unintended negative consequences.

Finally, many natives are great plants, and they have much to offer us functionally and aesthetically. For decades, the landscape trade has held an unconscious bias against natives, and these species are still hard to find in local nursery stores. Holding a preference for natives—that is, looking to natives first—can help rectify this history of neglect and lack of familiarity. However, a natives-only or antiexotics bias is now developing strongly in some quarters. Ultimately, we need to get beyond biases in any direction and think clearly about what plants we want to use, and why. Knee-jerk reactions won't serve us very long. Conscious design is our best hope now.

Consider using exotic species when a native species does not fit the site conditions, your functional needs, or your planting goals. The evolutionary history of North America has given the flora of the continent short shrift in some community niches, such as among the nitrogen-fixers. When you need a plant with a set of traits for which you cannot find a suitable native species, then look to exotic species to meet your needs. Many extremely useful, multifunctional, nonnative plants so far appear to have little potential to become nuisance species. We humans have also bred exotic plants as food crops far more than we have bred natives. Limiting ourselves to natives-only forest gardens will prevent us from reaching the full potential of forest gardening, and keep us more dependent on conventional agriculture and industrial inputs over the long run. And remember, every plant is native somewhere! We propose a few caveats to the use of nonnatives, however.

When using any plant, "native" or "exotic," beware of plants considered "invasive" or "opportunistic," planting them only in areas where the potential impact is low. Let's make explicit the two underlying pieces of this point: we must consider the characteristics of both the plant and the environment.

First, consider *any* species' opportunism—its expansiveness, dispersal strategies, and persistence—before bringing it to your site. Expansive plants, those that disperse by vegetative propagation and rapid physical enlargement, may be less of a problem in some sites and for some purposes than dispersive plants that spread by seed carried by wind, birds, or other animals. Dispersive species may not be a problem on your site, but they may spread throughout the neighborhood. An expansive species may spread less in your neighborhood than a dispersive one, but it may be too dominating for your garden purposes unless you are willing to manage it by, for example, using repeated cutting or rhizome barriers. Running bamboos, Japanese butterbur or sweet coltsfoot (*Petasites japonica*), and hot tuna (*Houttuynia cordata*) are useful, nonnative, vigorously expansive plants. Many natives can also be challenging in this regard, such as groundnut (*Apios americana*), Jerusalem artichoke (*Helianthus tuberosus*), and native raspberries or roses. Dispersive plants include exotics such as Norway maple (*Acer platanoides*) and garlic mustard (*Alliaria petiolara*). Both are considered major invasives, though garlic mustard is a tasty edible. Native dispersives include miner's lettuce (*Montia perfoliata*), a western native, and fireweed (*Epilobium angustifolium*), an eastern native, both yielding edible greens. The most challenging species are those that exhibit expansive, dispersive, and persistent behaviors, for they can spread rapidly regionally as well as locally and are hard to eliminate once established. Japanese knotweed (*Reynoutria japonica*) is one of those judged most problematic in New England, though there is evidence that it establishes primarily in disturbed areas.[79] Unfortunately, coltsfoot (*Tussilago farfara*), a well-known shade-tolerant medicinal plant and an early-season beneficial-insect nectar plant, also falls in this category, which is why it does not appear in volume 2, appendix 1. For a useful species such as this, we must make a value judgment as to whether its spread is a nuisance or a benefit. That debate is unlikely to be resolved anytime soon in the culture at large. We urge people to err on the side of caution, since opportunistic plants are difficult, if not impossible, to eradicate if we determine that they are indeed a problem. Our actions can effect our neighbors' and friends' gardens for decades to come. Don't be the one to let the cat out of the bag unless you are committed to putting it back in if it turns out to be a problem.

Second, consider the site and its context: do not introduce a plant that has strongly expansive, dispersive, or persistent characteristics, or a species currently on an invasive species list, to a site or region near healthy wild lands or where it is not already established. So-called invasives have some track record of becoming a nuisance, at least in human eyes. If you desire to plant goumi (*Eleagnus multiflora*), a developed nitrogen-fixing crop plant from Asia, or any of its cousins in the same genus (e.g., autumn olive, *E. commutata*, or Russian olive, *E. angustifolia*), be aware that the genus appears to have a habit of dominating large areas of land and spreading by bird-dispersed seed. Then again, it is definitely possible that the practice of highway departments planting huge areas of *Eleagnus* has increased the seed pressure in surrounding areas, increasing the likelihood that the plants would spread in the neighborhood. If you happen to live in such a neighborhood, then your planting of a goumi cultivar will likely do little damage. However, if you live in a place near healthy natural areas with few opportunist plants, then you should probably be more careful in your plant selection. See the "Nuisances" column of the Plant Species Matrix (volume 2, appendix 1) for information on opportunist issues in the listed species. Volume 2 also includes a "Watch List" of useful species that we considered too risky to put in the Plant Species Matrix.

be. How can we refine these blunt instruments so we can more precisely design social structures that will work to our advantage?

Guilds and polycultures are primary tools for social structure design. Our two views of community social structure, from the perspective of building blocks (species niches) and from the perspective of the whole system (community niches), lead to two corresponding guild and polyculture design strategies. We can weave guilds and polycultures strand by strand by selecting species to perform specific functions and partition specific resources. Alternatively, we can cut polycultures and guilds from whole cloth by using specific plant communities as models and substituting ecologically analogous species for the less useful species of the natural community.

The following subsection explores key principles, ideas, and definitions relevant to the above topics. Though in some ways these discussions are more appropriate for volume 2, they summarize much of this chapter and lay some groundwork so we can focus on the mechanics of designing guilds and polycultures in chapter 4 of volume 2.

THE ANCHORS OF SOCIAL STRUCTURE

Three elements form the principal anchors of forest garden social structure: predator habitat elements, healthy soil, and plants. We will touch on these briefly below.

Predator Anchors

The herbivores in any ecosystem generally have no problem finding suitable habitat to make some sort of living, for plants are everywhere. While decreasing herbivore habitat is a useful pest-control strategy, it is equally or more important to ensure that predator insects, birds, amphibians, and reptiles can meet their habitat requirements (see figure 4.8). These requirements vary tremendously from predator to predator, so we will discuss them only superficially here. See volume 2, appendix 5 for details.

Generally, predator insects need sources of

FIGURE 4.8. Garden ponds are excellent predator habitat elements, providing water for numerous beneficials and habitat for many others. This pond at Charlie Headington's forest garden (see case study 1, page 54) is fed primarily by roof runoff; note the bamboo downspout at right. *Photo by Dave Jacke.*

nectar, pollen, water, and alternative prey; sites for perching, nesting, and overwintering; and wind protection. We mentioned earlier in the chapter the kinds of nectar sources that predators and parasitoids prefer. Insects do not need much water. Small garden ponds or roof runoff containers should do fine, though larger pools will accommodate dragonflies more easily. However, plants, debris, sticks, or rocks jutting from the surface provide all insects safer access to the water.

Most insects benefit from undisturbed vegetation in proximity to the garden, or patches of undisturbed vegetation mixed into the garden. Provide

FIGURE 4.9: The different architectures of these ferns and their surrounding Labrador violets (*Viola labradorica*) allow this polyculture to exist with minimal competition between its component species. They partition space and the soil and light resources because of their varying forms (upright arching versus prostrate) and habits (clumping versus mat-forming). The violets also provide weed control and edible greens and flowers. *Photo by Eric Toensmeier.*

perching sites at varying heights to support different species if your garden lacks some vegetation layers. Undisturbed woods' edges, hedgerows, and meadow are good candidates for overwintering sites, ideally facing more than one direction relative to the sun so different insects can find their preferred habitats (volume 2, appendix 5 provides some information on specific plants that beneficials like to hibernate near). Many forest gardens will *be* this kind of vegetation, so there should be little problem achieving viable habitat.

Some insects like to nest in sunny, dry soil or in deadwood or hibernate in dead flower heads, empty seed capsules, hollow reeds, or other dead plant stems, so providing these features should help as well. Don't deadhead all your flowers, at least late in the season: you destroy valuable hibernation sites for spiders and other beneficials when you do so!

Birds require food, water, nesting and perching sites, and shelter. Insects, seeds, and berries, particularly winter seeds and berries, provide good foods generally, though food preferences vary by species. Dripping water attracts many birds, whether from a hose into a bucket or in a fancy sculptural feature. Nesting locations vary by species. Standing dead trees, poles, and posts work for perches, even attracting raptors at times. Thick brush and evergreen trees offer good shelter. Fewer outdoor cats and dogs aren't a requirement, but their absence does help the birds. Particular bird species will do specific work in your garden. It is worth researching which species to attract and providing their specific requirements in your forest garden.

Frogs and toads do a large amount of insect eating, most on the ground and some in the trees. Small to large pools or slow streams with sloping sides for easy in-out access and deep mud for winter are essential for many of these species. Good ground cover protects them from their predators, and moist, diverse environs provide them the food they need. They like to hide under logs and rocks to keep cool and moist. In urban and suburban areas, you may need to import these amphibians, in which case you should make sure to provide the best habitat you can for them so they can establish and reproduce.

Newts and salamanders do their nighttime predation quietly and in obscure fashion. Loose, moist soils with mulch, shady forest habitats, and water for breeding are ideal. These critters also enjoy old logs and rocks to hide under by day.

Snakes require good ground cover, spots to sun themselves, and access to water where they can't fall in and drown. Mulch, loose ground, and rock or brush piles offer nesting and overwintering sites.

Do not overlook these organisms and their requirements. Make sure you design these elements into your forest garden at least generally. Ideally, you will research the local animals that will do good work for you and satisfy their specific requirements.

Soil Anchors

Healthy soil is essential to a healthy ecosystem and to the control of insect explosions in forest canopies, as our earlier discussion of birds relying on energy from the soil food web showed (page 148). Healthy soil biology depends upon the plants that live in the soil ecosystem, a ready supply of organic matter to decompose, and a good mix of organisms. Supplying these soil factors will help create a strong aboveground social system, as well as a healthy belowground system. Chapter 5 discusses soil food webs in more detail.

Plants: Green Anchors

Plants play the paramount social-structure anchoring role for a host of reasons. Besides their function as primary producers of food energy upon which all other life depends, they create the physical architecture of virtually every terrestrial community. The dominant plants influence every aspect of community character, from soil to light, as discussed in chapter 3. The diversity of plants therefore determines the life-strategy opportunities available to every other form of life above- and belowground.

The five elements of vegetation architecture discussed in chapter 3 all relate to creating good social structure. Key among the five elements of architecture is diversity. The most critical plant diversity features that anchor social structure include:

- species, genetic variation within species, and deadwood legacies (compositional diversity);
- layers, age structure, and successional patchworks (structural diversity); and
- the specific functions or niches of each plant within food webs and guilds, such as supporting

beneficial insects or soil microbes (functional diversity).

Through these characteristics, plant diversity affects the diversity of microbes, predatory birds, and insects and helps create a stable, resilient social structure. One of the key ways plants anchor social structure is by anchoring insect predator and pollinator populations. However, it is important that "rather than seeking to increase crop diversity per se, agroecosytems be designed to provide natural enemies with specific resources that augment their efficiency."[80] Providing specific diverse resources for natural enemies and pollinators is the key to anchoring these aspects of forest garden social structure.

As mentioned earlier, many insect pest predators and parasites use flower nectar as a source of energy while they search for prey, whose bodies they use as protein sources or egg-laying sites. Given their biting or sucking mouthparts, they can get nectar only from the tiny, easily accessed flowers of the families Apiaceae, Asteraceae, and some of the Lamiaceae (umbels, composites, and mints). They need these flowers close by throughout the growing season.

"Close by" is relative. Predator species vary from region to region, each insect has different habits, their mobility varies tremendously, and they range in size from too small to see to large wasps. We therefore cannot generalize about the patterns in which to plant their preferred nectar sources, or how far they will fly from nectar source to crop plants in search of prey. The best we can say without getting into far too much detail is to plant these nectar sources everywhere, and make sure you have them blooming throughout the growing season! This will ensure you have the beneficials where and when you need them. Planting nectar plants in patches, drifts, and clumps will help the beneficials find and make use of them. They are less likely to find and use solitary plants.

The same strategy works for pollinators, too: plant nectar- and pollen-producing plants all over the place, and have them flowering throughout the

FIGURE 4.10: Flowers that grow in umbels, like the yellow flowers of this fennel (*Foeniculum vulgare*), are among the best specialist nectary plants around. Each such Apiaceae family flower head produces dozens, if not hundreds, of individual tiny flowers that mature over a long bloom season and have short tubes allowing predators to access their nectar. Fennel also provides excellent anise-flavored leaves, stems, and seeds, and the seeds also have medicinal value. In the background one can see the flowers of *Echinacea* sp. and *Monarda fistulosa*, each a good nectar plant in its own right. *Photo by Jonathon Bates.*

year. Many of the same flowers aid the predators and parasites mentioned above. Early spring and late fall flowers are especially important to help pollinators through lean times. For both the pollinators and the predators, it is important also to provide other habitat elements that allow them to rear young and overwinter.

Plants are the main anchors of social structure in two ways: as anchors of predator diversity and by strongly influencing soil health. Plants are also the main element we gardeners directly design and manage. Therefore, plants are the central subjects of our guild and polyculture design work.

GUILDS AND POLYCULTURES: PRIMARY SOCIAL-STRUCTURE DESIGN TOOLS

Polycultures are a human-created analog of natural communities, a viceroy butterfly mimicking nature's monarch. Technically speaking, a polyculture is any mixed assembly of species cultivated together in one growing space at the same time. Some polycultures more effectively achieve our key goals of diverse high productivity, self-maintenance, and ecological health, stability, and resilience than others do. What makes a group of species an effective polyculture? We'll define this more fully in chapter 1 of volume 2. Here we'll focus on the question of yield, specifically additive yielding or overyielding, as a means of drawing useful conclusions to undergird our discussion of guild and polyculture design strategies.

Necessary Conditions for Overyielding Polycultures: Guilds

European foresters have noticed that they get higher production in mixed forest stands than in monocultures if the polyculture meets one or both of the following conditions:

- the polyculture has more resources available to it, either because the mix more fully uses the available resources or because one or more species increases the availability of a scarce resource; or
- climatic fluctuations, pests, diseases, or other stresses affect the polyculture less because it is more stable and resilient.[81]

In short, additive yielding in polycultures results from resource-sharing and mutual-support guilds, with an added twist: not only do effective polycultures partition resources and create stability through functional interconnection, they *use more resources more fully by exploiting more niches.*

Polycultures can exhibit more complete use of resources in a number of ways. For example, mixtures of shade-tolerant and shade-intolerant canopy tree species can use a higher percentage of available sunshine. Such mixtures therefore often show higher productivity than shade-intolerant canopy species alone, though shade-tolerant species alone can be as productive as the mix.[82] Multiple vegetation layers also use sunlight more completely than a single-layer stand. Since the rooting patterns of plants vary in both time and space, mixes may more fully occupy the soil than monocultures (see "Plant Roots" in chapter 5, page 189). Different plants need nutrients and water in different proportions and at different times of the year, so mixing plants with different strategies and needs can make better use of these resources.

Similarly, species can enhance resource availability in many ways. Nitrogen-fixing and dynamic-accumulator plants are obvious examples. In drought periods, maple and apple trees can reportedly pump water from deep roots to shallow roots at night, creating a store of water for daytime use. Some of this water "leaks" into the surrounding soil and helps keep neighboring plants and the root-zone food web alive. Mixing deciduous trees into evergreen forests improves the decomposition of leaf litter, thereby enhancing nutrient cycling for all community members. It appears that nutrient cycling and litter decomposition happen faster in mixed forest stands of all types, either because the litter is complementary somehow or because diverse litter increases diversity in soil critter populations, and hence increases soil critter productivity. Willows and other water-loving plants can lower the water table in wet areas, increasing the oxygen supply in wet soils. This can result in improved rooting depth and nutrition for other plants.

Polycultures demonstrate increased stability in the face of pests, pathogens, climatic variations, and other stresses by building a better food web, providing more species diversity to respond to climatic and other fluctuations, and offering more diverse species to replace dead community members. Stability may not be evident until a time of catastrophe, or you may never see its effect since it prevents a crisis. This makes assessing stability-induced productivity increases difficult.

Not All Guilds Are Polycultures, but All Effective Polycultures Use Guilds

The earlier example of blackberries, grapes, their leafhopper pests, and their shared leafhopper predator shows that not all guilds require close proximity between members, particularly those involving animal intermediaries. Some of the guilds composing your forest garden will need the species growing in the same space, in polyculture, to work. Some will not. This depends on the resources being partitioned or the support being given. It is important, therefore, to distinguish between the separate but related work of building guilds and of designing polycultures when designing. In general, mutual-support guilds have more spatial flexibility than resource-partitioning guilds.

The polyculture partitioning principle (box 4.7) states that for a polyculture to work the species within it must be members of a resource-sharing guild. In addition, we want the plants and animals within our polycultures to generate mutualistic, facilitative, or neutral relationships as much as possible, both for their own sake and to minimize the effects of any competition that does occur in the planting. At the same time, we want the polyculture as a whole to use competition and inhibition against undesirable organisms to assist the polyculture's productivity and minimize its maintenance. Such interactions constitute a mutual-support guild.

Polycultures May Be Completely Novel Plant Assemblies

As we assemble groups of useful species that work together for mutual benefit and maximum yield, we are likely to bring together organisms that may have never or only rarely grown together before. Our polycultures may therefore exhibit unique structure and composition. This is both an advantage and a disadvantage: more possibilities for creativity exist,

Box 4.7: The Polyculture Partitioning Principle

*Polycultures have the highest chance of additive yielding
when their component species occupy divergent niches,
especially with respect to the most limiting resources.*

When two species occupy similar niches and live together, they compete. The competitive exclusion principle states that in this situation, one will always compete the other to extinction unless the other has an escape of some kind or the cropping principle comes into play (box 4.5). Therefore, for a polyculture to work at all, its species must occupy different niches. They must partition resources among themselves, use different resources, use the same resources at different times, or any combination thereof. The most limiting resources will generate the greatest potential for competition, so the components of the polyculture must partition these resources most effectively. This is especially true if we want the polyculture to yield more than the species growing separately in monoculture.

On a practical level, this means we need to understand the resource conditions our plants will encounter in some detail. It also means the plants within the polyculture should have different forms, sizes, and root patterns; different light, water, and nutrient needs; and varied seasonal patterns of development (see figure 4.9). Which of these characteristics should diverge the most among the members of the polyculture depends on what resources are the most limiting.

FIGURE 4.11. Plant form or architecture is one guide to working out which species are least likely to compete. This combination of a plum tree (*Prunus* sp.), a hardy kiwi vine (*Actinidia arguta*), and coltsfoot (*Tussilago farfara*) will probably work well because the species have very different niches. They partition light, and they probably partition the soil profile as well. *Photo by Dave Jacke.*

but a lack of coevolution between species may result in more interactions that are negative.

So if polycultures are more likely to overyield when they consist of resource-sharing and mutual-support guilds, how do we go about creating guilds and polycultures? How can we minimize the chances of negative interactions in our designed polycultures? The concepts of species niche and community niche provide two possible approaches: guild-build and habitat mimicry using ecological analogs.

WEAVING THE STRANDS: BUILDING GUILDS AND POLYCULTURES

Guild-build is the name we use for the process of building guilds and polycultures species by species based on the design's functional requirements, site conditions, and the species niches of candidate plants and animals. Guild-build involves careful definition of those functional requirements first and foremost, followed by careful site analysis to determine growing conditions and limiting factors and the selection of species that will perform those functions at all the times and in all the habitat conditions necessary. The designer must attempt to discern which species will grow well together as resource-sharing partners in a polyculture, as well as which should grow together as a mutual-support team in a polyculture. The designer must also attempt to create patterns, both within and outside of the polyculture patches, that create working guilds throughout the whole garden.

As you might imagine, this is interesting and challenging work, though sometimes tedious and, for large or highly varied designs, perhaps a bit grueling. Guild building has the potential to generate many new and interesting plant combinations to test in the real world. It also has the potential to create plant combinations with undesirable negative interactions, since many of the species may have never grown together before. However, the guild-build process is likely to result in more viable polycultures more quickly than simple random combinations. Not that random combinations are always a bad idea! However, if we want our polycultures to achieve certain goals, then guild-build is a reasonable process to use, at least temporarily.

Guild and polyculture design theories are recent, and we humans have limited experience with edible perennial polycultures in temperate climates. We have much to learn. The guild-build process described here and in volume 2, chapter 4 will give us good direction for real-world polyculture testing and development, region by region. However, trial, error, and observation will still provide us with important knowledge, both for your specific site and for other forest gardeners. Luckily, the need for lots of this grunt work should be relatively short-lived.

Once we have gone through the guild-build process some number of times in a region with a given set of plants, and we have tested the resulting plant combinations under different conditions, workable polycultures and guilds should become clear. The empirical process will take over and the need for guild building by manual labor should decrease. Each region will develop typical polycultures, and gardeners will experiment and expand from there, occasionally doing the grunt work of guild-build to figure out new possibilities from scratch. Guild-build might also continue to be necessary to design unique forest gardens for unusual goals or site conditions.

Effective use of the guild-build process requires at least three things: clear objectives, knowledge of the site's limiting factors, and an understanding of the species niches of the species you are working with. Clear purposes will help you select your species appropriately. Guild and polyculture design objectives arise from the needs and yields of the species you want to grow, and from site conditions. Common intentions include pest population balance, soil fertility improvement, weed control, diverse yields, aesthetic benefits, and ecosystem health.

One of the keys to resource partitioning, and therefore guild and polyculture design, is an understanding of limiting factors on your particular site. This will guide the selection of plants that partition the most limiting resources or help make more of those resources available. In fact, limiting factors act as one of the most important initial filters to help you eliminate candidate species for your forest garden. In this way, limiting factors can be a blessing, for they could greatly simplify your species choices for polyculture design from an overwhelming array of possibilities to a bewildering assortment or perhaps simply to a manageable selection.

Obviously, we cannot select species for certain ecosystem functions unless we know they perform them—hence, appendix 1 in volume 2! Your own knowledge and observations are just as, if not more, important than our Plant Species Matrix, however.

Clear objectives provide direction for the guild-build process, helping you determine what functions you need performed. Good site analysis helps you understand the varied conditions in which the guild members must grow and what resources most need partitioning. Good species information will help you select species to fill the necessary functions in all the growing conditions you expect to encounter. You can then select from this list of species to design each patch in the garden. This is how we design polycultures and guilds with the highest chance of achieving our objectives.

Guild-build provides for innovation, increased understanding, and an increased probability of meeting our objectives in polyculture design. However, that innovation increases the risk of negative interactions because many species have never grown together before. How might we minimize this risk in our polycultures?

WORKING FROM WHOLE CLOTH: HABITAT MIMICRY USING ECOLOGICAL ANALOGS

Theoretically, because species in natural communities coevolve to some degree, they have a better chance of having developed functioning guilds than do completely novel plant assemblies. Therefore, locally native communities (e.g., oak-hickory forest, Southeastern floodplain forest) and their component species can make good models for designing forest gardens. You can include native species from such local "original" habitats in your garden if they have known ecological functions or direct human uses. Yet many of those species will not have human uses or clearly desired ecological functions. The problem is that not including these species will leave holes in the ecological fabric of the mimic community's social structure. If we want to imitate natural communities structurally and functionally while increasing their usefulness to us, what do we do?

Luckily, coevolution is mostly diffuse, so the components of the model ecosystem are mostly rough guides, not precise templates. We can look for ecological analogs of the less useful native species by seeking more advantageous species that fill a comparable community niche in similar communities from the same or other regions (see box 4.8).

Assuming the above assumptions are correct, this approach saves a lot of design work as compared to the guild-build process. Nature has theoretically already done that design work, so why should we duplicate it? We know that the species in local native ecosystems survived in our locale, so we should mimic that ecosystem as directly as possible, right down to the species if possible. This should give us the best assurance that the forest garden will work as a functional ecosystem with minimal competition. Even if we don't know how the species in the native ecosystem function, using them or their analogs should provide our gardens with many of the benefits we seek.

Unfortunately, because there is a lot of debate about coevolution, it is difficult to say how many benefits, and of what kind, habitat mimicry using ecological analogs will confer on our gardens. Nonetheless, it is one reasonable approach to test in our forest gardens. In any case, this is only an approach to design. The proof will be in the pudding. We'll find out what works and what doesn't after we plant.

GUIDELINES FOR DESIGNING ECOLOGICAL ANALOGS

Making species and community analogies is a simple task on the surface, but it becomes more complex the more you delve into it.

Local native plant communities are the best, but not the only, models. Locally existing native plant communities represent centuries of evolutionary and coevolutionary history among species, and between organisms and the particular landscape they inhabit. Determine the characteristics of your soils and site, find out what kind of precolonial ecosystem grew there, and then look for actual

Box 4.8: Ecological Analogs

Ecologists have recognized that widely separated ecosystems in similar climates frequently contain taxonomically distinct species that nonetheless exhibit very similar form and function. They call this phenomenon convergent evolution, and the species that exhibit these similarities are called ecological equivalents. The term *ecological analog* has a somewhat different but related meaning, however. An ecological analog is a species or variety substituted for another ecologically similar species or variety for a specific reason, with the degree of similarity depending on the purposes of the designer and the species available for substitution. The idea of convergence and the concept of ecological equivalents guide our understanding of how to use ecological analogs. However, please remember two important cautions.

First, while recognizing convergence and using the term *ecological equivalents*, many ecologists also argue that "cases of species-for-species matching do not stand up under close scrutiny. . . . Detailed studies of convergence are as likely to turn up remarkable differences between the plants and animals in superficially similar environments."[83] This results from the forces of coevolution and the unique evolutionary background of each species, as well as the unique evolutionary backgrounds and combinations of the species within coevolving groups. In addition, no two environments are exactly alike climatically, or otherwise. Expecting species in similar community niches in distant but similar environments to perform in exactly the same way given all these variables is highly unrealistic.

This reality has numerous implications. For one, we prefer the term *ecological analogs* because *equivalent* denotes a much closer resemblance than seems ecologically possible. Second, we should use native species in our polycultures whenever possible, for they have evolved together and in the local environment for some time, and this gives us theoretical advantages. Third, when we substitute a different species for a native, we should try to substitute as closely as possible, both ecologically and taxonomically, to minimize the ecological differences between the native and mimic communities. This means using species with a similar community niche, from a similar climate, and possibly with similar taxonomy. This will maximize our chances of recreating the guilds that the native community evolved over time, and it will minimize the chances of creating negative interactions in our polycultures.

---

examples or written references to the species that lived in such habitats. You can also look to the existing "wild" vegetation on your site or in your region to see what is growing there now. In most cases, existing vegetation will include more non-native species than the historical plant communities, and these are less likely to represent the kind of coevolutionary processes that native communities should. However, they can still offer guidance for what will grow well in your garden given current site, climate, and disturbance conditions. The structure, species composition, and patterns of vegetation in the models are all important things to consider mimicking.

Create similar architectures with the same or analogous species. While weaving the polyculture web by building guilds may create completely novel plant assemblies in structure and composition, habitat mimicry using ecological analogs should create a structure similar to the model, probably with at least some different species. The closeness of the resemblance depends upon how closely you make the species and pattern analogies.

No two species are exactly analogous, so keep useful natives. Even when you are very careful about your substitutions—using species with similar form, function, and taxonomy—the ecology and function of the substitute will be different from that of the model. This potential loss of community functions in critical times or circumstances leads to the general principle that we should use native species and guilds in our polycultures whenever possible, not just because of the problems exotics may pose, but also to support the necessary functions of the community. Including useful native species in your forest garden will help retain or recreate parts of the local food web and guild structures. Using locally native plants should also increase the chances of plant survival and reduce maintenance needs in your garden. Research the functions and uses of the species in the original ecosystem, and determine whether the native plants will help you achieve your gardening goals. Keep those species that provide you or the garden with useful yields or functions.

Community niches make the translation. When you need to make substitutions, define the community niche filled by each model species and look for useful species that best fill that niche. Is the species a thin-crowned canopy mast producer (like a bitternut hickory, *Carya cordiformis*), a suckering shade-tolerant flowering shrub of mid- to late succession (such as pagoda dogwood, *Cornus alternifolia*), or an annual ruderal of disturbed sites (like tower mustard, *Arabis glabra*)? Abstracting the roles a species plays will help you find analogous species.

Plant form indicates niche. Structural similarities between species provide a measure of ecological similarity. "The general principle that an organism's structure is adapted to the particular environment it inhabits is well established."[84] This extends beyond the general form of tree, shrub, and herb to rooting patterns, leaf and stem patterns, dispersal patterns, and flower and fruit structure. You can use the structural form of a model species as a guide to selecting ecological analogs, along with other useful information such as its soil, water, and shade tolerances, its time niches, and so on. We can learn much just from finding examples of the plants in question and observing their architecture. Rooting pattern, one of the most important architectural features of plants, is perhaps one of the hardest to discover.

Native region climate is a critical factor. Ecological similarity should increase in proportion to the similarity of the climates in which the model and analog species evolved. Obviously, a desert-adapted plant is less likely to do well in a moist climate, while species from northeastern Asia tend to do well in northeastern North America since the climates are similar. However, the highly variable spring weather of our region, with its multiple freeze-thaw cycles, does confuse and confound many Asian species, leading to weather-related plant injuries and loss of productivity from freezing of flower buds.

Taxonomy relates to ecological roles. Taxonomically related species tend to fill similar ecological roles. For example, many edible plants in the lily family grow edible bulbs or corms and take the role of spring ephemerals or summer green herbs. On the other hand, differences between species even in the same genus can be considerable. Root-pattern variability among the oaks (*Quercus* spp.) is rather high, for instance, including flat-, heart- and tap-rooted species. Meanwhile, all or virtually all hickories are tap rooted. It pays to know your plants and your taxonomy in this business!

ECOLOGICAL ANALOGS AND GUILD-BUILD: NOT MUTUALLY EXCLUSIVE

Native plant communities are not "perfect." Just because species may have coevolved for centuries doesn't mean that every niche, every community function, every need in the community has been filled. Some regions are blessed with high diversity from which to draw, and others are less blessed. Even if we desire to create an edible forest garden closely mimicking the native ecosystem, it behooves us to use the guild-build process to review the species in the native community, looking for holes in the fabric. Maybe there's a gap in the availability of predatory insect nectar at some point in the season. Maybe one of our substitute species has a need that the natives and analogs don't quite fill. Doing some amount of guild analysis will help make sure the mimic performs well by the standards we have set for its design.

CHAPTER SUMMARY

A species' niche expresses its inherent characteristics in all realms and forms the basis of all interactions between that species and its surrounding environment and species associates. An organism's core strategy for surviving and reproducing places that organism into particular roles within its community. Each species fills a community niche, or function, as it goes about making its living in its unique way. Niche forms the foundation of social structures.

Relationships between species take a number of forms ranging from predation to neutralism, often with several kinds of interactions taking place at once between the same two species. These relationships form the frameworks of social structures.

When multiple species interact, they form food webs that regulate their populations and distribute energy and nutrients throughout the community. A well-functioning food web creates a self-regulating community by creating functional interconnection among species. Resource-sharing guilds create redundancy of function that stabilizes community processes and helps ensure continued balance as guild members reduce competition by partitioning their shared resources. Mutual-support guilds create a second layer of functional interconnection within and outside the food web that further stabilizes and binds together community members. All of these social structures develop to their fullest over evolutionary timescales as species adjust to each other. Yet social structure is fluid, invisible, and hard to design, so we must focus on the design elements that anchor and stabilize it.

Providing predator-habitat requirements and healthy soil biology helps anchor forest garden social structures in important ways. Yet plants function as the paramount social-structure anchors. Their compositional, structural, and functional diversity lay the groundwork for a healthy, stable, and resilient social ecology. As a result, we focus our design efforts on plants as we create guilds and polycultures.

We can attempt consciously to mimic social structures and gain the advantages of self-regulation and stability in two ways: by building guilds and polycultures from species niches and relationships, and by creating mimics of native plant communities using suitable native plants and ecological analogs of native community members. Habitat mimicry using ecological analogs takes fullest advantage of coevolutionary processes. Guild building allows the greatest innovation and the highest chance of achieving defined design objectives. We can use these approaches separately or together.

1. Perry, 1994, page 172.
2. Colinvaux, 1986, page 31.
3. Bazzaz, 1996, page 15.
4. Bazzaz, 1996, page 261.
5. Bugg et al., 1998.
6. Riechert, 1998, pages 211–12.
7. Riechert, 1998, page 211.
8. Riechert, 1998.
9. Nentwig, 1998, page 62.
10. Bazzaz, 1996, pages 158–59.

11. Bazzaz, 1996, pages 159–60.
12. Adapted from Mollison, 1988, page 32.
13. Bazzaz, 1996, page 119.
14. Bazzaz, 1996, pages 119–20, 142–43.
15. Colinvaux, 1986, page 31.
16. Modified from Kourik, 1986, page 35.
17. See Kourik, 1986, and other resources in the appendices for more discussion.
18. Perry, 1994, page 182.
19. Pickett, Collins, and Armesto, 1987, page 363.
20. Perry, 1994, page 227.
21. Perry, 1994, page 226.
22. Perry, 1994, page 229.
23. Perry, 1994, page 231.
24. Perry, Bell, and Amaranthus, 1992; Soil Foodweb Inc., 1999; Luoma, 1999.
25. Perry, 1994, pages 233–34.
26. Perry, 1994, page 242; Perry, Bell, and Amaranthus, 1992, page 152; Luoma, 1999, page 125.
27. Colinvaux, 1986, page 638.
28. Luoma, 1999; Perry, 1994, page 239.
29. Soil Foodweb Inc., http://www.soilfoodweb.com.
30. Buchman and Nabhan, 1996, page 24.
31. Perry, 1994, page 236; Northern Nut Grower's Association, 1979, page 220.
32. Much of the following information comes from Perry, 1994, pages 236–37.
33. Sauer and Andropogon Assoc., 1998, page 33.
34. Sauer and Andropogon Assoc., 1998, page 33.
35. Perry, 1994, page 238.
36. Perry, 1994, page 238.
37. Steve Breyer, Tripple Brook Farm, Southampton, MA, personal communication by phone.
38. This list of modes of facilitation is adapted from Hunter and Aarsen, 1988.
39. Luoma, 1999; Perry, 1994.
40. Soil Foodweb Inc., 1999, Web-site article.
41. Perry, 1994, pages 151–53.
42. Colinvaux, 1986, page 30.
43. Colinvaux, 1986, page 31.
44. Colinvaux, 1986, page 31.
45. Soule and Piper, 1992, page 108.
46. Colinvaux, 1986, page 22.
47. Häni et al., 1998, pages 185–86.
48. Altieri, 1995, page 300.
49. Stamets, 1993, page 420.
50. See chapter 7 and Paul Stamets's *Growing Gourmet and Medicinal Mushrooms* or *The Mushroom Cultivator* by Stamets and J. S. Chilton, for more information.
51. Perry, 1994, page 159.
52. Mollison, 1988, page 60.
53. Perry, 1994, page 183.
54. Foster, 1984, page 154.
55. Altieri, 1995, page 276.
56. Unfortunately, Dave lost track of this reference, but believes it was in an article in the *Permaculture Activist*.
57. Atsatt and O'Dowd, 1976.
58. Perry, 1994, pages 260–65.
59. Roughgarden, 1983.
60. Fox, 1988.
61. Ricklefs, 1979, page 678.
62. Bennett, 1997, pages 108–15.
63. See Bennett, 1997, for a well-developed "postmodern" view of evolution and Stanley, Van Valkenburgh, and Steneck, 1983, for evidence of episodic evolution.
64. Flannery, 2001, page 93; Stewart and Rothwell, 1993, pages 480–82.
65. Flannery, 2001, page 36.
66. Stewart and Rothwell, 1993, page 7; see also Barbour, Burk, and Pitts, 1987, page 177.
67. Ricklefs, 1979, page 379.
68. Graham, 1972; Stewart and Rothwell, 1993; Flannery, 2001.
69. Orians and Paine, 1983, page 432.
70. Orians and Paine, 1983.
71. Barbour, Burk, and Pitts, 1987, pages 177–80.
72. Theodoropoulos, 2003, for example, is very much in the individualistic camp, and this strongly influences his take on the natives, exotics, and invasives debate.
73. Ophuls, 1977.
74. Pimentel et al., 2000.
75. Sauer and Andropogon Assoc., 1998, page 49.
76. Quammen, 1998.
77. Holmgren, 1996.
78. Holmgren, 1997.
79. Theodoropoulos, 2003, page 36; Beerling, 1991.
80. Colle, 1998, page 111.
81. These results depend heavily on environmental context and the particular species involved; Perry, 1994, page 304.
82. Perry, 1994, page 305.
83. Ricklefs, 1979, page 682.
84. Ricklefs, 1979, page 747.

5

Structures of the Underground Economy

Plants and soil exist in a tightly linked partnership. Just as plant growth cannot be understood without reference to soil, neither can soil structure or the processes occurring within soil be understood without reference to plants.

—DAVID PERRY, *Forest Ecosystems*

Thus when a soil loses fertility we pour on fertilizer, or at best alter its tame flora and fauna, without considering the fact that its wild flora and fauna, which built the soil to begin with, may likewise be important to its maintenance.

—ALDO LEOPOLD

In many countries, the black market or "underground economy" dwarfs the "official" economy by an order of magnitude or more. The same goes in forest ecosystems. Yet we know so little about this dark world that various aspects of it deserve a chapter of their own. We are trying to mimic the structures of forest ecosystems. What are some of the key structures of the underground economy?

We have described the five elements of forest physical architecture and the social structure of ecosystems, and some of their implications for a range of forest garden design and management issues. However, these subjects only graze the topic of nutrient cycling and conservation as a whole system, and we have discussed primarily only aboveground architecture and social structures. We now approach the structure of nutrient flows, root systems, and the soil food web head-on to see what we can learn for our use and mimicry.

THE ANATOMY OF SELF-RENEWING FERTILITY

The cosmic abundance of the elements is quite different from the abundance of elements in living things. Burning any sample of life—a tree, a mouse, or a box full of bacteria—yields ashes that are remarkably similar to each other chemically, yet all with elemental concentrations quite unlike the mineral crust of the earth or a solar flare. Living things, therefore, select from the elements about them. They have little use for really abundant elements like silicon, aluminum, magnesium, and iron, but concentrate the relatively rare elements phosphorus, potassium, and calcium.

—PAUL COLINVAUX, *Ecology*

Soil development is the most important aim of biological agriculture. . . . However, an organic approach that "robs Peter to pay Paul" cannot be justified as sustainable. Importation of nutrients must be an investment in biological capital rather than a perpetual input necessary to maintain output.

—David Holmgren,
Hepburn Permaculture Gardens

Much farm and garden nutrition currently derives from nutrient minerals imported to a given site from far away at high energy and environmental cost. Most of these are "a perpetual input necessary to maintain output," not an investment in biological capital. As the cost of this input continues to rise in the coming decades, self-renewing fertility will become more and more of an issue. Healthy forest ecosystems tend to generate and maintain their own fertility as an inherent community function. They build the soil into a key legacy for the future and a major capital asset. When we learn how they do this and mimic the process, we gain practical advantages over the long haul. We may as well begin learning how to accomplish this long-term feat without compromising our short-term goals. Protracted and thoughtful observation will help us avoid protracted and thoughtless labor; this section gathers observations for us to use in our forest gardening process.

The anatomy of self-renewing fertility consists of the continuous, transformative living-mineral-chemical cycles (biogeochemical cycles) of plant nutrients. These cycles occur through the interaction between the physical ecosystem architecture, the ecosystem social structure, and the geological constituents of landscapes. Nutrients weave in and out of these structural elements of the ecosystem and tie them together. What nutrients are we talking about, and how do they behave? Where do they come from, where do they get stored, and where do they go? How can we constructively support these biogeochemical cycles to build the natural-capital value of our garden soils over time with minimum labor and cost?

This section further examines this third structural facet of forest ecosystems to see what we can learn for our forest gardens. Other authors cover much of the basic information on plant nutrition, the required balances between different minerals, signs of nutrient deficiency, and so on (see appendix 3). Despite their importance, we will not discuss these issues here. Our focus is the structures of nutrient flow and how to generate self-renewing fertility. We will look at the different kinds of nutrients, their sources and containers, how they leak out of ecosystems, and what plugs nature has evolved to stop those leaks. When we create gardens that tap those sources, enlarge those containers, and plug those leaks, we will have cocreated self-renewing fertility.

Nutrient Characteristics and Sources

Plants require at least eighteen essential elements to thrive, most of which they obtain primarily from the soil. We can conveniently divide these eighteen nutrients into four groups based on their ecological and physiological characteristics (table 5.1). Nine macronutrients (Groups 1 through 3) constitute the vast majority—99.5 percent—of plant biomass. Nine micronutrients (Group 4) make up very small proportions of living matter, yet plants cannot function without them because they play specific physiological roles.

Group 1 nutrients (carbon, oxygen, and hydrogen: C, O, H) constitute the bulk of living matter, because they are the primary components of all organic molecules, from sugars to fats and proteins. These building blocks of the physical infrastructure of all living things are very common elements. They dissolve easily in water, in both their gaseous and their ionic forms. The chemical bonds between these three elements constitute the primary storage of solar energy within all living matter. These elements cycle at a global scale, and their abundance means that they usually do not limit productivity.

Though Group 2 nutrients (nitrogen, phosphorus, and sulfur: N, P, S) constitute a small percentage of organic matter, two of them also tend to be in shortest supply to living organisms. Therefore,

TABLE 5.1. Major plant nutrients: characteristics, sources, and functions. *After Barbour, Burk, and Pitts, 1987, and Perry, 1994.*

Group / Nutrient	Common Ion	Leach-ability*	% Dry Wt.[†]	Sources[††]	Ecological Functions (Healthy Systems)	Physiological Functions
Group 1:						
C carbon	CO_3^{2-}	gas/hi	45	air	Cycled globally, not locally, these elements are readily available. Most other nutrients cycled mostly locally, except in agriculture.	Primary framework of all organic molecules, together constituting ± 96% of plant biomass.
O oxygen	O_2	gas	45	air, water		
H hydrogen	H^+	low	6	water, ion		
Group 2:						
N nitrogen	NO_3^-	gas/hi	1.5	air, atmos	Tightly cycled, but N and S cycle globally. Demand often exceeds supply: most likely to limit productivity. Stored in organic matter; decomposition releases. Acid rain supplies excess S and N.	Key parts of organic matter, proteins, enzymes, and other fundamental metabolic constituents.
P phosphorus	PO_4^{2-}	low	0.2	rock		
S sulfur	SO_4^{2-}	gas/hi	0.1	rock, atmos		
Group 3:						
K potassium	K^+	med	1.0	rock, atmos	Often, but not always, available in parent material. Tightly cycled, easily leached. Scarce in sandy, low-organic matter, or old soils. Not a constituent of organic matter. Held by organic matter, clay, and B horizon secondary minerals.	Involved in numerous metabolic processes, including photo-synthesis, osmosis, stomatal behavior, membrane integrity, enzyme activation.
Ca calcium	Ca^{++}	med	0.5	rock, atmos		
Mg magnesium	Mg^{++}	med	0.2	rock, atmos		
Group 4:						
Cl chlorine	Cl^-	hi	0.01	rock, atmos	Occur in very small amounts in most parent materials (except Fe, which is usually abundant). Low solubility at moderate pH can limit availability to plants unless chelated into organic molecules by plants, mycorrhizas, microbes, or organic acids. Thin line between "enough" and "toxic." Low pH can easily increase availability to toxic overdose.	Required in small amounts by plants, play numerous roles as activators and mediators of physiologic processes. Toxic in overdose. "Micronutrient deficiencies do occur and may be more widespread than we realize."[i]
Fe iron	Fe^{++}, Fe_3^+	lo	0.01	rock		
Mn manganese	Mn^{++}	lo	0.005	rock		
B boron	$B_4O_7^{2-}$	lo	0.002	rock		
Zn zinc	Zn^{++}	lo	0.002	rock		
Cu copper	Cu^{++}	lo	0.0001	rock		
Mo molybdenum	MoO_4^{2-}	lo	0.0001	rock		
Co cobalt	Co^{++}	lo	?	rock		
Ni nickel	Ni	lo	?	rock		

* Ease of leaching in its most common ionic or mineral form under normal soil temperatures and pH.

† Approximate concentrations of elements within higher plants as a percentage of dry weight.

†† Main sources of nutrient input to ecosystems: air — absorbed by plants directly from the air; water — stripped out of water molecules; ion — a free ion in the soil; atmos — dry deposition from the atmosphere or carried in rainfall; rock — a constituent of parent material (bedrock or mineral particles). Organic matter is not a source of input to the ecosystem, but a storage of nutrients within it.

i Perry, 1994, page 343.

lack of nitrogen is the most frequent limit on ecosystem productivity, followed by lack of phosphorus. Sulfur, whose sources include both rocks and the atmosphere, rarely limits plant growth, especially in these days of acid rain.

Nitrogen enters ecosystems from the air through nitrogen fixation by microbes (usually in association with plants), by falling in rain, or as dry particle deposition from the atmosphere. Some ecologists hold that leaves absorb more nitrogen (up to 10 percent of needs) directly from the air or rain than was previously believed.[1] Other research shows that free-living microbes in decaying wood, on the forest floor, in the root zones of plants, and even in the aboveground stems of living plants can fix small amounts of nitrogen from the air, even though the microbes are not plant mutualists.[2] Lichens in the canopy can be major nitrogen-fixers in old-growth forests.[3] Late-succession forests may therefore be able to accumulate some nitrogen, or make up for limited losses from their nitrogen stores, without legumes or other nitrogen-fixing

Box 5.1: The Concept of Limiting Factors

The presence and success of an organism or group of organisms depends upon a complex of conditions. Any condition that approaches or exceeds the limits of tolerance is said to be a limiting condition or a limiting factor.[4]

A single environmental condition (e.g., winter temperatures) occurring outside an organism's range of tolerance may prevent its effective survival, growth, and production. A single resource (e.g., a plant nutrient) in limited supply may do the same. It does not matter whether the resource is a minor one, whether other important resources are amply supplied, or whether other conditions are well within tolerance range. On the other hand, some resources or conditions can reduce growth and survival when they exceed needs, such as trace minerals, heat, and water.

If we want an organism to survive and thrive, therefore, we must make sure its needs are met. Hence, we must assess the niche characteristics of a species and understand the resources and conditions in our landscapes so we can determine what limiting factors or conditions may exist for that species. We can then select different species or modify the site conditions to increase our chances of success. Knowing which nutrients tend to limit plant growth, as discussed in this section, is a first step in this process.

Generally, when we address the primary limiting factor, survival, growth, and productivity radically increase. Beware, though: there may be multiple limiting resources or conditions to address, not just one! In addition, different factors may interact to create a complex of limiting conditions. For example, when soil pH is low (too acidic), many nutrients become unavailable to plants and some become toxic, forming a complex of challenges for plants. Adding more nutrients does not help; you must first address the acidity problem.

plants. These late-succession nitrogen-fixing pathways probably cannot meet the nitrogen needs of annually bearing nut trees, for example, but they can significantly contribute to decomposition processes. Therefore, it appears that most of the nitrogen in mature ecosystems accumulates from nitrogen-fixers in early succession. It then cycles conservatively through organic matter and back into organisms again, as long as the system is healthy, stable, and relatively mature.

Phosphorus derives almost exclusively from parent materials (very small amounts fall from the atmosphere). Its soil chemistry is complex: it often exists in forms that are not soluble or available to plants even when it is present in quantity. Phosphorus limitation is therefore most frequently a question of *lack of availability* rather than a lack of phosphorus in the soil. Soil organisms are extremely important in making phosphorus available to plants.

All these Group 2 elements reside within dead organic matter. Organic matter decay releases them. They generally cycle tightly within local ecosystems, though nitrogen and sulfur can also escape in their gaseous forms. These days, acid rain and acid particle deposition can supply nitrogen and sulfur in excess, especially within or anywhere downwind of urban or industrial areas.

The Group 3 cations (potassium, calcium, and magnesium, all positively charged: K^+, Ca^{++}, Mg^{++}) are all quite soluble. They can quickly leach out of organisms, dead or alive, so they do not stay *within* organic matter for very long. Potassium and calcium are the next most frequently limiting nutrients in ecosystems, after nitrogen and phosphorus. Potassium is a common ingredient of most fertilizer blends for this reason. Most deciduous trees and many evergreens require significant levels of calcium. Magnesium leaches easily, but because it is a key ingredient of secondary mineral clays that form in the B horizon, the soil usually recaptures it effectively. The same is often true of potassium, as well.[5] However, once these nutrients become embedded in the secondary minerals they are not directly available to plants except through the action of soil organisms such as mycorrhizal fungi.

All three Group 3 elements originate from rocks and atmospheric particles, mainly the former. However, some rocks contain only small amounts of one or more of these nutrients. If parent materials contain few of these elements, atmospheric deposition may be their only natural source. In this case, only very tight nutrient conservation will allow the ecosystem to build up adequate supplies.

As cations, potassium, calcium, and magnesium possess positive electrical charges. As a result, they adsorb onto the negatively charged surfaces of organic matter and mineral particles, meaning that they "hover" with a weak electrochemical bond. Plant roots can exchange hydrogen ions (H^+) for the nutrient cations, but adsorption holds the nutrients against leaching. Therefore, the more surface area a soil contains, the more cation exchange sites the soil contains, and the more Group 3 nutrients the soil can store. Therefore, sandy or low-organic matter soils cannot hold many of these nutrients, whereas finer-textured soils or those higher in organic matter can hold more. Older, more highly weathered soils tend to contain few of these nutrients as well, because they have had long periods to leach away, leading to depletion of the reserves in the parent material. Acid rain has increased the leaching of all nutrient cations as much as 200 to 300 percent in forests in eastern Tennessee, with calcium and magnesium being most vulnerable to replacement by hydrogen cations from the acid.[6] This is probably also occurring in other acid rain–affected areas.

All micronutrients fall into Group 4. Plants require these essential elements in extremely small quantities to support metabolic processes. Most micronutrients become more available to plants at a lower pH (more acidic). However, excess amounts of micronutrients can be toxic to plants, animals, and microbes, and the line between enough and too much can be very thin. Biological activity and biochemicals can chelate metal ions such as the micronutrients zinc, copper, cobalt, manganese, molybdenum, and others, meaning that the atoms become surrounded by a ring of complex organic compounds that render them more soluble and available to plants. Chelation can also make some metals less toxic. It is one means of rendering soils contaminated with lead, mercury, and cadmium safer for gardening. Mycorrhizal fungi and other soil microbes are the main known producers of chelators in the soil.

All the macronutrients easily dissolve in water in their common ionic forms. While high solubility makes these elements available to plant roots, it also exposes them to a high risk of leaching. Since the macronutrients can either leach away easily or turn to gas and disappear, it would seem that plants and other organisms should experience great difficulty meeting their nutritional needs. This is especially true when one considers that plant photosynthesis captures only about 2 percent of annual solar radiation,[7] and that it takes much energy simply to maintain high concentrations of elements that have a tendency to disperse and diffuse. Obviously, ecosystems have found ways of maintaining nutrient concentrations vastly different from what nonliving soils would maintain. How do they do it?

NUTRIENT CONTAINERS, FLOWS, LEAKS, AND PLUGS

Nutrients do not move through living systems in smooth, even-flowing transition, but in pulses, jerks and floods. The cycling of matter is inherent in the functioning of ecosystems, and is integral to their structure. Both essential and non-essential materials move in cyclic fashion.

—BARBOUR, BURK, AND PITTS,
Terrestrial Plant Ecology

Imagine six containers of nutrient elements: bedrock, mineral soil particles, soil water, organic matter, soil organisms, and plants (figure 5.1). The bedrock and mineral particles (collectively called the soil parent materials) have a nutrient composition

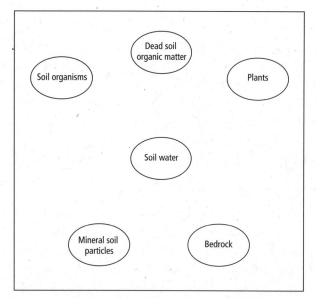

FIGURE 5.1. The anatomy of self-renewing fertility: the six primary nutrient containers of terrestrial ecosystems.

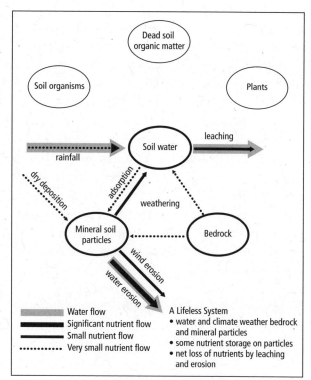

FIGURE 5.2. Nutrient flows in a lifeless ecosystem. Water and climate weather the bedrock and mineral particles to release nutrients. Rainfall and dry deposition add small amounts to the system as well. Mineral particles store some nutrients on their cation exchange sites. Nonetheless, leaching and erosion remove nutrients from the soil water and mineral particle containers to create a linear flow of nutrients out of the system.

determined by the kind of rock from which they arose. The soil water holds nutrients in chemical solution and as suspended particles. The soil organisms and plants hold nutrients in their bodies as living or dead tissues and body fluids. The organic matter contains nutrients in its structure and also has cation exchange sites that hold nutrients on its surface. While not one of the six containers, the surrounding atmosphere contains nutrients in gases, dust particles, and suspended drops of water. Each container can link to the others through various physical, chemical, or biological interactions, represented by arrows in the following diagrams. How do these nutrient containers interact in different situations to lose or conserve nutrients?

A Lifeless Ecosystem

In a lifeless ecosystem (figure 5.2), three of these containers would hold nutrients: the bedrock, the mineral soil particles, and the soil water. Physical processes and chemicals (e.g., freezing, thawing, and naturally occurring weak acids in soil water) would degrade or weather the mineral soil particles, releasing nutrients into the soil water solution. The bedrock would also weather and release nutrients,

though usually slowly over geologic timescales. The nutrients in the air enter the soil at low rates through gas exchange, dry-particle deposition, and rainfall. Some of the nutrient ions in the soil adsorb onto the soil particles at cation exchange sites. However, percolating water eventually leaches away most nutrients, at least in humid climates.

This lifeless soil system has three sources of nutrients (mineral soil particles, bedrock, and the atmosphere) and two plant-available nutrient storages (soil water and cation exchange sites on mineral particles). The nutrients rapidly flow out of this system, from both leaching and erosion. Leaching is a major nutrient leak in all humid ecosystems, even when vegetated: 45 to 65 percent of the soluble calcium and potassium can leach out of grassland soils

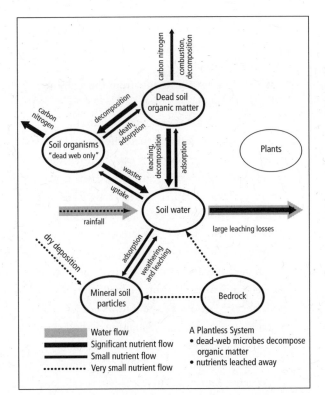

FIGURE 5.3. Nutrient flows on a clear-cut site or fallow agricultural field with no living plants. The addition of organic matter provides more nutrients and energy to the system, as well as decomposer organisms, but decomposition and leaching run the system down. Such a system is not self-renewing but is dependent on external sources of nutrients.

FIGURE 5.4. Leaching losses in winter in the eastern United States range from insignificant (1) in the prairies to high (4) in the Southeast. Leaching losses are therefore moderate to high throughout most of the eastern deciduous forest bioregion. When the landscape is structured as in figure 5.3, ecosystems in areas with significant winter leaching losses will lose nutrients for many months each year, making self-renewal all the more challenging. *Adapted from Brady, 1974.*

and litter in as little as four hours.[8] With no vegetative cover, wind and water erosion also cause major nutrient losses from this kind of system.

Nutrient Flows in a Plantless Ecosystem

Let's say we add two more nutrient containers to the above lifeless system: a large quantity of organic matter, including undecomposed and partially decomposed organic matter as well as humus, along with a range of soil organisms (figure 5.3). The links between the two mineral containers and the soil water would remain essentially unchanged, except that the rate of mineral weathering would increase because the organic matter and its decomposition releases additional acids, and the organisms do so as well. The organic matter would increase the soil's

water-holding capacity and aggregation, thereby reducing the rates of erosion and leaching. The organic matter container represents a supply of stored energy and nutrients, mainly in nutrient Groups 1 and 2, on which the soil organisms will feed. The organic matter also possesses additional cation exchange sites, and this additional cation exchange capacity (CEC) helps the soil grab and hold onto more nutrients. However, of all the organisms we added, the only survivors will be those that make a living by decomposing organic matter or that feed on the decomposers: the decomposer food web, or what we shall call the "dead web." Therefore, the system will tend to run down: the soil organisms will feed on the organic matter, releasing nutrients and decreasing the CEC over time, and the net flow of nutrients will be into the soil water and then out of the system by leaching (how fast leaching occurs depends, in part, on climate; see

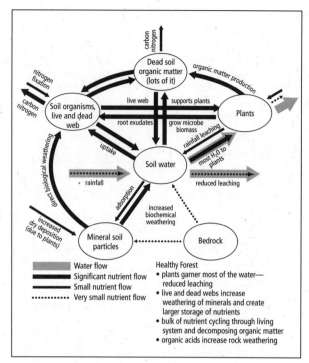

FIGURE 5.5. Nutrient flows in a healthy forest are self-renewing because of the addition of plants to the system. Plants energize the system, control water flows, add organic matter, and alter the soil food web, among other things. These changes shift the system into a nutrient-conserving and nutrient-gathering mode.

figure 5.4). Some nutrients will also pass into the air during decomposition and by direct breakdown in the heat of the sun. This is essentially what happens in a fallow agricultural field or a clear-cut forest before revegetation.

How Plants Change Nutrient Dynamics

Plants alter soil nutrient dynamics in a number of important ways (see figure 5.5), all of which lead to nutrient conservation. Perennial plant communities accentuate these effects:

- As the primary source of organic matter in the system, plants provide most of the energy that runs the soil food web. They expand the organic matter nutrient container, both in organic matter mass and in cation exchange capacity, by litterfall and by feeding soil organisms. Some

ecologists estimate that root dieback contributes more organic matter to the soil on a yearly basis than leaf litterfall.[9]

- Plant roots extract nutrients from the soil water before they can leach away.
- Plants garner soil water for transpiration, reducing percolation and therefore the chances of losing whatever nutrients exist in leachable form. With this mechanism, a sufficient quantity of vegetation can reduce leaching losses to nearly zero during the growing season. Forests usually contain enough vegetation to do this. Most agricultural communities do not.
- Plants radically increase the diversity and abundance of soil organisms by feeding soil microbes with energy-rich root secretions or exudates. As a result, five to ten times more fungi and ten to fifty times more bacteria live in root-zone versus non-root-zone soil,[10] and other organisms increase as well. This stores more nutrients in the soil organism container right within the root zone and creates a "live-web" complement to the dead-web soil microbes (see "The Soil Food Web" later in this chapter). Trees and other perennials release a pulse of root exudates in the early spring. This creates a microbial population explosion that stores large amounts of nutrients at a time when leaching losses are high due to winter decomposition combined with spring rains and snowmelt.[11]
- The mutualism between root-zone microbes and plants increases the movement of nutrients directly from organic matter and mineral particles to plants without the nutrients going through a leachable phase within the soil water. Mycorrhizal fungi are particularly important in this regard. The stability of root-zone microbe populations engendered by perennial plants facilitates this nutrient pathway.
- Perennial plants absorb nutrients in the fall, and sometimes during winter, for use the following year. This smoothes out the peaks and valleys of nutrient availability during the year and allows

for rapid growth based on nutrients stored within plant tissues during periods of high nutrient demand, such as spring.

- Forests increase the quantity of nutrients entering the system from the atmosphere relative to other plant communities by capturing more dust particles, mist, and rainfall.

By increasing the size of the organic matter and soil organism containers, directly storing nutrients themselves, improving direct nutrient transfer from OM and soil particles to plants, and reducing the amount of water available for leaching away nutrients, perennial plants create a nutrient system that is conservative in the true sense of that word. Note that *it is not the plants alone that conserve nutrients*. The interconnected system of plants, organic matter, and soil organisms, especially root-zone mutualists, creates this nutrient-conserving ecosystem. The plants *energize* the nutrient-conserving system and alter its composition, structure, and dynamics. Over time, more and more nutrients get bound up in organic matter, changing the nutrient balance of the soil from one like the parent material to one more appropriate for keeping an ecosystem running.

The longer a soil-plant community develops and evolves, the more efficient it gets at conserving nutrients: "climax communities have fewer leaks in nutrient cycles and more efficiently hold the nutrients in the plant-soil-plant cycle."[12] This is because the networked system of organic matter, organisms, and plants has had time to develop the links necessary for effective functioning. Soil development, therefore, is a process of mineral nutrients becoming increasingly bound up in organic matter as ecosystems mature, and being increasingly cycled within and between living organisms. Soil development occurs primarily within the A and B horizons of the soil profile, where the most life, roots, and nutrients become concentrated. The synthesis and accumulation of secondary minerals in the B horizon are also characteristic of soil development processes. These also help conserve mineral nutrients. Over time, the topsoil layers accumulate more and more minerals critical to life processes, to the point that the topsoil becomes rich in nutrients and relatively independent of the parent material. In healthy temperate forests, the trees use only a small percentage of the nutrients stored in the soil in any given year.[13] The temperate soil ecosystem holds and cycles the rest, providing plenty of backup supply in case of catastrophe (not so in tropical systems). Nutrient budgets of temperate forest ecosystems indicate that healthy forests lose about as many nutrients from leaching as they gain from deep weathering of parent materials.[14] *This means that our forest gardens could be free of outside nutrient-inputs at maturity if we get them right.*

The Fertility Structure of Conventional Agriculture

The above is not the linear "throughput" model of conventional agriculture, which adds nutrients to the soil as highly available fertilizer, a large percentage of which leaches away into groundwater and streams (figure 5.6). The management strategies of conventional agriculture generally decrease the size of the soil organism and organic matter nutrient containers. Chemical fertilizers oxidize (that is, chemically burn) organic matter and kill soil organisms. Every pesticide or herbicide tested so far negatively affects nontarget soil life.[15] Even on organic farms, every time we disturb the soil by tilling, plowing, or killing vegetation, we disrupt and set back these natural nutrient conservation processes and the development of the soil organism community. Lack of perennial plants leaves the soil in a condition similar to the clear-cut situation described earlier for at least part of the year, so the system begins to run down, eating the organic matter and releasing nutrients for leaching. These actions disturb the links creating an interconnected, year-round, nutrient-conserving soil community. The burden then shifts to the intervenor: we have to work to bring the soil back to a healthful, fertile, nutrient-conserving state and keep adding back the nutrients the system loses.

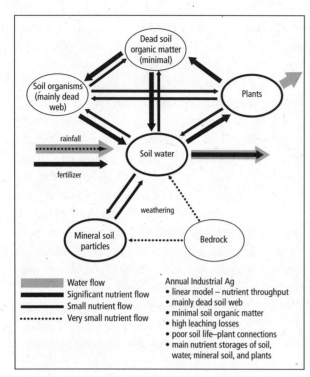

| Water flow |
| Significant nutrient flow |
| Small nutrient flow |
| Very small nutrient flow |

Annual Industrial Ag
• linear model – nutrient throughput
• mainly dead soil web
• minimal soil organic matter
• high leaching losses
• poor soil life–plant connections
• main nutrient storages of soil,
  water, mineral soil, and plants

FIGURE 5.6. In annual industrial agriculture, nutrient flows are still mainly linear because organic matter is minimized and the soil food web is damaged by typical industrial farming practices. High leaching losses are the norm, and annual plants just can't function the way that perennials do, particularly early in the season and during winter.

Natural systems strive toward health and fertility. When we ignore how they create this state, mentally sidelining the soil organisms and the soil organic matter, focusing only on the plants and mineral particles, we create work for ourselves and damage the ecosystem that sustains us.

The Anatomy of Self-Renewing Fertility

Biomass is the keeper of organization.

—RAMON MARGALEF

The preceding discussion helps us understand that healthy soils have two sources of mineral nutrition, the parent material and the atmosphere, and consist of six interconnected nutrient containers. The base of the system consists of the parent material, mineral

---

TABLE 5.2. Nutrient leaks and nutrient plugs.

Nutrient leaks:
• Leaching
• Transforming nutrients into their gaseous phase (N, S, C, O, H)
• Erosion (wind and water)

Nutrient plugs:
• Plants extracting nutrients from soil water
• Plants preventing erosion
• Plants transpiring water, reducing the amount of nutrient leaching
• Plants adding to soil organic matter, increasing CEC and within-organic matter storage
• Plants feeding soil organisms (in root zone and via organic matter), increasing container size
• Creating a network of nutrient flows between plants, soil organisms, and organic matter
• Plants cooling the soil microclimate and thereby slowing decomposition and combustion of organic matter
• Primary mineral soil particles holding nutrients on cation exchange sites
• Secondary mineral clays in the B horizon catching nutrients that do leach

---

soil particles, and the soil water, in which the primary nutrient flows move from parent material and mineral particles toward the soil water, with some temporary storage on cation exchange sites on the mineral particles. The top of the system consists of plants, soil organisms, organic matter, and, again, the soil water. Two-way nutrient flows between each pair of containers network these four elements together. The primary nutrient leaks (table 5.2) include leaching of nutrients in the soil water (potentially all elements) and losses of some nutrients to the atmosphere when various, mostly biological processes turn them to gases (mostly Group 1 and 2 elements). Soil ecosystems also lose significant nutrients from erosion, especially when unvegetated.

Plants plug these leaks in three ways on their own. First, they imbibe nutrients and store them for their own use. Second, they prevent erosion of the soil by wind and water. Third, a sufficient quantity of plants will garner the majority of water flow through the system for transpiration. This radically reduces the amount of water available to leach soluble nutrients. The latter function is one of the most important factors limiting nutrient leaching in forest ecosystems.

Plants cooperate with the rest of the system to plug leaks by adding energy to enlarge the organic matter and soil organism pools. They also create strong links within the top of the nutrient container system that conserve the nutrients and pass them between containers with minimal risk of leaching. This networked and enlarged system is the other most important nutrient-loss-reducing factor in forests. The cooler soil microclimate that plants create slows down the loss of nutrients by slowing decomposition. Secondary mineral synthesis in the B horizon forms another plug to nutrient loss, capturing leaching nutrients as they pass to the lower soil horizons. When earthworms and other organisms carry and churn these secondary minerals into the soil surface, they add to still another plug, the cation exchange capacity of the mineral particles themselves. If you look at these nine plugs, as outlined in table 5.2, you will see that all but mineral synthesis in the B horizon relate to the functions of living and nonliving biomass. We can see, therefore, that at least in the case of self-renewing fertility, Ramon Margalef was right: biomass *is* the keeper of organization.

A Few Comments on the Roles of Plants in Nutrient Cycling

The multifarious roles of plants in ecosystem nutrient dynamics could fill more than one book. Nevertheless, let's examine some more specific ideas about what plants do for nutrient cycles.

Understory Plants Cycle More Nutrients

In the late 1970s a researcher in British Columbia decided to explore the contribution of understory and overstory vegetation to forest nutrient cycling.[16] His work shows that the understory vegetation contributed only 3 to 11 percent of the total yearly aboveground litterfall, yet it had a much higher nutrient concentration than the overstory vegetation. As a result, this small amount of biomass accounted for a disproportionately high percentage

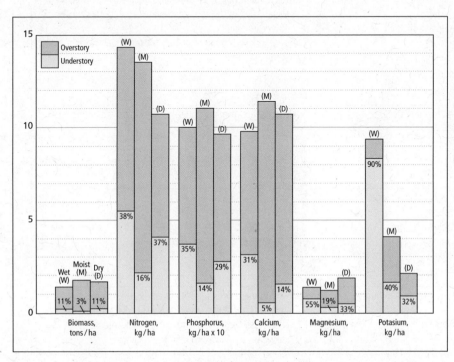

FIGURE 5.7. The contribution of understory vegetation to nutrient flows in forests is far greater than its diminutive size might indicate. Compare the percentage of biomass the understory contributes to the forest as a whole (left) to the percentage of various nutrients that that small amount of biomass contains (other columns). This breakdown is true across all levels of soil moisture. Careful design of the understory is key to creating self-renewing fertility! The numbers at left are the units shown below the bars, such as kilograms per hectare (kg/ha). *Adapted from Yarie, 1980. Used with permission.*

Feature Article 4:
Parent Materials: The Soil's Nutritional Constitution

Most of the macronutrients (Groups 2 and 3, table 5.1) and all the micronutrients derive principally from rock sources that weather into mineral parti-

cles. The kind of bedrock parent material, then, largely determines soil nutrient content and productivity: like our own parents, the soil's parent material

TABLE 5.3. Parent materials and soil nutrient constitution. *After Perry, 1994, pages 274–6, and Wilde, 1958, page 537.*

Parent Material Group (where found in U.S.)	Common Rock or Parent Material Types	General Soil and Nutrient Characteristics
Group 1:		
Siliceous rocks (scattered throughout)	- conglomerates - metamorphic quartzites - sandstones - siliceous shales	- Frequently sandy. Poor in all nutrients. - Low cation exchange capacity. - Not productive unless cemented by calcareous materials. - Lose biomass, organic matter = lose nutrients.
Group 2:		
Orthoclase-feldspathic rocks (scattered throughout)	- gneiss - granite - granitic porphyry - orthoclase felsites - syenite	- Usually sandy loams and loams. - Generally well supplied with potassium. - Usually low in calcium and magnesium. - Often acidic.
Group 3:		
Ferromagnesian rocks (scattered throughout)	- andesite - basalt - diabase - diorite - gabbro - hornblende gneiss	- These rocks rapidly weather into deep, fine-textured soils. - Usually rich in calcium, iron, magnesium, potassium, and other nutrients. - Can be low in potassium, but this rarely decreases the fertility of these soils.
Group 4:		
Calcareous rocks (scattered throughout)	- calcareous shales - chalk - dolomitic limestone - limestone	- Fertility greatly varies due to amount of weathering, clay content, and climate. - Deep, clay-rich soils are productive; shallow, pure limestone or chalk soils are a problem.
Group 5:		
Volcanic ash deposits (Pacific NW, California)	Mostly loose material with pieces of volcanic glass, feldspars, ferromagnesian minerals, quartz. Bedrock sometimes pumice stone.	- Quite fertile in most cases. - Tend to accumulate organic matter, to retain large quantities of water and nutrients, and to have low soil density (easy root penetration).
Group 6:		
Highly weathered soils (ultisols; SE U.S., subtropics)	- Any parent material that is highly weathered well below the root zone.	- Very nutrient-poor parent materials. - In tropics, most nutrients held and cycled within living biomass. Loss of biomass = loss of nutrients. This is less true of ultisols, though still a concern.

forms the "genetic basis" or "constitution" of the overlying soil. The living processes described here then modify this constitutional foundation, concentrating the minerals necessary for life within the topsoil. The nutrient constitution of the parent material therefore significantly affects our strategies for developing self-renewing fertility, as well as the nutritional resilience of the soil and the nutritional content of our plants.[17] This is especially true when the topsoil and its associated nutrient containers have been damaged and many nutrients have leaked out of the system. Which minerals does the parent material contain? (See table 5.3).

Parent materials project much more influence on ecosystems in relatively young soils than in older, more weathered soils.[18] Young soils develop in mountainous, volcanic, and glaciated areas, on river deposits, and in geologically active continental margins where ocean floors are being uplifted onto land (such as the West Coast of the United States). In these areas, the parent material is an important resource for building and maintaining the fertility of overlying soils. Plant roots can generally obtain these nutrients.

As soils age, the integrity and health of the ecosystem the soil supports becomes increasingly important to site fertility. The oldest, most weathered soils on the planet—some of those in Africa and South America—have parent materials so deeply weathered that they have much less nutrient value left for plants. There, the living tissues of the ecosystem hold the majority of nutrients. Destruction of the living tissues leads to rapid nutrient losses.

The United States contains some areas of soils, called "ultisols" in the U.S. classification system (see figure 5.8), that have not experienced glaciation in recent geological time, are found in warm, humid climates, and have a fairly long history of weathering. Ultisols are younger and less weathered than the most depleted African and South American soils; however, we should consider them more "at risk" for nutrient deficiency than the even younger materials found in the rest of the United States. On these soils, "clearcutting can break the biological chain that maintains nutrients within the rooting zone and lead to sharp declines in fertility."[19]

Ideally, once your forest garden is up and running, it will need few, if any, fertilizer inputs. Young parent materials can go a long way toward ensuring such self-renewing fertility. When the parent material contains nutrients in abundance, it should be relatively easy to renew the topsoil's nutrient content, and to keep renewing it, even when past mismanagement has leached its nutrients out. If, however, the parent materials do not contain one or more nutrients in abundance, this task will be much harder. A healthy forest garden in these soils may require larger inputs of nutrients in the beginning, the development of a tightly knit nutrient-recycling system in the garden for the long haul, and periodic fertilizer to keep it going. In any case, nutrients scarce in the parent material will need special attention for conservation over the long haul.

The bottom line is that it pays to look at the nutrient content of parent materials as well as that of the topsoil so you can determine your long-term nutritional strategies. Table 5.3 is only a general guide to this. You will need specific local information to formulate good strategies (see volume 2, chapter 3).

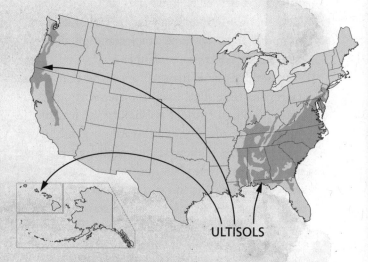

ULTISOLS

FIGURE 5.8. Highly weathered ultisol soils in the United States are places where self-renewing fertility will be the hardest to create and maintain. These soils are already very low in nutrient content because of their geological history. They will probably need careful nourishment during early forest garden succession and tight nutrient cycling for the duration. *Adapted from Brady, 1974.*

of five major nutrient elements in total annual aboveground litter (figure 5.7). Understory plants not only often contain higher nutrient concentrations than overstory trees, but they "turn over" (grow, die, decompose, and grow into new biomass) much more quickly. These factors help spur the decomposition of more decay-resistant litter, prime the engines of soil decomposers, and help prevent bottlenecks in the cycling of nutrients from dead organic matter to living plants. "The beneficial effect on stand productivity of maintaining a light understory has long been recognized by European silviculturists."[20] We can consciously support this process by choosing what plants grow when and where.

Ephemeral Plants as "Vernal Dams" Holding Back Nutrients

Another researcher in the 1970s, this time in a New Hampshire northern hardwood forest, studied many aspects of yellow trout lily (*Erythronium americanum*) ecology, including its nutrient dynamics. Trout lily is a delicate but not particularly useful plant, at least on the surface: it is edible only after prolonged boiling, and it may cause vomiting, which is one of its medicinal uses. It is, however, emblematic of all spring ephemeral wildflowers in another way.

Ephemerals have adapted to a niche that is very short on time but long on nutrient and sun resources. High nutrient availability and leaching in the spring results from cold-season organic matter decomposition followed by high rainfall and snowmelt, at a time when most plants have not yet started to grow. The sun is strong, but not for long, as the trees will soon leaf out. In response to this environment, ephemerals quickly grow, flower, fruit, and store reserves for the following year's dormancy and growth. All of this requires many nutrients.

This researcher looked at the nutrient dynamics of trout lily over a whole watershed to assess its impact on an ecosystem scale. He compared the nutrient intake of all the trout lily plants in the watershed to the total leaching losses from the watershed. It turns out that potassium uptake by trout lily equaled 82

percent of the amount lost to streams in the spring, and 53 percent of the total lost for the whole year. For nitrogen, the amounts were 91 percent of spring losses and 21 percent of yearly losses. By guzzling these nutrients and then releasing many of them as readily decomposed litter a short while later, when other plants are actively growing, trout lily becomes a "vernal dam" that holds nutrients back from leaching away in the spring.[21] We can assume that other ephemerals function in a similar way, though we don't know for sure. However, many ephemerals are highly nutritious spring edibles, and this supports the assumption.

Both of these studies point us toward herbaceous plants as key actors in the nutrient dynamics of forest gardens and support the strategy of using dynamic accumulator plants to help gather and conserve nutrients in our gardens.

Plants as Dynamic Nutrient Accumulators

As the two studies discussed above indicate, plants, especially herbaceous plants, greatly contribute to soil fertility by drawing nutrients out of the soil, storing them, and releasing them as they die. Some plants do this more actively than others, accumulating nutrients in their tissues to concentrations higher than those found in the soil or than usually found in the average plant. We can use these dynamic accumulators to conserve and improve soil fertility in our forest gardens.

Much folklore surrounds dynamic accumulators, as well as the use of plants to indicate different soil conditions. These traditional beliefs frequently lack rigor, accuracy, or broad applicability. However, solid evidence from the field of geobotany (mineral prospecting using plants) shows that specific plants or plant communities can indicate the presence of copper, uranium, selenium, zinc, silver, and other economically important minerals.[22] Many of these indicator plants also actively concentrate these minerals to higher levels than are found in the soil, though not all do. According to geobotanist R. R. Brooks, most mineral concentrators are herbaceous plants, an observation that parallels those of the studies discussed earlier. However, this field appears wide open for a great deal of basic research, since so little testing has taken place. In the meantime, volume 2, appendices 1 and 3 include lists of dynamic accumulators from reasonably reliable sources, the best plants of which we summarize in table 5.4.

Like most nitrogen-fixers, many dynamic accumulators aggressively colonize sites as any early- to midsuccession species would. Their ability to mine the soil for nutrients allows them to survive in a nutrient-poor environment, or to catch and hold rapidly leaching nutrients in a disturbed environment. Many dynamic accumulators are deep-rooted plants, so you can use them to concentrate minerals scarce in your topsoil but less scarce in your parent material, or to catch and recycle leaching nutrients before the system loses them completely. Whether they can accumulate minerals scarce in both your topsoil and your parent material is unclear, and

probably depends on the species you are using. Most forest gardens should probably include plants that accumulate the most leachable limiting nutrients (N, P, K, Ca) as a matter of course, unless they are abundant in the parent material.

The comfreys (*Symphytum* spp.) reign as kings of the dynamic accumulators.[23] Comfreys accumulate six different minerals (including N, K, and Ca) to higher than average levels, they produce abundant biomass, and their leaves decompose rapidly. They absorb large amounts of nitrogen and can recycle nutrients from wastewater and human excrement into usable farm products. Their roots are extremely persistent, however, so the plants are hard to remove once in place, and most species will "walk" around the garden to at least some degree. Russian comfrey (*Symphytum* x *uplandicum*) will not walk, however, and stays in its place. Michael Phillips, orchardist and author of *The Apple Grower*, recently started using comfrey under his apple trees. He says that it creates excellent soil and allows the trees' roots to come to the surface to feed,[24] unlike grass ground covers.[25] The comfreys produce beautiful flowers and provide overwintering sites for many beneficial insects and spiders.

Nettles (*Urtica dioica*) are another excellent dynamic accumulator (of seven nutrients, including N, K, and Ca) and are commonly used along with comfrey in English forest gardens for mulch, compost, fertilizing "teas" (see "Compost Tea" in volume 2, chapter 5), and animal fodder. Nettles also produce nutritious spring greens and high-quality fiber for paper or cloth. Their stinging hairs, their tendency to spread by seed and rhizomes, and the fact that some botanists consider nettles an invasive exotic make it advisable to plant with caution, however. Our native nettles relative, the shade-loving wood nettle (*Laportea canadensis*), has many similar uses and is a prime candidate for dynamic accumulator research.

Though understory plants generally contain more nutrients, trees can also act as dynamic accumulators. Flowering dogwood trees (*Cornus florida*)

TABLE 5.4. Best dynamic-accumulator plants currently known, and the nutrients they gather. All accumulate the most critical nutrients: potassium, phosphorus, and calcium. See volume 2, appendices 1 and 3 for many more species, in both the main Plant Species Matrix and the Species by Function tables. Na=sodium; Si=silica. For other nutrient symbols see table 5.1.

Latin Name	Common Name	Nutrients Accumulated
Betula lenta	black birch	Ca, K, P
Carya ovata	shagbark hickory	Ca, K, P
Chamaemelum nobile	German chamomile	Ca, K, P
Cornus florida	flowering dogwood	Ca, K, P
Juglans nigra	Black walnut	Ca, K, P
Nasturtium officinale	watercress	Ca, K, P, Mg, Fe, Na, S
Rumex spp.	sorrels and docks	Ca, K, P, Fe, Na
Symphytum spp.	comfreys	Ca, K, P, Fe, Mg, Si
Taraxacum officinale	dandelion	Ca, K, P, Cu, Fe, Mg, Si
Urtica dioica	nettles	Ca, K, S, Cu, Fe, Na, N

selectively absorb calcium at high levels, with the element accounting for between 2 and 4 percent of total leaf weight.[26] While dogwood leaf litter can slowly build soil calcium levels as a result, we also know that within twenty-four hours, rainfall can leach up to 50 percent of the calcium and more than 80 percent of the potassium out of apple leaves still on the tree.[27] Researchers in Sweden found that old oak trees took calcium from deep in the soil profile and returned it to the ground during rainstorms as it leached from leaves. The rainwater became enriched with calcium as it dripped through the branches and leaves (throughfall) or ran down the branches and stem to the ground (stemflow). Nutrient-demanding herbs frequently grew near the base of oak trees large enough to produce appreciable stemflow.[28] A large percentage of the nutrients captured by understory vegetation can be from canopy throughfall, either directly absorbed into understory leaves or taken up from the soil.[29] In this way, the understory plants capture formerly deep soil nutrients before they can leach back into deep soil layers again.

A Note on Time, Nitrogen-Fixers, and Dynamic Accumulators

Organic farming advocates and scientists claim that most of the nitrogen fixed by legumes in a rotation is not available to other plants until the legumes die or get tilled into the soil, since the legume uses most of the nitrogen for its own growth. The nitrogen then becomes available to the following crop after the dead legumes decompose. In perennial woody systems, the situation is somewhat different because we generally do not till the soil.

By many accounts, it takes years or decades for the benefits of dynamic accumulators and nitrogen-fixers to reach non-dynamic accumulators and non-nitrogen-fixers. By these accounts, the simplest explanation for the transmission of nitrogen to non-nitrogen-fixers is through leaf litter, rather than through root grafting, mycorrhizas, or accumulation in the soil from root exu-

dates. At least one researcher says "no evidence exists" demonstrating these pathways.[30] The same may be true of dynamic accumulators. Three points cast doubt on these doubts.

First, given the importance and volume of root shedding in forest soils, it seems appropriate to consider the impact of this pathway for transmitting nutrients to other species (we'll discuss root shedding in the next section). Second, since nutrients can leach so quickly from tree leaves to the understory and soil, then why not from herbaceous dynamic accumulators and nitrogen-fixers? Both these pathways could pass nutrients into the soil ecosystem at faster and higher rates than annual leaf litterfall, particularly when one considers that pruning plants causes both root shedding and leaf litterfall at the same time. Third, perhaps the most immediate benefit to the system, if not to the crop plants themselves, is that dynamic accumulators catch leaching nutrients before they get away and bring them back into play. Plugging nutrient leaks is no small matter from an ecological and system perspective.

So, while it may take time to increase soil fertility using dynamic accumulators and nitrogen-fixers, these plants probably play a key role in preventing losses that the system would have to make up before any gains could register. This benefit probably begins accruing at a system level once the dynamic accumulators are fully rooted, while improved nutrition to other plants may not show up for a while. In the meantime, cutting back dynamic accumulators and nitrogen-fixers for use as mulch will spread the nutrients they gather. Cutting also releases nutrients into the soil from root dieback. You can also compost the plants or use them to make fermented fertilizing teas. However, depending on your soil test results, you should probably not abandon the application of slow-release fertilizers in the establishment phase of your forest garden, given that it takes time to get these nutrient cycles going.

Since we want to mimic the anatomy of healthy, self-renewing forest fertility, we need to work with and understand the system as a whole and how to foster all nine of these nutrient plugs. Though mineral cation exchange capacity and the dynamics of soil organic matter greatly affect nutrient conservation, these processes are generally well known, at least within the organic farming and gardening community. We will leave the in-depth discussion of these topics to other authors. We will also let rest the subject of secondary mineral clay synthesis in the B horizon and its role in nutrient retention. We will, however, take a closer look below at the roles of soil organisms and plants. Since plants play multiple keystone roles in the soil ecosystem, we will discuss them first.[31]

PLANT ROOTS: ENGINES OF THE UNDERGROUND ECONOMY

The student of plant production should have a vivid, mental picture of the plant as a whole. It is just as much a biological unit as an animal. The animal is visible as an entity and behaves as one. If any part is injured, reactions and disturbance of the whole organism are expected. But in the plant, our mental conception is blurred by the fact that one of the most important structures is underground. Nor is the plant usually treated as an entity; it is often mutilated by pruning, cutting, and injuring the root system, frequently without much regard to the effect upon the remaining portion.

—JOHN WEAVER AND WILLIAM BRUNER, *Root Development of Vegetable Crops* (1927)

Many people imagine that a tree's root structure is a mirror image of its aboveground trunk and branches; one sees such images presented in many places. Is it true, though? In addition, most gardeners grow annuals or perennials whose roots, many assume, don't go very deep. In this case, one may reason that we need only concern ourselves with the upper 1 or maybe 2 feet (30 to 60 cm) of soil, for that is where

we can have the most impact and where our efforts make the most difference. It is a good idea to question our assumptions occasionally, and to see what we can learn from the exercise. Which of our "deep-rooted myths"[32] have dynamite under them, and which stand on solid ground?

It makes sense that the dark and hidden world of soil and roots would generate myths and controversy, even among scientists who study such things. For example, in his 1927 work plant ecologist John Weaver wrote:

An intimate knowledge of the habits of growth of the root systems of . . . crops will enable the grower to space plants to better advantage. It should also permit him to intercrop or grow in succession crops or mixtures [so] that the soil volume will have a better distribution of roots and thus permit methods of more intensive cultivation.[33]

Decades later, in his 1989 work, plant ecologist Thomas O. Perry wrote:

Plant roots can grow anywhere—in the soil, on the surface of the soil, in the water, and even in the air. Except for the first formed roots that respond positively to gravity, most roots do not grow toward anything or in any particular direction. Root growth is essentially *opportunistic* in its timing and its orientation. It takes place whenever and wherever the environment provides the water, oxygen, minerals, support, and warmth necessary for growth.[34]

Notice the apparent difference of opinion between Weaver's and Perry's statements above: Weaver assumes that plants have habits of root growth, while Perry believes they are completely opportunistic and exhibit no consistent patterns. Both scientists base their statements upon direct observation and experience. What are we to make of that? Of course, the answer is that this is not an either-or question; both assertions are true to a degree that varies depending on the species in question, as well as the circumstances in which the plants find themselves. Once again, we find there are few or no simple answers, only a whole new realm to explore. Let us begin that exploration, for, as Weaver says, understanding patterns of root distribution in the soil will help us design polycultures more effectively. Meanwhile, their opportunism can tell us things about the soil that only the plants know and can help our forest gardens overcome our oversights and mistakes.

Our exploration will focus on the following questions:

- In what patterns do plant roots grow, and why?
- What functions and effects do plant roots have?
- How do our answers to the above affect our design and management decisions?

We'll begin by examining rooting patterns in trees and shrubs, since more information exists about them and they form the core of our forest-garden plant palette.

Tree and Shrub Root Structure, Patterns, and Function

The first important point to make is that most tree and shrub roots grow *horizontally* through the soil near the surface, not vertically or in a mirror image of the tree branches. "The general direction of the framework system of roots is radial and horizontal."[35] The top 1 to 2 feet (30 to 60 cm) of soil typically contains 60 to 80 percent of tree roots by weight, and the top 3 feet (1 m) up to 99 percent of root mass, according to a large number of researchers.[36] This is particularly true in humid climates, whereas the roots of prairie trees and herbs go much deeper on a regular basis. The large, highly visible, perennial roots of trees may possess a less horizontal pattern (see below); however, most of a tree's root mass consists of small-diameter lateral roots, as well as spongy root fans and fine "feeder" roots less than $1/16$ inch (1 mm) thick

searching for the nutrients concentrated in the top-soil. It is difficult to represent accurately the mass of fine roots in the topsoil because they are simply too small and too numerous to show. The large distances tree roots cover, and the root-size changes from the trunk base to the most far-flung fine roots, make accurate representation of whole root systems extremely difficult. Remember this as you peruse the illustrations of tree root systems in this chapter.

Major tree roots near the trunk may start as thick as 12 inches (30 cm) in diameter and rapidly decrease in thickness as they branch and rebranch in the first 3 to 15 horizontal feet (1 to 5 m). The resulting ropelike $1/4$- to 1-inch-thick (10 to 25 mm thick) main laterals spread everywhere, branching more often in good soils and growing straight through less fertile or already occupied areas (see figure 5.9). From these main laterals, the fine root fans grow outward and upward, forming large fibrous mats of very small roots often called "feeder" or "absorbing" roots (figure 5.10).[37] Do not let the names confuse you, though: several researchers have shown that *all* tree roots can absorb water and nutrients about equally on a surface-area basis. Even fat, woody roots contribute significant amounts of calcium, phosphorus, water, and other nutrients to trees.[38] However, while the surface area of trees' root systems is usually greater than the surface area of their leaves,[39] the majority of this area consists of fine roots. The greater surface area of fine roots, plus the much larger populations of mycorrhizal fungi on them, increases the relative importance of younger, small-diameter roots for absorption. Fine roots and root mats are also important because they are ephemeral.

Root Systems Grow and Die on Their Own Schedule
Most research shows that tree roots grow on a different annual schedule than aboveground tissues. The fine roots and spongy root fans that wild forest trees put out grow and die on an annual or even

FIGURE 5.9. A single tree root can spread dozens of feet from the trunk and head in multiple directions as it branches among other trees. These red maple roots continue somewhat farther than is shown since some of the root tips were not found. Note that each of the other trees shown are doing the same thing in the same space. Root competition in this stand is therefore rather intense. *Adapted from Lyford and Wilson, 1964.*

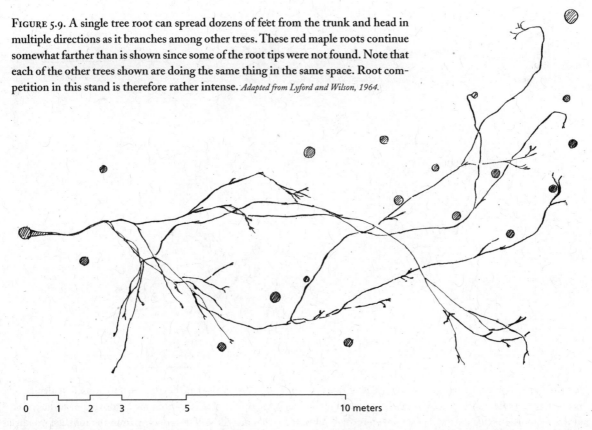

0 1   2   3   5   10 meters

more frequent basis, depending on climate and soil conditions: "the population and concentration of roots in the soil are as dynamic as the population of leaves in the air, if not more so."[40] When soil conditions are favorable, fine roots grow. When they aren't, the fine roots die. Trees may shed a root because it gets injured, because that root is receiving heavy competition or herbivory, because the soil resources in the area the root explores have petered out, or because the tree needs the nutrients and energy stored in that root for shoot growth or fruiting. Lack of rainfall is a frequent cause of surface root dieback, and roots often die for no apparent reason. This growth-and-death cycle can occur more than once in a growing season. It feeds the soil food web a tremendous amount of organic matter and nutrients each year, representing perhaps twice as much nutrient loss from trees as the annual leaf litterfall.[41] A large percentage of tree

nutrient uptake simply replaces losses such as these, as well as leaching losses from leaves.[42] Root shedding and regrowth also take a lot of energy from the tree. Maintaining good soil conditions will aid crop production by limiting root shedding to only that which is healthy and natural, as opposed to shedding caused by stress.

The ephemeral roots also help the tree adapt to dynamic, patchy forest resources. For example, the patterns of tree canopy leaves and branches may concentrate rain throughfall in one area. The soil under this spot will receive more nutrients and water, but this resource may not be in the same place the next year, or it may disappear altogether. Ephemeral roots help trees adapt to these changing circumstances. In addition, fine roots can act as a scouting party. They can tell a tree how big and tasty your new compost pile is so it can decide whether to create permanent roots to seize on the opportunity.

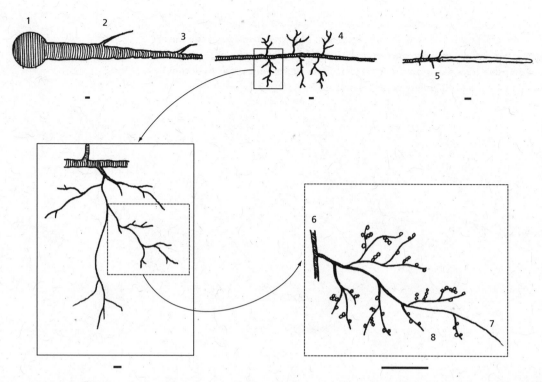

FIGURE 5.10. Tree roots range across so many scales of size over such large distances that they are hard to accurately depict. This schematic diagram offers a view of the whole root system including 1) the trunk; 2) adventitious roots growing near the trunk; 3) lateral woody roots growing off the tapering main root; 4) nonwoody, ephemeral root fans growing from the ropelike woody lateral; 5) budding first-order nonwoody roots behind the woody root tip; 6) second- and third-order nonwoody roots growing from the first-order nonwoody roots; 7) nonmycorrhizal soft root tip with root hairs; and 8) mycorrhizal fourth-order nonwoody roots. The horizontal bar beneath each image represents about 1 centimeter (0.4 inch). *Adapted from Lyford and Wilson, 1964.*

Overall root-system growth generally begins well before shoot growth in spring. Most trees in most years grow roots at their fastest clip in spring and early summer, with root growth ending as shoot growth peaks. Weather can delay, shorten, or stop this growth spurt, as can pruning nondormant trees, carrying a heavy fruit crop, or defoliation by insects. In most cases, root growth slows or stops in midsummer and picks up again in the late summer or fall after shoot growth or fruiting is complete, or as the weather moistens. These patterns appear to vary by species as well: some trees may have more than two root-growth peaks in a year (as is the case for some apples), and some only one in the spring (as is the case for pear, plum, and cherry). Apricot roots appear to grow most of the year.[43]

Spring shoot- and root-growth rates usually exceed a plant's nutrient uptake capacity. Therefore, autumn root growth and nutrient absorption appear critical for building nutrient reserves for the following year's growth and production. Trees build these reserves primarily in the fall after fruiting is over and leaves have fallen off the tree. Roots can actively grow and soak up nutrients all winter long if soil temperatures remain above 40°F (5°C).[44] Well-mulched soil can prolong the winter period where this is true.

A Reprise: Roots Spread Well Past the Tree Crown
It bears repeating here that tree roots spread well beyond the dripline of the tree crown, to between one and one half and three times the diameter of fruit-tree canopies (less in deep, fertile soils more in

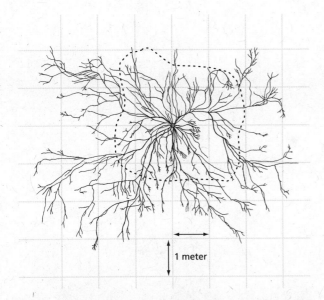

FIGURE 5.11. Numerous studies have shown that tree roots spread well beyond a tree's crown or dripline. They also do not necessarily spread equally in all directions. The dotted line is this fruit tree's crown. The squares are 1 meter (3.3 feet) on a side. *Adapted from Rogers and Vyvyan, 1934.*

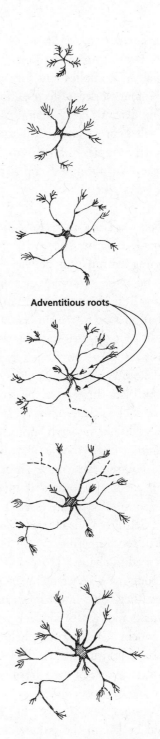

FIGURE 5.12. As a tree grows, the fine roots grow outward in an expanding circle. Eventually, as roots age and die (dashed lines), the tree grows younger adventitious roots starting at or near the trunk. It behooves us to attend to soil health under our trees as much as we do out from the crown if we want to give these roots the best soil possible.

shallow or infertile soils; see figure 5.11), or between one and four times the tree height for native forest trees. Fruit tree roots cover a horizontal area about five times the horizontal area of the tree's crown, or between four and seven times the crown area for native forest trees.[45] These ratios of crown to root spread vary somewhat from species to species and soil type to soil type, but they are good average figures. Also notice that the tree roots in figure 5.11 do not spread equally in all directions: researchers have found that up to half of the roots of apple trees may grow in one-quarter of the circle around the tree.[46]

Innies and Outies: Concentric Root Growth

As trees grow, the area of profuse fine-root growth moves outward along the main laterals (see figure 5.12), usually staying *outside* the dripline of the tree crown. As the tree ages, this outer ring of fine roots expands further and further. Eventually, adventitious roots begin to grow out from the base of the trunk to fill in the space left without fine roots near the trunk. As these "innies" develop, the tree often begins to shed portions, or even whole branches, of "outie" lateral roots.[47] These patterns of root growth over a tree's life span have implications for the patterns of soil-improvement work and fertilization we undertake. Keeping dynamic accumulators growing under fruit trees will improve the soil as the tree grows. Then, when the "innies" start to grow later in the tree's life, they will meet soil enriched during the intervening years.

Minglers, Bonders, and Loners: Root Interlacing, Grafting, and Avoidance

Root mingling within and between tree species appears to be rather common, though scientists seem to know little about the extent of vertical partitioning that goes on in the process. For example, native forest root systems overlap and interlace tremendously as they "go for an explore in the woods," to quote Winnie the Pooh (see figure 5.9; note that the black circles are the stems of other trees, whose root systems also occupy the space shown). In addition, research indicates that pear trees will mingle their roots with those of other pears.[48] Of course, even such "minglers" avoid mixing their roots with others' if they can, especially when confronted with closely packed stems (as in figure 5.13). It thus appears that necessity is the mother of root mingling.

As mentioned in chapter 1, over 160 tree species graft their roots with other members of the same species when they come into contact underground, and some make root grafts with members of other species or genera. Grafting may help balance out nutrient imbalances within a stand, as well as aiding plant communication through hormones for bud break, flowering, defense, and so on. One Finnish researcher recommends "that the old roots [of cut trees] should be left in the ground, since . . . the roots of a felled tree can continue to live and nourish a neighboring and still living tree with the roots of which they are in contact."[49] Known "bonders" include some wild nut tree species (table 5.5), but

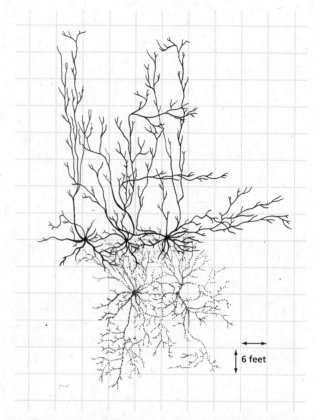

6 feet

FIGURE 5.13. Mingling of tree roots happens all the time. In this nine-year-old planting of Asiatic elm (solid lines) and osage orange (dashed lines) hedgerow, the area of mingling was about 29 percent of the total root area, even though the roots had plenty of room to grow elsewhere. Each square is about 6 feet (2 m) per side. *Adapted from Bunger and Thomson, 1938.*

few studies of root grafting deal with useful crop trees. Native eastern deciduous forest trees generally bond at least within species, though interspecies grafting is reportedly common.

At the other extreme, some "loner" trees not only will *not* root graft with other trees of their own species, but also avoid mingling their roots with them altogether. For example, research indicates that apple, persimmon, and peach roots usually do not intermingle with roots from others of their own species.[50] However, as far as we know loners will usually intermingle their roots with those of *other* species (figure 5.14).

Some speculate that apple roots don't intermingle

TABLE 5.5. Known root-grafting species of interest to edible forest gardeners, including eastern deciduous forest natives, common landscape trees, and species listed in the Plant Species Matrix of volume 2. What affects one tree may affect another grafted to it, including diseases, pollutants, and herbicides. Self-grafting is when a tree grafts to its own roots. Intraspecies grafts occur between two trees of the same species. Interspecies grafts occur between different species. R = rare; O = occasionally; C = common; X = observed by researchers, frequency not noted; varies = variable by species (some do, some don't); ? = researcher believes it does, but no firm evidence. *Data from Graham and Bormann, 1966.*

Latin name	Common name	Self	Intraspp.	Interspp.	Notes/Spp. known to graft with
Abies spp.	firs	X	O	C	
Acer platanoides	Norway maple			X	*Acer negundo*
Acer rubrum	red maple	C			
Acer saccharinum	silver maple	C			
Acer saccharum	sugar maple	C			
Betula alleghaniensis	yellow birch	X	X	?	
Betula lenta	black birch	X	C	?	
Betula nigra	river birch	X			
Betula papyrifera	paper birch				
Carya spp.	hickories			X	*Quercus nigra, Q. stellata, Ulmus* spp.
Fagus grandifolia	American beech	C	C		
Fagus sylvatica	European beech	X	X		
Fraxinus americana	white ash		C		
Larix laricina	larch	C	C		
Liquidambar styraciflua	sweetgum	C	C		
Picea spp.	spruces		O-C		*P. glauca, P. mariana* do not graft.
Pinus cembra var. *sibirica*	Siberian stone pine		C		
Pinus jeffreyi	Jeffrey pine		C		
Pinus strobus	white pine	C	C		
Pinus spp.	pines	varies	varies	R	many graft within species
Populus spp.	aspens, cottonwood	X	C		
Quercus acutissima	sawtooth oak		X		
Quercus alba	white oak	R	O-C	X	*Quercus rubra*
Quercus macrocarpa	bur oak	R–C	R–C		
Quercus spp.	oaks	R	R–C	varies	mostly other oaks when it happens
Rhus copallina	winged sumac		C?		
Robinia pseudoacacia	black locust		X		
Sassafras albidum	sassafras		C?		
Sophora japonica	Japanese pagoda tree		X		
Tilia americana	basswood	C			
Tilia spp.	lindens			X?	
Tsuga canadensis	eastern hemlock	C	C		
Ulmus spp.	elms			X	*Carya* spp.

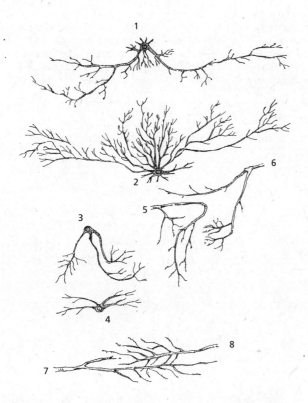

FIGURE 5.14. Some trees prefer not to mingle their roots with each other under any circumstances. They will go out of their way to avoid it, especially if they are of the same species. Trees 1 and 2 are peaches, 3 through 7 are apples, and 8 is a sweet cherry. Note that the apple and sweet cherry are mingling, though the apple has few rootlets on the side of the cherry.
Adapted from Kolesnikov, 1971.

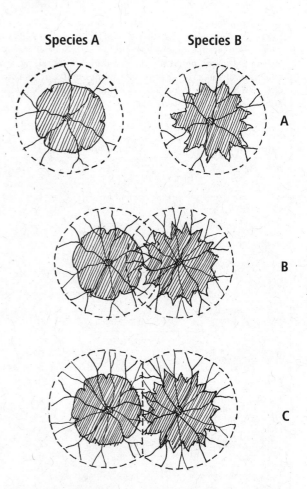

Species A   **Species B**

A

B

C

FIGURE 5.15A–C. Do root areas add or fold together in polycultures? Assume species A and B each have a 30-foot root diameter when grown alone (a: 706 sq. ft. root area each; total for two trees 1,412 sq. ft.). What happens when they grow close to each other? Do the root areas overlap (b: exclusive root area 538 sq. ft. each, shared area 168 sq. ft. each, total area 1,244 sq. ft.)? Or do they just shift their root areas away from each other (c: resulting in the same root areas as diagram a)? Obviously it depends on whether the species are minglers or loners. In either case, it would be good to know to help us design most effectively.

because of specific replant disease (see box 5.2). However, since individuals of the same species have the same resource requirements, they compete more intensely with each other than with trees of different species. Fruit trees tend to be very demanding of nutrients; so avoiding competition may contribute to a lack of desire to commingle roots. When planted densely, loners make greater use of the subsoil at an earlier age than less densely planted trees, *if the soil allows.*[51]

We need much more research to gauge how much intermingling is too much and how much trees can tolerate without losing productivity to root competition. Do the required root areas of trees add together or "fold" into one another when we are designing polycultures (figure 5.15)? Our expectation is that loners such as apples or peaches planted in monoculture will have additive root areas, while minglers will fold together to some degree, allowing denser plantings without sacrificing production. We still have much to learn to work out the practical specifics of these interactions. The rooting patterns

Box 5.2: Specific Replant Disease

Specific replant disease (also called apple decline, peach tree short life, and so on) is a mysterious syndrome that reduces tree vigor and shortens tree life when the same species or type of fruit grows in the same spot for more than one generation. The problem mainly affects large-scale growers, but it can cause problems for backyard orchards, too. The causes are unknown, symptoms vary from one place to the next, and the effects last in soil for up to fifteen years. Both biological and nonbiological factors appear to be involved in this problem, but the combinations of factors appear to vary with different crop species and regions.[52]

If you experience reduced vigor in trees planted where similar crops grew previously, moving the new trees can lead to recovery. The easiest preventive measure is to rotate your tree crops. Plant stone fruits (cherries, plums, prunes, peaches, apricots, nectarines) and pome fruits (apples, pears, quinces, hawthorns) in different places in each generation. Since animals probably dispersed these fruits far and wide in their natural setting, tree rotation mimics this natural disease-avoidance strategy. Researcher Dr. Elaine Ingham claims that specific replant disease results from changes in the soil food web as fruit trees mature, and that reinvigorating the soil food web will prevent the disease.[53] Work at Pennsylvania State University indicates that root nematodes transmit some forms of this disease. Planting cover crops of mustard family plants such as rape can reduce the nematode population.

Rooting Patterns and Depths Vary by Tree Species and Soil Conditions

Tree rooting patterns fall into three primary categories: taprooted, heart rooted, and flat rooted (see figure 5.16).[54] These three types have variations within them, with taprooted trees growing lateral roots to variable degrees, and flat-rooted trees growing short taproots or vertical roots called sinkers or strikers to a greater or lesser extent.

Of the 122 native trees cataloged by landscape architect Gary Hightshoe, not quite half are flat rooted, while about 30 percent are taprooted and another 30 percent are heart rooted. About 10 percent show more than one root type.[55] Whether these percentages hold for nonnative plants is another question. Species in the same genus (e.g., most hickories) often show similar root patterns. However, related species may also have completely different rooting patterns as one way they distinguish niches from each other (e.g., bur oak is taprooted while other oaks are heart or flat rooted). Only 9 percent of native trees cataloged by Hightshoe spread vegetatively, almost all of these by suckering.

Vegetative dispersal patterns arise from three methods: rhizomes, stolons, and root suckers. There is some confusion about these terms, and their use in the botanical literature varies, particularly with regard to shrubs. A rhizome is a modified stem that grows horizontally below the soil surface and from which new roots and shoots sprout; mints spread via rhizomes. A stolon is also a stem that grows horizontally from the mother plant and from which new shoots sprout and root, but stolons grow either on or above the soil surface, as in the case of strawberries, or above the soil but below the litter layer, as poison ivy sometimes does. Root suckers are shoots that grow from a true root belowground, either at the base of the plant or away from it. In this book, including the "habit" and "root pattern" columns of the Plant Species Matrix in volume 2, we call any woody rhizomatous or root-suckering plant a *suckering* plant if its shoots arise away from the base of the stem. These plants

of the various species can guide our design choices in this regard, but factors besides plant genetics help determine these patterns. Unfortunately, we know little or nothing about such root behavior among the vast majority of tree crops. Which species are loners, which are minglers, and which are bonders? It would be nice to know.

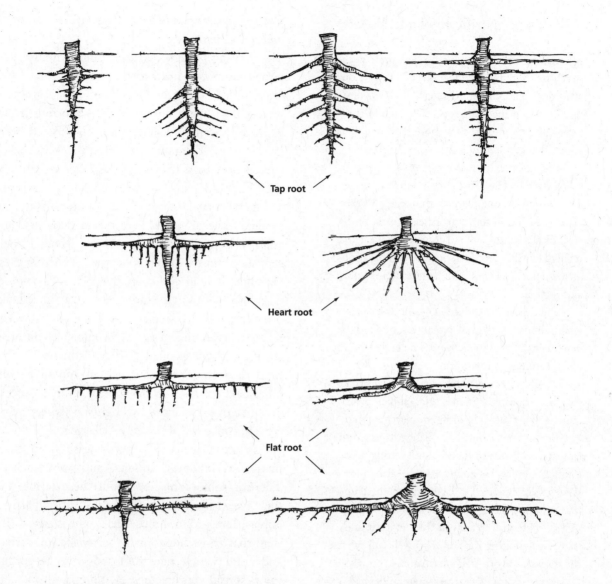

Tap root

Heart root

Flat root

FIGURE 5.16. Basic tree root patterns include taprooted, heart rooted, and flat rooted, but patterns vary from there. *Adapted from Kimmins, 1997, and Kolesnikov, 1971.*

have a thicket-forming or mat-forming habit. We also use the term stoloniferous when referring to root patterns, but stoloniferous woody plants may also have either thicket-forming or mat-forming habits. When a tree's extra shoots form only near the base of the stem, we say it has a *sprouting* habit, whether those sprouts arise from a rhizome, a root, or the crown of the plant (in shrubs, this is called a *multistemmed* habit). A number of trees we discuss

in this book are suckering, including American plum (*Prunus americana*), black locust (*Robinia pseudoacacia*), pawpaw (*Asimina triloba*), American persimmon (*Diospyros virginiana*), and sassafras (*Sassafras albidum*). The best examples of sprouting trees are the lindens (*Tilia* spp.).

While genetics may strictly determine root pattern in some plant species, soil and "social" conditions may carry more influence in other, more

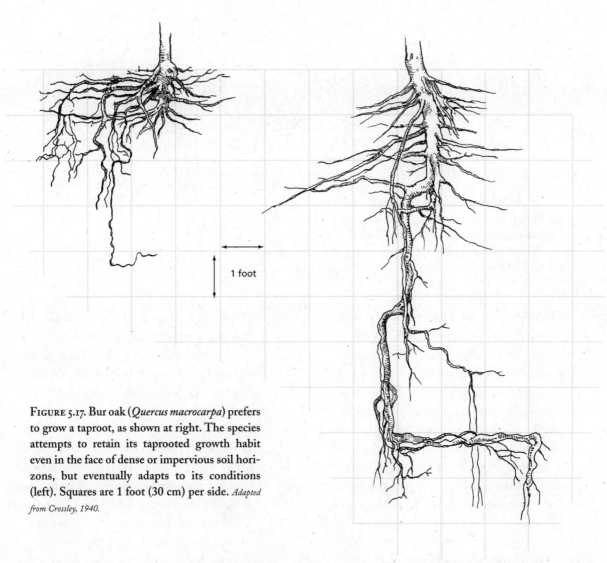

1 foot

FIGURE 5.17. Bur oak (*Quercus macrocarpa*) prefers to grow a taproot, as shown at right. The species attempts to retain its taprooted growth habit even in the face of dense or impervious soil horizons, but eventually adapts to its conditions (left). Squares are 1 foot (30 cm) per side. *Adapted from Crossley, 1940.*

adaptable species. Even in species with flexible root patterns, juvenile tree roots express a characteristic form that adapts to soil conditions only after a set time that, again, varies by species. Hence, bur oak struggles to express its taprooted nature well into "adolescence" even in heavily compacted soils, but eventually it adapts to become more heart rooted (figure 5.17), while red maple roots adapt to soil conditions almost right out of the seed.[56] These differences in rooting habit and root-pattern flexibility influence the distribution and success of the species in different environments. Unfortunately, we know little about the rooting ecology of most trees, shrubs, and herbs.

We do know that these factors influence tree rooting patterns and depth:[57]

- Physical barriers, such as compact layers or unfractured bedrock, limit rooting depth (figure 5.18). If a layer is unfavorable and roots can get below it, they may proliferate in the deeper layers (figure 5.19).
- Roots tend to branch more often in fine soils than in sandy soils, though clay soils can become limiting.
- Wetness or poor soil aeration kills roots due to lack of oxygen and the buildup of toxic compounds and hence can also limit rooting

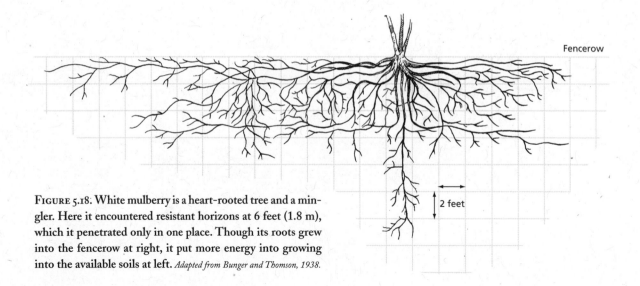

Fencerow

2 feet

FIGURE 5.18: White mulberry is a heart-rooted tree and a min-
gler. Here it encountered resistant horizons at 6 feet (1.8 m),
which it penetrated only in one place. Though its roots grew
into the fencerow at right, it put more energy into growing
into the available soils at left. *Adapted from Bunger and Thomson, 1938.*

depth. Seasonal high water tables that limit
rooting depth can lead, paradoxically, to
drought stress during periods of low rainfall
because roots are shallow.

- Cold soil temperatures slow root growth, so
  that deeper layers in cooler climates may not
  have as many roots as upper layers, which warm
  faster in the spring. The opposite may be true
  in southern areas: deeper layers may not freeze,
  and therefore deep roots may grow all winter.

- Fertile soil speeds root growth and can either
  promote more fine roots at all depths, or lead to
  root growth only in the fertile layers. Infertile
  soils slow root growth and foster shallow fine-
  root systems. If water is very scarce, however,
  there may be no root pattern differences
  between fertile and infertile soils.

- Interactions with other plants, such as root
  grafting, avoidance, and allelopathy, will change
  root patterns. Competition or the dynamics of
  the soil food web can limit tree roots to deeper
  layers or prevent them from growing into a particular area (notice the fencerow to the right side
  in figure 5.18). Dense planting, especially a
  monoculture of loner trees, pushes roots to grow
  into deeper layers if they can. Whether that is a
  good thing depends on soil, water, and climate
  conditions.

- Chemicals in the soil, such as aluminum and
  manganese toxicity from acid rain, may limit or
  alter root growth. Damaged or poorly developed
  soil food webs can lead to poor decomposition
  of pesticides or of natural wastes from plants
  and soil organisms. These chemicals can inhibit
  root growth.[58]

- Dry-summer climates can induce deep rooting as
  plants search for water, while plants in regions
  with frequent summer showers may tend toward
  shallower root systems. John Weaver's work with
  native prairie perennials and vegetable crops
  showed very deep rooting, deeper than many
  reported tree-root depths in more humid climates. Weaver concluded that the high evaporation rates and dry summers of the prairie induced
  these deep rooting habits: "the amount of water
  lost from the aboveground parts reflects itself in
  the development and extent of the absorbing
  organs."[59] We must take climatic and soil factors
  into account when comparing root-pattern data.

- Irrigation can induce shallow rooting, according
  to some authors, while other research indicates
  that consistently irrigated crops send their roots
  deeper, and light irrigation does the opposite.[60]
  When released from water stress, apparently
  plants will seek nutrients wherever they can
  find them.

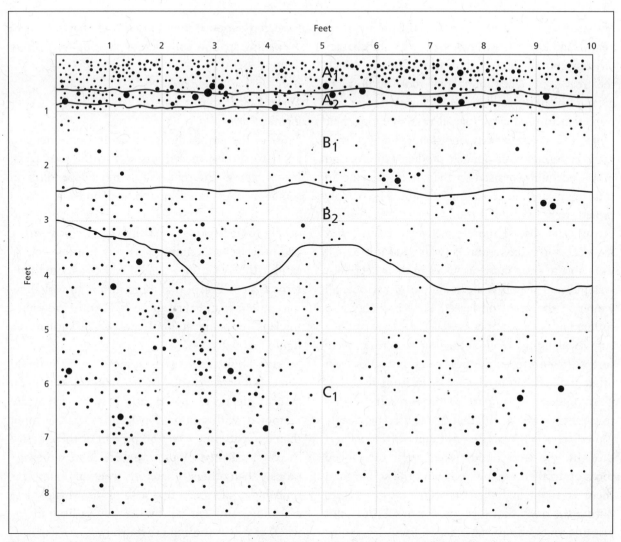

FIGURE 5.19. Even if restrictive layers are present (layer B_1), tree roots can sometimes proliferate below them. Each circle on this drawing represents an apple tree root where it crosses the wall of a soil pit in an orchard in upstate New York. *Adapted from Oskamp and Batjer, 1932.*

• Plants growing in full sun have more energy available to promote deep rooting than do those growing in partial or full shade.

Under good soil conditions, tree roots will grow as deep as 50 feet (15 m),[61] and they commonly grow to depths exceeding 10 to 12 feet (3 to 4 m) when they can and the right species are present. Researchers have found apple tree roots extending deeper than 12 feet (4 m), though some authors claim apples are shallow rooted. How do these findings fit with the other findings that most roots lie within 2 to 3 feet (60 to 90 cm) of the surface? Are these deep roots as unimportant as some authors suggest?

Deeply Rooted Trees Do It Better
A. T. Sweet did a lot of digging in his day. In the late 1920s he spent several years assessing apple orchards on different soils in the Ozark Mountains of Arkansas and Missouri, and then later in western New York. Oskamp and Batjer complemented his work with extensive investigations in New York a

few years later.[62] They all correlated the productivity, health, and longevity of apple trees with the characteristics and layering of the various soils in which the trees grew. They found that most apple roots grew in the upper soil horizons. However, trees that were able to send even a small percentage of their roots into deep, aerated, moist-but-not-wet soils grew larger, survived longer, produced more, and produced more consistently than trees growing in soils with a limited rooting depth. The deeply rooted trees withstood the vagaries of weather, insects, and disease more effectively because they had access to more resources (water and nutrients), were able to store more resources in their deep root systems, and may have been able to grow roots all winter in the deep soil layers. They probably also suffered less competition, as well, since these monoculture plantings of nonmingling tree roots were sure to create stress if the trees could not avoid each other and get their needs met at the same time.

An interesting support to these results is that researchers have found that at least some deeply rooted trees can practice "hydraulic lift" during a drought: the trees pump water from their deep roots up to their shallow roots and the soil around them at night and then draw on these reserves during the day.[63] Since we know that all roots, not just fine roots, absorb water and nutrients, we know that deep roots can function to meet these needs. "The deeper portions of the root system are often particularly active as the crop approaches maturity. Nutrients absorbed by them may produce a pronounced effect both upon the quantity and quality of the crop yield."[64]

So it appears that deep soils are important for healthy, productive trees even though most roots grow near the surface. Deep soils allow deeper rooting, and therefore better nutrition and moisture supplies, and therefore higher and more stable yields, healthier and longer-lived trees, and better nutrient cycling for the system as a whole. Shallow soils have the opposite effects, and trees planted in them need more space to reduce competition.

Research supports the supposition that manually deepening shallow soils before planting trees offers major benefits.[65]

Shrub Root Patterns: Same as Trees, Plus Thicket Formers

Most of the points discussed about tree roots also apply to shrubs: most roots stay in the top layers; plants express different root patterns depending on some mix of genetic, climatic, and soil factors; roots grow on a different schedule than shoots; and deeply rooted plants resist the vagaries of weather and other stresses more effectively. Shrubs tend to exhibit the same tap-, heart-, and flat-rooted patterns as trees, except that more shrubs grow shallow root systems, and they more frequently grow into thickets by being stoloniferous or suckering (see figure 5.20b and c).

Gary Hightshoe's work indicates that over 80 percent of native shrubs are flat rooted, less than 20 percent are heart rooted, and only 5 percent are taprooted, with around 5 percent exhibiting more than one pattern.[66] Over 50 percent of these native shrubs spread by stolons or suckers, some more vigorously than others. Therefore, when in doubt, it is probably a safe guess that a shrub has shallow lateral roots. You can tell by the way a shrub grows whether it is spreading vegetatively.

Suckering or stoloniferous shrubs tend to form thickets and frequently develop beautiful rounded forms in oldfields as they spread outward from their point of origin. Shrubs use these vegetative expansion strategies to expand their territory into high-competition grassland or meadow environments. Unfortunately, much of the literature on shrubs calls them stoloniferous even when they are actually rhizomatous or root suckering or vice versa. While the growth patterns resulting from rhizomatous stoloniferous, and suckering habits are more or less the same, underground rhizome barriers may not hold back stoloniferous shrubs as easily as they do rhizomatous or root-suckering shrubs, so the distinctions can be important for design.

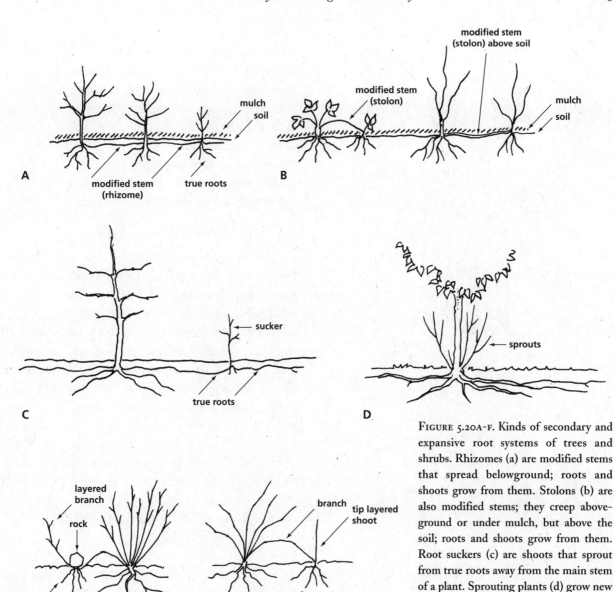

FIGURE 5.20A–F. Kinds of secondary and expansive root systems of trees and shrubs. Rhizomes (a) are modified stems that spread belowground; roots and shoots grow from them. Stolons (b) are also modified stems; they creep aboveground or under mulch, but above the soil; roots and shoots grow from them. Root suckers (c) are shoots that sprout from true roots away from the main stem of a plant. Sprouting plants (d) grow new shoots from the base of the stem or root crown. Layering (e) occurs when stems or branches root where they touch ground. Tip layering (f) is when a branch tip roots where it touches the ground.

Adventitious or secondary roots propagate from places other than the primary seed root or primary root crown, such as on branches or branch tips that touch the ground or become buried (as is the case for currants, gooseberries, and raspberries; see figure 5.20e), or as "innies" growing from the root crown or main roots. Floodplain trees such as pawpaw (*Asimina triloba*) can grow adventitious roots from stems buried by flooding. Shrubs root from branches and stems more frequently than trees. This fact makes various forms of layering a means of plant propagation both naturally and for human purposes. Layering works well with gooseberries and currants (*Ribes* spp.), for example. Shrubs that grow adventitious roots also frequently form thickets.

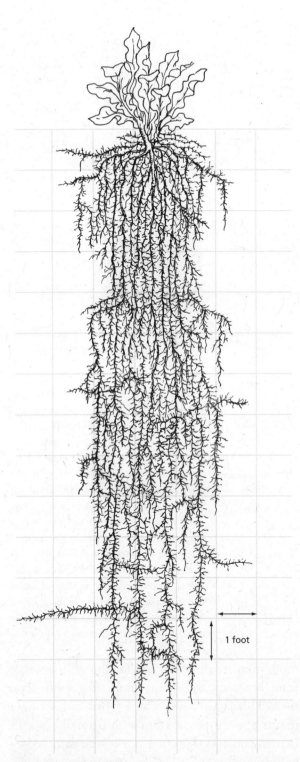

1 foot

FIGURE 5.21. Mature taproot system of a ten-year-old horse-radish plant (*Armoracia rusticana*) growing in semiarid conditions and deep soils. *Adapted from Weaver and Bruner, 1927.*

Since shrubs proliferate during midsuccession and after disturbance, it makes sense that many of them use vegetative propagation strategies to compete with grasses and forbs. Allowing thicket formers to form thickets within reason will reduce our work in management and reduce stress on the plants that want to grow that way. The challenge is finding ways to make these patterns work for us rather than complicating maintenance.

THE ROOTS OF HERBS

In contrast to trees and shrubs, one would think herbs would have much less flexibility when it comes to reaching out to find supplies. Their diminutive size and limited resources restrict their ability to go where no root has gone before, or at least it would seem that way. Surprisingly, the few studies on herbaceous perennial roots that our research turned up indicate these plants really can go places, both deep and wide, if they want. Yet only certain root structures allow widespread resource gathering, while others promote a "stand-and-deliver" approach. Understanding these structures will help us effectively partner perennial plants in our polycultures.

Roots, Rhizomes, Tubers, Corms, and Bulbs: A Brief Anatomy

Herbaceous perennial roots come in six basic packages, divided into roots and rootstocks. Roots take two different forms (taproots and fibrous roots), while the four kinds of rootstocks are actually modified stems or leaves. We shall briefly define each kind of root system and list a few of the better-known edibles that use them:

• Taproots, like their woody cousins, drive strongly downward, with secondary roots radiating outward from the central tap. Often forming as thick, fleshy storage organs, they usually contain high amounts of starch, which is why most of our root crops come from this category, including carrots, beets, parsnips, parsley, horseradish (figure 5.21), burdock, dandelion, chicory, and ginseng.

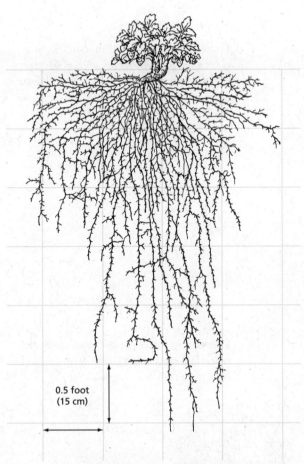

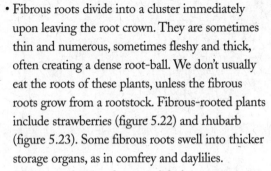

0.5 foot
(15 cm)

FIGURE 5.22. Fibrous roots of a three-year-old strawberry (*Fragaria virginiana*) in June after flowering and fruiting, in semiarid, deep soils. *Adapted from Weaver and Bruner, 1927.*

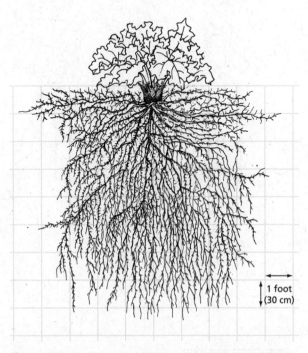

1 foot
(30 cm)

FIGURE 5.23. Fibrous roots of a four-year-old rhubarb (*Rheum* × *cultorum*) plant grown in deep, semiarid soils. Some of the roots grew beyond 10 feet (3 m), but the plant has many absorbing roots near the surface, too. *Adapted from Weaver and Bruner, 1927.*

- Fibrous roots divide into a cluster immediately upon leaving the root crown. They are sometimes thin and numerous, sometimes fleshy and thick, often creating a dense root-ball. We don't usually eat the roots of these plants, unless the fibrous roots grow from a rootstock. Fibrous-rooted plants include strawberries (figure 5.22) and rhubarb (figure 5.23). Some fibrous roots swell into thicker storage organs, as in comfrey and daylilies.
- Rhizomes develop from modified stems creeping horizontally through the soil. Roots and shoots sprout from the rhizome, and "leaves" on this "stem" usually take the form of scales that protect

the rhizome from the soil environment. Many woodland plants use rhizomes to creep around and find resource patches in the forest, creating large networks of seemingly separate plants. Though the rhizomes themselves may be at or near the soil surface, the roots can extend rather far down. Examples include asparagus (figure 5.24), ginger, licorice, and cattails.
- Tubers, technically the swollen tips of rhizomes, compose several of our common root crops and some good uncommon crops as well. Potatoes, sweet potatoes (figure 5.25), groundnuts, and Jerusalem artichokes all have tubers.

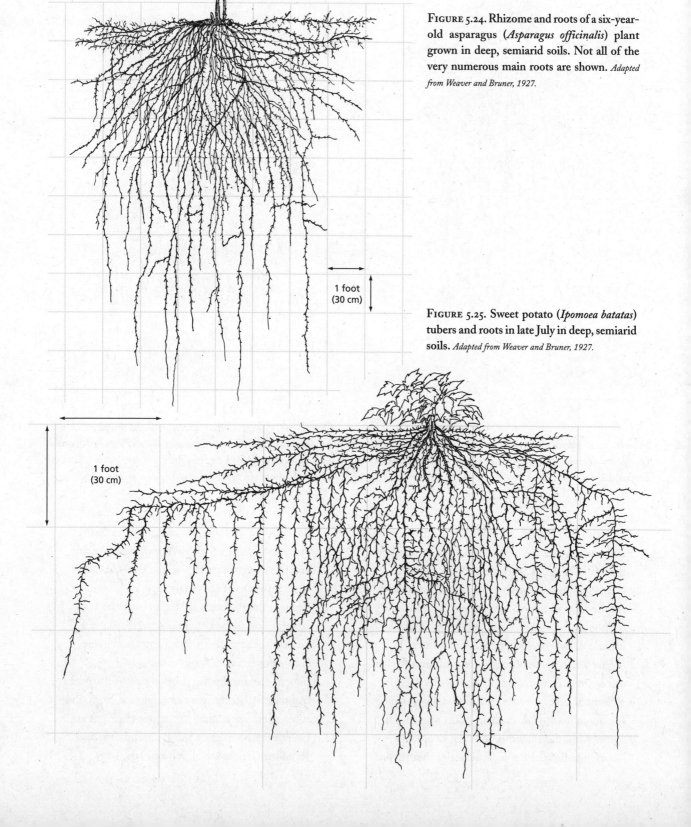

FIGURE 5.24. Rhizome and roots of a six-year-old asparagus (*Asparagus officinalis*) plant grown in deep, semiarid soils. Not all of the very numerous main roots are shown. *Adapted from Weaver and Bruner, 1927.*

1 foot
(30 cm)

FIGURE 5.25. Sweet potato (*Ipomoea batatas*) tubers and roots in late July in deep, semiarid soils. *Adapted from Weaver and Bruner, 1927.*

1 foot
(30 cm)

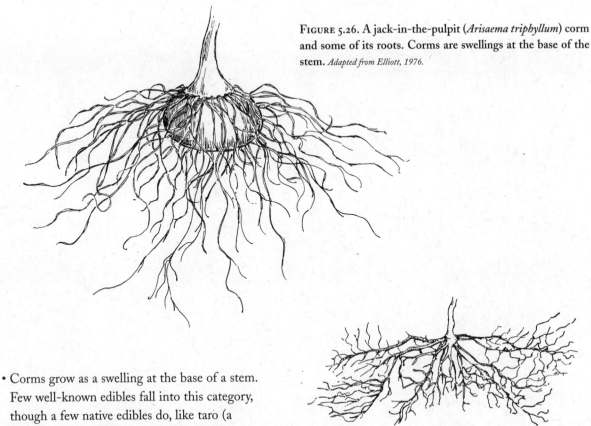

FIGURE 5.26. A jack-in-the-pulpit (*Arisaema triphyllum*) corm and some of its roots. Corms are swellings at the base of the stem. *Adapted from Elliott, 1976.*

FIGURE 5.27. Onions, like this nodding wild onion (*Allium cernuum*), form bulbs that consist of modified leaves as storage organs. *Adapted from Weaver, 1919.*

- Corms grow as a swelling at the base of a stem. Few well-known edibles fall into this category, though a few native edibles do, like taro (a better-known tropical food), jack-in-the-pulpit (figure 5.26), and spring beauty.
- Bulbs, made of layers of fleshy leaves that store nutrients and water, frequently produce a fibrous root system from their base. Most know bulbs such as garlic and onions, while nodding wild onion (figure 5.27), ramps, Turk's-cap lily, and wood lily are less well-known.

We recommend two things here: finding a copy of Douglas Elliott's *Wild Roots* for excellent illustrations of many edible and medicinal roots and rootstocks, and carefully excavating a few plants once in a while to get a picture in your mind of the entire organism with which you are dealing.

Run, Rhizome, Run: Horizontal Patterns

A plant's root form is integral to, and strongly influences, the plant's means of dispersal. It affects the horizontal patterns within which the plants grow. In this regard, we could say that rhizomes run, bulbs divide and conquer, tubers mass, taproots scatter, fibrous roots clump, and corms colonize.

Not all rhizomes run. Some walk, some crawl, some cruise. Some die at the back end as they grow forward. Others just continue to amass stems and roots along much of their length, forking and reforking into a crowd, or a smattering, of leaves and stems that seem like different plants (see figure 5.28). Linking disparate parts of themselves with rhizomes, and sometimes stolons, allows the herbs to cobble together a living on the forest floor, gathering water from one place, nitrogen from another, and sunlight from another. They may also move

A

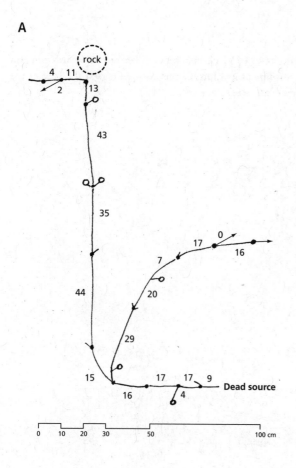

B

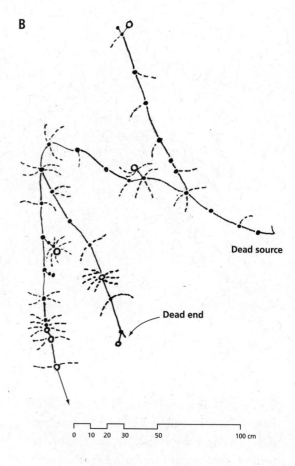

C

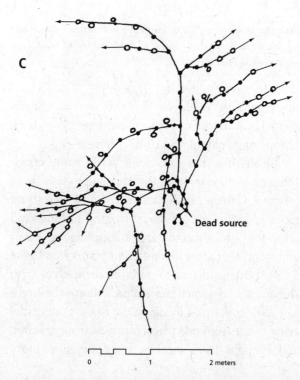

FIGURE 5.28A–C. Rhizomes like these run in different patterns, rooting and shooting along the way. If shown, o indicates the locations of leaves or shoots; dashed lines the locations of roots; numbers the number of roots along a segment; and dots the end of an annual growth increment. The "dead source" is the origin of growth. The varied locations of these different organs help the plant cobble together a living on the patchy forest floor. Species shown: a) vanilla leaf (*Achlys triphylla*), b) queencup (*Clintonia uniflora*), c) starflower (*Smilacina stellata*).
Adapted from Antos and Zobel, 1984.

like a slow-moving brush fire, using up resources in one area and then moving on.

Bulbs divide, and redivide, and redivide, often forming large patches or masses of separate but related plants—one big, happy family. Hillsides in Vermont sometimes have delicious ramps (*Allium tricoccum*) growing in huge patches up to 30 feet (9 m) in diameter. The solid, rich green carpets scatter here and there along the slopes in the dappled light and late spring snow. The more they divide, the more they conquer, and more power to them!

Tuberous plants often grow in masses as new shoots sprout from tubers each year, creating more tubers, which then sprout. Jerusalem artichoke (*Helianthus tuberosus*) is a classic example, one that some people have found rather pestiferous. Once these babies get their tubers full of stored sunlight, they are hard to get out of the ground, and any little piece you leave when you dig can come back to haunt you (pleasantly, we hope!). The easiest time to eliminate Jerusalem artichokes, or any tuberous plant if you should want to do so, is usually in summer after the rush of spring growth is complete, preferably during flowering. Then the roots are piddling affairs, easily uprooted and lacking persistence, at least in Jerusalem artichoke's case.

Taprooted herbs frequently have no means of transport except by seed, hence they scatter. Many of these plants are biennials; a number are vines. Many belong to the parsley family (Apiaceae, formerly the Umbelliferae), whose umbels of numerous tiny flowers become umbels of numerous tiny seeds. Others of this root type derive from the aster family (Asteraceae, formerly the Compositae) and have similar flowering and seeding habits. This seeding habit usually results in drifts of these plants scattered among other species.

Clumpy roots make for clumpy plants. Fibrous roots radiate from a core, the same core from which the shoots propagate. These clumps enlarge over time. Many clumpers reach a size and age where they may benefit from being sliced into two or more pieces and replanted, if that works for the particular species. Otherwise they devolve, ostensibly leaving room for their seed-born progeny to take their place.

Corms colonize. They may grow standing singly, at least to start, but they usually spread into clumps, masses, or carpets. Animals of one sort or another probably disperse the small numbers of large seeds many of them produce, but they often also create offsets belowground that spread into a colony from one plant standing alone.

Rooting Depths of Herbaceous Perennials

As figures 5.21 through 5.25 show, most of the cultivated perennial vegetables excavated by Weaver and friends in the 1920s rooted rather deeply (more than 3 feet, or 1 m), with the exception of strawberries, which generally root shallowly. Note that Weaver conducted this work in Nebraska and Oklahoma, both environments with high evaporation rates, and periods of moderate drought during the studies. The soils were deep, fertile loams with no major limiting layers, deeply charged with water from winter rains, and all plants grew in full sun. All of these factors promoted deep root growth, and the plants responded to them. The bulk of these plants' roots lay in the upper 3 to 4 feet (1 to 1.3 m) of soil, except for the horseradish, and the deep rooting almost certainly helped these plants to thrive in this environment.

Weaver found similar root depths for annual crops such as corn, beets, lettuce, and carrots under these conditions.[67] Of course, the annuals' roots spend less time in deep soil than those of perennials, and this affects plant nutrition and soil nutrient cycles. Also note, however, that all of these plants grew in monocultures, so gauging the effect of polyculture conditions on root patterns is difficult.

Root-distribution studies similar to Oskamp and Batjer's work with apples in New York, but undertaken in mixed natural forests, indicate the same "bulk of roots in the topsoil" reality we discussed for trees. The problem with these studies is that the researchers did not separate and identify the roots they found by species, and they often did not dig down very far either, which casts some doubt on these statements.[68] However, that doesn't help us design underground polycultures; we need species-by-species root patterns for that. No one, as far as we know, has studied the rooting habits of most forest-garden-type plants in a manner like Weaver (tracing the roots of individual plants), either separately or in polycultures. It is safe to assume that the soil factors that affect tree rooting patterns will affect herb roots as well. Beyond that, we have to punt, using our knowledge of soil and climate factors and the little we know about herb, shrub, and tree roots. So how do we pull all of this together into some reasonably coherent approach to perennial polycultures? Let's start by looking at a well-studied natural herbaceous polyculture to see what we can learn, and then discuss all the implications.

ROOTS AND POLYCULTURES: PARTITIONING THE DARK WORLD

We talked in chapter 4 about how the species in resource-sharing guilds divide resources among themselves to reduce competition by occupying different niches in time, space, or kind. Vertical layering of vegetation aboveground is one manifestation of this principle. It makes sense that forest plants would do the same thing regarding soil and water resources. What evidence of root-system partitioning exists? Unfortunately, relatively few good studies of root systems exist anywhere, including for temperate deciduous forests. On this question, John Weaver comes to the fore again.

Dividing the Soil Profile:
Prairie and Mountain Forest Observations
At a time when thousands of men were digging trenches to defend Europe in World War I, plant ecologist John Weaver and his colleagues traveled the dry Western plains and Rocky Mountains digging trenches, too. But they were mapping the root patterns of about 140 prairie, savanna, and forest plant species. They excavated more than 1,150

individual trees, shrubs, grasses, and herbs in a four-year period.[69]

In the case of prairie plants, Weaver did not limit himself to studies of the plants in isolation. He also studied natural polycultures. This work showed that the roots of more than half the prairie plants studied grew deeper than 5 feet (1.5 m), even as deep as 13 to 20 feet (4 to 6 m; they dug some of these trenches in clay!). The roots of about half the rest grew to depths between 2 and 5 feet (0.6 to 1.5 m). The balance, including most of the cool-season grasses, kept their roots in the top 2 feet (0.6 m) of soil. The deeper-rooted plants often had little branching and few absorptive roots in the upper soil horizons, leaving that space available for shallower-rooted species (figure 5.29). This partitioning of the soil by plants in the perennial polyculture "reduces competition and permits the growth of a larger number of species."[70] The species' root patterns also corresponded to their aboveground life history (or phenology): the shallow-rooted species tended to go dormant in the hotter, drier months, while the deepest-rooted species tended to be community dominants. This evidence of resource partitioning in a natural polyculture is tantalizing when one ponders the possibilities for designing edible forest gardens. What about forests?

Weaver's work in the Rocky Mountains included studies of root patterns in evergreen forests (dominant trees included ponderosa pine, Engelmann spruce, and Douglas fir). There he found that virtually all the forest plants grew most of their roots in the top 18 inches (45 cm) of soil. This apparently confirms reports that most plant roots stay in the top 2 feet (0.6 m) of soil, even in humid eastern forests and orchards. Could it be that prairies partition the soil while forests do not? We must be careful here.

Partitioning Limited Resources
At times during the growing season, the arid climate of the prairie completely depletes water reserves in the top 4 to 5 feet (1.2 to 1.5 m) of soil.

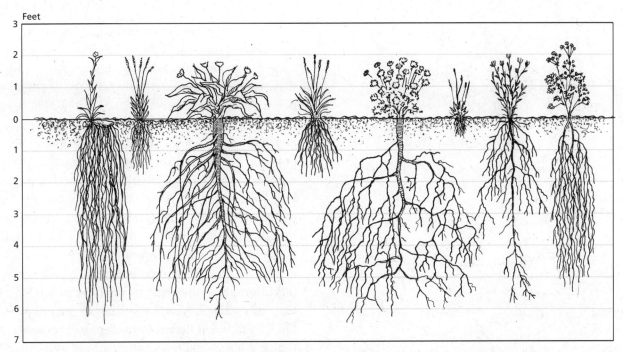

FIGURE 5.29. A natural polyculture of prairie species that functions as a resource-sharing guild. John Weaver found that half of the prairie species he researched had main absorbing roots deeper than 5 feet (1.6 m), one quarter had them between 2 feet and 5 feet (60 to 160 cm), and one quarter had them less than 2 feet deep (60 cm). The deepest-rooted plants were community dominants in the dry season. *Adapted from Weaver, 1919.*

But winter rains and spring snowmelt usually replenish the soil's water reserves. In addition, many prairie soils used to have topsoil several feet deep (until Western agriculture came along), so roots could grow far down without losing access to living soil. Thousands of years of coevolution may have also permitted competitive exclusion to create niche divergence among associated species.

The evergreen forests Weaver studied grew in the rain shadow on the eastern slope of the Rockies, so the climate was also dry. Though soil-moisture levels were never high in the thin topsoils Weaver found there, the surface 6 inches (15 cm) held the most moisture, with the soil getting drier with depth. Frequent summer showers kept surface moisture replenished, while the trees reduced soil temperatures, evaporation, and air movement so the surface wouldn't dry out. As Weaver said, "in general root position conformed strikingly with the distribution of soil moisture."[71] The obvious vertical soil partitioning of the prairies and the associated aboveground plant behaviors, as well as the surface roots of the mountain forest plants, reflect a response to a primary resource that is commonly scarce—water. So, does similar soil-profile partitioning happen in humid-climate forest soils? Given the paucity of serious studies like Weaver's in humid forest environments or any sort of humid perennial polyculture, we can only speculate and offer general guidelines at best.

Possibilities of Partitioning in Humid Forests

Obviously, a humid climate will not have the same resource limitations as an arid climate. We know that temperate deciduous forest soils tend to accumulate more nutrients than the plants need in a given year, and that more abundant rainfall is available to these forests. Therefore, the pressure to separate niches should be less than in the prairies. In some cases, there may be a primary limiting factor, such as water or nitrogen in sandy soils. In others, a mosaic of limiting factors may change over time.

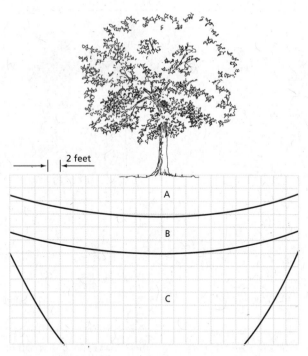

2 feet

A

B

C

FIGURE 5.30. The soil zones available to flat-rooted (A), heart-rooted (B), and taprooted (C) trees. Good polyculture design will maximize the soil zones used while minimizing competition between species by partitioning soil resources.

Therefore, resource partitioning will likely take place in a different form or may be muted. Even so, there will be some benefit to reducing competition between species by partitioning resources. What might it look like?

The limited vertical space available in mostly thin deciduous forest topsoils compresses, and probably diminishes, opportunities for partitioning of the soil profile by roots. Yet annual plants from early succession within the eastern deciduous forest region have been shown to partition the soil profile in both time and space.[72] In addition, anecdotal evidence suggests that at least some native forest trees locate their main lateral roots in specific soil horizons.[73] Do some run their root fans into the O horizon, while others prefer the A horizon? The only note Norbert Scully made about the root pattern of any particular species in his Wisconsin root distribution study was that the roots of the vine Virginia creeper (*Parthenocissus*

quinquefolia) grew almost exclusively in the upper part of the E horizon.[74] What other species, if any, have similar preferences? If we knew such things, they would help us design polycultures more effectively. Shovels, anyone?

In addition, the different patterns of tree, shrub, and herb root systems discussed earlier offer the possibility of vertical partitioning. Taprooted trees use the soil surface to a large degree, *and* they put a large percentage of roots into deep soil. Heart-rooted plants most often use a shallower portion of the profile than taprooted plants. Flat-rooted plants use the shallowest (see figure 5.30).[75] Besides helping us match our tree selections to our sites, this information may help us mix root patterns for reduced competition and fuller use of the soil profile. The different herb root types probably use vertical and horizontal space differently, as well. All of these rooting variations probably complement each other in various combinations if soil conditions permit (see figure 5.31). Yet we still do not have much decent information on the rooting habits of most of the useful edible-forest-garden plants, nor many replicates of the good data we do have to determine species variations under different conditions. Shovels, anyone?

The intermingling of roots of most forest trees might make it appear that trees do not partition the soil much horizontally. However, it is likely that horizontal partitioning does take place. It is just a question of at what scale. Two trees may have main laterals in the same space, but where and when do they put out their fine root fans? Proper spacing of plants is a simplistic approach to partitioning the soil horizontally—one that works. If we get more sophisticated about it, what limits might we be able to push? How much more productivity might we gain? If plants partition the soil and the aboveground layers vertically, then we should be able to pack them more closely horizontally, until we start running into limits set by light and shade tolerance, as well as total-system water and nutrient demands. This would allow the root areas to "fold" into one

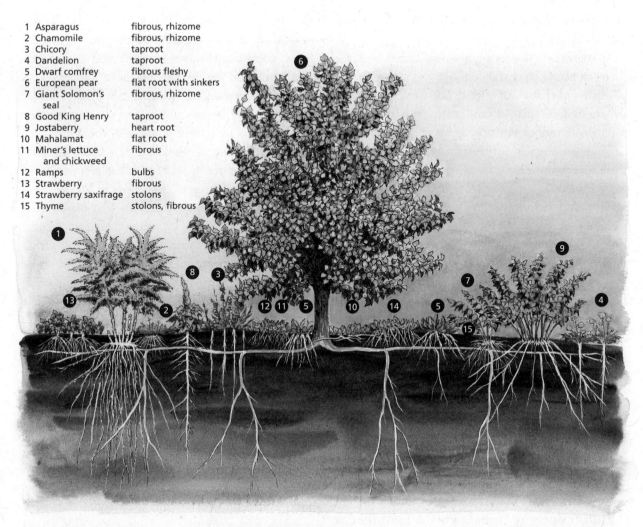

1 Asparagus   fibrous, rhizome
2 Chamomile   fibrous, rhizome
3 Chicory   taproot
4 Dandelion   taproot
5 Dwarf comfrey   fibrous fleshy
6 European pear   flat root with sinkers
7 Giant Solomon's   fibrous, rhizome
    seal
8 Good King Henry   taproot
9 Jostaberry   heart root
10 Mahalamat   flat root
11 Miner's lettuce   fibrous
    and chickweed
12 Ramps   bulbs
13 Strawberry   fibrous
14 Strawberry saxifrage stolons
15 Thyme   stolons, fibrous

FIGURE 5.31. This polyculture of trees, shrubs, and herbs shows mixtures of root types in one small space. The species and scheme are adapted from figure 2.14's microforest garden (page 44).

another, rather than to add together linearly. Again, we need more observations to help us test these theories and to begin to develop guidelines for design. Shovels, anyone?

There is good evidence of partitioning in time by spring ephemeral plants, and possibly by the pulses in growth and shedding of the ephemeral roots of trees and shrubs. What are the growth and shedding cycles of various plants with different rooting strategies? Do herbaceous perennial roots pulse to maximum extent at their time of flowering, followed by dieback (as with ephemerals), or is the opposite per-

haps the case, as plants use up resources stored in their roots to flower and go to seed? We know that the storage organs of perennial herbs tend to grow through the season as winter approaches. If so, the shared soil mass in a polyculture of herbs might have successive waves of roots from different plants over the growing season, waves that relate to the aboveground phenology and survival strategies of the plants. Might it be useful to plant companions with our tree or shrub crops whose roots grow and die in such a way that our main crops have the least root competition, while still gaining the benefits of dynamic accumulation, beneficial insect attraction, and additional crops?

Animals can more easily diversify niches by kind than can plants, since they can adapt to use resources at different levels of the food web. However, dynamic accumulators and nitrogen-fixers offer some possibility of partitioning by kind, as they may depend on a slightly different suite of nutrients than their neighbors. They may also reduce competition in the system as a whole over time by improving soil fertility and reducing scarcity. The disproportionately high nutritional content of understory vegetation adds to this line of thinking, since canopy trees might, in relative terms, need fewer nutrients even as they require more water in response to their full sun exposure.

Despite the lack of information on root-system complementarity, it would appear that mixing plants with different root pattern types, aboveground phenology, and nutritional profiles will lead to fuller use of the soil profile—and hence, reduced competition and increased production. We must guess quite a bit about these realities at this point, but educated guesses are better than random choices. At least we have an opportunity to test them, learn from them, and refine them.

ENGINES OF THE UNDERGROUND ECONOMY

Now that we have at least some understanding of how and where the roots of plants live underground, let's briefly review how they act as the engines of the underground economy and extend what we have already discussed.

Nutrients move dissolved in water in the mineral parts of their cycles, and this makes them susceptible to leaching. Healthy ecosystems conserve and accumulate nutrients by stripping them from the soil water and mineral particles and putting them into three kinds of organic matter—the living, the dead, and the very dead,[76] that is living organisms, active organic matter, and stable humus. Plants and their photosynthesizing kin, as the ultimate earthly source of energy that fuels all ecosystem processes

through the organic molecules that store sunlight,[77] spawn all of this organic matter. So in healthy forest ecosystems, nutrients cycle and gather primarily in and on living and dead tissues. This means that managing nutrients in living systems fundamentally means nourishing and interacting with life, not applying chemicals or rock dust.

Plant roots act as pipelines that bring the raw materials of nutrients and water to green, airborne factories. The distribution of roots in the soil tells us that most of the raw materials that plants need are concentrated in the topsoil under most circumstances. However, those few essential roots that explore the deeper reaches of the dark world stabilize the productivity of the whole system, in part by replenishing the stores of nutrients lost to the forces of nature and humanity.

But these pipelines work in more than one direction. They also distribute energy from the sun to those places the plants deem fit to spend it. Different plants spend their energy differently. Annual weeds direct about 20 percent of their solar energy into their roots. Grasses direct about 60 percent to their roots. Deciduous and coniferous trees send about 80 percent of their photosynthate into their root systems. Plants may exude fully half this energy into the soil around their roots as sugars, complex carbohydrates, and proteins.[78] Up to 40 percent of a plant's photosynthate goes into root exudates. Why?

Plant Roots and Soil Life:
Mutual Dependence in the Extreme

Root exudates create a booming economy in the root zone, the area right around the roots of plants and their mycorrhizal associates. Only a few millimeters to a few centimeters thick, the root zone contains the most life of any part of the soil: ten to fifty times the numbers of bacteria and many times the amount of fungi of soils outside the root zone.[79] Between eleven thousand and fifteen thousand species of bacteria live in the root zone per teaspoon of soil, compared to several hundred per teaspoon outside it, and there are several *miles* of mycorrhizal threads per teaspoon of root-zone soil, compared to several meters per teaspoon outside.[80] This commitment by plants of their hard-earned solar energy to support a bunch of freeloaders down there in the soil must have a payoff, right? How important are these little critters to the trees?

Because of this energy transfer, "nutrient retention and cycling, soil physical structure, and the composition of the soil community are directly tied to the presence of plants and (in some cases) to particular types of plants. This bioregulation of soil processes and properties by plants benefits plant growth, and plants and soils become tied together by mutually reinforcing positive feedback. When trees or ecological equivalent plants are removed from forest ecosystems for a long enough period, the ability of soils to support those plants deteriorates."[81]

In the 1960s, loggers clear-cut a number of forested areas in the Siskiyou Mountains of southwestern Oregon. Most clear-cuts regenerated well, but every one of four or five replantings at the "Cedar Camp" clear-cut failed. Twenty years after the cutting, ecologists studied the soil structure and biology at Cedar Camp and found a degraded soil ecosystem. Cedar Camp soils were structureless, "like beach sands," while nearby forests contained well-structured and aggregated soils with diverse pore sizes. Greater numbers of bacteria and harmful fungi, and fewer mycorrhizal fungi, inhabited the Cedar Camp soils. Compounds called siderophores, which are created by beneficial microbes and which help plants resist pathogens and gather iron, existed in much lower numbers. Populations of mites and other tiny arthropods that graze on bacteria and fungi were also low.[82]

The scientists replanted the site, this time adding about ³/₄ cup (150 ml) of soil from established forests to the tree holes at planting time. The results were dramatic (see figure 5.32). "Seedlings given soil from young forests grew roots faster, formed more mycorrhizas and survived and grew better than seedlings receiving no soil transfers. Soil transfers from older

FIGURE 5.32. The Douglas-fir seedling on the left received 150 ml of forest soil in its hole when it was planted at the Cedar Camp clear-cut; the two at right received none. You be the judge of the effects on root system growth! *Photo courtesy of David Perry. Reprinted with permission of the Johns Hopkins University Press.*

forests improved seedling growth, but not survival and mycorrhiza formation. Forest soils (especially those from younger forests) contained something (or 'somethings') that had been lost from the clearcut, and that loss effectively destroyed system resiliency."[83]

The researchers aren't sure exactly what happened, in either the problem or the solution. They hypothesized that the loss of energy from root exudates so changed the food web structure of the soil community that nutrient cycling caused by grazing soil organisms pooping out digested microbes effectively ceased. With no mycorrhizas, the trees had no other mechanism for gathering nutrients. The loss of soil aggregates compounded the problems by altering the physical and chemical structure of the soil. These and many other factors, including the harshness of the site, prevented reestablishment of trees. We don't quite know how generally we can apply the results of this work. Some things do become clear, though.

The mutual interdependence of plants and the soil community, especially in extreme environments, is obvious. Soil biology is key to nutrient cycles and plant health, and plants are key to soil biology and health. The worse your soils, the more attention you should pay to soil biology, but even those of us with decent soils should not garden in complete ignorance. We disregard the soil community at our peril, and our lack of respect can come back to haunt us. Not only pollution and chemical additives can damage the soil community, but also the "simple" change from forest to grassland modifies the soil community immensely, affecting crop production, crop survival, and our workload.

If the trees are paying so much attention to the soil microbes, why aren't we? We should not plant trees. We should plant ecologies.[84] This means polycultures, not only of plants, but also of all the living elements of a healthy soil food web.

THE SOIL FOOD WEB

With some exceptions, nutrients are input to ecosystems at rates far below tree growth requirements, and productivity is closely tied to nutrient cycling, or the rate at which nutrients are released from dead organic matter.

—DAVID PERRY, *Forest Ecosystems*

Everybody's interested these days in this notion of long-term site productivity. I think that once you scrape away the politics and the rhetoric, you're going to get down to the fact that the fauna of the soil is maybe *the* most crucial issue in determining long-term site productivity.

—ANDY MOLDENKE, SOIL TAXONOMIST, AS QUOTED IN *The Hidden Forest*, BY JON R. LOUMA

Each of the thousands of organisms in healthy soil has its own way of making a living. As with aboveground organisms, this diversity, paradoxically, ties these beings together in an interconnected web that lives and breathes, builds and destroys, grows and dies. What organisms make up the soil food web, how do they help us and our plant allies, and how can we support this web for our mutual benefit? As we work to mimic natural ecosystems, we must become savvy to the workings of this most important social structure. As motivation for exploring this unfamiliar territory, let us consider the gifts our little friends have to give us if we treat them right.

THE GIFTS OF A HEALTHY SOIL FOOD WEB

When we treat our neighbors and friends with respect and caring, we position ourselves to receive the gifts they hold and freely offer to us. These gifts come from their essence, and they support us at an essential level. Our buddies in the soil are no different. The following list of seven gifts has been adapted from the work of Dr. Elaine Ingham.[85]

Gift 1: Increased Nutrient Retention, Cycling, and Availability to Plants

Healthy, happy soils have large, stable, and dynamic soil-organism "containers" that retain nutrients, as discussed earlier. For example, bacteria are the most nitrogen-hungry organisms on the planet, and fungi can grab and hold up to 95 percent of the soluble calcium in a healthy soil.[86] Retention of these nutrients is only half the battle, though.

Once the soil community retains these nutrients, it needs to release them in the right place at the right time in the right form. It turns out that our plant and microbe friends know just how to do this. If we support them in doing what comes naturally, then we don't have to work so hard at it ourselves. Mycorrhizas unleash phosphorus tied up in organic matter and mineral particles and transport it to plants. Various organisms that graze on bacteria and fungi release the nutrients stored there. Since most soil life lives in plant root zones, these nutrients are in the right place. Since these releases come in the form of mineralized or easily decomposed bodily wastes, they are in the right form or soon will be.[87] But what about timing?

Remember the root exudates? Each specific variety of plant puts out its own unique mix of sugars, complex carbohydrates, and proteins, which attract and support a unique mix of soil organisms. Moreover, the plants vary their menu to encourage specific organisms at specific times! The plants are in control of the root-zone community because they provide the lunch, and that determines the kind of garbage the guests leave behind. It just so happens that the lunch guests' garbage is the plant's dinner! The improved nutrient retention and cycling generated by a healthy soil food web can greatly decrease the need for imported fertilizers. As David Perry notes in the opening quote for this section, most nutrients enter ecosystems at rates far below the needs of plants. If we mimic and support the soil food web, we can reduce nutrient inputs and rely instead on nature's recycling system.

Gift 2: Improved Crop Quality

Anecdotal evidence indicates that the improved nutrition a healthy soil food web supplies creates healthier, more nutritious crops. Dr. Ingham has stated that strawberries grown in healthy soil food webs contain three to seven times more protein than strawberries from poor soil food webs, and this protein improves sweetness and flavor dramatically. In addition, she says that wine grapes colonized with the wrong mycorrhizas (arbuscular mycorrhizas) make good wine. Yet when the grapes' preferred mycorrhizas (ectomycorrhizas) colonize them, the grapes not only contain more micronutrients but also make award-winning wine.[88]

Gift 3: Pest and Disease Suppression

"In nature, plant disease is the exception, rather than the rule."[89] The diverse organisms of a healthy soil food web include many species that compete with disease organisms for niche space or directly consume them. These competitors can mask the chemical signals given off by plant roots that pathogens use to find their hosts, physically block access to plant roots, prevent the pathogens from getting food resources, or produce chemicals that inhibit or kill them.[90] After all, in ecological terms an enemy of your friend is your enemy, so it makes sense that organisms dependent on root exudates would offer some protection to plants.

In a study of cucumber diseases, it took twelve different beneficial bacteria species to control one pathogen over the course of one growing season. In a different growing season, with different weather and soil conditions, it might take twelve or more completely different species to achieve control of this one pathogen.[91] Healthy soil food webs suppress diseases and other herbivores by providing diverse species of beneficials to eat, compete with, and defeat the bad guys.

The vast majority of soil organisms are beneficial. The good guys tend to have more specialized niche requirements. Many of them live off root exudates and cannot live long without plants around. They tend not to like soil disturbance, lack of oxygen, excessive wetness, or high nitrate or chemical levels. Every pesticide tested so far negatively affects nontarget soil organisms. According to Dr. Ingham, applying more than 100 pounds per acre (45 kg per ha) of inorganic fertilizer at once kills off large portions of the soil food web.[92]

Meanwhile, the bad guys tolerate a wider range of conditions, including harshness, disturbance, chemicals, drought, wet, and so on. Many of our standard gardening practices, therefore, select for the bad guys. When we try to control them with more harsh practices, we get more of them in the end. To paraphrase Edmund Burke, all it takes for evil to triumph is for the good folks to do nothing, or to just go away.

Gift 4: Improved Soil Structure: Drainage, Aeration, Water Holding, Habitat

The not-so-common wisdom says that increased organic matter content in soil improves the tilth and structure of the soil, improving drainage, aeration, and water-holding capacity. In reality, it is not the organic matter content per se but the degree of aggregation of soil particles that counts. Though organic matter content *is* important, soil organisms are critical for achieving the benefits of good aggregation. We have seen the difference that good compost makes compared to not-so-good compost when added to soil: good, living compost improves soil structure much more effectively than dead organic matter. Why?

It takes the work of many organisms to make soil aggregates and to shape them into good soil structure. Tiny bacteria secrete polysaccharide glues to attach themselves to whatever surfaces they grow upon. Roots and fungi also secrete polysaccharides. These glues stick soil particles together into "microaggregates." Fungal threads bind these microaggregates together into "macroaggregates." Larger invertebrates and worms burrow through the soil, forming these aggregates into visible crumbs. They also eat soil particles and poop them out along with more stickiness and more microbes. Each scale of structure creates "rooms" of different sizes. These rooms provide living and hiding spaces for different organisms, allow air and water to move in and out more freely, and at the same time trap more water more effectively (see figure 5.33). The high surface area of aggregates and aggregate interiors improves nutrient retention by offering more cation exchange sites.

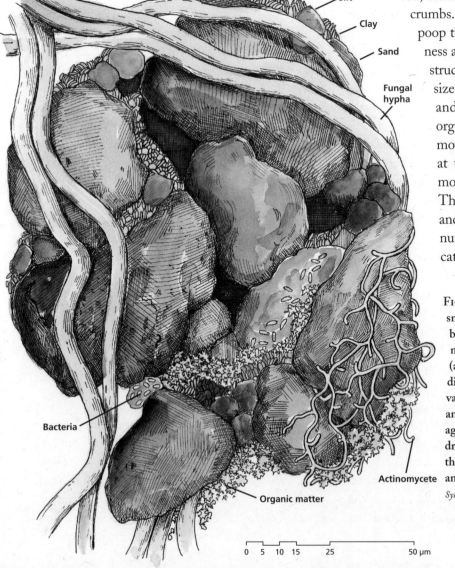

Silt
Clay
Sand
Fungal hypha
Bacteria
Organic matter
Actinomycete

0 5 10 15 25 50 µm

FIGURE 5.33. Soil aggregates consist of smaller aggregates and soil particles bound together by organic matter, microorganisms, and other materials (all drawn to scale here). They offer diverse microsites to suit the needs of various organisms. They hold both air and water more effectively than non-aggregated soil and also improve soil drainage. Microbes are key to creating them, and microbe populations increase and diversify in their presence. *Adapted from Sylvia et al., 1998.*

Improved soil aggregation also decreases the loss of soil due to erosion. For soil particles to erode they must first detach from other particles, and then they must move. Well-aggregated soils resist detachment much more effectively, and this makes the particles harder to transport.

Gift 5: Production of Plant Growth Factors

In the dance of mutual beneficence, both parties get to play the same game. Plants feed the root-zone organisms in return for benefits; the more feeding, the more benefits. Some bacteria produce chemical compounds that directly increase plant growth, apparently as a means of getting more root exudates! These compounds include a variety of hormones, chelators, and enzymes. Other bacteria—even some not living inside the roots of legumes—fix nitrogen. Many of these live in the root zone, using the energy supplied by root exudates to transform gaseous nitrogen into the mineral forms plants can use.

Gift 6: Decomposition of Toxic Chemicals and Pollutants

Who else but the microbes would know how to degrade the stuff we create? From pesticides and fertilizers to airborne chemicals "oiling" soils in urban areas, many pollutants damage the soil food web, particularly the soil arthropods, nematodes, and other organisms at higher trophic levels. Besides the stuff that humans put in the soil, plants, microbes, and animals also create bodily wastes that can inhibit growth if they become too abundant. Creating healthy soil requires the decomposition of all these toxins. Soil communities with limited diversity may not contain the organisms necessary to break down toxins at each stage of decomposition. A diverse, functioning soil food web contains sufficient microbes to break them down into just so much carbon, hydrogen, and oxygen.

Gift 7: A Cleaner Environment

All the gifts above add up to a cleaner environment. Fewer needed pesticides and fertilizers, better nutrient capture and cycling, as well as more effective toxin decomposition all mean less contamination of groundwater and streams. Reduced erosion means better water quality as well as healthier soils and plants. It's just that simple!

So, just who *are* these organisms bearing all these great gifts, and where do they live?

MEET YOUR FRIENDLY NEIGHBORHOOD SOIL ORGANISMS

Soil organisms live within, on, and around plant roots, in litter on the soil surface, on organic matter in the soil, on the surfaces of soil particles and aggregates, and within the air and water in the spaces between particles.[93] Like plant roots, the bulk of the biomass of soil organisms lives in the top layers of soil, especially the litter layer. However, Elaine Ingham has found aerobic microbes as far as 10 miles (16 km) below the earth's surface. She also says that wherever plant roots go, there goes the soil food web.[94]

Bacteria

- These single-celled organisms are usually less than 4/100,000 inch in size (1 micrometer or μm) and are spherical or rod shaped. Bacteria and clay particles are about the same size (figure 5.34). Bacteria attach themselves to whatever surfaces are available, including the skin of other organisms.
- Bacteria work mostly as organic matter decomposers, plant mutualists feeding on root exudates, and pathogens feeding on plant roots or other organisms. Some "chemical eaters" use nitrogen, iron, hydrogen, and sulfur compounds as an energy source, thereby cycling these nutrients (e.g., nitrifying bacteria, which convert ammonium nitrogen—NH_4—to nitrate and nitrite nitrogen, NO_3 and NO_2). Photosynthesizing cyanobacteria (blue-greens) initiate succession in bare soil but live in developed soils as well.
- Total bacterial biomass ranges from 1 to 13 tons per acre (0.4 to 5 metric tons per ha) in

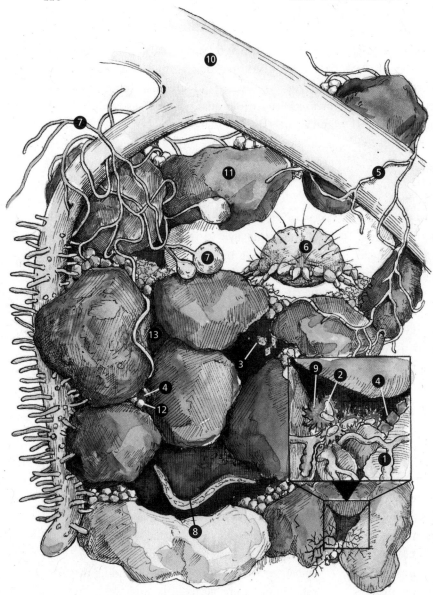

1   actinomycetes
2   bacteria
3   ciliate protozoa
4   clay
5   hyphae of a saprophytic fungus
6   mite
7   mycorrhizal spores and hyphae
8   nematode
9   organic matter
10 plant root with root hairs
11 sand
12 silt
13 water

FIGURE 5.34. At a larger scale than figure 5.33, one can see how soil aggregates interact with larger soil life forms, including plant roots, fungi, and arthropods such as mites. The soil can have tremendous diversity in a tiny area: while this drawing encompasses less than 1 millimeter square, it may have sites ranging from acid to alkaline, dry to wet, and oxygen rich to oxygen poor. *Adapted from Sylvia et al., 1998.*

healthy soil—equal to between two and twenty-six cows![95]

- They tend to feed on easily decomposable organic material (fresh, green matter) or root exudates, except the *Actinomycetes* group. *Actinomycetes* grow in strands as fungi do and can digest resistant organic matter (see figure 5.34). Many bacteria decompose toxic organic chemicals.

- Bacteria store, release, and cycle nutrients, especially in the root zone; degrade pollutants; secrete glues that bind soil particles into microaggregates; compete with disease-causing organisms; become food for other members of the soil food web; and produce plant-growth-regulating hormones, as well as antibiotics. Some bacteria are pathogenic, but the vast majority are beneficial.

Fungi

- Most fungi are microscopic multicelled organisms growing in threads called hyphae, which are 20 to 40/100,000 inch (5 to 10 μm) thick and a few cells to several yards long (figure 5.34).

Hyphae can grow singularly (invisible to the naked eye), in ropelike bunches called mycelium, or they can form the fruiting bodies we call mushrooms. "A single individual fungus can include many fruiting bodies scattered across an area as large as a baseball diamond."[96] Some fungi grow as single cells, such as yeasts. Fungi therefore tend to grow in a variety of soil habitats, including in, on, and around roots, in the litter layer, through pore spaces, and on aggregates and organic matter, and sometimes all of these at once!

- Fungi are mainly decomposers, mutualists (mycorrhizal fungi), and pathogens. Some fungi trap and kill nematodes, feed on insects, or suppress disease-causing fungi. Many can digest toxic organic chemicals. Decomposer fungi attack resistant organic matter that other organisms cannot, such as lignin and cellulose in wood. Some decomposers also act as facultative parasites, meaning they attack sick or dying trees and support their death process, though they will not attack and kill healthy plants, as do pathogens. Mycorrhizal fungi rarely act as parasites. Species of all three kinds of fungi frequently prefer certain kinds of wood or trees as substrates.
- Mycorrhizas can strip nutrients, phosphorus in particular, directly from organic matter and mineral particles and transport them long distances to roots. The total surface area of mycorrhizal hyphae can be ten to one hundred times more than the surface area of leaves in a forest.[97] They grow most prolifically in the root zone, where a gram of soil may contain miles of hyphae, as compared to the yards contained in a gram from outside the root zone (figure 5.34 does not do this reality justice, as mycorrhizas at their true density would obscure the roots completely). "Harvest Mutualisms" in chapter 4 (page 135) discusses mycorrhizas in some detail.
- Most cultivable edible mushrooms are decomposers, and many are also facultative parasites.

- A few edible mushrooms are mycorrhizal, but these are very hard to cultivate (see volume 2, appendix 2 for a table of cultivable mushrooms and their culture requirements).
- Fungal abundance increases through succession, with forests exhibiting the highest fungal biomass (up to 40 miles of hyphae per teaspoon [64 km per gram] of soil in coniferous forests).
- Because they form an interconnected network, fungi resist drought better than bacteria, maintaining growth, decomposition, and nutrient cycling when bacteria have gone dormant. Fungi require oxygen: waterlogged or compacted soils cannot support fungi for very long.
- Fungi store more calcium than any other soil organism in the form of calcium oxalate crystals on their hyphae (figure 5.35). Grazing mites, springtails, and nematodes make the calcium available to other organisms.
- Fungi decompose resistant organic matter; store, release, and transport nutrients and water,

FIGURE 5.35. Fungi are critical calcium conservers in soil ecosystems. They can quickly catch and store large amounts of calcium by forming calcium oxalate crystals on their surfaces. Maximizing fungal biomass in your soil conserves this highly mobile nutrient that is frequently a limiting factor for forest garden productivity. *Scanning electron micrograph by Alan Pooley, used courtesy of Kermit Cromack, Oregon State University.*

especially calcium and phosphorus; can strip
nutrients directly from organic matter and mineral particles with minimal risk of leaching;
physically bind soil particles and microaggregates together into larger aggregates, thereby
improving soil structure, aeration, drainage, and
habitat; serve as key food sources for other
organisms in the food web; protect plant roots
from pathogens, pollutants, and herbivores;
decompose pollutants; and release organic acids
that weather minerals. Glyphosate herbicide
(Roundup) kills fungi as well as plants.[98]

Protozoans

- Protozoans are mobile, microscopic, single-
  celled animals, several times larger than the
  bacteria upon which they primarily feed
  (1/5,000 to 1/50 inch, or 5 to 500 μm). All live
  within the soil water in pore spaces and the
  watery films of particle surfaces. Flagellates, the
  smallest protozoans, use one or more whiplike
  tails to move their spherical, banana-, or pear-
  shaped bodies. Some amoebas can change shape
  at will and use this ability to create temporary
  "feet" to push themselves around or to encircle
  and eat their food. Other amoebas have oval
  shells with holes from which they can extend
  their feet to move. Ciliates are covered with
  very tiny hairs that move in waves like oars for
  propulsion. All protozoans require water in
  which to live and move (see figure 5.34).
  Flagellates eat only bacteria, while ciliates and
  amoebas eat bacteria and other protozoans.
  Since they eat microbes, they live where the
  microbes are, and that's mostly in the root zone.
- Protozoans release nutrients stored in microorganisms by grazing upon them; increase
  organic matter decomposition rates because
  their grazing stimulates bacterial activity; help
  control pathogenic bacteria by grazing on them;
  become food for larger organisms; and regulate
  bacterial populations by predation.

Nematodes

- These hairlike, nonsegmented worms are 1/500
  inch (50 μm) in diameter and 1/20 inch (1 mm)
  or less long and not quite visible to the naked
  eye (a hand lens helps). Nematodes also live
  within the soil water. They are among the most
  numerous animals in the world, with up to 10
  to 20 million per square meter of surface soil,[99]
  and constitute up to 90 percent of multicellular
  soil animals.[100] They live and move in soil water
  (see figure 5.34).
- Nematodes occupy many niche groups. They
  act as fungal feeders, bacterial feeders, root
  feeders, omnivores, and predators. Plant parasitic root nematodes are the most well known
  and give the others an undeserved bad name.
- Bacterial- and fungal-feeding nematodes release
  nutrients when they graze, especially nitrogen,
  because they burn a portion of the carbon they
  ingest. They also have a higher carbon:nitrogen
  ratio (about 10:1) than bacteria (about 6:1), creating free nitrogen with every mouthful.
- Less-disturbed soils commonly contain more
  predatory nematodes and fewer disease-causing
  species than disturbed or agricultural soils.[101]
- Nematodes regulate the populations of other
  organisms by preying upon them; release nutrients from fungal and bacterial storage; control
  populations of disease-causing organisms,
  including root-feeding nematodes; provide food
  for larger organisms; and inoculate soils by carrying fungal spores, bacteria, and protozoans on
  or in their bodies and dispersing them. A small
  number (about 10 percent) of nematode species
  damage plant-nutrient and water-transport systems by feeding on their roots and cause disease
  by transmitting viruses in the process.

Soil Arthropods

- The group of animals called arthropods teems
  with a wide variety of organisms. In the soil,
  these include insects, arachnids (e.g., spiders

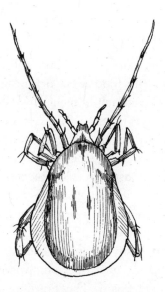 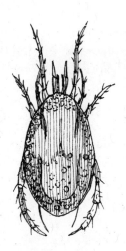 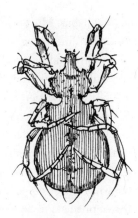

FIGURE 5.36. Mites fill a wide range of community niches in both soil and aboveground ecosystems. They grind organic matter, feed on plants, eat each other, and control populations of other organisms, including pests. They also carry microbes around the soil habitat and help form soil aggregates by moving through the soil. *Adapted from Brown, 1978.*

and mites), crustaceans (e.g., sow or pill bugs), and myriapods (including millipedes and centipedes). They range from microscopic mites and springtails (the Collembola) to millipedes and centipedes so big you wouldn't want to step on them. Small arthropods live in the pore spaces of the soil. Larger ones burrow or live in the litter layer.

- Healthy soil contains many, many species and numberless individuals of both mites (figure 5.36) and springtails. They are important grazers of bacteria and fungi and also act as organic matter shredders. Mites play key predator roles. A few mites give the rest a bad name by attacking crop plants.

- Arthropod shredders and decomposers include pill or sow bugs, millipedes, beetles, ants, earwigs, and many insect larvae, as well as mites and collembolans. Most of these eat feces—their own and of other animals. Their strategy is basically to break down organic matter, moisten it, and poop it out, leaving it for microbes, protozoans, and nematodes to digest

by the wayside. They will then come along and eat it again to ingest the released nutrients. Shredders thus make large or resistant organic matter available to microbial decomposers and inoculate the resulting feces—and soil—with microbes.

- Predatory arthropods tend to be larger, though many mites fill this niche. Beetles, both adults and larvae, compose one of the major kinds of large invertebrate predators in soils. Centipedes and spiders also play key predator roles in the litter and topsoil. These predators help maintain balance in the food web by controlling populations of other organisms.

- Most arthropods, especially the bigger ones, engineer the soil by burrowing, creating the "walls" and "rooms" of soil structure out of macroaggregates.[102] These workers can decompress soil squished by feet and some vehicles,[103] though they cannot loosen heavily compacted soil. The smallest arthropods cannot burrow effectively and must use the pores created by other organisms.

Earthworms and Potworms

- Everyone knows what earthworms are; however, the myths about them do not do justice to their true food habits. Most people think earthworms eat only leaf litter or organic matter. Though they do shred and eat organic materials and ingest soil as they burrow, they actually derive much of their nutrition from the microbes and small animals that live on and in these materials. Some earthworms prefer to burrow in organic layers of soil, some prefer mineral layers, and others use both. Some create burrows, while others do not.

- Earthworms tend to be more abundant in light and medium-loamy soils, in irrigated soils, and in soils with higher levels of organic matter. They become less common with soil disturbance and chemical use.

- There has been some recent evidence and concern that exotic earthworm species are now spreading in the continental United States. These species rapidly decompose leaf litter, so the litter layer is disappearing completely in some forests. This is altering nutrient cycles, soil microclimates, native plant germination rates, and bird nesting habitats, among other things. Please do not release your bait and vermicompost worms into the environment! They are most likely exotic species.

- Small cousins of the earthworms, potworms or whiteworms (*enchytraeids*) grow to $^3/4$ inch (15 to 20 mm) or less in size and live as generalist decomposers and grazers. They help create soil structure as they move through the soil.

- Earthworms and potworms bury and shred plant residues; stimulate microbial activity by eating and inoculating soil and organic matter; mix and aggregate soil; increase infiltration and water-holding capacity; and provide channels for root growth.

STRUCTURE AND FUNCTIONS OF THE SOIL FOOD WEB

As we did for the aboveground food web, we can roughly classify soil food web organisms into trophic levels and community niches by their food sources and functions (figure 5.37). The organisms in each community niche perform characteristic functions that tie them together in a healthy, balanced, functioning ecosystem (see table 5.6).

You will note similarities between the aboveground food web shown in figure 4.4 and the soil food web shown in figure 5.37: the spindle shape, with decreasing diversity as one ascends to higher trophic levels, and the increasing omnivory as one moves up the food chain. The functions of the trophic levels are also similar, though perhaps the soil food web performs a more complex set.

The numbers of these different organisms vary in different ecosystems and at different times (table 5.7). More individuals of all kinds of soil organisms, as well as more species and more functional groups, typically inhabit forest soils as compared to agricultural or prairie soils.[104] This results in more diversity and functional interconnection. Soil food webs with more diversity and functional interconnection offer more of the gifts discussed in the last section than soil food webs with less. A relative lack of disturbance over an extended time allows forest soil food webs to develop more niches and more links between them. In addition, the tendency for soil fertility to increase as forests mature provides more resources to support more diverse soil communities.

Not surprisingly, plant diversity directly affects soil food web diversity. Since plants form the basis for the support of most soil organisms through their root exudates, and each kind of plant supports a unique flora and fauna with its unique root exudates, the more diverse the plants in an ecosystem, the more diverse will be the soil food web.[105] In addition, diverse decomposer foods, that is, forest floor litter composed of various materials from different species, help build diverse soil food webs.

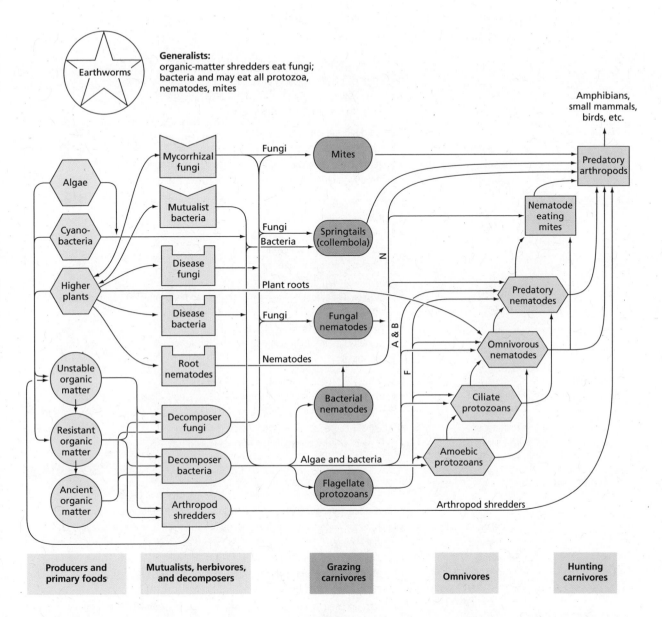

FIGURE 5.37. A schematic diagram of a soil food web. Like aboveground food webs, soil food webs have a spindle shape with high diversity and high populations of herbivores, plant mutualists, and decomposers and decreasing populations of the higher trophic levels. Each functional group of organisms plays critical roles; we need all of them for healthy soil. Earthworms are generalists eating most everything else shown here, so drawing their connections would hopelessly confuse the drawing. *Adapted from Natural Resources Conservation Service, 1999.*

"Complex litters supported a higher fungal and bacterial biomass, and a higher abundance of nematodes. In particular, abundance and diversity of omnivores and predators were significantly higher in complex litters."[106]

Though the soil food web is truly an interconnected whole, the producer and herbivore levels appear to separate into two relatively distinct food webs.[107] The plentiful "living web" organisms that live in the root zones of plants depend primarily on

TABLE 5.6. Community niches and functions of the soil food web. OM = organic matter *Adapted from Natural Resources Conservation Service, 1999.*

Niche	Kinds of Organisms/OM	Functions
Producers		Capture energy and create organic matter.
	• Algae	• Capture and store solar energy.
	• Cyanobacteria	• Create organic matter and add it to the soil.
	• Higher plants	• Exude photosynthates into the root zone.
Primary Foods		Store and release energy and nutrients.
	• Fresh and active OM	• Provide energy and nutrients to decomposers.
	• Resistant OM	• Store nutrients within and on their surface (cation exchange sites).
	• Ancient OM	• Improve soil aggregation, drainage, aeration, and habitat.
Mutualists		Enhance plant growth and cycle nutrients.
	• Fungi	• Protect roots from disease and herbivory.
	• Bacteria	• Fix nitrogen (bacteria).
		• Garner nutrients and water for roots.
		• Produce plant growth hormones.
		• Store nutrients in their own bodies.
		• Improve soil aggregation, drainage, aeration, and habitat with binding glues or fungal hyphae.
		• Provide food for higher trophic levels.
		• Degrade pollutants and chelate toxins and micronutrients.
		• Buffer soil pH.
Herbivores, Plant Pathogens		Consume plant roots, especially those of the weak.
	• Fungi	• Feed on plant roots, root cells, and other parts, promoting disease and death.
	• Bacteria	• Thin the plant community of weak or sick individuals.
	• Nematodes	• Potentially cause significant crop losses.
	• Microarthropods	• Indicate poor ecosystem balance when overabundant.
	• Macroarthropods	
Decomposers, Shredders		Break down organic matter.
	• Fungi	• Retain and immobilize nutrients in their biomass, preventing leaching losses.
	• Bacteria	• Create new compounds that are sources of nutrition for other organisms.
	• Arthropod shredders	• Improve soil aggregation, drainage, aeration, and habitat with binding glues or fungal hyphae.
	• Earthworms	• Provide food for higher trophic levels.
	• Potworms	• Degrade pollutants and chelate toxins and micronutrients.
		• Buffer soil pH.
		• Convert nitrogen and other compounds into mineral, plant-available forms or into gases.
		• Compete with or inhibit disease-causing organisms.
		• Shred organic materials into pieces accessible to microbes.
		• Provide bacterial habitat in guts and feces.
		• Shredders improve soil structure with fecal pellets and as they burrow through soil.
Grazing Carnivores		Release nutrients by consuming bacteria and fungi.
	• Flagellates	• Release nutrients bound up in herbivores, mutualists, and pathogens as plant-available "waste products."
	• Nematodes	
	• Mites	• Limit populations of many root-feeding and disease-causing organisms.
	• Springtails	• Stimulate the growth and activity of fungal and bacterial populations by moderate grazing.
	• Earthworms	

(table 6.2, continued)

Niche	Kinds of Organisms/OM	Functions
Omnivores, Predators, Generalists	• Amoebas • Ciliates • Nematodes • Mites • Arthropods • Earthworms	Control populations and structure soil. • Prevent overharvesting of fungi and bacteria by controlling populations of grazers. • Larger organisms improve soil structure by burrowing. • Large organisms carry small organisms long distances, inoculate soil with microbes, and promote diversity. • See page 224 for functions of earthworms. • Provide food for larger animals aboveground.

TABLE 5.7. Typical numbers of soil organisms in healthy ecosystems. Numbers are per gram (about 1 teaspoon) of dry soil unless otherwise stated. *From Natural Resources Conservation Service, 1999.*

Organism	Agricultural Soils	Prairie Soils	Forest Soils
Bacteria	100 million to 1 billion	100 million to 1 billion	100 million to 1 billion
Fungi	Several yards. Mostly arbuscular mycorrhizal fungi.	Tens to hundreds of yards. Mostly arbuscular mycorrhizal fungi.	Several hundred yards in deciduous forest. One to forty miles in coniferous forests. Mostly ectomycorrhizal fungi.
Protozoans	Several thousand flagellates and amoebas. One hundred to several hundred ciliates.	Several thousand flagellates and amoebas. One hundred to several hundred ciliates.	Several hundred thousand amoebas. Fewer flagellates.
Nematodes	Ten to twenty bacterial feeders. A few fungal feeders. A few predatory nematodes.	Tens to several hundred.	Several hundred bacterial and fungal feeders. Many predatory nematodes.
Arthropods (per sq. ft.)	Up to one hundred.	Five hundred to two thousand.	Ten to twenty-five thousand. Many more species than in agricultural soils.
Earthworms (per sq. ft.)	Five to thirty. More in soils high in organic matter.	Ten to fifty. Arid or semiarid areas may have none.	Ten to fifty in deciduous woodlands. Very few in coniferous forests.

plant root secretions for energy, while the "dead web" decomposers dominate outside root zones. The dynamic living web includes a wide range of organisms (mutualists and decomposers) that support plants in various ways, while the dead-web microbes exhibit slower growth and more tolerance for environmental variation, stress, and dormant periods. Most disease-causing organisms are dead-web microbes, while most plant-protective organisms are living-web microbes. The majority of microbes lives in root zones, so grazers and predators at higher trophic levels that control microbes, release nutrients, and reduce disease depend heavily on the living web to support their populations.

Annual plants have a hard time continuously supporting the living web because they die back every year, while perennials, whose roots sometimes grow through the winter, keep the living web going year-round. Perennial plants, especially trees, appear to be critical for maintaining healthy soil flora and fauna, so simply using perennials, especially woody perennials, should help develop and maintain an active, healthy soil community.

Understanding the functions that the different organisms play in the soil food web can help us diagnose specific problems in the garden. A friend has been adding calcium to his calcium-deficient, circle-mulched, grass-lane orchard for several years, yet foliar tests show that it never seems to show up in his trees. Since fungi store large amounts of calcium as calcium oxalate crystals, it could be that the orchard soils lack the fungal grazers that would release this calcium to the plant roots, or that the trees have insufficient mycorrhizas to transport the calcium to the roots. It could also be that the calcium is leaching away because, at least according to Dr. Ingham, grass ground covers favor bacterial dominance in soil and discourage fungi. We need more information to assess the problem. We can obtain it by sending soil samples to a lab to test both the soil nutrients and the soil food web (see volume 2, appendix 7 for details).

Managing Mycorrhizas: A Few Pointers

We can hardly overstate the importance of mycorrhizas to healthy ecosystem function. The most basic and prominent component of the living web, mycorrhizal fungi constitute up to 70 percent of soil microbial biomass[108] and colonize 70 percent to 80 percent of plant species. Researcher and restoration ecologist Ted St. John says:

> As the first organ of nutrient uptake, the mycorrhizal network mediates nutrient cycling. As the instrument of rapid root colonization, it determines the plant species composition of the community. As the medium of soil structure, it determines the flow of water, nutrients, and air, directs the pathways of root growth, and opens channels for the movement of soil animals. As the moderator of the microbial community, it determines the metabolic processes of the soil. In other words, **the mycorrhizal network is practically synonymous with *ecosystem function*** [emphasis in the original].[109]

Known benefits of healthy mycorrhizas include improved nutrient uptake (especially of phosphorus), faster plant growth, increased plant survival, better drought and disease resistance, reduction in weed populations, and improvements in soil aggregation and overall microbiology. Never

measure the success of mycorrhizal development by plant growth alone, though. Dramatic growth increases are less likely to occur in the field than in greenhouse experiments with sterile soil controls. Even so, the other benefits and the functions mycorrhizas perform make them highly important to forest gardening. Clearly, if we want to mimic forest ecosystem structure and function, we need to ensure mycorrhizas thrive. Luckily, that usually isn't hard.

Most healthy, undisturbed temperate forest soils contain sufficient fungal hyphae and spores to colonize any sterile host plants attempting to establish in them. Most nonforested soils in forested regions should have sufficient numbers of spores and active fungi to colonize sterile host plants, too. Contrary to the developing mythology about mycorrhizal inoculants, *most sites in the eastern forest region probably do not need inoculation with mycorrhizal fungi because native mycorrhizal fungi are already there.* Most mycorrhizal fungi are more selective about soil and site conditions than they are about plant host species, so most of our plants should partner with what is already there. On the other hand, not all sites have the necessary fungi.

Sites will probably have insufficient native mycorrhizal fungi if:

- grading has taken place, especially recently (earth moving shreds fungal networks and kills many other soil organisms outright);
- the soil has been tilled or disced two or more times per year;
- no topsoil exists due to grading or erosion, or topsoil that was stockpiled for more than a few weeks has been spread (some spores remain viable for one to two years, depending on the manner of stockpiling, but active hyphae die out quickly without plant hosts);
- the site has experienced a very hot surface fire or a fire in the ground;
- chemical fertilizers, pesticides, herbicides, or other toxics have been applied at any time, especially fungicides;

- soils are wet, periodically flooded, compacted, or seriously overgrazed;
- no vegetation exists, or the land has had long fallow periods; or
- vegetation consists solely or largely of nonhosts, such as mustard or goosefoot family plants (Brassicaceae or Chenopodiaceae) or sedges. Some authors suggest that annual or opportunist perennial weeds will have fewer mycorrhizas as well.

Some research also indicates that urban and suburban soils have compromised fungal communities resulting from air pollutants, including elevated nitrogen levels in polluted rainfall. Further research is needed to determine the level of damage and how to make up for it.

Planting radically different plants from the vegetation that already exists on site may also be problematic. An evergreen forest may not have the proper fungi for herbs and fruit or nut trees, for example, or a site with diverse deciduous woodies and herbs may not support fungi for ericaceous plants such as blueberries and their kin. We would be wise to group our plants based at least partly on their fungal associates to aid management and improve productivity. The basic breakdown here is between plants that partner with arbuscular mycorrhizal, ectomycorrhizal, and ericoid or other more rare mycorrhizal fungi (see volume 2, chapter 5).

The most common form of mycorrhizal fungi, arbuscular mycorrhizal fungi (see "Harvest Mutualisms," page 135), do not disperse very fast or very far. They make their large, hard-to-disperse spores underground. They move only by growing into an area through the soil (0.5 to 1 meter per year when associated with host plants[110]) or by traveling on the backs or in the guts of soil arthropods or earthworms. If a site lacks the right conditions, arbuscular mycorrhizal fungi may never move in. While ectomycorrhizal fungi disperse more readily than arbuscular mycorrhizal fungi due to their smaller spores, dispersal can take a significant chunk of time. This time lag after disturbance can affect plant survival and competition against nonmycorrhizal weeds. We often create conditions that militate against mycorrhiza development or destroy the very fungi we should support.

Consequently, we bear the burden of reinstating mycorrhizal fungi, especially arbuscular mycorrhizal species, when we have caused their decline. Our gardens also stand to gain the benefits of us doing so. For example, restoration ecologists have shown that rapid mycorrhiza development can dramatically reduce nonmycorrhizal weed problems, increase survival after planting, and improve soil aggregation, drainage, porosity, water-holding capacity, and biology.[111] If mycorrhizas are present, but not in sufficient numbers, such as in urban and suburban soils damaged by pollution, managing nutrients and other factors to support the fungi is probably the best approach. In the other circumstances described in the previous bulleted points, we will probably need to inoculate the soil, the plants, or both with mycorrhizal fungi. A few approaches to mycorrhizal inoculation exist, though as far as we know none have received extensive scientific scrutiny to assure their effectiveness. Let's quickly review some key techniques, while saving how-to details for volume 2, chapter 5.

Since mycorrhizal fungi (especially arbuscular mycorrhizal species) cannot remain active and viable without a plant associate, the best approach is for nurseries to inoculate their stock and use practices that maintain mycorrhiza viability throughout production, sale, and shipping. This practice is currently rare. However, it provides the most assurance of mycorrhizal viability after transplanting, it increases the chances of plant survival in the field, and it decreases the need for fertilizer. It should also improve soil conditions as the fungi extend into the soil surrounding their partner plants. We hope that more nurseries will take up the practice in the coming years.

You can also inoculate by placing soil from a healthy ecosystem into your planting holes. This method has a decent track record of moving native mycorrhizal fungi to new and deserving plant hosts. Such "soil inoculation" is, however, also a broad-spectrum technique for transplanting many different organisms of the soil food web. This technique may carry disease-causing organisms to your site. It will also damage the donor site some, since you need a significant amount of topsoil to ensure mycorrhizal inoculation—especially if you are inoculating many plants (see "Native Fungi Transplants" and "Soil Inoculation" in volume 2, chapter 5).

Commercial inoculants come in a number of forms, from powders to pellets to gel mixes, containing propagules such as spores, living mycelium, or colonized root fragments. Each product may have a different application method. We cover these in more detail in volume 2's chapter 5, under "Mycorrhizal Inoculation."

Some have raised concerns about monocultures of "exotic fungi" spreading through commercial inoculants. Most companies use the same fungi species in their products. These species, especially *Glomus intraradices*, are the most adaptable arbuscular mycorrhizal fungi known, working well in most soils in most regions for most plants. This would seem the usual recipe for an "invasive exotic nightmare." So far, though, scientists have found that these arbuscular mycorrhizal fungi usually cannot outcompete locally adapted natives *once the mycorrhizal network establishes itself and soil conditions improve*. In other words, the generalist species may act as early-succession mycorrhizas that create the conditions for their own demise and give way to native species. The few observations of this dynamic do not mean that exotic fungi problems will not appear in the future, but most scientists seem to feel that such a scenario is unlikely (let's hope those are not "famous last words"). However, prudence might suggest using local soil inoculation as the method of choice when you need inoculum, if you can afford the time and can minimize or mend the impact of taking soil from a healthy ecosystem.

The other soil food web management practices discussed in volume 2, chapter 5 have little direct effect on mycorrhizal inoculation as far as we know. The use of healthy compost or compost tea may not provide mycorrhizal fungi inoculum, though it will create better conditions for plants and soil microbes generally. Compost is an excellent fertilizer to use after inoculating with mycorrhizal fungi, or to prevent harm to existing mycorrhizas. Chemical fertilizers, especially readily available phosphorus, limit colonization by the fungi. Some kill fungi and other organisms outright. Native fungi transplants can effectively inoculate a new site with decomposer fungi but probably will not transplant mycorrhizal fungi, particularly arbuscular mycorrhizal species (see volume 2, chapter 5 for the distinction between the "soil inoculation" and "native fungal transplant" techniques). Ectomycorrhizal and ericoid fungi have been shown to act as decomposers, so a few of their propagules may be transferred by this method, though probably not enough to colonize plants. Most of the plants in which we are interested require arbuscular mycorrhizal fungi anyway.

Aside from inoculating soils that need it, protecting the existing native mycorrhizas is the best approach. Minimizing disturbance, especially large-scale grading or tilling, is key to this effort. Also avoid using chemical fertilizers and pesticides, minimize compaction, and prevent compaction, water-logging, and overgrazing. Maintaining permanent vegetative cover of the right plants is the most basic thing. Without plants, mycorrhizas are just a bunch of dead fungi.

INOCULANTS FOR NITROGEN-FIXERS

Nitrogen-fixing plants are a critical component of any forest garden system, and understanding their relationship to soil microbes is critical to maximizing their performance as soil-improving plants. "Nitrogen-fixing" plants don't actually fix any nitrogen themselves; instead, they form a symbiotic relationship with soil organisms that do the job for them, exchanging sugars for nitrogen. Without those soil organisms present, the plants cannot fix nitrogen. Nitrogen-fixing microbes can live freely in the soil but often form a mutualistic relationship with plant hosts. When this occurs, the plants form nodules on their roots, within which the bacteria live. Nodules are small, round, ball- or beadlike structures visible to the naked eye. In legumes, they are pink or red inside when actively fixing nitrogen.

Each kind of nitrogen-fixing plant interacts with certain groups of nitrogen-fixing organisms, some with more specificity than others. Groups of plants that can cross-infect each other with the proper bacteria are called cross-inoculation groups. Knowing these groups is critical to properly inoculating your nitrogen-fixing plants should you need to do so. In volume 2, appendix 3, the "Nitrogen-Fixers" table lists all the nitrogen-fixing species in the Plant Species Matrix, while the "Nitrogen-Fixer Inoculants" table provides cross-inoculation group information for all those species. Within a cross-inoculation group, each plant species can use the nitrogen-fixing bacteria of all other members, with one exception: plants in the cowpea group cannot cross-infect each other.

Two basic kinds of nitrogen-fixing plants exist: legumes and actinorhizal plants. Legumes are the familiar pea-family plants we all know and love. Actinorhizal plants hail from a variety of plant families. These two groups form partnerships with different kinds of organisms, and their inoculation issues therefore differ in a few respects. We will treat these two groups separately below.

Legumes (Family Fabaceae)
Most gardeners assume that all legumes fix nitrogen, when only about 90 percent actually do so. Of the sixty-two legumes in the Plant Species Matrix, only two do not fix nitrogen: honey locust (*Gleditsia triacanthos*) and redbud (*Cercis canadensis*). The nitrogen fixing bacteria that associate with legumes are all from the genus *Rhizobium*. Some legume species can associate with many different *Rhizobium* species, while others will nodulate only with a specific strain.

However, even though the plants may be capable of associating with more than one *Rhizobium* species, *all* nitrogen-fixing legumes can associate with only one *Rhizobium* bacteria species at a time.

With regard to the other side of the legume-*Rhizobium* relationship, many species and strains of *Rhizobium* bacteria exist, and most will infect a number of different legume species from the same cross-inoculation group. Many rhizobia are present in healthy soils, so inoculation is often not an issue. In general, you should inoculate your legumes if you are growing from seed; if your legumes are from a cross-inoculation group without local representatives; or if you are planting in highly disturbed, poor, or "dead" soils.

You can examine legumes in your garden or purchased from a nursery to see whether they have been inoculated. Inoculated legumes have a deep green leaf color. Their roots will have nodules, and these should be pink or red inside (cut them open). If your legumes do not meet the above criteria, you should inoculate. Nodules can exist but not be actively fixing nitrogen: if they are not pink or red inside, then you should inoculate.

Volume 2, appendix 7 lists several commercial sources of inoculants. Just make sure to buy the right *Rhizobium* strain for your plants (again, see volume 2, appendix 3). Mix inoculant with seed just before planting. You can use inoculants in your soil mix when potting or as a soil amendment when planting. You can also mix inoculants with water and pour the mixture on the roots or root-ball as a slurry, or you can use it as a preplanting soak for plant roots. Alternatively, you can dig up some soil from the root zones of nearby legumes in the same cross-inoculation group and work it into the root zone of your plants in any of the ways described above.

Actinorhizal Plants
These nonleguminous nitrogen-fixers come from a wide range of plant families and are mostly temperate-zone plants. What they have in common is that they interact with members of the genus

Frankia, a group of actinomycetes—organisms that are something of a mix between bacteria and fungi. Most actinorhizal plants will form nodules with a great many strains of *Frankia*. Individual actinorhizal plants may associate with multiple strains of *Frankia*—twenty species or more—at once. Scientists call the most prolific of these "promiscuous," while other plants are more moderate, preferring a tighter circle of associates at any given time.

In most cases, many strains of *Frankia* already live independently in the soil. Therefore, inoculation of actinorhizal species is not much of a concern. However, if your soil is highly disturbed or biologically inactive, or if your plants do not appear to be nodulated, you may want to inoculate just to be sure. Commercial *Frankia* inocula are not currently available, however. Check for nodulation among other local actinorhizal plants (dig up some roots and look). If they have active nodules, collect some soil from beneath them and add it to the root zone of your aspiring nitrogen-fixers. If you need to inoculate, be sure to use soil from plants in the same cross-inoculation group.

Sleeping Beauties and Princes Charming of the Underground World

We have discussed the importance of soil microbes to the underground economy and their increased numbers and activity in the root-zone environment. However, especially outside the root zone, "microbial communities are both numerous and diverse, but they are largely dormant. Their inability to move in the compact soil environment limits their activity to the immediate microsite in which they reside."[112] Soil microbes have the ability to create a new generation of organisms in about twenty hours, yet the actual time it takes them to do this in the soil averages one to one and a half years.[113] Why? Their activity is limited by conditions frequently inhospitable to their lifestyle. Yet, even outside the root zone, microbes play key roles in the soil ecosystem. Thus, microbes are like Sleeping Beauty, waiting for that wonderful kiss to

wake them up so they can resume their life-enhancing activities.[114] We already know that plant roots play a critical role in this regard. Who else activates them and how? Who else plays Prince Charming?

Soil invertebrates, that's who. Large soil invertebrates include earthworms, of course, but also termites, potworms, beetles and their grubs, fly larvae, centipedes, and, to a lesser degree, ants. Smaller invertebrates include mostly mites and springtails. The smaller invertebrates digest organic matter externally by shredding and moistening it, inoculating it with microbes, and pooping it out. Larger invertebrates have mutualist microbes living in their guts that break things down on their way through and also inoculate the feces.

All these animals kiss and awaken Sleeping Beauty in a number of ways, by:

- providing a rich, moist environment for the microbes inside their bodies and in their fecal pellets;
- spreading nutrient-rich substrates, that is, feces, throughout the soil as they move around, bringing food to the starving microbial masses, who are locked away in their microsites and unable to move;
- shredding decay-resistant organic matter and making it available to organisms, including plants, that would otherwise be unable to access its resources;
- creating a diverse abundance of stable soil structures (galleries, burrows, and chambers), improving infiltration, aeration, soil density, and so on; and
- aggregating soil particles with their fecal pellets and their burrowing activities.

The research indicates that the soil zones affected by earthworms and other invertebrates are regulators of soil biological processes equal to roots and root zones. Plants experience much higher growth rates and better nutrition when soil ecosystems have healthy populations of soil invertebrates doing their thing. How can we foster the development of these animal communities?

In forest gardening, we have a distinct advantage. Simply by making a forest garden, you will create virtually ideal conditions for the Princes Charming of the underground world. Mulching the soil, disturbing it infrequently, keeping it shaded and moist with constant vegetative cover, and providing perennial plants to supply deep, well-developed root zones will foster all of these organisms and their activities. In the most extreme sites you may have to break up preexisting compaction, inoculate with healthy soil, or undertake other forms of site preparation to get things started, but after that it should be a self-renewing, self-regulating, self-maintaining system.

Fungal-Bacterial Balance: A Defining Characteristic?

While plants manage soil microbes in the root zone by controlling root exudates, it is also possible that the ratio of fungal biomass to bacterial biomass in the soil as a whole influences the kinds of plants that can grow there. According to a theory advocated by Dr. Elaine Ingham, important processes of succession and plant survival depend upon this ratio: Bacterial-dominated soils inhibit many perennials and most woody plants, and fungal-dominated soils inhibit most grasses and annual weeds. Shrubs and pioneer trees tend to tolerate bacterial soils but convert them to fungal soils. Soils can shift from being fungal dominated to being bacterial dominated in as little as 6 inches (15 cm) vertically or horizontally.[115] While there is dispute about this theory, let's explore how it might work.

A major piece of this puzzle revolves around the kinds of organic matter that bacteria and fungi can decompose. Bacteria thrive on green, easily decomposed, high-nitrogen organic material, especially when mixed into the soil profile. On the other hand, litter left on the soil surface fosters fungi because it tends to dry out and lose nitrogen,

leaving a higher carbon substrate. Only fungi can decompose resistant organic matter, such as woody roots, branches, and twigs, even if it is below the soil surface. Tree leaves also tend to contain higher amounts of resistant organic matter than grasses and forbs. Nitrogen and coevolution also play important roles here.

Very early-succession soils—those with only mineral particles and no plants or organic matter—have few or no fungi in them, for there is nothing to decompose nor any root exudates. Bacteria, specifically photosynthetic bacteria such as cyanobacteria (formerly called blue-green algae), initiate succession by colonizing and beginning to add low-carbon organic matter to barren soil. This creates a niche for decomposer bacteria. Eventually the organic matter and soil biology build to a point where plants can grow, usually grasses and annual weeds at first. However, the biomass of bacteria is greater than the biomass of fungi in early-succession soils. Fungal to bacterial biomass ratios (F:B ratios) can range from 1:1 in highly productive agricultural systems to 1:10 or 1:40 in native grasslands (ten to forty times more bacteria than fungi).[116] Therefore, bacterial grazers dominate the soil food web grazing niche, and they release excess nitrogen when they eat bacteria, in the form of ammonium (NH_4^+).

The alkaline polysaccharide glues that bacteria secrete to attach themselves to soil particles help maintain a high soil pH, especially in the microzones where bacteria proliferate. Nitrifying bacteria abound in high-pH environments. They quickly burn any ammonium nitrogen released by microbe grazers as a source of energy, converting it to nitrate (NO_3^-). Nitrate is therefore the dominant form of nitrogen in bacterial soils. However, not all plants will flourish on nitrate as a nitrogen source. Grasses, weeds, annuals, and some perennials prefer nitrate nitrogen. Most perennials and woody plants do not thrive on nitrate nitrogen, though they may grudgingly survive on it. Therefore, the bacterial-adapted plants that prefer nitrate more easily outcompete them.

Fungi tend to dominate forest ecosystems, with F:B ratios of 5:1 to 10:1 in deciduous forests and 100:1 to 1,000:1 in coniferous forests. Fungi secrete organic acids that Ingham claims tend to maintain a soil pH lower than what nitrifying bacteria prefer. Therefore, ammonium nitrogen takes prominence in fungal-dominated soils. Woody plants and most perennials thrive on ammonium as a source of nitrogen and can therefore more easily outcompete grasses and other bacterial-associated plants in fungal-dominated soils.

This mutual dependence between fungi and woody plants makes sense. Woody plants create resistant organic matter containing nutrients that no organisms except fungi can break down. This creates mutually reinforcing feedback. Grasses and other early successional species have adapted to early-succession environments where the kinds and amounts of organic matter present do not support large numbers of fungi. It would follow that the species of fungi, bacteria, grazers, and predators within these different soil food webs would also differ. This means that growing plants in soils with their preferred F:B ratio should lead to improved mutualism, disease resistance, nutrient cycling, and plant health.

Dr. Ingham, who has spent her career studying soil food webs and is the most vocal proponent of the above information, says that the F:B biomass ratio can also determine the rooting behavior of trees. Apparently, the roots of trees preferring strongly fungal soil frequently will not venture into bacterial soils at all. Conventional wisdom says that competition, or perhaps allelopathic chemicals, drive orchard tree roots below grass ground covers. Ingham says that the roots are actually avoiding the bacteria-dominated surface soils. She also says that many inhibitory interactions believed due to allelopathic chemicals are really due to these fundamental differences in soil food web composition.[117] Such food web differences may play a role in the success of suckering and stoloniferous strategies in pioneering shrubs. These plants can carry their soil

food web with them, with backup support from "behind the lines." If Ingham's theory is true, F:B ratios should be a key criterion for choosing plant associates for polycultures.

The challenge is that though Dr. Ingham has done much work on fungal-bacterial balance, this theory is still controversial. She has so far published little documenting the soil food web preferences of various plants. Luckily, native habitat is a good guide: early-succession species tend to prefer bacteria-dominated soils, midsuccession species tend to thrive in a more balanced F:B ratio, and trees tend toward fungal soils. Pioneer woody plants, such as shrubs and pioneer trees, tend to tolerate bacterial soils but will push them toward fungal dominance. Native habitat can also guide design for perennial herbs: woodland herbs probably prefer fungal soils, while earlier-succession species probably prefer bacteria-dominated soils. Mixing plants that prefer bacterial and fungal soils is less likely to result in a happy plant-soil community.

SOIL FOOD WEB SUMMARY

We have spent many centuries using and abusing the soil without clearly understanding the role that soil organisms play, as functional groups or as a whole, in developing and maintaining soil fertility, structure, and health and in plant protection and production. Now that we are beginning to unravel some of these mysteries, the awe-inspiring interconnectedness of these belowground ecosystems becomes palpable. Each kind of organism plays at least one key role in balancing and maintaining the soil ecosystem. It behooves us to know our neighbors, to treat them with respect, support them, and nourish them, both as a whole and as specific functional groups. Then we may receive the gifts they have to offer. Luckily for us forest gardeners, once we get a healthy soil food web going, the chances of it getting out of whack are slim, since we generally will not be applying chemicals or tilling the soil on a regular basis.

DABBLING IN THE UNDERGROUND ECONOMY

A large proportion of plant biomass—often more than half—lives belowground. More than half of most plants' energy goes in the same direction. The vast majority of nonplant biomass lives belowground, too, in seething, writhing masses of little critters we mostly can't even see. On the backs of this hidden world we stand and walk, live and die, grow our food and eat it. All we can really do, in some ways, is to dabble in this realm that is both completely within and yet totally outside our grasp. Yet dabble we must if we are to succeed in our goal of establishing healthy, self-maintaining, high-productivity, forest-mimicking gardens. At the very least we should dabble with care and respect and so create the conditions to receive the soil's gifts without force or cunning, but with wisdom and consideration.

Self-renewing fertility depends upon following the same strategies devised by nature: nutrient conservation and accumulation. The most vital plant nutrients move much faster in ecosystems than most of us believe, leaching out of leaves in the rain, falling to the ground only to be absorbed again, and so on. Stopping these flows is impossible, yet we can plug the leaks from the system as a whole. The interconnected network of plants, soil organic matter, and soil organisms conserves and accumulates nutrients and stops leaching, the primary nutrient leak from all terrestrial ecosystems. Selecting dynamic accumulators and nitrogen-fixers as understory vegetation speeds nutrient accumulation and can redress imbalances in topsoil nutrient composition. Abundant vegetation garners soil water and strips nutrients from the soil, while organic matter and organisms store nutrients and transfer them to plants through their roots.

Plants energize the underground economy by creating organic matter that feeds decomposers and by exuding photosynthates from their roots to support the soil food web. Root systems grow and die at a faster rate than most of us realize, too, adding large quantities of organic matter to soils and responding to changing soil conditions rapidly. Most plant roots live in the top few feet of the soil profile, but trees whose roots run deeper tend to live longer and healthier lives, produce more, produce more consistently, and aid the transfer of nutrients from the subsoil to the topsoil. While soil conditions may limit plant root growth, different species may exhibit different rooting patterns when conditions allow. Mixing different root patterns in our polycultures holds the possibility of decreased competition, more thorough use of soil resources, and increased forest-garden productivity. Mingling plants that partition the soil horizontally or in time also holds this promise. Fuller understanding of both soil conditions and plant root habits will further these goals and allow us to better design our plant guilds.

The previously unrecognized contributions of soil organisms to plant production and health should go unrecognized no longer. The gifts these beings offer when we treat them well are manifold, arise naturally out of ecological principles and interactions, and save us work and energy. Forest gardens by their nature support the soil food web more effectively than most other farming or gardening systems. Learning to rebuild the web and to support it through time will offer us continued productivity and health over the long term. Planting trees, shrubs, and herbs means planting micro-ecologies along with them. As Ingham says, in a forest-garden scheme we can "set up a healthy soil, and let it go, no need to intervene. Unfortunately, given what we have done to the soil in the last 60 years, a bit of work is required to get the organisms back. But once back, let the plants do the work!"[118]

1. Kimmins, 1997, page 80.
2. Kimmins, 1997, page 80.
3. Kimmins, 1997, page 104; Luoma, 1999.
4. Odum and Odum, 1955, quoted in Colinvaux, 1986, page 34.
5. Perry, 1994, page 273.
6. Perry, 1994, pages. 380–81.
7. Perry, 1994, page 310.
8. Barbour, Burk, and Pitts, 1987, page 304.
9. Atkinson, 1980a, page 439; Kimmins, 1997, pages 92–93.
10. Richards, 1987, page 399.
11. Perry, 1994, pages 434–35.
12. Barbour, Burk, and Pitts, 1987, page 168.
13. Colinvaux, 1986, pages 427–29.
14. Colinvaux, 1986, page 433.
15. Elaine Ingham, Soil Food Web workshop and interview, Maine Organic Farmer's and Gardener's Association, Unity, Maine, March 18, 2000.
16. Yarie, 1980.
17. Kimmins, 1997, page 78.
18. Perry, 1994, page 273.
19. Perry, 1994, page 276.
20. Kimmins, 1997, page 99.
21. Muller, 1978.
22. Brooks, 1972.
23. See Lawrence Hills's *Comfrey: Past, Present and Future* for a great summary of research and uses.
24. Michael Phillips, personal communication, 2000.
25. Coker, 1958.
26. Kimmins, 1997, page 88.
27. Kimmins, 1997, page 90.
28. Kimmins, 1997, page 91.
29. Yarie, 1980.
30. Binkley, 1992.
31. For a more complete and technical discussion of all the flows and links between nutrient containers in forest ecosystems, see Kimmins, 1997, and Perry, 1994.
32. Kourik, 1986.
33. Weaver and Bruner, 1927, page 6.
34. Perry, 1989, page 3.
35. Perry, 1989.
36. Perry, 1989; Oskamp and Batjer, 1932; and many others.
37. Perry, 1989.
38. Atkinson, 1980b, page 172.
39. Perry, 1989, page 5.
40. Perry, 1989, page 9.
41. Atkinson, 1980a, page 439; Kimmins, 1997, pages 92–93.
42. Kimmins, 1997, page 90.
43. Atkinson, 1980b.
44. Perry, 1989, page 15.
45. Perry, 1989; Kourik, 1986; Atkinson, 1980a; Kolesnikov, 1971.
46. Rogers and Vyvyan, 1934.
47. Perry, 1989; Kolesnikov, 1971.
48. Atkinson, Naylor, and Coldrick, 1976.
49. Graham and Bormann, 1966, page 258.
50. Atkinson, Naylor, and Coldrick, 1976.
51. Atkinson, 1980a.
52. Yadava and Doud, 1980.
53. Soil Food Web, Inc., 2001.
54. Kimmins, 1997, page 248.
55. Hightshoe, 1988.
56. Weaver and Bruner, 1927, page 4.
57. Adapted mostly from Kimmins, 1997, pages 248–49. Many other authors confirmed and contributed to this list.
58. Elaine Ingham, Soil Food Web workshop and interview, Maine Organic Farmer's and Gardener's Association, Unity, Maine, March 18, 2000.
59. Weaver and Bruner, 1927, page 13
60. Kourik, 1986; Yeager, 1935; Jean and Weaver, 1924.
61. Perry, 1989, page 13.
62. Sweet, 1929; Sweet, 1933; Oskamp and Batjer, 1932; Oskamp, 1933.
63. Glenn and Welker, 1993, page 365.
64. Weaver and Bruner, 1927, page 7.
65. Atkinson, 1980a, page 466.
66. Hightshoe, 1988.
67. See Kourik's *Designing and Maintaining Your Edible Landscape* (1986) for those pictures.
68. For example, see Scully, 1942.
69. Weaver, 1919; Weaver, 1920.
70. Weaver, 1919, page 123.
71. Weaver, 1919, page 127.
72. Bazzaz, 1996, pages 155 and 157.
73. Perry, 1989, page 2.
74. Scully, 1942.
75. Bunger and Thomson, 1938.
76. Fred Magdoff, University of Vermont, quoted by Elaine Ingham, Soil Food Web workshop and interview, Maine Organic Farmer's and Gardener's Association, Unity, Maine, March 18, 2000.
77. Perry, 1994, page 267.
78. Food Soil Web, Inc., 1999.
79. Perry, 1994, page 286.
80. Luoma, 1999, page 123.
81. Perry, 1994, page 493.
82. Perry, 1994, page 493.
83. Perry, 1994, page 496.
84. Nöel, 1994.
85. This subsection based on Martens, 2000; Soil Food Web, Inc., 1999; Natural Resources Conservation Service, 1999; Perry, 1994; and Elaine Ingham, Soil Food Web workshop and interview, Maine Organic Farmer's and Gardener's Association, Unity, Maine, March 18, 2000.

86. Martens, 2000; Elaine Ingham, Soil Food Web workshop and interview, Maine Organic Farmer's and Gardener's Association, Unity, Maine, March 18, 2000.
87. Martens, 2000; Soil Food Web, Inc., 1999; Natural Resources Conservation Service, 1999.
88. Elaine Ingham, Soil Food Web workshop and interview, Maine Organic Farmer's and Gardener's Association, Unity, Maine, March 18, 2000.
89. Dickman, 1993, page 177.
90. Natural Resources Conservation Service, 1999.
91. Soil Food Web, Inc., 1999.
92. Elaine Ingham, Soil Food Web workshop and interview, Maine Organic Farmer's and Gardener's Association, Unity, Maine, March 18, 2000.
93. Sources include Natural Resources Conservation Service, 1999; Soil Food Web, Inc., 1999; Elaine Ingham, Soil Food Web workshop and interview, Maine Organic Farmer's and Gardener's Association, Unity, Maine, March 18, 2000; Lynch, 1990; Sylvia et al., 1998; Brown, 1978.
94. Elaine Ingham, Soil Food Web workshop and interview, Maine Organic Farmer's and Gardener's Association, Unity, Maine, March 18, 2000.
95. Natural Resources Conservation Service, 1999, pages C-1 and B-1.
96. Natural Resources Conservation Service, 1999, page D-1.
97. Perry, 1994, page 281.
98. Sauer and Andropogon Assoc., 1998.
99. Brown, 1978, page 41.
100. Elaine R. Ingham, in Sylvia et al., 1998, page 119.
101. Natural Resources Conservation Service, 1999, page F-3.
102. Elaine Ingham, Soil Food Web workshop and interview, Maine Organic Farmer's and Gardener's Association, Unity, Maine, March 18, 2000.
103. Elaine Ingham, Soil Food Web workshop and interview, Maine Organic Farmer's and Gardener's Association, Unity, Maine, March 18, 2000.
104. Natural Resources Conservation Service, 1999, page B-5.
105. Martens, 2000.
106. Ettema and Hansen, 1997.
107. Perry, 1994, page 503.
108. St. John, 2000, page 1.
109. St. John, 2000, page 11. For more information on mycorrhizal fungi, visit St. John's Web site, http://www.mycorrhiza.org.
110. St. John, 2000, page 24.
111. St. John, 1998.
112. Lavelle, 1997, page 97.
113. Lavelle, 1997, page 97.
114. Lavelle et al., 1994.
115. Elaine Ingham, Soil Food Web workshop and interview, Maine Organic Farmer's and Gardener's Association, Unity, Maine, March 18, 2000.
116. Natural Resources Conservation Service, 1999.
117. Elaine Ingham, Soil Food Web workshop and interview, Maine Organic Farmer's and Gardener's Association, Unity, Maine, March 18, 2000.
118. Elaine Ingham, March 26, 2000, email communication.

Succession: Four Perspectives on Vegetation Dynamics

Succession is one of the oldest, most basic, yet still in some ways, most confounded ecological concepts. Since its formalization as the premier ecological theory by H. C. Cowles and F. E. Clements in the early 1900s, thousands of descriptions of, commentaries about, and interpretations of succession have been published, and extended inconclusive controversy has been generated.

—R. P. McIntosh, "The Relationship between Succession and the Recovery Process in Ecosystems"

The conclusion to be reached is that it is highly unlikely that a single theory about succession will apply equally well everywhere.

—J. P. Kimmins, *Forest Ecology*

No matter what forms we observe, but particularly in the organic, we shall find nowhere anything enduring, resting, completed, but rather that everything is in continuous motion.

—Goethe

Changes in plant community composition and structure over time are about as mysterious as the wind: successional forces tend to "blow" in certain directions but can go almost any which way depending on the circumstances. The buildings and landscape patterns we create change the direction, speed, and character of the wind in our environments, with or without conscious intent on our part. Similarly, we can influence the direction, speed, and character of vegetation change, and often do so without consciously realizing or intending it. In this chapter, we bring the forces, patterns, and processes of plant community dynamics to the forefront so we can work directly and consciously as agents of succession. What is plant succession? What causes it? How can we work with the process and the forces that cause it to achieve our own purposes?

Social and personal belief systems have frequently shaped our ideas of plant community change. The first formal theories of plant succession used analogies to human development from childhood to maturity and were thereby founded upon a linear viewpoint. These classical theories and their underlying linear perspective persisted through almost sixty years of debate and study. Then, in the late twentieth century, three new perspectives on succession developed in a quick sequence. These new theories looked progressively deeper at the dynamics and causes behind the patterns that the classical theory attempted to describe. They have moved progressively closer to the messy truth of how and why ecosystems change. Many people still hold the early ideas of linear succession and climax. Meanwhile, the newest theories of vegetation dynamics have begun their journey from formulation to testing and refinement. Ecologists have carried forward some of the original ideas that still hold validity, in one form or another. They have dropped other elements, including the analogy to human development.

This chapter presents four perspectives on vegetation dynamics: classical linear succession to a stable climax; linear succession to a shifting mosaic; nonlinear, nonequilibrium patch dynamics; and a theory of successional causes that we will call the unified oldfield theory. It may appear that each of these perspectives represents a separate set of ideas, research, and theories. In reality, they have arisen as a developing flow, much as the "phases" of succession transform from one to another. Hence, this chapter is structured in a way that reflects the successional process itself. We hope that you will see how the legacies of the earlier theories directed the developmental path of the later theories, just like the legacies of prior ecosystems affect succession in the field. Each perspective contains elements of the others, and each is valid under certain conditions: there is no absolutely right or wrong theory. Each forms a possible template for forest garden design, and each helps guide our design and management decisions.

Succession concerns changes over time in the structure and composition of plant communities at two scales: at a specific site, and within the landscape as a whole. For this book, we focus on sites as large as your backyard, up to several acres at the very most. At a landscape scale (tens to hundreds or even thousands of acres), many more dynamics come into play that relate to succession but that have little bearing for forest gardeners. We will discuss these larger-scale issues only to the degree necessary to explain the emerging paradigm of vegetation dynamics and how our small sites fit into it. The same applies to questions of timescale. Vegetation dynamics challenge us to look beyond our narrow time frames and ponder the larger picture. These bigger pictures inform what we do on a small scale in both time and space.

CLASSICAL LINEAR SUCCESSION AND CLIMAX

Early ecologists studied ecosystems primarily as static communities until Frederick Clements formalized his theory of plant succession in 1916.[1] In what many now consider the classical view, succession is an "orderly, directional, and predictable"[2] progression of plant community types from early or pioneer stages to a permanent, stable, repeatable climax. According to this model, each stage has characteristic species for a given region with a given climate. Like much of our cultural paradigm, the classical school viewed ecosystem change through the lens of linearity. It also fixated on climax as the "adult form" of an ecosystem for any given region.

Clements believed that plant communities form a coherent whole, a "superorganism," that embodies some of the characteristics of true organisms. He likened succession to the growth and development of human beings from youth to maturity. He saw communities that somehow persisted in "immature" successional stages as dysfunctional "disclimaxes." A number of these ideas endure to this day, although the evidence supporting many of them is weak or nonexistent. People still use terms such as *mature*, *climax*, and *early succession* that arose as part of this perspective. The organism analogy certainly persists in popular culture, although it stands on shaky ground, if indeed it stands at all.

Ecologist H. A. Gleason, Clements's contemporary, rejected the superorganism theory in favor of an individualistic view. As Gleason said, "Every species of plant is a law unto itself, the distribution of which in space depends upon its peculiarities of migration and environmental requirements. . . . The behavior of the plant offers in itself no reason at all for the segregation of definite communities."[3] Gleason believed that randomness plays a central role in determining which species find their way to a particular spot. Plant communities, in this view, simply result from more or less random associations of species that share similar site requirements and possess overlapping ranges. A climax forest in the same region at different times therefore may not include the same species, or, if it does, it does so by chance as it interacts with environmental conditions and the tolerances and preferences of plants. Gleason's beliefs did not capture the popular imagination as much as Clements's did and so did not hold as much currency in popular culture.

The debate between these two theories fueled succession researchers for a large chunk of the past century. As a result, few ecologists now believe, and the data do not support, the superorganism analogy. However, as we discussed in chapter 4, plants are not entirely "laws unto themselves" either, but live in a complex community of interdependent individuals and species with varying degrees of interaction. Simple analogies just don't cut the mustard when it comes to understanding ecosystems. Ecosystems are not organisms, and they aren't a random free-for-all either. As usual, "the 'truth' (at least as we understand it today) contains elements of both viewpoints, but it is adequately captured by neither."[4]

FOUNDATIONS

Let's review some key aspects of the classical theories. We will focus here on those ideas that still offer value to forest gardeners. However, we shall also discuss key elements of the classical view that scientists have since rejected or modified as their understanding has grown. If we think of these ideas as if they were species in an abandoned field undergoing succession, then these now-rejected concepts would be like perennial grasses that may have dominated for a while but ultimately lost out to understandings that are, like shrubs or trees, more sophisticated and more encompassing.

Primary and Secondary Succession

Classically, succession takes two basic forms: primary and secondary. Primary succession occurs on lifeless rock and mineral particles with no living or nonliving legacies from a preexisting plant or soil community. This happens when glaciers recede, landslides occur, very severe erosion or fires sweep through, or heavy equipment moves large amounts of earth. The initial stages of most primary successions tend to involve bacteria, algae, lichens, and mosses, rather than higher plants, and to take long periods of time. The later stages of primary succession often follow a scheme similar to that for secondary succession: from annual herbs to perennial herbs to shrubs to trees. The organisms initiating primary succession, or any subsequent successional stage, are called pioneers. The first trees that grow in an oldfield succession, such as white or black birch, white pine, aspen, and so on, are pioneer trees. The later species are what this successional theory calls climax species.

Secondary succession takes place when a lesser disturbance disrupts the preexisting plant community but leaves some sort of legacy that influences the pace and pattern of succession. Legacies may include stores of nutrients, organic matter, soil organisms, plants, or plant propagules (any plant part that can grow into a new individual). Any of these will speed the regeneration of the community and influence its species composition. David Perry calls legacies "threads of continuity" that "constrain change and maintain a course leading back to the original community composition."[5] The fact that secondary successions often have a similar successional pattern of species in a given region is due, in part, to legacies.

Consequently, primary successions rarely occur, for the power of biological legacies looms large. Even the intense disturbance from the 1980 eruption of Washington State's Mount Saint Helens resulted in only the volcanic crater itself undergoing primary succession. Within the area hit by blast deposits and mudflows, ground-dwelling rodents, fallen logs, surviving roots and seeds, et cetera, provided powerful legacies for the new ecosystem. Within only three years, 230 of the pre-existing plant species reemerged—90 percent of the preeruption plants.[6] Assessment of biological legacies and strategies for dealing with them are a critical part of forest garden design and management!

The vast majority of forest gardeners will be dealing with secondary successions. In this case, we must either commandeer the power of biological legacies, using them for our own purposes, or overcome them to direct the system where we want it to go. The understandings gained from this chapter should help us to do either of these.

In forest gardening, the most likely event leading to something close to primary succession will be intense ground disturbance by heavy equipment. Even this kind of work usually leaves some legacies from the prior community, though they can be minimal. However, formerly forested sites maintained as lawn or agricultural fields for many years may act in some ways more like primary successions (see "Passing the Baton" later in this chapter).

Patterns of Change in Community Composition

The typical pattern of an "orderly, directional, and predictable"[7] successional sequence in the eastern deciduous forest goes from annual herbs to perennial herbs to shrubs to trees. However, this map does not include the earliest stages of succession from bare ground, does not discuss the climax stage, and does not represent the fullness of variation that can occur. Let's look a little more deeply.

Please remember that the "steps" or "stages" we discuss are, in reality, flows or fits and starts. Periods of waiting may occur at any point, such as when one phase reaches "old age" and begins to decay, but the next stage has not yet started and may not start for a while. Change may also completely transform a community in a few years.

Primary Succession

Barren mineral substrate (bare rock or mineral particles) is a tough environment, and only the toughest organisms can survive there. Bacteria, lichens, and mosses form the first living organic matter in these environments, dominating the scene for years or centuries, depending on climate and substrate (see figure 6.1; see also "Fungal-Bacterial Balance" in chapter 5, page 233 for a discussion of the changes in the soil food web during succession). Much of the organic matter created by these successional trail-blazers erodes away or gets burned in the sun before it can do any soil building of significance. Eventually, though, the accumulation of enough organic matter and organisms creates a living soil.

Once the soil becomes hospitable enough, tough pioneer plants (often mainly annual and perennial grasses and weeds) take over and the rate of soil building increases. These plants build soil by adding additional organic matter, which prevents erosion and improves the soil microclimate. Many early-succession plants are not obligate mycorrhizal species. However, they can still foster the diversification of the soil food web with root exudates and feed the soil food web with their root dieback. Early primary-succession soils tend to contain few nutrients, especially nitrogen. Therefore, many early-stage plants fix nitrogen or accumulate or conserve the nutrients they absorb. This leads to further soil improvements as they die or drop leaves. Many early-succession plants also grow deep, strong roots that help break up hard layers of soil and bring deep nutrients to the surface.

While soil building continues throughout succession until climax, the early stages are the most critical in the development of primary successions. Skipping stages may lead to faster attainment of climax but can radically lower ecosystem productivity over the long run because of poor or incomplete soil development. This is especially true if stages that include nitrogen-fixing plants are omitted.[8] *Careful attention to all aspects of soil development—physical, chemical, and biological—is critical to successful guidance of successional changes, particularly for soils that are barren.* Always include nitrogen-fixers and dynamic accumulators in your

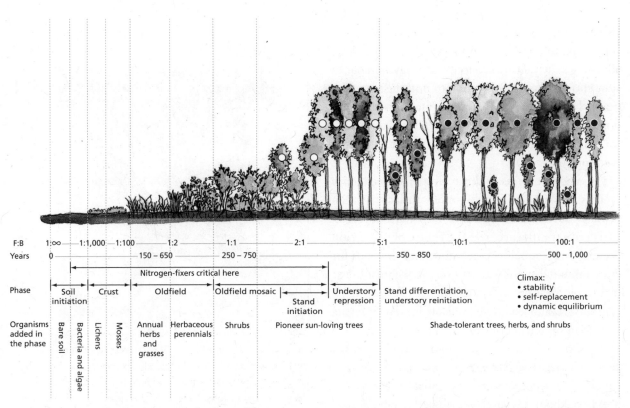

F:B	1:∞	1:1,000	1:100	1:2	1:1	2:1	5:1	10:1	100:1
Years	0		150 – 650		250 – 750		350 – 850		500 – 1,000

FIGURE 6.1. Primary linear succession to climax involves progressive soil and community development from bare, lifeless earth to climax forest containing a rich variety of organisms. Here, open circles indicate sun-loving species and dark circles shade-tolerant species. Secondary succession involves a disturbance that cycles the system from somewhere along the successional continuum back to any earlier stage except bare, lifeless earth. If the system starts with bare earth completely lacking in legacies from earlier living systems, it is a primary succession.

forest garden, as discussed in chapter 5, but especially in the early stages after a disturbance.

Once soil development reaches a certain point, the pattern of species changes may begin to follow typical patterns for a given region. However, particularly in secondary succession, this is one of those generalizations to which there are many exceptions.

Secondary Succession after Disturbance

Many variations occur within the standard pattern of oldfield succession to temperate forest (herbs, shrubs, and trees), depending on a number of factors:

- the history of, and species present in, the pre-disturbance community;
- the timing, kind, and intensity of disturbance and the legacies left behind;

- the species present in the surrounding area, where they are located, and their means of dispersal; and
- the vigor and competitive strengths of the plants established at any given time during the successional sequence.

Some examples: Pioneer or even climax trees may dominate a site very soon after disturbance if they dominated previously, and if the disturbance was not too intense. Years of agricultural use deplete fields of the seed banks of forest species, so trees must disperse from elsewhere, and the herbs and shrubs will likely persist in the fields longer. If a fire occurs just after the black birches (*Betula nigra*) drop their seed in May and June, but before the white pines (*Pinus strobus*) drop theirs in August and September, the pines will have an advantage in colonizing the site. If grasses gain an overwhelming advantage early in succession, they may be able to slow shrub or tree colonization to nothing for many years. They do this both by maintaining bacterial dominance in the soil food web and by competing for light, water, and nutrients against woody seedlings.

The above expresses the reality that secondary successions tend to exhibit more variability than primary successions. The factors listed above can exert greater influence over the course of succession because environmental constraints and the need for environmental modification exert less control over plant colonization and performance. Fewer plants can survive and compete well on barren, infertile soils than on fertile soils.

The fact that secondary successions vary more than primary successions gives us more freedom to design secondary successional sequences. Secondary succession is not a cookbook exercise. No single archetypal pattern governs what is ecologically sound. However, just as with primary successions, skipping stages in secondary successions can reduce long-term site productivity through lack of complete soil development. *Solid soil assessment is key to determining the developmental needs of the ecosystem.* Good preparation is essential to achieving a healthy, productive climax.

Climax: Stability, Self-Replacement, and Dynamic Equilibrium

In the classical view, every ecosystem eventually progresses to a climax, a "stable community in dynamic equilibrium that replaces itself."[9] Theoretically, climate factors largely determine the typical species composition of a given region's climax community, so that all dry, wet, and moist sites eventually converge on the same climax plant community. In regions with adequate rainfall and a long-enough growing season, the climax is some form of temperate deciduous forest: the "oak-hickory forest," the "northern hardwoods forest," or some other variation (see figure 6.2). We can use these climax plant com-

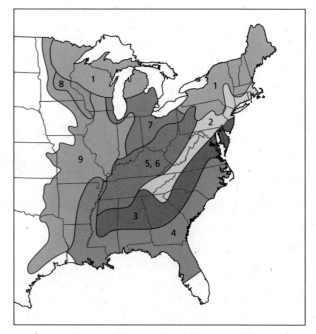

FIGURE 6.2. The nine basic "climax" forest types of the eastern deciduous forest region. While climax theory has been discredited, maps such as this can guide us in our forest garden design deliberations by offering ecological analogs. The climax forest types are: 1) Hemlock–white pine–northern hardwoods forest; 2) Oak-chestnut forest; 3) Oak-pine forest; 4) Southeastern evergreen–mixed southern hardwood forest; 5, 6) Mixed and western mesophytic forests; 7) Beech-maple forest; 8) Maple-basswood forest, and; 9) Oak-hickory forest. *Adapted from Robichaud and Buell, 1973.*

munities as models for habitat mimicry in forest gardening. However, stability, dynamic equilibrium, and self-replacement are the key criteria in the definition of climax for all regions.

In this context, stability means "resistance to change." Theoretically, once a forest achieves climax, internal forces maintain the status quo and only very strong "external" forces can change it. Hence, the total biomass, species composition, and architecture of climax forests would vary little over long periods (figure 6.3), as long as the climate is stable and no major disturbances occur. This ecosystem stability results mainly from species self-replacement.

Self-replacement refers to the idea that once shade-tolerant trees dominate the forest canopy, their offspring will continually replace them. This

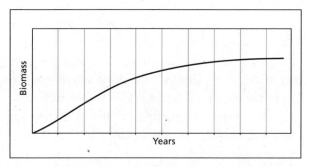

FIGURE 6.3. According to early theories of succession and climax, the total amount of biomass in a forest during succession was thought to increase to a maximum and stabilize there. Contrast this with figure 6.8.

effectively excludes shade-intolerant species from the forest on a continuous basis. Accordingly, the character, structure, and species composition of the community would remain essentially unchanged (equilibrium), though the individual members of the community would grow, die, and be replaced by their offspring over time (dynamism). So theoretically, self-replacement leads not only to stability, but also to dynamic equilibrium. We should remember, however, that *successional climax is a theory, not an observed reality*. Stability, self-replacement, and dynamic equilibrium are challenging to measure, and few sites remain undisturbed by human influences in the present day.

ENVIRONMENTAL MODIFICATION DURING SUCCESSION

A central tenet of the classical view of succession is that succession results *in*, and at least partly *from*, changes in the environment within which the succession is taking place. While many environmental changes take place during succession, we will touch on only three of the most important: soil fertility (organic matter and nutrient content, especially nitrogen), the soil moisture regime, and light.[10]

Soil Fertility: Organic Matter and Nutrient Storage

As discussed in chapter 5, the nutrient containers at the "top" of the soil ecosystem (plants, dead organic matter, and soil organisms) play critical roles in

building the nutrient content of soils. Since all forms of biomass increase in all three of these containers during succession, the amount of nutrients stored by the ecosystem increases as succession proceeds. This is especially true of nitrogen, particularly in primary succession.[11] Nitrogen is the primary nutrient that limits plant growth in old-fields and on disturbed sites.[12] So we know that natural successions increase nitrogen storage in ecosystems over time. What happens if we try to speed up that process with fertilizers?

Experiments conducted on oldfield successions suggest that adding fertilizer, especially nitrogen, tends to *increase the growth of early-succession species* such as annuals and grasses (especially perennial, nonnative grasses) at the expense of midsuccession herbs and woodies. A single fertilizer pulse allowed the later-succession plants to eventually rebound, while continued fertilization led to grass dominance.[13] "Clearly more research is needed . . . [but] fertilization may indeed be a way of reversing succession in oldfields."[14] Hence, fertilization does not appear to speed up succession as we forest gardeners might sometimes prefer. At the same time, researchers have observed that shrub and tree establishment can increase the nitrogen and phosphorus content of the upper soil layers, allowing later colonization by species with high demands for nutrients.[15]

It would appear, then, that how the system proceeds or what form the nutrients come in are as important as the measured nutrient content in the soil when it comes to the system's successional path. Readily available nutrients (fertilizer) seem to encourage early-succession plants adapted to rapidly corner the market on the flush of nutrients available after a disturbance.[16] Presumably, slowly released nutrients bound up in organic matter would encourage species adapted to creating mycorrhizas or to allying with other organisms to get nutrients from organic matter, such as competitor-strategists, stress tolerators, or stress-tolerant competitors (see "Plant Strategies and Life Histories" later in this chapter). This is how nature does it, so why not us? Mulch, nitrogen-fixers, and dynamic accumulators would therefore seem important means to spur succession toward later stages.

Moisture Regime

The idea that successions on dry, wet, and moist soils eventually converge on a single climatic climax has little credibility these days. However, ecologists generally accept that as succession proceeds, wet soils tend to become drier, dry soils tend to become moister, and moist soils tend to stay that way. These effects result from a variety of factors, mainly increases in soil organic matter. However, they may take decades or centuries to manifest.

In oldfield succession experiments, researchers found that, again, grasses responded better than forbs to broadcast irrigation.[17] These effects were short-lived and expensive to achieve, so broadcast irrigation appears to be an ineffective means of "pushing" a forest garden succession along or of directing its path, unless you want to encourage grasses. Drip irrigation probably works better for our purposes, though it may have similar effects.

Light and Shade

The assumption of the classical view is that shade gets progressively deeper during forest succession, achieving its deepest depths at climax. This is probably not true because true climax occurs so rarely, which we will explain shortly. In many natural successions, shade is often the deepest at a phase of succession called understory repression. This phase occurs when vigorously growing young trees close ranks as a relatively low, extremely dense canopy. The depth of shade this creates usually kills the last vestiges of the sun-loving herbs and shrubs that remain from early succession. The canopy opens up again as the tree stand differentiates in age and structure, creating a mosaic of light and shade throughout the woods. Shade-tolerant plants can then move in to take over the new territory. We can design such a phase into our successions to help us transform our understory from sun-loving to shade-loving plants.

Light and shade conditions also depend upon the size of the stand. According to British researchers, clumps of trees must cover at least 16,000 square feet (0.37 acres or 0.15 ha) to produce enough shade for woodland herbs.[18] Given that they conducted this research in Britain, it is probable that the minimum area would be larger in the stronger sun of lower latitudes.

RATES OF SUCCESSION VARY

How fast ecosystems change during succession depends upon a number of factors. Nevertheless, having some estimate of the total time for succession to climax can give us an idea of what to expect for our designs.

Factors Affecting Successional Speed

The speed with which plant communities change depends on several interacting factors, some of which we can influence, and others of which we can't:

- climate and soil conditions;
- the amount of environmental change required during succession;
- how fast organisms alter the environment;
- the growth rate and life span of dominant plants;
- the ability of the existing community to dominate the site and resist invasion; and
- the intensity and frequency of disturbance.[19]

Succession goes faster in warmer or well-watered climates than in cooler or drier climates. Dry, wet, or infertile sites succeed more slowly than moist, fertile sites. Not surprisingly, primary successions take longer to reach climax than secondary successions because they require more environmental modification from beginning to end. Plants and microbes that rapidly produce large amounts of organic matter or quickly change the soil environment will speed succession. Fast-growing plants and plants that produce fast-decomposing organic matter will also speed up succession. Long-lived plants slow down succession, because it takes longer for them to die and be replaced.

Not only does the total time from initiation to climax vary, but also the rate of community change at different successional stages varies. In the eastern forest, early successional stages often move faster than later stages, because early-succession plants tend to be shorter lived than late-succession plants. However, even these tendencies vary from situation to situation. Observations in Michigan, Ontario, and Britain show that it can take fifty years or more for significant tree establishment to occur in old fields, even when nearby woodlands toss seed at the fields every year.[20] Succession can even stop altogether for long periods.

Work under power lines in New England has shown that shrub communities with continuous, thick canopies and dense spacing can resist tree establishment for over thirty years, and probably more.[21] Herbaceous perennials can do the same, not only by growing in dense stands, but also by using allelopathic substances or by associating with soil organisms that resist fungi and their woody-plant associates. The initial flora plays a huge role in creating such situations, as does the intensity of the dispersal pressure from outside (duration, number of seeds, species of plant). In the power-line shrublands, the researchers judiciously used herbicides to kill establishing trees, but once the continuous shrub canopy formed, they did nothing else. Obviously, even such a stable shrubland will change, potentially very rapidly, if severe enough disturbances occur. It all depends on the species present, their density and pattern, the age structure of the populations, and so on.

When we choose plants and the patterns within which we plant them, we influence the probable successional sequence and timeline, whether we know it or not. The plants' life span, their density and vigor, the ease with which their organic matter decomposes, their effects on soil fertility, and their level of competitiveness will all affect the plant community's rate of change. Dense, vigorous, or exclusionary

plants tend to slow succession by inhibiting colonization by later-succession species. Decay-resistant litter slows succession; it may build into a germination-inhibiting mulch, and it may prevent new plants from gaining access to needed nutrients.

Similarly, our management efforts affect the rate of succession. Are we continually turning up bare ground? This sets succession back but also creates opportunities for new species to colonize. Are we thinning stands of desired plants when we weed, which then allows other plants to move in? Are we assisting the demise of plants by too much or too little fertilizing or irrigating or by improper pruning? Such practices injure the individual plants, but they also may provide openings for new plants to influence the community's developmental direction. The point is this: we can affect the rate of succession in our forest gardens if we pay attention to these factors and plan ahead.

Some evidence suggests that a lack of synchronization between the soil and plant communities may impede successional development or alter its direction. The soil may be highly bacterial from topsoil importation or manure or fertilizer applications, inhibiting plants that require a more fungal-dominated soil environment, for example.

Estimated Total Length of Successions

While we are on the subject of time in a successional context, let us look at the bigger picture. How long does it take for a complete classical succession to occur? What does this mean for us forest gardeners?

In cool, humid coastal British Columbia, primary successions on dry sites may take 500 to 1,000 years to reach climax. Meanwhile, primary successions in wet sites (theoretically, succeeding from standing water to moist climax forest) may take as long as 10,000 years. In contrast, the 100 to 500 years required for primary succession on moist sites in that region seems short.[22] Secondary succession of northern hardwood forest in New Hampshire may take up to 350 years to stabilize.[23] Presumably, warmer climates or sites that are more fertile will succeed more quickly.

In the face of such estimates, it would appear that assuming we can grow a "climax" forest garden in our lifetime is preposterous. In addition, most of our crop trees are not climax species and are not, therefore, self-replacing. Since the term *climax* means a stable, self-replacing ecosystem in dynamic equilibrium, we probably should not use the word when we speak about designing forest gardens. We suggest using the term *horizon* or *horizon habitat* to denote the furthest future ecosystem we are designing, and reserving the word *climax* for times and places where it is truly appropriate. Who knows? Perhaps someday we will learn how to design true climax forest gardens: stable, self-replacing, food-producing ecosystems sound great, don't they? Nonetheless, since we are talking about forest gardening as a metaphor and about using all stages of succession to grow food, we can still achieve useful "forest" mimics in our lifetimes.

MECHANISMS OF CHANGE IN THE CLASSICAL PARADIGM

Ecologists have laid out many theories about the mechanisms of succession over the years. Here we will spotlight three that seem to have the most relevance to our discussion.

Passing the Baton: Relay Floristics and Environmental Modification

As we stated earlier, bacteria, algae, and lichens form the initial stages of primary succession because only they can tolerate such extreme environments. Over many decades they modify the environment until mosses can survive. The mosses accelerate the process of soil formation until herbaceous plants can grow. Soil building continues even as shrubs and trees take over, well into the wooded stages of succession. Throughout this process, the soil food web develops in concert, from being bacteria dominated to being fungi dominated, as discussed in the last section of chapter 5.

Observations of processes such as this led to one of the original aspects of successional theory: the belief that early-succession species modified site conditions so the environment became more favorable for later-succession species. The assumption was that later species colonized the site as conditions became favorable, and that they did not exist on the site until that time. This "tag team" of plants modifying a site until they "work themselves out of a job" then passing on the baton to the next set of species is called relay floristics (see figure 6.4).

Researchers now believe that relay floristics operates more during primary successions than during secondary successions because of the varying need for environmental modification. Propagule dispersal and successful plant colonization are also key factors in relay floristics. Hence, the plants around a given site help determine the successional pathway taken. If trees grow nearby and their seeds get blown onto the site, a primary succession may skip some middle or later stages, with the consequent risk of lower ecosystem productivity over the long run.

The Initial Flora Influences the Successional Pathway

Imagine that we stage a footrace that includes sprinters, middle-distance runners, and marathoners. When the gun goes off, the pack is tight, but the sprinters almost immediately take the lead. A little later, the sprinters reach their limits of training and start to peter out, but the middle-distance runners are hitting their stride, and the marathoners are just warming up behind them. If new runners were to now try entering the race, they would have a lot of catching up to do; few would succeed at this strategy. In the meantime, the sprinters fall gasping to the ground, and the middle-distance runners take the lead, with the marathoners still pacing themselves, conserving their energy. Eventually, the middle-distance runners collapse, and the marathoners finish the race alone. One or two latecomers might finish the race too, but generally they would not finish near the head of the pack.

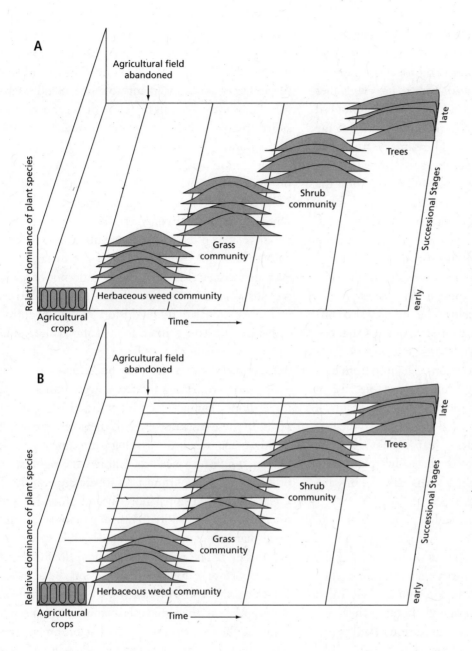

FIGURE 6.4A–B. A conceptual representation of species behavior during (a) relay floristics and (b) initial floristic composition succession dynamics. In relay floristics, species arrive at a site and establish when conditions are ripe for them to do so. In initial floristic composition, all the species present during a successional sequence are there at the beginning, but they show themselves only when the time is ripe. Most successions exhibit both of these behaviors to one degree or another. *Adapted from Egler, 1954. Used with permission.*

We could stage this race a number of times with a different mix of racers—say, all marathoners, or mostly middle-distance runners with a few marathoners and one or two sprinters, or any other combination—and each time the pattern of who takes the lead when would change. With fewer contestants starting at the gun, more latecomers would be able to get in on the race with some chance of success. *The character of the race would depend upon the initial composition of the pack and the running strategy for which each racer has trained.* In the case of plants, we call the sprinters, middle-distance runners, and marathoners by the names of ruderals, competitors, and stress tolerators, respectively (see the following section, as well as "Basic Plant Strategies" in chapter 4, page 126).

When legacies of soil and plants exist on a site, the initial composition of the pack plays a defining role in the character of the successional race. Many of the woodies, perennials, and biennials found in oldfield successions after the annuals die out *were already there even though we may not have seen them.* Either they grow the first or second year as tiny, unnoticed seedlings, or the seeds lie in the soil waiting for the right conditions to sprout. The same is true of at least some of the shrubs and trees that grow later on.

Most gardeners know about soil seed banks, the literally millions of plant seeds that lie dormant in the soil, sometimes for decades, before germinating when the right conditions occur. Farmers expend much effort to defend against this seed bank. Forests contain soil seed banks, too (again, with millions of seeds per acre), though the species present differ from those in oldfields. The soil may also contain stem sections, buds, roots, and stumps that can quickly regenerate whole plants. Because of these resources, secondary successions can jump from bare ground to self-replacing climax forest directly, or they may include any number of other shortcuts, if the right propagules are present and the soil legacy suffices. In a clear-cutting experiment in New Hampshire, 95 percent of the individual plants that regenerated on the site already existed there in some form before the clear-cutting.[24]

We must therefore assume that practically any site already contains seeds or other propagules of a wide range of species. These species possess varying life histories and ages to maturity that determine when they come to dominate a stand. Annuals appear first after a disturbance, for example, because they germinate under disturbed conditions and grow quickly. Perennials appear next because they take longer to grow to maturity. Also, it may take up to three years for perennial seeds to experience the specific sequences of conditions they sometimes require to germinate. Shrub and tree seeds often prefer to germinate in less harsh conditions than the previous plants, so some wait—but some don't. Once they sprout, they often grow more slowly and take more time to develop and dominate than the annuals and perennials. The theory of initial floristic composi-

tion assumes that the initial flora largely determines the successional stages the site goes through, and how quickly (figure 6.4). The initial flora also affects the ability of additional plants to move in and establish themselves. We can therefore direct the successional pathway by controlling or managing the initial flora.

Our forest gardens will initially include many plants we did not select that got there before us. When plants occupy a site, they reduce the ability of other plants to seed in or spread. Even if other plants do arrive, they often have a competitive disadvantage because they got there last. This is not to say, however, that dispersal and colonization do not occur in secondary successions. Farm fields, suburban lawns, and other sites with a long history of continual disturbance will have a more limited initial flora, and immigration will play a larger role. Neighboring trees, shrubs, and herbs with numerous seeds can exert an overwhelming influence, even with a dense initial flora. Animals also disperse and plant many seeds. In these cases, however, the newcomers can get an advantage only if the existing community is weak or thin, if a disturbance occurs at just the right time, or if they act as opportunists or supercompetitors.

Cataloging the initial flora in and around a site offers us the opportunity to plan site preparation and weed management and to invite desirable species to stick around. The power of the initial flora gives us the opportunity to direct succession by densely planting useful species for each stage of succession all at once. We can then guide the community to keep it going in the direction we want. Establishment and maintenance of the garden as a whole will be made easier by planting a wide range of successional species at one time. In that process, we must be aware of the strategies each species uses to survive and spread.

Plant Strategies and Life Histories

The theory of initial floristic composition raises plant strategies and life histories as critical factors in determining the composition of each successional stage. As the footrace envisioned above illus-

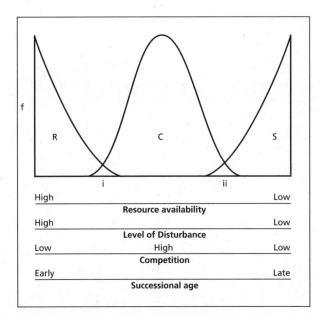

FIGURE 6.5. The frequency (f) of ruderal, competitor, and stress-tolerant species varies depending on resource availability, the level of disturbance, and competition. These factors change from the beginning to the end of succession such that ruderals dominate first, competitors second, and stress tolerators at the end of succession. At point 'i' disturbance is low enough that competition becomes the most adaptive strategy. At point 'ii' resource limitations make stress tolerance more adaptive than competition. *Adapted with permission from J. P. Grime,* American Naturalist *111:1169-94. Copyright © 1977 by the University of Chicago Press.*

Box 6.1: The Principle of Allocation

Different species allocate their limited energy to different structures and functions in their effort to survive and reproduce. When genetically coded, these allocation patterns define an organism's adaptive strategy. Each adaptive strategy has different architectural and behavioral implications for the plant or animal in question.[26]

We all must choose where and when to spend our time and energy. When we develop habits in that regard, we have adopted a strategy to get us through life. In plants and animals these strategies are genetically coded to at least some degree, and that code determines the organism's structure and functions. Does a given plant allocate its energy mostly to reproduction and dispersal, to growth and competition, or to defense and maintenance? Does it have broad environmental tolerances, or does it have specific, narrow requirements? Is a given predator a specialist or a generalist? Which strategy a plant or animal chooses will determine in which environments it will perform the best. It will also influence its usefulness to us, both in kind and in quantity, and how, where, when, and why we can use that species in our forest garden.

When we choose plants for our garden, we are choosing to use their strategies. We should make sure that we manage and use plants in ways that are in harmony with their essential life strategy and their resulting architecture or form. Plants that emphasize reproduction will likely yield more seed than those that emphasize maintenance or those that emphasize growth and competition, for example. Trying to force high yields of fruit from plants that use maintenance as a primary strategy will be an uphill battle, while harvesting leafy greens from a plant that emphasizes growth and competition makes good sense. However, plant breeding often alters a plant's fundamental strategy and therefore alters its ecology, successional role, and resource or maintenance demands.

trates, ruderals, competitors, and stress tolerators take different places in the successional sequence. The adaptiveness of the various plant strategies and life histories varies as succession moves forward, which assists the change in species populations over time (see figure 6.5).[25] All of this is based on the principle of allocation (box 6.1).

Early-succession plants mostly use the ruderal strategy. These plants, exclusively herbaceous annuals and biennials (table 6.1), allocate most of their energy to reproduction. They live short lives, yet their seed remains viable in the soil for long periods. This adapts them to take advantage of disturbed conditions that appear randomly and infrequently, and that change quickly. They spend little energy on resource gathering (root or shoot growth)

TABLE 6.1. Selected characteristics of ruderal, competitor, and stress-tolerator plants. *Adapted from J. P. Grime*, Plant Strategies, Vegetation Processes, and Ecosystem Properties. *Copyright © 2001 John Wiley & Sons Ltd. Reproduced with permission.*

Characteristic	Ruderal	Competitor	Stress Tolerator
Life form	Annual and biennial herbs	Perennial herbs, shrubs, trees	Perennial herbs, shrubs, trees
Shoot architecture	Small stature; limited lateral spread	High, dense canopy; wide spread	Extremely varied
Life span	Very short	Long or relatively short	Long to very long
Leaf and root life span	Short	Relatively short	Long
Flowering frequency	High, sometimes more than once per year	Typically yearly once established	Intermittent over a long life
Amount of energy devoted to seeds	Large	Small	Small
Regenerative strategies	Seasonal regeneration in gaps; many small wind-dispersed seeds/spores; persistent seed banks	Vegetative expansion; seasonal regeneration in gaps; many small wind-dispersed seeds/spores; persistent seed banks	Vegetative expansion; persistent seedling bank
Maximum potential growth rate	Rapid	Rapid	Slow
Response to stress	Rapid curbing of growth; energy diverted to flowering	Maximizing vegetative growth	Responses slow and small in size
Timing of nutrient uptake and photosynthesis	Opportunistic, coinciding with vegetative growth	Strongly seasonal; coincides with long period of continuous vegetative growth	Opportunistic, often uncoupled from vegetative growth
Energy and nutrient storage	Confined to seeds	Most built into plant structure; some stored for following year	Stored in leaves, stems, and/or roots
Litter	Sparse, not usually persistent	Copious, not usually persistent	Sparse, sometimes persistent
Palatability to generalist herbivores	Usually high	Various	Low

because disturbed environments tend to exhibit flushes of nutrients and greater water availability. Ruderals also have little need for defense: their pop-up-and-go strategy is a good defense in itself. Their nomadic habits help them avoid competition but afford them little opportunity to dominate anything other than early succession, immediately after disturbance. They frequently grow in masses.

Ruderals prevent fertility loss by capturing and holding nutrients mobilized by disturbances. They quickly generate large quantities of organic matter, mostly because of their number, since ruderal plants typically have a small stature and limited lateral spread. We can use them as mulch plants and nutrient conservers, but we must use them as such *immediately* after a disturbance or else the nutrients they need will leach away. Many common food

crops and cover crops are ruderals, which is why we need to give them so many nutrients and set back succession all the time.

As other plants begin to colonize a disturbed site, or disturbance becomes less frequent, ruderal strategies become less adaptive for plant success. Competitor plants devote themselves to resource gathering and rapid growth, with reproduction a secondary concern. They quickly take up as much space as possible so they have the best shot at reproducing later. They generally turn whatever resources they can grab into plant tissue very quickly but put little energy into building longevity into those tissues. They store only what energy and nutrients they need to get going next year. They spread using all available means: vegetative expansion (root and shoot growth), wind-dispersed seed, and seed banking. They some-

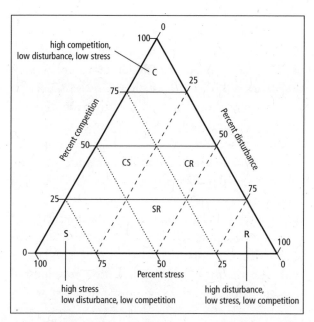

FIGURE 6.6. Few plants fall clearly into one of the three life-strategy categories laid out by the RCS theory. When you see disturbance, competition, and stress each as a continuum, you arrive at a chart like this to describe plant strategies. Species with intermediate strategies then become competitive stress tolerators (CS), competitive ruderals (CR), or stress-tolerant ruderals (SR). *Adapted with permission from J.P Grime,* American Naturalist *111:1169-94. Copyright © 1977 the University of Chicago Press.*

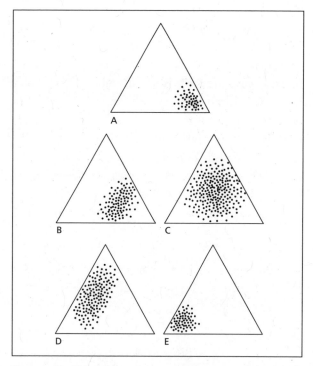

FIGURE 6.7. Using figure 6.6 as a guide, we can then classify plant life forms and see where they fall: A) annual herbs; B) biennial herbs; C) perennial herbs and ferns; D) trees and shrubs; and E) lichens. *Adapted with permission from J.P Grime,* American Naturalist *111:1169-94. Copyright © 1977 the University of Chicago Press.*

times compete and defend themselves against competition using chemical warfare (allelopathy). They can be trees, shrubs, or perennial herbs (see table 6.1). They frequently grow in clumps and drifts.

As succession continues, living and dead organic matter bind up more and more free nutrients, and fewer and fewer nutrients are easily available to plants. This leaves plants that grow rapidly at a disadvantage compared to those adapted to tolerate resource limitation. Stress tolerators put their energy into maintenance and mutualism. They grow slowly because they create tissues that withstand the test of time. They can absorb and store nutrients when they aren't growing, whereas most competitors and all ruderals can absorb nutrients only when they are actively growing. Stress tolerators eventually overtop competitors and shade them out. They also develop mutualistic relation-

ships with fungi and other organisms to help them overcome resource limitations. On moderately moist sites with temperate seasons, deciduous trees are the most adaptive plant life forms. Trees are also the most stress tolerant, at least partly because they influence the environment around them so much.

While the above discussion seems pretty cut-and-dried, the plant world clearly is not. Most plants fall somewhere between these three points of the triangle, showing characteristics of more than one strategy (figure 6.6). Some of our common annual food crops express competitor strategies, even though annuals generally fall at the ruderal end of the spectrum. These we call competitive ruderals. Stress-tolerant ruderals include plants that colonize early primary successions on poor sites. We can consider pioneer trees to be competitive stress tolerators.

While it is difficult to locate any one species exactly

on the R-C-S diagram, the various plant groups do tend to fall in certain parts of the triad (figure 6.7). Perennial herbs form the main exception to this rule, because their life form is so adaptable. This in part helps us understand why the different life forms dominate at the stages of succession that they do. It can also help us select plants exhibiting the right attributes for our designed successional sequences. But where are these sequences going? Do they end at some stable dynamic equilibrium or not? How valid is the climax concept?

EMPEROR CLIMAX HAS NO CLOTHES

Although generally accepted by plant ecologists until 1970, the hypothesis that a forest developed to a fixed climax was difficult to test, and in fact . . . was incorrect.

—DANIEL BOTKIN, *Forest Dynamics*

Many ecologists now consider the classical theory of a stable, permanent endpoint of succession to be a nakedly simplistic and perhaps embarrassing fallacy, at least for most forests. We could consider the three underpinnings of the theory (stability, self-replacement, and dynamic equilibrium) to be clothes made for Emperor Climax, ruler of all successions. These clothes, of course, turn out not to exist. Nevertheless, while the emperor may not have any clothes on, we still have an emperor, at least for now. He just looks different without all those robes. Stable, self-replacing climax occurs far less often than previously thought, and only under specific conditions. Some forests do achieve it, but it is not as broadly applicable or controlling as we used to think. However, all the concepts, theories, and observations of succession discussed above that arose during Emperor Climax's reign remain valid: primary and secondary succession, legacies, environmental modification, timescales, relay floristics, initial floristic composition, and plant strategies.

In any case, the climax concept still holds some value. It provided useful structure for ecological research for many years. It organized vegetation

mapping and classification, which helps us create habitat mimics for our forest gardens. We can still use climax as a theoretical endpoint for forest garden design, even though it's not always the best, nor is it the only model out there. What other models exist for the long-term future of our forest gardens?

The next section explores a second model of vegetation dynamics that amplifies our understanding of successional processes at an ecosystem level. This model still assumes the linear progression of classical succession. However, it replaces the theory of climax as a stable, self-replacing dynamic equilibrium with a theory that shares some similarities with the theory behind typical crop rotations in organic gardening: shifting mosaic steady state.

PROGRESSIVE SUCCESSION TO SHIFTING-MOSAIC STEADY STATE

In the late 1970s, a series of long-term, multidisciplinary, ecosystem-scale forest-succession experiments came to fruition at the Hubbard Brook Experiment Station in New Hampshire's White Mountains.[27] These experiments involved clearcutting whole watersheds previously covered with northern hardwood forest (beech-birch-maple). The researchers then compared the successional dynamics of species composition and nutrient, water, and energy flows in the denuded and nearby untouched watersheds.

At the same time, work began to gel on computer simulations of forest succession.[28] These simulations formalized complex sets of interacting theories and assumptions about tree niches, tree growth, competition, nutrients, and other factors. The acid test of a computer model is whether it can reasonably approximate the behavior of real forests. These simulations did so, based on data from real ecosystems, including the Hubbard Brook experiments. They gave credence to the assumptions and theories built into the computer program (and supported H. A. Gleason's individualistic theories of plant communities). It also offered researchers the ability to "grow" a virtual forest for three hundred to five hundred years under different conditions and see what happens.

These two pieces of research elaborated on and clarified many understandings of the classical succession model, including the causes of succession, and especially the dynamics occurring within the typical early and middle stages of linear forest succession, for which we have the most real-world data. Much of what we have discussed in the previous section remains as part of this second succession model. However, these two pieces of research also caused significant shifts in perspective concerning the nature of climax and equilibrium. This research helps us see the relationship between succession dynamics at the ecosystem scale and at the site scale. Understanding this relationship is key to understanding succession as a whole system.

In this successional model, linear succession leads to a shifting-mosaic steady state in which any particular site within the forest undergoes continuous cycles of succession and disturbance. The disturbances in this case come about by the simple death and replacement of trees in a process called gap dynamics. Therefore, some portion of the forest is *always at early-successional stages*, but the location of these early-succession sites shifts over time. The same is true of all other stages of succession, and this creates a mosaic of patches at different successional stages, all of which change location as the system ages. Yet at the landscape scale, the forest as a whole maintains more or less the same species composition, energy and nutrient dynamics, and so on: a shifting-mosaic steady state.

One major difference between shifting mosaic and classical climax is that while the species composition at the landscape scale doesn't change much over time, *the shifting mosaic includes species from all stages of succession.* Conversely, a classical climax, by definition, includes only self-replacing species of late succession, e.g., shade-tolerant trees that can grow in the shade of their own elders.

PHASES AND DYNAMICS OF SECONDARY SUCCESSION

Different authors describe the various "stages" of succession differently, depending on what kind of system they are describing. Often these descriptions involve ecosystem architecture or what kinds of plants dominate (the "shrub stage"), the presuccession state of the system ("oldfield"), or some sense of timing ("midsuccession"). Here we will discuss the phases of succession in terms of ecosystem dynamics instead of species, plant types, history, or architecture.

The Hubbard Brook experiments involved a series of small watersheds on impervious granite bedrock.[29] Researchers left some watersheds untouched and experimentally manipulated others for comparison. The impervious bedrock allowed the reasonably accurate measurement and calculation of energy, water, and nutrient budgets for each watershed before, during, and after the experimental clear-cuts.

In the autumn of 1965, loggers cut all trees larger than about 1 inch (2 cm) in diameter to the ground within a 38-acre (15.6 ha) watershed that they named W2. They left all the wood in place and cut slash and brush to within 5 feet (1.5 m) of the ground. They built no roads or skid trails in the process, thus minimizing soil disturbance and erosion. For three subsequent growing seasons, researchers used herbicides to keep vegetative growth from rebounding, and then they let the ecosystem do its thing. The herbicide treatment allowed the researchers to separate the effects of nutrient releases due to disturbance from the effects of nutrient and water uptake by plants during regrowth.

F. Herbert Bormann and Gene Likens used the above experiment to define four phases of secondary succession: reorganization, aggradation (the opposite of degradation), transition, and steady state (see figure 6.8). To these four we add disturbance as a key phase defining the sequence of events that follows. The basic measure used to define these phases is the total biomass, living and dead, within the

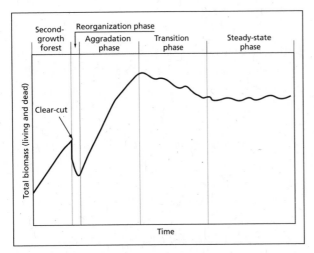

FIGURE 6.8. The four phases of secondary succession as defined by Bormann and Likens include reorganization, aggradation, transition, and steady state. Each is defined by the behavior of the system with respect to the levels of biomass in the ecosystem. *Adapted from Bormann and Likens, 1979. Used with permission.*

ecosystem. *The assumption here is that there was a preexisting ecosystem that underwent some form of disturbance, leading to a renewed successional process.* Therefore, this perspective does not apply in whole to primary successions, though many aspects of it are certainly relevant.

Basically, it all boils down to this: the story of disturbance and succession is essentially the story of plant communities losing, gaining, and then again partially losing control over the potentially destructive forces that nature throws at them.

The Predisturbance Condition:
An Aggrading Ecosystem

The preclear-cut forest of W2 was a second-growth northern hardwood forest dominated by beech, sugar maple, and yellow birch (*Fagus grandifolia, Acer saccharum,* and *Betula alleghaniensis,* respectively). Several years of baseline monitoring showed that when the experiment began the ecosystem was still recovering from thinnings and cuttings in the late 1800s and early 1900s. This means the nutrient containers in the system looked more or less like those in figure 5.5 (page 180). The system showed

an ongoing increase in the living and dead biomass at the top of the nutrient container system, which means it was storing more and more nutrients in the topsoil and vegetation over time. The system was aggrading.

Aggradation essentially means that the system is building abundance. In ecological terms, aggradation is the building of increased living and dead biomass, soil fertility, and physical and biological complexity. An ecosystem can create these forms of natural capital only by controlling the potentially destructive forces of water, wind, and solar energy. *Ecosystems exert maximum control over these forces during the aggradation phase, thereby controlling the system's energy, water, and nutrient flows.*

Aggrading ecosystems control these forces and flows by building living and dead architecture. We discussed in chapter 5 how plants plug nutrient leaks by directing water through their bodies to garner nutrients and thereby limit the water available for leaching away nutrients. Plants accomplish this essential work by building biological infrastructure that also controls the flows of solar energy.

Plants convert sunlight to biomass at a very low efficiency. Only 1 to 2 percent of the solar energy that falls on a forest gets used in photosynthesis. However, "the trick that makes this small energy flux so important is to use it for physical construction. A temperate forest controls wind, water, and soil movement by what amounts to mass engineering, and the forces of chaos in a habitat are checked as the floods of a great river are checked—by a few subtle engineering works."[30] By building biological infrastructure, plants end up using around 40 percent of the sun's energy to evaporate water, pumping it from the soil into the air, thus gaining control over water, nutrients, and sunlight in one fell swoop. This coup d'état allows the forest to build abundance patiently, one leaf, one stem, one drop of water, one year at a time.[31] This is what watershed W2 was doing at the beginning of the Hubbard Brook experiments.

Then the chainsaws came.

Disturbance: Loss of Infrastructure Means Loss of Control

We will discuss disturbance in more detail below; however, let us briefly consider what we mean by the word. Pickett and White define a disturbance as "any relatively discrete event in time that disrupts ecosystem, community, or population structure and changes resources, substrate availability, or the physical environment."[32] A disturbance can arise from any destructive event, such as a hurricane, ice storm, fire, insect outbreak, the death of a single tree, or the thinning or clear-cutting of a whole forest. Environmental fluctuations, such as climate changes, rising water tables, and the like may also cause disturbance. In the case of this model of succession, once the chainsaws and herbicides left W2, the assumption was that the only disturbances that would occur within the ecosystem were those generated from within the ecosystem itself. In other words, no hurricanes, fires, clear-cutting, or climate changes—only the normal life spans of trees and the interactions between them and their environment.[33]

When the chainsaws and herbicides came to W2, they took the system in figure 5.5 and made it into figure 5.3. They destroyed the living infrastructure, shutting down the water and nutrient controls the system previously had had. The plants stopped photosynthesizing, shutting off the energy supply to the living-web microbes in the soil. The dead-web microbes, on the other hand, had a veritable feast. Dead organic matter increased radically, and to top it off, soil temperatures climbed due to the loss of plant cover. This sped up everybody's metabolism and led to a dead organic matter feeding frenzy. In the case of W2, researchers observed a weight loss of 23 percent in the forest floor as biomass decomposed during three years of herbicide treatment.[34] *Disturbances convert biomass and other resources from one form to another.* How much and what gets converted depends on the kind, timing, and intensity of the disturbance.

With no plants taking up water and putting it in the air, Hubbard Brook stream flows increased from 25 to 40 percent overall, and storm flows increased by as much as 300 percent. The amount of rain entering the ground increased, helping keep the decomposer feast going and washing away the garbage the feasting left behind. Unfortunately for the soil, that garbage was a large quantity of nutrients previously stored up through many years of slow, patient labor by the ecosystem. Total nutrient losses in stream water increased by a factor of *eight* during the devegetation period, peaking in the second year and then dropping off. The drop was due to the easily available nutrients and readily decomposed organic matter being exhausted, so that further decomposition of resistant organic matter was necessary to release more nutrients. *It took only two years to exhaust the supply of readily available nutrients in the soil ecosystem.*[35] Delaying revegetation after a disturbance leads to large losses of nutrients.

Keeping the plants dead for three years shut down the natural recycling system of the forest, prolonging the disturbance and deepening its impact. It also altered the microclimate, exposing the remnants of the system to the forces of nature. The more intense the disturbance, the more the threads of continuity—legacies from the preexisting ecosystem—get cut. As Bormann and Likens said:

> In a sense, the disturbance opens the [forest] system to those potentially destructive forces that are ever-present in its environment: rain, running water, wind, heat, and gravity. The longer these forces operate in an uncontrolled way, the more the ecosystem is degraded, and the longer the time necessary for the ecosystem to recover to pre-disturbance conditions, if indeed recovery is possible.[36]

Reorganization: Recovering Control by Drawing on Natural Capital

In the reorganization phase, the ecosystem "comes to terms" with the disturbance event and eventually reestablishes control over the water and nutrient flows within it. To reorganize itself and reestablish its infrastructure, the system draws on the natural capital it had previously built up. The more natural capital the system has to draw on, the faster it will recover. The more intense the disturbance, the longer recovery will take. The greater the nutrient losses before the beginning of recovery, the slower the process.

Once a disturbance is over, the processes of increased decomposition of biomass and loss of nutrients continue unabated for a time (as long as supplies last). These processes do have a side benefit, though: easily available nutrients become abundant in the soil water. The soil water is often more available as well, since there is less transpiration. Combine that with plenty of sunshine and warmer soil temperatures and you have a perfect environment for ruderal plants, whose seeds either have been lying in the soil for years waiting for just this opportunity or can blow in from the neighborhood.

Designed for rapid growth, ruderals rapidly begin taking up nutrients, building infrastructure, and modifying microclimates. Other plants also come into play: root and stump sprouts, formerly suppressed seedlings, and surviving trees, shrubs, and herbs all respond to the new conditions. The marathon of initial floristic composition is on! How many racers crowd the race track and what kind of runners they are depend on the legacies left over from the previous system. They must act quickly to prevent nutrient losses from mounting, however, for they have only a few short years before the readily available nutrients become exhausted.

It can take ten to twenty years for the ecosystem to again assert the control over the forces of wind, water, and sun that it once had. This means nutrient leaks remain large and nutrient plugs small for a significant time. As a result, the curve in figure 6.8 shows the biomass level decreasing through the reorganization period, even though there are quick gains in living biomass in the early years. Decomposition still exceeds production, so biomass drops and a net loss of nutrients and energy from the system occurs.

While the rapid growth of ruderals may make it look as if the soil is fertile, this can be deceiving. The flush of vegetation is more a response to nutrient *availability and losses* than to soil fertility.[37]

Imagine now that we continually disrupt the ecosystem over a long period. We release a flush of nutrients by turning over the soil and destroying the vegetation, then let it lie fallow for a while as ruderals take over, only to disrupt it again and repeat that process. Obviously, we thereby maintain the system in a state of disturbance and reorganization, with the consequent losses of nutrients, biomass, and complexity over time. Trying to maintain or even improve the natural capital of such a system takes a tremendous amount of work. This is exactly what we do in conventional agriculture: fight a continuous uphill battle. We can instead use the processes of natural systems to build natural capital.

Aggradation: The Period of Peak Control over Ecosystem Processes

Aggradation is the period of highest stability (i.e., constancy of ecosystem functions) in forest ecosystems. Forests in this phase maximally buffer the vagaries of wind, water, and weather to control the flows of the key elements essential to ecosystem health and productivity. The aggradation phase begins when total biomass levels start to increase again (fifteen to twenty years after the clear-cutting at Hubbard Brook) and ends when biomass stops accumulating (projected to be 150 to 250 years after the clear-cutting at Hubbard Brook). Biomass accumulates rapidly at first, then more slowly later in the phase.

As the ecosystem accumulates biomass, the living system strongly regulates the flows of energy, water, and nutrients. The chemistry of drainage waters varies little even as drainage flow rates vary a lot. The soil's resistance to erosion increases dramatically. The cation exchange capacity of the soil increases as organic matter accumulates, literally doubling the depth of the forest floor in the first sixty years.[38] The ecosystem controls the internal flows of water by controlling evapotranspiration and by increasing the ability of the soil to hold water. Stream flow rates decrease, reducing leaching and erosion. Ultimately, the rate of nutrient losses from the aggrading Hubbard Brook watershed came to equal *or fall below* the amount of nutrients entering the system by atmospheric deposition and the weathering of rock and mineral soil.[39]

The aggradation phase may last around two hundred years in northern hardwood forests, building biomass the whole time. Eventually, the ecosystem accumulates so much living and dead biomass that the energetic cost of maintaining that biomass rises high enough to equal biomass production. This is when the aggradation phase ends and the transition to steady state begins.

Transition: The System Seeks Balance

Little real-world data exists for the last two phases of succession in this model, transition and steady state. According to computer simulations, the transition to steady state starts about two hundred years after clear-cutting, and may last as long as two hundred years.

This succession model assumes a single clear-cut disturbance that begins a renewed successional sequence. Consequently, the resulting trees are all the same age, at least initially. For this reason, we can talk about the ecosystem in the reorganization and aggradation phases as if the whole system is in one phase, for it is. From transition phase on, we can no longer do that, for the ecosystem begins to differentiate at two levels: site and landscape.

To understand what occurs in the transition phase, let's look at the four phases of succession at both scales. Imagine you have one hundred plastic plant pots sitting in your backyard, laid out in ten rows of ten pots each. Each pot represents a site within an aggrading forest like the preclear-cut watershed at Hubbard Brook. You plant one seedling of a self-sowing annual plant in every pot. One hundred percent of the pots now contain a low amount of living biomass—one tiny seedling (figure 6.9a).

The plants draw on the accumulated reserves of nutrients and energy in their pots to begin building living biomass. The nutrient and organic matter reserves of the soil in the pots drops as they do so. As the weeks go by, the plants get bigger. Since all the plants are the same age, they all reach a moderate level of living biomass at about the same time, but some are maturing faster than others. As they age more and grow more, the variation in size and maturity increases, but they all achieve a high level of living biomass at about the same time. Then some plants begin to flower and die, sowing seeds that immediately sprout and begin growing (figure 6.9b). When this occurs, each particular pot goes from a high level of living biomass to a low level of living biomass and then begins growing living biomass again. As time goes on, more plants flower, die, and reproduce, but the age structure of the population gets more diverse because of their varying growth rates. The system goes from all the pots containing roughly the same amount of living biomass to some pots containing a little, some moderate amounts, and some high amounts. The percentage of pots at the different levels of living biomass begins to vary. Some pots have tiny sprouts, some have flowering mature plants, others are somewhere in between, and which pots are in which condition varies over time. Eventually, the system comes to a steady state where the proportion of pots at each level of living biomass more or less stabilizes (figure 6.9c).

This is what happens in a clear-cut forest allowed to succeed. In the reorganization phase, every site in the landscape has low levels of living biomass. The living biomass at every site within the whole landscape then grows at about the same rate throughout aggradation. In the transition phase, the even-aged structure of the stand begins to break down as trees die and succession begins again at particular sites in the landscape. That begins creating the shifting mosaic.

The decline in total biomass during transition shown in figure 6.8 occurs because as old trees die, more and more patches of the forest go back to

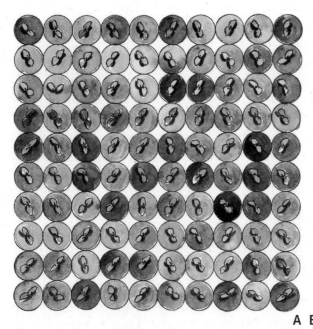

A B

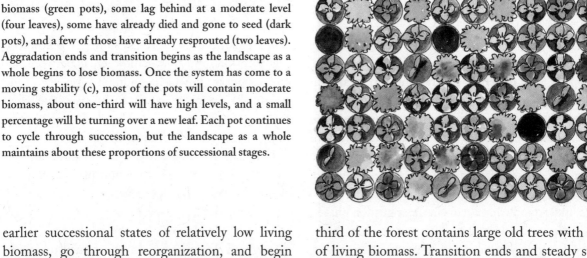

C

FIGURE 6.9A–C. A landscape of plant pots with self-sowing annuals in them could follow the pattern of succession laid out in the shifting-mosaic model. At first (a), 100 percent of the pots contain low levels of living biomass just after the first seeds have sprouted. The plants grow at slightly different rates (b), so that while most pots contain high amounts of living biomass (green pots), some lag behind at a moderate level (four leaves), some have already died and gone to seed (dark pots), and a few of those have already resprouted (two leaves). Aggradation ends and transition begins as the landscape as a whole begins to lose biomass. Once the system has come to a moving stability (c), most of the pots will contain moderate biomass, about one-third will have high levels, and a small percentage will be turning over a new leaf. Each pot continues to cycle through succession, but the landscape as a whole maintains about these proportions of successional stages.

earlier successional states of relatively low living biomass, go through reorganization, and begin aggrading again. As the transition phase continues, the proportions of the forest in the various biomass categories settle toward a sort of moving balance (figures 6.10 and 6.11). Sites with moderate living biomass dominate (about 60 percent of the landscape). A small percentage of the forest has low living biomass (just after trees die), and about a third of the forest contains large old trees with lots of living biomass. Transition ends and steady state begins when this process results in relative stability at a landscape level, even as gap dynamics create new disturbances every year to keep the shifting mosaic going. Can you imagine how we might mimic this in our forest gardens? Can you see how Native American agroforestry and slash-and-burn agriculture (see chapter 1) mimicked this process?

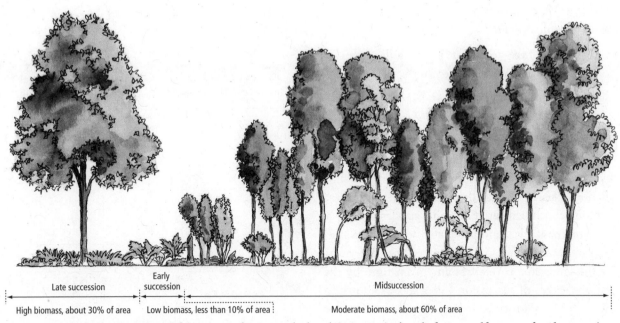

Late succession — High biomass, about 30% of area

Early succession — Low biomass, less than 10% of area

Midsuccession — Moderate biomass, about 60% of area

FIGURE 6.10. A section through a shifting-mosaic forest reveals that the community has shady areas, old trees, and early succession sites. This allows species from all stages of succession to survive indefinitely. Though midsuccession dominates, there is diversity in these sites, with varying tree and tree-stand ages and lumpy texture because each patch is at a different stage of midsuccession.

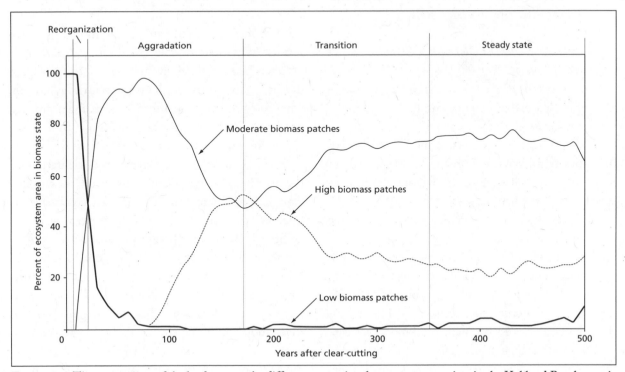

FIGURE 6.11. The proportions of the landscape at the different successional stages vary over time in the Hubbard Brook experiments. Eventually, they settle to a moving balance of about 2/3 of the landscape at moderate biomass (midsuccession), 1/3 at high biomass (late succession), and a small fraction at low biomass (early succession, just after disturbance). This is the steady state, even though the mosaic shifts over time. *Adapted from Borman and Likens, 1999. Used with permisssion.*

Shifting-Mosaic Steady State: Cycles of Succession and Wobbling Stability

> The idea of the steady state is among the more controversial of ecological constructs.

> —F. H. BORMANN AND G. E. LIKENS,
> *Pattern and Process in a Forested Landscape*

Bormann and Likens used the term *steady state* with some trepidation. Shifting-mosaic steady state is no clean, straight-line equilibrium. The computer simulations clearly suggest that the steady-state phase exhibits continued variation in its species composition, biomass level, and productivity, but this variation stays near some sort of average. The percentage of the landscape covered at any given time by the various stages of succession varies too, as shown in figure 6.11 and discussed above. Steady state in this model is a wobbling sort of stability at both the large and small scales: gap dynamics causes succession cycles at small scale, and random variation around a mean occurs at a large scale.

Gap Dynamics: Cycles, Not Steady States, at Small Scale

When a tree falls in the forest it leaves a gap: a vertical open space that extends through the vegetation layers from the canopy down to the top of the herb layer (6 feet, or 2 meters, or more).[40] Since gap dynamics will likely affect many forest gardens in some way, we will explore the factors involved in significant detail here.

The forest by its nature generates gaps from tree falls due to old age. Wind and ice storms assist this process, causing old or weak trees to break or fall. As trees grow larger and larger with age, and especially in shallow or wet soils, "domino effect" multiple tree falls occur more frequently. These gaps then undergo succession, with the kind of succession depending on gap size and disturbance intensity. Gap dynamics involve only this small-scale, tree-by-tree replacement within a forest, driven by the death of individual trees or small groups of them. Gap dynamics dominate succession only in

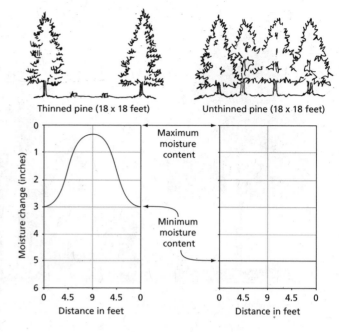

FIGURE 6.12. Soil moisture levels in gaps increase near the center of the gap. Nutrient and light levels increase in gaps too, spurring the system to regrowth. *Adapted from Douglas, 1967.*

certain managed ecosystems or in old-growth forests "where large-scale tree-killing disturbance occurs infrequently relative to tree longevity."[41] Gap dynamics always do occur in forests, though, even when they don't dominate the successional process as they do in the steady-state phase.

The microclimate within gaps depends largely upon gap size, though the shape and orientation of the opening also have some influence. For example, gaps exhibit increased wind speeds, temperature fluctuations, light levels, and soil moisture availability (figure 6.12). Though the *amount* of the soil moisture increase appears to depend on factors other than gap size, the increase in soil moisture lasts *longer* in larger gaps. Nutrient availability does not appear to shift significantly in gaps smaller than about 3,300 square feet (57 by 57 feet, or about 300 square meters).[42] Light is probably the most important factor determining plant behavior and survival in gaps.

Light availability depends mostly upon the ratio between the diameter of the gap and the canopy

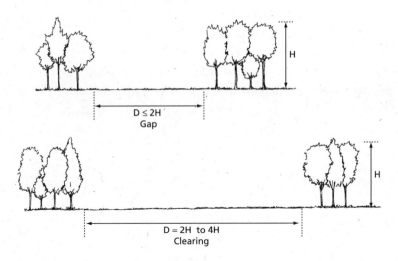

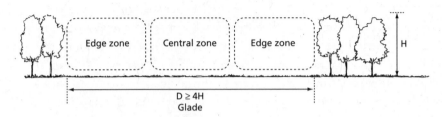

FIGURE 6.13. We define gaps as discrete holes in a forest from the canopy down to near the forest floor whose diameter is less than twice the height of surrounding trees (D ≤ 2H). Clearings are holes whose diameter ranges from two to four times the tree height (D = 2H to 4H). Glades are four or more times wider than their surrounding trees' height (D ≥ 4H), and have a substantial central space with a different microclimate than that of the glade's edges.

height (the D/H ratio), though latitude also plays a role. When canopies and latitudes are high or widths are small, less light gets to the gap floor. Conversely, short canopies, low latitudes, and wide gaps allow more light to the gap floor. Light levels generally increase with an increasing D/H ratio until D/H is about 2. These differences in light penetration persist year-round.[43]

Since the D/H ratio has such a strong effect on the availability of this defining resource, we use D/H to define the following terms: The D/H ratio of a gap is less than 2 (e.g., a hole 100 feet or less in diameter within 50-foot trees), while the D/H of a clearing ranges from 2 to 4 (a 100- to 200-foot hole within 50-foot trees). A glade is an open space, surrounded by woods, with a D/H larger than 4. Above a D/H of 4, the space begins to feel open rather than enclosed[44] and contains a substantial central space whose microclimate differs significantly from that of the edges (figure 6.13). Gaps and clearings exhibit similar dynamics and characteristics and constitute essentially a single habitat.

On the other hand, glades are so large that it is better to consider their edges and centers as separate habitats. The term *gap dynamics* here refers to the successional behavior of both gaps and clearings, but not of glades.

Plant growth habits and tolerances also affect gap dynamics. The horizontal outgrowth of surrounding trees' side branches averages 2 to 6 inches (4 to 14 cm) per year and ranges up to 8 to 10 inches (20 to 26 cm) per year.[45] Since it occurs on all sides of a gap, horizontal outgrowth can close small gaps within a few years. In larger gaps or clearings, while outgrowth does occur, upgrowth takes on more importance. Upgrowth can arise from new individuals starting from seed in the seed bank or from stump or root sprouts. Upgrowth may also arise from "advance regeneration" of preexisting shade-tolerant seedlings, saplings, or stump or root sprouts suppressed by the previous canopy.[46] Higher disturbance intensity results in less advance regeneration and more new individuals, because the existing vegetation gets killed or wounded.

Small gaps tend to favor the regeneration of stress-tolerant, late-succession plants, while larger gaps, clearings, and glades favor the regeneration of competitor pioneer trees or ruderal and competitor herbs and shrubs. Stress-tolerant trees tend to withstand low light levels and high root competition, while pioneers require open conditions for germination and can grow faster at higher light levels than can stress tolerators.[47] The pioneer trees thus dominate upgrowth in larger openings, while stress tolerators do best in small gaps. Research indicates that shade-tolerant trees rarely grow much, if at all, when suppressed and make it to the canopy only by way of successive growth spurts created by a series of gap events in their lifetimes.[48]

As a result of these microclimatic and plant-growth factors, the amount of successional regression within a gap depends mainly on the size of the hole and the intensity of disturbance. If we want to establish forest gardens in gaps or clearings, we must ponder the appropriate gap size and disturbance intensity to support our desired species and mimic the desired structure.

In natural systems, gap size and disturbance intensity depend on a number of factors, including tree species, tree age, soil conditions, and the cause of death or disturbance. Late-succession deciduous trees tend to grow rather large as they age, spreading widely and weighing many tons. Old, late-succession deciduous trees therefore often create large, multitree gaps when they fall. Generally, as deciduous trees age, the gaps they create when they fall grow larger and succession gets set back further when gaps occur. On the other hand, some late-succession western evergreens (e.g., western hemlock, *Tsuga heterophylla*) grow in such narrow spires that they almost never create gaps large enough to allow shade-intolerant species to grow. This can lead to the attainment of a classic stable, self-replacing climax condition, as long as major disturbances occur infrequently.[49] These conditions appear to occur rarely, however.

Windstorms, ice storms, insect attacks, and fires all have different impacts on the level of disturbance. The root mass of shallow-rooted or dying trees may turn from horizontal to vertical in shallow or wet soils or during windstorms, leaving pits up to a meter deep and mounds of a similar or larger stature. This diversifies the soil profile, sets succession far back in small areas, and eventually results in the pit and mound topography discussed in chapters 1 and 3. Ice storms and insect attacks tend to break deeply rooted trees piecemeal rather than toppling them, thus reducing soil disturbance and gap size. Obviously, ground fires cause less disruption than fires in tree crowns, and fires burning deeply into dry soil disturb more intensely than fires running fast over wet soils.

Scientists have estimated average gap formation rates of 1 percent per year in many kinds of forests, with a range of 0.5 to 2 percent. This means that any given site in a steady-state forest will form a gap every fifty to two hundred years. Average temperate-tree life spans range from three hundred to five hundred years. Therefore, at any given time most of the forest is undergoing regeneration or is next to a regenerating gap. Most of a forest therefore experiences at least some edge effects all the time.[50] The upshot is this: Even with stable climates and low rates of large-scale or intense disturbance, *at a small scale (plots up to about 5 acres or 2 hectares[51]), many or most forested sites will not exhibit a steady-state or dynamic-equilibrium condition. Instead, any given site in a forest, even in old growth, will cycle irregularly but continuously between a disturbed condition and a regenerating condition.* Over time on a large scale, gaps therefore generate a shifting mosaic of patches, with these patches at all different stages of succession.

Shifting Mosaics: Wobbling toward Stability at Large Scale

Essentially, the shifting mosaic represents a forested landscape going through "rotations" similar to those of standard organic farming. Large-scale farmers rotate their fields between soybeans and grains or corn, for example. Gardeners may classify crops as "heavy feeders" (e.g., corn, lettuce, and tomatoes), "light feeders" (all root crops), and "heavy givers" (nitrogen-fixers).[52] They then grow them in series over time, shifting their location so that each year each plot within the garden gets different crops that feed or exhaust the soil at different rates, and that have different pathogens and pests. By shifting these crops around, the garden as a whole remains in a "steady state" of production, with about the same proportions of each crop each year, even though their location changes. So it is with the forest in the shifting-mosaic stage, at least theoretically: the architecture and social structure of the forest as a whole remains about the same, but the stage of succession at any particular location varies over time. "The structure of the forest would range from openings to all degrees of stratification, with dead trees concentrated on the forest floor in areas of recent disturbance. The forest stand would be considered all-aged and would contain a representation of most species, including some early-succession species, on a continuing basis."[53] This would appear to offer the kind of structural and compositional diversity we desire for our forest gardens.

The garden rotation analogy makes it sound more orderly than it is in natural systems, however. The proportions of the different stages of succession within shifting mosaics vary over time in an irregular pattern. However, while they vary, they vary within a certain range, and they always stay near a certain average proportion (as in figure 6.11). The same occurs with other overall ecosystem characteristics, such as total biomass. The system isn't completely stable or at equilibrium, but it isn't completely chaotic either.

Likewise, the forest and its internal dynamics generate tendencies toward balance. However, chance interacts with these tendencies to create random variation around an average. Because there is an average, researchers have called the shifting mosaic a "steady state," but it is an unsteady steady state. Maybe a better analogy is a drunken man trying to walk a straight line. He wobbles toward stability, and if not too drunk, he generally maintains his balance. Steady-state forests are like drunken men: they wobble through a balancing act, perhaps not staying on the line, but approximating it somehow.

We can carry the analogy a bit further, too: like a drunken man, if the forest sways too far from its usual upright steady-state position, it falls over. The random catastrophes that all life forms must deal with from time to time, if severe enough, can push an ecosystem outside the limits of recovery. For example, after a series of fires in the 1800s, soil losses on the formerly forested summit of Mount Monadnock in southwestern New Hampshire created a bare rock summit that may take hundreds of years to become forested again, if it ever does.

CHANGES IN ECOSYSTEM CHARACTERISTICS THROUGH SUCCESSION

Many ecologists have made statements and guesses about general trends in ecosystem characteristics through succession, and many of these ecologists disagree about what the trends are. However, enough agreement exists on some of these trends to make a few useful conclusions regarding forest garden design. We will also comment on those trends that many believe exist but that the data do not support.

Biomass, Nutrient Flow Control, and Soil Fertility: Peaking in Aggradation

The basic diagrams from the foregoing discussion show the trends in the accumulation of biomass throughout succession: rising rapidly in early succession, peaking as transition occurs, then falling somewhat as steady state kicks in. A related pattern occurs in the system's control over nutrient cycling, and there is no mistake in this. As biomass accumulates, nutrients get taken out of mineral form and put into organic matter. Once biomass accumulation stops, control over nutrient flows weakens. As a result, the soil's nitrogen and carbon content generally rises during aggradation, with fertility theoretically dropping some in steady state. A number of studies confirm these general patterns in a number of different ecosystems.[54] *Part of our strategy for self-renewing fertility, therefore, is to create more aggradation and less disturbance and reorganization.*

Biodiversity: Midsuccession Often More Diverse

Many people believe that ecosystem diversity increases through succession. In fact, no consistent trend appears to occur with diversity during succession across different environments. What kind of trend one sees depends on what kind of diversity one is talking about.

Frederick Clements believed that, as a rule, species diversity was low in early succession, high in midsuccession, and low again at climax.[55] He was only partly right: Diversity fell by half from pioneer weeds to "climax" prairie in an Oklahoma succession.[56] Yet in forests, observers have seen peaks in diversity occur in the early or middle stages of succession, sometimes near the end of the middle, but rarely at the climax or steady-state stages. The computer modeling we mentioned earlier predicts species diversity peaking at midsuccession along with biomass.[57] "Plant species diversity increases throughout early succession, but it decreases in the temperate zone in late succession as the canopy closes and a few species become major dominants. Thus, in the temperate zone, a periodic local disturbance that sets succession back to earlier stages is necessary to maintain maximum diversity."[58] Of course, in the shifting-mosaic model, periodic disturbances happen naturally through gap dynamics, and this leads Bormann and Likens to the belief that biodiversity will reach its highest peak during steady state. The combination of patches containing old trees with many patches in aggradation phase provides habitat for sun-loving and shade-tolerant species in all vegetation layers.

At the larger scale, habitat diversity should also increase through succession (at least in the shifting-mosaic model). Since the model is based on a catastrophic disturbance resulting in an even-aged stand, diversity between habitats is low until transition begins. As the stand differentiates, habitat diversity climbs, reaching a maximum during steady state because of the diverse shifting-mosaic architecture.

Native North Americans seemed to understand these facts about both kinds of diversity, as shown by their forest management practices. They didn't necessarily let the forest reach shifting mosaic, but they *created* a mosaic with their fires and other efforts. They weren't only after diversity, however: they also wanted productivity.

Productivity Frequently Peaks at Midsuccession

Making generalizations about ecosystem productivity trends during succession is probably the most difficult task of all. The question of productivity also constitutes one of the core of issues in forest garden design. So here's our best shot at it in brief.

Most reports state that ecosystem productivity, both net and gross, peak in midsuccession. However, this can be at a shrub stage, a pioneer-tree stage, an early hardwood or early conifer stage, or even in early "climax," depending on whom you cite and where they are working. Clearly, however, the most frequent observation is that productivity peaks somewhere in midsuccession.

Bormann and Likens observed that clear-cut watersheds gained very rapidly in productivity in the early years of recovery. Within two years after cutting (no herbicides this time), net primary productivity averaged about 38 percent of that of a fifty-five-year-old intact forest, and between years four and six sometimes rose above that of intact forest. They believe this was mainly because the "sprinter" trees took over so fast, had such highly available resources, and expressed very "exploitive" (ruderal and competitor) strategies. They also found that there was often a drop in production after year six before it climbed again later, staying high until year fifty. They speculate that net primary productivity would be low in the mature system.[59]

General Conclusion: Design for Midsuccession or Shifting Mosaic

All of these trends lead us to consider midsuccession as the ideal stage of succession to design for: biomass gain, nutrient flow control, soil fertility improvement, species diversity, and ecosystem productivity all peak at this stage. When designed and managed correctly, midsuccession environments can also exhibit high habitat diversity.

We can also take this data to indicate that we should design forest gardens as shifting-mosaic mimics. The majority of sites in a shifting mosaic are at midsuccession, with a small percentage at early succession and about a third at mature stages. Therefore, shifting mosaic mostly creates the ideal midsuccession phase, but it also offers more habitats for us to play with.

QUESTIONS ABOUT THE CLIMAX AND STEADY-STATE CONCEPTS

In a strict sense, there can be no absolute steady state, but only a system undergoing slow long-term change.

—F. H. BORMANN AND G. E. LIKENS, *Pattern and Process in a Forested Ecosystem*

The theory of linear succession to climax held its ground for a good many years, and the belief in some sort of equilibrium in part led Bormann and Likens to develop their theory of shifting-mosaic steady state. However, by the last decade of the twentieth century, a body of evidence had accumulated showing the limitations of both of these ideas. The analogy of the steady-state forest to a drunken man raises the question, how long can the forest wobble along without changing direction?

Though a forest may reach some sort of wobbling shifting mosaic or climax at the "end" of a successional sequence, slow, long-term changes always appear to be afoot, wreaking havoc upon the simple theories of mice and men. The following factors limit the applicability of both the theory of climax equilibrium and the theory of steady state:

- "Small landscape units definitely are unstable,"[60] particularly in deciduous forests. Gap dynamics represent "internal" disturbances generated from within the system that create this instability. In deciduous forests in particular, where old trees can attain great size, many of the gaps that form are so large that sun-loving species can survive indefinitely as part of the forest mix (this may not be true in some coniferous forests, where there is better evidence of true self-replacing climax). This recognition led to the theory of shifting mosaic and away from climax theory. In this context, perhaps we should think of climax more as a state of "ripeness" that passes into decay and renewal than as a permanent, stable dynamic equilibrium.

- Pollen records indicate that, for example, American chestnut (*Castanea dentata*) arrived in the northern parts of its preblight range only about two thousand years ago.[61] It took eight thousand years for the species to move north after the last glaciers melted (figure 6.14). The postglacial migration of trees, shrubs, and herbs still isn't over: many woodland herbaceous species that *could* live in the Northeast haven't gotten here yet by natural means. This means that the potential climax or steady-state communities still may not have stabilized.

- Succession to climax or steady state takes longer than the apparent natural frequency of major climatic shifts, and it takes long periods for vegetation to respond to these shifts.[62] "It is quite probable that the ranges of some trees are still changing in response to recent climate shifts, such as the 'Little Ice Age,'[63] which ended in the eighteenth century."

- Humans have affected the existing forests on the planet in many ways, including cutting; introducing exotic plants, pests, and diseases; creating pollution; and disrupting natural disturbance regimes. These human influences have disrupted any equilibrium that may have been possible before the human population explosion.[64] Our

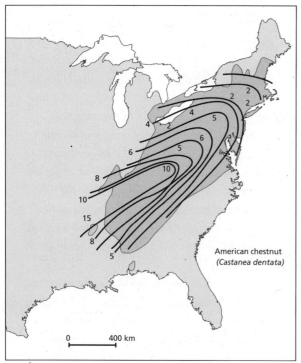

FIGURE 6.14. The lines on this map show the estimated range of the American chestnut at different times after the melting of the last glaciers in North America. Numbers are radio-carbon dates (in thousands of years before present) of the first appearance of the species on a site, based on pollen records. The gray area is the species' current range. The chestnut took several thousand years to move north and east, only arriving in New England two thousand years ago. With such realities facing us, how can we believe that the forest could reach a steady state or climax? *Adapted from Davis, 1982.*

recent understandings of human-induced global climate changes add another layer to this.

- Researchers have cataloged the history of fires and other "outside" disturbances in precolonial North American forests using archaeological methods. This work shows that severe "external" disturbances occur frequently enough in most forests to prevent climax or steady state from ever occurring (certain parts of the northern hardwood forest region may be an exception).[65]

These points, especially the frequency of disturbance in most environments, bring the whole idea of "linear succession to anything" into question. It would appear that the idea of a shifting-mosaic steady state or a permanent, equilibrium climax is just about dead at any practical level; this despite the fact that the fundamental ecosystem phases and dynamics described by the shifting-mosaic theory remain valid.

It turns out that the nature, timing, and intensity of disturbance dramatically affect the pattern and composition of a successional sequence. These disturbances occur in a patchy distribution in time and space, not in a "monoculture" form as did the Hubbard Brook experiments. Might ecosystems function more like aimless wanderers than like maturing superorganisms or drunken men? Might they simply change direction in reaction to chance occurrences? Again we offer the usual ecologist's answer to such a question: it depends.

PATCH DYNAMICS: OUT OF LINE AND OUT OF BALANCE

The term "succession" does not necessarily require the progressive development to a climax or mature state.

—R. P. McIntosh, "The Relationship between Succession and the Recovery Process in Ecosystems"

More recent views of succession claim that succession is a multidirectional, probabilistic process which can have more than one endpoint.

—F. A. Bazzaz, *Plants in Changing Environments*

The two earlier models of vegetation dynamics both assume ecosystem development with no "outside" disturbances over long time spans with a consistent climate. The recognition that these two conditions rarely pertain forces us to consider alternative views. Indeed, those two models assume no human interaction with the ecosystem for hundreds of years, perpetuating the erroneous myth separating humans from nature. The idea of successional linearity, with definite stages and certain species in each stage leading to a certain conclusion, is also suspect, though many ideas derived from the linear models appear sound. This is particularly true in human-influenced environments. What might a nonlinear, nonequilibrium view of vegetation change look like? If succession can go in many directions, is ruled at least partly by probability, and has many potential endpoints, how might that influence our way of designing and managing forest gardens? Or to put it more simply, how can we load the "successional dice" in our favor?

The challenge of a nonlinear, nonequilibrium view is that few situations exist that can indicate "this pattern is how succession generally happens." Our question changes from "Where does succession (in general) go?" to "Where is this particular succession going?" To answer this question (without getting into far too much detail about a specific piece of land at a specific time), we must look progressively deeper at the underlying structure of vegetation change. In this section, we take one step into this underlying structure, before we plunge into the realm of causation in the next section.

Patch-dynamics researchers recognize that the environment and the resources in it are patchy in nature. Not only that, but the events that change the availability of those resources (disturbances) add patchiness to that patchiness. The ecosystem then responds to these patterns with further patchiness by distributing seeds, plants, leaf litter, dead bodies, rainfall, and whatever else you might think of in additional patches. Many of the ecosystem's patches correspond to the environment's patches, but some do not. These patches change over time, that is, they go through succession. However, each patch follows a somewhat different successional path because the dynamics of each patch differ: the individuals and species present differ, the timing and intensity of disturbance differ, and the environmental conditions differ. In natural forests, the result is probably something like the shifting mosaic of the previous succession model, except that patch dynamics does not assume the system as

a whole will necessarily achieve steady state or equilibrium. However, the cyclic succession that occurs in the gap dynamics of shifting mosaic forms a fundamental foundation to the viewpoint of patch dynamics.

In this section we will discuss four aspects of patch dynamics: patches, disturbances, nonlinear pathways, and nonequilibrium. We should point out, however, that this field of study is so new that observations and hypotheses dominate the discussion; the work of developing research methods has only begun, and few developed or proven theories exist. Hence, some of this discussion comes from our own observations and may not represent the "official" ideas within the field.

PATCHES

If you have ever seen a map of soil types, you know the irregular patterns that soils form in the landscape. These patterns occur at all scales: wet spots, dry spots, steep slopes, flat areas, different kinds of bedrock and substrata, different kinds of vegetation—all of these and more compose and respond to the patchiness of the world around us. When you walk in the woods or through oldfields, you can easily observe the patchy nature of ecosystems as they interweave with their environment. In forests we find patches such as tree falls with young saplings, areas where the shrub layer makes passage impossible, or open groves of large trees with no understory. Oldfields contain masses of goldenrod and other forbs interspersed with shrub mounds, tree clumps, and grassy drifts (figure 6.15). All of this supports the claim that "[b]iological systems, on some level, are patchy."[66]

Site analysis and assessment work on design projects often reveal the patchy nature of the landscape. The underlying logic to these patterns frequently emerges only when the patterns are sorted and laid on top of one another in graphic form. We have a hard time seeing these patterns in part because we manage the landscape in ways that obscure or fight them rather than embracing and harmonizing with

FIGURE 6.15. Oldfield successions demonstrate the patchiness of ecosystems, with clumps of shrubs, trees, and herbs scattered all around. *Photo by Dave Jacke.*

them. Monoculture mind generally ignores and overrides the rich textures of our world.

Patches have fairly definite edges in space, but the definitiveness of those edges can vary a lot. Patches may be of any size and may have any level of consistency or variability of texture within them. The word *patch* implies a relationship of one patch to another in space and to the surrounding unaffected or less affected matrix."[67] We can find patchy patterns in every key resource for plants and production: light, air, water, and soil. Patches can exist in any layer of vegetation. Patches come and go with time. The practical definition of a patch will vary depending on the kind of ecosystem with which you are working, the resources in which you are interested, and scale. Here are a few examples:

- The gaps left by fallen trees in mature forests are patches (all gaps are patches, but not all patches are gaps).
- When ground fires sweep through a forest, they generally do not burn the whole area at the same level of intensity. They leave mosaics of unburned patches amid lightly, moderately, and heavily burned patches.
- The lumpy texture of forest vegetation creates horizontal *and vertical* patches.
- Windstorms affect forests patchily, depending on the wind direction and topography, as well as the age and species of a tree stand. The wind affects some spots intensely, others less so.
- The canopy and forest floor distribute water patchily in rainstorms.

These textures create patchworks of light and dark and dry and wet as the canopy and layer densities and soil conditions vary.

The essential things to note about patches are that:

- patches of various sizes constitute one of the fundamental units of ecosystem structure;
- they exhibit various qualities of size, shape, texture, and discreteness;
- they can be patches of resources or elements in the environment (e.g., soils, light, air, water) or patches in the architecture of the living ecosystem (e.g., vegetation density or species composition);
- patches occur within a broader matrix of environment and ecosystem;
- they need to be defined specifically for any particular ecosystem to be studied, designed, or managed;
- patches are dynamic: both their "contents" and their size, shape, texture, and discreteness change through time; and
- succession occurs in each patch somewhat independently; in other words, the history and successional pathway of each patch differ from those of its matrix and neighboring patches, depending on the specific conditions within and around each patch.

We can use the concept of patches as a key organizing idea for forest garden design and management. Thinking in patches allows us to "chunk down" the design and management of the forest garden into manageable "bite-size" pieces. We can design a patchwork of polycultures to simplify the potentially mind-boggling complexity of our garden ecosystem, without losing diversity. *Designing in patches increases diversity in our gardens by helping us create lumpy texture in the aboveground architecture.*

Look at the photos in figures 3.20 and 3.21 (page 106). The natural forest in the first photo has a lumpy texture. Here we find patches of open understory with a dense ground layer, patches of dense

shrub layer with no ground layer, and so on. This is structural diversity, caused by natural forces acting upon systems undergoing succession. If the first photo represented a chunky stew, the second photo would be more like smooth split-pea soup. The polyculture spreads together throughout the forest garden, with fewer patches of any kind and density in all layers. Though there is full use of all the layers, there is little structural diversity to this ecosystem. Remember that structural diversity benefits both the beneficial insects in the forest canopy and the beneficial birds, both of which help control the pests we don't want. Lumpy texture promotes biological diversity, which promotes balanced ecosystems. Patch dynamics promote lumpy texture.

Maybe the best way to sum all this up is: patches happen! But what causes patches in the first place? Besides the overall randomness of the environment, one of the primary causes of patches is disturbance, and the succession that takes place afterward. What we find, however, is that we cannot separate the successional process from the disturbances that precede it. Disturbance and succession form a fundamental, inseparable whole, creating the species and community patterns that we see in natural and managed systems.

DISTURBANCES

Several hypotheses . . . have proposed that, historically, forest ecosystems have been destroyed and restarted at irregular but relatively short intervals by catastrophic disturbances.

—BORMANN AND LIKENS,
Pattern and Process in a Forested Ecosystem

Thus the ultimate fate of a never-disturbed forest is to go downhill biologically.

—DANIEL BOTKIN, *Forest Dynamics*

The native peoples of North America knew how essential disturbance was for maintaining the productivity and diversity of the plant communities their livelihoods depended upon. Is disturbance a fundamental factor in vegetation change? The more we look at this question, the more clearly the answer is yes, even in natural systems, but especially so in managed systems. Disturbance is not "bad." Disturbance was here before we humans arrived, and it will be here long after we're gone. *Disturbance is a key part of succession, and it influences the trajectory of every ecosystem.*

Disturbances play many roles in ecosystems:

• "Disturbances reduce the dominance of a site by established individuals and create openings for colonization and growth by new individuals."[68] This applies to both plants and animals and can lead to the dominance of the community by different species than were dominant before.
• They can promote or prevent the establishment of certain life forms or species.
• They can temporarily increase the availability of water, light, or nutrients by reducing rates of uptake or use due to loss of biomass and by increasing the decomposition of organic matter.[69]
• Disturbances alter the flows of energy within ecosystems.
• They frequently occur in a patchwise manner, adding to the ecosystem's structural diversity.
• The life-history patterns and adaptations of plants and animals are often, at least in part, an evolutionary response to disturbance patterns. The life-history strategies we discussed earlier in this chapter are a good example. As one writer said, "The European origin of the majority of weeds in the USA probably derives from the much longer time for evolution of disturbance-adapted species in Europe."[70] The reality is that plants in the United States are also adapted to disturbance, but that of a different regime than that typical of the European—and now American—cultural and agricultural landscape.
• When disturbances are severe enough, they can reduce water and nutrient supplies by destroying legacies, degrading the site, and disrupting nutrient cycles.

• Disturbances affect the direction, pattern, and timing of succession. "The most obvious role that disturbance plays in ecosystems is in the deflection of a community from some otherwise predictable successional path."[71] The timing of a disturbance, what kind of disturbance it is, and its intensity, severity, and pattern, influence the effects it will have on the successional pathway an ecosystem takes afterward.
• If disturbances occur frequently enough, they can induce a "disturbance climax" where the ecosystem maintains an equilibrium condition because the disturbances prevent change from occurring. For example, frequent fires maintain the longleaf pine (*Pinus palustris*) forests of the southeastern United States. Hardwoods become dominant when humans suppress these fires, upon which longleaf pine is dependent. Lawns are also disturbance climaxes.

Clearly, disturbance is important to ecosystems. It affects a wide variety of ecosystems in all parts of the world, the successional paths of those ecosystems, all levels of their food webs, and the evolutionary paths of species within them. We use disturbances all the time as we manage ecosystems, yet we don't have a common frame of reference from which to observe and understand their effects. Creating such a framework should help us better decide why, when, how, and what kind of disturbances to create. This section reflects only the beginnings of that framework.

Disturbance Defined

Ecologists P. S. White and S. T. A. Pickett define a disturbance as "any relatively discrete event in time that disrupts ecosystem, community, or population structure, and changes resources, substrate availability, or the physical environment."[72] They define it so generally because we must specify the scale and processes of disturbance for each particular situation. Mowing the lawn, for example, disrupts the structure of the ecosystem by shortening the grass and preventing flower stalks from succeeding in their task. This favors rhizomatous plants over seed-dispersed plants. Depending on the height of the cutting blades, mowing alters the availability of light on the soil surface, as well as the amount of water being used by and the nutrient balance of the plants. The effects on the soil food web vary depending on whether the clippings fall back on the ground or are bagged and carried away. Here, as in other disturbance scenarios, the details of how, when, and what kind of disturbance takes place influence the effects of the disturbance on the system.

We should distinguish between the intensity of a disturbance and its severity: intensity refers to the amount of energy expended during the disturbance (the heat of a fire or the force of a wind), while severity refers to its actual level of impact on a given species or community. For example, herbicide application is less intense than cutting of oak saplings, yet the severity of herbicides is higher, since oak saplings can regenerate from the stump after cutting, but not if the herbicide kills the roots. The severity of a disturbance varies by species, too; for instance, grasses find mowing less severe than do seedling trees. Whether targeted severity is better than broad-scale intensity depends on your goals.

The phrase *disturbance regime* refers to the pattern of patch disturbance in space, in time, and in intensity and severity.[73] How frequently do disturbances occur? What kind of disturbance(s) are they? How intense and severe are they? How large an area do they affect, where, and in what pattern? How do they affect the occurrence of other disturbances (e.g., erosion after soil cultivation, or fire after blowdowns of insect-damaged trees)? Researchers are still gathering this kind of information for most natural ecosystems, and the few generalizations emerging from this work still need testing.[74] For example, moist temperate forests appear to develop a constant rate of gap creation and filling (as in a shifting mosaic), with any particular site in the forest forming a gap once every

fifty to two hundred years, on average.[75] Ecologists consider gap dynamics an internally generated disturbance, but there are other kinds, too.

Ecologists have tried to distinguish between disturbances generated from within the ecosystem and those coming from "outside" the system. Internal disturbances would include things like gap formation by the death of old trees or insect outbreaks, while external disturbances would include hurricanes, ice storms, and maybe fires. We have used and will use these terms, but remember that the internal dynamics of the community influence the likelihood or severity of external disturbances and vice versa. An insect outbreak may later increase the chances or intensity of a fire or increase the severity of a windstorm, for example.

Whether human-caused disturbances are internal or external to the ecosystem depends on our outlook and relationship to the system. Exploitive or destructive disturbances signal a mindset of separation. As forest gardeners, we must treat the garden as participants in the community, choosing our disturbances wisely for the good of the whole and *living with the consequences*. We need to think proactively about the specific effects we seek to achieve, rather than unthinkingly mowing because we have a mower, or cutting because we happen to have a chainsaw in our hands.

Emerging Hypotheses of Disturbance

Since the study of disturbance is so new, we have only two basic hypotheses concerning the effects of disturbance on ecosystems to guide us: the intermediate disturbance hypothesis and the disturbance frequency hypothesis. However, they are useful management guidelines.

The intermediate disturbance hypothesis states that "species richness will be greatest in communities experiencing [an] intermediate level of disturbance" in intensity and extent.[76] Yet the definition of "intermediate intensity and extent of disturbance" varies depending on the condition of the community and the species present. What size of patch and what kind and level of disturbance will maintain the diversity we prefer? Unfortunately, we have little practical information with which to answer this question—you will have to feel this out and experiment for yourself. This vagueness does not, however, diminish the value of this hypothesis as a guideline.

The disturbance frequency hypothesis runs parallel with the first: "where disturbance recurs more frequently than the time required for competitive exclusion, richness should be maintained."[77] This essentially restates the cropping principle in a more specific case (see box 4.5, page 134). The time required for competitive exclusion to occur depends on the fertility and climate of the site and the species involved: their vigor, their rates of growth, and their life span. In grasslands, mowing or a fire once per year promotes higher diversity, whereas mowing once per week reduces it. For forests, a fire, blowdown, patch, or gap once every ten decades on average promotes higher diversity. As mentioned in the introduction, coppice forestry plots in Britain went through a nine- to twenty-five-year cycle that allowed sun-loving herbs to thrive for a few years before shade slowly suppressed them. Meanwhile, the shade-tolerant herbs suffered for a while, then came back as the shade deepened. Neither group ever won out over the other because a disturbance (cutting the coppice) occurred just frequently enough to maintain the richness of the forest floor. Though it may be difficult to imagine doing this to our crops, it may be useful every so often to whack back our forest gardens, or patches of them, to maintain diversity.

Please note that the first hypothesis discusses intensity and extent, while the second discusses frequency. Both are likely important. Robert Hart used his sickle or hedge shears to cut back vigorous plants every so often. This protected the less vigorous plants that grew nearby from competitive exclusion. The disturbance was also intermediate in intensity and extent; he didn't rip out the vigorous plants, and he cut only the patches that needed it. This elegantly simple practice embodies the hypotheses stated by ecologists. However, we can take this fur-ther by defining our patches—size, texture, species, and disturbance regime—based on these two guidelines and thereby simplify or reduce the work required to manage the system. For example, when we learn which crop-yielding ground covers grow well together and need the same disturbance regime (whether that is cutting back, mulching, or yearly burning) we can design "polyculture patches" around these plant associations. Developing specific practical suggestions for various polycultures in this regard will require much experimentation.

Finally, we should note that ecosystems rarely experience just one form of disturbance over time, and that "the interplay of disturbances of different sizes is probably more important than the existence of a single intermediate type" of disturbance for generating or maintaining species diversity and other community attributes.[78] In other words, diversity of disturbance (scale, timing, and kind) may promote diversity of architecture and composition.

Factors Affecting Disturbance Severity

The same kind of disturbance of the same intensity occurring in two different ecosystems will probably have different levels of severity and varied consequences. What factors affect the severity of disturbance on a given ecosystem?[79]

Aboveground versus Belowground Dominance. This refers to how much biomass within the community lies above or below the soil surface. Aboveground disturbances will less strongly affect plant communities in which most species put their energy into root production and storage than those in which most species emphasize shoot production. Aboveground disturbances may not affect the soil food web much at all, depending on their severity, whereas they will greatly affect the canopy animal community.

Resource Base. Communities with greater resource bases are less affected by disturbances and recover faster. Tree cutting of an intensity or frequency that would only briefly affect a moist, fertile site may well devastate the nutrient supplies and cycles on dry, infertile sites. The definition of "intermediate" disturbance depends partly on the resource base of the community.

Niche Strategies of Species. The strategies of the species present or available to a site will determine the response of the community to a disturbance. If few rapidly growing species survive in a site's seed banks, recovery will take longer. Disturbance regimes also influence the strategies of the species present: high frequencies of forest disturbance should favor short-lived trees that grow fast and reproduce early, for example.[80] Another example: "[e]arly and copious production of light, wind-dispersed seeds is generally correlated to the ability to respond to large disturbances."[81]

Relative Competitive Abilities. Most ecologists assume that, within any group of plants growing in one place, some plants are more competitive than others. They call this a "competitive hierarchy." This range of competitiveness must exist for disturbance to have any impact on species richness, as in the two hypotheses discussed above. If a community or patch consists only of species of similar competitiveness, then the effects of disturbance will be more random than these hypotheses suggest.

Landscape Characteristics. The topography, soils, microclimate, and size of the landscape or habitat greatly influence the effects of disturbances on the ecosystem. Varied topography may reduce the impact of windstorms on some areas and increase it in others. Soil conditions affect the resource base, and their pattern and variation within the landscape thereby influence disturbance effects. Both of these factors alter microclimates and therefore growing conditions.

Scale. When the area affected by disturbances is small compared to the habitat area (e.g., gap dynamics in northern hardwoods forest), then the

probability of the landscape achieving a steady state or equilibrium condition are the highest. Relatively large disturbances tend to prevent equilibrium from occurring.

Clearly this is a complex business. All these factors interact, and we must consider all of them for each site to have any chance of predicting the outcome of a disturbance. If we are to manage our forest gardens well, we must really get to know our context in time and space. Though there may be some science to this, plainly we are dealing more in the realm of art and craft. With few or no masters, we are all apprentices in the workshop of forest gardening and patch dynamics.

NONLINEAR PATHS OF SUCCESSION

The classical succession model assumes linear succession. The shifting-mosaic model also assumes linear succession, yet the ultimate fate of forests in that model is a shifting mosaic created by a cyclic successional process called gap dynamics. Patch dynamics takes this a step further.

We can summarize the difference in viewpoint here as a question of how big a picture we see. The basic idea of directional, linear succession continues to hold some validity. However, as we expand our vision, we find that what seemed like a line is actually part of a larger circle (remember how the world used to be flat?). Disturbance completes the circle. "Linear" succession frequently sets an ecosystem up for disturbance to occur; gap dynamics clearly illustrate this, but it is also true for fires in dry regions, among other things. Thus it would seem that most successions cycle from disturbance through recovery to disturbance again. Indeed, this is how many ecosystems operate at a small scale. Yet not only are cyclic successional pathways entirely possible, even common, from the patch-dynamics perspective, but branching pathways are common as well.

Given the variety of factors influencing successional pathways, it would seem that no clear linear direction is likely except perhaps in the broadest sense. If shrubs take over an oldfield and succession slows or stops as a thicket, that pathway is different from that of an oldfield that succeeds to a mosaic of trees, shrubs, and herbs, then becomes a woodland, then a forest. Yet a disturbance at any given time may alter either pathway. Research on the succession of dunes at Lake Michigan showed that a variety of pathways are possible given varying sites, conditions, and disturbances (see figure 6.16). Figure 6.17 shows a variety of generalized successional pathways observed by researchers in different places. "Real successions may be composed of combinations of these simplified pathways."[82]

The main point to this section is to advocate a shift in worldview: succession is not linear. It only looks that way when we don't see the big picture. We see cycles in many aspects of natural systems, and we see branching patterns in many aspects of natural systems, so why not in successional

processes, as well? Nature is much more complex and variable than many people are willing to admit. Few simple, clear successional realities exist for us to mimic. The successional future of a particular patch contains many possible realities. Events and our choices will determine which reality comes to pass. Ecosystems, and we, are much more free to move and change than our mythology tells us. The same is true for another big myth about natural systems: the belief that everything is in balance.

Nonequilibrium

Earlier in this chapter, we used the analogies of rotations in organic farming and gardening and annuals growing in one hundred flowerpots to explain the shifting-mosaic steady state. In a rotation, the farmer divides a field into several areas, each with a different crop. The crops then rotate through each field area from year to year. The key

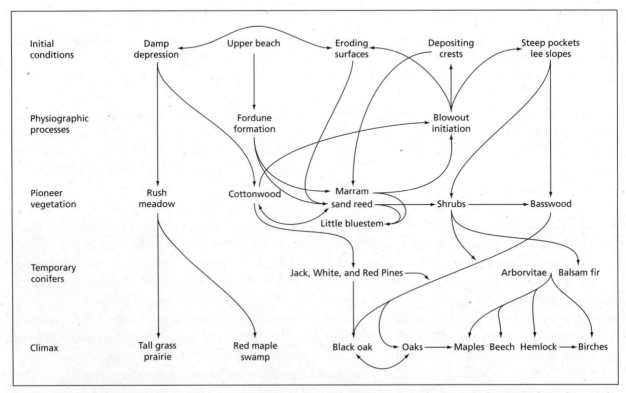

FIGURE 6.16. Successional pathways are clearly not always linear. In fact, they can wander in many directions depending on the circumstances. This diagram shows alternative successional pathways on dunes near Lake Michigan. *Adapted from Olson, 1958, via Pickett, Collins, and Armesto, 1987.*

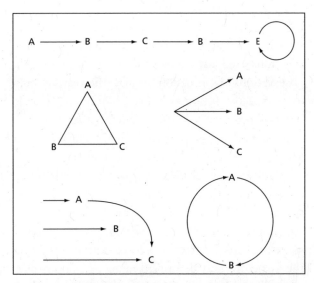

FIGURE 6.17. Successional pathways may be linear to a predetermined and self-replacing end state; bounce in any direction among a limited number of possible states; have multiple possible outcomes; have one outcome but different ways of getting there; or cycle between two or more states on a continuous basis. *Adapted from Pickett, Collins, and Armesto, 1987.*

thing here is that the proportions of the field in each crop remain the same from year to year, so the system remains in equilibrium. With the flowerpots, each pot cycled through the growth, flowering, and death of its inhabitant, while the group of flower pots as a whole maintained more or less the same proportion of pots at any given level of living biomass. In a shifting-mosaic steady state, the proportions of the forest at any given stage of succession remain more or less the same, even though the locations of the areas in each stage change over time (see figures 6.10 and 6.11).

In patch-dynamics theory, not only do the locations of the different successional stages vary over time, but the proportions of the landscape at any given stage vary too. This variation combines the semidirectional trends of successional sequences with the randomness of disturbances and patchy environments. Half the forest could be in reorganization stage for a time, while the rest splits evenly between early and late aggradation. As succession proceeds, that balance would shift to half being in

early aggradation while the rest has continued to succeed to later aggradation or has begun forming gaps to cycle back to the beginning. Yet because of various disturbances, some portion gets set back again "before its time." Succession occurs in a directional manner as before, but patchwise interruptions in the "normal" flow prevent the forest from ever achieving a proportional balance of successional stages.

This view does not exclude the possibility of equilibrium, though patch-dynamics researchers currently consider this the exception rather than the rule.[83] Indeed, it appears that the internal dynamics of forests pull them toward a shifting-mosaic steady state. However, the random occurrences we call disturbances tend to keep the system from achieving it.

Many parts of the eastern deciduous forest have experienced intermittent or periodic disturbances such as fire, large-scale storms (hurricanes, nor'-easters), frequent and numerous small-scale storms (thunderstorms, tornadoes), drought, insect outbreaks, and human management. In most regions, these disturbances, though irregular, have been intense enough and wide ranging enough to set succession back seriously over large areas or in many patches. This occurs frequently enough to prevent the forest from ever reaching steady-state or climax stage.[84] The same is rather likely to be true in our forest gardens.

The nonequilibrium model gives us much more room to play. We don't need to follow a linear succession toward some climax system, nor do we have to follow a rotational scheme that mimics a shifting mosaic (though that might be a good idea). We can choose our goals and direction and then see how it goes. We can change our minds and the garden's direction. Mess with one patch, and then another, and see what happens. As long as we understand the rules of the game, we can play with relative freedom and abandon, mimicking ecological systems and dynamics the whole way. But what are the rules of the game?

A UNIFIED OLDFIELD THEORY: SUCCESSIONAL CAUSES

A simple mechanistic explanation of succession is not possible. Truly there is a rich array of possible mechanisms to explain succession.

—F. B. GOLLEY, (1977), as quoted in "The Relationship between Succession and the Recovery Process in Ecosystems," by R. P. McIntosh

For many decades, physicists have sought a "unified field theory" that would predict all physical phenomena using one grand equation embodying the essential workings of the universe. Ecologists trying to understand succession have made a similar effort to understand the mechanisms of succession. We

forest gardeners need to design and manage succession in our gardens, not just understand it. We therefore need a framework to unify all the proven observations of succession through the years, to help us predict the future of a succession, and to guide succession design and management. We could call such a package a unified oldfield theory (with tongue firmly planted in cheek, of course).

In 1989, Steward Pickett and Mark McDonnell created what they called a "hierarchy of successional causes" or a "theory of successional forces." The foundation of their work includes two laws, some principles, and all the forces proven to act on the structure and composition of vegetation over time. Their theory underlies and unifies the three successional perspectives presented earlier in this chapter. Extending it to include additional prob-

TABLE 6.2. A unified oldfield theory: the causes of plant succession and means of succession management. The importance of each contributing process or condition and defining factor will vary from time to time and place to place. *Modified from Pickett and McDonnell, 1989, and inspired by Luken, 1990.*

Causes of Community Change	Contributing Processes or Conditions	Defining Factors	Guidance Strategies D = Design M = Management	Succession Guidance Approaches
Site or niche availability	Disturbance	• Kind of disturbance • Scale and size • Pattern • Intensity and severity • Timing and frequency	D: site selection and design M: designed disturbance	Deliberate site and niche availability
	Niche availability	• Timing and quantity of resources available: light, water, nutrients, pollinators, etc. • Resource use and niche overlap of species present (their niche, size, form, density, pattern, vigor, resource demand, etc.)	D: community design M: designed disturbance M: proactive planting M: resource management M: soil food web mgt.	
Differential species availability (propagule survival and dispersal)	Propagule pool	• Size of pool • Nature of propagule (species; seed, bud, advance regeneration; size, weight, etc.) • Propagule viability over time • Disturbance regime and land use and mgt. pattern, as they affect propagule viability • Preexisting species (e.g., soil seed bank)	D: site selection D: species selection M: designed disturbance M: proactive planting M: soil food web mgt.	Directed species availability
	Propagule dispersal	• Landscape structure and pattern • Dispersal agents behavior and ecology (wind, animals)	D: site selection and design D: community design M: designed disturbance M: proactive planting	

(continued next page)

(table 6.2, continued)

Causes of Community Change	Contributing Processes or Conditions	Defining Factors	Guidance Strategies D = Design M = Management	Succession Guidance Approaches
Differential species performance (colonization, vigor, persistence, and reproduction)	Resource availability and environmental conditions	• Nutrient, water, and light availability • Topography • Microclimate • Soil character	D: site selection and design D: community design M: designed disturbance M: resource management M: soil food web mgt.	Facilitated species performance
	Random environmental stresses	• Climate cycles and extremes • Site history and prior occupants • Pollution events	D: site selection and design	
	Plant tolerances, requirements and capacities	• Germination requirements • Growth and assimilation rates and timing • Soil, water, and climate tolerances and requirements	D: species selection	
	Life history and strategy	• Energy and biomass allocation pattern (RCS), form, and habit • Life span and reproductive timing and mode	D: species selection	
	Herbivory (including disease and predation)	• Plant defenses, resistance, and vigor • Climate cycles and variation • Community architecture and texture • Population cycles and food-web interactions	D: species selection D: community design M: designed disturbance M: soil food web mgt.	
	Competition	• Competitors' identity, niche, numbers, and relative size and vigor • Resource supplies • Competition intensity and for what resources • Competitors' herbivores and mutualists • Competitors' environmental tolerances and conditions	D: species selection D: community design M: designed disturbance M: proactive planting M: resource management M: soil food web mgt.	
	Mutualism (and facilitation)	• Partners' identity, niche, numbers, and vigor • Level and kind of support • Partners' predators, herbivores, and allies • Partners' environmental tolerances, and conditions	D: species selection D: community design M: designed disturbance M: soil food web mgt.	
	Inhibition (plus allelopathy and self-poisoning)	• Soil conditions • Prior occupants and current neighbors • Soil food web composition • Fungal: bacterial balance	D: species selection D: community design M: designed disturbance M: soil food web mgt.	

able successional forces as well as succession design and management strategies creates our unified old-field theory (table 6.2).

The unified oldfield theory identifies *the* three general causes of succession as: (1) site or niche availability; (2) differential species availability to that site; and (3) differential species performance (see box 6.2). Several processes or conditions contribute to each of these three causes, and various factors define each contributing process or condition, as shown in table 6.2. These three layers of increasing detail define the complete universe of possible factors causing plant succession. For example, disturbance is the contributing process

Box 6.2: The Law of Vegetation Dynamics

If a site or niche becomes available, and if species are differentially available at that site, or if species perform differentially at that site, then vegetation structure or composition will change through time.[86]

According to Pickett and McDonnell, site availability, differential species availability, and differential species performance describe the complete universe of causes of plant community change. They feel this generalization is powerful and universal enough that they call it a law, one that applies to individual species as well as to groups of different plants growing together. While we agree with them in general, we believe that niche availability is an equally important part of the first primary cause of vegetation change, site or niche availability. Clearly, if a site is available in an ecosystem, a new species has an opportunity to become established. But why niche availability?

It is possible to have an ecosystem where disturbance has not happened for a long period, yet the plant community still has niches open for exploitation. For example, North America has relatively few native nitrogen-fixers. In some environments, this niche remains open even when the full complement of native species is present. Particularly in designed ecosystems, it is likely we will discover that open niches exist, even if a "site" per se is not available. Niches in the environment basically represent resources not being utilized and, hence, lost potential yields. They also represent opportunities for

unwanted plants to establish and shift the successional pathway.

If a site or niche is available, then changes in species composition depend first on the ability of new species to reach that site. The propagules of different species will vary in their ability to reach that site at the given time; that's differential species availability. The ability of the available plants to thrive there varies, and it varies through time as conditions change. If the new species thrive more than the preexisting plants, community structure and composition will change. If not, then they won't. The three primary causes of succession make it that simple. It gets more complex from there, though.

A wide range of processes or conditions contributes to each of these three causes of plant community change. An even wider range of specific factors defines each contributing condition (see table 6.2). Each of these specific factors varies in influence and importance in time and space. Hence, the law is both profoundly simple and profoundly challenging. The simplicity of the three causes of succession clarifies how we can design and manage our forest gardens. The complexity will keep us on our toes as we dance with our created ecosystems into the future.

that makes sites available for plants to colonize. Specific factors define what sites a disturbance makes available, in which locations, at what times, and in what manner. These factors include the kind of disturbance, when it occurred, its intensity and severity, and so on. The different layers of factors nest into one other to define the availability of sites or niches, which help cause plant succession. These nesting layers are why Pickett and McDonnell call their theory a "hierarchy of successional causes."[85]

Essentially, the hierarchy of successional causes

represents a set of interacting forces. We know from physics that if two equal forces push in opposite directions upon an object, the object will remain in the same location. If, however, one of the forces becomes stronger than the other, the object will move until the forces acting upon it come into balance again. This applies to bodies in motion, too: if an object is moving at a certain speed in a given direction, it will continue to do so until some other force changes its trajectory. So it is with successional change in ecosystems. When the forces described in

Box 6.3: The Law of Dynamic Tolerance

An assemblage of species having different tolerance to the [nonliving] environment and differing capacities for interaction through resource use will sort through time in order of their tolerance.[87]

Every species has evolved a given set of tolerances to and preferences for its environment. Each has evolved a given strategy for survival that determines how it allocates its resources (e.g., ruderals, competitors, and stress tolerators). Given the assembly of species gathered in a patch, those that tolerate the current conditions and whose strategies work best in those conditions will dominate the site first. As environmental conditions change, the most adaptive strategies and tolerances will change as well, leading to a change in the dominant plants. The ruderals have the advantage at first, so they dominate initially. The competitors and stress tolerators wait until the time and environment are ripe to take over in their turn, if plants with all of these strategies are available to the site. The species present "sort through time" in the order in which they can tolerate and thrive in the conditions present as succession proceeds. Yet dynamic tolerance involves many other factors as well, especially the social factors of competition, mutualism, inhibition, and so on (see table 6.2).

Understanding and using this law is essential to species selection and management for designed successions, and indeed for the design of useful perennial polycultures.

table 6.2 are in balance, no net force moves the system from one state to another. When these forces become imbalanced, ecosystem change occurs. Hence Pickett and McDonnell also call this a "theory of successional forces."

The strength of the various forces outlined in table 6.2 varies in time and space. The forces interact with each other. Many are hard to separate from each other when observed experimentally. Researchers have demonstrated that some act as factors driving succession (those included in the original theory).[88] We added others because we believe they play a role, though this has not necessarily been fully documented. All these forces or factors are likely important at one time and place or another. However, one of the three primary causes of vegetation dynamics is qualitatively different from the others.

The availability of a site or niche describes an initial condition of the ecosystem. So does the differing availability of species to a given site. This leaves the variation in species performance at a given site as the "core process" of plant succession—the process that drives species replacements over time. That fact led Pickett and McDonnell to state the law of dynamic tolerance (box 6.3). Once provided with a specific set of initial conditions (an available site or niche and a set of species), the law of dynamic tolerance takes over the successional process. This law underlies the marathon of initial floristic composition and the baton passing of relay floristics discussed earlier.

Obviously, the understanding of successional causes expressed in table 6.2 is no simplistic analogy. It represents a process-oriented approach, rather than a pattern-oriented approach, focusing on mechanisms rather than pathways of succession. This makes it more broadly applicable for design and management in different climates, regions, and kinds of gardens. Though we won't discuss the details here, we urge you to study table 6.2 carefully, for it summarizes much of the ecology discussed in this book. It also summarizes the possible approaches and strategies for influencing successional pathways in our forest gardens, which helps us plan inquiry and action. We will discuss these in more detail in volume 2, including details of succession design, site preparation, and succession management. The following subsection lays the groundwork for those discussions, using the unified oldfield theory, the previous sections of this chapter, and other information provided in this book.

Feature Article 5:
"Invasive" Plants and the Unified Oldfield Theory

> There currently exists an enormously rich literature of succession ecology that is being virtually ignored by many researchers studying invasions.
>
> —M. A. DAVIS, K. THOMPSON, AND J. P. GRIME,
> "Charles S. Elton and the Dissociation of Invasion
> Ecology from the Rest of Ecology"

The term *invasion*, as used in ecology, denotes the dispersal of plant propagules or animals to a new site and their successful establishment and spread in their new home. Clearly plant invasion is, by definition, a vegetation dynamic or successional change. The term has become increasingly associated with invasion by exotic species, however, and the field of "invasion biology" has sprung up to study exotic species invasions. However, invasion biology has so far seemed unable to document a reasonable basis for predicting or even understanding the true causes of invasion.

David Theodoropoulos (see feature article 3) believes this is because invasion biology is a pseudoscience and its underlying theory has no credible basis.[89] Even if we disregard that strong statement, Davis, Thompson, and Grime make a case that invasion biology has dissociated itself from succession ecology. Now that we have some theoretical context for succession, let us try to link invasion biology and succession ecology. How can the unified oldfield theory illuminate the debate about invasives or, as we call them, opportunists? How does this debate illuminate the unified oldfield theory?

Much invasion biology literature, and indeed the term *invasive species* itself, lays the blame for invasions squarely at the feet of the species themselves. The public hype about invasive plants does this quite clearly, and the work people are doing to remove such species indicates they are acting on this belief. However, when we look at the unified oldfield theory, we see that the first cause of vegetation change is the availability of a site or niche. If this successional theory is correct, then "invasion" cannot be attributable to opportunistic plants alone.

In an attempt to place the discussion in a conventional ecological context, plant ecologist J. P. Grime reviewed much of the scientific literature on plant invasions in his 2001 book *Plant Strategies, Vegetation Processes, and Ecosystem Properties*. He began by examining evidence for similarity among invaders in their "functional type" and modes of regeneration and dispersal. He, and others he cites, found that "invaders comprise a diverse assortment of plant functional types with widely different methods of regeneration and dispersal." Despite this lack of similarity, he also found that "a prerequisite for . . . invasion is the production of large numbers of propagules."[90] At first blush this may indicate that the plants are indeed "at fault," because they produce prodigious amounts of seed. While this may fit with the second primary cause of succession, differential species availability, we are still left with the issue of how the propagules find a site or niche. Since the "invaders" have no common means of dispersal or regeneration, and noninvaders share the same means, we cannot conclude that the plants are entirely at fault.

Theodoropoulos claims that disturbance, human or natural, is a precursor to all invasions, which fits the unified oldfield theory. One can easily observe that many opportunist plants appear to gravitate toward, and spread rapidly within, habitats with major or regular disturbance, such as riverbanks, roadsides, railways, field edges, and other human-influenced landscapes. Additional anecdotal evidence supports this idea, and indeed some authors believe that invasive plants do not spread into healthy natural ecosystems.[91] However, Grime states that "evidence is accumulating" that "successful establishments by [exotics] in relatively undisturbed habitats" is increasing in frequency, having been "highly intermittent" previously.[92] Perhaps disturbance alone is not a necessary precursor.

Grime goes on to explore a new theory of "community invasibility": "a plant community becomes more susceptible to invasion when there is an increase in the amount of available resources."[93] He says, "This theory rests on the assumption that an invading species must have access to available resources, e.g., light, nutrients, and water, and that a species will enjoy greater success in invading a community if it does not encounter intense competition for these resources from resident species."[94] Increased resource availability can result from an increased supply of resources (such as nitrogen-enriched rainfall from human air pollution), from reduced uptake of resources by resident species (such as that due to death or wounding of resident individuals from disturbance), or both. "The elusive nature of the invasion process appears to arise from the fact that it depends upon conditions of resource enrichment or release that have a variety of causes but occur only intermittently and, to result in invasion, must coincide with an availability of invading propagules."[95]

One can clearly see the connections with the unified oldfield theory, as revised with the addition of niche availability, in the scenario Grime describes. Once these two initial conditions are met, the differences in species performance take over as the controlling factor in whether an "invader" can spread effectively. Most of the opportunist species of highest concern to biologists are plants that use the competitor strategy; they rapidly grow to dominate space and resources.

The discussion above supports our contention that the term *invasive species* is a bit of a misnomer, and that *opportunist* is a better word. The behavior of plants and ecosystems that many have labeled the "invasive species crisis" is most likely not a result of plant characteristics alone. If the theory of community invasibility is true, resource fluctuations—that is, niche availability—and disturbances underlie and support rampant plant behavior. Without such fluctuations or disturbances, "invasion" could not occur.

This discussion also supports our revision of Pickett and McDonnell's law of vegetation dynamics by adding niche availability to the first primary cause of succession. Under this theory, one could have a plant community packed full of species that resists invasion until the community experiences, for example, a particularly wet year or experimental irrigation. Indeed, Grime cites examples of studies where just this has occurred.

What lessons can we draw from this for our forest gardens? Invasibility is not an inherent, unchanging characteristic of plant communities but something that changes over time. While ground covers may prevent "weeds" from colonizing your garden in most years, some invisible resource shift could alter the dynamics to allow a new plant to join your garden community. In addition, when an opportunist plant arrives, you need to assess the whole ecosystem to evaluate your action options. Blaming the plant is not necessarily the right way to go, and certainly disturbing the site by removing it will not always be a long-term solution. Evaluate the resource conditions in the garden and the niche the opportunist fills. Find a way to get a useful yield from the resource the opportunist is using—to fill the niche it is occupying. When you remove a plant or plants from your garden, or anywhere else, for that matter, consider what to replace it with before you remove it. If you leave an open site or niche, you can expect another species, perhaps an opportunist, to take up the opportunity you are leaving by the wayside.

SUCCESSION DESIGN: USING THE FOUR MODELS

The phrase *succession design* could be a misnomer, for any number of reasons. Isn't it a bit arrogant and controlling to "design" a succession, when nature does no such thing? Isn't it a lot of work? How can we "design" successions when the ecologists are still figuring out what succession is and how it works, anyway?

Succession design doesn't have to be an act of arrogance and control; it can embody playful engagement with nature, and fascination, which takes the word *work* right out of consideration. Besides, we can design successions in a variety of ways that demand more or less from us. In addition, designing successions based on the ecological theories, trying them in the real world, and evaluating the results is one of the best ways to test those theories, to learn what works and what doesn't. This takes ecology out of the realm of description and into the realm of prediction. We forest gardeners are potentially on the forefront of scientific inquiry here! Let's hope that the ecologists catch on to what we are doing and join the fun. So, how *do* you design successions? We'll lay some groundwork here. Succession design details follow in volume 2, chapter 4.

For any given situation there's more than one way to design a succession. You can design any number of successional pathways for a given circumstance, and you can take a number of different approaches to the succession design process, too.

The Usual Approach

Many landscape design plans are disconnected from any sense of temporal reality. This fosters a static view of the landscape: once the plan is realized, you work to keep it that way forever. Even if you don't hold this static view, you could create a plan with no thought for successional sequencing. This can create a lot of unnecessary work and a garden that doesn't mimic forest development through time. The best way to use this approach is

to make a plan, implement it, and periodically review what you did, evaluate how it succeeded, and make a new plan as needed. In other words, develop a scenario taking into consideration several years of vegetation growth, and plant plants that will work for the increasing shade, or improving soil, or other foreseeable changes in conditions. You can do more than this, though.

This chapter offers four models of succession. Which succession theory makes most sense to you and best fits your sense of your future? Answer that question and work from that place. Use that model to envision your garden's future. Combine your theory or outlook with your goals, site, and species information to develop a scenario (or two or three). Then design it, and try it out. Only trying it and observing the results will tell whether your application of the theory works the way the theory predicts. Unfortunately, there are no simple answers here, at least not yet. To help you out, though, some thoughts on how to design successions follow, based primarily on patch-dynamics theory. Please remember, though, that this is only one way to go about it, and perhaps the most design-oriented way. You can develop other methods based on your way of working with your garden.

Six Keys to Succession Design

Six key ideas structure and guide succession design. Three of these deal with time and three with space (see table 6.3). *Horizon* and *habitat* refer to the ecosystem at the "endpoint" of the designed sequence—as far as you can or want to imagine into the future. The horizon habitat is analogous to the climax, yet this endpoint is only temporary. Once you "get over the next hill," the successional horizon will recede farther ahead of you, and the habitat you'll see at that horizon will probably be different. The habitat at the horizon is where you're headed, and it draws the rest of the succession design onward.

Scenarios and *patterns* connect the future to the present in time and space. A scenario is a flow of

TABLE 6.3. Six keys to succession design.

	Time	Space
Temporary Endpoint:	Horizon	Habitat
Pattern That Connects:	Scenario	Pattern
Basic Unit of Design:	Phase	Patch

events, a description of the plant community's growth and development over time through relatively discrete phases. The pattern of patches characterizes and defines a habitat's broad-scale architecture at any given time. These patterns derive from patterns within the landscape (especially elements such as climate, landform, water, soils, and access) as well as from patterns in the vegetation itself. The patch patterns change through time to create the habitat's successional scenario.

Phases and *patches* compose the most basic units of succession design in time and space. "Chunking down" the habitat into a pattern of patches and the scenario into a pattern of phases allows us to integrate time and space considerations as we design. Once we design the various phases of succession for each patch, we can select species, design polycultures, and create action plans for each patch showing what to plant initially, when to disturb, and when to relay-plant, for example.

We can use these six key ideas to design any number of different succession scenarios based on the different succession theories.

KINDS OF SUCCESSION SCENARIOS

Each succession theory discussed in this chapter has possible uses in forest gardening, depending on the time frame you have in mind and the space available, as well as your philosophical approach.

Linear Succession to a Horizon

On heavily disturbed sites over most human time frames, the theory of linear succession to a climax closely approximates the reality we experience. This model particularly applies if you are willing to maintain the horizon habitat as a "self-replacing dynamic equilibrium," in this case including yourself as part of the ecosystem's "self-replacing self," of course. Alternatively, if your time frame is shorter than what it would take to reach a climax, you can design a linear succession to a horizon, leaving choices about habitats beyond that horizon to a future time. Ideal designed successions in these cases result in useful crops from the first year onward, with reduced maintenance and improving soil quality as time goes on. On sites close to primary-succession condition, the scenarios will likely follow the standard herbs-to-shrubs-to-trees phase progression envisioned in the linear climax theory.

Rotational Mosaics

Following the shifting-mosaic steady state succession model, we can design rotational mosaics in which patches succeed in circular fashion through either natural attrition or human intervention. A patch may follow a cycle of herbs-shrubs-trees and then back to herbs, or it may cycle over a shorter range of successional phases (shrubs-trees-shrubs-trees, for example, or herbs-shrubs-herbs-shrubs). The challenge here is finding the right proportions of patches at the various phases to maintain an equilibrium *and* yield sufficient quantities of appropriate crops as desired. Since the later successional phases tend to last for decades, some patches may have to repeat a series of early-successional phase cycles multiple times before moving into the mature stages.

Rotational mosaics may take up large areas, since the later phases of succession tend to involve rather large trees. Yet the possibility of stable yields of diverse crops urges us to give rotational mosaics a solid try. Rotations such as these should also offer disease-prevention benefits (especially concerning specific replant disease; see box 5.2 page 197), provide diverse habitats and lumpy texture, and, depending on species composition, may include soil-building phases so that each rotation cycle builds soil. We can also incorporate rotations into other successional schemes without designing the whole forest garden as a rotational mosaic.

FIGURE 6.18. The rounded shrub forms caused by vegetative expansion are beautifully shown in this oldfield succession in Gill, Massachusetts. Also notice the pure stand of seedling white pines against the wood's edge to the left. They must have blown in on the wind from the white pines farther down the edge to the right in the distance. *Photo by Dave Jacke.*

Gap Succession

Gap succession is a subset, and cause, of shifting-mosaic steady states, yet it has other uses, too. Rotational mosaics assume an equilibrium system in which we create gaps at a relatively constant rate. Yet gap successions don't necessarily imply such constancy. We can use gap successions to transform an existing forest from less useful species to more useful species. Or we can use an understanding of the resource patterns in gaps to design a forest garden succession within a small lot surrounded by trees or buildings. Setting back succession in a gap-wise manner is one option for rejuvenating mature forest gardens or for taking over old orchards where tree replacement may be a necessity. Succession within gaps may be more or less linear, or it may follow a multilateral pattern as in dynamic patches.

Dynamic Patches and the Ever-Present Now

As the most free-form of all the successional theories, patch dynamics offers us the most room to play, and the possibility of many approaches to succession design. Since each patch has its own successional pathway, we can intensively design all kinds of successional sequences within one forest garden, using all the above models if we want. We could also design a number of patches the same way initially, then direct them in different ways as they develop—planting into one, disturbing another regularly, letting another be and seeing what happens, and so on.

This way, we would be still planning ahead and remaining clear about where we want the system to go, but we would have options, variety, and flexibility.

We can also use the "ever-present now" approach, where we acknowledge the situation and potential of each patch in each moment, making design and management decisions as we go based on changing goals and situations. Hence, we rarely "design" full-blown future succession scenarios, but we do much pondering, scheming, and strategizing about next steps and near- and long-term futures as each patch develops. We implement and see what happens, then make more decisions later.

This approach is great if you want to play, but not necessarily so great if you need to plan on certain crops being around all the time for your business or for home use. It may be the closest approximation in a managed ecosystem to how succession really happens, though: a sequence of different disturbance, regeneration, and invasion events, interspersed with periods of plants performing as they do under the given conditions. Rolling with the punches. Not pushing the river. Going with the flow. The challenge here is trying to balance your vision of the future and your needs and desires with the present reality and letting the system take its own course to just the right degree. Not enough forethought, and you could end up with no food at some point. Too much forethought and attachment to outcomes, and you end up taking more control than you intended.

Aikido-ing Existing Successions

The martial art of aikido applies to self-defense the principle of nonresistance, of using your opponent's energy and force against him or her. If your opponent throws a punch, you grab his or her arm and keep moving in the same general direction, but you add your own energy to redirect the flow and throw your opponent on the floor.

To "aikido" an existing succession means to see what the ecosystem is doing, then add your own energy to redirect the flow. A grassland is beginning to grow wild blackberries, so you plant better black-berry varieties in the field or simply encourage the ones that are coming in. You see dogwoods invading, so you replace them with another multistemmed shrub that's more useful, like hazelnuts. Wild apples start to grow, so you graft good fruit varieties onto them, using the wildlings as rootstock. Aikido-ing a succession is less about design than it is about benevolent and skillful opportunism, but it works. This approach can lead to less than optimal productivity, slow succession, or poor soil development, however, if the species needed to build soil or break up hardpan do not show themselves, for example. Aikido-ing existing successions is most appropriate when the need for production is low or the resources available are minimal. This is not to say that productivity in these gardens is always low, however! It's just that you might not be able to count on high production in all circumstances.

As you might imagine, the details of how to design each of the above succession approaches will vary tremendously. We'll discuss them further in volume 2, chapter 4, though, since the intent here is simply to bring the theories we have discussed to a point of clarity and usefulness so we can move on.

SUMMARY: THE SIMULTANEITY OF THE FOUR MODELS

We have presented four perspectives on succession, more or less in the order that they developed in the field of ecology: classical linear succession to climax, linear succession to shifting mosaic, patch dynamics, and a hierarchy of successional causes (or unified oldfield theory). These four perspectives range from theories focused on patterns to theories focused on processes. A key story line in the chapter has been that aspects of the earlier theories have been dropped or were shown to be incorrect. Yet many of their fundamentals remain valid.

Linear succession is an observed reality. It occurs in a patchwise manner. Its species composition, rate of change, and pathway are influenced by all the factors outlined in the unified oldfield theory. When we leave a suite of plants to their own devices, they "sort through time" to become dominant in an order determined by their life span, their strategy, and their tolerance to conditions created and modified by their own existence, growth, and death. The strategies of annual herbs, perennial herbs, shrubs, and trees tend to optimize at specific phases of an ecosystem's development after disturbance. This makes succession look linear and repeatable, at least over a human life span. This is a useful construct for forest garden design.

The shifting-mosaic and patch-dynamics models assert that climax (stable, self-replacing dynamic equilibrium) does not occur, or if it does, it occurs only under rare special conditions. Therefore, if a temperate forest landscape develops for a long time with no major external disturbances, gap dynamics eventually lead to a patchwise cyclic succession at small scale and a shifting-mosaic steady state at the landscape scale. The analogy of this cyclic forest "rotation" to garden rotations also yields a useful construct that may guide forest garden design and management. However, the broad-scale "unsteady steady state" forests proposed in the shifting-mosaic model probably do not develop naturally in most cases, partly because patchy external disturbances *do* occur. Each disturbance sets back the successional clock to a degree depending on the disturbance's intensity and severity and the open niches and legacies it leaves behind. These legacies influence the following succession's direction, speed, and productivity. New plants join the fray, and the sorting through time starts over.

Patch-dynamics theory holds that disturbances are fundamental determinants of successional processes and are therefore integral aspects of succession rather than isolated, unnatural events. The theory also holds that patches are a fundamental unit of ecosystem structure. In addition, though succession in different patches often follows similar pathways and ends up in the same place, this is not always the case. Since the initial conditions and species present in each patch vary, and because the disturbance events in each patch differ in kind, time, and space, the successional path of each patch may be very different. Succession is a probabilistic process, not a deterministic one.

Therefore, the unified oldfield theory summarizes *all* the known or suspected causes, factors, and mechanisms governing vegetation dynamics and puts them into a wise and clarifying structure. Its perspective becomes exceedingly important as deterministic models of succession fall by the wayside. The more freedom we have to design, direct, and manage succession, the more we need to understand its inner workings. This model offers us tools for observation, inquiry, and management, not fixed prescriptions or patterns in time or space. Its power lies not in the summary table itself (table 6.2) but in the vision the table offers, the questions it helps us ask, and the actions it guides us to take. This chapter has barely scratched the surface of the unified oldfield theory. Volume 2 will return to it. Give it careful consideration as you design, plant, and manage your successions. There is much more there than meets the eye.

When we step back from the details, we can see that all of this means that, in a way, *all four models operate simultaneously*. Like Dorothy and her cohorts in Oz, which reality we see—fearful or brave lion, linear or nonlinear succession—depends on which way you look at it.

For backyard forest gardeners, understanding the larger context of succession helps us know how what we're doing fits into the bigger picture. Each of us gets to choose the perspective from which we look. At a practical level, the key prescriptions are these:

- Design and manage your forest garden as patches defined by functions, site conditions, and management needs.
- Carefully design disturbances, and learn to capitalize on unexpected ones.
- Invest in ecological legacies if you must to improve the performance of your designed

ecosystem and give you more options. This means improving natural capital, mainly through site preparation, but also through wise ecosystem design and management.

• Apply both the relay-floristics and initial-floristic-composition models, depending on your circumstances. Relay plantings are good if you have to build legacies or make major environmental modifications or transitions, such as from full sun to full shade. However, solidly establishing a well-designed initial flora and letting it succeed provides the most garden and yield with the least effort in the long run.

• Plant strategies (e.g., ruderals, competitors, and stress tolerators) play a key role in determining successional patterns as plants "sort through time." If you want to design successions, pay attention to the plants' sizes, growth rates, reproductive strategies, and longevity so you can place them appropriately in time and space.

• The nonlinear, nonequilibrium model of succession frees us from rigid and limiting mental models, letting us use the linear and rotational mosaic schemes more fluidly and optionally. You don't have to plan to play, but plan if you want to create a linear, branched, or rotational succession. If you don't want to plan your successions, go ahead and play in the eternal now of nonlinear, nonequilibrium succession! You may have to use relay plantings more frequently than you would otherwise, but that's okay. Just don't be afraid to cut things down. Become a wild, disturbing force of nature once in a while and see what happens!

• Human life spans are quite limited compared to successional time frames. Therefore, design each garden patch to a successional horizon that recedes ahead of you as you go and grow. This allows you to plan ahead, but also to change course when you come over a hill and can see a new horizon in the distance.

• Midsuccession offers the highest ecosystem productivity, highest biodiversity, highest rates

FIGURE 6.19: Even grazing can't necessarily hold back succession. Cattle like this one won't eat everything they find, so they create selective pressure favoring grazing-resistant plants such as junipers (*Juniperus communis* and *J. virginiana*) and thorny roses, raspberries, and Japanese barberry (*Berberis thunbergii*). The gentler slopes don't succeed because they are mowable and get heavier grazing pressure. *Photo by Dave Jacke.*

of biomass accumulation and soil fertility improvement, and the most control over nutrient, water, and sunlight flows. This is what we want to create if we are to achieve our forest gardening goals.

• From an ecological viewpoint, our goal for human-inhabited landscapes in the temperate forest biome should be to produce a landscape mosaic with most habitat patches in various stages of midsuccession (the aggradation phase), a few patches reorganizing after disturbance, and a significant number of old patches. This offers us the chance to maximize our local landscape's productivity and nutrient self-reliance and to minimize our need for distant landscapes to support us at high ecological cost. We can and should implement this vision one patch at a time, even when working at broad scale. Start with your own yard, and let it grow from there.

After a century of study, our perspectives on vegetation dynamics offer a reasonably grounded basis for practical application. However, these "practical theories" are not and probably will never be simple, sweeping generalizations that we rigidly parrot. We have more freedom and responsibility than that! Instead, they offer guidelines for observation, strategizing, and on-the-ground testing as we negotiate the currents of vegetation change. Effectively, this chapter gives us the knowledge we need to learn how to sail. When we sail, we wisely use the energy of the wind to propel us toward our goal by choosing our gear, planning our course, adopting a strategy to follow our course, and adapting to changing circumstances.

Case Study 3

E. F. Schumacher Forest Garden

Size: 2.1 acres (0.85 ha) ✦ Location: Dartington Estate, Totnes, Devon, England ✦
Designed 1993, planted 1994 and onward ✦ USDA Hardiness Zone: 9 ✦
Latitude: 50.5° N ✦ Growing Season: more than 240 days

When we traveled to Britain in 1997 to visit forest gardens there, we saw many gardens that were planted far too densely to be productive and healthy over the long haul. Near the end of our travels we went to see the E. F. Schumacher Forest Garden, the work of Martin Crawford, founder and Director of the Agroforestry Research Trust in south Devon. Martin's extensive publications on agroforestry had already been important references for us, and they remain so. We both held great anticipation about seeing Martin's place, yet we were also prepared for another disappointment. However, Eric's first comment upon walking into Martin's forest garden was "Wow! The trees are planted the right distance apart!" As we learned during our stay, Martin was doing many things right. Our time there proved to be one of the highlights of our trip, and his work remains a critical reference for the development of the field (photos of this garden appear in figures 2.16, 2.17, and 2.18, page 47).

The Schumacher Garden, formerly a pasture, now has three basic habitats: a small nursery, a small shrubby area, and the "woods." The woods consists of a mostly even-aged stand of trees planted in the early days of the garden, with a densely planted herbaceous and shrubby understory that has expanded every year since Martin started and will soon cover the whole understory. The canopy alone contains thirty-one families of woody plants, and the garden now has over 450 plant species, which is very high diversity for a 2.1-acre (0.85 ha) site. This reflects Martin's goal of testing a wide variety of species. However, many of

FIGURE C3.1. Martin Crawford stands next to a littleleaf linden (*Tilia cordata*), which he planted for its edible leaves and coppices to keep those leaves within reach. This photo was taken in 1997, in the early stages of his forest garden when it still looked fieldlike. Other photos of Martin's garden can be found in chapter 2. *Photo by Dave Jacke.*

these are minor crop species for research and demonstration; this is not a garden intended to maximize food production of salable crops. While the scale of this garden and its research focus make it inappropriate as an in-depth case study for this book, we felt it important to include Martin's experiences here. Dave conducted this interview with Mr. Crawford by e-mail and telephone in the spring of 2003, six years after we visited his garden, and seven years after he began planting it.

GOALS AND DESIGN

DAVE JACKE: What were your original goals for the Schumacher Forest Garden?
MARTIN CRAWFORD: Partly experimental, partly to show what can be done. The aim was to use a very wide diversity of species to be able to both test them out and show what a huge number of useful species there are. *Useful* here meant of use to people either directly (food, fiber, medicinal, dye, and so on) or indirectly (for example, nitrogen-fixers and mineral accumulators to benefit the system, bee plants, and the like).

DJ: Have your goals changed since then?
MC: Nope, they are the same.

DJ: How much design work did you do up front? How much of that design have you altered over time? What would you do more, less, or differently in the design phase?
MC: I designed only the top canopy layer to begin with. Not much of that has been changed over time—a few trees have been removed, a few have died, and a few different ones replanted. On this scale I felt it was not worth trying to design the shrub and herbaceous layers at the beginning because (1) I was going to grow most of the plants myself, and what I planted would partly depend on what I had available; and (2) the underplanting of shrubs and herbaceous plants would take eight to ten years and I was

inevitably going to learn over that time of good and bad planting combinations and the like and so alter what I plant accordingly. On a much smaller scale, I would probably design more layers at the beginning, but on my scale I would do the same again.

DJ: What were your main design aims?
MC: I wanted the canopy shorter to the south and graduating higher to the north, because the main storm winds come from the southwest and south. This is a very windy area. [*Note: He wanted to gradually deflect the winds higher rather than present a solid, high front to the very strong winds. The latter would result in stress and damage to the windbreak and create greater turbulence downwind of it. The former allowed him to use crop trees to deflect the wind, whereas crop trees usually do not perform well in typical windbreak designs.*] I also wanted more fruits than nuts because there are many gray squirrels in the adjacent woods, and I was afraid I wouldn't get anything if I planted nuts. The hazels are mostly for coppice. I may put in nuts if the soon-to-be-tested squirrel contraceptive works. [*Note: Gray squirrels are a recent import from the United States that are causing many new challenges in Britain.*]

DJ: How did you figure tree spacing for your design?
MC: In general I have allowed 30 percent space between tree canopies at their full potential size. To others I now advocate leaving a minimum of 25 percent space for enough light energy to get through to lower plants, and a maximum of 50 percent space to retain the feel of a forest or woodland. In my experience, at denser than 25 percent space there is not much opportunity for fruiting in the understory.

Some trees in the plan are designed at very close spacing for coppicing. Some are already getting coppiced, for example, I am coppicing lime trees [*also known as linden,* Tilia cordata] for edible leaves on roughly a ten-year rotation: nine to eleven years depending on tree size, effect on neighboring trees, et cetera. I also coppice eucalyptus and hazels.

DJ: What does "30 percent space" means?
MC: "Thirty percent space" means I put 30 percent extra space around *each* tree at maximum canopy size: that is, there is a space of 6 meters [*20 ft*] between two 10-meter-diameter [*33 ft*] trees. Fifty percent space means I add half the mature crown diameter around *each* tree, that is, there is space around each mature tree equal to the mature crown radius. [*Note: By this reckoning, 25 percent space is equivalent to 40 percent coverage, since the distance between trees would be equal to the average radius of the trees. This means that, technically speaking, Martin is designing savanna systems, not woodland or forest systems. See "Vegetation Density" in chapter 3, page 84.*]

DJ: If you were to do it over, would you plan to leave some gaps for more light? Your spacing plan would seem to create an even-textured ecosystem. We generally advocate having more varied spacing to create "lumpy texture" within the forest garden: dense tree clumps, gaps, more open tree stands, and so on. This provides varied microenvironments to support animal and understory plant diversity.
MC: Thirty percent spacing is working out well. In reality, my canopy is lumpier than the plan would suggest. Lumpy texture, as you call it, has evolved due to tree failures and planting positions not being very accurate. There are several areas with denser trees and shrubs and others with lots of light too.

DJ: Did you plan for succession past climax in the canopy?
MC: I didn't think, [and] I am not thinking, much beyond the "climax." I am aware of the need for replacement and am dealing with that as it occurs. I felt I couldn't plan for it and [so] didn't think about the longevity of the trees in the canopy in my design process.

DJ: We noticed that there were few nitrogen-fixers in the canopy. Did you plan for more in the ground cover layer than in the canopy?

MC: Many nitrogen-fixers are understory plants, for example shrubby alders and *Eleagnus* species. . . . I have alders scattered and clumped in the canopy, mainly for nitrogen fixation, plus for logs for mushrooms, and slash as scattered mulch. I could chip these, but I don't. I also coppice some alders.

DJ: How big is your nursery?
MC: My nursery area is 150 square meters [*about 1,500 sq ft*], which is sufficient to produce plants to plant out approximately 600 square meters [*6,500 sq ft*] per year of shrubs and herbaceous stuff, and to sell some too.

ESTABLISHMENT

DJ: When did you begin planting the forest garden? How did you plant it (in what order: trees and shrubs, then herbaceous)? How many species did you plant? How much did it cost? How much time did it take?
MC: Canopy layer was mostly planted in 1994 and 1995. I planted trees into existing old pasture with black plastic mulch mats. I put in about 250 trees of 150 species. Planting would take about a day per thirty to forty trees. Shrubs and herbaceous plants were then planted year by year with about 600 square meters [*6,500 sq. ft.*] planted per year into ground mulched with black woven landscape fabric for a year beforehand. Planting of 600 square meters in winter takes seven to ten days. Cost of trees about £1000 [*about $1,900 USD*]. I have about 450 species planted now.

DJ: Summarize your basic establishment strategies. How much help did you have?
MC: Trees established well using 2-meter by 2-meter mulch mats. These are removed either when the tree is large enough or when underplanting takes place.

With underplanting, for the first couple of years I did not mulch, but I hand weeded/hoed shrubs and herbaceous plants until complete cover established by late summer (nine to ten months after planting). Since then, in new plantings, I lay out black woven landscape fabric for a year to kill the established meadow. The landscape fabric lasts for about eight years before it starts to degrade. Having it down for a year kills couch grass [*Known in the United States as quackgrass,* Agropyron repens] and most docks/dandelions. What few do remain of the latter are easy to pull up by hand because they have only thin roots. When I take out the fabric, I put down coarse chipped bark mulch 1 inch [*2.5 cm*] deep, just deep enough to suppress weeds for the first year, and plant herbaceous species at a density to fill in over a year. The dense planting has usually resulted in good weed-suppressing cover by July or August. The exceptions are some of my experimental mixes, which did not always work as I expected. This has worked well and saved me a lot of time. With this approach I get a few herbaceous weeds, mainly nettles, docks, and dandelions. Most shrubs and herbaceous plants were grown in Rootrainer deep cells, which are quick to plant and take well. All work has been done by me with no help.

DJ: Did your strategy to plant the trees and figure out paths later work, or was it a mistake?
MC: I don't think it was a mistake. I planned the large access paths at the beginning, although there have been various smallish alterations as time went by. I continue to do without a network of permanent small paths; I just walk over the cover crop where I need to. Because of the scale of the garden and dispersed treading this works fine.

MAINTENANCE AND MANAGEMENT

DJ: What kind of maintenance are you doing? How much time are you spending?
MC: My major maintenance job is weeding in the spring and early summer. The main weeds I take out are weed trees (ash, willow, birch, sycamore), nettles (I have plenty of these in the hedges if I

need some), brambles (very important—I have seen forest gardens taken over by these), and cleavers (*Galium aparine*), which can distort young trees and shrubs. I pull these out if possible and cut docks and any other undesirables with garden shears. I am happy for these to regrow, as this increases their nutrient pump value. I tend to spend about six days per month in April, May, and June and two days in July and August on weeding patrols.[*Keep in mind this is a one-man operation on 2 acres*]

Mowing of grass paths and any remaining grass unplanted areas has been done by a contractor for the past five years. This takes about an hour every three weeks during the growing season.

DJ: Has self-maintenance really begun to take shape?
MC: Yes. Where the cover mix is growing well there is very little to do (for example, the *Rubus* ground covers—*R. nepalensis, R. tricolor, R.* 'Betty Ashburner'; and the mints—*Mentha suaveolens, M. longifolia*).

DJ: How much help have you had?
None.

DJ: What pest and disease problems have you had?
MC: Very few. Insect pests: none of note. Birds sometimes take some fruits, but I am happy to leave the *Berberis* (barberry) for them. Rabbits are fenced out. In the past couple of years, I have been getting more deer and now have to protect young shrubs from rubbing damage. Diseases: the only one of note is quince scab. No quince varieties appear to be resistant to this (which is often a problem even in open gardens in Devon) and I have now regrafted these with pears. [*Note: Britain appears to have many fewer pests and diseases than the United States, at least for stone and pome fruits.*]

DJ: Have you had any management problems with ground covers under fruits? We have been concerned that dense ground covers will make it difficult to do pest control by picking up fruit drops.

MC: This may be an issue. However, codling moths are really the only pest problem we have here, and you can still get half your crop even if you do no pest control. Under my apples I have horsemint and lemon balm about 4 feet [*1.3 m*] high. I could lay those over, and the fruit will fall on the plants and be relatively easy to pick up.

DJ: Are you still mulching?
MC: Only in preparation for underplanting.

DJ: Are the fertility strategies working? What soil changes have you noticed?
MC: They seem to be. Soil under permanent cover is becoming very friable and high in organic matter. After about five to six years, it was very apparent that almost everything was growing faster and more healthily (partly due to improved microclimate, no doubt). Soil pH appears to be stable after the initial application of calcified seaweed as a liming material.

DJ: What changes have you seen in the fauna, especially insects and birds?
MC: Large numbers of ground beetles seem to keep the slugs under control. A pond dug two years ago is also building a good frog population. Plenty of birds nesting in the hedges. Deer as mentioned above.

DJ: Have you had any "invasive" plant problems?
MC: No invasive problems as of yet—they're generally not a problem in Britain; there is nothing like kudzu. The English native flora is very poor, so we rely upon exotics to achieve a diversity of plants in general, especially useful plants. [*Note: The cool summer climate and high latitude may have something to do with the lack of "invasive" tendencies. The more vigorous species have less energy available with which to overcome their competitors.*]

DJ: How about "weed" problems? How have you dealt with them?

MC: My main weed problems are weed trees and brambles: ash and sycamore in specific areas where they seed in, and willow and birch, which have light, windblown seed. The willow and birch don't sprout through vigorous ground covers, though they can get a foothold in deciduous ground covers or gaps in the ground covers.

The only herbaceous weed of significance is creeping buttercup (*Ranunculus repens*). Where the ground cover is deciduous or not well established, this has occasionally invaded. An exceptionally mild, wet winter two years ago made the problem worse, as the buttercup kept growing all winter. If the cover crop is vigorous enough, it can usually outcompete the buttercup in the growing season; otherwise I deal with the problem by mulching the existing cover crop out and replanting with something more vigorous and/or evergreen. Bindweed (*Convolvulus* spp.) isn't killed by the plastic killing mulch used in establishment and can be a problem occasionally.

DJ: Have any planted plants become weed problems?
MC: No. The vigorous ground covers require some management, but this is easy enough.

DJ: How much and which plantings have wandered from where you planted things?
MC: Not very much. I am quite strict on where I will allow the really vigorous things (like *Rubus tricolor*) to wander. Others I am happy to see self-sow where they want—for example, comfrey species, claytonia, and lemon balm often self-sow in many places.

DJ: How have the vegetation dynamics changed over time?
MC: Where it is shady enough I am getting self-sowing of some species, like claytonia. In other places, where I have planted a mixture (such as soapwort and wild strawberry), the latter is becoming a higher percentage of the mixture as shade increases.

DJ: How much shade have you got now?
MC: About 40 percent-ish.

DJ: Which ground cover species are working well? Which combinations?
MC: Strawberries (*Fragaria vesca, Fragaria virginiana*, wild strawberries—*not* cultivated species, which are not a good ground cover) and *Duchesnea* work well with quite a few different things—they are evergreen all year. They work with things like:

- Siberian purslane (*Claytonia*) [*spring beauties*]
- comfreys
- sorrels (*Rumex* and *Oxyria*)
- perennial onions

I'm trying to find more evergreen ground covers. Winters are getting milder, and more weeds are growing year round than used to, so deciduous ground covers aren't as useful as they were.

DJ: Which species and species mixes are working for you in the herb layer?
MC: Mints and *Rubus* as mentioned above. Lemon balm is also excellent as a mass planting. *Claytonia*. Wild strawberries are good in mixtures, as they move to fill any gaps. False strawberry (*Duchesnea indica*) similarly. Comfreys. Periwinkle. Soapwort or *Sedum telephium* or *S. spectabile* mixed with runners. A nice mixture I have recently discovered is a vigorous mint (*Mentha suaveolens*) mixed with wood pea (*Lathyrus sylvestris*) for nitrogen input.

DJ: What are your favorite edibles at this point? What do you actually eat?
MC: Raw: lime tree leaves (*Tilia cordata*)—fabulous basis for salads; various mallows (*Malva* spp.)—again great leaves for salads; Siberian purslane [*spring beauty*] (*Claytonia sibirica*)—beet-flavored leaves; mountain sorrel (*Oxyria digyna*)—leaves of melting texture and lemony flavor; snowbell tree (*Halesia carolina*)—immature fruits have a wonderful crunchy texture and pea flavor; shallon (*Gaultheria shallon*); bamboo shoots (several

species); red valerian (*Centranthus ruber*)—broad-bean-flavored leaves; sweet cicely (*Myrrhis odorata*).
Fruits: medlars; hawthorns (*Crataegus schraderiana, C. durobrivensis, C. ellwangeriana*); blue bean (*Decaisnea fargesii*); mulberries; Chinese quince (*Pseudocydonia sinensis*); wild white strawberries; *Rubus* spp. (raspberry family).
Cooked: perennial Babington leek (*Allium babingtonii*); groundnut (*Apios americana*); good King Henry (*Chenopodium bonus-henricus*).
Spices: pepper trees (*Zanthoxylum schinifolium, Z. alatum*—Nepal pepper); American allspice (*Calycanthus floridus*).

DJ: Have you measured or assessed yields at all?
MC: No.

OVERALL

DJ: What were your big surprises?
MC: Rapid improvement in soil condition under permanent cover. Sudden increase in plant growth and health after five to six years due to microclimate and soil changes.

DJ: What is working out the way you thought it would?
MC: Most things: the self-fertility of the forest garden (everything is growing really healthily now, there's lots of nutrient cycling going on); yields; self-maintenance; it's a great place to be in, very beautiful.

DJ: Based on your experience, what are the three to five most important things to think about going in?
MC: Getting the tree spacing right, in my opinion the single most important thing; hedges and windbreaks for shelter; weeding out brambles and tree weeds regularly; and propagating your own plants, especially herbaceous, because you need a lot and it saves money.

DJ: What lessons does your experience offer to smaller-scale forest gardeners?
MC: All the main lessons, as above. It takes very little time to maintain, but *timing is critical*. Like most gardening, you need to do things at the right time to be efficient—you need to learn timing. If you don't get the timing right you can easily double the work.

At smaller scale be more careful about using really vigorous ground-cover plants—I use mown grass paths to hold them back. At smaller scale this might be difficult, but you still need moderately vigorous plants or you won't get a decent ground cover.

One-eighth acre [*500 sq. m.*] of forest garden would be pretty easy to maintain.

DJ: Any thoughts/recommendations for people doing broad-scale herbaceous stuff? You have said to propagate your own stock and plant intensively in smaller areas and grow from there.
MC: I often use what I call an "expanding edge technique" for expanding areas of herbaceous plants that have a spreading nature (mints, *Rubus*, strawberries). I mulch out an area parallel to an existing planted area with woven black plastic landscape fabric. While it is mulching, the existing area expands under or over the mulch fabric. When the fabric is removed, the ground underneath is either already colonized by underground runners or the over-ground growth can root straight into it.

DJ: What has been the biggest drag? The most difficult part?
MC: Difficult to answer. Lugging heavy wet bark mulch to the far end of the garden was a drag, but it only took a day or two. Mowing the grass wasn't much fun when I used to do it.

DJ: Are you having fun? What specifically is most fun?
MC: Yes! I love almost all the time I am in the garden. Walking through the fragrant ground-cover layers, picking a salad from trees, listening to the bamboos grow . . .

DJ: Sounds great! Thanks, Martin! Enjoy!
MC: You're welcome! I will. You too!

1. Pickett and McDonnell, 1989, page 241.
2. Pickett and McDonnell, 1989, page 241.
3. Gleason, 1926, quoted in Perry, 1994, page 129.
4. Perry, 1994, page 129.
5. Perry, 1994, page 141.
6. Perry, 1994, page 156.
7. Pickett and McDonnell, 1989, page 241.
8. Kimmins, 1997, page 427.
9. Pianka, 1988, quoted in Botkin, 1993, page 115.
10. Botkin, 1993, page 136.
11. Perry, 1994, page 268.
12. Luken, 1990, page 109.
13. Luken, 1990, page 109.
14. Luken, 1990, page 106.
15. Luken, 1990, page 114.
16. Luken, 1990, page 104.
17. Luken, 1990, page 116.
18. Buckley and Knight, 1989, cited in Harmer and Kerr, 1995, page 124.
19. Kimmins, 1997, pages 422–24.
20. Harmer and Kerr, 1995, page 116.
21. Niering et al., 1986.
22. Kimmins, 1997, page 405.
23. Bormann and Likens, 1979, page 167.
24. Bormann and Likens, 1979, pages 103–4.
25. This discussion is adapted from the work of J. P. Grime, 1977 and 1979, as reported by Barbour, Burk, and Pitts, 1987, pages 96–102.
26. Adapted from Pickett and McDonnell, 1989, page 243.
27. Bormann and Likens, 1979.
28. Botkin, 1993.
29. This whole discussion is based in large part on Bormann and Likens, 1979.
30. Colinvaux, 1986, page 437.
31. Most of the ideas for this paragraph came from Colinvaux, 1986, pages 436–37.
32. White and Pickett, 1985, page 7.
33. This actually turns out to be the case in the Hubbard Brook

forest except for the climate changes. See Bormann and Likens, 1979, chapter 7.

34. Bormann and Likens, 1979, page 89.
35. Bormann and Likens, 1979, pages 84–88.
36. Bormann and Likens, 1979, page 160.
37. Kimmins, 1997, page 120.
38. Bormann and Likens, 1979, page 49.
39. Bormann and Likens, 1979, various pages.
40. Definition adapted from Kimmins, 1997, page 433.
41. Kimmins, 1997, page 433.
42. Kimmins, 1997, page 434.
43. Runkle, 1985, page 19.
44. Harris and Dines, 1988, pages 340–44.
45. Runkle, 1985, page 22.
46. See Bormann and Likens, 1979, page 109 for more information.
47. Kimmins, 1997, page 433.
48. Runkle, 1985, pages 23–24.
49. Kimmins, 1997, page 426.
50. Runkle, 1985, page 18.
51. Bormann and Likens, 1979, pages 169–70.
52. Jeavons, 1995.
53. Bormann and Likens, 1979, page 175.
54. See Colinvaux, 1986, pages 608–9; Kimmins, 1997, pages 436–37.
55. McIntosh, 1980, page 19.
56. Perino and Risser, 1972, cited in Barbour, Burk, and Pitts, 1987, page 254.
57. Botkin, 1993, page 136.
58. Loucks, 1970, as summarized by Barbour, Burk, and Pitts, 1987, page 254.
59. Bormann and Likens, 1979, page 139.
60. Shugart, 1984, page 11.
61. Shugart, 1984, page 12.
62. Kimmins, 1997, page 405; Shugart, 1984, page 11.
63. Shugart, 1984, page 11.
64. Shugart, 1984, page 11.
65. Bormann and Likens, 1979, chapter 7.
66. White and Pickett, 1985, page 5.
67. White and Pickett, 1985, page 4.
68. Canham and Marks, 1985, page 198.
69. Canham and Marks, 1985, page 198.
70. Reiners, 1983, page 92.
71. Pickett and White, 1985b, page 373.
72. White and Pickett, 1985, page 7.
73. Pickett and White, 1985b, page 376.
74. Pickett and White, 1985b, page 376.
75. Runkle, 1985, page 18.
76. Pickett and White, 1985b, page 378; Cairns, 1980, page 3.
77. Pickett and White, 1985b, page 379.
78. Runkle, 1985, page 33.
79. This discussion is based on Pickett and White, 1985b, pages 379–83.
80. Runkle, 1985, page 18.
81. Canham and Marks, 1985, page 199.
82. Pickett, Collins, and Armesto, 1987, page 343.
83. White and Pickett, 1985, page 5.
84. Bormann and Likens, 1979, pages 192–212.
85. Pickett and McDonnell, 1989.
86. Modified from Pickett and McDonnell, 1989, page 243.
87. Pickett and McDonnell, 1989, page 243.
88. See Pickett, Collins, and Armesto, 1987, for the original table with references for those factors known to affect succession.
89. Theodoropoulos, 2003.
90. Grime, 2001, pages 227–29.
91. Brown, 1995, for example.
92. Grime, 2001, page 229. His work is well cited.
93. Grime, 2001, page 229.
94. Grime, 2001, page 229.
95. Grime, 2001, pages 229–30.

Conclusion:
Elements, Dynamics,
and Desired Conditions

The foregoing chapters have laid out the philosophical and theoretical underpinnings of forest gardening and ecological design. These underpinnings shape the behavior of ecosystems in general, and forests in particular. They also deepen our understanding of what forest gardening is and guide us in our design deliberations and management actions.

We saw in chapter 1 that the keystone of forest gardening is a paradigm shift in our own human consciousness—from monoculture mind to polyculture mind; from separation to unity; from exploitation and manipulation to respect and interdependence; from intervenor to ecosystem participant. As the Talmud reminds us: "We see things not as they are we see things as *we* are." If we do not make this paradigm shift, we will use our ecological understandings only to engage in further control and manipulation from an intervenor position. While this may blunt the trauma we thereby induce in ourselves and in the world, it won't solve the significant problems we face.

The forest-gardening vision offers us a chance to make this paradigm shift in a clear, conscious, and explicit way. In forest gardening we can explore the realities, nuances, and connections involved in applying the new paradigm in a small context with concrete, kinesthetic, gustatory feedback. We can make mistakes on paper and on the ground in a safe environment where the risks are low. In addition, the goals we have in forest gardening are themselves examples of the ecological paradigm, for they are mutually reinforcing. High, diverse yields of the whole garden ecosystem arise from a healthy community that exhibits functional interconnection and is thereby self-maintaining. This creates conditions that support our economic and physical well-being and nourishes our spirits with beauty and elegance. The entire process cultivates our perfection as human beings living in harmony with each other and our world—as free, whole, and wholesome people interrelated and interdependent with our surroundings. Once we grasp how these systems work in our backyards, we can begin to translate such relationship patterns into our family, our neighborhood, our culture and society, and our inner life.

Upon hearing and feeling these goals it is easy to want to jump right in. Yet forest gardening asks us to look, listen, and feel before we act, to proceed with deliberation and consideration. Therefore, this volume has examined the structure and function of forest ecosystems so we can be clear about which aspects of natural ecosystems we want to mimic, and which we do not, and so we can design with awareness of all the pieces with which we work.

The five elements of ecosystem architecture—vegetation layers, soil horizons, and plant density, patterning, and diversity—each have specific functions in and influences on the ecosystems we design. Not only should we interact with and use all vegetation layers, but we must understand that their density, patterning, and diversity affect the performance and quality of the ecosystem both above- and belowground. For example, knowing that the canopy receives the most sunlight and generates the highest production helps us focus on which species to put in the canopy, without neglecting the benefits of understory layers for nutrient cycling, food web structure, ecosystem stability, and, yes, additional food and medicine production. These five elements of architecture frame the design of our forest gardens.

Understanding the social structure of ecosystems—species niches, species relationships, community niches, food web structure, and guild structures—is critical if we are to build a garden that functions as we would like. Diverse, high yields and self-maintenance are not chance events. The better we understand how to create mutually supporting and resource-partitioning guilds and polycultures, the more likely we are to achieve both high yields and self-maintenance, as well as ecosystem health. This requires that we learn the niches of the species with which we work and play in a much more robust way than most of us have before. That we have more than one approach to creating such ecosystems—building guilds by rote and using ecological analogs—gives us hope and room to play in discovering how to create this new reality.

It is easy for us to forget, too, that all of the things just said apply to the "underground economy" as well as the aboveground economy of the forest and the garden. The vast majority of woodland organisms make their living in a dark world that is so close to us, yet so far from our minds most of the time. Creating self-renewing fertility requires that we understand the anatomy of this hidden world. The central role of plants and soil organisms in this economy alerts us to the fact that creating self-renewing fertility means interacting with living things—managing belowground microherds, partitioning the soil profile with plant roots, and feeding the soil from the top down *and* the bottom up with mulch and root exudates. Learn underground economics from the inside by digging holes, researching the root patterns of plants, meeting your friendly neighborhood soil organisms, and thinking of plants as a whole beings, not only as what we perceive with our eyeballs. Our sense of wonder about this dark world can help us cultivate awe and humility toward the rest of our world. This can only help us engage more fully in our backyard ecosystems and develop the kind of relationships that forest gardening is all about.

Finally, we must also look beyond our own "here and now" to envision our ecosystem and our gardens as they grow and change over time. The model of linear succession to a stable, self-replacing dynamic equilibrium known as climax represents the "flat earth" view we get from keeping our time-space sense anchored in our limited experience of the day-to-day paradigm. The model has some utility for forest gardeners, but its utility is limited, and it has the highest probability of keeping us in command-and-control mode. The shifting-mosaic–steady state model begins the shift from the monolith into a more dynamic rotational mosaic with interesting design possibilities that bear full exploration. Yet even this limits our perspective and the potential. Knowing that ecosystems are organized in patches, that disturbance is an inherent part of succession, and that ecosystems probably rarely experience equilibrium completes the circle and gives us a sense of total freedom. Yet to succeed in using that freedom wisely, we must delve more deeply into the dynamics of plant communities. The unified old-field theory offers us the ability to ride the waves of the succession river with skill, élan, and verve moment by moment. All that remains is to begin the adventure.

From here, the forest garden journey has two main components. Though the ecological passage we have taken in volume 1 has been extensive, we still have more to learn. The promising and relevant theory presented here needs further testing and refinement in a forest-garden context. We also must turn what we have learned into a toolbox that the designer and gardener can use. These two paths are interrelated.

This volume's presentation of forest ecology provides a framework for developing numerous testable questions for at least a generation of students, researchers, and backyard enthusiasts to explore. What kinds of yields do forest gardens achieve? How many calories of energy go into and come out of such systems? What percentage of the net primary productivity of such systems is yield, and how can we increase that percentage? What kinds of pest and beneficial organisms inhabit forest gardens, and in what kind of food web structure? How can we tweak the system to improve its self-management of pest populations? Which species and varieties work best as beneficial insect nectary plants, overwintering habitats, and so on? Anecdotal evidence from Martin Crawford and Charlie Headington indicates that self-renewing fertility does seem to develop in these systems. Is this true? How close have they come to achieving this state? Can dynamic accumulators do the job we think they can? Which species and cultivars act as the best dynamic accumulators? What are their actual nutrient dynamics? What are the root patterns of various crop and ecosystem support plants in different soil environments? Do root areas fold into one another, or do they add when plants grow in polycultures? We could go on, and on, and on. We urge you to begin exploring questions such as these, and to let the rest of us know your results.

As for the gardener's toolbox, that is the subject of volume 2 of this work. Volume 1's ecological analysis has brought to light numerous design and management directions for forest gardeners. However, these directions arose in a pattern that relates more to ecology than it does to the practical requirements of a designer or gardener. This has always been the challenge in ecological design: the information of ecology is patterned in a way that makes that information difficult for a practitioner to use. In our case, we have a bridge: the forest garden concept.

We want to design a garden ecosystem that mimics forest structure and function to generate a limited set of desired conditions. Primary among these desired conditions are high, diverse yields; self-maintenance; and a healthy ecosystem. To achieve these goals as a result of its inherent nature, the garden's design must create specific dynamics within the garden ecosystem. These ecosystem dynamics must, by their very nature, generate our desired conditions and deal with all of the gardener's typical problems and challenges—weed control, plant health, water supply, pests and diseases, and so on. Our ecological analysis has certainly brought to light information about ecosystem dynamics that addresses these gardeners' issues and desired conditions. It has also identified the key design elements with which we must work to create these ecosystem dynamics. We can therefore say that in a successful forest garden the *design elements create ecosystem dynamics, which yield our desired conditions.*

Design elements create ecosystem dynamics, yielding desired conditions: this statement is a more refined expression of what forest gardening is about, of what is ecosystem mimicry. Figure 7.1 presents the details that lie behind this sentence. What are these design elements? What are the ecosystem dynamics? We hope this diagram stimulates connections to what you have read so far. Consider it a summary of what we have learned in volume 1 and how we can apply it in practice, for it forms the basis for our discussions in volume 2. It links ecology and design in a clear, concise manner. It helps us understand exactly what we are doing in forest gardening, and why. And it provides a turning point for *Edible Forest Gardens*, allowing us to put the ecology to bed and pick up the design and management discussion in volume 2.

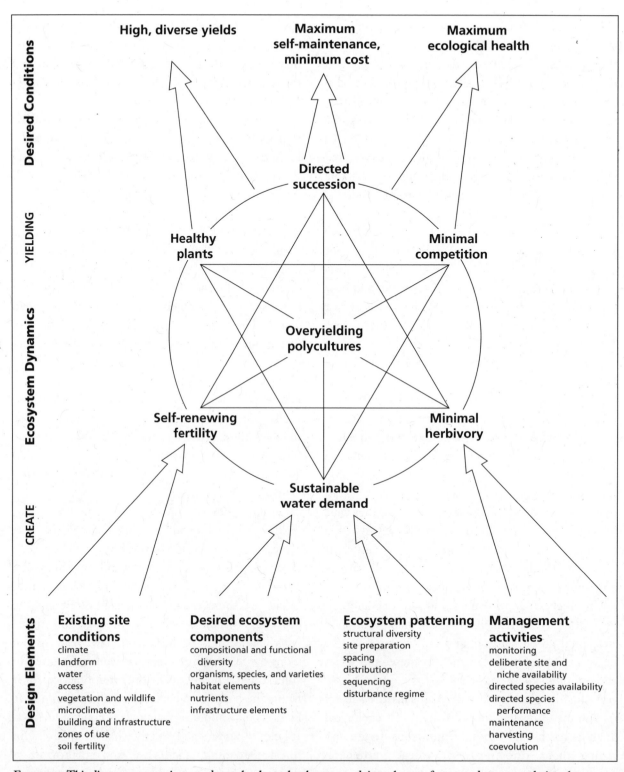

Desired Conditions

High, diverse yields   Maximum self-maintenance, minimum cost   Maximum ecological health

YIELDING

Directed succession

Healthy plants   Minimal competition

Ecosystem Dynamics

Overyielding polycultures

Self-renewing fertility   Minimal herbivory

CREATE

Sustainable water demand

Design Elements

Existing site conditions
climate
landform
water
access
vegetation and wildlife
microclimates
building and infrastructure
zones of use
soil fertility

Desired ecosystem components
compositional and functional
  diversity
organisms, species, and varieties
habitat elements
nutrients
infrastructure elements

Ecosystem patterning
structural diversity
site preparation
spacing
distribution
sequencing
disturbance regime

Management activities
monitoring
deliberate site and
  niche availability
directed species availability
directed species
  performance
maintenance
harvesting
coevolution

FIGURE 7.1. This diagram summarizes at a deeper level exactly what we are doing when we forest-garden: we use design elements to create ecosystem dynamics that, by their inherent nature, achieve our desired conditions. Volume 2 of this work delves into specifically how to use these design elements to create these ecosystem dynamics so our forest gardens generate our desired conditions.

Remember, forest gardening is simple at its essence, involving choosing plants and deciding when and where to place them in the garden. From these seemingly simple choices, we seek to generate forestlike structures that achieve our design goals. If we are to succeed at this task, the simple act of putting a plant in the ground must be rife with the right implications and potentialities. Protracted and thoughtful observation and design is better than protracted and thoughtless labor. The more consciously we can make these simple choices, the more successful we will be at creating the awesome interactions that make healthy ecosystems what they are. The conceptual tools presented in this volume are probably more important to this success than your shovel and wheelbarrow. Now let's take these conceptual tools and put them to work. Welcome to the adventure!

FIGURE 7.2. Welcome to the adventure! Martin Crawford's forest garden in Devon, England, beckons. *Photo by Martin Crawford.*

APPENDIX ONE

Forest Gardening's "Top 100" Species

Of the hundreds of useful species covered in volume 2 this book, a subset stand out as those "most likely to succeed" in forest gardens. Here we profile species that:

• we know will grow easily over all or most of the eastern deciduous forest region;
• are the best at what they do (the most delicious fruits, the best ground covers, the best species for attracting beneficial insects or building soils); or
• are highly functional multipurpose plants (such as soil-building beneficial-insect-attracting ground covers or nitrogen-fixing plants with edible fruits)..

We have grown, or observed in nature or gardens, each of the "Top 100" species. We have also tasted almost all of them, if not discovered a number of ways to eat and enjoy them. We believe these species to be among the best the world has to offer for our region at this time.

We introduce you to these plants to assist you with species selection. Each profile includes information on the form, habit, uses, and functions of the plants. We explain why we think each of these plants is deserving of "Top 100" status and provide design tips to help you think about how to use them in your edible forest garden. We also provide a short list of the best mushrooms for cultivation in forest garden systems. For more detailed information to help you determine which species are best suited to your site, design, and goals, see the Plant Species Matrix and the Species by Use and Function tables in volume 2's appendices.

We have neither the room nor the expertise to describe planting, pruning, propagation, and the other aspects of caring for these species here. See the books and organizations in the appendix 3 of this volume to learn how to grow these exemplary plants and fungi. The nurseries and seed companies in volume 2, appendix 7 also offer valuable practical information (in addition to selling plant and fungal material).

When dealing with edible and medicinal plants, it is of utmost importance to exercise due caution. Most gardeners will find many of the food plants listed here new or unfamiliar, and you must proceed carefully to make sure you have the proper plant part of the right species at the right time of year prepared correctly. This book is not a guide to wild edibles. Use other references to correctly identify any species you intend to eat before you eat it, even if you purchased it labeled from a nursery. Eat only the parts listed as edible in the ways the references suggest; even common foods such as apples have toxic parts (the seeds) that we should not eat, and proper preparation of some plants makes them not only edible but delicious! The first time you eat a new plant, take one small bite and then wait a little while to see what happens. Many people have allergies without knowing it, and these can be life threatening. If nothing happens on your first try, increase your intake at a reasonable pace and pay attention to your body's signals before proceeding further. Deliberate and thoughtful experimentation brings great rewards with minimal risks.

We have arranged the species from large woodies (trees) to herbaceous plants, alphabetically by Latin name within each category. The profiles use the following format:

Common name – *Latin Name*
Hardiness zone, light preferences, habit and form, height x width, uses and functions

LARGE TREES

Sugar Maple – *Acer saccharum*
Hardiness zone 3, sun to shade, standard (single trunk) tree, 75–100 ft. x 75–100 ft., edible sap for syrup

This stately and beautiful native tree is the source of maple syrup. While planting sugar maples for sap production is a long-term investment (you will not be able to tap your trees for many years), your trees may outlast your house and will probably produce sweet sap for your great-grandchildren. You should plant several trees to have enough sap to make syrup: typically, you need 40 gallons of sap to make 1 gallon of syrup. For small plantings, we definitely recommend using the new improved varieties that have higher sugar content. You can plant sugar maples much closer together than fruit and nut trees, making them an ideal choice for creating shady forest garden conditions. Unbeknownst to most people, you can tap most of the other maples for syrup, including the much-maligned box elder (*Acer negundo*).

FIGURE A.1. Pecans (*Carya illinoinensis*) are generally considered a southern nut, but hardy varieties are being developed. Such "northern pecans" can ripen in as little as 120 to 140 days, yielding crops as far north as Michigan. *Photo by Oikos Tree Crops.*

HICKORIES AND NORTHERN PECAN (*Carya* SPP.)

Northern Pecan – *Carya illinoinensis*
Hardiness zone 6, full sun, standard (single trunk) tree, 75–120 ft. x 75–120 ft., edible nuts

Shellbark Hickory – *Carya laciniosa*
Hardiness zone 6, full sun, standard (single trunk) tree, 70–85 ft. x 30–50 ft., edible nuts

Shagbark Hickory – *Carya ovata*
Hardiness zone 4, full sun, standard (single trunk) tree, 70–85 ft. x 30–50 ft., edible nuts

If you have room for long-lived, low-maintenance nut producers, consider pecans and hickories. The genus *Carya*, to which hickories and pecans belong, contains some of the most delicious nuts in the world. While wild seedlings of these native trees tend to have more shell than nut, grafted trees of improved varieties are available. Your patience in waiting for them to bear will return rewards in the form of decades—even centuries—of harvests. You should have at least two trees to ensure pollination, unless there are native hickories nearby.

Dedicated members of the Northern Nut Growers Association (NNGA) have traveled to the northern wild range of the pecan and collected nuts and grafting stock from the hardiest trees. The resulting varieties can fruit far out of the native range of the pecan—some as far north as the Great Lakes, Iowa, and New Jersey. None are yet fully reliable in New England due to the highly variable weather there. Northern pecan varieties have smaller nuts than commercial pecans, with a richer flavor. Crossing pecans with other hickories has produced hardy "hicans," which tend to have large nuts but do not bear heavily.

Shellbark hickory is also known as kingnut due to the fine flavor and large size of its nuts. It is not quite as hardy as the shagbark, but many regard it as an even finer nut. Again, we recommend grafted varieties. Shellbarks tend to grow in lowlands and river bottoms, and they can tolerate seasonal inundation.

Shagbark hickory is a hardy, beautiful tree with great flakes of bark peeling off the trunk. Nuts from seedling trees are usually hard to crack, but nuts from grafted trees open more easily. The flavor of all is excellent. Shagbarks are an upland species, intolerant of flooding.

WALNUTS (*Juglans* SPP.)

Heartnut – *Juglans ailantifolia* var. *cordifolia*
Hardiness zone 5, full sun, standard (single trunk) tree, 60 ft. x 60 ft., edible nuts

Butternut – *Juglans cinerea*
Hardiness zone 3, full sun, standard (single trunk) tree, 50–75 ft. x 50–75 ft., edible nuts

Black Walnut – *Juglans nigra*
Hardiness zone 4, full sun, standard (single trunk) tree, 75–100 ft. x 75–100 ft., edible nuts, dynamic accumulator

Carpathian Walnut – *Juglans regia*
Hardiness zone 5, full sun, standard (single trunk) tree, 100 ft. x 75–100 ft., edible nuts

Walnuts are among the most majestic of nut trees. The walnuts we buy in the store are Persian walnuts (*Juglans regia*). These have shells so thin you can crack them by hand. The walnuts we can grow here in the eastern forest region are wilder, with thicker shells, but their flavor is delicious. Grafted varieties are highly recommended, as these tend toward easy cracking and you can get whole nuts from the shell. Grafted plants will also begin to produce nuts much more quickly. While seedlings generally do not share these desirable characteristics, they are significantly less expensive to buy. Some cultivars are self-fertile, but others require cross-pollination.

Black walnut is a native nut with a strong, delicious flavor. It produces an allelopathic chemical, juglone, that poisons some species of plants, thereby reducing competition. However, many plants can and do thrive under the light shade cast by black walnut. See the table on juglone-tolerant and juglone-susceptible plants for more information (volume 2, appendix 3). Black walnut is an excellent dynamic accumulator, building potassium, phosphorus, and calcium content in soils.

Butternut is another native species with tasty nuts. The nuts can keep for many years in their shells. Unfortunately, a blight is currently killing many of these trees in the wild, and in gardens, too. Evidence indicates that native Americans burned butternut groves every three years; perhaps this would help with pests and diseases (see chapter 1).

Carpathian walnuts are a hardy strain of the store-bought Persian walnut. Collected in the Carpathian Mountains of eastern Europe, one of the coldest parts of the species' range, they allow gardeners in cold climates to enjoy the flavor of Persian walnuts, if not the easy cracking.

Heartnut is the most perfectly formed nut for our region. Grafted varieties crack out tasty, whole, heart-shaped nuts, though seedlings often do not. An Asian native, it succeeds well here. Breeders have also hybridized the heartnut with the butternut to create the "buartnut," which generally has high productivity but loses the heartnut's perfect cracking.

Korean Nut Pine – *Pinus koraiensis*
Hardiness zone 3 or 4, full sun, evergreen standard (single truck) tree, 30–100 ft. x 15–50 ft., edible nuts

Unfortunately, none of the eastern forest region's many important native pines produces edible nuts. However, many edible species are hardy here. Of these, the Korean is the most widely adaptable and proven nut producer. Most of the "Italian pine nuts" we buy in stores are really Korean pine nuts, grown on Chinese plantations. Generally, nut pines are slow to grow and slow to bear but then produce for many, many years. Grafting Korean nut pines onto white pine roots makes them grow faster. Nut pines hold great importance in forest gardens in this region, since we have so few edible evergreen trees from which to choose. Thus, nut pines are a likely choice for windbreaks, privacy screens, and wildlife cover.

Figure A.2. Of the nut-producing pines, Korean nut pine (*Pinus koraiensis*) is the best choice for our region, with reasonably large pine nuts and a look similar to the native white pine (*P. strobus*). *Photo by Dave Jacke, courtesy of the Tripple Brook Farm.*

Edible Acorn Oaks (*Quercus* spp.)

Swamp White Oak – *Quercus bicolor*
Hardiness zone 6, full sun, standard (single trunk) tree, 75–100 ft. x 75–100 ft., edible nuts

Holm Oak – *Quercus ilex*
Hardiness zone 7, full sun, standard (single trunk) tree, 75 ft. x 75 ft., edible nut

Bur Oak – *Quercus macrocarpa*
Hardiness zone 2, full sun, standard (single trunk) tree, 75–100 ft. x 75–100 ft., edible nut

Schuette's Oak – *Quercus* x *schuettei*
Hardiness zone 4b, full sun, standard (single trunk) tree, 70 ft. x 70 ft., edible nut

Oaks stand as one of the most important tree genera in the eastern forest region, blessing us with an incredible diversity of species. Though we can rarely eat acorns fresh due to their bitter tannins, we can process and grind them into flour or meal. Acorn flour has an earthy, nutty flavor and tastes great when added to wheat flour in baking (blueberry-acorn muffins are especially good). See appendix 3 for information on processing and cooking with acorns. Some have said that in the history of humanity, we have eaten far more acorns than we have modern staples like wheat and potatoes.

J. Russell Smith, in his classic book *Tree Crops: A Permanent Agriculture*, makes a powerful case for selecting and improving sweet, high-yielding oaks as an eventual replacement for much of the annual grain we eat today—a "corn tree." All of the oak species listed in volume 2's Plant Species Matrix have relatively sweet (low-tannin) acorns. The matrix lists species with acorns of every size and shape and for virtually every imaginable site condition. Like many nut and fruit trees, some oaks bear heavily only every other or every few years. Oaks require cross-pollination, but as long as there is an oak of some species nearby (and there usually is!), this should not be a problem.

Bur oak is a tough native, able to grow in virtually any situation—it tolerates a wide soil pH range, will grow in wet or dry soils, and tolerates temperatures approaching -50°F (-68°C)! Several varieties are available with low-tannin acorns, including some with truly enormous acorns. This oak is the best choice for the Midwest.

Holm oak, also known as the ilex oak or holly oak, hails from Europe, where its acorns are used as human and livestock food in some places. Although it is not hardy in most of our range, its almost almond-flavored acorns definitely make it worth growing where possible.

Schuette's oak is a naturally occurring hybrid of bur and swamp white oak found where the two species overlap. It has large, sweet acorns. Like this species, many of the hybrid oaks available tend to grow rapidly and produce copious amounts of acorns.

Swamp white oak is a native tree growing in wet areas, but it can grow on mesic sites as well. It is the best oak for human food for the East Coast region.

MEDIUM TREES

ALDERS (*Alnus* SPP.)

Italian Alder – *Alnus cordata*
Hardiness zone 5, full sun to part shade, standard (single trunk) tree, 30–50 ft. x 20–35 ft., fixes nitrogen

Grey Alder – *Alnus incana*
Hardiness zone 2, full sun to part shade, standard (single trunk) tree, 40–60 ft. x 25–40 ft., fixes nitrogen

Speckled Alder – *Alnus rugosa*
Hardiness zone 2–6, full sun to part shade, multistemmed shrub, 20–35 ft. x 20–35 ft., fixes nitrogen

Smooth Alder – *Alnus serrulata*
Hardiness zone 5–8, full sun to part shade, multistemmed shrub, 12–20 ft. x 12–20 ft., fixes nitrogen

This group of nonleguminous nitrogen-fixers lives in cold and temperate climates throughout the northern hemisphere. We have several native multistemmed species that require wet conditions, including speckled alder and smooth alder. Two Eurasian species, Italian alder and grey alder, thrive in mesic and even droughty soils, making them excellent candidates for forest garden nitrogen fixation. Italian alder is a lovely ornamental, closely resembling a pear tree. All alders coppice well and make good substrates for mushroom production. Martin Crawford of the Agroforestry Research Trust advocates planting dry-tolerant alders for nitrogen fixation in forest gardens, with regular coppicing to keep them from shading out fruit trees.

Pawpaw – *Asimina triloba*
Hardiness zone 5b, full sun to part shade, suckering tree, 20–35 ft. x 20–35 ft., edible fruit

This underutilized native is a relative of the luscious tropical fruit cherimoya. The pawpaw is an understory tree in native forests with black walnut, pecan, canebrake bamboo, and other useful species. It forms long-lived thickets; it is conceivable that a single individual could live for thousands of years by sending up new shoots to replace the old. Pawpaw fruits are large, with creamy white or yellow flesh that you eat with a spoon. The flavor is like a mix of avocado and pear, sometimes described as vanilla custard with hints of banana, mango, and papaya. The trees can fruit well even in partial shade. Pawpaws are a great choice for forest gardens—not only do they have few pest problems, their foliage can function as an insecticide! Active efforts are under way to select and breed improved pawpaws. Plant at least two for pollination.

FIGURE A.3. The pawpaw (*Asimina triloba*) is an easily grown native of floodplain forest understories. Its large, custard-flavored fruit is highly nutritious. *Photo by One Green World.*

Chinese Chestnut – *Castanea mollissima*
Hardiness zone 5, full sun, standard (single trunk) tree, 25–35 ft. x 25–35 ft., edible nuts

The Chinese chestnut is a productive, low-maintenance nut tree. It thrives even in soils too sandy and poor for most crop trees. The only work these trees really require is harvesting—which should be done with thick leather gloves, since the nuts come encased in prickly husks. The Chinese chestnut's moderate size makes it more appropriate for the forest garden than most nut trees. The hearty flavor of baked chestnuts is one of the great pleasures of autumn. Many of the chestnut trees on the market are hybrids, often of several species. Make sure that the trees you buy are resistant to chestnut blight—many hybrids, even many Chinese varieties, are not. Unlike the case with most nut trees, it is not essential to purchase grafted chestnuts. Badgersett Research Farm has developed chestnuts adapted to coppicing every three years in rotation. This might be a way to fit chestnuts into small gardens, especially because you need at least two for pollination. Also, stay tuned for the release of blight-resistant American chestnuts: we keep hearing this will occur soon.

FIGURE A.4. Chinese chestnut (*Castanea mollissima*) is productive and tasty, even on sandy acid soils. *Photo by One Green World.*

PERSIMMONS – *Diospyros* SPP.

Asian Persimmon – *Diospyros kaki*
Hardiness zone 7 (some to 6), full sun, standard (single trunk) tree, 25–40 ft. x 25–40 ft., edible fruit

FIGURE A.5. The Asian persimmon (*Diospyros kaki*) is among the most popular fruits in China. Its fruit is larger than that of the American persimmon, but the species is hardy only to zone 6 or 7. This cultivar is a hybrid called 'Nikita's Gift' that combines the size of the Asian species with the increased hardiness of the American species (up to zone 6). *Photo by One Green World.*

American Persimmon – *Diospyros virginiana*
Hardiness zone 5, full sun, suckering tree, 50–75 ft. x 50–75 ft., edible fruit

FIGURE A.6. American persimmon (*Diospyros virginiana*) is a low-maintenance native tree whose delicious fruits ripen in late fall. It is adapted to midsuccession in zones 5 through 9. This cultivar, 'Early Golden', produces fruits that approach dates in flavor. *Photo by One Green World.*

Hybrid Persimmon
Hardiness zone 5 or 6, full sun, may sucker, height variable, edible fruit

The Asian or kaki persimmon is one of the most popular fruits in the world, having been cultivated for untold centuries. However, few in the United States have ever eaten one. A fully ripe Asian persimmon is as luscious and sweet as anything you can imagine, with the consistency of an overripe tomato. In contrast, the unripe fruit of most varieties tastes unbelievably horrible—metallic, chalky, and bitter. Unfortunately, most cultivars of this fruit are hardy only to zone 7, though a few varieties are hardy to zone 6. Most varieties need a male pollinator, although some are self-pollinating.

Luckily, the native American persimmon is hardy into zone 5, and perhaps even farther north. People consider this fruit tree a weed through much of its range in the Southeast and Midwest. It grows well in poor, sandy, acid soils and is an early midsuccession species. The fruits are smaller than those of the Asian species, up to medium plum size, but extremely delicious when ripe (unripe fruits, like the kaki, taste terrible). The fruit of many varieties partially dry on the tree and will remain on the branches until December. This is a species only recently brought into cultivation—many of the best cultivars, like the famed 'Early Golden', are actually individuals that were selected from the wild for their superior flavor. We believe that these native, delicious, low-maintenance fruits are one of the very best choices for the edible forest garden. You will need a male persimmon for every eight or so females. The cultivar 'Szukis' is self-pollinating. Note that the two species will not pollinate each other.

After many attempts, breeders have recently developed hybrid persimmons. They seem to combine the best of both worlds, retaining the hardiness of American persimmons while increasing fruit size. Some hybrids are naturally dwarfed.

MULBERRIES (*Morus* SPP.)
Hardiness zone 5, full sun to part shade, standard (single trunk) tree, 30–50 ft. x 30–50 ft., edible fruit

FIGURE A.7: Improved varieties of mulberry (*Morus* spp.) have excellent flavor and other desirable characteristics, including hardiness to zone 5. Shown is *Morus alba* 'Pakistan', a white mulberry cultivar with some of the largest fruits available (zone 6). *Photo by Rob Cardillo, courtesy of Edible Landscaping.*

Often an underestimated crop, the mulberry is a reliable, low-maintenance fruit producer. While many mulberries have a bland flavor, a good cultivar has both acid and sweetness—and there are many fine cultivars from which to choose. They are excellent candidates for home production, as they ripen over a long period. Mulberries are better than most fruits at setting fruit in partial shade. People grow mainly three species in the United States: the native red mulberry and the black and white mulberries. Despite the common names, fruit color does not indicate species (white mulberry fruits are often purple, for example). Most cultivars, as well as most trees you will find in the wild, are hybrids between two or more of these species. Most of the best varieties are hybrids. Some mulberries are self-fertile, while others require a pollinator. A dwarf cultivar, 'Geraldi Dwarf', holds interesting promise for smaller gardens.

FIGURE A.8A. The fast-growing native chickasaw plum (*Prunus angustifolia*) spreads to fill southern oldfields. September brings small, very tart red plums on plants up to 12 feet (4 m) high. *Photo by Oikos Tree Crops.*

FIGURE A.8B. Native plums have much to offer for little effort. The beach plum (*Prunus maritima*) hails from eastern seashores and can produce tremendous yields of small fruit excellent for jam and extremely dense blooms of white flowers. This is a precocious open-pollinated dwarf selection called 'Nana.' *Photo by Oikos Tree Crops.*

NATIVE PLUMS (*Prunus* SPP.)

American Plum – *Prunus americana*
Hardiness zone 3, full sun, suckering tree, 20–35 ft. x 20–35 ft., edible fruit

Canada Plum – *Prunus americana* var. *nigra*
Hardiness zone 3, full sun, suckering tree, 6–20 ft. x 6–20 ft., edible fruit

Chickasaw Plum – *Prunus angustifolia*
Hardiness zone 5, full sun, thicket-forming shrub, 8–10 ft. x 8–10 ft., edible fruit

Hog Plum – *Prunus hortulana*
Hardiness zone 5, full sun, suckering tree, 12–30 ft. x 12–30 ft., edible fruit

Beach Plum – *Prunus maritima*
Hardiness zone 3, full sun, multistemmed shrub, 8–12 ft. x 8–12 ft., edible fruit

Wild Goose Plum – *Prunus munsoniana*
Hardiness zone 5, full sun, clumping thicket former, suckering shrub, 10 ft. x 10 ft., edible fruit

A great many native plum species exist whose flavor can be quite good, though it varies from tree to tree. However, some improved varieties are available, as well as hybrids with cultivated plums. Many of the wild seedlings do not bear fruit every year—either because of a biennial bearing habit or because of late frosts killing the flowers. We have not heard reports of this problem with the improved varieties. Surely we should not ignore such an abundant resource of native edible species as those listed above! There are of course a number of excellent plums from Europe and Asia as well, and a great number of hybrids between American-, European-, and Asian-type plums. Note that native plums, while often resistant, are not immune to the vast array of insects and diseases attacking plums, including the dreaded plum curculio. Depending on pest pressure in your area, they may require attention for pest and disease control. Their dense thickets provide important habitat for many beneficial wildlife species. Plant at least two for cross-pollination; different species can cross-pollinate each other as long as they flower at the same time.

PEAR (*Pyrus* SPP.)

Asian Pear – *Pyrus bretschneideris*
Hardiness zone 4, full sun, standard (single trunk) tree, 25–30 ft. x 25 ft., edible fruit

European Pear – *Pyrus communis*
Hardiness zone 3 or 4, full sun, standard (single trunk) tree, 8–40 ft. x 10–25 ft. (depending on rootstock), edible fruit

Pears are one of the best fruits we can grow in the forest garden. In most of the eastern forest region, apples have intense pressure from pests and diseases. Pears, in contrast, are far easier and more

FIGURE A.10. Pears (*Pyrus communis*) are much more easily grown than apples in forest garden systems, with fewer pests and diseases to contend with. *Photo by Eric Toensmeier.*

FIGURE A.9. The Asian pear (*Pyrus bretschneideris*) is much underappreciated in the United States. At their gourmet best when homegrown, these fruits are generally pest and disease resistant, easy to grow, and hardy to zone 4. The trustworthy Japanese cultivar 'Chojuro' ripens in early to mid-September and offers a full, sweet flavor. *Photo by One Green World.*

rewarding to grow in a low-maintenance regime. Although they do not store as well as apples, pears are certainly among the world's finest fruits. Their flavor ranges from melting, buttery European pear cultivar like 'Seckel' to crisp, juicy, applelike Asian pears like '20th Century'. One disease problem is worth noting: fireblight is a very serious problem that can quickly decimate susceptible trees. Obtain fireblight-resistant varieties as insurance. Even if the disease has not yet reached your area, it is moving across the region and may well arrive within the lifetime of your trees. Pears are available in full, dwarf, and semidwarf sizes. There are also enormous pear varieties available that yield small, hard fruits used to make a pear cider, known as 'perry.' Plant at least two pears for pollination. Not all varieties within a species will pollinate each other, and some—but not all—Asian and European pears will pollinate each other. See a nursery catalog for details.

WOODY VINES

HARDY KIWIFRUIT (*Actinidia* SPP.)

Hardy Kiwifruit – *Actinidia arguta*
Hardiness zone 4, full sun, climber, 20–100 ft., edible fruit

Super-Hardy Kiwifruit – *Actinidia kolomikta*
Hardiness zone 3, full sun, climber, 20–100 ft., edible fruit

Purple Hardy Kiwifruit – *Actinidia purpurea*
Hardiness zone 4, full sun, climber, 20–100 ft., edible fruit

Hardy kiwifruits are among the most promising low-maintenance fruits for our climate. These woody vines are in the same genus as the kiwifruit you buy in the supermarket but yield smaller fruit (about the size of a large grape) that have smooth skin instead of fuzz and taste much sweeter. A fresh hardy kiwi off the vine is one of the world's finest fruits.

Hardy kiwifruits are native to forest edges in eastern Asia. These species can take a few years to establish. They are vulnerable to late frosts when young. Once they are up and running they become highly productive. Under ideal conditions, they can produce up to 100 pounds of fruit per vine annually. Hardy kiwifruit vines are vigorous sprawlers; you should not let them grow on trees about whose form you care. Capable of growing to great heights, they are best grown on large, established trees or kept well maintained on a trellis. Although trellising requires more work (building the trellis,

FIGURE A.11: The hardy kiwifruit (*Actinidia arguta*) is a delicious fruit that should be much more widely grown. This deciduous vine evolved growing in wood's edges in northeastern China. Male and female flowers are on separate plants in most varieties. *Photo by Dave Jacke, courtesy Tripple Brook Farm.*

forest region, where European grapes (*V. vinifera*) can experience great difficulty with pests and diseases. Improved varieties of native grapes tend to have a fruitier "grape jelly" flavor compared to the *vinifera* grapes you find in the supermarket. Such delicious and trouble-free native fruits are certainly worth including in the forest garden. You can intensively prune and trellis them for high production or allow them to climb on trees or other structures, trading lower yields for ease of management. Grapes require a warm microclimate in the late summer for fruit ripening, so a west-facing slope or edge is ideal.

The fox grape is cultivated throughout the northeast, and many varieties and hybrids are available, including "Concord"-type fresh and juice varieties, seedless types for fresh eating, and wine varieties. Fox grapes are self-pollinating.

The muscadine grape, or scuppernong, is the ultimate low-maintenance grape—the plants are practically immune to pests and diseases. The flavor is strong and delicious and really cools you down on a hot day. Scuppernongs are hardy only to zone 7, however. Muscadine pollination can be complicated—plants can be male or female or can have both male and female flowers. Consult a nursery catalog for information on the pollination needs of specific varieties.

intensive annual pruning), it is the best way to maximize yields. Ripe fruit falling from tall trees is still perfectly edible, but it will not store very well. Because of their high vitamin C content, carefully harvested fruit can last for weeks in a simple box or bucket in your cellar. Male and female flowers grow on separate plants. You need to have one male for every eight or so females to set fruit. The cultivar 'Issai' is self-pollinating but not reliably hardy in zone 5 or even zone 6.

Hardy kiwifruit is the most commonly grown hardy *Actinidia*, with green grape-size fruit. Super-hardy kiwifruit is significantly hardier, with smaller but still delicious fruits. Purple hardy kiwifruit is essentially a purple-skinned *A. arguta*.

NATIVE GRAPES (*Vitis* SPP.)

Fox Grape – *Vitis labrusca*
Hardiness zone 3–9, full sun, woody vine, 35+ ft., edible fruit

Muscadine Grape –*Vitis rotundifolia*
Hardiness zone 7–9, full sun, woody vine, 12–20 ft., edible fruit
Humans have taken several native grape species into cultivation. These vines thrive in the eastern

SHRUBS (SMALL TO LARGE)

SASKATOON & JUNEBERRIES (*Amelanchier* SPP.)

Saskatoon – *Amelanchier alnifolia*
Hardiness zone 2, full sun, multistemmed shrub, 5–15 ft. x 5–15 ft., edible fruit

Allegheny Shadbush – *Amelanchier lamarkii*
Hardiness zone 4–8, full sun, standard (single truck) tree, 12–30 ft. x 12–35 ft., edible fruit

Running Juneberry – *Amelanchier stolonifera*
Hardiness zone 4, full sun, running thicket former shrub, 4–6 ft. x indefinitely spreading, edible fruit

Figure A.12. The North American *Amelanchier* species (juneberry, saskatoon, shadbush) have blueberry-almond–flavored fruits that ripen before blueberries. They come in tree and multistemmed shrub forms, depending on species and variety. *Photo by Eric Toensmeier.*

This is a large genus of underutilized and often delicious natives. They range in size from 6 feet (2 m) (some saskatoon varieties) to close to 50 feet (15 m) (tree-form varieties). They generally form graceful multistemmed shrubs. As one of the earliest blooming flowers in spring, they are becoming widely planted as ornamentals. Their berries (in some areas ripening in June, thus the name) are similar to blueberries but less acid and with a bit of an almond flavor from the small seeds. *Amelanchier* species are very hardy and adaptable. There are native species in every state in our range. They flourish in such diverse habitats as swamps, sand plains, and rocky outcrops on windy mountainsides. They seem to have some disease problems, including fireblight, a devastating disease that they can spread to their fellow members of the Rose Family, including pears and apples. They are definitely worth incorporating as a rugged, low-maintenance, early-fruiting member of your forest garden. All *Amelanchier* species are self-pollinating.

The saskatoon is now cultivated in large areas of cold prairie in Canada as a new commercial crop. Many cultivars of saskatoon are available, including 'Regent', notable for its excellent fruit and somewhat dwarf growth habit. Some developed varieties in Canada are yielding up to 7 tons of fruit per acre (15 metric tons per ha)! This species seems to prefer drier soils similar to those of its native prairie habitat.

Allegheny shadbush is typical of several treelike *Amelanchier* species. It is difficult to harvest berries from the top of a 30-foot (9 m) tree, but the birds will enjoy the fruits you cannot reach. Running juneberry is a promising species for sunny forest garden patches and phases. It forms a low thicket and spreads indefinitely, perhaps finding its way to sunny patches as conditions change in the forest garden over time.

Edible Shoot Bamboos (*Arundinaria, Phyllostachys, Sasa,* and *Semiarundinaria* spp.)

Canebrake Bamboo – *Arundinaria gigantea*
Hardiness zone 6, full sun to part shade, evergreen running bamboo, 10–20 ft. x indefinitely spreading, edible shoots

Dwarf Canebrake Bamboo – *Arundinaria gigantea tecta*
Hardiness zone 6, full sun to part shade, evergreen running bamboo, 6 ft. x indefinitely spreading, edible shoots

Sweetshoot Bamboo – *Phyllostachys dulcis*
Hardiness zone 7, full sun to part shade, evergreen running bamboo, 20–40 ft. x indefinitely spreading, edible shoots

Stone Bamboo – *Phyllostachys nuda*
Hardiness zone 6, full sun to part shade, evergreen running bamboo, 20–35 ft. x indefinitely spreading, edible shoots

Blue-green Glaucous Bamboo – *Phyllostachys viridi-glaucescens*
Hardiness zone 6b, full sun to part shade, evergreen running bamboo, 20–35 ft. x indefinitely spreading, edible shoots

Chishima-zasa Bamboo – *Sasa kurilensis*
Hardiness zone 7, full sun to part shade, evergreen running bamboo, 10 ft. x indefinitely spreading, edible shoots

Temple Bamboo – *Semiarundinaria fastuosa*
Hardiness zone 6b, full sun to part shade, evergreen running bamboo, 20–35 ft. x indefinitely spreading, edible shoots

Bamboos are among the most beautiful and useful of plants. People around the world use them in thousands of ways. In the relatively cold climate of the eastern deciduous forest, we can grow only running bamboos, and only short species within that group. However, we can grow many of the most delicious species for edible shoots, and the flexible poles they provide are extremely useful in the garden. Running bamboos can easily take over a garden—for this reason we highly recommend using a strong rhizome barrier to keep them in place (see volume 2, chapter 5). While their running habit may cause trouble in the garden, bamboos rarely set seed. They are thus highly unlikely to naturalize extensively at the ecosystem level. This example reminds us that highly expansive plants are not necessarily dispersive.

The hardiness zones listed above are approximate temperatures for killing the evergreen leaves, though the plants will leaf out again in spring or come back from the roots in the case of much greater cold. Bamboo will not reach its full height as it approaches its hardiness limits. The shoots are usually cooked, but the nonnative species listed here are among the "sweetest": they lack bitterness enough that some people eat them raw. Worth noting are the canebrake bamboos (*Arundinaria gigantea* and the dwarf *A. gigantea tecta*), which are native to the southeast and once formed huge thickets in floodplains. Their flavor is inferior to that of the other species listed here, but the prospect of keeping these native bamboos alive (they are now rare in the wild) should entice many gardeners to find a place for them.

Siberian Pea Shrub – *Caragana arborescens*
Hardiness zone 2–7, sun, multistemmed shrub, 8–20 ft. x 12–18 ft., fixes nitrogen

This nitrogen-fixing shrub has proven itself both hardy and noninvasive throughout the eastern deciduous forest region. It hails from northeastern Asia, including Siberia, and is extremely cold tolerant. Both bees and humans enjoy Siberian pea shrub's pretty yellow pealike flowers. The pods that follow contain edible beans; however, these are quite small and generally not worth the effort of picking (chickens will eat them, though). The Plant Species Matrix in volume 2 lists several smaller species in the genus, but we know little about their reliability in our conditions. Luckily, this larger legume has demonstrated itself to be well mannered and a superb choice for the eastern forest region.

FIGURE A.13. The Siberian pea shrub (*Caragana arborescens*) is a hardy and reliable nitrogen-fixer. While its "peas" are edible, they are small and hard to harvest, but chickens love them. It is a good screen and nurse plant. *Photo by Dave Jacke.*

Chinquapin – *Castanea pumila*
Hardiness zone 5b, full sun, multistemmed shrub, 6–20 ft. x 6–20 ft., edible nuts

Chinquapin (or chinkapin) is a native shrubby cousin of American chestnut. It has great potential as a shrubby nut producer for forest gardens. It grows throughout the southern portion of our region but is hardy into the warmer parts of zone 5. Chinquapins bear only one nut in each bur, and the nuts do not ripen at the same time. For these reasons it is not well suited to commercial production, but it still works for backyard growing. Chinquapins are somewhat resistant to chestnut blight, and because they grow in multistemmed thickets, losing a few older stems to blight is not such a problem. One improved cultivar, 'Golden', is available. Chinquapins need a cross-pollinator, so seedlings should work fine, either together or to pollinate 'Golden'.

FIGURE A.14. Hybrid hazelnuts (*Corylus* spp.) are productive and tasty. The multistemmed shrubs make good screens and windbreaks. *Photo by Dave Jacke, courtesy Tripple Brook Farm.*

FIGURE A.15. Though popular in the Russian Far East, Japan, and China, goumi (*Eleagnus multiflora*) is virtually unknown in the West. Its fruit is edible and medicinal, ripening in late June on a 6-foot (2 m) plant and fruiting reasonably well in the shade. It is potentially opportunistic, but perhaps worth trying in areas where its *Eleagnus* relatives autumn and Russian olive are already well established. All *Eleagnus* species are nitrogen-fixers. *Photo by One Green World.*

Hybrid Hazel – *Corylus* spp.
Hardiness zone 3, full sun, clumping thicket former shrub, 12–20 ft. x 12–15 ft., edible nuts

Hazels are another good choice for nut production in small and midsize gardens. They grow easily and can yield profusely—if you can beat the squirrels to the nuts! Hazels grow in dense thickets, providing cover for birds and other wildlife. European filberts (*C. avellana*) have large nuts and are easy to crack, but they are susceptible to eastern filbert blight. The native species, American hazelnut (*C. americana*), is resistant to the blight, but has smaller, thick-shelled nuts. Hybrid varieties (sometimes known as "hazelberts" or "filazels") combine the best of both worlds and are the best choice for forest gardens in eastern North America. Plant at least two different varieties for pollination. According to reports we have heard, you need at least 500 feet (150 m) of tree-free meadow on all sides to prevent squirrels from harvesting your hazelnuts for you. Plant extra and enjoy watching the wildlife.

Goumi – *Eleagnus multiflora*
Hardiness zone 5–8, full sun to part shade, multistemmed shrub, 6–8 ft. x 6–8 ft., edible fruit, fixes nitrogen

The goumi is one of the best candidates for edible forest gardens, except for one possible problem. It fixes nitrogen and produces tasty edible berries, even fruiting well in partial shade. Improved varieties from the former Soviet Union have recently become available here. Goumi is the best-flavored nitrogen-fixer with edible fruit and is especially valuable in gardens with limited space, where it would be difficult to sacrifice space to nonedible nitrogen-fixing shrubs. Some cultivars are self-fertile. Others require a pollinator.

The problem is that goumi is a member of the genus *Eleagnus* which features a number of nitrogen-fixing shrubs with edible fruit. Several Eurasian *Eleagnus* species have naturalized extensively. Their ability to fix nitrogen makes them well suited to disturbed and degraded sites, and birds disperse their seeds by consuming their fruit. Many consider these other *Eleagnus* species opportunistic or "invasive," while others question whether this is due only to the nature of the plants themselves. The fact that highway departments planted tens of thousands of these plants across the country's degraded landscape probably helped them disperse so rapidly. Though we do not know goumi to be highly dispersive in our region, it certainly may have the potential to act so. You can decide what you think about including this species in your garden. Please read feature article 3 (page 156) to gain an understanding of our proposed policy on native and exotic species.

BUSH CHERRIES (*Prunus* SPP.)

Mongolian Bush Cherry – *Prunus fruticosa*
Hardiness zone 2, full sun, multistemmed shrub, 3 ft. x 3 ft., edible fruit

Japanese Bush Cherry – *Prunus japonica*
Hardiness zone 4, full sun, clumping thicket former shrub, 8 ft. x 8 ft., edible fruit

Dwarf Bush Cherry Hybrids – *Prunus japonica* x *jacquemontii*
Hardiness zone 3–8, full sun, multistemmed shrub, 3–4 ft. x 3–4 ft., edible fruit

Nanking Cherry – *Prunus tomentosa*
Hardiness zone 3, full sun, multistemmed shrub, 6–10 ft. x 6–8 ft., edible fruit

Many, many species could be included here. The genus *Prunus* is enormous and includes many edible cherries. The shrub species are useful in the forest garden, as they do not take up much space. These plants include some of the hardiest of all

FIGURE A.16. Bush cherries come from a variety of species. Nanking cherry (*Prunus tomentosa*) hails from Asia and produces abundant subacid to sweet red or white fruits that can be eaten raw or in preserves. The dense, 6- to 8-foot (2 to 3 m) plants are excellent for hedging, with profuse white blooms in spring. *Photo by Edible Landscaping.*

fruiting plants. All bush cherries require a cross-pollinator.

Dwarf bush cherry hybrids 'Jan', 'Joy', and 'Joel' have good sour flavor and grow to 3 to 4 feet (1 to 1.3 m) high. The late professor Elwyn Meader, one of the great fruit breeders of our time, developed these hybrids over the course of twenty-five years. They are resistant to pests, diseases, birds, and even Japanese beetles! Mongolian bush cherry forms a 3- to 4-foot (1 to 1.3 m) suckering bush. The fruits work great for pies but taste quite tart raw. It is hardy to the unbelievable zone 2. Japanese bush cherry is another shrubby cherry species. Variety *nakai* has fruits up to 2 inches (5 cm) in diameter with good flavor, while the regular species has fine fruits as well. Nanking cherry is one of the more common bush cherries. It is hardy to zone 3 and drought tolerant with small, tasty cherries.

GOOSEBERRY, JOSTABERRY, AND CURRANT (*Ribes* SPP.)

Jostaberry – *Ribes* x *culverwellii*
Hardiness zone 3–7, full sun to part shade, multistemmed shrub, 4–8 ft. x 4–8 ft., edible fruit

Black Currant – *Ribes nigrum*
Hardiness zone 4–7, full sun to part shade, multistemmed shrub, 3–5 ft. x 3–5 ft., edible fruit

Clove Currant – *Ribes odoratum*
Hardiness zone 3b–7, full sun to part shade, multistemmed shrub, 6–12 ft. x 6–12 ft., edible fruit

Red and White Currant – *Ribes silvestre*
Hardiness zone 2–7, full sun to part shade, multistemmed shrub, 3–5 ft. x 3–5 ft., edible fruit

Gooseberry – *Ribes uva-crispa*
Hardiness zone 3–7, full sun to part shade, clumping thicket former shrub, 3–5 ft. x 3–5 ft., edible fruit

This genus is as popular in Europe as blueberries are here, but North Americans currently know little about its members. People destroyed many plantings and wild stands in the early twentieth century because many *Ribes* act as alternate hosts for white pine blister rust. This disease kills white pines, an important timber species here. However, many

FIGURE A.18. Gooseberries (*Ribes uva-crispa*) are an excellent fruit for full or part-day shade. The cultivar 'Winham's Industry' is particularly prolific. *Photo by One Green World.*

FIGURE A.17. Like their *Ribes* cousins, red currants (*R. silvestre*) also grow well in full or partial sun. Their clusters of bright red sweet-tart berries stand out on the plant, the table, and the tongue. This cultivar is known as 'Cherry Red'. *Photo by One Green World.*

resistant varieties are now available, and it turns out that many species do not carry the rust at all. Nonetheless, it is still illegal to grow them in some states and counties—you may want to look into this before ordering plants, particularly if there are white pines in your area.

All of these species are especially useful for edible forest gardens because they fruit well in partial shade. They are also extremely cold hardy. There are native and nonnative *Ribes*, and many of the commercial varieties are hybrids. All are multi-stemmed or thicket-forming smallish shrubs, except the taller, more upright jostaberry. All *Ribes* are self-pollinating.

Gooseberries are low, thorny shrubs forming dense, thicketlike clumps, although you can prune them to a single-stem form. They have the largest *Ribes* fruit, and most varieties are rust-resistant. Good gooseberry varieties are as fine a fruit as any, rivaling the sweetest grapes for flavor. Jostaberries are hybrids of currants and gooseberries, with vigorous growth and more height than either. Jostaberries are thornless and rust resistant, and the berries are very good, resembling tart, fruity blueberries. Currants come in many colors and species. They have a range of rust resistances, so be careful when you order varieties. Generally, they are too tart for fresh eating, but they make some of the world's finest jellies and beverages. Currants are thornless. Red and white currants are low maintenance, very productive, and generally rust resistant. Native clove currants have a sweet, musky flavor. Black currants are the group of currants most susceptible to rust, although resistant cultivars like 'Consort' are available. They have a strong flavor, which most people find makes great preserves but is a bit strong for fresh eating.

BRAMBLES – *Rubus* SPP.

Red Raspberry – *Rubus idaeus*
Hardiness zone 3–9, full sun, running thicket former shrub, 4–6 ft. x
   indefinitely spreading, edible fruit

Black Raspberry – *Rubus occidentalis*
Hardiness zone 4, full sun, running thicket former shrub, 3–6 ft. x
   indefinitely spreading, edible fruit

These popular berries are perhaps best suited for pockets of monoculture production within the forest garden. Their thorny thickets and vigorous expansion limit the number of species with which they can interact sociably. There are hundreds of species in the genus *Rubus*, including native, non-native, and hybrid types. Improved varieties are available of a number of native species. All brambles are self-pollinating. The general categories of brambles for fruit production in the east are raspberries, with shorter canes and red fruits; dewberries, with trailing, often thornless canes and blackberry-like fruit; and black raspberries, with arching purple canes that root at the tip to form tangled thickets and tasty purple or black, slightly dry berries. Blackberries, though delicious and productive, are too vigorously expansive to be good neighbors in a forest garden.

Elderberry – *Sambucus canadensis*
Hardiness zone 3–10, full sun to part shade, multistemmed shrub,
   6–12 ft. x 6–12 ft., edible fruit, tea plant, specialist nectary

This unassuming native shrub does not at first present itself as an extraordinary selection for forest gardens. However, it turns out to be a marvelous multipurpose plant. The fruits are edible, but generally only for cooking or making beverages such as elderberry wine. The flowers make a soothing tea, which some people use medicinally. They are also a valuable early-season nectar source for attracting specialist beneficial insects. Elderberries are low maintenance and widely adaptable. They thrive in wet areas most fruits cannot abide. They form good thickets for bird cover and provide them with berries as well. A few named cultivar with superior fruit are available, notably 'Yates'. Elderberries require a pollinator.

HIGHBUSH BLUEBERRY AND RABBITEYE BLUEBERRY (*Vaccinium* SPP.)

Rabbiteye Blueberry – *Vaccinium ashei*
Hardiness zone 7–9, full sun, multistemmed shrub, 4–18 ft. x 4–18
   ft., edible fruit

Highbush Blueberry – *Vaccinium corymbosum*
Hardiness zone 4–7, full sun, multistemmed shrub, 6–12 ft. x 6–12
   ft., edible fruit

These native shrubs are among the most delicious fruits in the world. They are low maintenance and quite long lived. Blueberries require strongly acid soils (below pH 5.5) and need good drainage (although they can be found growing on small raised mounds in bogs). Many people with good garden soils will go to a lot of trouble to acidify them to grow these delectable berries. The recent "half-high" blueberry introductions are hardier and tastier cultivars resulting from backcrossing commercial stock with wild plants ('Northsky' and 'Northblue' are two examples). Toward the southern end of our range (zone 7), the taller but otherwise similar rabbiteye blueberries replace the hardier highbush types. *Vaccinium* species are self-pollinating but set more fruit with cross-pollination.

LOW SHRUBS
(UNDER 18 INCHES/45 CM)

WOODY LEGUME GROUND COVERS (*Cytisus, Genista,* AND *Indigofera* SPP.)

Prostrate Broom – *Cytisus decumbens*
Hardiness zone 6–8, full sun, clumping mat former shrub, 8 in. x 3+
   ft., ground cover, fixes nitrogen

Silky-Leaf Woodwaxen – *Genista pilosa*
Hardiness zone 6–8, full sun to part shade, multistemmed shrub,
   1 ft. x 3–4 ft., ground cover, fixes nitrogen

Trailing Silky-Leaf Woodwaxen – *Genista pilosa procumbens*
Hardiness zone 6–8, full sun to part shade, clumping mat former
   shrub, 2 in. x 3 ft., ground cover, fixes nitrogen

Arrow Broom – *Genista sagittalis*
Hardiness zone 3–8, full sun to part shade, clumping mat former
   shrub, 3–18 in. x 2–3 ft., ground cover, fixes nitrogen

Chinese Indigo – *Indigofera decora*
Hardiness zone 5, full sun, multistemmed shrub, 18 in. x 6–8 ft.,
 ground cover, fixes nitrogen

These low-growing nitrogen-fixing shrubs make ideal ground covers for sunny spots (or phases) in forest gardens. The genus *Genista* contains a number of worthy species, all of which clothe themselves in gorgeous yellow pealike flowers in season. Silky-leaf woodwaxen grows 1 foot high and 3 to 4 feet wide (30 x 100–130 cm), while its shorter cousin, trailing silky-leaf woodwaxen, grows just 2 inches high and 3 feet wide (5 x 90 cm). How is that for a perfect ornamental nitrogen-fixing ground cover? Arrow broom is similar but grows 4 to 18 inches by 2 to 3 feet (10–45 x 60–90 cm), forming a compact mound. Chinese indigo is in the same genus as the famous dye plant also called indigo. It grows up to 18 inches high and 6–8 feet across (45 x 200–240 cm), providing an excellent way to fill sunny spaces between young trees. It produces attractive purple flowers. Prostrate broom is another fine mat-forming, nitrogen-fixing, shrubby ground cover. Other *Cytisus* species have naturalized extensively on the West Coast, but we do not know this species to be dispersive.

LOWBUSH BLUEBERRY AND OTHER LOW ERICADS (*Gaultheria* AND *Vaccinium* SPP.)

Wintergreen – *Gaultheria procumbens*
Hardiness zone 3, full sun to part shade, evergreen running mat
 former, 2–6 in. x indefinitely spreading, edible fruit, edible tea,
 ground cover

Lowbush Blueberry – *Vaccinium angustifolium*
Hardiness zone 2, full sun, clumping thicket former, 2 ft. x 3+ ft.,
 edible fruit, ground cover

Creeping Blueberry – *Vaccinium crassifolium*
Hardiness zone 6, full sun to part shade, evergreen clumping mat
 former shrub, 2–6 in. x 5+ ft., edible fruit, ground cover

Lingonberry – *Vaccinium vitis-idaea*
Hardiness zone 4, full sun, evergreen multistemmed shrub, 6–12 in.
 x 2 ft., edible fruit, ground cover

In acid soils, these native, low-growing members of the heath family (Ericaceae) are highly desirable.

As a group, they are useful as ground covers that produce tasty berries. *Vaccinium* and *Gaultheria* species are self-pollinating but set more fruit with a pollinator.

Lowbush blueberry is a source of superb blueberries. While it is not dense enough to make a completely weed-suppressing ground cover, you can grow it as part of a ground cover polyculture—for example, with *Carex pensylvanica* or other species. Anyone in zone 6 or warmer with acid soils should definitely be growing creeping blueberry. This excellent ground cover forms a dense, wide, evergreen mat and bears delicious blueberries. Top it off with beautiful red fall color and you have an excellent multipurpose native plant. Lingonberry grows in alpine and arctic areas throughout the northern parts of the world. Its berries are quite similar to cranberries, but it thrives in drier soils than that bog-loving species. Lingonberries form small, dense, evergreen clumps. Europeans cultivate this species (it is also native there), and improved varieties are now arriving here. Wintergreen is a beloved wild edible of oak and pine forests. The fragrant evergreen leaves make a refreshing tea (which needs honey or sugar), and the berries have a sweet wintergreen flavor. The cultivar 'Christmas' bears large numbers of extra-large fruit. The plant tolerates heavy shade but grows more densely and sets more fruit in sun.

HERBACEOUS VINES

Groundnut – *Apios americana*
Hardiness zone 3, full sun to part shade, sprawler, to 6 ft., edible
 tubers, fixes nitrogen

This important wild and semicultivated food for American Indians and early European settlers is native throughout our range. Breeders at Southern Louisiana State University are now developing it as a commercial crop. Undeveloped plants bear a number of tubers—up to a small egg in size—on long, stringy roots. The improved varieties have

FIGURE A.20. Groundnut (*Apios americana*) produces "strings" of tubers under vigorous herbaceous vines. New varieties under development produce significantly larger tubers, but even the large-grape-size tubers of unimproved plants taste good and can produce well. *Photo by Oikos Tree Crops.*

FIGURE A.19. Groundnut (*Apios americana*) is a native, nitrogen-fixing, herbaceous vine that is being domesticated as a new crop. Its large, pealike leaves and deep purple flowers are shown here as it climbs on Jerusalem artichoke (*Helianthus tuberosus*), another native with edible tubers. The tubers of these species are shown in figures A.20 and A.34. *Photo by Eric Toensmeier.*

fewer and larger tubers, with yields comparable to those of potatoes, but very high in protein. The tubers taste earthy, nutty, and starchy—quite nice when cooked like ordinary root crops. Groundnut is also a nitrogen-fixer. It grows as an herbaceous climber, trellised or sprawling over nearby plants. Though they can be slow to establish, groundnuts can become quite vigorous in the right conditions. New plants can sprout several feet away from the parent tuber. Design with groundnuts must account

for their expansive growth and vigorous sprawling. They are not right for all polycultures, perhaps requiring rhizome barriers in some contexts.

Jinenjo Yam – *Dioscorea japonica*
Hardiness zone 4–10, full sun to part shade, sprawler, to 10 ft., edible roots, edible shoots

Jinenjo is a hardy and productive perennial root crop and an important vegetable in Japan. The tubers grow at the base of the vines like a cluster of sweet potatoes. To maintain them as perennials, either leave at least one tuber in the ground or cut the top third off one or two tubers and replant them. The young shoots are also edible. Give jinenjo room to climb or sprawl, and place it so that harvesting the tubers does not disturb the roots of neighboring plants. Jinenjo is an attractive ornamental. The related Chinese yam (*D. batatas*) is highly dispersive in the southern portion of our range, where many regard it as a pest.

Maypop – *Passiflora incarnata*
Hardiness zone 6–10, full sun, suckering sprawler, 10–30 ft., edible fruit

Maypops are a hardy passionflower native to the Southeast. Their flowers are extraordinarily beau-

FIGURE A.21. Our native passionflower, maypop (*Passiflora incarnata*), has beautiful flowers and sweet, tangy fruit. *Photo by Dave Jacke.*

tiful, and the fruit of good varieties has a sweet, tart, rich flavor. Unfortunately, finding the right niche for maypops can be tricky. The vines die back to the ground each fall and do not emerge until early summer. Then they take off, growing up to 30 feet (9 m) in southern areas (much less in the Mid-Atlantic and North). The plants also produce suckers at a distance from the parent plant. This expansive growth habit can cause trouble. Perhaps one could safely grow maypops by allowing them to climb on bamboo or suckering, expansive shrubs within the protection of a strong rhizome barrier. Maypops require a cross-pollinator.

CLUMPING HERBS
(ABOVE 6 INCHES/15 CM)

MINT RELATIVES (*Agastache, Melissa, Monarda,* AND *Pycnanthemum*)

Anise Hyssop – *Agastache foeniculum*
Hardiness zone 3, full sun to part shade, clumping herb, 2–4 ft. x 1–2 ft., tea

FIGURE A.22. The lilac flowers of anise hyssop (*Agastache foeniculum*) have a wonderful licorice-mint aroma and are great in teas. The plant is also one of the best nectary species around, attracting a wide range of generalist and specialist insects over a long flowering period. Also shown is blue-flowered borage (*Borago officinalis*) to the left, and black-eyed Susan (*Rudbeckia hirta*) in back, both nectary plants. *Photo by Jonathon Bates.*

Lemon Balm – *Melissa officinalis*
Hardiness zone 5, full sun to part shade, clumping herb, 1–3 ft. x 1–3 ft., tea

Bee Balm – *Monarda didyma*
Hardiness zone 4, full sun to part shade, running herb, 3–4 ft. x 2-4 ft., tea

Mountain Mint – *Pycnanthemum* spp.
Hardiness zone 5, full sun to part shade, running herb, 1–3 ft. x indefinitely spreading, tea, ground cover

These members of the mint family work superbly in forest gardens. All thrive in sun or part shade and make pleasant teas or additions to salads. They also attract beneficial insects and act as "aromatic pest confusers" to confound pests in their quest for food plants.

Anise hyssop is native to western North America. Another of its common names, licorice mint, aptly describes its aroma and flavor. The flowers bloom for a long period. A great diversity of both beneficial and pest insects find the flowers popular, visiting in great numbers. In fact, the entire plant seems like a "community center" for insects of all kinds, thus functioning as both a generalist nectary and an important shelter and habitat plant for invertebrates. Bee balm is a native with beautiful red flowers that are popular with hummingbirds. It has a strong mint scent. It forms large clumps that move around the garden like a slow-motion brush fire. Lemon balm is a wonderful garden plant with a lemony-mint scent. It forms nice clumps and will not spread. Lemon balm should find a home in many forest gardens because it makes a great generalist nectary plant. Mountain mints are native herbs with a potent mint scent. They run in the garden somewhat but not as aggressively as *Mentha* mints. *Pycnanthemums* seem to grow best with a little soil disturbance. Mountain mint flowers are extremely popular with beneficial insects, making them one of the best generalist nectary plants.

Perennial Onions (*Allium* spp.)

Multiplier Onion – *Allium cepa aggregatum*
Hardiness zone 5, full sun, clumping, 2 ft. x 1 ft., edible bulb, aromatic pest confuser

Egyptian Walking Onion – *Allium cepa proliferum*
Hardiness zone 5, full sun to part shade, running, 2 ft. x indefinitely spreading, edible greens and top bulbs, aromatic pest confuser

Nodding Wild Onion – *Allium cernuum*
Hardiness zone 3, full sun to part shade, clumping, 1–2 ft. x 1–2 ft., culinary, aromatic pest confuser

Welsh Onion – *Allium fistulosum*
Hardiness zone 4, full sun, clumping, 2–3 ft. x 1–2 ft., edible scallion and greens, aromatic pest confuser

Chives – *Allium schoenoprasum*
Hardiness zone 5, full sun to part shade, clumping, 6–20 in. x 6–20 in., culinary, dynamic accumulator, aromatic pest confuser

FIGURE A.23. The perennial multiplier onion (*Allium cepa aggregatum*) is one of the most productive of all root crops. *Photo by Eric Toensmeier.*

Garlic Chives – *Allium tuberosum*
Hardiness zone 3, full sun, clumping, 18 in. x 12 in., culinary, aromatic pest confuser

Many species of perennial onions are ideal for forest gardens. Their edible parts include greens, flowers, and bulbs. Spring clumps can be divided for a harvest of scallions. Alliums function as aromatic pest confusers when scattered around the garden. Flowering species make good generalist nectaries.

Chives are a well-known culinary herb with edible greens and flowers; they thrive in full sun to partial shade. Multiplier or potato onions and shallots are productive, perennial bulb-forming alliums. Annually dividing the clumps provides gourmet bulbs with good storing qualities. Young greens or whole plants of Welsh onions, garlic chives, and our native nodding wild onion make good scallions and tender greens. Garlic chives also have pungent edible flowers that are popular with beneficial insects. The Egyptian walking onion, besides being a fine scallion, produces tiny edible bulbs at the top of its stalks. When the stalk falls over, new plants grow—so it "walks" around the garden. This novel plant-dispersal strategy can get out of hand if you let it go long enough. If so, eat more! They are tasty, especially early in the season.

FIGURE A.24. Ramps (*Allium tricoccum*), superb wild onions, naturalize to form large colonies in shade. For a close-up of this spring ephemeral, see figure 3.4. *Photo by Eric Toensmeier.*

FIGURE A.25. Eric Toensmeier holding a branch of milkvetch (*Astragalus glycyphyllos*), a nitrogen-fixing ground cover. This polyculture also contains, to the left of Eric, sea kale (*Crambe maritima*); front left, dwarf comfrey (*Symphytum grandiflorum*); front right, perennial ground cherry (*Physalis subglabrata*) and Egyptian onion (*Allium cepa proliferum*). *Photo by Dave Jacke.*

Ramps – *Allium tricoccum*
Hardiness zone 4, part to full shade, clumping, 1 ft. x 1 ft., edible greens and bulbs, aromatic pest confuser

While a perennial allium like the above species, ramps (also known as wild leek) stand out as a vegetable uniquely suited to forest gardens. Ramps are a native wild edible, growing as a spring ephemeral in moist, deciduous woods. In spring, these onions emerge briefly and disappear by the time the tree canopy fully leafs out. The large, tender leaves taste sweet and pungent, while the bulbs have a strong onion flavor. In North Carolina, ramp festivals happen every spring to celebrate this delicious plant. Interplant ramps with something to take up the space after they die back (wild ginger works well). They are one of the few truly excellent food crops that can grow in full shade.

Asparagus – *Asparagus officinalis*
Hardiness zone 3, full sun, clumping, 3–5 ft. x 18–36 in., edible shoots

This popular perennial vegetable needs no introduction. In forest gardens, asparagus is probably best suited to sunny glades. Its tall, feathery foliage, pliable stems, and sensitive roots do not compete well with vigorous species or deal well with windy conditions. Build polycultures around its need for rich soils and minimal competition, or grow it in small monoculture patches.

Milkvetch – *Astragalus glycyphyllos*
Hardiness zone 4, full sun to part shade, clumping, 6–12 in. x 4–5 ft., fixes nitrogen

This nitrogen-fixer is a fantastic polyculture companion. It tends to grow hugging low to the ground and spreads to form a wide, dense mat. This *Astragalus* species is attractive and tough, while permitting taller plants to grow up through its foliage. We could use more nitrogen-fixers like this! Milkvetch is a great example of a plant that has never achieved popularity based on its looks but may someday be much more common as we begin to appreciate functional plants. Note that several thousand species populate this genus, with wildly varying characteristics. Make sure to get this species if you want a good ground cover.

WILD INDIGO (*Baptisia* SPP.)

Blue Wild Indigo – *Baptisia australis*
Hardiness zone 4, full sun to part shade, clumping, 2–4 ft. x 3–5 ft., fixes nitrogen.

Yellow Wild Indigo – *Baptisia tinctoria*
Hardiness zone 3, full sun to part shade, clumping, 2–3 ft. x 2–5 ft., fixes nitrogen

These native legumes are popular garden plants. They are also fine nitrogen-fixers. Wild indigos are

FIGURE A.27. Good King Henry (*Chenopodium bonus-henricus*) is a versatile perennial vegetable grown for shoots, leaves, flower buds, and seeds. *Photo by Eric Toensmeier.*

FIGURE A.26. Blue wild indigo (*Baptisia australis*) is a lovely native nitrogen-fixer. *Photo by Eric Toensmeier, courtesy of Tripple Brook Farm.*

large plants that take up a good bit of space, particularly because their stalks tend to collapse and sprawl on surrounding plants once their seedpods form. Place them where you need a large nitrogen-fixer. Many useful species exist in addition to the native blue and yellow wild indigos featured here. Some dwarf varieties are available.

Good King Henry – *Chenopodium bonus-henricus*
Hardiness zone 3, full sun to part shade, clumping, 1–3 ft. x 12–18 in., edible leaves, shoots, buds, and seeds

Besides having one of the best Latin names around, this perennial vegetable is a prime candidate for the forest garden. It is in the same family as spinach and somewhat resembles it in form and taste. The British eat the shoots in spring, calling them Lincolnshire asparagus. They also cook the young

leaves like spinach; they are too bitter to eat raw. The flower buds taste remarkably like broccoli. The seeds are also edible—in fact, the Europeans once cultivated His Majesty as a grain crop. This shade-tolerant multipurpose perennial vegetable is good, but breeding could improve it further so it could become a new perennial forest garden broccoli, spinach, or seed crop.

CHICORY & DANDELION

Chicory – *Cichorium intybus*
Hardiness zone 3, full sun to part shade, clumping, 1–4 ft. x 1–2 ft., edible leaves, dynamic accumulator

Dandelion – *Taraxacum officinale*
Hardiness zone 3, full sun to part shade, clumping, 6–24 in. x 6–24 in., edible leaves and flowers, dynamic accumulator

These common edible weeds have entered into cultivation—improved varieties are available for use in gourmet salads. Both are excellent dynamic accumulators and have some effectiveness as generalist nectary plants. Along with sorrels (below), these two species are among the best edible dynamic accumulators for the forest garden. The roots of both species can yield coffee substitutes.

Chicory has a slightly bitter flavor, which is an essential part of mesclun salad mix. A number of varieties are perennial, but not all. Perennial types include 'Sweet Trieste', 'Spadona', 'Ceriolo', 'Dentarella', and 'Red Rib'. Many foragers have

FIGURE A.28. The "dynamic duo": two excellent edible dynamic accumulators, chicory (*Cichorium intybus*, right) and French sorrel (*Rumex acetosa*, left). *Photo by Eric Toensmeier.*

FIGURE A.29. Sweet cicely (*Myrrhis odorata*) is a specialist nectary. The unripe (green) seeds taste like licorice candy. *Photo by Eric Toensmeier.*

eaten the nutty, bitter, spring leaves of the dandelion. Breeders have selected domesticated dandelions for larger leaves and reduced bitterness, but the wild ones, when pampered in the garden, are almost indistinguishable. You can eat the flowers as fritters and use them to make dandelion wine. Moreover, we can guarantee that dandelions will take care of themselves in your garden!

Sea Kale – *Crambe maritima*
Hardiness zone 4, full sun to part shade, clumping, 2–3 ft. x 3 ft., edible broccolis, leaves, and shoots

This traditional perennial vegetable grows wild along European seacoasts. Sea kale is cultivated for its large spring shoots, which gardeners blanch and eat. Also delicious but less well-known are the mild and delicious broccoli-like flower buds. Plant breeder Carol Deppe, author of *Breed Your Own Vegetable Varieties*, thinks sea kale has potential for development into a new perennial broccoli-like vegetable. The leaves of plants too young to have flowered taste remarkably like collard greens. See figure A.25.

Lovage – *Levisticum officinale*
Hardiness zone 4, full sun to part shade, clumping, 4–8 ft. x 4–8 ft., edible leaves and stalks

A traditional herb and vegetable from Europe, lovage plants resemble enormous clumps of celery. Their leaves and young stalks are among the first to grow in spring, with a taste unbeatable in soups. Once the plant has reached about 2 feet (60 cm) tall, the flavor becomes too intense for most people, but you can blanch the plants like celery for a milder taste. You can use sections of the stalk as flavored straws. All parts of the plant have a strong lemon-celery flavor. After flowering, the stalks collapse and can smother neighboring plants. Either cut back the flowering stalks, or provide lovage with neighbors that can tolerate the disturbance. Lovage is reliable, a fine specialist nectary plant, and low maintenance. Every forest garden would do well to have at least one plant.

Sweet Cicely – *Myrrhis odorata*
Hardiness zone 4, full sun to part shade, clumping, 3 ft. x 3 ft., edible leaves and seeds

Sweet cicely is one of the finest edible specialist nectary plants. The anise-flavored foliage has provided a sweetener for centuries in Europe, where it was often cooked with rhubarb before the wide availability of sugar. The real taste treat, though, is the fresh green seeds, which have the flavor of anise and sunflower seeds—eat them like candy. Sweet cicely thrives in sun or partial shade.

Rhubarb – *Rheum* spp.

Himalayan Rhubarb – *Rheum australe*
Hardiness zone 6–9, full sun, clumping, 5–8 ft. x 5 ft., edible leafstalks

Rhubarb – *Rheum* x *cultorum*
Hardiness zone 1, full sun, clumping, 3–5 ft. x 3–5 ft., edible leafstalks

Turkey Rhubarb – *Rheum palmatum*
Hardiness zone 6–9, full sun, clumping, 5–8 ft. x 5 ft., edible leafstalks

Rhubarb is one of the few commonly grown perennial vegetables—it is large and persistent once planted. Cook the leafstalks for their sour flavor, which goes particularly well with strawberries in pie. You can also use rhubarb leafstalks as a vegetable, something like tart celery. Remember that the stalks must be cooked, and do not eat the leaves and roots as they are quite poisonous. Rhubarb is a bold plant in the garden and needs a nice, sunny spot and rich soil. In addition to the familiar species, you may also want to try the enormous—but tasty—6-foot (2 m) stalks of Turkey rhubarb or the apple-flavored leafstalks of Himalayan rhubarb.

Sorrels (*Oxyria* and *Rumex* spp.)

Mountain Sorrel – *Oxyria digyna*
Hardiness zone 2, full sun to part shade, clumping, 2–12 in. x 12 in., edible leaves

French Sorrel – *Rumex acetosa*
Hardiness zone 3, full sun to part shade, clumping, 1–3 ft. x 1 ft., edible leaves, dynamic accumulator.

Buckler-Leaved Sorrel – *Rumex scutatus*
Hardiness zone 3, full sun to part shade, clumping, 1 ft. x 1–2 ft., edible leaves, dynamic accumulator, ground cover

This closely related group of perennial vegetables shares a delicious lemony flavor. Sorrels are particularly tasty in spring soups—try them with lovage! Besides being gourmet vegetables, sorrels are one of the best dynamic accumulators, mining the subsoil for calcium, phosphorus, and potassium. Given their edible leaves, love of partial shade, and role as dynamic accumulators, sorrels should be one of the most widely used forest garden plants in our region.

French sorrel is a popular perennial vegetable. The cultivar called 'Profusion' never flowers, and you can thus eat it all year (like most greens, sorrels become less palatable when flowering). It also never forms a tall flower stalk and remains tidily under 1 foot (30 cm) tall. 'Profusion' sorrel is truly a must-have for any forest garden. You can also cultivate buckler-leaved sorrel for its leaves. It, too, makes an excellent ground cover, forming a low mound up to 2 feet (60 cm) across. Though an alpine species, mountain sorrel is very similar to its close relatives the *Rumex* sorrels. It shares the same lemony flavor. The leaves grow considerably larger in partial shade. It seems likely that mountain sorrel is also a good dynamic accumulator.

Scorzonera, Oyster Plant – *Scorzonera hispanica*
Hardiness zone 4–9, full sun to part shade, clumping herb, 1–3 ft. x 1–2 ft., edible roots and leaves, specialist nectary

Gardeners usually grow scorzonera as an annual root crop for its gourmet, oyster-flavored taproots. In forest gardens, however, scorzonera is best valued as a perennial leaf crop. You can eat the leaves raw and enjoy their lettucelike flavor. Some backyard breeders are working to bring scorzonera fully into its own as a perennial leaf crop. Meanwhile, it is still a fine choice both for its edible leaves and as a specialist nectary plant.

Skirret – *Sium sisarum*
Hardiness zone 5–9, full sun to part shade, clumping, 3 ft. x 1–2 ft., edible roots, specialist nectary

Skirret is a productive root crop and specialist nectary plant for the sunnier parts of the forest garden. Its roots have long been cultivated in Eurasia but fell out of favor in the twentieth century. This is probably because the pencil- to finger-thick taproots, which grow as a dense cluster, often have a fibrous or woody core, at least in unnamed varieties. Fortunately, improved varieties that entirely lack this trait are now available and can be vegetatively propagated. The cooked roots are sweet and filling, like a blend of parsnip and potato. This productive

FIGURE A.30. Skirret (*Sium sisarum*) is a productive root crop. *Photo by Eric Toensmeier.*

FIGURE A.31. Skirret is also a specialist and generalist nectary plant from the family Apiaceae. In addition, skirret provides foliage habitat for parasitic wasps and egg-laying sites for lacewings. *Photo by Jonathon Bates.*

and low-maintenance vegetable may enjoy a renaissance as we come to appreciate the role of multipurpose perennials in forest gardens and other edible landscaping systems.

Sweet Goldenrod – *Solidago odora*
Hardiness zone 3, full sun to part shade, clumping, 2–4 ft. x 2–4 ft., edible tea, specialist nectary

Goldenrods are ubiquitous species in the oldfield stage of succession throughout the eastern forest region. As a group, goldenrods are important for beneficial insects as a fall nectar source and a place to aggregate and then spread into the garden. Sweet goldenrod has the added benefit of being one of our finest native tea plants. Blue mountain tea, a beverage made from the leaves and flowers, has a licorice-like flavor. The leaves also make a nice nibble. As goldenrods go, this species is not very aggressive, mostly staying in place as a clump. A few sweet goldenrods in the sunnier phases or areas of your garden will provide many benefits with little care.

COMFREYS (*Symphytum* SPP.)

Large-flowered Comfrey – *Symphytum grandiflorum*
Hardiness zone 4, full sun to part shade, clumping, 8–12 in. x 18 in., dynamic accumulator, ground cover, beneficial habitat

Russian Comfrey – *Symphytum* X *uplandicum*
Hardiness zone 6, full sun to part shade, clumping, 1–4 ft. x 3 ft., dynamic accumulator, beneficial habitat

Comfreys are fantastic functional plants for the forest garden. They are perhaps the best of all the dynamic accumulators. They grow extremely well in most conditions, and you can cut them for nutrient-rich mulch several times each season. They also excel at attracting beneficial insects, providing a preferred egg-laying and overwintering site for many species. Comfreys are also beloved by spiders, hosting as many as 240 per square meter in the soil below them during winter, according to one study. The challenge is that comfreys are incredibly persistent—once planted, they are virtually impossible to eliminate. A tiny root piece left in the ground will start a new plant. In addition, the species most commonly grown spreads by seed. Comfrey has taken over many gardens—don't let it happen to you!

One way to avoid this is to plant Russian comfrey, a sterile hybrid of two species, meaning it cannot make viable seed and, thus, cannot be weedy by seed. It is just as persistent as the common species, however. Large-flowered comfrey is a ground-covering species that forms a low mound. It will spread vegetatively and to a certain degree by

FIGURE A.33. Yarrow (*Achillea millefolium*) is truly multifunctional: it is a specialist nectary, dynamic accumulator, and preferred habitat for many beneficial insects. *Photo by Jonathon Bates*

FIGURE A.32. Hybrid Russian comfrey (*Symphytum* x *uplandicum*) is the queen of dynamic accumulators, concentrating up to six important minerals in its leaves and releasing them to the topsoil. It provides great foliage habitat for spiders, parasitic wasps and lacewing egg-laying, and spiders overwinter en masse in the soil under it. *Photo by Eric Toensmeier.*

seed. Large-flowered comfrey is a fantastic soil-building ground cover for partial shade.

RUNNING HERBS
(ABOVE 6 INCHES/15 CM)

Yarrow – *Achillea millefolium*
Hardiness zone 3, full sun to part shade, running, 8–36 in. x indefinitely spreading, ground cover, dynamic accumulator, beneficial habitat, specialist nectary

This low-maintenance workhorse is one of the premier multipurpose support plants for the forest garden. It forms clumps but sends out vigorous runners to form new clumps. Many assume that yarrow is in the Apiaceae, due to its umbel-shaped heads, but it is in fact a member of the aster family (Asteraceae). Regardless, it is a fine specialist nectary plant. It also provides foliage habitat and egg-laying sites for ladybugs, spiders, lacewings, Carabid beetles, and parasitoid insects. It dynamically accumulates phosphorus and potassium, among other nutrients, and, of course, it is a popular ornamental, drought tolerant, and medicinal too! Although a bit aggressive, yarrow has much to offer as a multifunctional plant for the edible forest garden.

Pink Tickseed – *Coreopsis rosea*
Hardiness zone 3–9, full sun, running, 1–2 ft. x indefinitely spreading, ground cover, specialist nectary

This native wildflower is a popular and attractive ornamental and a low-maintenance, multipurpose forest-garden plant. It forms a moderately dense ground cover and spreads rapidly. This specialist nectary blooms profusely from July to September, providing much fuel for beneficial insects. Growing the wild type, rather than named cultivars, may provide the highest nectar yield for beneficials, as plant breeding for ornamental qualities often unintentionally decreases nectar production by flowers. Note that the related clumping *Coreopsis* species are also fine choices for the forest garden.

FIGURE A.34. The tubers of our native Jerusalem artichoke (*Helianthus tuberosus*) are rich in carbohydrates, crispness, and nutty flavor. A number of varieties are available with different characteristics. These highly productive plants can persist vigorously, so plant them where you can let them stay. *Photo by Oikos Tree Crops.*

Jerusalem Artichoke – *Helianthus tuberosus*
Hardiness zone 2, full sun to part shade, running, 6–12 ft. x indefinitely spreading, edible roots

This enormous perennial sunflower relative is among our best native wild edibles. Jerusalem artichokes produce truly enormous quantities of tubers. They are generally somewhat smaller than potatoes and taste crisp and sweet. Jerusalem artichoke is one of the few commercially grown perennial vegetables, and one of the very best low-maintenance food crops for our climate. For some people the roots can cause flatulence, particularly when eaten raw. Keep trying; your body will adjust if you eat them frequently. Jerusalem artichoke grows in dense stands. Either respect it and give it plenty of room to spread, or fence it in with rhizome barriers. Dwarf varieties may be somewhat more manageable, or at least less competitive. Annual harvesting invigorates the plants and leads to higher yields. Jerusalem artichoke has a reputation for being quite persistent, even weedy, but apparently if you uproot the plants in July when they are flowering, they will not come back. At least not as much!

Daylily – *Hemerocallis* spp.
Hardiness zone 2 or 3, full sun to part shade, running, 1–5 ft. x indefinitely spreading, edible flowers, buds, and tubers

Daylilies certainly have a role to play in the forest garden, although contemporary landscaping clearly overuses them. The flowers and flower buds are a popular vegetable in northern Asia, and those in the know in the United States and Canada eat them, too. The tubers are also edible, and quite productive. They can cause a bit of digestive upset for those who are not accustomed to them, so use them with caution. Daylily does not fit this book's definition of a ground cover (it is too tall), but it is a great ground cover nonetheless. The challenge is that daylilies are too large and vigorous to be a good companion to most herbs. Daylilies are a good low-maintenance choice for an area of your garden to which you don't want to have to pay any attention.

Ostrich Fern – *Matteuccia struthiopteris*
Hardiness zone 2, part to full shade, running, 4–6 ft. x indefinitely spreading, edible shoots

Each spring, markets in New England offer the strange, tightly curled shoots of ostrich fern, known as fiddleheads. This is one of the most well-known and beloved native wild edibles of the eastern forest. It is also an attractive ornamental, reaching 4 to 6 feet (1.2 to 1.8 m) or more and forming extensive colonies in moist soil and part to full shade. The distance between crowns leaves room for low-growing, shade-tolerant companions. Steam or boil the fiddleheads for at least ten minutes to remove toxins. They taste delicious when boiled and served with butter.

Mints – *Mentha* spp.
Hardiness zone 3, full sun to part shade, running, 1–3 ft. x indefinitely spreading, edible tea, culinary, aromatic

The numerous species and hybrids of mint are highly adapted for the forest garden. They were among the most prevalent understory species in Robert Hart's garden. Unfortunately, as he was quick to admit, they were among the more troublesome weeds in his garden as well. Mints tend to be vigorous runners, colonizing new areas but never staying in one area for too many years. They will outcompete many other herbs, except for large, tough, well-established clumpers. Their foliage is wonderful in teas, fresh or dried, and in small amounts in salads. The flowers are excellent generalist nectaries, attracting many beneficial insects, and the strong scent of the foliage confuses pests in their search for their favorite foods. A new cultivar called 'Marilyn's Salad Mint' is said to have milder-flavored leaves and is a promising new running perennial vegetable for partial shade.

Giant Solomon's Seal – *Polygonatum biflorum* var. *commutatum*
Hardiness zone 3, full sun to part shade, running, 3–5 ft. x indefinitely spreading, edible shoots

This beautiful, native wildflower of the lily family sends up slender 3 to 5 foot (0.9–1.6 m) stalks in drifts and spreads by rhizomes. It is commendable for its adaptability—giant Solomon's seal grows in full sun all the way to full shade. Cut and use its edible shoots in the spring, like asparagus; they taste quite good, though the leaf cluster at the top of the shoot may taste somewhat bitter. Giant Solomon's seal is another example of an underutilized native that is highly adapted to the forest garden model.

Chinese Artichoke – *Stachys affinis*
Hardiness zone 5, full sun to part shade, running, 18 in. x indefinitely spreading, edible tubers

This running ground cover is in the mint family. It is native to eastern Asia, but people now grow it

FIGURE A.35. Giant Solomon's seal (*Polygonatum biflorum* var. *commutatum*) is a native with edible shoots that can be picked and cooked like asparagus in springtime. *Photo by Dave Jacke.*

FIGURE A.36. When mature, giant Solomon's seal (*Polygonatum biflorum* var. *commutatum*) arches gracefully over its neighbors, sometimes reaching 5 feet (1.6 m) in height. *Photo by Dave Jacke.*

FIGURE A.37. Chinese artichoke (*Stachys affinis*) makes an excellent ground cover and produces numerous small, minty, edible tubers. We have used it with success in our three-sisters perennial polyculture. *Photo by Dave Jacke, courtesy of Tripple Brook Farm.*

FIGURE A.38. The native wood nettle (*Laportaea canadensis*) is a shade-loving vegetable. Like its sun-loving cousin, stinging nettle (*Urtica dioica*), it stings until cooked. *Photo by Dave Jacke.*

throughout the cold climates of the world. It produces small (1 inch/3 cm) tubers, in good quantity. The tubers are crisp, with a light mint flavor, but they are also bumpy and somewhat difficult to clean. They taste good raw in salads and can be cooked in a variety of ways. Chinese artichoke makes a moderately dense cover. Annual harvest results in higher yields. Harvest all you can find, because enough will always elude discovery to ensure a vigorous stand the following year.

NETTLES (*Laportaea* AND *Urtica* SPP.)

Wood Nettle – *Laportaea canadensis*
Hardiness zone 3, part to full shade, running, 1–3 ft. x indefinitely spreading, edible leaves

Stinging Nettle – *Urtica dioica*
Hardiness zone 4, full sun to part shade, running, 3–4 ft. x indefinitely spreading, edible leaves, dynamic accumulator

Nettles in a forest garden? Why would we welcome a plant that causes painful stings? Believe it or not, nettles are among the most beneficial plants for the forest garden. For starters, both of these closely related species produce delicious and hearty greens—when cooked (make sure to harvest with gloves on). Even a minute of steaming is enough to deactivate the sting. If you have never had them, the delightful taste of the greens will surprise you. Both plants form large colonies through seed and rhizomes. Use rhizome barriers, and be sure to locate

your nettles where you will not accidentally brush against them.

Stinging nettle is one of the most nutritious leafy greens in the world, as well as being a fabulous dynamic accumulator and a wonderful compost plant. Research indicates that it increases the volatile oil content of herbs grown alongside it, making them more aromatic. Stinging nettles have naturalized in most of the United States, often in situations closely resembling forest gardens. The variety *gracilis* is native to North America. Our native wood nettle is also a delicious potherb and may be a dynamic accumulator like its cousin. Wood nettle grows in full shade and seems to thrive in the understory of old-growth forests.

PROSTRATE HERBS

WILD GINGER (*Asarum* SPP.)

Wild Ginger – *Asarum canadense*
Hardiness zone 3, part to full shade, running mat former, 4–8 in. x indefinitely spreading, ground cover, edible root

Shuttleworth's Wild Ginger – *Asarum shuttleworthii*
Hardiness zone 6, part to full shade, evergreen clumping mat former, 4–8 in. x 14 in., ground cover

Wild ginger is one of our best native ground covers. These dense, low-growing species spread indefinitely. They make lovely ornamentals, especially

FIGURE A.39. Wild gingers (*Asarum* spp.) are lovely edible native ground covers for shade. Shown here is *Asarum canadense*, the most common eastern species, growing under sugar maple (*Acer saccharum*) in a stand of Massachusetts old-growth forest. *Photo by Dave Jacke.*

FIGURE A.40. A native ground cover and specialist nectary, green and gold (*Chrysogonum virginianum*) provides bright yellow flowers throughout the spring season. *Photo by Eric Toensmeier, courtesy Tripple Brook Farm.*

evergreen species such as Shuttleworth's wild ginger. The roots of some species, including wild ginger, supposedly substitute for cultivated ginger. In our experience, the flavor is not nearly as pleasant as that of ginger—it has a bit of a medicinal flavor. Nevertheless, wild gingers are an outstanding choice for a native shade-loving ground cover.

Green and Gold – *Chrysogonum virginianum*
Hardiness zone 4, full sun to part shade, evergreen clumping mat former, 3–6 in. x 18in., specialist nectary, ground cover

Also known as golden star, this is another fantastic native ground cover. While not fast growing, this slow and steady mat former is a reliable low-maintenance species for sun to partial shade. It forms low, dense evergreen mats that are covered by beautiful yellow daisylike flowers in spring and early summer. Goldenstar flowers in the early part of the year—the crucial period when the forest garden needs beneficial insects but few other specialist nectaries are available. This trait, combined with green and gold's excellence as a ground cover, makes it a great choice for forest gardens.

STRAWBERRIES (*Fragaria* SPP.)

Garden Strawberry – *Fragaria* x *ananassa*
Hardiness zone 3, full sun, evergreen running, 6–12 in. x indefinitely spreading, edible fruit, ground cover

Beach Strawberry – *Fragaria chiloensis*
Hardiness zone 7, full sun, evergreen running, 6 in. x indefinitely spreading, edible fruit, ground cover

Musk Strawberry – *Fragaria moschata*
Hardiness zone 5, full sun to part shade, evergreen running, 6–12 in. x indefinitely spreading, edible fruit, ground cover

Alpine Strawberry – *Fragaria vesca alpina*
Hardiness zone 3, full sun to part shade, evergreen clumping, 10 in. x 10 in., edible fruit

Wild Strawberry – *Fragaria virginiana*
Hardiness zone 4, full sun to part shade, evergreen running, 4–12 in. x indefinitely spreading, edible fruit, ground cover

As a group, strawberries generally make excellent edibles and only moderate ground covers. They are well suited to sunny pockets of production or to being interwoven with clumping species in polycultures. Most spread indefinitely as runners and are self-pollinating. A few varieties do require a pollinator.

Beach strawberry is native from California to Chile on the Pacific coast. Fruit quality is allegedly good but not great. Unlike most strawberries, it makes a dense, evergreen ground cover. Unfortunately, it is not very hardy. Musk strawberry is an underutilized species that, while not very productive, bears delicious fruit said to taste of raspberry and pineapple. Alpine strawberry is unusual in that it forms a single clump and does not spread. It is a great candidate for the edges of garden pathways because it ripens just a few small fruit at a time, but does so throughout the growing season. Thus if you walk by every day you can make the most of what it has to offer—and there is more strawberry flavor packed into one of these tiny fruits than in any number of enormous store-bought hybrids! Wild strawberry, our native wild species, bears small, sweet fruits. It is not much of a ground cover, but it intermingles well with grasses and wildflowers in meadows here in New England. We could use it similarly in the forest garden. Garden strawberry is the common cultivated form, a hybrid of several of the above species. You can't beat it for productivity, and many cultivars have excellent flavor. This is a perfect species for pockets of production, but it might want to have its patch rotated every few years for disease prevention. Strawberry-rhubarb pie is sure to be a favorite product of the forest garden!

Galax – *Galax urceolata*
Hardiness zone 4, part to full shade, evergreen running, 6–12 in. x indefinitely spreading, ground cover

This native evergreen ground cover is an excellent choice for forest gardens with some shade. It spreads, but not overly vigorously, forming a dense colony of tight clumps. Galax is another underutilized native deserving of attention. We are happy it is becoming more available as an ornamental.

Miner's Lettuce (*Montia* spp.)

Miner's Lettuce – *Montia perfoliata*
Hardiness zone 4, full sun to part shade, clumping, self-seeds, 6–12 in. x 6–12 in., edible leaves, ground cover

Siberian Miner's Lettuce – *Montia siberica*
Hardiness zone 4, full sun to part shade, clumping, self-seeds, 8–12 in. x 8–12 in., edible leaves, ground cover

Greg Tilford, in his excellent *Edible and Medicinal Plants of the West*, says, "Of all edible [wild] plants, miner's lettuce stands out as one of the most palat-

FIGURE A.41: A native northwestern wild edible, miners' lettuce (*Montia perfoliata*) is a great salad plant for sun or shade. It obviously also makes a good groundcover! *Photo by Jonathon Bates.*

able . . . the leaves and stems of this group of plants taste almost identical to lettuce . . . Miner's lettuce stays tender and sweet throughout its growth cycle."[1] In addition to its delectable status, miner's lettuce makes a fine ground cover in moist soils with partial to very dense shade. Both species listed here are native to western North America. Miner's lettuce is an annual or short-lived perennial that self-sows to form a dense carpet. This species is cultivated commercially as a salad green with a truly delicious flavor. It tolerates somewhat dry soils, unlike Siberian miner's lettuce, a clumping perennial that spreads freely by seed. Its leaves taste good, except when the plant is flowering.

Foamflower – *Tiarella cordifolia*
Hardiness zone 3, part to full shade, running, 6–12 in. x indefinitely
   spreading, ground cover, specialist nectary

This beautiful shade-loving plant is one of our best native ground covers. It forms attractive clumps and drifts, spreading indefinitely. Foamflower is a specialist nectary, attracting beneficial insects in spring. You can find foamflower in rich woods throughout our region.

White Clover – *Trifolium repens*
Hardiness zone 4, full sun to part shade, running, 4–10 in. x indefinitely spreading, fixes nitrogen, ground cover, edible leaves

This tireless workhorse deserves a place in virtually every forest garden. It is a fine candidate for sunny pathways, as it will tolerate substantial foot traffic. It is (somewhat) edible, and it fixes nitrogen like a champ. The stems creep and root as they go, forming mats. White clover is well suited as a ground-covering polyculture companion to accompany crop shrubs or larger herbs. It is a good generalist nectary and a preferred cover and egg-laying site for many beneficial insects. Unlike many forest garden species, white clover is widely available. You can easily start it from seed right in the ground where you want it. Inoculate to ensure nitrogen fixation.

VIOLETS (*Viola* SPP.)

Canada Violet – *Viola canadensis*
Hardiness zone 4, full sun to part shade, running, 6–16 in. x indefinitely spreading, edible leaves and flowers

Labrador Violet – *Viola labradorica*
Hardiness zone 3, full sun to part shade, evergreen running, 4 in. x
   indefinitely spreading, edible leaves and flowers

Sweet Violet – *Viola odorata*
Hardiness zone 4, full sun to part shade, evergreen running, 6–8 in. x
   indefinitely spreading, edible leaves and flowers

These attractive little flowers are excellent understory species for forest gardens. All have edible leaves and flowers, but let us warn you, some taste much better than others do. As a rule, yellow-flowering types have more bitterness. Nonetheless, good-tasting violets exist for almost any site condition you may have. We have listed only a few; learn your own native species! In addition to the runners profiled

here, there are also many nice clumping types. Labrador violet, from chilly northern New England and Canada, makes an excellent ground cover: it is semievergreen, dense, and matlike. Unfortunately, the somewhat woolly leaves are not particularly palatable. Sweet violet makes a good, vigorous, evergreen ground cover. The leaves are by far the sweetest of any violet we have tried. It functions best in areas free of scorching hot summers. Canada violet is a fine native with good-flavored leaves and flowers.

Barren Strawberry – *Waldsteinia fragarioides*
Hardiness zone 4–7, full sun to part shade, evergreen running, 4–8
   in. x indefinitely spreading, ground cover

Barren strawberry is another fantastic native ground cover. It spreads rapidly and forms a dense carpet, and it is one of the best evergreen ground covers for full sun. The plants closely resemble strawberries, to which they are closely related, but their small, green fruit is not edible.

FUNGI

Shiitake – *Lentinula edodes*
Many farmers and gardeners in our region grow shiitake mushrooms. Their cultivation is fairly simple and reliable. Shiitakes will grow on logs or stumps. Their rich flavor and firm texture make shiitakes a popular gourmet mushroom. Many Asian cultures also consider them medicinal.

Oyster Mushroom – *Pleurotus ostreatus*
Oysters grow easily in a variety of substrates. Cultivators usually grow them on logs or stumps, but they can also grow in compost piles, straw mulch, or almost any carbonaceous material. They are voracious decomposers and are even used to clean up and digest toxic oil spills. Their gourmet flavor does, in fact, resemble that of oysters.

Chicken-of-the-Woods – *Polyporus sulphureus*
Chicken-of-the-woods mushrooms provide exceptional quality food. They exhibit a Day-Glo orange

FIGURE A.42. Shiitake mushrooms (*Lentinula edodes*) are easily grown on logs, preferably oak. The mushrooms are tasty and reportedly have great medicinal value as well. *Photo by Dave Jacke.*

FIGURE A.43. Chicken-of-the-woods (*Polyporus sulphureus*), the mushroom that really does taste just like chicken! These mushrooms were found growing wild by the side of the road. *Photo by Eric Toensmeier.*

color and actually do taste just like chicken. Chicken-of-the-woods grows best on stumps but can also grow on partially buried logs.

King Stropharia – *Stropharia rugoso-annulata*

King stropharias are large, gourmet mushrooms. Their flavor resembles that of potatoes cooked with wine. Stropharias are well suited to cultivation in straw or wood-chip mulch—in fact, they commonly pop up uninvited in bark mulch used for landscaping. When overmature, the caps can exceed 12 inches (30 cm) in diameter.

FIGURE A.44. Another tasty mushroom, the king stropharia (*Stropharia rugoso-annulata*) thrives in wood-chip and bark mulch, producing large mushrooms in quantity. *Photo by Jonathon Bates.*

1. Tilford, 1997, page 98.

APPENDIX TWO

Plant Hardiness Zone Maps

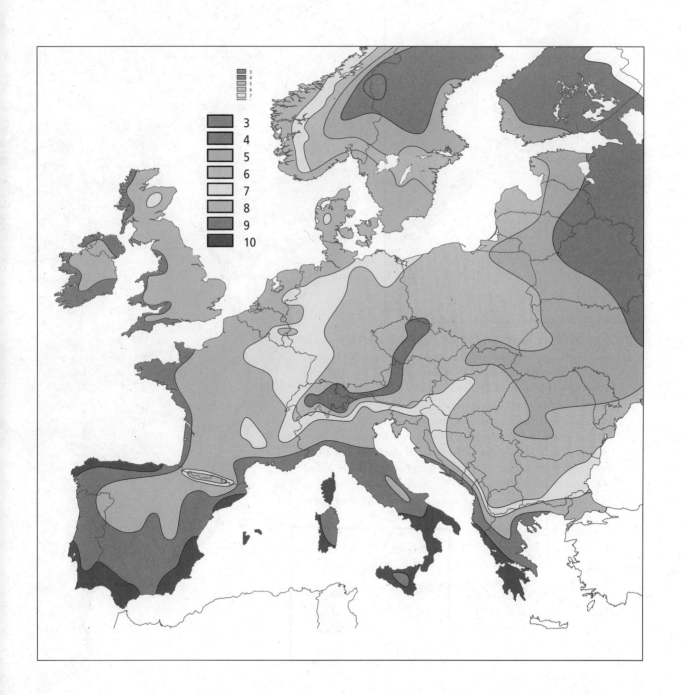

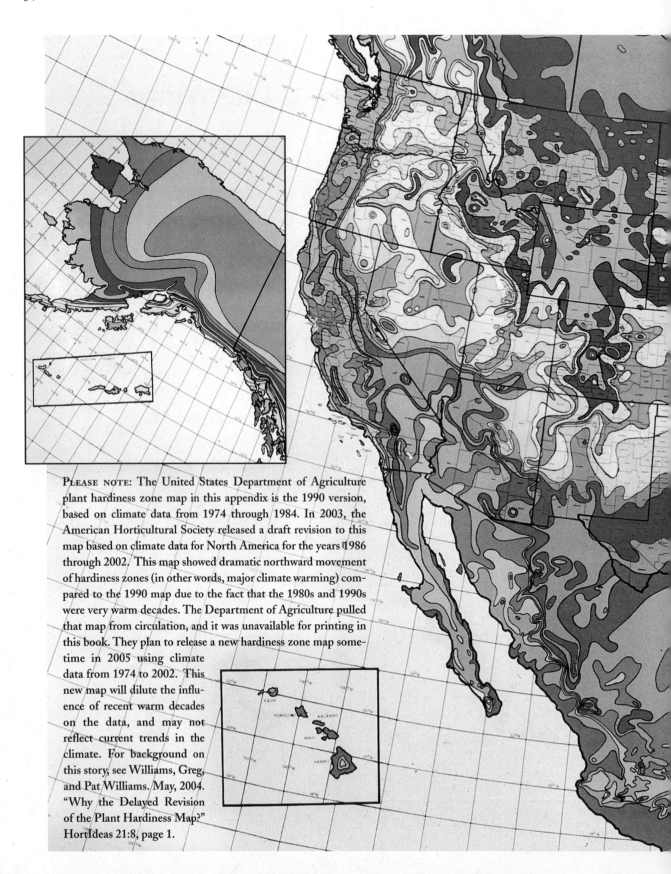

PLEASE NOTE: The United States Department of Agriculture plant hardiness zone map in this appendix is the 1990 version, based on climate data from 1974 through 1984. In 2003, the American Horticultural Society released a draft revision to this map based on climate data for North America for the years 1986 through 2002. This map showed dramatic northward movement of hardiness zones (in other words, major climate warming) compared to the 1990 map due to the fact that the 1980s and 1990s were very warm decades. The Department of Agriculture pulled that map from circulation, and it was unavailable for printing in this book. They plan to release a new hardiness zone map sometime in 2005 using climate data from 1974 to 2002. This new map will dilute the influence of recent warm decades on the data, and may not reflect current trends in the climate. For background on this story, see Williams, Greg, and Pat Williams. May, 2004. "Why the Delayed Revision of the Plant Hardiness Map?" HortIdeas 21:8, page 1.

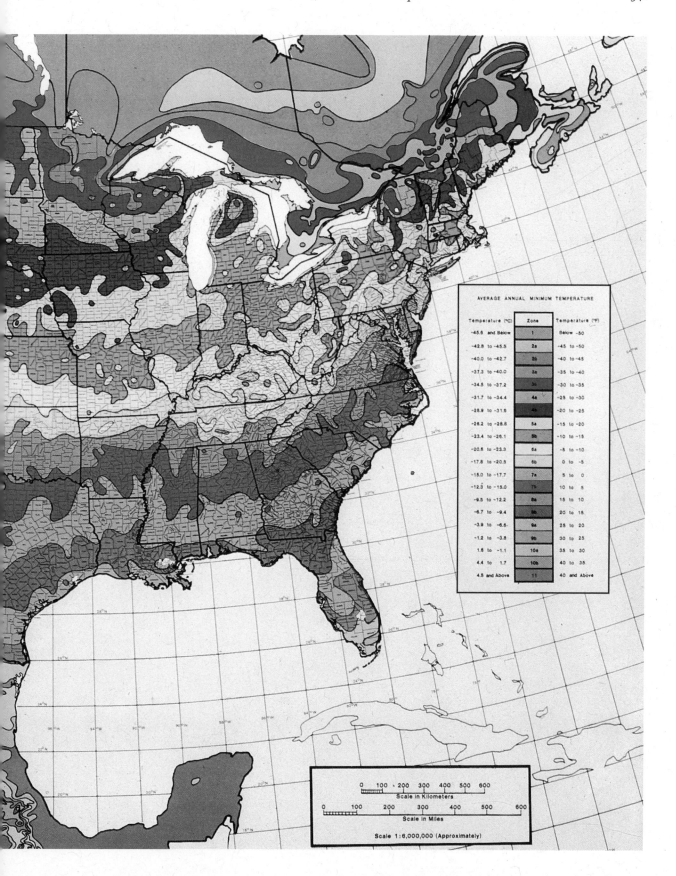

AVERAGE ANNUAL MINIMUM TEMPERATURE

Temperature (°C)	Zone	Temperature (°F)
-45.6 and Below	1	Below -50
-42.8 to -45.5	2a	-45 to -50
-40.0 to -42.7	2b	-40 to -45
-37.3 to -40.0	3a	-35 to -40
-34.5 to -37.2	3b	-30 to -35
-31.7 to -34.4	4a	-25 to -30
-28.9 to -31.6	4b	-20 to -25
-26.2 to -28.8	5a	-15 to -20
-23.4 to -26.1	5b	-10 to -15
-20.6 to -23.3	6a	-5 to -10
-17.8 to -20.5	6b	0 to -5
-15.0 to -17.7	7a	5 to 0
-12.3 to -15.0	7b	10 to 5
-9.5 to -12.2	8a	15 to 10
-6.7 to -9.4	8b	20 to 15
-3.9 to -6.6	9a	25 to 20
-1.2 to -3.8	9b	30 to 25
1.6 to -1.1	10a	35 to 30
4.4 to 1.7	10b	40 to 35
4.5 and Above	11	40 and Above

0 100 200 300 400 500 600
Scale in Kilometers

0 100 200 300 400 500 600
Scale in Miles

Scale 1:6,000,000 (Approximately)

APPENDIX THREE

Publications and Organizations

PUBLICATIONS

FOREST GARDENING & PERENNIAL POLYCULTURES

Agroforestry News.
A quarterly magazine from the Agroforestry Research Trust featuring articles on forest garden design and profiles of useful plants for Britain. Available from the Agroforestry Research Trust (see under "Organizations"), and through the *Permaculture Activist* (see below).

Apios Institute for Regenerative Perennial Agriculture online database
Online resource featuring user-generated reports on forest garden species, polycultures, and garden designs. Online at www.apiosinstitute.org.

Creating a Forest Garden: Perennial Crops for a Changing Climate. MARTIN CRAWFORD.
Guide to forest gardening by director of the Agroforestry Research Trust, an international leader in temperate-climate perennial polycultures.

Designing and Maintaining Your Edible Landscape Naturally. ROBERT KOURIK.
A critical reference for forest gardeners, covering design, site preparation and planting, pest control, fertility, mulching, and more. Excellent. Definitely worth pursuing.

Farming in Nature's Image. JUDITH SOULE AND JON PIPER.
An important work on the science of perennial polycultures. Chapters 4 and 5 are required reading! They discuss the authors' work with the Land Institute to develop perennial polycultures modeled on the prairie ecosystem.

Forest Gardening. ROBERT HART.
The book that started it all, describing Hart's experiments in adapting the tropical forest polyculture model to his temperate climate. Inspirational, but not terribly informative.

How to Make a Forest Garden. PATRICK WHITEFIELD.
Fills in much of the practical information that Hart's book lacks. A useful handbook for forest gardening in the British climate.

Tree Crops: A Permanent Agriculture. J. RUSSELL SMITH.
Written in 1927, this classic book is one of the foundations of permaculture. Describes a tree-based agricultural model to provide food for humans and livestock.

A Year in a Forest Garden. MARTIN CRAWFORD.
Video presenting four seasons in Martin Crawford's forest garden, demonstrating species, theory, and practices like coppicing and harvesting.

USEFUL PLANTS & FUNGI

Cornucopia: A Source Book of Edible Plants. STEPHEN FACCIOLA.
Describes over three thousand species of edible plants, with sources to order each and every one! A powerful tool in the hands of an adventurous gardener.

Edible Wild Plants of Eastern North America. LEE ALLEN PETERSON.
Describes many plants that might be included in forest gardens. Particularly useful are the tables in the back describing useful plant species for a range of habitats and successional stages.

Growing Gourmet and Medicinal Mushrooms. PAUL STAMETS.
The bible of mushroom production. Though focused on indoor culture techniques, it includes information on the outdoor cultivation of mushrooms on logs, stumps, compost piles, and mulch.

Growing Unusual Vegetables. SIMON HICKMOTT.
Provides growing and use information on interesting vegetables, including many perennials. Focuses on British climate.

A Guide to Nut Tree Culture in North America, volume 1. DENNIS FULBRIGHT, EDITOR.
Comprehensive tome on nut production. Covers most hardy nut species, except walnuts (which will be covered in the forthcoming second volume).

Landscaping With Fruit: Strawberry Ground Covers, Blueberry Hedges, Grape Arbors, and 39 Other Luscious Fruits to Make Your Yard an Edible Paradise. LEE REICH.
Mouth-watering guide to cold-climate edible-landscaping fruits, with great information of productivity and level of maintenance.

Mycelium Running: How Mushrooms Can Help Save the World. PAUL STAMETS
Guide to growing and using mushrooms for food, forestry, and remediation of environmental problems from clear-cuts to oil spills.

Nitrogen-Fixing Plants for Temperate Climates. MARTIN CRAWFORD.
Excellent reference for selecting nitrogen-fixing plants. A British focus, but very relevant to eastern North America.

Perennial Ground Covers. DAVID MACKENZIE.
By far the best guide to ground covers we have seen.

Perennial Vegetables: From Artichoke to "Zuiki" Taro, a Gardener's Guide to Over 100 Delicious, Easy-to-Grow Edibles. ERIC TOENSMEIER
Detailed profiles of perennial vegetable crops including many temperate species, with design and management strategies.

Plants for a Future. KEN FERN.
Remarkable guide to useful plants from an author with over one thousand useful species in his collection. Focus on British climate. Beware: Ken Fern enjoys plant flavors that we find distasteful.

Plants for a Future online database.
Information on over seven thousand useful species for temperate climates, with wild habitat, propagation, edible and medicinal uses, and much, much more. Incredibly useful and free! Online at http://www.pfaf.org.

Uncommon Fruits for Every Garden. LEE REICH.
Well-written guide to low-maintenance, delicious, hardy fruits.

Wild Edible Plants of Western North America. DONALD KIRK.
Covers the full range of edible plants of the West, from the Sonoran desert to the Yukon Territory.

NATIVE PLANTS

Gardening with Native Wildflowers. SAMUEL JONES AND LEONARD FOOTE.
An excellent guide to growing southeastern natives.

Growing and Propagating Native Wildflowers of the U.S. & Canada. WILLIAM CULLINA.
Beautiful and informative, with hard-to-find propagation information from Cullina's years of experience with the New England Wildflower Society.

Native Trees, Shrubs, & Vines. WILLIAM CULLINA.
Another fantastic reference from Cullina.

Native Trees, Shrubs and Vines for Urban and Rural America: A Planting Design Manual for Environmental Designers. GARY HIGHTSHOE.
This mind-blowingly comprehensive book is for the hard-core designer. A remarkable range of information about each species, including rooting type, pollution tolerance, and native range by county! A great investment.

COOKBOOKS FOR FOREST GARDEN PLANTS & FUNGI

Billie Joe Tatum's Wild Foods Field Guide and Cookbook. BILLIE JOE TATUM.
Features great recipes for many wild edible plants and mushrooms. Also a good field guide.

Edible Wild Mushrooms of North America: A Field-to-Kitchen Guide. ALAN BESSETTE, ARLEEN BESSETTE, AND DAVID FISCHER.
Useful field guide with mouthwatering photos and recipes.

Native Harvests: American Indian Wild Foods & Mushrooms. E. BARRIE KAVASCH.
This is an expanded twentieth anniversary edition of Kavasch's earlier celebrated book. Contains many great recipes for many native wild edibles.

Vegetables from Amaranth to Zucchini: The Essential Reference. ELIZABETH SCHNEIDER.
Information and recipes, including many for forest garden vegetables and mushrooms.

ECOLOGY AND EASTERN NORTH AMERICAN ECOSYSTEMS

1491: New Revelations of the Americas Before Columbus. CHARLES MANN.
Mind-opening information on the complex and populous pre-Columbian societies in the New World. Much coverage of agriculture and land-management practices.

Changes in the Land: Indians, Colonists, and the Ecology of New England. WILLIAM CRONON.
Fascinating history of the New England forest. Provides insights on the broader history of the eastern forest region in the past millennium.

Deciduous Forests of Eastern North America. E. LUCY BRAUN.
This classic 1950 book is one of the most comprehensive surveys of the vegetation of the eastern deciduous forest. It relates vegetation to climate and landform and gives species lists and relative abundances to help describe the plant communities. A great source for model ecosystem information.

Ecology. PAUL COLINVAUX.
This textbook provides an excellent in-depth review of the full breadth of the science of ecology as it stood in the mid-1980s. Colinvaux believes strongly in Gleason's individualistic view of plant communities.

Ecology of Eastern Forests. JOHN KRICHER AND GORDON MORRISON.
This Peterson guide packs much useful information into a field-guide-size reference.

The Eternal Frontier: An Ecological History of North America and Its People. TIM FLANNERY.
An engaging natural and social history of the last 65 million years of North America that underlines the fluid nature of ecosystems as they change over time. We recommend reading this before taking on Theodoropoulos's *Invasion Biology: Critique of a Pseudoscience* (page 345).

Forest Ecosystems. DAVID PERRY.
This book was a key reference for *Edible Forest Gardens*. Perry provides solid scientific footing and a well-integrated systems view of both the big picture of forest ecosystems and the critical details.

The Forgotten Pollinators. STEPHEN BUCHMANN AND GARY PAUL NABHAN.
A groundbreaking book for lay readers. Elucidates the importance of pollination in ecosystems and the effects of the loss of pollinators due to human disturbance.

Ghosts of Evolution: Nonsensical Fruit, Missing Partners, and Other Ecological Anachronisms. CONNIE BARLOW.
Illuminates the botanical aftermath from the evolutionarily "recent" loss of the giant sloth, mammoth, mastodon, and other "megafauna" from the eastern forest region. It changed our thinking about "native" ecosystems. Another prerequisite for Theodoropoulos's *Invasion Biology*.

Landscape Restoration Handbook. DONALD HARKER, SHERRI EVANS, MARC EVANS, AND KAY HARKER.
Lists native "climax" species for all regions of the continental U.S. Very helpful for ecological analog design.

New England Wildlife: Habitat, Natural History, and Distribution. RICHARD DEGRAAF AND MARIKO YAMASAKI.
An excellent reference on the ecology of the region's native birds, mammals, reptiles, and amphibians. The earlier version (by DeGraaf and Rudis and published by the US Forest Service) is out of print but is available online as a download at http://www.fs.fed.us/ne/newtown_square/publications/popular-publications.shtml

Old Growth in the East: A Survey. MARY BYRD DAVIS.
Describes the characteristics of eastern old growth. Documents numerous existing stands and fragments of old growth you can visit for each state east of the Mississippi.

Soil Biology Primer. NATURAL RESOURCES CONSERVATION SERVICE (NRCS).
This short handbook describes the basics of soil food web ecology and the roles of various organisms in the soil ecosystem. A good introduction, and the online version is free. Visit http://www.soils.usda.gov/sqi/soil_quality/soil_biology/soil_biology_primer.html. For hard copies go to http://www.swcs.org/en/publications/books/soil_biology_primer.cfm.

Some Ecological Aspects of Northeastern American Indian Agroforestry Practices. KARL DAVIES.
This article was ahead of its time in describing the sophisticated eastern North American Indian agroforestry practices, particularly prescribed burning to encourage nut, berry, and wildlife production. More evidence that there has not been a "primeval forest" in our region for thousands of years. Online at http://www.daviesand.com.

Tending the Wild: Native American Knowledge and the Management of California's Natural Resources. M. KAT ANDERSON.
Details sophisticated indigenous land management of California over a 12,000 year period before European arrival. Fantastic models for long-term sustainable ecosystem management.

NATIVES AND EXOTICS

Invasion Biology. MARK DAVIS.
This scientific text is a skeptical review of invasion biology, questioning assumptions in a less polemical style than Theodoropoulos.

Invasion Biology: Critique of a Pseudoscience. DAVID THEODOROPOULOS.
Proposes that the "invasive species" movement is based on bad science, and that it misses the true causes of the environmental crisis. Raises many, many important questions. It truly changed the way we think and see. Required reading, but read the following first to prime you well: *The Eternal Frontier* (Flannery); *Guns, Germs, and Steel* (Diamond); and *Ghosts of Evolution* (Barlow).

The Once and Future Forest: A Guide to Forest Restoration Strategies. LESLIE JONES SAUER AND ANDROPOGON ASSOCIATES.
This is a good book by a recognized authority in ecological design and restoration, but it is also alarmist in tone. Many good strategies, and decent information on the ecological health of the eastern forest, but beware of the invasion biology.

Stalking the Wild Amaranth. JANET MARINELLI.
Along with Sauer's book above, this one is a good contrast to David Theodoropoulos. Raises good questions about how we might garden "in the age of extinction."

FIELD GUIDES

Field Guide to Trees and Shrubs. GEORGE PETRIDES.
A guide to eastern woody plants. One of the few field guides that includes both trees and shrubs. The botanical keys are usually helpful to those who know the lingo, but the drawings could be better.

Garden Insects of North America: The Ultimate Guide to Backyard Bugs. WHITNEY CRANSHAW.
This is a good identification guide to the herbivores, predators, and pollinators in your garden, but it provides minimal information on the ecology and management of the pests described. Use along with *The Organic Gardener's Handbook of Natural Insect and Disease Control* (Ellis and Bradley).

Insect, Disease, and Weed ID Guide. JILL CEBENKO AND DEB
    MARTIN.
A welcome overview of unwelcome organisms.

Mushrooms of Northeastern North America. ALAN BESSETTE,
    ARLEEN BESSETTE, AND DAVID FISCHER.
An excellent field guide to eastern mushrooms, including edi-
bility.

Newcomb's Wildflower Guide. LAWRENCE NEWCOMB.
Our favorite wildflower and flowering-shrub identification
guide for the eastern region.

Weeds of the Northeast. RICHARD UVA, JOSEPH NEAL, AND
    JOSEPH DITOMASO.
Excellent guide to annual and perennial weeds (including many
useful species).

PERMACULTURE

Gaia's Garden: A Guide to Home-Scale Permaculture. TOBY
    HEMENWAY.
A good introduction for North American gardeners.

Introduction to Permaculture. BILL MOLLISON AND RENY MIA
    SLAY.
Mollison's most readable overview of permaculture.

Permaculture: Principles and Pathways beyond Sustainability.
    DAVID HOLMGREN.
Larger view of permaculture and humanity's post-petroleum
future, within a framework of practical principles for design.

The Permaculture Activist.
Quarterly magazine for North American permaculture enthusi-
asts. Articles on forest gardens, useful plants, and more.
Available from http://www.permacultureactivist.net.

Permaculture Magazine.
This British permaculture magazine includes articles on forest
gardens, useful plants, et cetera. Available from
http://www.permaculture.co.uk.

Water for Every Farm: Using the Keyline Plan. P. A. YEOMANS.
The basic book on keyline planning, one of the foundations of
permaculture.

GARDENING AND FARMING IN THE FOREST

*The American Woodland Garden: Capturing the Spirit of the
    Deciduous Forest.* RICK DARKE.
The author of this book undertook a photo essay following one
specific patch of forest through twenty years. The book also
describes many ornamental aspects of woodland gardening in
the eastern forest and provides a catalog of numerous woodland
natives and their ornamental uses.

*Beth Chatto's Woodland Garden: Shade-Loving Plants for Year-
    Round Interest.* BETH CHATTO.
For the ornamental woodland gardener, especially in Britain,
this book is wonderful. Great pictures, good information, and
an engaging style.

Ecoforestry: The Art and Science of Sustainable Forestry. ALAN
    DRENGSON AND DUNCAN TAYLOR, EDITORS.
A wealth of essays on the scientific, philosophical, economic, and
practical issues of sustainable forestry, from researchers, practitioners, and theorists.

*Restoration Forestry: An International Guide to Sustainable
    Forestry Practices.* MICHAEL PILARSKI.
A wide-ranging collection of essays, contacts, and information
for using forestry as a means of ecological healing.

The Silvicultural Basis of Agroforestry Systems. MARK ASHTON
    AND FLORENCIA MONTAGNINI, EDITORS.
The contributors put some solid scientific footing under agroforestry, examining plant-environment interactions, plant-plant
interactions, nutrient dynamics, and so on.

Temperate Agroforestry Systems. ANDREW M. GORDON AND
    STEVEN M. NEWMAN, EDITORS.
Reviews the status of agroforestry systems used in temperate
climates throughout the world. An excellent global overview.

*The Woodland Way: A Permaculture Approach to Sustainable
    Woodlot Management.* BEN LAW.
How to make a living from the woods while living in and
caring for it. Based on Ben's life cutting coppice, making char-
coal, and building crafts in rural Britain.

ECOLOGICAL GARDENING,
FARMING, AND LANDSCAPING

*American Horticultural Society Plant Propagation: The Fully
    Illustrated Plant-by-Plant Manual of Practical Techniques.*
    ALAN TOOGOOD, EDITOR.
An easy-to-use, comprehensive guide to the full range of propagation techniques.

*Arboriculture: Integrated Management of Trees, Shrubs, and
    Vines.* RICHARD HARRIS, JAMES CLARK, AND NELDA
    MATHENY.
An excellent reference on the subject, with solid footing in
research and practice. Highly recommended.

Biotechnical Slope Protection and Erosion Control. DONALD
    GRAY AND ANDREW LEISER.
An excellent technical manual on using plants and other means
besides concrete to stabilize slopes. A must-see for anyone with
a challenging site or doing professional design.

*Breed Your Own Vegetable Varieties: The Gardener's and Farmer's
    Guide to Plant Breeding and Seed Saving.* CAROL DEPPE.
Crucial guide to backyard breeding for vegetables and more.
Includes information on domesticating wild edibles.

Building Soils for Better Crops. FRED MAGDOFF.
Good overview of ecological soil care.

Drip Irrigation for Every Landscape and All Climates. ROBERT
KOURIK.
As the title suggests, this book tells all.

*How to Grow More Vegetables (and Fruits, Nuts, Berries, Grains,
and Other Crops) Than You Ever Thought Possible, On Less
Land Than You Can Imagine.* JOHN JEAVONS.
The bible of intensive gardening and mini-farming, with lots of
information on double-digging techniques.

*The Instant Expert Guide to Mycorrhiza: The Connection for
Functional Ecosystems.* TED ST. JOHN.
The best summary we've found so far on mycorrhizas.
Available in .pdf format at http://www.mycorrhiza.org.

Lasagna Gardening. PATRICIA LANZA.
A manual on sheet-mulch gardening.

Northeast Cover Crop Handbook. MARIANNE SARRANTONIO.
Very nice guide to cover cropping for the eastern forest region.

*The Organic Gardener's Handbook of Natural Insect and Disease
Control.* BARBARA ELLIS AND FERN MARSHALL BRADLEY.
Identification and organic remedies for pests and diseases.

Start with the Soil. GRACE GERSHUNY.
Excellent introductory guide to soils.

Soil Foodweb, Inc.
www.soilfoodweb.com
Great online resource for soil biology information.

Rainwater Harvesting for Drylands and Beyond Volume One.
BRAD LANCASTER.
Practical overview to capturing rainwater and using it produc-
tively in the home and landscape.

CLIMATE INFORMATION

*Climatological Summaries—Climatography of the U.S. National
Oceanic and Atmospheric Administration. 1950–present.* No.
20, NATIONAL CLIMATE DATA CENTER, Asheville, NC.

*Annual Degree Days to Selected Bases Derived from 1951–1980
Normals. Supplement 1* to *Climatography of the U. S. no. 81.*
NATIONAL OCEANIC AND ATMOSPHERIC ADMINISTRATION.
1982. National Climate Data Center, Asheville, NC.

Climatic Atlas of the United States. NATIONAL OCEANIC AND
ATMOSPHERIC ADMINISTRATION. 1980. National Climate
Data Center, Asheville, NC.

ORGANIZATIONS

Agroforestry Research Trust
46 Hunters Moon
Dartington, Totnes
Devon TQ9 6JT
United Kingdom
(++44) (0)1803 840776
www.agroforestry.co.uk
The world's leading temperate forest garden research institu-
tion. Excellent publications, including *Agroforestry News.*

American Bamboo Society
750 Krumkill Rd.
Albany, NY 12203-5976
www.americanbamboo.org
Amateur and professional bamboo enthusiasts.

American Chestnut Foundation
469 Main Street, Suite 1
PO Box 4044
Bennington, VT 05201-4044
(802) 447-0110
www.acf.org
Dedicated to restoring the American chestnut through
breeding and other efforts.

Apios Institute for Regenerative Perennial Agriculture
www.apiosinsitute.org

Promoting development of edible forest gardens and other
perennial production systems. Projects include online user-generated profiles of species, polycultures, and site designs.

Association for Temperate Agroforestry
203 ABNR Bldg.
University of Missouri
Columbia, MO 65211
(573) 882-9866
www.aftaweb.org
Promoting agroforestry including forest farming.

Ecological Agriculture Projects
McGill University (Macdonald Campus)
Ste-Anne-de-Bellevue, QC H9X 3V9
Canada
(514) 398-7771
Fax: (514) 398-7621
Email: info@eap.mcgill.ca
www.eap.mcgill.ca
One of the world's best collections of materials on sustainable
food and agriculture systems, probably the best in North
America. Many of the materials are unpublished or out of
print, or otherwise difficult to obtain. Check out their virtual
library online!

Edibleforestgardens.com
www.edibleforestgardens.com
The place for updates, networking, and additional information
on forest gardens. Hosted by the authors of the tome you are
reading.

The International Ribes Association
PO Box 428
Booneville, CA 95415
(707) 895-2811
Information and networking for professional and backyard
growers of *Ribes* fruits (currants, gooseberries, and jostaberries).

The Land Institute
2440 E. Water Well Rd.
Salina, KS 67401
(785) 823-5376
www.landinstitute.org
Researching "natural systems agriculture," perennial polycultures modeled on prairie vegetation. Breeding new perennial
grain and legume crops. Awesome!

North American Fruit Explorers (NAFEX)
1716 Apples Rd.
Chapin, IL 62628
www.nafex.org
Association of fruit enthusiasts. Their journal *Pomona* reports
on members' experiences with breeding, hardiness trials, and
work with rare or unusual species and varieties.

North American Mycological Association
6615 Tudor Ct.
Gladstone, OR 97027-1032
(503) 657-7358
www.namyco.org
Amateur and professional mushroom enthusiasts. Can connect
you with one of the many regional mycological associations.
For both wild collectors and growers of mushrooms.

North American Native Plant Society
PO Box 84, Station D
Etobicoke, ON M9A 4X1
Canada
(416) 680-6280
www.nanps.org
Native plant enthusiasts from the U.S. and Canada. Can connect you with one of the many regional native plant
associations.

Northern Nut Growers Association
PO Box 427
648 Oak Hill School Rd.
Townsend, DE 19734-0427
www.icserv.com/nnga
Network of researchers, commercial producers, and backyard
enthusiasts growing nut trees (plus persimmon and pawpaw).

The PawPaw Foundation
c/o Pawpaw Research
147 Atwood Research Facility
Kentucky State University
Frankfort, KY 40601
www.pawpaw.kysu.edu/ppf/default.htm
Work to popularize the pawpaw (*Asimina triloba*).

Plants for a Future
Blagdon Cross
Ashwater, Beaworthy
Devon EX21 5DF
United Kingdom
01208 872 963
Organization promoting useful perennial plants, especially edi-
bles. Their Web site, including their indispensable database, is
a fantastic resource.

Seed Savers Exchange
3076 North Win Rd.
Decorah, IA 52101
(563) 382-5990
www.seedsavers.org
Remarkable organization whose members exchange seeds and
plant material of vegetables, fruits, nuts, herbs, and flowers.

Society for Ecological Restoration
285 W. 18th Street, Suite 1
Tucson, AZ 85701
(520) 622-5485
www.ser.org
Organization dedicated to repairing damaged ecosystems.
Many of their techniques are of interest to forest gardeners.

United Plant Savers
PO Box 400
East Barre, VT 05649
(802) 479-9825
www.unitedplantsavers.org
Encourages preservation and restoration of native medicinal
plants.

GLOSSARY

additive yielding: also called *overyielding*; when the yield of two or more crops grown in polyculture is more than that of equivalent areas of the two crops grown in monoculture; in some contexts, additive yielding also includes the system yield, that is, when yields of one or more crops are lower than when grown in monoculture, but the diverse yields of the polyculture add together for a higher total yield.

adsorbed: held in a thin layer of molecules on the surface of a solid body or liquid, usually by electrochemical attraction.

adventitious: describes roots growing from a stem or other upper part of a plant, rather than the root crown or another root.

aggrade: to build biological capital within an ecosystem during succession; the opposite of degrade.

agroforestry: the growing of agricultural products using trees and other woody plants, often in combination with typical annual crops or other common agricultural systems; specifically includes systems such as *alley cropping*, nut and fruit orchards, forest gardening, animal fodder systems (a.k.a. *silvopastoral* systems), windbreaks, etc. Different from forestry in that agroforestry integrates agricultural production, whereas forestry is concerned specifically with growing trees for lumber, pulp, or other wood products.

allelochemicals: chemicals produced by plants, animals, or microbes not for metabolic functioning but to serve ecological purposes such as defense against herbivores or competitors.

allelopathy: the inhibition of one plant by another through the use of chemical compounds, usually as a means of defense against competition.

alley cropping: growing annual crops between widely spaced rows of tree crops.

anion: a negatively charged ion.

aspect: the direction a site, slope, or *microclimate* faces relative to the sun.

between-patch guild: a guild that does not require its plant members to grow within the same patch for the guild to function.

biogeochemical cycles: cycles of chemical elements, including nutrients, through the ecosystem, transforming the elements into living (bio), mineral (geo), and chemical forms as they go.

biomass: literally "life matter"; living or dead tissues, chemicals, or other organic material produced by plants, animals, microbes, or other living things; when dead, it becomes organic matter, though it is still biomass.

bulb: a short underground stem with fleshy leaves or scales; actually a modified leaf bud serving as a storage organ.

canopy: the uppermost spreading branchy layer of a forest; the topmost of any vegetative layer overhead, usually with more or less continuous cover. The canopy can be very high, or it can be relatively low, as long as it is above the shrub layer (12 feet/3.6 m).

carnivores, primary and secondary: organisms that gain their needed energy from other nonproducer organisms; primary carnivores eat *herbivores*, and secondary carnivores eat primary carnivores.

cation: a positively charged ion.

cation exchange capacity: the quantity of cations the soil can hold or the relative number of cation exchange sites within a soil; the higher the cation exchange capacity, the more cationic nutrients the soil can hold for nutrient uptake by plants and other organisms.

cation exchange sites: negatively charged sites on soil particles and organic matter within soil that hold *cations*; the more cation exchange sites a soil contains, the higher is its *cation exchange capacity*.

chelate: to form a compound consisting of a metal atom surrounded by a molecule, usually an organic molecule; chelation makes many toxic metals less toxic and makes others more available to plants.

clearing: a vertical open space within a forest matrix extending through the vegetation layers from the canopy to the top of the herb layer (6 feet or 2 meters high), with a diameter-to-height ratio between 2 and 4.

climax: the "endpoint" of a successional sequence, usually thought of as a specific forest type for each part of eastern North America. See chapter 6 for a more thorough explanation.

codominant: those fewest species whose combined cover value composes the majority of the vegetation for their layer or, for the community as a whole, the overstory; to be codominant, species must usually have a cover value of at least 20 to 30 percent.

community niche: an ecological role within a community, e.g., "canopy foliage herbivore," "lignin decomposer," "late-succession understory tree"; community niches may be filled by numerous species.

competitor: in the context of the core strategies of species niches, a competitor species allocates most of its resources toward growth and competition, rather than reproduction or stress tolerance.

consistence: see *soil consistence*.

consumers: organisms that must gain their needed energy from another organism and cannot obtain it directly from a nonbiological source; contrast with *producers*.

coppice: the woody material regrowing from the stump or roots of a tree or shrub after it is cut down; a.k.a. "stump sprouts."

corm: an enlarged, fleshy, but solid bulblike base of a stem, lacking the fleshy leaves of a true bulb; not a modified leaf bud but part of the stem, serving as a storage organ.

corridor: plant and animal communities surrounded by an area with a dissimilar community structure and composition, while being long and narrow.

coverage, cover value, or **percent cover:** the percentage of an area beneath the canopy of a given species or set of species.

cross-inoculation groups: groups of nitrogen-fixing plants that can inoculate each other with the proper bacteria for nitrogen fixation; named for the kinds of plants in the group, e.g., the "cowpea" group or the "pea" group.

crown density: the concentration of opaque matter in a tree, shrub, or herb crown as it affects the transmission of light to the vegetation layers below.

deciduous: denotes plants that drop their leaves for a period each year, such as during the winter in temperate climates or the dry season in the tropics.

decomposers: organisms that gain their needed energy by breaking down biomass lost as waste from other organisms or left over from already-dead organisms.

diffuse mutualism: a mutualist strategy in which a species can cooperate with an array of potential partners; the opposite of *pairwise mutualism*.

dispersive: plants that spread rapidly and far by seed, borne by either animals or wind; we use this value-neutral term rather than words like *invasive*, which both is inaccurate and presumes that "invasiveness" is a characteristic resulting only from plant characteristics, and not the interaction between the plant and its environment.

disturbance: any relatively discrete event in time that disrupts ecosystem, community, or population structure and changes resources, substrate availability, or the physical environment.

dominant: the dominant species of a community is that overstory species that contributes the most cover to the community, compared to other overstory species; dominance usually occurs when the species has a cover value of over 50 percent. May also refer to the dominant species within a particular vegetation layer. The community or layer is often named for the dominant species. Many people object to the term *dominant* for political/ideological reasons. We use the term despite its problems because we want to maintain an interface with concepts from vegetation ecology.

ecological analogs: species or groups of species selected by humans for specific reasons to perform functions, fill niches, create a habitat, or exhibit a form similar to a model species or species group.

ecological equivalents: species or groups of species that evolved to perform functions, fill niches, create a habitat, or exhibit a form similar or equivalent to a species or species group in an ecologically similar or equivalent habitat.

ecological time: timescales at which ecosystems change but for which evolutionary change is a minimal influence; for forest ecosystems, ecological time is on the order of years, decades, and centuries. Beyond that we get into the realm of evolutionary time.

edge environments: transition zones between two distinct habitats, where the edge contains species from both neighboring habitats as well as species specifically adapted to the transition zone.

eluviation: the transportation of dissolved or suspended material within the soil by the movement of water when rainfall exceeds evaporation; a.k.a. *leaching*.

emergent property: a characteristic, quality, or behavior that emerges from the interactions between elements, such that the property can be said to belong only to the interacting elements as a whole system, not the elements themselves.

endophytes: organisms, typically fungi, living within the leaves and stems of plants, usually within the plant cells, as plant mutualists gaining sugars from the plant in return for protecting the plant from pests and diseases.

environment niche: a suite of ecological conditions within which a given species can exploit an energy source effectively enough to reproduce and colonize similar conditions; the mirror image of the *species niche*.

ephemeral: a plant that leafs out, flowers, and fruits and then goes dormant for the rest of the growing season; this strategy is most common in spring, hence the name *spring ephemeral*.

exotic: a plant that arrived in North America after European contact, either as a self-propelled or accidental immigrant or imported intentionally by humans.

expansive: particularly vigorous plants that spread vegetatively by rhizomes, stolons, or other means; we use this value-neutral term instead of words like *rampant*, *aggressive*, or *invasive*, especially the last, which presumes that "invasiveness" is a characteristic resulting only from plant characteristics, and not from the interaction between plants and their environment.

exudates: compounds released by plants from their roots (or other places); plants use root exudates to feed and manage the root-zone food web, drastically increasing the plants' nutrient uptake and overall health.

facilitation: an ecological interaction between two species where one species is unaffected by the fact that it benefits the other.

facultative: not obligated to use a typical niche strategy, lifestyle, or behavior, but may use it under some conditions; e.g., "facultative mycorrhizal plants" use mycorrhizal fungi only when soil nutrients are limited.

facultative parasite: a organism that parasitizes hosts that are already sick or dying.

farmaceutical: homegrown or farm-grown medicinal crops; this is the opposite of, and does not include, anything involving genetically engineered plants for producing chemical drugs, which the pharmaceutical industry calls "pharming."

floristics: relating to the study of the distribution of plants within an area.

fodder: coarse food fed to domestic animals, especially cattle, horses, and sheep, but other animals such as goats, rabbits, chickens, llamas, ostriches, yaks, and water buffalo are included. Fodder is usually cut and fed directly or cut and stored for later use.

forb: any nongrassy herbaceous plant, such as ferns, perennial flowers, wildflowers, bulbs, herbaceous vines, etc.

forest: stands of trees with 100 percent canopy coverage and interlocking crowns.

fractured partial shade: shade cast periodically throughout the day by various objects, but interspersed with sunny periods.

friable: literally "spongy"; with reference to *soil consistence*, easily crumbled or pulverized.

gap: a vertical open space within a forest matrix extending through the vegetation layers from the canopy to the top of the herb layer (6 feet or 2 meters high), with a diameter-to-height ratio less than 2.

gap dynamics: the successional processes that occur when trees die within a forest matrix, leaving a gap or clearing.

generalist herbivores: herbivores that eat whatever plant foods they can find and are palatable; contrast with *specialist herbivore*.

genotype: the genetic constitution of an individual organism; the genotype interacts with the environment to produce the observable or expressed characteristics of the individual, a.k.a. its phenotype.

girdling: cutting through the living parts of a tree's or shrub's bark into the older, nonliving wood around the stem's whole circumference, but not cutting the plant down; allows the plant to remain standing for a time, but kills it.

glade: a vertical open space within a forest matrix extending through the vegetation layers from the canopy to the top of the herb layer (6 feet or 2 meters high), with a diameter-to-height ratio greater than 4.

gross primary production: the total amount of solar energy captured in photosynthesis by a plant or ecosystem; compare to *net primary production (NPP)*.

guilds: groups of species that partition resources or create networks of mutual support.

habit: a plant's behavior as it is reflected architecturally; determined by the pattern the plant produces as it grows, reproduces, and spreads, e.g., mat forming, standard tree, clumping herb, etc.

habitat: a place or type of place that provides food, water, or refuge to a species or individual; usually characterized by vegetation type or other dominant ecosystem features.

herbivores: organisms that gain their needed energy from the products of producers, that is, plants, by either eating, parasitizing, or forming mutualistic relationships with them.

high shade: shade produced by a high canopy, which usually allows some light to enter from the sides and causes light levels to be even across the space due to scattering.

hydric: wet or very wet; containing plenty of moisture; compare to *mesic* and *xeric*.

hyphae: the thin, branching filaments that make up the *mycelium* of a fungus.

inhibition: an ecological interaction between two species where one species either benefits from or is unaffected by its suppression or limiting of the establishment, growth, reproduction, or activities of the other.

initial floristic composition: the theory that the flora of a community undergoing succession changes due only to variation in which species are dominant at a given time, not because the different species arrive as conditions change. This theory stands on the idea that all or most of the site's flora is present at the beginning of the successional sequence, and that the successional pathway is influenced primarily by that initial flora, not recruitment during the sequence.

insectary plant: a plant providing food or shelter to beneficial insects.

insectivorous: insect eating.

intensity (of disturbance): the amount of energy expended during a disturbance.

invasive: a plant, animal, or other species considered a threat to ecosystem integrity or human values due to its expansive or dispersive behavior within certain environmental contexts; this term is usually used in a way that indicates the user believes the species so named is the source of the threat;

we do not use this term to describe plants because it ascribes characteristics to plants that can result only from the interaction between a plant and its environment.

ion: an atom or molecule with a net electrical charge due to the loss or gain of one or more electrons.

landform: in design, the shape and slope of the earth's surface, as well as the composition and pattern of its bedrock and surficial geology.

layering: a means of propagation or plant dispersal where the plant forms roots along a branch or stem that is placed in a small trench by humans or that touches the ground of its own accord.

leaching: the transportation of dissolved or suspended material within the soil by the movement of water when rainfall exceeds evaporation; a.k.a. *eluviation*.

legacy: a biological, mineral, or chemical inheritance passed down from one ecosystem to the next; usually refers to legacies remaining after disturbance resets the successional clock.

light saturation: the intensity of light (usually expressed as percent of full sun) at which a plant's rate of photosynthesis can no longer increase.

macronutrients: the nine nutrients that constitute the vast majority (99.5 percent) of plant biomass: C, O, H, N, P, S, K, Ca, and Mg.

mesic: containing a moderate amount of moisture; compare to *hydric* and *xeric*.

microclimate: the climate of a small site, area, or habitat; a microclimate can be as small as a kitchen table or as large as the side of a mountain, as long as its conditions are essentially uniform and significantly different from the overall climate and neighboring microclimates.

micronutrients: the nine plant nutrients that are required by plants to function but make up only 0.5 percent of plant biomass: Cl, Fe, Mn, B, Zn, Cu, Mo, Co, and Ni.

mimicry: the close external resemblance of an animal, plant, or inanimate object (or part of one) to another animal, plant, or inanimate object; in forest gardening, the structural and functional resemblance of a designed garden to a model ecosystem.

monoculture: in agriculture, the growing of one species or crop variety in one area; in culture, the homogenization of cultural expression to a single or narrow set of values, behaviors, social structures, and ways of being; in psychology, the limiting of perspective such that one sees the world as composed of elements that have only one purpose, function, feature, or value.

mottles: spots or patches of soil color significantly different from the color of surrounding soil; usually an indicator of the estimated seasonal high water table.

multistemmed: having more than one stem arising from the root crown; usually refers to shrubs; in trees this habit is called *sprouting*.

mutualism: an ecological interaction between two species where both species benefit from the interaction; may be *obligate* or *facultative* and *diffuse* or *pairwise*.

mutual-support guild: a group of species from different *trophic levels* that interact in such a way as to support each other; these species meet each other's intrinsic needs by using each other's intrinsic by-products, that is, they functionally interconnect.

mycelium: the vegetative parts of a fungus, consisting of a network of fine white filaments (*hyphae*).

mycorrhiza: (plural, mycorrhizas); a mutualistic relationship between a plant and a fungus, where the plant gives the fungus sugars in return for water, nutrients, and, often, protection from soil-borne pests.

native: a species that established itself on the North American continent before European contact.

nectary plant: a plant providing nectar to beneficial insects as a source of calories; may be divided into specialist nectary and generalist nectary, depending on the kinds of insects that use the nectar (generalist and specialist insects have different kinds of mouthparts).

net primary production (NPP): the amount of energy captured by plants during photosynthesis that is not used for respiration; NPP represents the amount of solar energy converted into *biomass*.

neutralism: an ecological relationship between two species where neither species affects the other.

niche: a general term denoting "ecological space"; see definitions for the three kinds of niches: *species niche, community niche,* and *environment niche*.

niche analysis: enumerating the characteristics of a species, community, or environment niche as far as is possible by breaking it into its component parts, such as, for a *species niche,* needs, products, behaviors, intrinsic characteristics, evolutionary history and associates, and so on.

nodulation: the formation of nodules caused by the mutualism between nitrogen-fixing bacteria (*Rhizobium* spp. or *Frankia* spp.) and their plant hosts.

nodules: small, round beads or balls containing nitrogen-fixing bacteria that grow on the roots of nitrogen-fixing plants. If they are pink or red inside when you cut them open, nitrogen fixation is happening.

nonnative: see *exotic*.

NPP: see *net primary production*.

obligate: restricted to one niche strategy or particularly characteristic mode of life or behavior, e.g., obligate mycorrhizal fungi can survive only as mutualists of plants.

oldfield: a former agricultural field, pasture, hayland, meadow, or lawn that has been abandoned and is undergoing *succession*; usually refers to the middle stages of succession, when the ecosystem consists of a patchy mosaic of herbs, shrubs, trees, and vines.

OM: organic matter.

omnivores: organisms that gain their needed energy from more than one *trophic level*.

opportunist: formerly known as *invasive*; a species that exhibits highly *dispersive* or *expansive* behavior. Some of these, especially "exotic" species, are perceived by humans as a threat to ecosystem integrity; we use this term rather than *invasive* to include the environment as a component of the dynamic called "invasion."

overstory: the topmost layer of a plant community; usually called a canopy unless the overstory is under 12 feet (3.6 m) high.

overyielding: see *additive yielding*.

oviposition: "egg-laying location"; usually refers to insect egg location requirements; each insect species has different oviposition requirements, which can be quite specific as to substrate or plant host, microclimate, and location upon the host plant or substrate.

pairwise mutualism: a mutualistic relationship between two species where they cooperate only with each other, and not with any other partners; the opposite of *diffuse mutualism*.

parasitoid insects: insects whose adults lay their eggs in or on host insects (usually pests), and whose young eat the host when they hatch.

parent material: the underlying rock or other mineral material within and upon which soils form; forms the "constitution" of the overlying soil, strongly influencing its *texture, structure, consistence,* and nutrient content.

part-day shade: shade that occurs only in part of the day, while the rest of the day is sunny.

patch: a plant and animal community surrounded by an area with a dissimilar community structure or composition.

percent cover: see *coverage*.

perennial: a plant growing back every year without starting from seed.

permaculture: the conscious design and cocreative evolution of human cultures, settlements, and agricultural systems, using ecological principles and indigenous wisdom to mimic the diversity, stability, and resilience of natural systems; a contraction of "permanent agriculture" and "permanent culture" coined by David Holmgren and Bill Mollison in Australia in the late 1970s.

phenology: the study of cyclic and seasonal natural phenomena, especially in relation to climate, plants, and animal life.

pioneer: the first plants to colonize a new site or to begin the change from one successional stage to another; pioneer trees are the first to invade a grassland, for example.

pollarding: cutting a woody plant so it coppices, but cutting it well above ground level to keep fresh shoots out of reach of livestock.

polyculture: the growing of more than one species or crop variety in a patch or space at one time; contrast with *monoculture*.

predatory insects: an insect whose adult or larval stages directly catch and eat other insects; contrast with *parasitoid insects*.

primary succession: succession that begins with bare soil or rock, with no biological legacies from the predisturbance ecosystem.

producers: organisms that transform energy from sunlight (or, rarely, some other nonbiological source) into biomass.

propagule: any plant part that can produce a new individual of the species, such as a seed, a viable root or stem fragment, or a bud.

relay floristics: the theory that the flora of a site undergoing succession changes as conditions shift due to the recruitment of new species to the community and the dying out of existing ones; that is, that the species arrive and depart in waves as conditions change; contrast with *initial floristic composition*.

resource-partitioning guild: see *resource-sharing guild*.

resource-sharing guild: a group of species from the same *trophic level* that use the same resource in a similar way but avoid competition by specializing and differentiating when, where, or how they use the resource.

rhizomatous: a plant that spreads by means of *rhizomes*.

rhizome: a rootlike structure, actually a modified stem, that spreads through the soil and from which shoots and roots grow to form new, interconnected "plants."

rhizosphere: the root zone of the soil; primarily refers to the very thin layers of soil adjacent to roots that is influenced by root *exudates* and is full of microbial life; some authors use the term to describe the soil horizons where roots primarily live, that is, the O, A, and B horizons.

richness or **species richness**: the total number of species in a given area; richness is different from diversity, in the ecologist's sense of the word: Diversity also measures the relative abundance of the species, not just how many species there are.

root: the part of a plant that grows in the opposite direction from the stem, usually underground, lacking nodes.

root density: the concentration of roots in a given area of soil.

root sucker: a shoot arising from a true root, not a *rhizome* or *stolon*, at a distance from the plant's main stem.

root suckering: denotes a plant that grows *root suckers*.

root zone: the area of intensive microbial activity and diversity within a few millimeters or centimeters of plant roots; this activity is caused in great part by root *exudates*.

ruderal: literally from Latin, "rubble"; in the context of the core strategies of *species niches*, a ruderal species allocates most of its resources toward reproduction and dealing with disturbance, rather than stress tolerance or growth and competition.

savanna: a transition plant community between prairie and forest consisting primarily of prairie plants and deep-rooted trees, with tree cover generally between 25 and 40 percent.

secondary succession: succession that begins after a disturbance to a preexisting ecosystem, so that the direction of the following succession is influenced by the biological legacies from the previous ecosystem.

seed bank: the total inventory of viable seeds stored in the soil, leaf litter, streambed, or lakebed of an ecosystem, some old and decay resistant, some newer and not as long-lasting; the seed bank may contain literally millions of seeds per acre, including numerous plant species; these numbers accumulate in forest soils and litter as well as in agricultural and suburban soils.

self-maintenance: when an entity or system maintains itself, performing all the work needed to run the system, such as providing nutrients and water, mulching, and so on.

self-management: when a system or entity envisions its future and marshals the forces needed to achieve that vision; includes guiding succession and evolution.

self-regulation: part of self-maintenance, wherein an entity or system regulates itself; in the garden this includes keeping populations of insects, animals, diseases, and plants in balance.

severity (of disturbance): the actual level of impact a disturbance has on a given species or community.

shifting-mosaic steady state: a theoretical ecosystem condition where each *patch* of the landscape is constantly cycling from gap disturbances to mature forest and back again, while at the larger scale the landscape exhibits relative stability in its vegetation characteristics.

shrub: a woody plant of limited height with multiple stems arising at or near the ground; usually shorter than a tree, although some dwarf trees are smaller than some large shrubs.

shrubland: a shrub-dominated plant community where shrub layer coverage is greater than 40 percent but less than 99 percent, and there is less than 40 percent tree cover above it.

silvopastoral systems: agroforestry systems integrating tree crops with grazed pasturelands. The trees provide food, fuel, fiber, fodder, or fertilizer production, as well as benefits such as wind reduction, soil salinity control, humidification of the air, shade, and improved grazing-animal weight gain due to microclimate improvements.

sinkers: roots that grow downward from a location along a horizontal root, rather than from the root crown.

soil consistence: the relative firmness or looseness of the soil in its undisturbed condition, ranging from loose to very firm.

soil horizon: a generally horizontal stratum of soil with uniform and distinct characteristics, including texture, structure, consistence, and color, and a dominant or predominant ecological function or characteristic, such as organic matter accumulation and decomposition, assimilation, leaching, etc.

soil profile: the vertical pattern of soil horizons: their depth, texture, structure, consistence, and color.

soil structure: the shape, alignment, and patterning of soil particles, e.g., blocky, platy, massive, or granular.

soil texture: the fineness or coarseness of a soil, determined by the percentage of different particle sizes (sand, silt, and clay) composing the soil.

species niche: the relationship of an organism to food and enemies; its core strategy for making a living, and its multiple inherent needs, products, characteristics, functions, and tolerances.

species strategy: the core of the species niche; a genetically coded pattern or suite of adaptations evolved by a species that allows it to make a living in a certain way under certain conditions.

spring ephemerals: see *ephemeral*.

sprouting: a term used as a class of tree habit or behavior in this book and denoting a tree having shoots form at the base of the stem or trunk; these shoots may arise from rhizomes, buds on the crown, or root suckers, but they are nonetheless at the base of the plant.

stemflow: the flow of rain down the stems of trees and other plants; stemflow collects rainfall and may contain high concentrations of nutrients and plant chemicals, including *allelochemicals*; the amount of stemflow a plant produces depends on its size and branching pattern.

stolon: a modified stem that grows horizontally above the ground or below the mulch but above the soil, from which a plant forms new shoots and roots as a means of expansion.

stoloniferous: a plant that spreads by means of *stolons*.

stool: a tree stump that grows regularly cut coppice.

stress tolerator: in the context of the core strategies of species niches, a stress tolerator allocates most of its resources toward resisting stress, rather than reproduction or growth and competition.

strikers: see *sinkers*.

structure: see *soil structure*.

succession: the progressive change from one ecosystem or habitat type to another by natural processes of soil and community development and colonization; in the eastern United States, usually refers to the transformation of bare soil or disturbed lands back to forest, but in other climates and circumstances succession can mean other outcomes. See chapter 6.

suckering: plants that spread by means of *rhizomes* or *root suckers*, with stems or shoots arising at a distance from the main stem or trunk.

texture: see *soil texture*.

thicket: a shrub-dominated plant community with little or no tree cover where the crowns of the shrubs interlock and cover 100 percent of the area.

threshold level: the pest population level at which you will take a specific pest management action; the threshold level and the management action should be determined in advance, and you should have a monitoring program that will help you determine the population size and tell you when the threshold is reached.

throughfall: rain that hits leaves but falls through them to the ground, rather than gathering and flowing down stems as *stemflow*; throughfall may contain nutrients and other chemicals leached out of leaves, including *allelochemicals*.

trophic level: one of the different levels of the food web, e.g., *producer*, *herbivore*, *primary carnivore*, and so on; "trophic" literally means "nursing" in Greek; each species on the same trophic level operates on a common feeding plan.

tuber: a fleshy, thickened part of a rhizome, usually at the end, serving as a storage organ. Most often bears buds, or "eyes," as on potatoes.

umbel: numerous tiny flowers that, taken together, compose a flower that forms a flattened, umbrella-shaped disk.

understory: any layer of vegetation underlying the canopy or overstory. Ecologists also use the term to describe a specific ecological niche of trees adapted to grow and reproduce in the shade of the canopy, e.g., "understory trees."

understory repression: a stage of succession where dense pioneer tree saplings shade out sun-loving shrubs and herbs, and the understory often becomes barren. Understory repression is followed by the development of a shade-loving herbaceous layer and a more varied canopy structure as competition between the saplings kills off some of their number, and shade-tolerant trees, shrubs, and herbs colonize and grow below them.

uniform deep shade: dark conditions created by complete coverage of a dense canopy or shade structure.

uniform partial shade: half-sunny or dappled-shade conditions created from complete coverage by a light-permeable material, such as a pergola or a canopy of thin-crowned trees.

varmint: a vertebrate animal, usually wild, that competes for the crops we grow or otherwise causes trouble in our garden ecosystem.

weathering: the physical disintegration and chemical decomposition of materials at or near the earth's surface.

within-patch guild: a set of plants that must grow together in a patch for the guild to become operative.

woodland: a tree-dominated plant community where tree cover is greater than 40 percent, but less than 100 percent

xeric: dry or containing little water; compare to *hydric* and *mesic*.

yield: useful product; in a forest garden context, yield is usually defined as the system yield, or the yield of the whole system, not just one species or plant within the system.

BIBLIOGRAPHY

Aaltonen, V. T. 1926. "On the space arrangement of trees and root competition." *Journal of Forestry* 24: 627–44.

Allen, O. N., and Ethel Allen. 1981. *The Leguminosae: A Sourcebook of Characteristics, Uses, and Nodulation.* Madison, WI: University of Wisconsin Press.

Altieri, Miguel. 1995. *Agroecology: The Science of Sustainable Agriculture*, 2nd ed. Boulder, CO: Westview Press.

Antos, Joseph E., and Donald B. Zobel. 1984. "Ecological implications of below ground morphology of nine coniferous forest herbs." *Botanical Gazette* 145(4): 508–17.

Armson, K. A. 1977. *Forest Soils: Properties and Processes.* Toronto: University of Toronto Press.

Ashton, Mark S., and Florencia Montagnini, eds. 2000. *The Silvicultural Basis of Agroforestry Systems.* New York: CRC Press.

Atkinson, David. 1980a. "The distribution and effectiveness of the roots of tree crops." *Horticultural Reviews* 2: 424–90.

Atkinson, David. 1980b. "The growth and activity of fruit tree root systems under simulated orchard conditions." In *Environment and Root Behavior*, ed. David N. Sen. Jodhpur, India: Geobios International, pp. 171–85.

Atkinson, David, Denise Naylor, and Gwyneth Coldrick. 1976. "The effect of tree spacing on the apple root system." *Horticultural Research* 16: 89–105.

Atsatt, Peter R., and Dennis J. O'Dowd. 1976. "Plant defense guilds." *Science* 193: 24–29.

Audubon, John James. 1827–1838. On the Passenger Pigeon. In *Birds of America.* http://www.ulala.org/P_Pigeon/ Audubon_Pigeon.html (accessed September 2, 2004).

Barbour, Michael G., Jack H. Burk, and Wanna D. Pitts. 1987. *Terrestrial Plant Ecology*, 2nd ed. Reading, MA: Benjamin/Cummings Publishing Company, Inc.

Barkman, J. J. 1992. "Canopies and microclimate of tree species mixtures." In *The Ecology of Mixed-Species Stands of Trees,* eds. M. G. R. Connell, D. C. Malcolm, and P. A. Robertson. Special publication #11 of the British Ecological Society. Boston: Blackwell Scientific Publications, pp. 181–88.

Barlow, Connie. 2000. *Ghosts of Evolution: Nonsensical Fruit, Missing Partners, and Other Ecological Anachronisms.* New York: Basic Books.

Bazzaz, F. A. 1996. *Plants in Changing Environments: Linking Physiological, Population and Community Ecology.* New York: Cambridge University Press.

Beerling, D. J. 1991. "The effect of riparian land use on the occurrence and abundance of Japanese knotweed *Reynoutria japonica* on selected rivers in South Wales." *Biological Conservation* 55: 329–37.

Bennett, K. D. 1997. *Evolution and Ecology: The Pace of Life.* New York: Cambridge University Press.

Bessette, Alan, Arleen Bessette, and David Fischer. 1997. *Mushrooms of Northeastern North America.* Syracuse, NY: Syracuse University Press.

Binkley, D. 1992. "Mixtures of N_2-fixing and non-N_2-fixing tree species." In *The Ecology of Mixed-Species Stands of Trees*, eds. M. G. R. Connell, D. C. Malcolm, and P. A. Robertson. Special publication #11 of the British Ecological Society. Boston: Blackwell Scientific Publications, pp. 99–124.

Biswell, Harold H. 1935. "Effects of the environment upon the root habits of certain deciduous forest trees." *Botanical Gazette* 96 (June): 637–708.

Bormann, F. H., and G. E. Likens. 1979. *Pattern and Process in a Forested Ecosystem.* New York: Springer-Verlag.

Botkin, Daniel B. 1993. *Forest Dynamics: An Ecological Model.* New York: Oxford University Press.

Brady, Nyle C. 1974. *The Nature and Properties of Soils*, 8th ed. New York: Macmillan Co.

Brand, Stewart. 1994. *How Buildings Learn*. New York: Viking Press.

Braun, E. Lucy. 1950. *Deciduous Forests of Eastern North America*. Philadelphia: Blakiston.

Brooks, R. R. 1972. *Geobotany and Biogeochemistry in Mineral Exploration*. New York: Harper & Row.

Brown, Alison Leadley. 1978. *Ecology of Soil Organisms*. London: Heineman Educational Books.

Brown, J. H. 1995. *Macroecology*. Chicago: University of Chicago Press.

Buchman, Stephen L., and Gary Paul Nabhan. 1996. *The Forgotten Pollinators*. Washington, DC: Island Press/Shearwater Books.

Bugg, Robert L., John H. Anderson, Craig D. Thomsen, and Jeff Chandler. 1998. "Farmscaping in California: Managing hedgerows, roadside and wetland plantings, and wild plants for biointensive pest management." In *Enhancing Biological Control*, eds. Charles H. Pickett and Robert L. Bugg. Berkeley: University of California Press, pp. 339–74.

Bunger, Myron T., and Hugh J. Thomson. 1938. "Root development as a factor in the success or failure of windbreak trees in the southern high plains." *Journal of Forestry* 36: 790–803.

Burrell, C. Colston. 1995. "The rhythm of the forest: From spring wildflowers to fall foliage." In *Woodland Gardens: Shade Gets Chic*, ed. C. Colston Burrell. Brooklyn, NY: Brooklyn Botanical Garden, pp. 17–24.

Burrell, C. Colston. 1997. *A Gardener's Encyclopedia of Wildflowers*. Emmaus, PA: Rodale Press.

Cairns, John. 1980. *The Recovery Process in Damaged Ecosystems*. Ann Arbor, MI: Ann Arbor Science Publishers, Inc.

Campbell, Bernard. 1983. *Human Ecology: The Story of Our Place in Nature from Prehistory to the Present*. New York: Aldine Publishing Co.

Canham, Charles D., and P. L. Marks. 1985. "The response of woody plants to disturbance: Patterns of establishment and growth." In *The Ecology of Natural Disturbance and Patch Dynamics*, eds. S. T. A. Picket and P. S. White. Orlando, FL: Academic Press, pp. 197–217.

Carpenter, I. W., and A. T. Guard. 1954. "Anatomy and morphology of the seedling roots of four species of the genus *Quercus*." *Journal of Forestry* 52 (April): 269–74.

Cebenko, Jill, and Deb Martin. 2001. *Insect, Disease, and Weed ID Guide*. Emmaus, PA: Rodale Press.

Chatto, Beth. 2002. *Beth Chatto's Woodland Garden: Shade-Loving Plants for Year-Round Interest*. London: Cassell Illustrated.

Coker, E. G. 1958. "Root studies, XII: Root systems of apple on Malling rootstocks on five soil series." *Journal of Horticultural Science* 33(2): 71–79.

Colinvaux, Paul. 1986. *Ecology*. New York: John Wiley & Sons.

Colle, Moshe. 1998. "Parasitoid activity and plant species composition in intercropped systems." In *Enhancing Biological Control*, eds. Charles H. Pickett and Robert L. Bugg. Berkeley: University of California Press, pp. 85-120.

Covey, Stephen R. 1989. *The Seven Habits of Highly Effective People*. New York: Simon & Schuster.

Cranshaw, Whitney. 2004. *Garden Insects of North America: The Ultimate Guide to Backyard Bugs*. Princeton, NJ: Princeton University Press.

Crawford, Martin. 1995. "Forest gardening: Edges." *Agroforestry News* 3(2): 12–16.

Crawford, Martin. 1997a. *Cherries: Production and Culture*. Dartington, Totnes, Devon, UK: Agroforestry Research Trust.

Crawford, Martin. 1997b. *Currants and Gooseberries: Production and Culture*. Dartington, Totnes, Devon, UK: Agroforestry Research Trust.

Crawford, Martin. 1997c. "Forest gardening: Groundcover polycultures." *Agroforestry News* 6(1): 5–12.

Crawford, Martin. 1997d. *Groundcover Plants*. Dartington, Totnes, Devon, UK: Agroforestry Research Trust.

Crawford, Martin. 1998. *Nitrogen-fixing Plants for Temperate Climates*. Dartington, Totnes, Devon, UK: Agroforestry Research Trust.

Crawford, Martin. 1999. "Forest gardening: Polycultures and matrix planting." *Agroforestry News*: 7(2): 37–40.

Cronon, William. 1983. *Changes in the Land: Indians, Colonists, and the Ecology of New England*. New York: Hill & Wang.

Crossley, D. I. 1940. "The effect of a compact subsoil horizon on root penetration." *Journal of Forestry* 38: 794–96.

Cullina, William. 2000. *The New England Wildflower Society Guide to Growing and Propagating Wildflowers of the United States and Canada*. New York: Houghton Mifflin.

Cullina, William. 2002. *Native Trees, Shrubs and Vines: A Guide to Using, Growing, and Propagating North American Woody Plants*. New York: Houghton Mifflin.

Dansereau, Pierre. 1957. *Biogeography: An Ecological Perspective*. New York: The Ronald Press Co.

Darke, Rick. 2002. *The American Woodland Garden: Capturing the Spirit of the Deciduous Forest*. Portland, OR: Timber Press.

Davies, Karl. 1984. "Some ecological aspects of northeastern Indian agroforestry practices." Student paper written for Cornell University's Tree Crops Research Project, Ithaca, NY. Can be found at www.daviesand.com

Davies, K. M., Jr. 1990. "Microclimate evaluation and modification for northern nut tree plantings." In *Annual Report of the Northern Nut Growers Association,* vol. 81. Also available at www.daviesand.com

Davies, K. M., Jr. 1995. "Non-traditional tree crops for northern climates." Can be found at www.daviesand.com

Davis, Mark A., Ken Thompson, and J. Philip Grime. 2001. "Charles S. Elton and the dissociation of invasion ecology from the rest of ecology." *Diversity and Distributions* 7:97–102.

Davis, M. B. 1981. "Quaternary history and the stability of forest communities." In *Forest Succession: Concepts and Application.* eds. D. C. West, H. H. Shugart, and D. B. Botkin. New York: Springer-Verlag, pp. 132–53.

Davis, M. B. 1982. "Holocene vegetational history of the eastern United States." In *Late-Quaternary Environments of the United States,* ed. H. E. Wright Jr. Minneapolis: University of Minnesota Press, pp. 166–81.

Davis, Mary Byrd. 1993. *Old Growth in the East: A Survey.* Richmond, VT: Wild Earth Press.

DeGraaf, Richard M., and Deborah D. Rudis. 1983. *New England Wildlife: Habitat, Natural History, and Distribution.* U.S. Department of Agriculture, Forest Service, Northeast Forest Experiment Station, General Technical Report NE-108. Out of print, but available online as a .pdf download at http://www.srs.fs.usda.gov/pubs

DeGraaf, Richard M., and Mariko Yamasaki. 2001. *New England Wildlife: Habitat, Natural History, and Distribution.* Hanover, NH: University Press of New England.

Deppe, Carol. 2000. *Breed Your Own Vegetable Varieties: The Gardener's and Farmer's Guide to Plant Breeding and Seed Saving.* White River Junction, VT: Chelsea Green.

Diamond, Jared. 1997. *Guns, Germs, and Steel: The Fates of Human Societies.* New York: W. W. Norton & Co.

Dickman, Martin. 1993. "Molecular biology of plant-parasite relations." In *Soil Microbial Ecology: Applications in Agricultural and Environmental Management.* New York: Marcel Dekker, Inc., pp. 177–202.

Douglas, J. Sholto, and Robert A. de J. Hart. 1984. *Forest Farming: Towards a Solution to Problems of World Hunger and Conservation.* London: Intermediate Technology Publications.

Douglass, J. E. 1967. "Effects of species and arrangement of forests on evapotranspiration." In *Proceedings of the International Symposium on Forest Hydrology.* New York: Pergamon Press.

Dramstad, Wenche E., James D. Olson, and Richard T. T. Forman. 1996. *Landscape Ecology Principles in Landscape Architecture and Land-Use Planning.* Washington, DC: Island Press.

Drengson, Alan, and Duncan Taylor, eds. 1997. *Ecoforestry: The Art and Science of Sustainable Forest Use.* Stony Creek, CT: New Society Publishers.

Elliott, Douglas B. 1976. *Roots: An Underground Botany and Forager's Guide.* Old Greenwich, CT: The Chatham Press.

Ellis, Barbara, and Fern Marshall Bradley. 1996. *The Organic Gardener's Handbook of Natural Insect and Disease Control.* Emmaus, PA: Rodale Press.

Ettema, C. H., and R. A. Hansen. 1997. "Nematode diversity in litter of varying complexity." *Soil Ecology Abstracts.* http://www.ksu.edu/biology/bio/meetings/abstracts.html (accessed April 27, 2005).

Facciola, Stephen. 1990. *Cornucopia: A Sourcebook of Edible Plants.* Vista, CA: Kampong Publications.

Facciola, Stephen. 1998. *Cornucopia II: A Sourcebook of Edible Plants.* Vista, CA: Kampong Publications.

Fern, Ken. 1997. *Plants for a Future: Edible and Useful Plants for a Healthier World.* Hampshire, England: Permanent Publications.

Flannery, Tim. 2001. *The Eternal Frontier: An Ecological History of North America and Its Peoples.* New York: Atlantic Monthly Press.

Foster, Steven. 1984. *Herbal Renaissance.* Salt Lake City, UT: Gibbs-Smith Publishers.

Foster, Steven, and James A. Duke. 1990. *A Field Guide to Medicinal Plants: Eastern and Central North America.* Peterson Field Guide Series, #40. Boston: Houghton Mifflin Company.

Fox, L. R. 1988. "Diffuse coevolution in complex communities." *Ecology* 69: 906–07.

Friends of the Trees. 1992. *Kiwi Fruit Enthusiast's Journal,* vol. 6. Michael Pilarski, ed. Tonasket, WA: Friends of the Trees.

Fukuoka, Masanobu. 1978. *The One-Straw Revolution: An Introduction to Natural Farming.* Emmaus, PA: Rodale Press.

Fulbright, Dennis, ed. *A Guide to Nut Tree Culture in North America,* vol 1. Townsend, DE: Northern Nut Grower's Association.

Futuyma, Douglas J., and Montgomery Slatkin, eds. 1983. *Coevolution.* Sunderland, MA: Sinauer Associates.

Giono, Jean. 1985. *The Man Who Planted Trees*. White River Junction, VT: Chelsea Green.

Glenn, D. M., and W. V. Welker. 1993. "Root development patterns in field grown peach trees." *Journal of the American Horticultural Society* 118(3): 362–65.

Gordon, Andrew M., and Steven M. Newman, eds. 1997. *Temperate Agroforestry Systems*. New York: Center for Agriculture and Biosciences International.

Gosz, J. R., R. T. Holmes, G. E. Likens, and F. H. Bormann. 1978. "The flow of energy in a forest ecosystem." *Scientific American* 238: 93–101.

Graham, Alan, ed. 1972. *Floristics and Paleofloristics of Asia and Eastern North America*. New York: Elsevier.

Graham, B. F., Jr., and F. H. Bormann. 1966. "Natural root grafts." *The Botanical Review* 32(3): 255–92.

Gray, Donald H., and Andrew T. Leiser. 1989. *Biotechnical Slope Protection and Erosion Control*. Malabar, FL: Krieger.

Grime, J. P. 1977. "Evidence for the existence of three primary strategies in plants and its relevance to ecological and evolutionary theory." *American Naturalist* 111: 1169–94.

Grime, J. P. 1979. *Plant Strategies and Vegetation Processes*. New York: Wiley & Sons.

Grime, J. Philip. 2001. *Plant Strategies, Vegetation Processes, and Ecosystem Properties*, 2nd ed. New York: John Wiley & Sons.

Häni, Fritz J., Ernst F. Boller, and Siegfried Keller. 1998. "Natural regulation at the farm level." In *Enhancing Biological Control*, eds. Charles H. Pickett and Robert C. Bugg. Berkeley, CA: University of California Press, pp. 161–210.

Harker, Donald, Sherri Evans, Marc Evans, and Kay Harker. 1993. *Landscape Restoration Handbook*. Boca Raton, FL: Lewis Publishers.

Harmer, R., and G. Kerr. 1995. "Creating woodlands: To plant trees or not?" In *The Ecology of Woodland Creation*, ed. Richard Ferris-Kaan. New York: John Wiley & Sons, pp. 113–28.

Harris, Charles W., and Nicholas T. Dines. 1988. *Time-Saver Standards for Landscape Architecture*. New York: McGraw-Hill.

Harris, J. A., and T. C. J. Hill. 1995. "Soil biotic communities and new woodland." In *The Ecology of Woodland Creation*. ed. Richard Ferris-Kaan. New York: John Wiley & Sons, pp. 91–112.

Harris, Richard N., James R. Clark, and Nelda P. Matheny. *Arboriculture: The Integrated Management of Landscape Trees, Shrubs and Vines*, 3rd ed. Upper Saddle River, NJ: Prentice-Hall.

Hart, Robert A. de J. 1991. *Forest Gardening*. Totnes, Devon, UK: Green Books.

Hemenway, Toby. 2001. *Gaia's Garden: A Guide to Home-Scale Permaculture*. White River Junction, VT: Chelsea Green.

Hickmott, Simon. 2003. *Growing Unusual Vegetables: Weird and Wonderful Vegetables and How to Grow Them*. Bristol, England: Eco-Logic Books.

Hightshoe, Gary L. 1988. *Native Trees, Shrubs and Vines for Urban and Rural America: A Planting Design Manual for Environmental Designers*. New York: Van Nostrand-Reinhold.

Hills, Lawrence. 1976. *Comfrey: Past, Present, and Future*. London, England: Faber and Faber.

Holch, A. E. 1931. "Development of roots and shoots of certain deciduous tree seedlings in different forest sites." *Ecology* 12(2): 259–98.

Holling, C. S. 1998. "The renewal, growth, birth and death of ecological communities." *Whole Earth Review* 93: 32–35.

Holmgren, David. 1995. *Hepburn Permaculture Gardens: 10 Years of Sustainable Living*. Hepburn, Victoria, Australia: Holmgren Design Services.

Holmgren, David. 1996. *The Role of Native Vegetation in Back Yard Permaculture*. Hepburn, Victoria, Australia: Holmgren Design Services. Available at http://www.holmgren.com.au (accessed January 2004.)

Holmgren, David. 1997. "Weeds or Wild Nature?" *Permaculture International Journal* 61. Available at http://www.holmgren.com.au (accessed January 2004.)

Holmgren, David. 2002. *Permaculture: Principles and Pathways beyond Sustainability*. Hepburn, Victoria, Australia: Holmgren Design Services.

Hopkins, H. T., Jr., and R. L. Donahue. 1939. "Forest tree root development as related to soil morphology." *Proceedings of the Soil Science Society of America* 4: 353.

Hunter, A. F., and L. W. Aarsen. 1988. "Plants helping plants." *Bioscience* 38: 34–40.

Jean, Frank C., and John E. Weaver. 1924. *Root Behavior and Crop Yield Under Irrigation*. Washington, DC: Carnegie Institute of Washington.

Jeavons, John. 1995. *How to Grow More Vegetables Than You Ever Thought Possible on Less Land Than You Can Imagine*, 5th ed. Berkeley, CA: Ten Speed Press.

Jones, Samuel B., Jr., and Leonard E. Foote. 1990. *Gardening with Native Wildflowers*. Portland, OR: Timber Press.

Jorgensen, Neil. 1978. *A Sierra Club Naturalist's Guide: Southern New England*. San Francisco: Sierra Club Books.

Kavasch, Barrie. 1999. *Native Harvests: Recipes and Botanicals of the American Indian,* 2nd ed. New York: Vintage Books.

Kimmins, J. P. 1997. *Forest Ecology: A Foundation for Sustainable Management.* Upper Saddle River, NJ: Prentice-Hall.

Kirk, Donald. 1975. *Wild Edible Plants of Western North America.* Happy Camp, CA: Naturegraph Publishers.

Kolesnikov, V. 1971. *The Root System of Fruit Plants.* Moscow: Mir Publishers.

Kormondy, Edward J. 1976. *Concepts of Ecology,* 2nd ed. Englewood Cliffs, NJ: Prentice-Hall.

Kourik, Robert. 1986. *Designing and Maintaining Your Edible Landscape, Naturally.* Santa Rosa, CA: Metamorphic Press.

Kourik, Robert. 1992. *Drip Irrigation for Every Landscape and All Climates.* Santa Rosa, CA: Metamorphic Press.

Kricher, John C., and Gordon Morrison. 1988. *Ecology of Eastern Forests.* Peterson Field Guides no. 37. Boston: Houghton Mifflin Company.

Lanza, Patricia. 1998. *Lasagna Gardening.* Emmaus, PA: Rodale Press.

Lavelle, P. 1997. "Faunal activities and soil processes: Adaptive strategies that determine ecosystem function." *Advances in Ecological Research.* 27: 93–132.

Lavelle, P., C. Lattaud, D. Trigo, and I. Barois. 1994. "Mutualism and biodiversity in soils." *Plant and Soil* 170(1): 23–33.

Lavelle, Patrick, and Alister V. Spain. 2001. *Soil Ecology.* Boston: Kluwer Academic Publishers.

Law, Ben. 2001. *The Woodland Way: A Permaculture Approach to Sustainable Woodland Management.* East Meon, Hampshire, England: Permanent Publications.

Laycock, William A. 1967. *Distribution of Roots and Rhizomes in Different Soil Types in the Pine Barrens of New Jersey.* Washington, DC: U.S. Geological Survey, Professional Paper 563-C.

Le Guin, Ursula K. 1985. *Always Coming Home.* New York: Bantam Books.

Leopold, Aldo. 1966. *A Sand County Almanac with Essays from Round River.* New York: Oxford University Press/Sierra Club/Ballantine Books.

Li, Fumin, D. Jordan, Felix Ponder Jr., Edwin Berry, Victoria Hubbard, and Kil Yong Kim. 1997. "Earthworm and microbial activity in a central hardwood forest after compaction and organic matter removal." *Soil Ecology Society Abstracts.* http://www.ksu.edu/biology/bio/meetings/abstracts.html (accessed April 27, 2005).

Liebman, Matt. 1995. "Polyculture cropping systems." In *Agroecology: The Science of Sustainable Agriculture,* 2nd ed. ed. Miguel Altieri. Boulder, CO: Westview Press, pp. 205–18.

Luken, James O. 1990. *Directing Ecological Succession.* New York: Chapman & Hall.

Luoma, Jon R. 1999. *The Hidden Forest: The Biogeography of an Ecosystem.* New York: Henry Holt & Co.

Lutz, Harold F., Joseph Ely Jr., and Silas Little Jr. 1937. *The influence of Soil Profile Horizons on Root Distribution of Eastern White Pine.* New Haven, CT: Yale University School of Forestry, Bulletin 44.

Lyford, W. H., and B. F. Wilson. 1964. *Development of the Root System of* Acer rubrum L. Harvard Forest Papers, no. 10. Petersham, MA: Harvard Forest.

Lynch, J. M., ed. 1990. *The Rhizosphere.* New York: Wiley-Interscience, John Wiley & Sons.

MacArthur, R. H., and J. W. MacArthur. 1961. "On bird species diversity." *Ecology* 42(3): 594–98.

MacKenzie, David S. 1997. *Perennial Groundcovers.* Portland, OR: Timber Press.

Magdoff, Fred. 2000. *Building Soils for Better Crops.* Washington, DC: Sustainable Agriculture Network.

Marinelli, Janet. 1998. *Stalking the Wild Amaranth: Gardening in the Age of Extinction.* New York: Henry Holt & Co.

Martens, Mary-Howell. 2000. "The soil food web: Tuning into the world beneath our feet." *Acres, USA* 30(4), April 2000.

Martin, Glen. 1996. "Keepers of the Oaks." *Discover,* August 1996 pp. 44–50.

McDonnell, Mark J., and Steward T. A. Pickett, eds. 1993. *Humans as Components of Ecosystems: The Ecology of Subtle Human Effects and Populated Areas.* New York: Springer-Verlag.

McIntosh, R. P. 1980. "The relationship between succession and the recovery process in ecosystems." In *The Recovery Process in Damaged Ecosystems,* ed. J. Cairns Jr. Ann Arbor, MI: Ann Arbor Science Publications, pp. 11–62.

Mollison, Bill. 1979. *Permaculture Two: Practical Design for Town and Country in Permanent Agriculture.* Stanley, Tasmania: Tagari Books.

Mollison, Bill. 1988. *Permaculture: A Designer's Manual.* Tyalgum, Australia: Tagari Publications.

Mollison, Bill, and David Holmgren. 1978. *Permaculture One: A Perennial Agriculture for Human Settlements.* Melbourne, Australia: Corgi Books, Transworld Publishers.

Mollison, Bill, with Reny Mia Slay. 1991. *Introduction to Permaculture*, 2nd ed. Tyalgum, Australia: Tagari Publications.

Morrison, Susan Dudley. 1989. *The Passenger Pigeon*. Gone Forever Series, Crestwood House. New York: MacMillan Publishing Company.

Muller, Robert N. 1978. "The phenology, growth and ecosystem dynamics of *Erythronium americanum* in the northern hardwood forest." *Ecological Monographs* 48: 1–20.

National Oceanic and Atmospheric Administration (NOAA). 1974. *Climates of the States*. Port Washington, NY: Water Information Center, Inc.

Nentwig, Wolfgang. 1998. "Weedy plant species and their beneficial arthropods: Potential for manipulation in food crops." In *Enhancing Biological Control*, eds. Charles H. Pickett and Robert L. Bugg. Berkeley: University of California Press, pp. 49–71.

Newcomb, Lawrence. 1977. *Newcomb's Wildflower Guide*. New York: Little, Brown & Co.

New Hampshire Water Supply and Pollution Control Commission and New Hampshire State Conservation Commission. 1984. *Soil Manual for Site Evaluations in New Hampshire*, 3rd printing. Concord, NH: New Hampshire Water Supply and Pollution Control Commission and New Hampshire State Conservation Commission.

Niering, W. A., G. D. Dreyer, F. E. Egler, and J. P. Anderson Jr. 1986. "Stability of a *Viburnum lentago* shrub community after 30 years." *Bulletin of The Torrey Botanical Club* 113: 23–27.

Niering, W. A., and R. H. Goodwin. 1974. "Creation of relatively stable shrublands with herbicides: Arresting 'succession' on rights-of-way and pastureland." *Ecology* 55: 784–95.

Nöel, David. 1994. "Don't plant trees . . . (plant microecologies)." *Permaculture Activist* 30-A: 1–3.

Northern Nut Grower's Association. 1979. *Nut Tree Culture in North America*. Hamden, CT: Northern Nut Grower's Association.

Natural Resources Conservation Service. 1999. *Soil Ecology Primer*. U.S. Department of Agriculture, Natural Resources Conservation Service, Soil Quality Institute, Publication PA-1637, August 1999.

Nutting, Helen Cushing. 1925. *To Monadnock: The Records of a Mountain in New Hampshire through Three Centuries*. New York: Stratford Press.

Odum, Eugene P. 1971. *Fundamentals of Ecology*. Philadelphia: W. B. Saunders Co.

Ophuls, William. 1977. *Ecology and the Politics of Scarcity: Prologue to a Political Theory of the Steady State*. San Francisco: W. H. Freeman & Co.

Orians, Gordon H., and Robert T. Paine. 1983. "Convergent evolution at the community level." In *Coevolution*, eds. Douglas J. Futuyma, and Montgomery Slatkin. Sunderland, MA: Sinauer Associates, pp. 431–58.

Oskamp, Joseph. 1933. "Rooting habits of deciduous fruits on different soils." *Proceedings of the American Society for Horticultural Science* 29: 213-19.

Oskamp, Joseph, and L. P. Batjer. 1932. *Soils in Relation to Fruit Growing in New York, Part II: Size, Production, and Rooting Habit of Apple Trees on Different Soil Types in the Hilton and Morton Areas, Monroe County*. Ithaca, NY: Cornell Agricultural Experiment Station, Bulletin 550.

Packham, J. R., D. J. L. Harding, G. M. Hilton, and R. A. Stuttard. 1992. *Functional Ecology of Woodlands and Forests*. New York: Chapman and Hall.

Parnall, Ruth. 1998. *Vegetation and Land Use History of Nine Mesophytic Forest Stands in Western Franklin County, MA*. Master's thesis, Connecticut College, New London, CT.

Paul, E. A., and F. E. Clark. 1989. *Soil Microbiology and Chemistry*. New York: Academic Press.

Perry, David A. 1994. *Forest Ecosystems*. Baltimore, MD: Johns Hopkins University Press.

Perry, D. A., T. Bell, and M. P. Amaranthus. 1992. "Mycorrhizal fungi in mixed species forests and other tales of positive feedback, redundancy and stability." In *The Ecology of Mixed-Species Stands of Trees*, eds. M. G. R. Connell, D. C. Malcom, and P. A. Robertson. British Ecological Society Special Publication #11. Boston: Blackwell Scientific Publications, pp. 151–79.

Perry, T. O. 1989. "Tree roots—facts and fallacies." *Arnoldia* 49(4): 3-21.

Peterson, Lee Allen. 1977. *A Field Guide to Edible Wild Plants: Eastern and Central North America*. Peterson Field Guide Series, #23. Boston: Houghton Mifflin Company.

Petrides, George A. 1972. *A Field Guide to Trees and Shrubs*, 2nd ed. Peterson Field Guide Series, #11. Boston: Houghton Mifflin Company.

Pickett, Charles H., and Robert L. Bugg, eds. 1998. *Enhancing Biological Control: Habitat Mangement to Promote Natural Enemies of Agricultural Pests*. Berkeley: University of California Press.

Pickett, S. T. A., S. L. Collins, and J. J. Armesto. 1987. "Models, mechanisms and pathways of succession." *The Botanical Review* 53(3): 336–71.

Pickett, S. T. A., and M. J. McDonnell. 1989. "Changing perspectives in community dynamics: A theory of successional forces." *Trends in Ecology & Evolution* 4: 241–45.

Pickett, S. T. A., and P. S. White, eds. 1985a. *The Ecology of Natural Disturbance and Patch Dynamics*. New York: Academic Press.

Pickett, S. T. A., and P. S. White. 1985b. "Patch dynamics: A synthesis." In *The Ecology of Natural Disturbance and Patch Dynamics*, eds. S. T. A. Pickett, and P. S. White. New York: Academic Press, pp. 371–84.

Pilarski, Michael. 1994. *Restoration Forestry: An International Guide to Sustainable Forestry Practices*. Durango, CO: Kivaki Press.

Pimentel, David, Lori Lach, Rodolfo Zuniga, and Doug Morrison. 2000. "Environmental and economic costs of non-indigenous species in the United States." *Bioscience* 50(1): 53–5. Summarized in *Hortideas* 17(2).

Quammen, David. 1998. "Planet of weeds." *Harper's Magazine*, October 1998, pp. 57–69.

Rackham, Oliver. 1993. *Trees and Woodland in the British Landscape: The Complete History of Britain's Trees, Woods, and Hedgerows*. London: Weidenfield & Nicolson.

Reich, Lee. 2004. *Uncommon Fruits for Every Garden*. Portland, OR: Timber Press.

Reijntjes, Colin, Bertus Haverkort, and Ann Waters-Bayer. 1992. *Farming for the Future: An Introduction to Low-External-Input and Sustainable Agriculture*. London: Macmillan Press; Leusden, Netherlands: ILEISA.

Reiners, W. A. 1983. "Disturbance and basic properties of ecosystem energetics." In *Disturbance and Ecosystems: Components of Response,* eds. H. A. Mooney and M. Godron. New York: Springer-Verlag, pp. 83–98.

Richards, B. N. 1987. *The Microbiology of Terrestrial Ecosystems*. New York: John Wiley & Sons, Inc.

Ricklefs, Robert E. 1979. *Ecology*, 2nd ed. New York: Chiron Press, Inc.

Riechert, Susan E. 1998. "The role of spiders and their conservation in the agroecosystem." In *Enhancing Biological Control*, eds. Charles H. Pickett and Robert L. Bugg. Berkeley: University of California Press, pp. 211–37.

Robertson, Philip A., George T. Weaver, and James A. Cavanaugh. 1978. "Vegetation and tree species patterns near the northern terminus of the southern floodplain forest." *Ecological Monographs* 48: 249–67.

Robichaud, Beryl, and Murray F. Buell. 1973. *Vegetation of New Jersey: A Study of Landscape Diversity*. New Brunswick, NJ: Rutgers University Press.

Rodwell, J. S., and G. S. Patterson. 1995. "Vegetation classification systems as an aid to woodland creation." In *The Ecology of Woodland Creation*, ed. Richard Ferris-Kaan. New York: John Wiley & Sons, pp. 63–74.

Rogers, W. S., and M. C. Vyvyan. 1934. "Root studies, V: Rootstock and soil effects on apple root systems." *Journal of Pomology and Horticultural Science* 12: 110–50.

Roughgarden, Jonathon. 1983. "Coevolution between competitors." In *Coevolution*, eds. Douglas J. Futuyma, and Montgomery Slatkin. Sunderland, MA: Sinauer Associates, pp. 383–403.

Rudofsky, Bernard. 1955. "The conditioned outdoor room." In *Behind the Picture Window*. New York: Oxford University Press.

Runkle, James R. 1985. "Disturbance regimes in temperate forests." In *The Ecology of Natural Disturbance and Patch Dynamics*, eds. S. T. A. Pickett and P. S. White. New York: Academic Press, pp. 17–34.

St. John, Ted. 1992. "The importance of mycorrhizal fungi and other beneficial organisms in biodiversity projects." Paper presented at the Western Forest Nursery Association meeting, September 1992. Available in .pdf format at www.mycorrhiza.org

St. John, Ted. 1996. "Mycorrhizal inoculation: Advice for growers and restorationists." *Hortus West* 7(2): 1–4. Available in .pdf format at www.mycorrhiza.org

St. John, Ted. 1998. "Restoration at San Onofre State Beach, California." *Land and Water*, July/August 1998, pp. 15–17. Available in .pdf format at www.mycorrhiza.org

St. John, Ted. 2000. *The Instant Expert Guide to Mycorrhiza: The Connection for Functional Ecosystems*. Available in .pdf format at www.mycorrhiza.org

Sarrantonio, Marianne. 1994. *Northeast Cover Crop Handbook*. Emmaus, PA: Rodale Press.

Sauer, Jonathon D. 1988. *Plant Migration: The Dynamics of Geographic Patterning in Seed Plant Species*. Berkeley: University of California Press.

Sauer, Leslie Jones, and Andropogon Associates. 1998. *The Once and Future Forest: A Guide to Forest Restoration Strategies*. Washington, DC: Island Press.

Schneider, Elizabeth. 2001. *Vegetables from Amaranth to Zucchini: The Essential Reference*. New York: Morrow Cookbooks.

Schowalter, T. D. 1989. "Canopy arthropod community structure and herbivory in old-growth and regenerating forests in western Oregon." *Canadian Journal of Forest Research.* 19: 318–22.

Schwartz, Peter. 1996. *The Art of the Long View: Planning for the Future in an Uncertain World*. New York: Doubleday.

Scully, Norbert J. 1942. "Root distribution and environment in a maple-oak forest." *Botanical Gazette* 103: 492–517.

Senge, Peter, Richard Ross, Bryan Smith, Art Kleiner, and Charlotte Roberts. 1994. *The Fifth Discipline Fieldbook*. New York: Doubleday.

Shugart, H. H. 1984. *A Theory of Forest Dynamics: The Ecological Implication of Forest Succession Models*. New York: Springer-Verlag.

Simmons, E. A., and G. P. Buckley. 1992. "Ground vegetation under planted mixtures of trees." In *The Ecology of Mixed-Species Stands of Trees*, eds. M. G. R. Connell, D. C. Malcom, and P. A. Robertson. British Ecological Society Special Publication #11. Boston: Blackwell Scientific Publications, pp. 211–32.

Smith, J. Russell. 1950. *Tree Crops: A Permanent Agriculture*. New York: Harper & Row.

Soil Foodweb, Inc. 1999. *An Introduction to the Soil Foodweb*. CD lecture, #1 in a series of talks on the soil food web. Corvallis, OR: Unisun Communications.

Soil Foodweb, Inc. 2001. *A Plant Production Overview*. CD lecture, #2 in a series of talks on the soil food web. Corvallis, OR: Unisun Communications.

Soule, Judith D., and Jon K. Piper. 1992. *Farming in Nature's Image*. Washington, DC: Island Press.

Spellerberg, I. F. 1995. "Biogeography and woodland design." In *The Ecology of Woodland Creation*, ed. Richard Ferris-Kaan. New York: John Wiley & Sons, pp. 49–62.

Spencer, J. W. 1995. "To what extent can we recreate woodland?" In *The Ecology of Woodland Creation*, ed. Richard Ferris-Kaan. New York: John Wiley & Sons, pp. 1–16.

Spirn, Anne Whiston. 1998. *The Language of Landscape*. New Haven, CT: Yale University Press.

Sprackling, John A., and Ralph A. Read. 1979. *Tree Root Systems in Eastern Nebraska*. Nebraska Conservation Bulletin no. 37. Lincoln, NB: University of Nebraska—Lincoln, Institute of Agriculture and Natural Resources, Conservation and Survey Division.

Stamets, Paul. 1993. *Growing Gourmet and Medicinal Mushrooms*. Berkeley, CA: Ten Speed Press.

Stamets, Paul, and J. S. Chilton. 1983. *The Mushroom Cultivator*. Olympia, WA: Agarikon Press.

Stanley, Stephen M., Blaire Van Valkenburgh, and Robert S. Steneck. 1983. "Coevolution and the fossil record." In *Coevolution*, eds. Douglas J. Futuyma and Montgomery

Slatkin. Sunderland, MA: Sinauer Associates, Inc, pp. 328–49.

Stewart, Wilson, N., and Gar W. Rothwell. 1993. *Paleobotany and the Evolution of Plants*. New York: Cambridge University Press.

Sweet, A. T. 1929. *Subsoil: An Important Factor in the Growth of Apple Trees in the Ozarks*. Washington, DC: U.S. Department of Agriculture, Circular #95, pp. 1–12.

Sweet, A.T. 1933. *Soil Profile and Root Penetration as Indications of Apple Production in the Lake Shore District of Western New York*. Washington, DC: U.S. Department of Agriculture, Circular #303.

Sylvia, David, Jeffry Fuhrmann, Peter Hartel, and David Zuberer. 1998. *Principles and Applications of Soil Microbiology*. Upper Saddle River, NJ: Prentice Hall.

Tatum, Billie Joe. 1976. *Billie Joe Tatum's Wild Foods Field Guide and Cookbook*. New York: Workman Publishing.

Theodoropoulos, David I. 2003. *Invasion Biology: Critique of a Pseudoscience*. Blythe, CA: Avvar Books.

Tilford, Gregory. 1997. *Edible and Medicinal Plants of the West*. Missoula, MT: Mountain Press Publishing.

Tilman, David. 1988. *Plant Strategies and the Dynamics and Structure of Plant Communities*. Princeton, NJ: Princeton University Press.

Toensmeier, Eric. Forthcoming. *Perennial Vegetables*. White River Junction, VT: Chelsea Green.

Toogood, Alan, ed. 1999. *American Horticultural Society Plant Propagation: The Fully Illustrated Plant-by-Plant Manual of Practical Techniques*. New York: DK Publishing.

Tromp, J. 1983. "Nutrient reserves in roots of fruit trees, in particular carbohydrates and nitrogen." *Plant and Soil* 71: 401–13.

United Nations Educational Scientific Cultural Organization (UNESCO). 1973. *International Classification and Mapping of Vegetation*. Paris: United Nations Educational Scientific and Cultural Organization.

Uva, Richard H., Joseph C. Neal, and Joseph M. DiTomaso. 1997. *Weeds of the Northeast*. Ithaca, NY: Cornell University Press.

Watt, A. D. 1992. "Insect pest population dynamics: Effects of tree species diversity." In *The Ecology of Mixed-Species Stands of Trees*, eds. M .G. R. Cannell, D. C. Malcolm, and P. A. Robertson. Special publication #11 of the British Ecological Society. Boston: Blackwell Scientific Publications, pp. 267–76.

Weaver, John E. 1919. *The Ecological Relations of Roots.* Washington, DC: Carnegie Institute of Washington, Publication #286.

Weaver, John E. 1920. *Root Development in the Grassland Formation.* Washington, DC: Carnegie Institute of Washington, Publication #292.

Weaver, John E., and William E. Bruner. 1927. *Root Development of Vegetable Crops.* New York: McGraw-Hill.

Weaver, J. E., and Joseph Kramer. 1932. "Root system of *Quercus macrocarpa* in relation to the invasion of prairie." *Botanical Gazette* 94: 51–85.

White, P. S., and S. T. A. Pickett. 1985. "Natural disturbances and patch dynamics: An introduction." In *The Ecology of Natural Disturbance and Patch Dynamics*, eds. S. T. A. Pickett and P. S. White. New York: Academic Press, pp. 3–13.

Whitefield, Patrick. 1996. *How to Make a Forest Garden.* Clanfield, Hampshire, UK: Permanent Publications.

Whittaker, Robert H. 1970. *Communities and Ecosystems.* New York: Macmillan.

Wilde, S. A. 1958. *Forest Soils.* New York: The Ronald Press Co.

Williams, Michael. 1993. "An exceptionally powerful biotic factor." In *Humans as Components of Ecosystems: The Ecology of Subtle Human Effects and Populated Areas*, eds. Mark J. McDonnell and Steward T. A. Pickett. New York: Springer-Verlag, pp. 24–39.

Wolkpomir, Richard. 1995. "Bringing ancient ways to our farmers' fields." *Smithsonian Magazine* 26(8): 99–106.

Woodruff, J. G., and Naomi Woodruff. 1934. "Pecan root growth and development." *Journal of Agricultural Research* 49(6): 511–530.

Yadava, U. L., and S. L. Doud. 1980. "The short life and replant problems of deciduous fruit trees." *Horticultural Reviews* 2: 1–85.

Yahner, Richard H. 1995. *Eastern Deciduous Forest: Ecology and Wildlife Conservation.* Minneapolis: University of Minnesota Press.

Yarie, J. 1980. "The role of understory vegetation in the nutrient cycle of forested ecosystems in the mountain hemlock biogeoclimatic zone." *Ecology* 61: 1498–1514.

Yeager, A. F. 1935. "Root systems of certain trees and shrubs grown on prairie soils." *Journal of Agricultural Research* 51(12): 1085–92.

Yeomans, P. A. 1958. *The Challenge of Landscape: The Development and Practice of Keyline.* Sydney, Australia: Keyline Publishing Party, Ltd. Out of print. Can be found at the library of the U.S. Department of Agriculture in Washington, DC.

Yeomans, P. A. 1981. *Water for Every Farm: Using the Keyline Plan.* Adelaide, Australia: Griffin Press Limited.

Young, M. R. 1992. "Conserving insect communities in mixed woodlands." In *The Ecology of Mixed-Species Stands of Trees*, eds. M. G. R. Cannell, D. C. Malcolm, and P. A. Robertson. Special publication #11 of the British Ecological Society. Boston: Blackwell Scientific Publications, pp. 277–96.

INDEX

The field research for, and writing of, portions of this manuscript were undertaken under the auspices of the New England Small Farm Institute, Inc., Belchertown, Massachusetts.

The New England Small Farm Institute was founded in 1978. Its mission is to promote the viability of our region's small farms. It develops and delivers innovative, farmer-guided programs and resources; provides direct assistance to aspiring, new, and developing farmers; and advocates for new farmers and sustainable small-scale agriculture. The Institute manages Lampson Brook Agricultural Reserve—416 acres of public land designated as a National Historic Register heritage landscape—as a small farm demonstration and training center.

New England Small Farm Institute
PO Box 937, Belchertown MA 01007
(413) 323-4531 www.smallfarm.org